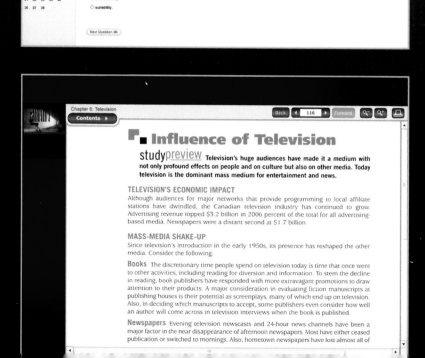

THE MEDIA OF MASS COMMUNICATION

JOHN VIVIAN
WINONA STATE UNIVERSITY

PETER J. MAURIN

FIFTH CANADIAN EDITION

PEARSON

AB
and

Toronto

Library and Archives Canada Cataloguing in Publication

Vivian, John
    The media of mass communication: with My mass comm lab / John Vivian,
Peter J. Maurin.—5th Canadian ed.

Includes indexes.
ISBN 978-0-205-49975-5

1. Mass media—Textbooks.   I. Maurin, Peter   II. Title.   III. Title: My mass comm lab.

P90.V58 2008   302.23   C2007-905517-6

ISBN-13: 978-0-205-49975-5
ISBN-10:   0-205-49975-9

Vice President, Editorial Director: Gary Bennett
Acquisitions Editor: Chris Helsby
Marketing Manager: Sally Aspinall
Developmental Editor: Emily Jardeleza
Production Editor: Pearl Saban
Copy Editor: Lenore Latta
Proofreader: Martin Townsend
Production Coordinator: Avinash Chandra
Composition: Integra
Photo Research: Amanda McCormick
Art Direction: Miguel Angel Acevedo
Cover Design: Miguel Angel Acevedo
Interior Design: Dave McKay
Cover Image: Getty Images

1 2 3 4 5   12 11 10 09 08

Printed and bound in the United States of America.

To Harold Vivian, my father,
who sparked my curiosity about the
mass media at age five by asking what
was black and white and read all over.

And to Elaine Vivian, my mother,
who nurtured this curiosity by keeping
the house stocked with books, magazines
and reading material of every sort.

J. V.

To my soulmate, Kim; thank you for all your
love, patience and understanding over the last
"twenty-five-plus" years. To my kids, Sonja and
Joshua. You are each gifted in your own way;
thank you for letting me be both your dad and
your friend. And always remember I love you more . . . .

This book is also dedicated to
the memory of my mother
and father, Peter and Blanka Maurin.

P. J. M.

Contents

chapter 9 **Public Relations**   **169**

chapter 10 **Advertising**   **187**

Preface

In the increasingly crowded field of introduction to mass communication books from which professors can choose, nothing is fresher than this Fifth Canadian Edition of *The Media of Mass Communication*. Based on feedback from instructors since the first edition back in 1997, this new edition also features three new chapters: Movies, Entertainment, and Mass Media and Governance. Change is ever constant in mass communication, and it is a textbook author's challenge to keep up with media events as they unfold. This updated version includes the latest changes in the Canadian and American media landscape.

How This Book Is Organized

THE MASS MEDIA

Chapter 1, "Mass Media Literacy," provides a foundation for understanding the mass media and the dynamics that affect the messages that mass media transmit. It also includes details on the process of mass communication. The next six chapters deal with each of the major mass media—print, sound recordings, movies, radio, television and the internet.

MASS MESSAGES

Then come chapters on the major content forms disseminated by the media to mass audiences. These include news, public relations, advertising and entertainment. Also included is a chapter on media research, with special attention to measuring the audience for mass messages.

MASS MEDIA ISSUES

The rest of the book focuses on specific issues, including media research, media law and ethics, media effects, the mass media and society, global mass media, and mass media and governance.

Using This Book

This edition retains many of the popular features that have helped your predecessors master the subject, as well as introduces some new ones.

- **Media in Theory.** Chapters open with theoretical questions that lay the foundation for issues explored later in the chapter.
- **Study Previews.** New to this edition, these previews will help you prepare for the material ahead, each major section beginning with a preview of the concepts to be covered there.
- **Media Online.** The margins contain hundreds of web addresses to guide your learning about the mass media beyond the textbook and the classroom.
- **Running Glossary.** Also new to this edition are glossary definitions in the margins, on the same page that the name or concept is introduced in the text.
- **Case Studies.** Some chapters include another new feature—a case study. These case studies illustrate an issue discussed in the chapter. Each also includes questions to help you sort through the problems presented.
- **Media People.** This feature introduces personalities who have had a major impact on the media or whose story illustrates a major point in media history.

- **Media Timeline.** This feature helps you to see the sequence of important media events and to put the events of the chapter in historical context.
- **Media Databank.** This feature contains tables to help you see certain facts about the mass media at a glance.
- **Questions for Review.** These questions are keyed to the major topics and themes in the chapter. Answer them for a quick assessment of whether you caught the major points.
- **Questions for Critical Thinking.** These questions ask you both to recall specific information and to use your imagination and critical-thinking abilities to restructure the material.
- **Deepening Your Media Literacy.** To put your learning to a practical application, Kay Turnbaugh has created a challenging exercise at the end of every chapter. This is a new feature for this Fifth Canadian Edition.
- **Keeping Up to Date.** These sections list professional and trade journals, magazines, newspapers and other periodical references to help you keep current on media developments and issues. Most of these periodicals are available in college and university libraries.
- **For Further Learning.** Every chapter ends with suggested additional readings to further your understanding. Included are seminal, pivotal and leading recent works.

Supplements

INSTRUCTOR'S RESOURCE CD-ROM

This resource CD-ROM includes the following supplements for instructors:

INSTRUCTOR'S RESOURCE MANUAL (IRM)

This manual is designed to ease time-consuming demands of instructional preparation, to enhance lectures, and to provide helpful suggestions to organize the course. The IRM contains helpful teaching resources and lecture enrichment, including outlines, synopses, and glossaries.

TEST BANK

The test bank includes multiple choice, true/false, matching, fill-in-the-blank, short answer and essay questions.

MYTEST

MyTest for *The Media of Mass Communication,* Fifth Canadian Edition from Pearson Education Canada, is a powerful assessment generation program that helps instructors easily create and print quizzes, tests, exams, as well as homework or practice handouts. Questions and tests can all be authored online, allowing instructors ultimate flexibility and the ability to efficiently manage assessments at anytime, from anywhere. Please visit **www.pearsonmytest.com/** to access MyTest.

POWERPOINT PRESENTATION PACKAGE

The PowerPoint slides created for this text outline the key points in each chapter and are ideal for lecture presentations.

These supplements are also available for downloading from a password-protected location on Pearson Education Canada's online catalogue, at **vig.pearsoned.ca.** See your local Pearson sales representative for details.

MYMASSCOMMLAB

This is where student and media connect. MyMassCommLab is an interactive and instructive online solution for mass communication courses that combines multimedia, video, activities, research support, tests and quizzes to make teaching and learning fun!

Acknowledgments

The Canadian author and publisher would like to thank the following reviewers who provided feedback and support during the development of this project: Maija Saari, Wilfrid Laurier University; Mike Dwyer, Mohawk College; Darryl Hartwick, Mohawk College; Ken Wallis, Mohawk College; Catherine Ozols, Mohawk College; Mary Francoli, Carleton University; Andre Champagne, University of Ottawa; Dale Bradley, Brock University; Mary Catherine Thompson, University of Lethbridge; Marc Belanger, Vanier College; Jay Wilson, University of Saskatchewan; Mahmoud Eid, University of Ottawa; David Young, McMaster University; and Lorraine Clarke, Vanier College.

The Canadian author would also like to thank the remarkable staff at Pearson Education: Christopher Helsby, Emily Jardeleza and Carolin Sweig. A special note of thanks to editor Lenore Latta, whose thorough and painstaking editing has made me a better writer.

Also, much thanks to John Vivian of Winona State University for providing the Canadian author with wonderful material to work with when adapting the text for the Canadian market.

Keeping Current

To you, the student, I want to emphasize that this book is a tool to help you become more intelligent and discerning as a media consumer. If you plan on a media career, the book is intended to orient you to the courses that will follow in your curriculum. This book, though, is only one of many tools for staying on top of the subject for many years to come. A feature at the end of every chapter, Keeping Up to Date, has tips on how to keep current even after your course is over.

—John Vivian and Peter J. Maurin

Mass Media Literacy

Media in Theory

Theories on How the Media Work

Media scholars have devised several ways to dissect and analyze the mass media. These include the ideas of the so-called "Toronto" or "Canadian School" of communication, which embodies the ideas of Harold Innis and Marshall McLuhan. Both men were determinists; they argued that the physical form of communication would determine the psychological and social outcome.

Marshall McLuhan: The Medium Is the Message

Marshall McLuhan examined how we perceive media messages: looking not only at the content of the message but also at the form of the message. He used the metaphor of a light bulb to explain his idea. He argued that while everyone notices the content of the light bulb (the light it provides), no one notices the form, that is, the bulb itself. The same holds true for content in the context of the media. People notice the content of the media (a speech on radio, a comedy on television) but not the medium that transmits the message. McLuhan came to believe that the characteristics of the medium influence how we perceive the message.

McLuhan's model divides media into hot and cool categories. Books, magazines, and newspapers are **hot media** because they require a high degree of thinking to use them. To read a book, for example, you must immerse yourself to derive anything from it. You must concentrate and tune out distractions. The relationship between you and the medium is intense—or hot. The same is true of magazines and newspapers, which require the audience to participate actively in the communication process.

Marshall McLuhan ■ Canadian who claimed the medium was the message.

hot media ■ Print media, which require more intimate audience involvement.

In contrast, some media allow the audience to be less actively involved, even passive. These are **cool media**. Television, for example, requires less intellectual involvement than do the hot media. In fact, television requires hardly any effort. When radio is played mostly as background, it doesn't require any active listener involvement at all. It's a cool medium. Radio is warmer, however, when it engages listeners' imaginations, as with radio drama.

Are movies hot or cold? In some ways, movies are like television, with simultaneous visual and audio components. But there are essential differences. Movies involve viewers completely. Huge screens command the viewers' full attention, and sealed, darkened movie-house auditoriums shut out distractions. On a hot–cool continuum, movies are hot. But what about a movie played at home on television? Cool.

Harold Innis: Time and Space

Harold Innis was a political economist at the University of Toronto whose communication model was based on what he referred to as **bias in communication**. This bias had effects in both time and space.

This analysis of time and space bias was examined in some detail in *Empire and Communication*, a book published in 1950. This book included a historical look at forms of communication that have helped in the rise and fall of civilizations. Innis's study reported on life from ancient Egypt up to and including North American society in the 1940s. His hypothesis was that the type of social organization in all these different societies was signified by the types of media that each used to communicate important information. In turn, those media were directly related to how those in power kept power through their "monopolies of knowledge."

By Innis's way of thinking, this communication bias is linked to the media of choice during each historical period and by each civilization. For example, stone and clay have a bias for time; that is, they can last a long time due to their material composition, and therefore can be passed down from generation to generation. Societies using these "time-based" media, according to Innis, were hierarchical and decentralized and based on tradition. On the other hand, paper has a bias for space; it's light and can be passed around from person to person. Cultures using this medium were less hierarchical and more centralized and more commercial than earlier civilizations. In short, media that were light and fast favoured control over space, while heavy, slow, and face-to-face media were better suited to keeping cultures stable over time.

The works of Innis and McLuhan should not be overlooked. Both men made "The 100 Most Important Canadians in History" list published by *Maclean's* magazine in 1998.

media TIMELINE

MEDIA TECHNOLOGY

1446 **Primal Event** Johannes Gutenberg devised movable metal type, permitting mass production of printed materials.

1455 **Books** Johannes Gutenberg printed the first of his Bibles using movable type.

1690 **Newspapers** Ben Harris printed *Publick Occurrences*, the first newspaper in the English colonies.

1741 **Magazines** Andrew Bradford printed *American Magazine* and Benjamin Franklin printed *General Magazine*, the first magazines in the English colonies.

1877 **Recording** Thomas Edison, with help from Montreal's Emile Berliner, introduced the phonograph, which could record and play back sound.

1888 **Movies** William Dickson devised the motion picture camera.

1906 **Radio** Canada's Reginald Fessenden broadcast to ships at sea.

1927 **Television** Philo Farnsworth invented the tube that picked up moving images for live transmission.

1969 **Web** The U.S. Department of Defense established the computer network that became the internet.

Other Media Models

study<u>preview</u> McLuhan and Innis aren't the only ones with theories on how the media work. There are almost as many theories on mass media as there are mass media choices.

ENTERTAINMENT AND INFORMATION

Many people find it helpful to define media by whether the thrust of their content is entertainment or information. By this definition, newspapers almost always are considered an information medium, and audio recordings and movies are considered entertainment. As a medium, books both inform and entertain. So do television and radio, although some networks, stations, and programs do more of one than the other. The same is true of magazines, with some titles geared more toward information, some more toward entertainment.

Dividing mass media into entertainment and information categories is becoming increasingly difficult as newspapers, usually considered the leading information medium, back away from hard-hitting content to woo readers with softer, entertaining material. For better or worse, this same shift is also taking place at *Time* and *Maclean's* magazines. This melding even has a name that's come into fashion: **infotainment**.

infotainment ■ Melding of media role as purveyor of information and entertainment.

Infotainment

Celebrities and their ordeals and antics have risen on the scale of newsworthiness as the gap between news and entertainment has narrowed. When an angle-seeking paparazzo squirted actor Tom Cruise with water from a handheld "microphone" in a London crowd, Cruise's confrontational response made newscasts everywhere.

ELITIST VERSUS POPULIST

An ongoing tension in the mass media exists between advancing social and cultural interests and giving broad segments of the population what they want. This tension, between extremes on a continuum, takes many forms. At one end of the continuum is serious media content that appeals to people who can be called **elitists** because they feel the mass media have a responsibility to contribute to a better society and a refinement of the culture, regardless of whether the media attract large audiences. At the other end of the continuum are **populists**, who are entirely oriented to the marketplace. Populists feel the mass media are at their best when they give people what they want. Most mass media in Canada are somewhere in the middle of the elitist–populist continuum. CBC offers some serious fare, but also offers Don Cherry on *Coach's Corner*.

elitists ■ Focus on media responsibility to society.

populists ■ Applaud media that attract a large following.

CONTENT-DISTRIBUTION MODEL

Many dynamics in mass media behaviour today can be visualized in a model that divides media functions into message creation and message distribution: the **content-distribution model**. Some companies are heavily focused on creating content, such as producing

content-distribution model ■ Divides functions of media companies into a creation category, such as producing a television program, and a distribution function, such as delivering the program on a cable system.

Marshall McLuhan

Marshall McLuhan

Born in Edmonton in 1911, Canadian communication theorist Marshall McLuhan taught at Assumption College in Windsor (now the University of Windsor) and at St. Michael's College at the University of Toronto. In 1954 he founded *Explorations*, a journal devoted to the analysis of popular media and culture. His ideas in the 1960s and 1970s took popular culture by storm. He was a frequent guest on talk shows in both Canada and the United States. He even appeared in a cameo role in the 1977 Woody Allen movie *Annie Hall*. McLuhan is also the patron saint of *Wired* magazine.

While the phrase "the medium is the message" is the most popular "McLuhanism," he did have some other attention-grabbing things to say on various aspects of mass media. For example:

- "Television is a serious medium, it's an inner oriented medium, you are the vanishing point, it goes inside you, you go on an inner trip, it is the prelude, the vestibule to LSD."
- "All news is fake. It's pseudo-event. It's created by the medium that is employed. Newspaper news has nothing to do with TV news."
- "Advertising is a service industry that provides its satisfactions quite independent of the product, and people are increasingly tending to get their satisfactions from the ad rather than the product."

movies, publishing books, and publishing magazines. Other companies are heavily focused on distribution, such as operating movie houses, bookstore chains, and cable systems. Some major players, including Canadian media companies, are building stakes in both content and distribution. Consider these examples:

Media Company	Content Units	Distribution Units
Time Warner	Cable News Network (CNN)	Time Warner Cable
Disney	Disney Studios	ABC
Rogers	Toronto Blue Jays	Rogers Sportsnet
Corus Entertainment	Nelvana	YTV and Treehouse TV

■ Importance of Mass Media

study<u>preview</u> **Mass media are usually thought of as sources of news and entertainment. They also carry messages of persuasion.**

PERVASIVENESS

Mass media are pervasive in modern life. Every day Canadians listen to one of 1 238 radio stations, read one of 100 daily newspapers, watch one of 662 TV services available and surf the internet for a little over two hours a day. Political candidates spend most of their campaign dollars on television ads to woo voters. The economy depends on advertising to create mass markets. With mass media so influential, we need to know as much as we can about how they work. Consider:

- Through the mass media we learn almost everything we know about the world beyond our immediate environs. What would you know about the execution of Saddam Hussein or the damage caused by Hurricane Katrina if it were not for newspapers, radio, television and other mass media?

Media Consumption

People spend an average of 40 percent of their day and 60 percent of their waking hours with the mass media. These data, extracted from research from Veronis Suhler, show slight shifts over the years. Most notable are growth in time spent with the web and recorded music and shrinkage in time spent with radio.

	1997	2001	2003
Television	4.3 hours	4.4 hours	4.4 hours
Radio	3.0 hours	2.8 hours	2.7 hours
Records	0.7 hour	0.8 hour	0.9 hour
Newspapers	0.4 hour	0.4 hour	0.4 hour
Books	0.3 hour	0.3 hour	0.3 hour
Movies (including home video)	0.2 hour	0.2 hour	0.2 hour
Magazines	0.2 hour	0.2 hour	0.2 hour
Web	0.1 hour	0.4 hour	0.5 hour
Totals	9.2 hours	9.5 hours	9.6 hours

- An informed and involved citizenry is possible in a modern democracy like Canada only when the mass media work well.
- People need the mass media to express their ideas widely. Without mass media your expression would be limited to people within earshot and those to whom you write letters.
- Powerful forces use the mass media to influence us with their ideologies and for their commercial purposes. The mass media are the main tools of propagandists, advertisers and other persuaders.

INFORMATION SOURCE

The most listened-for item in morning newscasts is the weather forecast. People want to know how to prepare for the day. The quality of their lives is at stake. Not knowing that rain is expected can mean getting wet on the way home or not being prepared for a slower commute on rain-slick roads.

The heart of the media's informing function lies in messages called **news**. Journalists themselves are hard pressed to agree on a definition of news. One useful definition is that news is reports about things that people want or need to know. In Canada, reporters usually tell the news without taking sides.

Advertising also is part of the mass media's information function. The media, especially newspapers, are bulletin boards for trade and commerce. People look to supermarket flyers for specials. Classified advertisements also provide useful information.

news ■ Nonfiction reports on what people want or need to know.

ENTERTAINMENT SOURCE

The mass media can be wonderful entertainers, bringing together huge audiences not otherwise possible. More people cried at the movie *Titanic* than read all of the dozens of books about the tragedy. More people hear Michael Bublé on CD or the radio than ever attend one of his concerts. Count the seats in Jimmy Buffett's bar in Myrtle Beach, South Carolina, and contrast that with the audience for his signature song, "Margaritaville," in even one television appearance on CMT Canada.

Almost all mass media have an entertainment component, although no medium is wholly entertainment. The thrust of the North American movie industry is almost all entertainment, but there can be a strong informational and persuasive element. Even the most serious newspaper has an occasional humour column. Most mass media are a mix of information and entertainment—and also persuasion.

PERSUASION FORUM

People form opinions from the information and interpretations to which they are exposed, which means that even news coverage has an element of persuasion. The media's attempts to persuade, however, are usually in editorials and commentaries whose persuasive purpose is obvious. Most news media separate material designed to persuade from news. Newspapers package their opinion articles in an editorial section. Commentary on television is introduced as opinion.

The most obvious of the media messages designed to persuade is advertising. **Advertisements** exhort the audience to action—to go out and buy toothpaste, cornflakes and automobiles. **Public relations** is subtler, seeking to persuade but usually not to induce immediate action. Public relations tries to shape attitudes, usually by persuading mass media audiences to see an institution or activity in a particular light.

advertisements ■ Messages intended to persuade people to buy.

public relations ■ Messages intended to win support.

⌐▪ Culture and Values

study<u>preview</u> Historically, mass media treatment of socially divisive issues has helped to create new consensus. This culturally binding media role may be fading. The exponential growth in fragmented (or demassified) media channels in recent years has created separate nests where like-minded people find enduring support for their perspectives and prejudices, which solidifies diversity at the expense of consensus.

BINDING INFLUENCE

The mass media bind communities together by giving messages that become a shared experience. A rural newspaper editor scrambling to get an issue out may not be thinking about how her work creates a common identity among readers, but it does. The town newspaper is something everyone in town has in common. In the same way, watching Team Canada at the Olympics gives Canadians something in common. A shared knowledge and a shared experience are created by mass media, and thus they create a base for community.

Stories on misdeeds help us figure out what we as a society regard as acceptable and as inexcusable. News coverage of the Canadian Gomery Inquiry into "AdScam" did this. So did coverage of major lapses in the government response to the Hurricane Katrina disaster in Louisiana, Mississippi and Alabama. At many levels the mass media are essential for the ongoing process whereby society identifies its values. The media act as agents of socialization.

GOVERNMENT REGULATION OF CULTURE

Due to the pervasiveness of American media on Canadian airwaves and the binding influence of media, the federal government formed an independent body to supervise and regulate broadcasting. The **CRTC** is the Canadian Radio-television and Telecommunications Commission. In the 21st century, the CRTC has the tenuous job of balancing the economic, cultural and social aspects of broadcasting while dealing with the influence of both the internet and the 500-channel universe. The CRTC's goals include making sure that Canadian radio and television stations can be profitable while ensuring that Canadians are seen and heard on Canadian media.

It's not just the CRTC that feels Canadian media should be Canadian. Ian Greenberg, president and CEO of Astral Media, the Canadian company that owns TMN, Mpix, Teletoon, and Family Channel, feels that Canadian media must be

CRTC ■ Canadian Radio-television and Telecommunications Commission. It ensures that Canadians are seen and heard on Canadian media.

Canadian. It's not just a matter of culture; it's a matter of economics. Greenberg says, "to ultimately deliver financial value, we first need to understand and reflect Canadian social and cultural beliefs. Not only do we express and reflect Canadian values, but we also help shape those values to a certain extent."

500-CHANNEL UNIVERSE

Less than a quarter century ago, for most people the choices for a daily news recap in Canada were the three major television networks (CBC, CTV and Global), a local newspaper, and radio headlines on local stations. The news in those not-so-distant days was edited for general audiences from a detached, neutral perspective. Those media sources still exist, largely in their traditional form. But three revolutionary technologies have changed the media environment dramatically:

- Satellite communication
- Digitized messages
- The internet

The explosion of media sources, called the **500-channel universe**, was first hailed for the way it added to the marketplace of messages and loosened the oligopoly of relatively few media sources. Darker questions have since arisen. Studies are finding that few people scan their new choices to expose themselves to the diverse content. It may be a 500-channel universe, but in the case of television few people go beyond the channels that coincide with their interests and biases. So instead of being the vehicle for social cohesion that the media used to be, the reality is that new channels, including thousands on the internet, reinforce what separates us on the cutting-edge issues by which society defines its values. The media may be becoming a vehicle less for the traditional consensus building than for building walls around societal niches.

Is there still room for Canadian television in the new 500-channel universe? Glen O'Farrell, President and CEO of the Canadian Association of Broadcasters, thinks there is. He says, "in the struggle between 'Me' media and 'mass' media, how can we ensure there's still a place for Canadian media? Canadians expect, and ultimately need, their media universe to continue resonating with Canadian voices, music and images that reflect the Canadian experience."

500-channel universe ■ Fanciful term for the growth in media channels available in recent years.

■ Primary Mass Media

study<u>preview</u> **Mass production of the written word became possible with an invention by Johannes Gutenberg in the 1440s, which transformed human existence in ways he never imagined. The legacy of Gutenberg's technology includes books, newspapers and magazines. Later came media rooted in chemical and electronic technology.**

PRINT TECHNOLOGY

The introduction of mass-produced books in the 15th century marked a turning point in human history. Before then, books were handwritten, usually by scribist monks who copied existing books onto blank sheets of paper letter by letter, one page at a time. These **scribists** could turn out only a few hand-lettered books in a lifetime of tedium.

In the mid-1400s **Johannes Gutenberg**, a tinkerer in what is now Germany, devised an innovation that made it possible to print pages using metal letters. Gutenberg's revolutionary contribution was in applying metallurgy to the printing process, which went back to ancient China. The idea for **movable metal type** occurred to Gutenberg in the mid-1430s. Instead of using wood, which often cracked in the pressing process, he experimented

scribists ■ Monks who copied books manually.

Johannes Gutenberg ■ Inventor of printing press which, in turn, made mass media and advertising possible.

movable metal type ■ Small blocks of type arranged into words, lines and pages.

with casting individual letters in a lead-based alloy. He built a frame the size of a book's page and then arranged the metal letters into words. Once a page was filled—with letters and words and sentences—he put the frame into a modified wine press, applied ink, laid paper and pressed. The process made it possible to produce dozens, even hundreds or thousands, of copies.

Gutenberg's impact cannot be overstated. The duplicative power of movable type put the written word into wide circulation and fueled quantum increases in literacy. One hundred years after Gutenberg, the state of communication in Europe had undergone a revolution. Elaborate postal systems were in place. Standardized maps produced by printing presses replaced hand-copied maps, with all their inaccuracies and idiosyncrasies. People began writing open letters to be distributed far and wide. Newspapers followed. The exchange of scientific discoveries was hastened through special publications. Johannes Gutenberg stands at a dividing point in the history of humankind. A scribist culture preceded him. The age of mass communication followed. His influence was so significant that in 2000, he was named A&E's Person of the Millennium for his invention of the printing press.

Books, **magazines** and **newspapers**, the primary **print media**, generally can be distinguished in the following four categories: binding, regularity, content, and timeliness.

	Books	Magazines	Newspapers
Binding	Stitched or glued	Stapled	Unbound
Regularity	Single issue	At least quarterly	At least weekly
Content	Single topic	Diverse topics	Diverse topics
Timeliness	Generally not timely	Timeliness not an issue	Timeliness important

Although these distinctions are helpful, they cannot be applied rigidly. For example, timeliness is critical to *Maclean's*, even though it's a magazine. Over the past 30 years, book publishers have found ways to produce "instant books" on major news events within a couple of weeks so that their topics can be timely.

CHEMICAL TECHNOLOGY

Movies are a medium based on photographic chemistry. Although a lot of video production, including some prime-time television, is shot on videotape and stored electronically, Hollywood still makes most movies on strips of transparent celluloid that are "pulled through the soup"—making movies a **chemical medium**, a technology that dates back to 1888.

In some respects, this chemical technology is not only archaic but also expensive. Studios make as many as 6000 copies of major releases and ship them from movie house to movie house in cumbersome metal boxes. The freight bills alone are astronomical. How much easier—and cheaper—it would be to transmit movies via satellite to movie houses, a system that would cut film and distribution costs by perhaps 85 percent.

As digital technology improves and costs come down, movies are shifting from chemical to electronic technology. But don't hold your breath.

ELECTRONIC TECHNOLOGY

Television, radio and sound recordings flash their messages electronically. Pioneer work on **electronic media** began in the late 1800s, but they are mostly a 20th-century development. Unlike print messages, television and radio messages disappear as soon as they are transmitted. Although it is true that messages can be stored on electronic disks and on tape and by other means, they usually reach listeners and viewers in a nonconcrete form. Television is especially distinctive because it engages several senses at once with sound, sight and movement.

The newest mass medium, the web, combines text, audio and visuals—both still and moving—in a global electronic network.

Technology Melds

study<u>preview</u> For more than 400 years the mass media were largely word-driven. The few visuals were carved woodcuts. An integration of photographic technology transformed the media in the late 1800s, changing dramatically how great numbers of people saw the world. Now digital technology is changing traditional media forms in new ways.

PRINT-VISUAL INTEGRATION

The chemical technology used in traditional photography was discovered almost 200 years ago. In 1727 experimenters realized that silver nitrate darkens when exposed to light. A hundred years later, in 1826, French scientist **Joseph Niépce** discovered he could create a fixed image by exposing a light-sensitive, silver-coated copper plate to iodine or mercury vapours. The discovery culminated centuries of experiments to capture and preserve an image. Although Niépce could create a photographic image, he didn't figure out how to make copies. Without copies, the images could not be communicated widely. The only visuals in the mass media of the time—books, magazines and newspapers—continued to be engraved line drawings, and there were not many of them. There was nothing photographic.

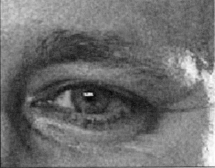

The breakthrough that melded the printing press with photographic technology came in 1878. **Frederic Ives** at Cornell University divided a photograph into a microscopic grid, each tiny square with a raised dot to register a separate tonal gray from a photograph; the bigger the dot, the more ink it would transfer to the paper and the darker the gray would be. The grid, cast into metal, was called a **halftone**. At the typical reading distance, 14

Inked Dots In the halftone process, invented by Frederic Ives in the 1870s, bigger dots transfer more ink to the printed page for dark parts of a halftone. Smaller dots are lighter. In some respects, the halftone grid is akin to computer-screen pixels with each dot, or pixel, contributing to the larger whole.

inches, the human eye couldn't make out the grid, but the eye could see the image created by the varying grays. Two years later, the New York *Daily Graphic*, a newspaper, adapted Ives's process to high-speed printing and published a halftone image. This was revolutionary. In numbers never before imagined, people could not only read about the world beyond their immediate horizon but also see it.

During this same period, work with motion pictures was coming together, largely at inventor Thomas Edison's laboratories in New Jersey. In 1891 Edison began producing movies. This compounded the impact of visuals as a component of the mass media. There is no better illustration of the impact of visuals than noting the way early moviegoers, in a wholly new experience, would duck in horror when a locomotive came at them on screen, no matter how jerky, scratchy and black-and-white the image was. **Visual literacy**, a sophistication in interpreting photographic images, would come slowly.

Frederic Ives

DIGITAL INTEGRATION

Digital technology was devised in the 1950s, first for telephone communication upgrades, but not until 1983, when recorded music was introduced on CDs, did the public perceive the significance. Suddenly, recorded music had unprecedented clarity. When **Marc Andreessen** introduced the **Netscape** internet browser in 1993, the number of people with home access to digitized media content swelled. Dazzled at new possibilities, entrepreneurs poured $1 trillion into an infrastructure to support the **dot-com** industry, named for the ".com" suffixes used by commercial sites on the internet.

The inflated dot-com bubble burst in 2000. In the crash, most upstart dot-com enterprises went belly up. Still, the potential of a new age of mass communication was obvious. Caught in the great dot-com implosion were book, magazine, newspaper, radio and television companies that already had begun moving content online. The most dramatic shift was in downloadable music, an area in which the technology of internet distribution so leapfrogged the existing recording industry infrastructure that some experts predicted that the industry would free-fall out of existence. The dive in CD sales leveled off, however, and by embracing the new technology, the recording industry began to recover.

Meanwhile, digitized technology is eclipsing the technological roots of the mass media. The legacy of Gutenberg, Ives, Edison and the others is no longer their technology but the business models and infrastructure that grew from their technology and shaped the corporate and culture icons of the modern mass media. Even when printing presses are gone, there will still be businesses whose products include the great novels, reference works, textbooks and news. Likewise, the digitization of broadcasting and Hollywood means merely a change in delivery of media messages.

■■ MSM and New Media

study<u>preview</u> **Mass media can be divided into mainstream and new media categories. The distinction is imperfect for purposes of neat, clean pigeonholing but can help to make some sense of changing ownership, content and audience patterns, and technology.**

MAINSTREAM MEDIA

The fragmentation of the mass media into new forms has blurred distinctions. There was a time when identifying a media product was relatively easy. Everybody knew what a newscast looked like. CBC and CTV offered the master models. Today the mass media comprise an oddball bevy of sources, from which massive percentages of people pick up their knowledge of the day's events. Young people opt more for Jon Stewart, Rick Mercer and David Letterman. Serious news junkies have CBC. Sports fans have their choice of TSN, Sportsnet or The Score.

The term **mainstream media**, sometimes abbreviated as MSM, has been coined to help navigate an evolving landscape. Although the term is rather elastic, it usually distinguishes traditional media forms and sources from new ones.

Ownership In terms of ownership, the major media companies—CanWest, Rogers, Corus and CTVglobemedia in Canada and Time Warner, Viacom, and Disney in the United States—are mainstream. In contrast are start-ups with novel business plans. Then there are anarchical arrays of products on the web, some of which are creating new moulds. **Blogs**, highly personalized and often quirky, definitely are not MSM. Satellite radio companies XM and Sirius, using technology in new ways, are hardly MSM with their potential to upend the radio industry as we've known it for three-quarters of a century.

Technology The term "MSM" also distinguishes technology-based platforms. Television and magazines are mainstream, clearly defined and traditional. Wi-Fi and other technology-wrought newcomers, definitely not MSM, sometimes are called **new media**.

NEW MEDIA

Innovation is not new to the mass media. The Beadle Brothers, who introduced dime novels before the Civil War, were the new media of their day, profoundly changing the U.S. book market. Today, innovations outside the mainstream include broad, sometimes fuzzy categories like alternative media, underground media and high-tech media.

Alternative Media Campus and community radio stations in Canada are geared to neighbourhood service with low-power transmitters and have made possible a level of interactivity with their audiences not possible for traditional stations that seek large audiences to draw advertising and pay the bills. These low-power stations, many staffed with volunteers, are alternative voices in the radio universe. There are currently almost 100 community radio stations in Canada, mostly in Quebec. There are an additional 53 campus stations across Canada. You probably have one on your campus.

Underground Media The generation-defined, antiestablishment press of the 1970s was one form of new media, living on in free-distribution weekly form. The emphasis is heavy on local, live entertainment, usually bar-centred; reformist social and political perspectives; outrageous, often ribald humour; and a high quotient of street vulgarities and sexual innuendo.

High-Tech Media Technology creates new possibilities. Think what iPods are doing to music stores and radio listenership. Cybercafes are giving way to Wi-Fi. For better or worse, internet bloggers have widened participation in public affairs journalism.

Economics of Mass Media

study<u>preview</u> **With few exceptions, the U.S. mass media are privately owned and must turn profits to stay in business. Except for books, sound recordings and movies, most media income is from advertising, with lesser amounts directly from media consumers. These economic realities are potent shapers of media content.**

ECONOMIC FOUNDATION

The mass media are expensive to set up and operate. The equipment and facilities require a major investment. Meeting the payroll requires a bankroll. Print media must buy paper by the ton. Broadcasters pay gigantic electricity bills to pump their messages through the ether.

To meet their expenses, the mass media sell their product in two ways. Either they derive their income from selling a product directly to mass audiences, as do the movie, record and book industries, or they derive their income from advertisers that place advertisements for mass audiences that the media provide, as do newspapers, magazines, radio and television. Newspapers and magazines are hybrids with both audience and advertising revenue streams. In short, the mass media operate in a capitalistic environment. With few exceptions they are in business to make money.

Advertising Revenue Advertisers pay the mass media for access to potential customers. From print media, advertisers buy space. From broadcasters they buy time.

Book publishers once relied solely on readers for revenue, but that has changed somewhat. Today, book publishers charge for film rights whenever Hollywood turns a book into a movie or a television program. Publishing houses now profit indirectly from the advertising revenue that television networks pull in from broadcasting movies.

Movies too have come to benefit from advertising. Until the 1950s, movies relied entirely on box-office receipts for profits, but moviemakers now calculate what profits they can realize not only from movie-house traffic but also from selling to television and the home video market. High-tech DVDs are replacing VHS tapes, increasing what was already the lion's share of movie producers' income. Today, moviemakers even pick up advertising directly by charging commercial companies to include their products in the scenes they shoot, a technique called product placement.

Circulation Revenue Although some advertising-supported mass media, such as network television, do not charge their audiences, others do. When income is derived from the audience, it's called **circulation** revenue. *Maclean's* may cost $4.95 at the corner store, but little if any of this newsrack charge ends up with Rogers, the parent company. Distribution is costly, and distributors all along the way take their cut. For some publications, however, subscription income makes the difference between profit and loss.

Direct audience payments have emerged in recent years in broadcasting. Cable and satellite subscribers pay a monthly fee. Audience support is the basis of subscription television such as commercial-free TMN or Mpix. Noncommercial broadcasting, including provincial broadcasters such as Saskatchewan's SCN and Ontario's TVO, rely heavily on viewer contributions.

Government Subsidies While the idea of government support for the mass media might seem to some a waste of public money, both the U.S. and Canadian governments support some form of public broadcasting. In Canada, the **Canadian Broadcasting Corporation (CBC)** is mandated by the government to promote Canadian culture to Canadians. Due to belt tightening since the 1990s, government support for public broadcasting seems to be dropping off, as both Canadian and U.S. government funds for public broadcasting have been cut drastically in the last few years. Despite the cutbacks, the CBC's yearly budget is approximately $1.3 billion or roughly $29 per Canadian.

Award-Winning Advertisements

To reach potential customers, advertisers buy space or time in mass media that can deliver audiences. It's the ads themselves, however, that drive home the sales pitch—but first they must get attention. Print ads that did this best in 2003 were "Rebirth" by the ad agency TBWA, Paris, for Sony PlayStation, honoured with the Grand Prix Award at the Cannes international advertising festival; and another by the agency Hopper Galton, for the Discovery Channel documentary *Age of Terror*, winner of the Cannes Golden Lion award.

Courtesy Discovery Networks Europe. Photo by Ernst Fischer.

TERRORISM HAS CHANGED THE WAY WE VIEW THE WORLD

'AGE OF TERROR' Global terrorism in context.
The first of four documentaries starts tonight at 9.30.

Discovery CHANNEL

ECONOMIC IMPERATIVE

Economics figures into which messages make it to print or to the airwaves. To realize their profit potential, the media that seek large audiences choose to deal with subjects of wide appeal and to present them in ways that attract great numbers of people. A subject interesting only to a small number of people does not make it into *Canadian Living* magazine. CTV drops programs that do not do well in the television ratings. This is a function of economics for those media that depend on advertising revenue to stay in business. The larger the audience, the more advertisers are willing to pay for time and space to pitch their goods and services.

Even media that seek narrow segments of the population need to reach as many people within those segments as possible to attract advertisers. Two Canadian digital channels, Edge TV and WTSN (Women's Television Sports Network), were not able to attract a large enough audience or advertisers. As a result, both stopped broadcasting in 2003.

UPSIDE AND DOWNSIDE

The drive to attract advertising can affect media messages in sinister ways. For example, the television station that overplays the ribbon-cutting ceremony at a new store is usually motivated more by a desire to please an advertiser than by a commitment to reporting news. The economic dependence of the mass media on advertising income gives considerable clout to advertisers, which may threaten to yank advertising out of a publication if a certain negative story appears. Such threats occur, though not frequently.

At a subtler level, lack of advertiser support can work against certain messages. During the 1950s, as racial injustice was emerging as an issue that would rip the nation apart a decade later, U.S. television avoided documentaries on the subject. No advertisers were interested.

DEMASSIFICATION

The idea that the mass audience is the largest number of people who can be assembled to hear mass messages is changing. Most media content today is aimed at narrow, albeit often still large, segments. This phenomenon is called **demassification**.

demassification ▪ Media focus on narrower audience segments.

This demassification process, the result of technological breakthroughs and economic pressures, is changing the mass media dramatically. Radio demassified early, in the 1950s, replacing formats designed to reach the largest possible audiences with formats aimed at sectors of audience. Magazines followed in the 1960s and the 1970s, and today most of the 12 000 consumer magazines in the United States cater only to the special interests of carefully targeted groups of readers. Today, with dozens of television program services via cable or satellite in most U.S. households, television also is going through demassification.

The effects of demassification are only beginning to emerge. At first, advertisers welcomed demassification because they could target their pitches to groups of their likeliest customers. The latest trend in demassification has advertisers producing their own media to carry their messages by mail to potential customers who, through computer sorting and other mechanisms, are more precisely targeted than magazines, newspapers, television and radio could ever do. The new **alternative media**, as they are called, include:

alternative media ▪ Emerging, narrowly focused advertising vehicles.

- Sponsored websites with games and other lures to attract return visits.
- Direct mail catalogues and flyers to selected addresses.
- Television commercials at the point of purchase, such as screens in grocery store shopping carts.
- Place-based media, such as magazines designed for distribution only in physicians' waiting rooms.
- Telemarketing, in which salespeople make their pitches by telephone to households determined by statistical profiles to be good potential customers.
- Email marketing, sometimes referred to as "spam."

If advertisers continue their shift to these and other alternative media, the revenue base of magazines, newspapers, radio and television will decline. Wholly new ways to structure the finances of these media will be necessary, probably with readers, listeners and viewers picking up the bill directly rather than indirectly by buying advertised products, which is the case today.

▗▖ Media Conglomeration

study**preview** Giant corporations with diverse interests have consolidated the mass media into relatively few hands. One result is that new talent and messengers have a harder time winning media attention.

MEDIA OWNERSHIP CONSOLIDATION

conglomeration ■ Combining of companies into larger companies.

The trend toward **conglomeration**, sometimes referred to by Canadian writers as "concentration of ownership," involves a process of mergers, acquisitions and buyouts that consolidates the ownership of the media into fewer and fewer companies. The deep pockets of a wealthy corporate parent can see a financially troubled media unit, such as a radio station, through a rough period, but there is a price. In time the corporate parent wants a financial return on its investment, and pressure builds on the station to generate more and more profit. This would not be so bad if the people running the radio station loved radio and had a sense of public service, but the process of conglomeration often doesn't work out that way. Parent corporations tend to replace media people with career-climbing, bottom-line managers whose motivation is looking good to their supervisors in faraway cities who are under serious pressure to increase profits. In radio, for example, management experts, not radio people, end up running the station, and the quality of media content suffers.

convergence ■ Early 21st-century model of media cross-ownership. Converged companies typically own print, broadcast, and internet holdings.

The other media trend is **convergence**. This term is used to describe media cross-ownership; some refer to it as "multi-platform media." It refers to the practice of one conglomerate with interests in publishing, broadcasting and the internet. Ted Rogers defined convergence in two different ways: "The computer and the TV set are coming together. You're putting together different media through one instrument. That's technological convergence. And then there's the convergence we might call marketing convergence, where you're packaging together people's needs in a way to make it easier for them. In Rogers's case it may be all the services—telephony, long distance, high speed internet, low speed internet, cable, paging, etc. . . ." It's interesting to note that Rogers made these comments in *Maclean's*—a magazine he owns.

It's the marketing opportunities that attracted CanWest Global Communications Corp. to purchase Alliance Atlantis, a Canadian production and distribution company. It also owned the specialty channels Showcase, History Television and Food Network Canada. When CanWest bought Alliance Atlantis in 2007, the Chief Executive for CanWest, Leonard Asper, explained the rationale for the purchase by saying the merging of the two companies offers new opportunities for cross-promotion of content. According to Asper, "by sharing

Media Convergence

The *CSI* franchise is co-produced and distributed by Canada's Alliance Atlantis. The success of the company in producing and distributing winning media content was one reason why it was purchased by CanWest Global in 2007.

programming across our multiple platforms, we see opportunities for ratings growth, which we expect will ultimately drive advertising revenue growth. Most importantly, in an increasingly competitive environment, this gives CanWest a great platform for growth in Canada." The merger gave CanWest greater control of the production, distribution and programming aspects of Canadian media content.

CONVERGENCE IN CANADA

How extensive is convergence in Canada? Consider the information on the six media rivals that have established themselves as the major players in Canada, as of 2007:

- CTVglobemedia is a multimedia company whose major holdings are CTV and *The Globe and Mail*. The company also owns The Comedy Network, CTV Newsnet, and Report on Business Television, and holds a majority interest in TSN. On the digital side, they also have interests in Discovery, Animal Planet, and the NHL Network. In 2006, they purchased CHUM, which included specialty channels MuchMusic, Bravo! and Book TV.

- CanWest Global is another Canadian media powerhouse with interests in print and television broadcasting. In addition to the Global Television Network, it owns 11 daily newspapers, including the *National Post*. It also owns several conventional and digital specialty channels, including TVtropolis, Deja View, and Lonestar. CanWest Global also has media holdings around the world, such as TV3 in Ireland and C4 in New Zealand. Online, it owns the Canada.com network, which allows surfers access to all the company's holdings. In 2007, it purchased Alliance Atlantis, pending CRTC approval.

- Quebecor owns TVA (the largest television network in Quebec), Sun Media (the second-largest Canadian newspaper group), and the Canoe.ca website. The company also has interests in 12 publishing houses and Vidéotron, a chain of video rental stores.

- Rogers Media has interests not only in cable TV distribution but also in programming with Sportsnet. In publishing, it owns *Maclean's*, *Chatelaine*, and *Flare* magazines. Its internet division includes Excite.ca, and Rogers owns radio and television stations in British Columbia, Alberta, Manitoba and Ontario. In addition to all of this, Rogers has a strong presence in wireless communication and owns the Toronto Blue Jays.

- Corus Entertainment's diverse interests include radio stations in western Canada, Ontario and Quebec. Its TV holdings include YTV, Teletoon, and CMT (Country Music Television). Corus is also involved in the production of content through Nelvana, a Canadian production company that produces such kids' fare as *Babar*, *Franklin* and *Beyblade*.

How significant is convergence? Dwayne Winseck, a journalism professor at Carleton University, says that while convergence and consolidation make sense from a business standpoint, "it is not good for journalism or democracy, where citizens continue to look to the media to reflect, extend and amplify public life."

While technologically possible, the economics of convergence has yet to be worked out. The effects of convergence are only now being felt. Even Matthew Fraser, media columnist for the *National Post*, writes, "convergence, it seems, will take some time to prove itself as a business model." The real impact of convergence for everyone—people working in the media, consumers, and media moguls—won't be felt for years. This opinion was confirmed by Kevin G. Wilson, who wrote in the Montreal *Gazette* that these large converged media companies "have yet to demonstrate that the patchwork of companies they have assembled are capable of generating any beneficial synergies." Even Leonard Asper, speaking after CanWest's purchase of Alliance Atlantis, felt it would be 2010 or 2011 before they would see any of the real effects of the merger.

DUBIOUS EFFECTS OF CONGLOMERATION

Critics such as **Ben Bagdikian** say that conglomeration affects the diversity of messages offered by the mass media. Speaking at the Madison Institute, Bagdikian portrayed conglomeration in bleak terms: "They are trying to buy control or market domination not just in one medium but in all the media. The aim is to control the entire process from an original manuscript or new series to its use in as many forms as possible. A magazine article owned by *the company* becomes a book owned by *the company*. That becomes a television program owned by *the company*, which then becomes a movie owned by *the company*. It is shown

media ONLINE

Converged Media Links to corporate profiles, annual reports, and detailed information for all of Canada's largest media companies.
www.ctvglobemedia.ca
www.canwestglobal.com
www.corusent.com
www.quebecor.com
www.rogers.com

Ben Bagdikian ■ Critic of media consolidation.

THE NEW MEDIA MONOPOLY

A COMPLETELY REVISED AND UPDATED EDITION WITH SEVEN NEW CHAPTERS

BEN H. BAGDIKIAN

"NO BOOK ON THE MEDIA HAS PROVED AS INFLUENTIAL TO OUR UNDERSTANDING OF THE DANGERS OF CORPORATE CONSOLIDATION TO DEMOCRACY AND THE MARKETPLACE OF IDEAS AS THE MEDIA MONOPOLY; THIS NEW EDITION BUILDS ON THAT WORK AND SURPASSES IT."—ERIC ALTERMAN, AUTHOR OF WHAT LIBERAL MEDIA

Media Critic Ben Bagdikian, called "one of the most considerate voices in journalism today," says that huge media companies are ever more profit-obsessed. Their corporate strategies, he says, often sacrifice high-quality content and public service on the altar of increasing profits. Bagdikian has amassed distressing data on conglomeration in his book *The New Media Monopoly*.

Ben Bagdikian

in theatres owned by *the company*, and the movie sound track is issued on a record label owned by *the company*, featuring the vocalist on the cover of one of *the company* magazines. It does not take an angel from heaven to tell us that *the company* will be less enthusiastic about outside ideas and production that it does not own, and more and more we will be dealing with closed circuits to control access to most of the public."

Nobody begrudges a company making a profit. The difficulty comes when the recycling displaces creative new entries in the mass media marketplace. NBC executive Don Ohlmeyer concedes that a vertically integrated network is disinclined "in even considering projects in which they don't own a financial interest." Independent Hollywood producers, who once competed to produce network shows, are finding themselves out of the loop. The result, says Gary Goldberg, creator of *Spin City* on ABC: "You see this blandness and similarity to the shows. Consumers are the ones who get hurt."

Quality Headquarters push subsidiaries to cut costs to increase profits, a trend that has devastated the quality of writing and editing. Fewer people do more work. At newspapers, for example, a reporter's story once went through several hands—editor, copy editor, headline writer, typesetter, proofreader. At every stage, the story could be improved. In today's streamlined newsrooms, proofreaders have been replaced by spell-check software, which not only introduces its own problems but also lacks the intelligence and judgment of a good proofer. The jobs of the reporter and the typesetter have been consolidated. In many newsrooms, so have the jobs of copy editors and headline writers.

Cross-Promotion Mega-media companies like NBC Universal are finding more ways to cross-promote their products. NBC tied teaser trailers to its Universal movies before launching its television reality series *The Apprentice* with Donald Trump.

Los Angeles *Times* reporter Tom Rosentiel, writing in the *Columbia Journalism Review*, tells how reporters, pressured to increase productivity, take shortcuts to generate more copy: "Newspapers and newsmagazine interviews today are increasingly conducted over the phone, with reporters assembling stories as much as reporting them, combining elements from electronic transcripts, data bases and television. A growing number of major events, reporters acknowledge, are covered without going to the scene. The stories . . . lack the advantage of serendipity or the authenticity of having been there."

In the book industry, media critic Jacob Weisberg has documented how several major publishers, including Simon & Schuster and Random House, have routinely eliminated important stages in the editing process to rush new titles to print and turn quicker profits. In a revealing article in the *New Republic*, Weisberg lists these results of the accelerated schedules:

- Factual errors, both major and minor, that in earlier times, he says, would have been caught by careful editing.
- Loose, flabby writing from deadline-pressured writers who once could rely on editors to tighten their work. Some books, Weisberg says, are running 100 pages longer than they should.

Sameness You can fly from the East to the West Coast on the same day and read the same Associated Press stories word for word. Newspaper publishers learned long ago that sharing stories via the AP could reduce costs. The resulting economics came at the cost of less diversity in content.

Cultural sociologists fret about the sameness. In recorded music, for example, major record companies often encourage artists to imitate what is already popular. The result is that derivative music squeezes original artists and material out of the marketplace or at least makes it more difficult for these artists to find an audience. Sociologists think that the movement of culture in new directions is slowed by this process.

Barry Diller, who created popular television programs at ABC and later at Fox, says that the problem is the profit-driven trend to recycle existing material for a quick buck. In a speech to magazine executives, Diller pointed out the short-sightedness of recycling: "Taking a movie like *Jurassic Park* and turning it into a video game, that's repackaging. Taking a bestseller and putting it on tape, that's repackaging. Taking magazine articles and slapping them on-line, word for word, that's repackaging." He then likened repackaging to strip mining: "After you've extracted the riches from the surface, there's nothing left."

Corporate Instability Conglomeration also has introduced instability. Profit-driven corporate parents are quick to sell subsidiaries that fall short of profit expectations even for a short term or just to raise cash. In 2003, AOL Time Warner realized that it had taken on more than it could handle and put Warner Books up for sale. However, bids were too low, and Time Warner reversed its decision. Typically in unstable situations, uncertainty diverts energy and focus from ongoing projects. Some projects are put on hold. There is uncertainty about new projects. Employees, with sudden career jitters, look for jobs elsewhere. None of this serves the media consumer well.

POSITIVE EFFECTS OF CONGLOMERATION

Is convergence good or bad? One industry insider says it's a good thing. Jack Tomik is the past president of CanWest Media Sales. He oversaw sales and marketing for all of CanWest's holdings in Canada. He was also involved in the branding of Global. Unlike critics such as Bagdikian, Tomik sees positive things coming out of convergence and conglomeration. He uses two television stations owned by CanWest to illustrate his point: CH-TV in Victoria and CH-TV in Hamilton are part of the same brand. They share the same logo and the same news intro. But that's where the sameness ends and the quality begins, according to Tomik: "I have a RAM truck. I know there are thousands of them out there, but this one's mine. I have ownership of it. It's the same with a brand. You can have the same look and the same feel, but the station is relevant to that community. It's about how you use a brand and how you service your viewers. It's less about the name and more about what it means to the viewers in that locale. If you're a person who lives on Vancouver Island, you have ownership of the CH brand. It's your local television station. People in Hamilton also have ownership of CH in that market." In 2007, CH-TV was rebranded as E!

There are other examples of the positive effects of convergence or conglomeration. At the end of World War II, the mainline book-publishing business was dominated by family-run publishing houses, all relatively small by today's standards. Although there are still hundreds of small publishers, consolidation has reduced the industry to six giants. Depending on whom you ask, the conglomeration has been a godsend or a disaster. If the effects are looked at positively, the book industry is financially stronger:

- Parent corporations have infused cash into their new subsidiaries, financing expensive initiatives that were not financially possible before, including multi-million-dollar deals with authors.
- Because parent corporations often own newspapers, magazines and broadcast companies, book publishers have ready partners for repackaging books in additional media forms.
- Many of the new parent corporations own book companies abroad, which helps to open up global markets.

In today's business climate, the lure of market dominance and profit, often on a global scale, keeps driving the concentration of media companies into fewer and fewer conglomerates.

CONGLOMERATION CRACKS

Pell-mell conglomeration among media companies might have peaked. Shareholders in Vivendi, the erstwhile French media conglomerate, discovered in 2002 that big isn't always better when, after rapid expansion, the empire verged on collapse. Vivendi sold off Universal to General Electric, which melded the movie studio into its NBC. Vivendi's Houghton Mifflin book-publishing unit was bought by an investor group. Other units went on the auction block too.

Although Vivendi's situation was extreme, it was not alone among troubled media giants that had grown through mergers and acquisitions in the 1980s and 1990s. The union of Time Warner and America Online (AOL) was heralded at the time for the anticipated synergies from which both partners would supposedly derive advantages. But Time Warner ended up trying to sell AOL when it not only underperformed on expectations but also yielded few offsetting benefits. Viacom executives have toyed with spinning off their fast-growth MTV Networks unit, which includes Nickelodeon and the BET network, rather than letting their future be hobbled by CBS and other Viacom entities whose growth has slowed.

Whether the era of giant conglomerates dominating the mass media is fading is not clear. It could be that recent sell-offs are fine-tuning adjustments of their holdings by parent companies, with subsidiaries merely moving from one mega corporate home to another. What is clear is that major media corporations are more cautious about finding acquisitions that are good fits than were Vivendi and Time Warner.

media TIMELINE

MASS COMMUNICATION THEORY

1916 Swiss linguist Ferdinand de Saussure explained that we communicate through signs.

1948 Claude Shannon and Warren Weaver developed a technical model for the study of communication.

1949 Wilbur Schramm defined mass communication as a field of study.

1954 Wilbur Schramm's *The Process and Effect of Mass Communication* was published.

1973 French philosopher Roland Barthes established the role of myth (or connotation) as a vehicle for cultural ideology through mass communication.

1974 The concentric circle model of communication was developed by Ray Hiebert, Donald Ungurait, and Thomas Bohn.

Wilbur Schramm

Wilbur Schramm

Some say Wilbur Schramm created mass communication as a hybrid academic discipline. There is no doubt that Schramm's two influential anthologies shaped two generations of mass comm scholars. His *Mass Communications*, compiled in 1949, combined seminal works in the social sciences with works by leading media practitioners and scholars. "It combined diversity of approach with unity of target," Schramm wrote in the introduction. That it did.

Enthusiastic word spread abroad, prompting requests from scholars for copies within a week of the book's release. Demand so outstripped supply that some used copies sold at triple the retail price. Schramm revised the trail-blazing book in 1959, again combining important work from anthropology, economics, political science, psychology and sociology with material from the growing field of mass communication studies.

In the meantime, in 1954, Schramm compiled another anthology, *The Process and Effect of Mass Communication*. Originally *P&E*, as it was known, was intended as a research methods primer for U.S. information agency employees, but as Schramm pulled material together, it was clear the book had a larger appeal. *P&E* was a worthy successor to the *Mass Communications* anthology, but both remained in demand, and the University of Illinois Press kept reprinting them.

Thirty-one years after *P&E*'s introduction, and with the second edition becoming outdated, the University of Illinois Press asked Schramm to do a third edition. His agenda full, Schramm declined but urged that someone do a revision. "The only obligation is to make a book that will be as good for the future as *P&E* was for its time," he said. Schramm was not being immodest. It was a fact, recognized everywhere, that *P&E* had become a mainstay in curricula of emerging mass communication departments throughout the country and abroad.

While Schramm's *Mass Communications* and *P&E* were major contributions, they were in a sense mere warm-ups. When Schramm died in 1987, his legacy included 30 books, 25 of them translated into other languages, and more than 120 research and scholarly papers and treatises. His personal papers, which his family holds, contain 18 722 pages.

The largest collection in his papers is 6158 pages for his final book, *The Story of Human Communications: Cave Painting to Microchip*, which was in press when he died. The scope of the book, the whole spectrum through history, seemed an appropriate ultimate work for Wilbur Schramm, who was then 80.

■ Types of Communication

study <u>preview</u> The communication in which the mass media engage is only one form of communication. One way to begin understanding the process of mass communication is to differentiate it from other forms of communication.

Intrapersonal Communication We engage in **intrapersonal communication** when we talk to ourselves to develop our thoughts and ideas. This intrapersonal communication precedes our speaking or acting.

Interpersonal Communication When people talk to each other, they are engaging in **interpersonal communication**. In its simplest form, interpersonal communication is between two people physically located in the same place. It can occur, however, if they are physically separated but emotionally connected, like lovers on cell phones.

The difference between the prefixes *intra-* and *inter-* is the key difference between intrapersonal and interpersonal communication. Just as *intra*mural athletic games are within a school, *intra*personal communication is within one's self. Just as *inter*collegiate games are between schools, *inter*personal communication is between individuals.

Wilbur Schramm A short biography of Wilbur Schramm.
www.bookrags.com/research/ schramm-wilbur-1907-1987- eci-03

Exploring Nonverbal Communication A scholarly look at communicating without words.
http://nonverbal.ucsc.edu

communication ■ Exchange of ideas, information.

intrapersonal communication ■ Talking to oneself.

interpersonal communication ■ Usually two people face to face.

Group Communication There comes a point when the number of people involved reduces the intimacy of the communication process. That's when the situation becomes **group communication**. A club meeting is an example. So is a speech to an audience in an auditorium.

group communication ■ More than two people; in person.

Group and Mass Communication When The Dixie Chicks go on stage, the members are engaging in group communication. A spontaneous relationship with their audience is part of their performance—their communication. In the recording studio, they have to adjust their performance intuitively to an audience they cannot see. This lack of immediate feedback is a characteristic of mass communication that separates it from interpersonal and group communication. It's also an example of what Canadian Marshall McLuhan meant when he said "the medium is the message."

mass communication ■ Many recipients; not face to face; a process.

Mass Communication Capable of reaching thousands, even millions, of people is **mass communication**, which is accomplished through a mass medium like television or newspapers. Mass communication can be defined as the process of using a mass medium to send messages to large audiences for the purpose of informing, entertaining or persuading.

In many respects, the process of mass communication and other communication forms is the same: Someone conceives a message, essentially an intrapersonal act. The message then is encoded into a common code, such as language. Then it's transmitted. Another person receives the message, decodes it and internalizes it. Internalizing a message is also an intrapersonal act.

In other respects, mass communication is distinctive. Crafting an effective message for thousands of people of diverse backgrounds and interests requires different skills than chatting with a friend across the table. Encoding the message is more complex because a device is always used—for example, a printing press, a camera or a recorder.

One aspect of mass communication that should not be a mystery is the spelling of the often-misused word *communication*. The word takes no "s" if you are using it to refer to a *process*. If you are referring to a communication as *a thing*, such as a letter, a movie, a telegram or a television program, rather than a process, the word is *communication* in singular form and *communications* in plural. When the term *mass communication* refers to a process, it is spelled without the "s."

■ Components of Mass Communication

study<u>preview</u> Mass communication is the process that mass communicators use to send their mass messages to mass audiences. They do this through the mass media. Think of these as the Five Ms: mass communicators, mass messages, mass media, mass communication and mass audience.

MASS COMMUNICATORS

The heart of mass communication is the people who produce the messages that are carried in the mass media. These people include journalists, scriptwriters, lyricists, television anchors, radio disc jockeys, public relations practitioners and advertising copywriters. The list could go on and on.

Mass communicators are unlike other communicators because they cannot see their audience. Kevin Newman knows that thousands of Canadians watch him every evening on *Global National*, but he cannot see them or hear their reactions. He receives no immediate feedback from his mass audience. This communicating with an unseen audience distinguishes mass communication from other forms of communication. Storytellers of yore told their stories face to face, and they could adjust their pacing and gestures and even their vocabulary according to how they sensed they were being received. Mass communicators don't have that advantage.

mass communicators ■ Message crafters.

MASS MESSAGES

A news item is a **mass message**, as are a movie, a novel, a recorded song and a billboard advertisement. The *message* is the most apparent part of our relationship to the mass media. It is for the messages that we pay attention to the media. We don't listen to the radio, for example, to marvel at the technology. We listen to hear the music or information.

mass message ■ What is communicated.

media ONLINE

Web Journal of Mass Communication Research Read some of the latest studies in the field.
www.scripps.ohiou.edu/wjmcr

MASS MEDIA

The **mass media** are the vehicles that carry messages. The primary mass media are books, magazines, newspapers, television, radio, sound recordings, movies and the web. Most theorists view media as neutral carriers of messages. The people who are experts at media include technicians who keep the presses running and who keep the television transmitters on the air. Media experts also are tinkerers and inventors who come up with technical improvements, such as compact discs, DVDs, satellite radio, and newspaper presses that can produce high-quality colour.

mass media ■ Vehicles that carry messages.

MASS COMMUNICATION

The process through which messages reach the audience via the mass media is called *mass communication*. This is a mysterious process about which we know far less than we should. Researchers and scholars have unraveled some of the mystery, but most of how it works remains a matter of wonderment. For example, why do people pay more attention to some messages than to others? How does one advertisement generate more sales than another? Is behaviour, including violent behaviour, triggered through the mass communication process? There is reason to believe that mass communication affects voting behaviour, but how does this work? Which is most correct—to say that people can be *controlled* by mass communication? Or *manipulated*? Or merely *influenced*? Nobody has the answer.

MASS AUDIENCES

The size and diversity of **mass audiences** add complexity to mass communication. Only indirectly do mass communicators learn whether their messages have been received. Mass communicators are never sure exactly of the size of audiences, let alone of the effect of their messages. Mass audiences are fickle. What attracts great attention one day may not the next. The challenge of trying to communicate to a mass audience is even more complex because people are tuning in and tuning out all the time, and when they are tuned in, it is with varying degrees of attentiveness.

mass audiences ■ Recipients of mass messages.

■ Communication Models

study<u>preview</u> **Scholars have devised models of the communication process in an attempt to understand how the process works. Like all models, these are simplifications and are imperfect. Even so, these models bring some illumination to the mysterious communication process.**

ROLE OF COMMUNICATION MODELS

Hobbyists build models of ships, planes, automobiles and all kinds of other things. These models help them see in different ways whatever they are modeling. Industrial engineers and scientists do the same thing, learning lessons from models before they actually build something to full scale. Communication models are similar. By creating a facsimile of the process, we hope to better understand the process.

A reality about models is that they are never perfect. This reality is especially true when the subject being modeled is complex. An architect, for example, may have a model of what the building will look like to passersby, but there also will be models of the building's heating system, traffic patterns and electrical, plumbing and ventilation systems. None of these models is complete or accurate in every detail, but all nonetheless are useful.

Communication models are like that. Different models illustrate different aspects of the process. The process itself is so complex that no single model can adequately cover it.

BASIC MODEL

Two Bell telephone engineers, **Claude Shannon** and **Warren Weaver**, laid out a **basic communication model** in 1948. They were working on advanced switching systems. The model, fundamentally a simple diagram, gave them a reference point for their work. That model has become a standard baseline for describing the communication process. The Shannon-Weaver model identifies six steps in the communication process (Figure 1.1):

- The human stimulation that results in a thought.
- The encoding of the thought into a message.
- The transmission of the message.
- The reception of the message.
- The decoding of the message by the recipient into a thought.
- The internalization of the message by the recipient.

NARRATIVE MODEL

Yale professor **Harold Lasswell**, an early mass communication theorist, developed a useful yet simple model that was all words—no diagram. Lasswell's **narrative model** poses four questions: Who says what? In which channel? To whom? With what effect?

You can easily apply the model. Pick any bylined story from the front page of a newspaper.

- Who says what? The newspaper reporter tells a story, often quoting someone who is especially knowledgeable on the subject.
- In which channel? In this case the story is told through the newspaper, a mass medium.
- To whom? The story is told to a newspaper reader.
- With what effect? The reader decides to vote for Candidate A or B, or perhaps readers just add the information to their reservoir of knowledge.

CONCENTRIC CIRCLE MODEL

The Shannon-Weaver model can be applied to all communication, but it misses some things that are unique to mass communication. In 1974, scholars Ray Hiebert, Donald Ungurait and **Thomas Bohn** presented an important new model—a series of concentric circles with the encoding source at the centre. One of the outer rings was the receiving audience. In between were several elements that are important in the mass communication process but less so in other communication processes.

The **concentric circle model** (Figure 1.2) is one of the most complete models for identifying elements in the mass communication process, but it misses many complexities. It takes only one message from its point of origin, but in reality thousands of messages are being issued simultaneously. Audiences receive many of these messages but not all of them, and the messages are received imperfectly. Feedback resonates back to communicators unevenly, often muted, often ill-based. Gatekeeping too is uneven. In short, there are so many variables that it is impossible to track what happens in any kind of comprehensive way.

Claude Shannon ■ Devised a basic communication model, with Warren Weaver.

Warren Weaver ■ Devised a basic communication model, with Claude Shannon.

basic communication model ■ Shows sender, encoding, transmission, decoding, receiver.

Harold Lasswell ■ Devised the narrative model.

narrative model ■ Describes process in words, not schematic.

Thomas Bohn ■ Devised the concentric circle model, with Ray Hiebert, Donald Ungurait.

concentric circle model ■ Useful radiating model of the mass communication process.

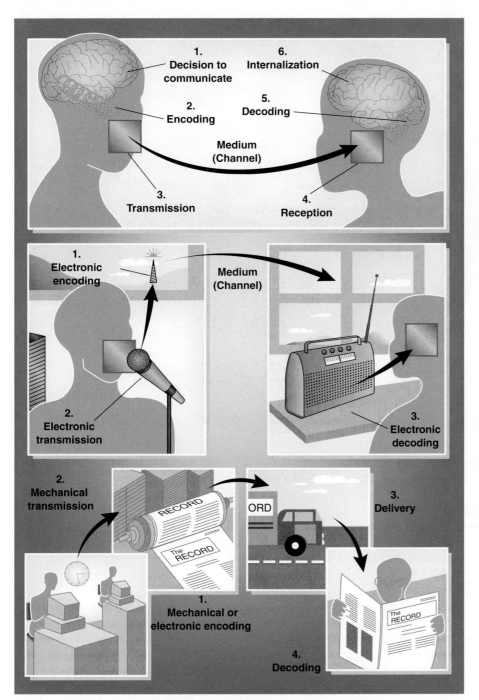

Figure 1.1 Fundamentals of the Process Claude Shannon and Warren Weaver reduced communication to fundamental elements in their classic model. Communication, they said, begins in the human mind. Messages are then encoded into language or gesture and transmitted. A recipient sees or hears the message and decodes from the language or other form in which it was transmitted and internalizes it. Those fundamental elements are also present in mass communication except that there is a double encoding and double decoding. In mass communication, not only does the communicator encode the message into language or another form to be communicated but also the message then is encoded technologically for transmission through a mass medium. In radio, for example, the words are encoded into electronic impulses. At the decoding site a piece of machinery—a radio receiver—decodes the impulses into words, which then are decoded again by the human recipient to internalize them. With print media the two steps in decoding are not as obvious because they are so integrated. One is reading the words. The other is converting those representations into concepts.

◾ Fundamentals in the Process

study<u>preview</u>　Most models for mass communication as well as other communication forms share some fundamental elements. The elements are sequential, beginning with whatever stimulates a person to want to communicate and continuing through encoding and transmission. To complete the communication process, the recipient of the message must decode and internalize it.

STIMULATION

Both the Shannon-Weaver model and the concentric circle model begin with a source who is stimulated to want to communicate a message. The **stimulation** can result from many things.

stimulation ◾ Stirs someone to communicate.

Figure 1.2 Concentric Circle Model The scholars who designed the concentric circle model suggest thinking of it as a pebble being dropped in still water. The ripples emanating outward from the communicator go through many barriers before reaching the audience or having any effect. The model takes note of feedback, media amplification, noise and distortion introduced by the media.

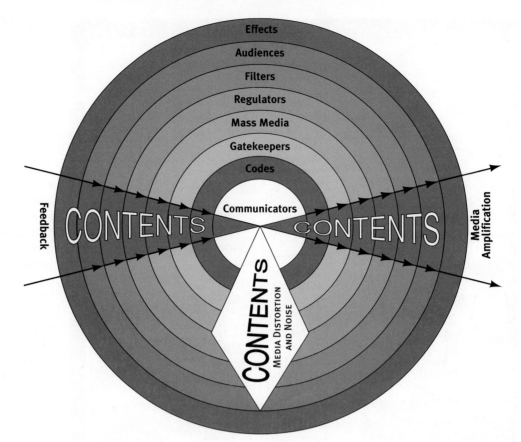

Emotions can be stimuli, as can something that is sensed. The stimulation can be as diverse as seeing a beautiful panorama, feeling a draft, hearing a child cry, or smelling dinner.

ENCODING

encoding ■ Putting something into symbols.

The second step is **encoding**. The source puts thoughts into symbols that can be understood by whoever is destined to receive the message. The symbols take many forms—for example, the written word, smoke signals or pictographs.

TRANSMISSION

transmission ■ Sending a message.

The message is the representation of the thought. In interpersonal communication the message is almost always delivered face to face. In mass communication, however, the message is encoded so that it is suitable for the equipment being used for **transmission**. Shannon and Weaver, being telephone engineers in the 1940s, offered the example of the sound pressure of a voice being changed into proportional electrical current for transmission over telephone lines. In technical terms, telephone lines were channels for Shannon and Weaver's messages. On a more conceptual basis the telephone lines were the *media*, in the same way as is the printed page or a broadcast signal.

DECODING

decoding ■ Translating a symbolic message.

The receiver picks up signals sent by the transmitter. In interpersonal communication the receiver is a person who hears the message, sees it, or both. An angry message encoded as a fist banging a table is heard and perhaps felt. An insulting message encoded as a puff of cigar smoke in the face is smelled. In mass communication, the first receiver of the message is not a person but the equipment that picks up and then reconstructs the message from the signal. This mechanical **decoding** is necessary so that the human receiver of the message can understand it. As Shannon and Weaver put it: "The receiver ordinarily performs the inverse operation that was done by the transmitter."

INTERNALIZATION

internalization ■ Making sense of a decoded message.

In mass communication a second kind of decoding occurs with the person who receives the message from the receiving equipment. This is an intrapersonal act, **internalizing** the message. For this second kind of decoding to work, the receiver must understand the communication form chosen by the source in encoding. Someone who reads only English will not be able to decode a message in Greek. Someone whose sensitivities are limited to punk rock will not understand Handel's *Water Music*. In other words, the source and the receiver must have enough in common for communication to occur. This common experience, which can be as simple as speaking the same tongue, is called **homophyly**. In mass communication the encoder must know the audience well enough to shape messages that can be decoded accurately and with the intended effect.

Internalization

A consumer who has seen and heard ads for a product retrieves those messages from memory to weigh whether or not to make a purchase. Those retrieved messages are considered with packaging messages, which are a form of mass communication.

▛ Players in the Process

study<u>preview</u> Two great influences on the mass communication process are gatekeepers and regulators. Gatekeepers are media people who influence messages. Regulators are nonmedia people who do the same.

GATEKEEPERS

The most visible people in the mass communication process are the communicators. These are the Christie Blatchfords, Sandie Rinaldos and Michael Landsbergs. But mass communication is not a solo endeavour. Dozens, sometimes hundreds, of individuals are involved. A Stephen King thriller passes through several editors before being published. When it's adapted as a screenplay, substantial modifications are made by many other individuals, all expert in the medium of the movie. Later, when it is adapted for television, experts in television as a mass medium make further changes, and so might the network program standards office. Any media person who can stop or alter a message en route to the audience is a **gatekeeper**. Newscast producers are gatekeepers because they decide what is aired and what is not. They make decisions about what to emphasize and what to deemphasize. Magazine and newspaper editors do the same, sorting through hundreds of stories to choose the relatively few that will fit in their publications.

Gatekeepers have tremendous responsibility because they shape the messages that reach us. They even decide which messages don't reach us. When gatekeepers make a mistake, both the communication process and the message suffer.

REGULATORS

Institutions that try to influence mass-communicated messages before they reach the audience are **regulators**. In Canada, broadcasters are regulated by the CRTC, while advertising is governed by the Competition Act, which is administered and enforced by Canada's Competition Bureau.

Regulators in the mass communication process also include **pressure groups**. In Canada, the Friends of Canadian Broadcasting lobbies for more Canadian content on our airwaves and more funding for Canadian TV and movies.

GATEKEEPER-REGULATOR HYBRIDS

There are also gatekeeper-regulator hybrids in the mass communication process. Media trade and professional organizations influence media content. Ethics codes of the Canadian Broadcast Standards Council (CBSC), a self-regulatory body made up of industry professionals, have had wide influence on what Canadians hear and see on our airwaves. Canadian advertisers have guidelines from Advertising Standards Canada, while the Radio-Television News Directors Association of Canada is a self-governing body for broadcast journalists.

Are organizations like the CBSC gatekeepers or regulators? Composed of media people, they would seem to be gatekeepers, but because they do not operate on the front line (that is, they do not make content decisions directly), they have many characteristics of regulators. They are, in fact, **gatekeeper-regulator hybrids** that institutionalize peer pressure among media people to influence media content.

■ Impediments to Communication

study<u>preview</u> **In any form of communication, the message sent isn't always the message received. Some models emphasize things that interfere with a message being communicated. Feedback can influence a communicator to change a message. Noise is transmission interference. Filters are recipient factors that interfere with an easy or correct reception of the message.**

NOISE

If speakers slur their words, the effectiveness of their messages is jeopardized. Slurring and other impediments in the communication process before the message reaches the audience are called **noise**. In mass communication, which is based on complex mechanical and electronic equipment, the opportunities for noise interference are countless because so many things can go wrong. Noise occurs in three forms: semantic noise, channel noise and environmental noise.

Semantic Noise Mass communicators themselves can interfere with the success of their own messages by sloppiness. This is called **semantic noise**. Sloppy wording is an example. Slurring is also a semantic impediment to communication.

Channel Noise When you're listening to an AM radio station and static interrupts the transmission, you are experiencing **channel noise**. Other forms of channel noise include smudged ink on a magazine page and a faulty microphone on a television anchor's lapel.

Environmental Noise An intrusion that occurs at the reception site is **environmental noise**. This would include a doorbell interrupting someone's reading of an article or noisy kids distracting a viewer from the six o'clock news, interfering with the decoding process.

Mass communicators go to special lengths to guard against noise interfering with their messages. For example, in encoding, broadcast scriptwriters avoid "s" sounds as much as possible because they can hiss gratingly if listeners are not tuned precisely to the frequency. Because words can be unintentionally dropped in typesetting, many newspaper reporters write that a verdict was "innocent" rather than "not guilty." It would be a serious matter if noise resulted in the deletion of "not."

To keep noise at a minimum, technicians strive to keep their equipment in top-notch condition. Even so, things can go wrong. Also, mass communicators cannot control noise that affects individual members of their audience—such as the siren of a passing fire truck, a migraine headache or the distraction of a pot boiling over on the stove. Clear expression, whether sharp writing in a magazine or clear pronunciation on the radio, can minimize such interference, but most noise is beyond the communicator's control.

Repetition is the mass communicator's best antidote against noise. If the message does not get through the first time, it is repeated. Rarely is an advertisement played only once. Radio newscasters repeat the same major news stories every hour, although they rehash the scripts so they will not bore people who heard the stories earlier.

FILTERS

Unwittingly, people who tune in to mass messages may themselves interfere with the success of the mass communication process. The causes of this interference are known as **filters**.

Informational Filters If someone doesn't understand the language or symbols a communicator uses, the communication process becomes flawed. It is a matter of lacking information to decipher a message, a deficiency called an **informational filter**. This filter can be partly the responsibility of the communicator, whose vocabulary may not be in tune with the audience's. More clearly, though, it is an audience deficiency.

Physical Filters When a receiver's mind is dimmed by fatigue, a **physical filter** is interfering with the mass communication process. A drunk person whose focus fades in and out also suffers from a physical filter. Mass communicators have little control over physical filters.

Psychological Filters If a receiver is a zealous animal rights activist, **psychological filters** likely will affect the reception of news on medical research involving animals. Being on a different wavelength can be a factor. Imagine two women friends going to the movie *Fatal Attraction* together. One woman is married and monogamous; the other is involved with a married man. Having different ideas about and experiences with marital fidelity, which is at the heart of the movie, the women hear the same words and see the same images but see two "different" movies.

The Lower case

Oozing corpses raising eyebrows
San Francisco Chronicle 5/27/05

Ted Waitt's grandmother guaranteed his loan to start Gateway.
The New York Times 5/20/05

Beautification process begins today for pope
Eau Claire (Wis.) Leader-Telegram 6/29/05

Legislators spurn domestic partners
Milwaukee Journal Sentinel 5/24/05

Some adults grow into blemishes
The Olympian (Olympia, Wash.) 7/9/05

Weather watchers keep eyes on the sky for meteorologists
Asheville (N.C.) Citizen-Times 7/15/05

Documentary filmmaker introduced students to AIDS
Sarasota Herald-Tribune 4/12/05

Former addict has resisted temptation to stay clean
Winona (Minn.) Daily News 6/5/05

Vicious animal law considered
The San Francisco Examiner 6/20/05

Police say finger in chili had been given to husband
Milwaukee Journal Sentinel 5/14/05

Endangered ape delivers child
The Indianapolis Star 7/14/05

CJR offers $25 for items published in The Lower case. Please send only original, unmutilated clippings suitable for reproduction, together with name and date of publication, and include your Social Security number for payment.

Semantic Noise

In every issue, the *Columbia Journalism Review* delights in reproducing bad headlines and other newspaper gaffes as a reminder to journalists to be more careful. These gaffes are examples of semantic noise, in which ambiguous wording and other poor word choices interfere with clear communication.

Reprinted from *Columbia Journalism Review*, September/October 2005. © 2005 by Columbia Journalism Review.

filters ▦ Receiver factor that impedes communication.

informational filter ▦ Receiver's knowledge limits impede deciphering symbols.

physical filter ▦ Receiver's alertness impedes deciphering symbols.

psychological filter ▦ Receiver's state of mind impedes deciphering symbols.

Results of Mass Communication

studypreview Because mass communication reaches such large audiences, the process amplifies messages like a giant megaphone. Things that are mass communicated stand a better chance of becoming important than things that are not. Mass communication has its greatest influence when it moves people to action.

AMPLIFICATION

The technology of the mass media gives mass communicators a megaphone. This is something other communicators don't have. A letter writer, for example, generally aims a message at one other person. A magazine writer, in contrast, has the printing press to reach thousands, if not millions, of readers. The printing press is a megaphone. Broadcasters have their transmission equipment. The equipment of the mass media allows the **amplification** of messages by mass communicators in ways that are not possible with interpersonal or even group communication.

Things that mass communicators choose to communicate have a status conferred on them. This is gatekeeping at work. Stories and views that don't survive the gatekeeping process have little chance of gaining widespread attention. Those that make it through the process have some inherent credibility just because they made it over so many hurdles.

Status conferral can work positively and negatively. For example, it appeared by 2004 that in going to war, the U.S. government had overreacted to suspicions that Iraq possessed weapons of mass destruction (WMD). News coverage of U.S. claims about the existence of the weapons, although sometimes sketchy, nonetheless fanned enthusiasm for war. Indeed, *WMD* became a household word that nobody would have recognized even a year earlier. Intensive media coverage of high-budget searches for the weapons after the war kept the issue on the front burner in the 2004 presidential campaigns and into the second term of the Bush Administration. In Canada, when Auditor General Sheila Fraser released her audit revealing that $100 million had been paid to various advertising agencies for little or no work, it raised the issue of how the Canadian government was wasting tax dollars. This information subsequently became an issue in the 2004 federal election.

Status conferral is not limited to the news media. Music can capture the public's imagination and keep an issue alive and even enlarge it. Crosby, Stills, Nash & Young's "Ohio" expressed some of the sentiments of those opposed to the war in Vietnam. In 2004, Green Day's "American Idiot" also spoke for those who had issues with the Bush Administration and the war in Iraq. Movies also have the power to move people and sustain issues. Sidney Poitier's movies of the 1960s, including *In the Heat of the Night*, helped to keep racial integration on the agenda. The 1988 movie *The Thin Blue Line* led to the exoneration of a death-row inmate.

FEEDBACK

Because mass communication is not the one-way street that the Shannon-Weaver model indicated, later theorists embellished the model by looping the process back on itself.

The recipient of a message, after decoding, responds. The original recipient then becomes the sender, encoding a response and sending it via a medium back to the original sender, who becomes the new destination and decodes the response. This reverse process is called **feedback**.

In interpersonal communication you know if your listener does not understand. If you hear "Uhh?" or see a puzzled look, you restate your point. In mass communication, feedback is delayed. It might be a week after an article is published before a reader's letter arrives in the newsroom. Because feedback is delayed and because there usually is not very much of it, precise expression in mass communication is especially important. There is little chance to restate the point immediately if the television viewer does not understand. A mass communicator cannot hear the "Uhh?"

An inherent disadvantage of mass communication when compared to interpersonal and group communication is delayed feedback. In interpersonal communication, feedback can be immediate: a quizzical arch of an eyebrow, a hand cupped around an ear to hear better, a fist in the face.

Technology has reduced delays in feedback, but feedback remains an impediment in mass communication that doesn't occur in face-to-face communication. Feedback left on a telephone answering machine, for example, will go unheard until somebody listens to the messages. Email can stack up. Faxes can go unread.

Despite feedback as a shortcoming in mass communication, there is an offsetting advantage: efficiency. Other forms of communication, including interpersonal and group,

---

amplification ■ Spreading a message.

status conferral ■ Credence that a topic or issue receives because of media attention.

feedback ■ Recipient's response to the sender.

media ONLINE

Kill Your Television Teacher and former journalist Ron Kaufman of Philadelphia, Pennsylvania, created this website as a guide to research on the effects of television viewing.
www.turnoffyourtv.com

may have the advantage of on-the-spot feedback, but they cannot reach the massive audience of mass communication.

EFFECTS

The whole point of communicating a message is to have an **effect**. A jokester wants to evoke at least a chuckle. A eulogist wants to inspire memories. A cheerleader wants to stir school spirit. The vast size of the mass communicator's audience compounds the potential for powerful effects. Because the potential effect is so great, we need to understand as much as possible about the process that leads to effects.

■ The Semiotic School

study<u>preview</u> The semiotic school of thought looks at the creation of meaning in communication. This approach to communication theory draws on the work of French cultural theorist Roland Barthes and the idea of signs, what they refer to, and the influence of culture on those references.

To understand what semiotics is and what signs are, it is important to see how the French semiotician **Roland Barthes** expanded on the work of Swiss linguist **Ferdinand de Saussure**. For de Saussure, the **sign** is composed of a signifier and a signified, as shown in the figure below.

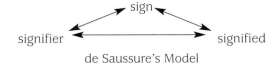
de Saussure's Model

For example, the words *maple leaf* constitute a sign. This sign is composed of a **signifier**, the letters in the words "m-a-p-l-e-l-e-a-f," and its **signified**, the mental concept of leaves from a maple tree that accompanies the words. Together, the signifier and signified form the sign of the "maple leaf." The relation between the signifier and its signified is entirely arbitrary. The words *maple leaf* denote what they do solely because of the linguistic conventions of the English language.

DENOTATION AND CONNOTATION

Barthes took this idea of signification one step further. For Barthes, there is not only one level of signification (the mental concept of "maple leaf"), but two: first- and second-order signified. He called these levels of meaning **denotation** and **connotation**, respectively. Barthes's conceptualization of signs is shown in the figure below.

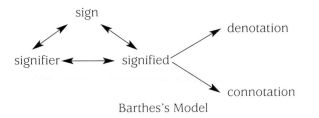
Barthes's Model

Denotation is the same as de Saussure's idea of the signified. It is what Barthes calls the simple, everyday meaning in the sign. For example, "maple leaf" signifies, or denotes, a type of leaf from a particular tree. But it can also mean many other things. There is a difference in its **connotation**, which deals with an additional level of meaning. For example, a maple leaf can signify Canada, or an NHL team, as well as a leaf from a maple tree. For Barthes, this second-level meaning is a vehicle for cultural ideology. It's only because we are Canadians that the maple leaf signifies Canada to

Symbols of Canadian Comedy

The Royal Canadian Air Farce has been poking fun at Canadian culture on the CBC since 1973.

C.S. Pierce ■ Classified signs into different categories.

icons ■ Signs that look like what they signify.

index ■ A sign that is connected to what it signifies.

symbol ■ A sign that has an arbitrary connection to what it signifies.

us. Hockey fans will interpret a maple leaf as signifying the team from Toronto. The multitude of meanings that can be associated with a sign is also arbitrary and depends largely on cultural conventions. That's what semiotics looks at—the many different types of meanings that are created by cultural influences.

By analyzing the relationship between denotation and connotation in popular culture, Barthes believed that hidden ideologies (or what he called "mythologies") could be uncovered. A myth can also be defined as a culture's belief system.

Not all signs are created equal. Communication theorist **C.S. Pierce** designed a way to classify signs according to their level of connotation or denotation. Pierce divided signs into three categories: **icons**, **indexes** and **symbols**.

- Icons are signs that resemble what they represent because the signifier looks like what is signified. For example, a map of Canada is an icon of Canada because it looks like the geographic layout of the country. A picture of Nickelback is an icon of the Canadian group. If the sign is denotative and not connotative, it is an icon.

- An index is directly related to what it represents. A popular example of an index is smoke, which usually indicates there is a fire. Smoke is an index of fire because smoke has a connection with fire. An index is a mixture of connotation and denotation. Smoke by itself is largely denotative, but it connotes something else: fire. A Mountie's hat is also an index; it not only is a hat but also has come to represent an RCMP officer. The late Prime Minister Pierre Trudeau always wore a rose in his lapel. The rose became an index of Trudeau.

- A symbol is a sign that is entirely connotative because there is no clear connection between the signifier and the signified. Words are symbolic of what they represent. The Canadian flag, the fleur-de-lis and the beaver are all Canadian symbols. They don't look like Canada, but they have all become symbolic of various aspects of our culture. Symbols develop their meaning over time through convention. The meaning given to symbols is arbitrary and can change.

CHAPTER 1 Wrap-Up

The mass media are the vehicles that carry messages to large audiences. These media—books, magazines, newspapers, records, movies, radio, television and the internet—are so pervasive in modern life that many people do not even notice their influence. Because of that influence, however, we should take time to understand the mass media so that we can better assess whether they are affecting us for better or worse.

Mass communication is a mysterious process. Many scholars have developed theories and models to help us understand some aspects of mass communication, but the process is so complex that we will never master it to the point of being able to predict reliably the outcome of the process. There are just too many variables. This does not mean, however, that the quest for understanding is pointless. The more we know about how mass communication works, the better mass communicators can use the process for good effects and the better media consumers can intelligently assess media messages before using them as a basis for action.

Questions for Review

1. How are the mass media pervasive in our everyday lives?
2. How do the mass media contribute to social consensus and also to divisiveness?
3. What are the three technologies on which the primary mass media are built?
4. What was the effect of the integration of printed mass media and photography? What was the effect of digitization?
5. What is the difference between mainstream media and new media?
6. How do media organizations make money to stay in business?
7. Define demassification, convergence and conglomeration. What effects are they having on the mass media?
8. How do gatekeepers and regulators influence media messages? How are they different from each other?
9. How do noise and filters impede mass communication?
10. Status conferral is one effect of mass media amplification. How does this work?
11. Why are Canadians McLuhan and Innis important figures in the study of media theory?
12. Explain the role of signs and semiotics in the communication process.

Questions for Critical Thinking

1. Which mass media best perform the informing purpose? The entertaining purpose? The persuading purpose? Which of these purposes is served by the advertising industry? By public relations?
2. The effectiveness of messages communicated through the mass media is shaped by the technical limitations of each medium. A limitation of radio is that it cannot accommodate pictures. Can you provide examples of content limitations of certain media? What are the audience limitations that are inherent in all mass media?
3. Some people are confused by the terms *cool media* and *hot media* because, in their experience, radios and television sets heat up and newspapers are always at room temperature. What is the other way of looking at hot and cool media?
4. Which is more important to the Canadian mass media: profits or doing social good?
5. Which mass media rely directly on consumer purchases for their economic survival? Advertising provides almost all the revenue for commercial radio and television stations, but indirectly consumer purchases are an important factor. In what way?

6. Do we need the CRTC to regulate broadcasting in the 21st century?
7. How is each of these types of communication—intrapersonal, interpersonal, group and mass—difficult to master?
8. All communication involves conceiving, encoding, transmitting, receiving and decoding, but some of these steps are more complicated for mass communication. Explain.
9. Different mass communication models offer different insights into the mass communication process. Describe the different perspectives of these models: Shannon-Weaver, concentric circle, narrative and semiotic.
10. From your own experience, describe a message that went awry as it moved through the mass communication process. Did the problem involve gatekeepers? Regulators? Noise? Filters?

Deepening Your media LITERACY

How do you become more media literate?

STEP 1 Think of your favourite commercial on television.

Dig Deeper

STEP 2 People who are media literate consume media with a critical eye. They evaluate sources, intended purposes, techniques and deeper meanings. Answer these questions about your favourite commercial:

1. Why is this ad effective? Write a list of the persuasion techniques it uses.
2. Who is the intended audience? Who will benefit from this commercial?
3. Does it sell more than a product?
4. Does it help you to identify any social values? Which ones? Does it glamorize a way of life? Does it bind a community?
5. How does it attempt to shape our perception of reality?
6. What is the elitist view of this TV ad? What is the populist view?
7. What signs (icons, indexes and symbols) are used in the ad?

What Do You Think?

STEP 3 Media are most powerful when they operate at an emotional level. Do you think most viewers would be able to separate fact from fantasy in this ad? Does your favourite commercial tell you anything truly useful about the product? Do you think it's fair for a commercial to attempt to shape our behaviour or attitudes?

Keeping Up to Date

Scholarly discussion on the communication process can be found in *Communication Yearbook*, published since 1977, and *Mass Communication Review Yearbook*, published since 1986.

The *Journal of Communication* and *The Canadian Journal of Communication* are quarterly scholarly publications.

For Further Learning

Ken Auletta. *Three Blind Mice: How the TV Networks Lost Their Way* (Random House, 1991).

Ben Bagdikian. *The Media Monopoly*, Fifth edition (Beacon, 1997).

Ben H. Bagdikian. "Special Issue: The Lords of the Global Village." *The Nation* 248 (June 12, 1989): 23, 805–20.

Erik Barnouw and others. *Conglomerates and the Media* (The New Press, 1998).

Roland Barthes. *Mythologies* (Paladin, 1973).

Paul Benedetti and Nancy DeHart. *On McLuhan: Forward Through the Rear View Mirror* (Prentice Hall, 1996).

Arthur Asa Berger. *Media USA: Process and Effect* (Longman, 1988).

"Broadcasters Must Be Canadian: Greenberg." *Broadcaster Magazine Alert* (March 9, 2004).

Andrew Cardozo. "Big Applications and the CRTC." *Broadcast Dialogue* (October 2006): 6.

Benjamin M. Compaine and Douglas Gomery. *Who Owns the Media? Competition and Concentration in the Mass Media Industry*, Third edition (Erlbaum, 2000).

CRTC. *Broadcast Policy Monitoring Report 2006*.

John Fiske. *Introduction to Communication Studies* (Routledge, 1990).

Matthew Fraser. "How Much Con in Convergence?" *National Post* (July 30, 2001).

Matthew Fraser. "Iron Law Brought Us Convergence, Heaven's Gate." *National Post* (June 11, 2001).

Thomas Friedman. *The World Is Flat: A Brief History of the 21st Century* (Farrar, Straus & Giroux, 2005).

Laurel Hyatt. "Letting the Genie out of the Bottle." *Broadcaster Magazine* (March 2001).

Harold Innis. *Empire and Communications* (Oxford Press, 1950).

Daphne Lavers. "deKerckhove." *Broadcast Dialogue* (September 1999).

Robert Lichter, Linda S. Richter and Stanley Rothman. *Watching America: What Television Tells Us about Our Lives* (Prentice Hall, 1991).

Stephen W. Littlejohn. *Theories of Human Communication*, Third edition (Wadsworth, 1989).

Michelle Martin. *Mainstream Models in Mass Communication Research from Communication and Mass Media: Culture, Domination and Opposition* (Prentice Hall Canada, 1997).

Eric McLuhan and Frank Zingrone. *Essential McLuhan* (Anansi, 1995).

Marshall McLuhan. *The Gutenberg Galaxy: The Making of Typographical Man* (University of Toronto Press, 1967).

Marshall McLuhan. *Understanding Media* (Signet, 1964).

Denis McQuail. *Mass Communication Theory* (Sage, 1987).

Denis McQuail and Sven Windahl. *Communication Models for the Study of Mass Communication* (Longman, 1981).

Mark Crispin Miller. "Can Viacom's Reporters Cover Viacom's Interests?" *Columbia Journalism Review* (November–December 1999): 48–50.

Mark Crispin Miller. "Free the Media." *Nation* (June 3, 1996): 9–28.

Glen O'Farrell. "What's to Become of Canadian Media?" *Broadcast Dialogue* (November 2006): 6.

Tara Perkins and Rick Westhead. "CanWest Buying Alliance." *Toronto Star* (January 11, 2007).

Sumner Redstone with Peter Knobler. *A Passion to Win* (Simon & Schuster, 2001).

Grant Robertson. "Biggest Risk in Alliance Deal is Global TV's Performance: Asper." *The Globe and Mail* (January 11, 2007).

Anthony Smith. *The Age of the Behemoths: The Globalization of Mass Media Firms* (Priority Press, 1991).

Susan Sontag. "One Culture and New Sensibility." *Against Interpretation* (Farrar, Straus & Giroux, 1966).

Bohdan Szuchewycz and Jeannette Sloniowski, eds. *Canadian Communications*, Second edition (Prentice Hall Canada, 2001).

Alexis S. Tan. *Mass Communication Theories and Research* (Macmillan, 1986).

James R. Taylor. "The Office of the Future: Weber and Innis Revisited." *Communications in Canadian Society*, Benjamin Singer, ed. (Addison-Wesley, 1983).

Kevin G. Wilson. "The Rise and Fall of Teleglobe." Montreal *Gazette* (May 18, 2002).

Samuel P. Winch. *Mapping the Cultural Space of Journalism: How Journalists Distinguish News from Entertainment* (Praeger, 1998).

Tony Wong. "Redrawing the Media Map." *Toronto Star* (July 13, 2006).

Antonia Zerbisias. "Ready or Not, CRTC Takes on Media Convergence." *Toronto Star* (April 14, 2001).

Wordless Society Ahead? No, says futurist George Gilder, not even the generation raised on MTV can communicate effectively without words. Visuals can enhance but not replace them, he says.

Print

Media in Theory

Wordless Society Ahead? Not Likely

Do newspapers and other word-based print media have a future? In a variation of Canadian Marshall McLuhan's "the medium is the message" theory, media seer **George Gilder** puts his money on word-based media over television, which relies on visuals to tell stories.

Futurist George Gilder says that not even the generation raised on MTV can communicate effectively without words. Visuals can enhance words, but not replace them, he says. As Gilder sees it, people who see the communication of the future as primarily video have missed the fact that video works better than words for only an extremely narrow range of messages: "Video is most effective in conveying shocks and sensations and appealing to prurient interests of large miscellaneous audiences. Images easily excel in blasting through to the glandular substances of the human community; there's nothing like a body naked or bloody or both to arrest the eye." However, human communication goes far beyond shock scenes and sensual appeals, he says, noting that people communicate mostly through words.

The printed product you receive on your doorstep every morning may seem like a technological dinosaur from Johannes Gutenberg's time. The fact, however, is that newspapers are well into the digital age. Reporters dip into digitized data for source material and write stories on computers. Editors edit stories and lay out pages electronically. It is in final production that old technology reigns, with multi-million-dollar presses that consume tons and tons of newsprint and barrels and barrels of ink. In delivery too, with minimum-wage carriers entrusted to get the product to readers, newspapers lag.

That is changing. In the vanguard of changing to electronic production, rather than printing, and to electronic delivery, rather than "carriers and the local newsstand," are newspapers ranging from modest circulation weeklies to major dailies. Some online editions offer only word-for-word versions of what is in the print editions or only selected

George Gilder ■ Claims wordless society not on the horizon and that words do much to anchor meaning.

stories, but some newspapers are repackaging stories to take advantage of opportunities that the internet offers. That includes online videos, podcasts and **blogs**. Still, true to their tradition, the online newspapers remain word-based. Visuals are a useful accoutrement but seldom the heart of the message.

media TIMELINE

THE PRINTED WORD

1844	George Brown founded *The Globe and Mail.*	**1967**	Jim Michaels founded the Los Angeles–based *Advocate*, the first gay newspaper.	**1998**	Conrad Black launched the *National Post.*
1905	*Busy Man's Magazine*, which would eventually be renamed *Maclean's*, was founded by John Baynes Maclean.	**1970**	Davey Committee examined Canadian newspapers.	**2001**	CanWest Global purchased the *National Post* from Conrad Black.
1955	Bohemian New York literati founded *The Village Voice.*	**1981**	Kent Commission: more investigation of Canadian newspaper ownership.	**2001**	Bell Globemedia, now known as CTVglobemedia, converged broadcasting and print.
1956	O'Leary Commission looked at magazine publishing in Canada.	**1996**	Magazines went online with Pathfinder and Time Warner. Others followed.		

■ Importance of Newspapers

studypreview Newspapers are the primary mass medium from which people receive news. In most cities no other news source comes close to the local newspaper's range and depth of coverage. This contributes to the popularity and influence of newspapers.

NEWSPAPER INDUSTRY DIMENSIONS

The newspaper industry dwarfs other news media by almost every measure. More than half of all adult Canadians read a newspaper every day. The data are staggering:

- 100 daily newspapers put out 4.7 million copies a day in Canada. Including weekend editions, 31 million daily newspapers are sold in Canada each week. In the United States there are 1570 daily newspapers.
- Weekly newspapers in Canada publish 12.8 million copies each week; 74 percent of Canadians read their local weekly newspaper.

Sources: The Canadian Newspaper Association's Canadian Daily Newspaper Circulation Data 2007 and Canadian Community Newspapers Association's Snapshot 2007.

Perhaps because television has stolen the glitz and romance that newspapers once had, the significance of newspapers is easy to miss. But the newspaper industry is large by every measure. In an article marveling at an issue of a newspaper as "the daily creation," *The Washington Post*'s Richard Harwood, writing about his own newspaper, said, "Roughly 11 000 people are involved in the production and distribution each day, enough bodies to fill all the billets of an Army light infantry division." Although Harwood stretched to include even the delivery boys and girls in his startling number, his point is valid: newspapers far outdistance other news media in the number of people who gather, edit and disseminate news.

There is no foreign ownership of Canadian newspapers. According to the Income Tax Act, a newspaper is Canadian if the type is set in Canada, it is printed in Canada, and it is published by Canadians.

CONTENT DIVERSITY AND DEPTH

In most communities, newspapers cover more news at greater depth than competing media. A metropolitan daily such as *The Vancouver Province* may carry hundreds of items—more than any British Columbia television or radio station and at greater length. Magazines, for example, offer more depth on selected stories, but the magazines are published relatively infrequently and run relatively few articles.

Newspapers have a rich mix of content—news, advice, comics, opinion, puzzles and data. It's all there to tap into at will. Some people go right for the stock market tables, others to sports or a favourite columnist. Unlike radio and television, you don't have to wait for what you want.

All this does not mean that the newspaper industry is not facing problems from competing media, new technology and ongoing lifestyle shifts. But to date, newspapers have reacted to change with surprising effectiveness. To offset television's inroads, newspapers have put new emphasis on being a visual medium and have shed their drab graphics for colour and aesthetics. To accommodate the work schedule transition in recent decades from factory jobs starting at 7 a.m. to service jobs starting at 9 a.m., newspapers

Cool Medium? The Canadian Newspaper Association's 1998 advertising campaign seems to be saying something about the value of reading a newspaper. Referring to the ideas of McLuhan discussed in Chapter 1, are newspapers a "hot" or "cool" medium?

media DATABANK

Who Owns What?

The landscape has changed dramatically since the Kent Commission in 1981. Most newspapers in Canada today are owned by one of fourteen different companies, many of them converged, multi-platform media companies. Newspapers are listed in terms of percent share of weekly circulation:

Owner	% Share of Weekly Circulation	Total Number of Papers
CanWest Publications	28%	13
Quebecor/Sun Media/Osprey	26%	37
Torstar	13.9%	4
Power Corporation	9.8%	7
CTVglobemedia	7.1%	1
FP CNLP	3.5%	2
Transcontinental	3.1%	11
Halifax-Herald News	2.2%	1
Brunswick News	2.1%	3
Glacier Canadian Newspapers	1.6%	9

In 2006, there were only four independently owned and operated newspapers in Canada: *L'Acadie Nouvelle* in Caraquet, *Le Devoir* in Montreal, *The Reminder* in Flin Flon, and the *Whitehorse Star*. Their combined circulation represented 0.9 percent of weekly newspaper circulation.

Source: Canadian Newspaper Association, Canadian Daily Newspaper Circulation Data 2007.

Top Newspapers in Canada

Here are the top newspapers in Canada, ranked by weekly circulation, according to the Canadian Newspaper Association.

Note the impact of conglomeration and convergence in terms of the ownership groups.

Newspaper	Weekly Circulation	Ownership Group
Toronto Star	3.3 million	Torstar
The Globe and Mail	2 million	CTVglobemedia
Le Journal de Montréal	1.9 million	Quebecor/Sun Media/Osprey
La Presse (Montreal)	1.5 million	Power Corporation
Toronto Sun	1.4 million	Quebecor/Sun Media
National Post	1.2 million	CanWest Publications
The Vancouver Sun	1 million	CanWest Publications
The Gazette (Montreal)	974 000	CanWest Publications
Ottawa Citizen	920 000	CanWest Publications
Winnipeg Free Press	886 000	FP CNLP

Source: Canadian Newspaper Association, Canadian Daily Newspaper Circulation Data 2007.

have emphasized morning editions, now that more people have a little extra time in the morning, and phased out afternoon editions, because more people are at work later in the day. Knowing that the days of ink-on-paper technology are limited, the newspaper industry is examining **electronic delivery** methods for the 21st century. For example, in 2006, the *Toronto Star* began publishing an electronic afternoon edition that was delivered right to the subscriber's email inbox.

Some problems are truly daunting, such as the aversion of many young people to newspapers. Also, chain ownership has raised fundamental questions about how well newspapers can do their work and still meet the profit expectations of distant shareholders.

electronic delivery ■ Sending news to readers' computer screens.

media ONLINE

Canadian Newspaper Association All the facts that are fit to print about Canadian daily newspapers.
www.cna-acj.ca

Canadian Community Newspapers Association (CCNA) The national voice for community newspapers in Canada.
www.ccna.ca

broadsheet ■ A newspaper format with full-size pages; typically six columns wide and 22 or 24 inches long.

■ Newspaper Products

study<u>preview</u> Over years, the size and formats of newspapers grew as printing technologies improved and paper and printing supplies became plentiful. In recent years the size has progressively shrunk as paper costs have risen and tastes have changed.

BROADSHEETS

The first modern newspapers in the penny press period (see Chapter 8) were pint size. Ben Day's pioneering *New York Sun* of 1833 was the size of a handbill. Canada's first newspaper, *The Halifax Gazette*, founded in 1752, was about half the size of a sheet of foolscap paper. As large, steam-powered presses were introduced and as paper supplies became plentiful, page sizes grew into what came to be called **broadsheets**. Some were so wide that pages had nine two-inch columns per page, although 50-inch paper, folded into 25-inch wide pages, became standard until the 1980s.

To save costs, the newspaper industry settled on a trimmer new size, called **SAU**, short for **standard advertising unit**, in the 1980s. The SAU format made it easier for big advertisers to place ads in multiple papers, all with standardized dimensions. The introduction of SAU precipitated an almost universal change to a six-column format, in contrast with the formerly dominant eight-column format. The saving in newsprint cost was significant. A downside was that there was less room for news and other content.

TABLOIDS

The word **tabloid** has a second-rate connotation from papers featuring eye-catching but tawdry headlines, but newspaper people use the word in a clinical sense for a half-size newspaper that is convenient to hold. Ironically, considering the association of the words *tabloid* and *sensationalism*, none of the papers in the sensationalistic yellow press period (which you will read about in Chapter 8) were tabloids—with the exception of a one-day experiment by New York publisher Joseph Pulitzer on the first day of the 20th century to illustrate the newspaper of the future.

In recent years, with continuing readership declines, especially among young adults, newspaper executives have discovered through surveys that people prefer compact newspapers. The world's leading newspaper designer, **Mario Garcia**, is traversing the country and the globe for comprehensive redesigns. Garcia's team is making two to three broadsheet-to-tabloid conversions a month. Laura Gordon, in charge of a Dallas *Morning News* tabloid variation called *Quick*, makes the point that tabloids are portable in ways that broadsheets aren't: "We call it the Taco Test, the idea that you can have a newspaper open and have a taco at Taco Bell without going into other people's space."

The tabloid format is gaining popularity in Canada. Many Canadian newspapers are changing formats. In 2006, 82 Canadian papers were broadsheets; the other 18 were tabloids. These 18 tabloids accounted for about a quarter of total newspaper circulation in Canada. This trend toward tabloids is expected to continue.

Still, the word *tabloid* carries a stigma. Garcia said in an interview with the trade journal *Editor & Publisher* that one of his newspaper publisher clients wanted a tabloid prototype designed but couldn't handle the word *tabloid*: "He told me, 'You can do a tabloid—but don't call it a tabloid.'" Alternatives include *compact newspaper* and *laptop newspaper*.

NEWSPAPER PRODUCTION

The Industrial Revolution, which began mechanizing manufacturing in the 1600s, reached the newspaper industry in the mid-1800s. Steam-powered presses became the rage. And paper, suddenly manufactured in rolls, not sheets, made press runs of thousands of copies an hour possible. Although the process has been refined, newspaper presses today, more than 150 years later, use the same technology—huge presses at central locations running hour after hour to get each day's issue into distribution. It's all labour intensive. Distribution itself is complex and also labour intensive—getting papers dropped at thousands of individual delivery points by, say, 6:30 a.m.

Digital printing may change all this. Instead of trucks fanning out at predawn from a single giant printing plant with hundreds of thousands of copies of the day's paper, imagine something like photocopiers scattered throughout the paper's circulation area. Each machine spits out only a few hundred copies.

Richard Rinehart, operations executive at the Raleigh, North Carolina, *News & Observer*, sees lots of untapped potential in digital printing beyond the economics. Digital printers at scattered sites, he says, can be programmed to augment their local

standard advertising unit (SAU) ■ A trimmer newspaper broadsheet format with standardized dimensions; introduced in the 1980s.

tabloid ■ A newspaper format with pages half the size of a broadsheet; typically five columns wide and 14 to 18 inches long; *tab* for short; not necessarily sensationalistic despite a connotation the term has acquired.

Mario Garcia ■ Newspaper design expert who champions tabloid formats.

Mario Garcia On the cutting edge of newspaper design. He has transformed many newspapers from broadsheets to tabloids. He believes that the layout and design of the newspaper, like the content itself, should "tell a story."

ONLINE

Garcia Media The design firm started by Mario Garcia to help clients develop effective visual tools and communication strategies.
www.mariogarcia.com

Q and A with Mario Garcia Online interview with Garcia from The Poynter Institute.
www.poynter.org/content/ content_view.asp?id=48680

Le Soleil This Quebec City newspaper converted to the tabloid format in 2006.
www.cyberpresse.ca/section/ CPSOLEIL

Smudgy Heritage The word *tabloid* is correct for any newspaper with half-size pages, but it picked up an unseemly connotation. The **New York** *Daily News*, launched in 1919, dwelled on sensational stories and flashy headlines that shouted for street sales—as with its exclusive, unauthorized photo of Ruth Snyder, the first woman executed in U.S. history. The word *tabloid* was sullied by papers like the *Daily News* that focused on the bizarre and sensational.

New York *Daily News* ■ Founded 1919; its focus on the bizarre defined *tabloid* in public thinking as a word for sensationalism.

news with subscriber-chosen add-ons—regional grocery ads included for 617 Maple Street, sports news and comics for 618, financial news and classified ads for 619, and so on.

■ Newspaper Chain Ownership

study preview Through the 20th century, newspapers have been incredibly profitable, which, for better or worse, encouraged chain ownership. Today, chains own most North American newspapers.

TREND TOWARD CHAINS

William Randolph Hearst ■ Chain owner who dictated contents of all his newspapers.

newspaper chain ■ Company that owns several newspapers.

Reasoning that he could multiply profits by owning multiple newspapers, **William Randolph Hearst** put together a chain of big-city newspapers in the late 1880s. Although Hearst's chain was not the first, his empire became the model in the public's mind for much that was both good and bad about **newspaper chains**. Like other chains, Hearst's expanded into magazines, radio and television. The trend toward chain ownership continues, and today 160 chains own four of every five dailies in the United States. Chain ownership is also coming to dominate weeklies, which had long been a bastion of independent ownership.

Is chain ownership good? The question raised in Hearst's time was whether diverse points of view were as likely to get into print if ownership were concentrated in fewer and fewer hands. While **local autonomy** is consistent with North American journalistic values, a corporate focus on profits raises a dark new question: Are chains so myopic about profits that they forget good journalism? These are the types of questions that were the basis of two royal commissions in Canada.

In 1970, a special Senate committee on the status of the mass media in Canada, headed by Senator Keith Davey, released its report about the state of Canadian newspapers. Part of the rationale for the **Davey Committee** was the growing concern regarding concentration of newspaper ownership in Canada. In its report, the committee noted that "the media is passing into fewer and fewer hands, and that the experts agree that this trend is likely to continue." The commission made many recommendations, including the creation of a press ownership review board, which would monitor ownership changes and proposed mergers. The government's reaction was lukewarm at best, and such a board was never created.

A little more than 10 years later, the situation had not improved. Ownership of Canada's newspapers, particularly in Quebec, had fallen into fewer and fewer hands. The 1981 **Kent Commission** into newspaper ownership in Canada, headed by Tom Kent, came about following an incident that was too convenient to be coincidental. On the same day in August 1980, the *Ottawa Journal*, which had been publishing for 94 years and was owned by the Thomson chain, and *The Winnipeg Tribune*, 90 years old and owned by the Southam chain, closed their doors and ceased publication, leaving Winnipeg and Ottawa as one-newspaper towns. Each city still had a daily newspaper—the *Winnipeg Free Press*, owned by Thomson, and the *Ottawa Citizen*, owned by Southam. Within a week, the Kent Commission was born. Its mandate was to look into the state of newspapers in Canada and to propose a course of action for the government. In a multi-volume report, the Kent Commission made the following recommendations:

- No owner could control more than 5 percent of Canada's total newspaper circulation.
- No owner could own more than five newspapers.
- No owner could own more than one newspaper within a radius of 500 kilometres.
- To stop the trend toward chains, several, including Thomson, would be ordered to "divest" themselves of some of their newspaper holdings.

As was the case with the Davey Committee, the Kent Commission's suggestions died before becoming law. In 1984, while the Newspaper Act was being debated in Parliament, an election was held. When Parliament reconvened, the bill died.

Why all the concern about **concentration of ownership** in Canada? After all, in a capitalist society, one should be able to venture into any enterprise one wants to. While the players have changed in the last 25 years, both Davey and Kent leave us with the following points to think about when discussing the effects of concentration of ownership in a democracy:

- News is a product that needs a variety of voices to be produced. Without this variety, newspapers "become more alike, less individual, less distinctive."
- As newspapers become part of a large corporation, the people who run them likely won't have a background in journalism but will have a background in business or management. Given this scenario, profits become more important than editorial content and the news-gathering and writing process.
- Too much power in too few hands contradicts the role of the press in a democracy. Concentration of press ownership in Canada may mean power without accountability.
- While it's true that newspapers face competition from radio and television, it's newspapers that have traditionally been used to record history.

The last word on this issue goes to David Estok of the University of Western Ontario: "The Kent Commission now seems quaint and old-fashioned, resembling a different time and place. But the issues it raised about media ownership, diversity of opinion and political and cultural control of our communications industries are as relevant as ever."

local autonomy ■
Independence from chain headquarters.

Davey Committee ■ 1970 Royal Commission into media ownership.

Kent Commission ■ 1981 Royal Commission into newspaper ownership.

concentration of ownership ■
Conglomeration and convergence of media into fewer and fewer hands.

ONLINE

The Globe and Mail Canada's oldest national daily newspaper.
www.theglobeandmail.com

National Post Browse the latest news or subscribe to the paper's online edition. You can also access CanWest's TV and radio properties through this website.
www.nationalpost.com

National Post

In 1998, Canada had its first "National" newspaper when Conrad Black launched the *National Post*. In 2000, Black sold 50 percent of the *Post* to CanWest Global. In 2001, he sold the paper outright to CanWest.

▪ National Dailies

study<u>preview</u> **Although a nation of mostly local newspapers, Canada has two firmly established dailies.**

THE GLOBE AND MAIL

The Globe and Mail was founded in 1844 in Toronto by Scottish immigrant **George Brown**. Although labeled as politically conservative, Brown was also somewhat of a publishing innovator. He expanded the format of the paper, and *The Globe* began publishing daily in 1853. He also published a weekly edition for readers living outside of Toronto. He was rewarded for his efforts; by 1872, circulation had almost tripled to 45 000. By the end of the 19th century, it had increased to 80 000. *The Globe* merged with the *Mail and Empire* in November 1936.

In 2001, *The Globe and Mail* became part of the multimedia platform owned by Bell Globemedia, now known as CTVglobemedia. It's still a widely read and respected paper, with circulation of about 2 million weekly.

NATIONAL POST

For a relatively new newspaper, the *National Post* has quite a history. In 1998, **Conrad Black** sold his interest in *The Hamilton Spectator*, *The Record* (Kitchener-Waterloo), the *Guelph Daily Mercury*, and the *Cambridge Reporter* to Sun Media for 80 percent of the *Financial Post* and $150 million. Then, on October 27, 1998, Black's Southam entered the national newspaper sweepstakes when it began publishing the *National Post*.

Then, in the summer of 2000, Canadian media history was made when CanWest Global, a broadcast media giant, paid $3.5 billion for a 50 percent interest in the *National Post*, plus 13 Canadian daily newspapers and 136 smaller newspapers. In the fall of 2001, CanWest purchased the remaining 50 percent interest in the *National Post*.

This new paper became a notable presence in the lucrative southern Ontario market. For example, in Toronto, it competes with *The Globe and Mail*, the *Toronto Star*, and the *Toronto Sun*. Although only in existence a few short years, the *National Post* has clearly established itself as an industry leader.

▪ Hometown Newspapers

study<u>preview</u> **Most newspapers in Canada are considered the voice of their hometown area, covering local news and carrying local advertising. Big-city dailies are the most visible hometown newspapers, but medium-sized and small dailies have made significant strides in quality in recent decades and have eroded the metro newspapers' outlying circulation.**

METROPOLITAN DAILIES

In every region of the United States there is a newspaper whose name is a household word. These are metropolitan dailies with extensive regional circulation. Vancouver, Montreal and Toronto feature strong metropolitan newspapers. The following is a snapshot of Canada's leading metropolitan daily, the *Toronto Star*.

Toronto Star The *Toronto Star* not only is a metropolitan daily, but also has the largest daily circulation of any newspaper in Canada: over 400 000 copies. The Star was founded in 1892 as the Toronto Star and Publishing Company. Its founding fathers were 21 printers who were on strike (or locked out, depending on who you believe). They had worked for the Toronto News until a new typesetting process threatened their jobs. Within days of losing their jobs, they borrowed old printing presses and, with each printer assuming the roles of writer, reporter, ad salesperson, and proofreader, the first Evening Star was printed on November 3, 1892. The masthead proclaimed "A paper for the people." It's this incident that gave rise to the Star being identified as a "liberal" paper for many years.

Today, the *Star* employs more than 4500 people, including almost 400 people in its newsroom. The *Star*'s press centre produces over 3.2 million newspapers per week, and the *Saturday Star* has a circulation of over 600 000. The *Star* is owned by Torstar Corporation. The company also owns the Metroland Media Group, which includes 105 weekly newspapers and a handful of hometown dailies. They also publish Harlequin Romances.

HOMETOWN DAILIES

With their aggressive reporting on national and regional issues, the metro dailies receive more attention than smaller dailies, but most people read **hometown dailies**. By and large, these locally oriented newspapers, most of them chain-owned, have been incredibly profitable while making significant journalistic progress since World War II.

hometown daily ■ Edited primarily for readers in a defined region.

Fifty years ago, people in small towns generally bought both a metropolitan daily and a local newspaper. Hometown dailies were thin, and coverage was hardly comprehensive. Editorial pages tended to offer only a single perspective. Readers had few alternative sources of information. Since then, these smaller dailies have hired better-prepared journalists, acquired new technology and strengthened their local advertising base.

■ Challenges for Daily Newspapers

study preview Even with fairly stable circulation figures, daily newspapers face major challenges. Traditional advertising revenue streams are in transition too. New efficiencies are being realized through shared newsrooms and production facilities and other cost-cutting measures. Is the future of newspapers on the internet? Stay tuned.

CIRCULATION

Except during the Depression of the 1930s, when almost every sector of the economy suffered, newspapers were among the most consistently profitable businesses of the 20th century. Even with circulation down slightly, the industry has continued to be profitable. Most of the major Canadian chains, which own almost every daily, have reported operating profits in the 13 to 15 percent range over the last few years.

Newspaper companies will survive. They are well positioned to dominate the future of news because, in almost every community, they have the largest, most sophisticated staffs for gathering and telling local news. Even with the benefits of convergence within a media company, that resource is unmatched by even the largest television or other news operation.

How can daily newspapers still be making so much money? In part, it's through cost cutting. Technology has facilitated production cost reductions. In many cases, reporting staffs have been trimmed—at the expense of old standards of news coverage. A monopoly on local readers has allowed local newspapers to adjust advertising rates upward without significant merchant resistance. Also, many papers have gone to narrower pages, which reduce paper costs, a significant raw-material expense. Some papers have compounded newsprint savings by printing fewer pages. But there is a significant downside: less room for news.

ADVERTISING

Retail consolidations have hurt newspaper advertising. Major competing department stores and groceries once were a mainstay of revenue for newspapers. Today this is less so. Chains have bought out their competitors, each acquisition eliminating a major local advertiser.

Also, national advertisers don't look much to newspapers anymore. Statistics Canada reports that national advertising accounts for only about a third of a newspaper's ad revenue; the rest are local ads. Magazines and network television deliver larger and more targeted audiences more cost effectively than general-interest hometown newspapers can. The exception has been **free-standing inserts**, the preprinted, usually slick paper advertising circulars that are tucked into newspapers. These FSIs, as they're called, are about all that's left of national advertising for newspapers. FSIs aren't nearly as lucrative as in-the-regular-paper ads. Newspapers have had to keep their FSI rates low, lest these advertisers find distribution less expensive through the postal system.

MARKETING DATABASES

As a condition for access to their news websites, a growing number of newspapers is requiring visitors to register. Access is free in exchange for personal information that enables the paper to create a single customer database for print subscribers and email subscribers as well as internet visitors for news and classifieds with breakdowns to identify personal interests.

Aside from selling almanacs and occasional other news-related products, newspapers have kept to their primary business: news. This may need to change if advertising revenue for newspapers declines, as expected, with the already occurring emergence of more competing outlets for advertisers to reach potential customers. As media visionary **Barry Diller** sees it, all of the major mass media will go to direct marketing of their own inventories of consumer products to create revenue streams to replace the loss of traditional advertising. Diller's own operations, including the Home Shopping Network on television, as well as his USA Television Network, already are a prototype for other media, including newspapers, to enter the business of retailing products alongside their traditional news and entertainment content.

INTERNET TRANSITION

Newspapers got into the ground floor of the internet in the 1990s by establishing news sites. Gradually, newspapers have sold online space as an add-on feature to advertisers that already buy space in the paper. Whether these sites will be a significant avenue for newspaper companies in the future is an open question, especially considering that the cost of admission to create a website is low and that lots of other companies, including local television and radio stations, have established competing sites.

▛ Weekly Newspapers

study<u>preview</u> **Many community weekly newspapers, especially in fast-growing suburbs, are thriving.**

COMMUNITY WEEKLIES

Weekly newspapers are making strong circulation gains, especially in suburban communities, and some have moved into publishing twice a week. In all, over 600 weekly newspapers are published in Canada, with total weekly circulation approaching 12 million, the majority of them tabloids.

To the discomfort of metro dailies, many advertisers are following their customers to the suburban weeklies. Advertisers have found that they can buy space in weeklies for less and reach their likeliest customers. Ralph Ingersoll, whose weeklies give fits to the daily Long Island *Newsday* in New York, explained it this way in an interview with *Forbes*: "If you're an automobile dealer on Long Island, you can pay, say, $14 000 for a tabloid page in *Newsday*, most of which is wasted because the people that get it will never buy a car in your neck of the woods, or you can go into one of the weekender publications and pay a few hundred dollars and reach just the people likely to drive over to your shop."

Some weeklies, particularly those in upscale suburbs, offer sophisticated coverage of community issues. Others feature a homey mix of reports on social events such as who visited whom for Sunday dinner. The success of these weeklies sometimes is

called **telephone book journalism** because of the emphasis on names, the somewhat over-drawn theory being that people buy papers to see their names in print. Weeklies have in common that they cover their communities with a detail that metro dailies have neither staff nor space to match. There is no alternative to keeping up with local news.

RURAL WEEKLIES

Rural weeklies generally have fallen on rough times. Part of their problem is the diminishing significance of agriculture in the national economy and the continuing depopulation of rural North America. In communities that remain retail centres, rural weeklies can maintain a strong advertising base. However, the Main Street of many small towns has declined as improved roads and the construction of major retail stores like Wal-Mart draw customers from miles away. In earlier days those customers patronized hometown retailers, who placed significant advertising in hometown weeklies. Today many of these Main Street retailers, unable to compete with giant discount stores, are out of business.

SHOPPERS

Free-distribution papers that carry only advertisements have become increasingly important as vehicles for classified advertising. In recent years, **shoppers** have attracted display advertising that earlier would have gone to regular newspapers. Almost all shoppers undercut daily newspapers on advertising rates.

By definition, shoppers are strictly advertising sheets, but beginning in the 1970s some shoppers added editorial content, usually material that came free over the transom, such as publicity items and occasional self-serving columns from legislators. Some shoppers have hired staff members to compile calendars and provide a modicum of news coverage. Most of these papers, however, remain ad sheets with little that is journalistic. Their news-gathering efforts and expenses are minuscule compared with those of a daily newspaper.

■ Alternative and Minority Newspapers

studypreview Most newspapers attempt broad coverage for a broad audience, but more specialized newspapers are important in the lives of many people. These include counterculture, ethnic and black newspapers, many of which are expanding and prospering today.

COUNTERCULTURE NEWSPAPERS

A group of friends in the Greenwich Village neighbourhood of New York, including novelist **Norman Mailer** and **Don Wolf**, decided to start a newspaper. Thus in 1955 was born *The Village Voice*, a free-wheeling weekly that became a prototype for a 1960s phenomenon called the **alternative press** that has continued to thrive.

In its early days, *The Village Voice* was a haven for bohemian writers of diverse competence who volunteered occasional pieces, some lengthy, many rambling. Many articles purported to be investigative examinations of hypocritical people and institutions, but, as *The Voice* veteran Nat Hentoff has noted, nobody ever bothered to check "noisome facts," let alone the "self-righteous author." *The Voice* seemed to scorn traditional, detached, neutral reporting. Despite its flaws, the amateurism gave *The Voice* a charm, and it picked up readership.

The Voice today is more polished and journalistically serious. The characteristics that made it distinctive in its early history, and that were picked up by other **counterculture newspapers**, include:

- Antiestablishment political coverage with a strong antimilitary slant.
- Cultural coverage that emphasizes contrarian music and art and exalts sex and drugs.
- Interpretive coverage focusing more on issues of special concern to alienated young people.
- Extensive entertainment coverage and listings of events.

telephone book journalism ■ Emphasizing readers' names in articles.

shopper ■ An advertising paper without news.

ONLINE

The Village Voice This alternative newsweekly has won numerous awards, including three Pulitzer Prizes. It maintains its no-holds-barred philosophy on which it was founded 50 years ago.
www.villagevoice.com

The Coast Check out Halifax's weekly alternative newspaper.
www.thecoast.ca

The Georgia Straight Surf over to Vancouver's weekly newspaper to see how it covers news and entertainment.
www.straight.com

Norman Mailer ■ Among the founders of *The Village Voice*.

Don Wolf ■ Among the founders of *The Village Voice*.

The Village Voice ■ Model for contemporary alternative press.

alternative press ■ Generally antiestablishment publication for a young alienated audience.

counterculture newspapers ■ Challenge, defy mainstream values.

- A conversational, sometimes crude style that includes four-letter words and gratuitous expletives for their shock value.
- Extensive personal ads for dating and sex liaisons.

ETHNIC NEWSPAPERS

Canada has been officially multicultural since 1971. The Canadian Multiculturalism Act passed in 1988 supports the idea that Canada is pluralist and that all cultures should be encouraged to maintain their heritage and traditions while living in Canada. Given this status as a multicultural country, it's not surprising that Canada is host to scores of ethnic newspapers. The Media Awareness Network says there are more than 250 ethnic newspapers in Canada serving more than 40 cultures. Seven of these ethnic newspapers are dailies.

The first ethnic newspaper in Canada was *Die Welt, und Neuschottländische Correspondenz*, which began publishing in 1788 in Halifax. Research on the ethnic press in Canada and the United States reflects ideological differences between the two countries. In the United States, the model is assimilation; in Canada, it's accommodation. One of the earliest studies on the role of the U.S. ethnic press was done by Robert Park in the early 1920s. He found that most immigrants said they planned to live in the States only temporarily and would return to their native country once they had earned enough money. On the other hand, in their 1990 study of the Portuguese community in Quebec, Alpalhao and Da Rosa found that in some areas of Quebec the existence of an ethnic means of mass communication, as well as other ethnic institutions (social services, churches, etc.), "permit a large percentage of the community to live as if they were still in the milieu of origin."

Black newspapers have been important in Canada since the days of slavery and the underground railroad into Canada. The Centre for the Study of Black Cultures in Canada at York University reports that the earliest black newspapers in Canada were *Voice of the Fugitive* in 1851 and *The Provincial Freeman* in 1853. Canada's largest ethnic newspaper is *Share*, which is devoted to both local and Caribbean news. *Share*'s publisher, Arnold A. Auguste, says, "*Share*'s focus is on Toronto. It is a community newspaper which covers our community, what we are doing here, in Toronto. *Share* is connected to the community at large." Auguste must be doing something right: *Share* reaches 130 000 readers each week.

▛▖ Evaluating Newspapers

study<u>preview</u> **Quantitative measures of a newspaper's success include circulation and penetration. How to judge quality? Rankings and awards are indicators, although they are imperfect. You yourself can evaluate whether the newspaper gives adequate resources to coverage.**

CIRCULATION AND PENETRATION

Once upon a time, measuring a newspaper's marketplace success against its competition was simple. The paper with the largest circulation won. Today, though, hardly any cities have competing dailies. Even so, numbers count. Is circulation growing? Declining? Because almost every newspaper reports its circulation to an auditing agency, circulation can be tracked year to year, even quarter to quarter.

Even more significant comparative data come from comparing **penetration**. Penetration is the percentage of people or households that get the paper. The Audit Bureau of Circulations (ABC) doesn't collect penetration data, but fairly reliable penetration is easy to calculate: Divide the population by the circulation. Seeking precise penetration data can get tricky. How you measure the circulation area, for example, can make a difference. There are other variables too. Even so, simple math can give you a good indicator of whether a newspaper's acceptance in the marketplace is improving.

QUALITY INDICATORS

While the Canadian Newspaper Association and the Canadian Community Newspapers Association both hold annual awards for excellence in newspaper publishing, there are

penetration ■ Percentage of persons or households that a newspaper reaches in its circulation area.

Bonnie Fuller

Bonnie Fuller

In charge at American Media publications, Canadian Bonnie Fuller unveiled her remake of the supermarket tabloid *Star* for a 2004 run against celebrity titles *People, Us Weekly* and *InStyle.* For respectability, Fuller threw out the classified advertising and most customer-direct advertising—about half of the magazine's ad pages. She promised advertisers a 116 page publication, compared to the previous 80, and set aside 40 pages for ads, compared to the previous 24. Fuller went cutesy with labels for some features, like "Star Bucks," with celebrities photographed in acts of public consumption; "The Stars Are Out," with celebrities at parties and occasions; and "Doctor to the Stars," with health and beauty tips.

As a magazine editor, Fuller has always had a magic touch. In her six years as editor, she turned *Flare* into the largest fashion magazine in Canada. Then, in New York, she relaunched *YM*, a magazine geared toward young women ages 15 to 24, more than doubling its circulation from 700 000 to more than 1.7 million. In 1994, Fuller joined Hearst Magazines where she launched the French fashion, beauty and lifestyle magazine *Marie Claire* for U.S. readers. Initial circulation of 250 000 rocketed past 500 000. Then Hearst put Fuller in charge of *Cosmopolitan*, which was still riding high on the sex-and-the-single-girl themes of Helen Gurley Brown after more than 30 years—quite an act to follow.

As the new *Cosmo* editor, Fuller used reader focus groups to guide her in making changes and additions. She included articles on AIDS and sexual harassment and, with no holds barred, any issue of concern and relevance to young women, at the same time maintaining the saucy, sexy Helen Gurley Brown tone. In Fuller's first year, *Cosmo* circulation flourished and drew more advertising. Fuller was named 1997 Editor of the Year by the trade journal *Advertising Age.* From 1998 to 2001 she served as editor of *Glamour.*

What next? Fuller took on the editorship of the celebrity magazine *Us Weekly*, which had floundered for years against Time Warner's *People.* Almost instantly, *Us* became a pop culture must-read.

At the risk of being labeled a serial job-hopper, in 2003 Fuller switched to tabloid publisher American Media. At American Media she not only was editing one title but was also editor-in-chief for all the company's magazines. It was a new level of responsibility. Said Fuller: "A chance to do this isn't going to necessarily come up in two years, in three years. It came up now." How could the era's most successful magazine editor stoop as low as American Media's *National Enquirer* and *Star?* Her stock answer in myriad interviews was the same: "Don't fool yourself. Every news outlet is doing tabloid stories."

A hands-on editor, Fuller first tackled American Media's supermarket pulp tabloid *Star.* Coverlines suddenly were less gee-whiz and more upbeat. To reposition *Star*, she had it printed on glossy paper. She shunned old *Star*-type scoops that, while tantalizing, often turned out to be untrue. A successful celebrity magazine, she said, needs credibility.

Would Fuller succeed? The circulation of the *Star* she inherited at first slipped below 1.2 million, but by 2005 it was up to 1.6 million in an increasingly competitive field of celebrity magazines. The question was whether, fully Fuller-ized, the magazine could top *People* at 3.5 million. Fuller was confident, saying that her target after *Star* would be to rejuvenate American Media's recently acquired *Men's Fitness* and *Muscle and Fitness* and a motley group of other titles, including Latino magazines, *Natural Health, Globe* and perhaps even American Media's flagship *National Enquirer.*

---

some quality indicators that you can generically use to evaluate your local paper. These are described below.

News Hole What percentage of space in the newspaper goes to news? This is called the **news hole**. From a reader's perspective the bigger the news hole, the better. Discount postal rates are available only to newspapers that cap advertising at 70 percent. Many publications push the limit to maximize revenue, sometimes shorting readers on news coverage, commentary and other non-ad content.

> **news hole** ■ Space for news in a newspaper after ads are inserted; also time in a newscast for news after ads.

Content Because local coverage is more costly than stories from news agencies, a good measure of quality is whether a newspaper has extensive local coverage or loads up with wire stories. Is local coverage thorough? Is it accurate? Does the newspaper have its own reporter to cover provincial politics? Its own Ottawa bureau?

Staff What kind of professionals report and edit the newspaper? Seasoned reporters who know the community well? Or beginners? Does the newspaper offer competitive salaries for the best talent? Salary scales are available on newspapers with collective-bargaining agreements.

Management Does top management have a permanent stake in the community? Or does leadership rotate in and out, with individuals focusing on making a name in order to move up in the corporate structure?

Influence of Magazines

study<u>preview</u> **Today, as through their whole history, the major magazines constitute a mass medium that targets a national audience. At their best, periodicals pack great literature and ideas into formats that, unlike books, almost anybody can afford. Magazines are also a national unifier because they offer manufacturers a nationwide audience for their goods.**

A NATIONAL ADVERTISING MEDIUM

Advertisers used magazines through the 19th century to build national markets for their products, which was an important factor in transforming North America from an agricultural economy to a modern one. This also contributed to a sense of nationhood. The other mass media could not do that as effectively. Few books carried advertisements, and newspapers, with few exceptions, delivered only local readership to advertisers. Today, advertising is still an important concern to Canadian magazine publishers. The majority of their total revenue is generated by advertisers.

MASSIVE MAGAZINE AUDIENCE

People have a tremendous appetite for magazines. There is a Canadian magazine for almost every city and region of the country and for almost any interest. While only 20 percent of magazines available on Canadian newsracks are actually homegrown, Canadians seem to prefer Canadian magazines over American ones because of the Canadian content. Canadian magazines are perceived by readers as being more relevant to the experiences of Canadian readers than are their U.S. counterparts. Here's a snapshot of the Canadian magazine industry from Statistics Canada:

- In 1993, there were 1678 Canadian magazine titles available; by 2003 there were almost 2400.
- Annual total circulation for all Canadian magazines is 778 million or roughly 320 000 sold for each Canadian periodical.
- Advertising revenue is close to a billion dollars a year.

PROTECTING CANADIAN MAGAZINES

June Callwood calls Canadian magazines "the only ones that will tell you how complex this country is, how interesting, how beautiful, where the troubled places are, they find our rascals and our heroes and they have become the fabric of our ordinary lives. We can look in a magazine and see ourselves." However, content and writing are not the only factors that make Canadian magazines successful. The Canadian government sees magazines as playing a "significant role in the cultural life of Canadians" by reflecting our own distinctive people, places, and lives. For more than a hundred years, the government has helped foster the growth and development of Canadian magazines through many different initiatives. For example, The **Postal Assistance Program (PAP)** helps Canadian magazine publishers offset the cost of distributing their periodicals by mail. This is particularly significant because the majority of Canadian magazines rely heavily on mail subscriptions. It helps about 1200 publications each year. The Department of Canadian Heritage also supports Canadian magazines with marketing, distribution and professional development through the **Canada Magazine Fund (CMF)**.

In 1999, in response to American arguments that **Canada's Bill C-55**, designed to protect the Canadian magazine industry, was unfair under both NAFTA and the WTO, the Canadian government made significant changes to the bill. Now, under the new **Foreign Publishers Advertising Services Act**, U.S. publishers could now begin to accept Canadian advertising and market what have become known as split-run publications. These split runs are American magazines published in Canada with up to 18 percent Canadian advertising. Plus, Canadian advertisers could now deduct the cost of this advertising as a business expense on their income tax forms, something that wasn't allowed prior to 1999. Now, 50 percent of the cost of the ad is tax deductible if the magazine features more than 80 percent foreign content; 100 percent is tax deductible if the magazine has more than 80 percent Canadian content.

Magazines as Media Innovators

studypreview Magazines have led other media with significant innovations in journalism, advertising and circulation. These include investigative reporting, in-depth personality profiles, and photojournalism.

INVESTIGATIVE REPORTING

Muckraking, usually called "investigative reporting" today, was honed by magazines as a journalistic approach in the first years of the 20th century. Magazines ran lengthy explorations of abusive institutions in the society. It was **Theodore Roosevelt**, the reform president, who coined the term *muckraking*. Roosevelt generally enjoyed investigative journalism, but one day in 1906, when the digging got too close to home, he likened it to the work of a character in a 17th-century novel who focused so much on raking muck that he missed the good news. The president meant the term derisively, but it came to be a badge of honour among journalists.

PERSONALITY PROFILES

The in-depth **personality profile** was a magazine invention. In the 1920s, **Harold Ross** of the *New Yorker* began pushing writers to a thoroughness that was new in journalism. They used multiple interviews with a range of sources—talking not only with the subject of the profile but also with just about everyone and anyone who could comment on the subject, including the subject's friends and enemies. Such depth required weeks, sometimes months, of journalistic digging. It's not uncommon now in newspapers, broadcasting or magazines, but before Harold Ross, it didn't exist.

Under **Hugh Hefner**, *Playboy* took the interview in new directions in 1962 with in-depth profiles developed from a highly structured question-and-answer format. This format became widely imitated. *Rolling Stone* uses Q-and-A's regularly, often creating news. In 2003, presidential hopeful Wesley Clark, a retired general, told *Rolling Stone* that a three-star general in the Pentagon had told him that the Iraq invasion was planned only as the beginning of further U.S. invasions in the Middle East and elsewhere, and Clark named the additional target countries. It was a bombshell assertion that made news. Other magazines meanwhile are boiling down the Q-and-A into quick takes. *Time* introduced the "10 Questions" feature in 2002, tightly editing pointed questions and answers to fit on a single page.

PHOTOJOURNALISM

Magazines brought visuals to the mass media in a way books never had. *Harper's Weekly* sent artists to draw Civil War battles, leading the way to journalism that went beyond words.

The young editor of the ***National Geographic***, Gilbert Grosvenor, drew a map proposing a route to the South Pole for an 1899 issue, putting the *Geographic* on the road to being a

Canada Magazine Fund (CMF) ■ Support for Canadian magazines through the Department of Canadian Heritage.

muckraking ■ Early 20th-century term for investigative reporting.

Theodore Roosevelt ■ Coined the term *muckraking*.

personality profile ■ In-depth, balanced biographical article.

Harold Ross ■ Pioneered the personality profile.

Hugh Hefner ■ Adapted the personality profile to Q-and-A.

Harper's Weekly ■ Pioneered magazine visuals.

National Geographic ■ Introduced photography in magazines.

National Geographic

The *Geographic* has remained in the vanguard of magazines photographically. For its 100th anniversary in 1988, the cover was the first hologram, a three-dimensional photograph, ever published in a mass-audience magazine. With a circulation of 6.7 million, the *Geographic* is not only among the oldest surviving U.S. magazines but also among the most read.

visually oriented magazine. For subsequent issues, Grosvenor borrowed government plates to reproduce photos, and he encouraged travelers to submit their photographs to the magazine. This was at a time when most magazines scorned photographs. However, Grosvenor was undeterred as an advocate for documentary photography, and membership in the National Geographic Society, a prerequisite for receiving the magazine, swelled. Eventually, the magazine assembled its own staff of photographers and gradually became a model for other publications that discovered they needed to play catch-up.

Aided by technological advances involving smaller, more portable cameras and faster film capable of recording images under extreme conditions, photographers working for the *Geographic* opened a whole new world of documentary coverage to their readers. Following are among *Geographic* accomplishments:

Seeing the News

Henry Luce's *Life* magazine pioneered photojournalism, beginning with Margaret Bourke-White's haunting shadows of the giant new Fort Peck Dam in Montana for the inaugural issue. When World War II came, *Life* dispatched Bourke-White and other photographers to capture the story, even the horrific details. With people eager for war news, circulation soared.

- A photo of a bare-breasted Filipino woman field worker shocked some *Geographic* readers in 1903, but Grosvenor persisted against Victorian sensitivities to show the peoples of the world as they lived.
- The first photographs from Tibet, by Russian explorers, appeared in 1905 in an 11-page spread—extraordinary visual coverage for the time that confirmed photography's role in journalism.
- A 17-page, 8-foot foldout panorama of the Canadian Rockies in 1911 showed that photojournalism need not be limited by format.
- The magazine's 100th anniversary cover in 1988 was the first hologram—a three-dimensional photograph—ever published in a mass-audience magazine. It was a significant production accomplishment.

Life magazine brought U.S. photojournalism to new importance in the 1930s. The oversize pages of the magazine gave new intensity to photographs, and the magazine, a weekly, demonstrated that newsworthy events could be covered consistently by camera. *Life* captured the spirit of the times photographically and demonstrated that the whole range of human experience could be recorded visually. Both real life and *Life* could be shocking. A 1938 *Life* spread on human birth was so shocking for the time that censors succeeded in banning the issue in 33 cities.

■ Consumer Magazines

study<u>preview</u> **The most visible category of magazines is general-interest magazines, which are available on newsracks and by subscription. Called consumer magazines, these include publications like *Reader's Digest* that try to offer something for everybody, but mostly they are magazines edited for narrower audiences.**

NEWSMAGAZINES

Although it is often compared to *Time*, **Maclean's**, "Canada's Weekly News Magazine," was founded in 1905 by John Bayne Maclean, almost 20 years before *Time* first appeared. However, the magazine we now know as *Maclean's* was called *Busy Man's Magazine* until 1911. Originally, it was a large-format magazine, about the size of *Life*, but in 1969 it was reduced to a standard size. In content, *Maclean's* is similar to *Time*, with an emphasis on in-depth coverage of national and international stories. Columnists like Peter C. Newman (a former editor of *Maclean's*), Barbara Amiel, and Allan Fotheringham have offered their perspectives to Canadians in the pages of this magazine. *Maclean's* even issues a national edition written in Chinese.

Fresh out of Yale in 1923, classmates **Henry Luce** and Briton Hadden begged and borrowed $86 000 from friends and relatives and launched a new kind of magazine: *Time*. The magazine provided summaries of news by categories such as national affairs, sports and business. It took four years for *Time* to turn a profit, and some people doubted that the magazine would ever make money, noting that it merely rehashed what daily newspapers had already reported. Readers, however, came to like the handy compilation and the sprightly, often irreverent writing style that set *Time* apart.

While *Time*, *Newsweek* and *U.S. News & World Report* cover a broad range of subjects, specialized newsmagazines focus on narrower subjects. The largest category is those featuring celebrity news, including the gossipy sort. The supermarket tabloid **National Enquirer** focuses on the rich and famous,

Special Issue 1998
CANADA'S WEEKLY NEWSMAGAZINE
Maclean's
NOVEMBER 23, 1998 ON DISPLAY UNTIL DECEMBER 13, 1998
The Eighth Annual Ranking
UNIVERSITIES

Newsmagazines
Canada's counterpart to *Time* magazine is *Maclean's*. It brings the Canadian journalism tradition of analysis to the newsstands.

Magazine Circulation Leaders: Canada

According to *Masthead Online*, here are the top Canadian magazines in 2006. Data were compiled by combining advertising revenue and circulation revenue.

Magazine	Total Estimated Revenue (Canadian dollars)
Chatelaine	50 million
Canadian Living	41 million
Reader's Digest	37 million
Maclean's	36 million
Time (Canada)	24 million
Canadian House and Home	22 million
7 Jours	21 million
Flare	17 million
TV Guide	17 million (no longer publishing newsrack edition)
Chatelaine	16 million (French Language Edition)

Source: MastheadOnline.com

Sarah Josepha Hale ■ Founded first women's magazine.

Seven Sisters ■ Leading women's magazines.

Demassification

Magazines were the first medium to demassify. *Chatelaine*, a magazine for Canadian homemakers, ranks as one of the best-selling magazines in Canada.

hyped-up medical research and sensational oddball news and is an incredible commercial success, with 2.1 million in circulation. Time Warner's *People* is at 3.6 million.

WOMEN'S MAGAZINES

The first U.S. magazine edited to interest only a portion of the mass audience, but otherwise to be of general interest, was *The Lady's Magazine*, which later became *Godey's Lady's Book*. **Sarah Josepha Hale** helped start the magazine in 1828 to uplift and glorify womanhood. Its advice on fashions, morals, taste, sewing and cooking developed a following, which peaked with a circulation of 150 000 in 1860.

The *Godey's* tradition is maintained today in the competing magazines *Better Homes and Gardens*, *Family Circle*, *Good Housekeeping*, *Ladies' Home Journal*, *Redbook*, *Woman's Day* and the erstwhile *Rosie* (née *McCall's*). While each sister can be distinguished from her siblings, there is a thematic connection: concern for home, family and high-quality living from a traditional woman's perspective.

These traditional women's magazines are sometimes called the **Seven Sisters**. An eighth sister is *Cosmopolitan*, although it may more aptly be called a distant cousin. Under Helen Gurley Brown and later Bonnie Fuller, *Cosmopolitan* has geared itself to a subcategory of women readers: young, unmarried and working. It's the most successful in a large group of women's magazines seeking narrow groups. Among them are *Elle*, focusing on fashion, and *Essence*, for black women. The teen girl market, dominated by *Seventeen* and *YM*, has become crowded with Little Sister spinoffs *Cosmogirl*, the leading newcomer with 1.1 million circulation in 2004, *ElleGirl* and *Teen Vogue*. In Canada, *Flare*, *Images*, and *Focus on Women* are also geared toward narrow audiences.

MEN'S MAGAZINES

Founded in 1933, *Esquire* was the first classy men's magazine. It was as famous for its pinups as for its literary content, which over the years has included articles from Ernest Hemingway, Hunter S. Thompson and P.J. O'Rourke. Fashion has also been a cornerstone in the *Esquire* content mix.

Esquire ■ First classy men's magazine.

Hugh Hefner learned about magazines as an *Esquire* staff member, and he applied those lessons when he created **Playboy** in 1953. With its lustier tone, *Playboy* quickly overtook *Esquire* in circulation. At its peak, *Playboy* sold 7 million copies a month. By 2004, however, *Playboy* seemed tired. Circulation was down to 3.2 million. The publisher of copycat *Penthouse* was in bankruptcy. Meanwhile, upstarts like *Maxim* at 2.5 million, *FHM* at 1.1 million and *Stuff* at 676 000 were in an ascendancy despite critics who objected to their raciness. Responding to critics, some retail outlets, notably giant retailer Wal-Mart, ceased stocking some men's titles as well as some women's magazines with provocative covers.

Playboy ■ Widely imitated girlie/lifestyle men's magazine.

Not all men's magazines dwell on sex. The outdoor life is exalted in *Field & Stream*, whose circulation tops 2 million. Fix-it magazines, led by *Popular Science* and *Popular Mechanics*, have a steady following.

Non-Newsrack Magazines

study<u>preview</u> **Many organizations publish magazines for their members. Although these sponsored magazines, including** *National Geographic*, **resemble consumer magazines, they generally are not available at newsracks. In fact, consumer magazines are far outnumbered by sponsored magazines and by trade journals.**

SPONSORED MAGAZINES

The founders of the National Geographic Society decided in 1888 to put out a magazine to promote the society and build membership. The idea was to entice people to join by bundling a subscription with membership and then to use the dues to finance the society's research and expeditions. Within a few years the *National Geographic* had become a phenomenal success both in generating membership and as a profit centre for the National Geographic Society. Today, more than 100 years old and with U.S. circulation at 6.7 million, the *Geographic* is the most widely recognized **sponsored magazine** in the nation. Other sponsored magazines include *CARP The Magazine*, published by the Canadian Association of Retired Persons for its members.

sponsored magazine ■ Generally non-newsrack magazine, often member-supported.

TRADE JOURNALS

Every profession or trade has at least one magazine, or **trade journal**, for keeping abreast of what is happening in the field. In entertainment, *Billboard* provides solid journalistic coverage on a broad range of subjects in music: new recording releases, new acts, new technology and new merger deals. *Billboard* is essential reading for people in the music industry. Trade journals covering the Canadian and American mass media include *Marketing* magazine for advertising and marketing, *The Publisher* for the newspaper industry, and *Broadcaster* and *Broadcast Dialogue* for the Canadian radio and television industries. About 4000 trade journals cover a mind-boggling range of businesses and trades. Consider the diversity in these titles: *Rock & Dirt*, *Progressive Grocer*, *Canadian Plastics*, *Hogs Today* and *Hardware Age*.

trade journal ■ Keeps members of profession or trade informed.

NEWSLETTERS

Even more focused than trade journals are subscription newsletters, a billion-dollar industry. These newsletters are expensive, generally $600 to $1000 a year, with some as much as $5000. Why do people pay that much? Where else could Chamber of Commerce executives find the information that's in *Downtown Promotion Reporter*? And no other publication duplicates what's in *Food Chemical News*, *Beverage Digest* and *Inside Mortgage Finance*. John Farley, vice-president of the largest newsletter company, Phillips

Publishing, contends that newsletters are the purest form of journalism because they carry little or no advertising: "We're answerable to no one but our subscribers." Today, more than 5000 subscription newsletters are published in the United States and Canada. Some newsletters now have subscription websites.

■ Magazine Demassification

studypreview Giant mass-audience magazines, led by *Life*, were major influences in their heyday, but television killed them off by offering larger audiences to advertisers. Today, the magazine industry thrives through demassification, the process of seeking audiences with narrow interests. Critics believe that demassification has changed the role of magazines in society for the worse.

ASSAULT FROM TELEVISION

The oversize mass-audience magazines do not exist today—at least not as they did in the old days. *Collier's*, having gone bankrupt, published its final issue in 1956. Hemorrhaging money despite a circulation of 4 million, *The Saturday Evening Post* ceased publication in 1969. In 1971 *Look* died. *Life* was not able to capitalize on the fact that it suddenly had less competition, and it went out of business the next year. It had lost $30 million over the previous three years. What had happened to the high-flying, oversize, mass-audience magazines? In a single word: television.

At its peak, *Life* had a circulation of 8.5 million, but in the 1950s the television networks had begun to deliver even bigger audiences to advertisers. The villain for the giant magazines was not merely television's audience size, but **CPM**—advertising jargon for cost per 1000 readers, listeners or viewers (the *M* standing for the Roman numeral for 1000). In 1970 a full-page advertisement in *Life* ran $65 000. For less money an advertiser could have one minute of network television and reach far more potential customers. CPM-conscious advertising agencies could not conscientiously recommend *Life*'s $7.75 CPM when the networks' CPM was $3.60, and advertisers shifted to television.

CPM ■ Cost per thousand; a tool to determine the cost effectiveness of different media.

A NARROWER FOCUS

With the demise of *Life*, doomsayers predicted that magazines were a dying breed of media. However, advertisers withdrew only from magazines with broad readerships. What they discovered was that although it was less expensive to use television to peddle universally used products such as detergents, grooming aids and packaged foods, television, geared at the time for mass audiences, was too expensive for products appealing to narrow groups. Today, relatively few magazines seek a truly mass audience. These include *Reader's Digest* and the Sunday magazine supplements.

Special-interest magazines, whose content focused on limited subjects and whose advertising rates were lower, fit the bill better than either television or the giant mass-audience magazines for reaching customers with special interests. For manufacturers of $7000 stereo systems, for example, it made sense to advertise in a narrowly focused audiophile magazine such as *Stereo Review*. In the same way, neither mass-audience magazines nor television was a medium of choice for top-of-the-line racing skis, but ski magazines were ideal. For fancy cookware, *Food & Wine* made sense.

CRITICS OF DEMASSIFICATION

Norman Cousins, once editor of the highbrow magazine *The Saturday Review*, criticized demassified magazines for betraying their traditional role of enriching the culture. Cousins said that specialization had diluted the intellectual role of magazines in the society. Advertisers, he said, were shaping magazines' journalistic content for their commercial purposes—in contrast to magazine editors independently deciding content with loftier purposes in mind.

Magazine Demassification Advertisers favour magazines that are edited to specific audience interests that coincide with the advertisers' products. Fewer and fewer magazines geared to a general audience remain in business today. In Canada, demassified magazines abound from *Going Natural*, a magazine published by the Federation of Canadian Naturists (nudists), and *The Antigonish Review*, for fans of poetry and prose.

Calvin and Hobbes
by Bill Watterson

Scholar Dennis Holder put this "unholy alliance" of advertisers and readers this way: "The readers see themselves as members of small, and in some sense, elite groups—joggers, for example, or cat lovers—and they want to be told that they are terribly neat people for being in those groups. Advertisers, of course, want to reinforce the so-called positive self-image too, because joggers who feel good about themselves tend to buy those ridiculous suits and cat lovers who believe lavishing affection on their felines is a sign of warmth and sincerity are the ones who purchase cute little cat sweaters, or are they cat's pajamas." Magazine editors and writers, Holder said, are caught in the symbiotic advertiser–reader alliance and have no choice but to go along.

Norman Cousins and Dennis Holder were right that most consumer magazines today tend to a frothy mix of light, upbeat features, with little that is thoughtful or hard-hitting. There is no question that demassification works against giving readers any kind of global view. However, most readers want to know about other people, particularly celebrities, and about a great many trendy topics. And advertisers want to reach those readers, preferably by steering clear of any controversial magazine coverage that might hurt sales. So profitability for most magazines and their advertisers is locked into providing information their target audiences are interested in rather than serving an indefinable "public interest," which might sometimes be controversial. The emphasis on profits and demassification saddens a number of people who believe that magazines have a higher calling than a cash register. These critics would agree with Cousins, who warned that emphasizing the superficial just because it sells magazines is a betrayal of the social trust that magazine publishers once held. "The purpose of a magazine," he said, "is not to tell you how to fix a leaky faucet, but to tell you what the world is about."

NEW COMPETITION

An ominous sign for magazines is the cable television industry, which is eating into magazine advertising with an array of demassified channels, such as TSN and CBC Newsworld. The demassified cable channels are picking up advertisers that once used magazines almost exclusively to reach narrow slices of the mass audience with a presumed interest in their products and services.

Another drain on magazine revenue is the growth of direct-mail advertising. Using sophisticated analysis of potential customer groups, advertisers can mail brochures, catalogues, flyers and other material, including video pitches, directly to potential customers at their homes or places of business. Every dollar that goes into direct-mail campaigns is a dollar that in an earlier period went into magazines and other traditional advertising media.

INTERNET MAGAZINES

Consumer and trade journals adapted quickly to digital delivery in the late 1990s with internet editions. The Canoe website in Canada offers links to magazines owned by Sun Media, while the Rogers site can connect you to *Maclean's*, *Chatelaine*, and other Rogers-owned publications. Meanwhile, the number of websites offering magazine-type content continues to grow.

Evaluating Magazines

study<u>preview</u> Circulation and advertising revenue are measures of a magazine's populist success. A new way of evaluating the impact of magazines focuses on the readers themselves.

READER USAGE MEASURE

A new way of gauging magazine quality, the **Reader Usage Measure**, or **RUM**, was created in 2003 by the magazine industry and Northwestern University media researchers. Thirty-nine statements are put to readers in carefully controlled surveys to ascertain positive and negative reactions. The statements are direct. Answering *Yes* to these statements contributes to a strong RUM score:

- I get value for my time and money.
- It makes me smarter.
- I often reflect on it.

Conversely, answering *Yes* to the following statements lowers the RUM score:

- It disappoints me.
- I dislike some of the ads.
- It leaves me feeling bad.

Ellen Oppenheim, a marketing executive with Magazine Publishers of America, said RUM data provide "a quantitative measure of qualitative information" that transcends circulation, ad pages and ad revenue—all of which are advertising-rooted measures. RUM is a reader-rooted measure that points to a magazine's connectedness to its audience.

The first RUM study included 4347 readers of 100 leading magazines, which was a large enough sample to provide demographic breakdowns. Black readers, for example, want magazines about which they can say, "It touched me" and "It grabbed me visually." Generation Y women, who came of age in the 1990s, gravitate to magazines that help them share experiences. Historically, the great magazines have been edited by people with an intuitive sense for their audiences. With RUM there is concrete information to supplement instinctive knowledge about what attracts an audience.

CHAPTER 2 Wrap-Up

Can newspapers and magazines survive? Even if people were to stop buying newspapers and magazines tomorrow, newspaper organizations would survive because they have an asset that competing media lack: the largest, most skilled newsroom staffs in their communities. The presses and the ink-on-newsprint medium for carrying the message may not have a long future, but newspapers' news-gathering capability will endure.

The magazine industry once was defined by giant general-interest magazines that offered something for everybody. Advertisers soured on these oversize giants when television offered more potential customers per advertising dollar. Magazines then shifted to more specialized packages. This focused approach worked. Magazines found advertisers who were seeking readers with narrow interests. Now, as other media—particularly television—are demassifying, magazines stand to lose advertisers, which poses new challenges.

Questions for Review

1. How did the mass production of the written word change society?
2. Describe the rise of newspaper chains and the trend toward conglomeration in Canada.
3. Why do most newspapers publish only morning editions now?
4. Why are community newspapers booming?
5. Why have alternative publications experienced increased readership?
6. Are magazines losing their influence as a shaper of the culture? Explain your answer.
7. How have magazines been innovative as a journalistic and a visual medium?
8. How has demassification affected both newspapers and magazines?

Questions for Critical Thinking

1. Did the Davey Committee and Kent Commission leave any legacies from which we can learn?
2. When U.S. magazines came into their own in the 1820s, they represented a mass medium that was distinct from the existing book and newspaper media. How were magazines different?
3. Is demassification good or bad for readers?
4. What will the effect of convergence be on newsroom staff?
5. Discuss the role of these innovators in contributing to magazines as a visual medium: Gilbert Grosvenor and Henry Luce.
6. The late Norman Cousins, a veteran social commentator and magazine editor, worried that trends in the magazine industry were undermining the historic role that magazines have had in enriching the culture. What is your response to Cousins's concerns?
7. There are no laws protecting Canadian newspapers, yet there are many government initiatives in place for magazines. Is this fair?

Deepening Your media LITERACY

NEWSPAPERS

Can a newspaper have a personality?

STEP 1 Get copies of two different newspapers, daily or weekly.

Dig Deeper

STEP 2 Make a list of the following characteristics for each publication:

1. How big is the news hole? An easy way to calculate this is to measure the total number of inches in each column of type, from the top of the page to the bottom, and multiply by the number of columns across the page. Multiply this number by the total number of pages. Then measure the number of inches of non-advertising material and figure the percentage of non-advertising content—that's your news hole.
2. How much of the news is staff-written? How much comes from news services?
3. How diverse is the opinion section?
4. Is the publication chain-owned or independent?
5. What word or phrase describes the overall look of the publication?
6. What kind of news does it carry? Local, sports, entertainment, other?

What Do You Think?

STEP 3 Write down a few words or a phrase that describes the personalities of the publications you investigated. Answer these questions: Can you determine the politics of the publisher or editor from reading the newspaper? What text or images led you to this conclusion? Can you determine who the perceived audience of a publication is by reading it? Can you determine what values it expresses? It is said that a truly successful newspaper belongs to the community. Do you think that's true for the newspapers you studied?

MAGAZINES

Should magazines try for universal appeal, or is it better to have a smaller, specialized audience?

STEP 1 Make a list of characteristics you think make a trade journal successful. Imagine that you are the publisher of a trade journal. Write down three things you would tell your editor to do to make the magazine successful. Now think about consumer magazines and make the same lists.

Dig Deeper

STEP 2 Pick a trade journal and a consumer magazine and make notes on the following characteristics:

1. If you are working with a printed magazine, approximately what percentage of the pages are devoted to advertising? If it is an online magazine, count the number of ads.
2. How many stories are in this issue? How long are they? How many are about controversial subjects?
3. How many photos or illustrations are there?
4. What are the demographics of the audience targeted by the style of the writing, the layout and the advertising? Do there seem to be any ties between advertising and the stories?
5. What else do you see that sets this magazine apart?

What Do You Think?

STEP 3 Compare the lists of attributes of a trade journal and a consumer magazine that you made in Step 2. How do they compare to your ideas in Step 1? Does one of the magazines you looked at do a better job than the others of appealing to its audience? If so, why? Does this correlate with how well a magazine reaches its readers? Do you think it is better to choose to serve a bigger audience or a smaller one?

Keeping Up to Date

CARD (Canadian Advertising Rates and Data) is a listing of newspapers and magazines published in Canada. It includes circulation data and current ad rates.

Editor & Publisher is a weekly trade journal for the newspaper industry.

Folio is a trade journal on magazine management. Among major newspapers that track magazine issues in a fairly consistent way are *The New York Times*, *The Wall Street Journal*, and *USA Today*.

NewsInc. is a monthly trade journal on newspaper management.

Newspaper Research Journal is a quarterly that deals mostly with applied research.

Presstime is published monthly by the Newspaper Association of America.

The Publisher covers community newspapers across Canada.

Many general-interest magazines, such as *Maclean's*, cover print media issues on a regular basis.

For Further Learning

James Adams. "A Good News, Bad News Issue." *The Globe and Mail* (July 25, 2006).

J. Antonio Alpalhao and Victor Da Rosa. *A Minority in a Changing Society: The Portuguese Communities of Quebec* (University of Ottawa Press, 1980).

Roland Barthes. "The Photographic Message." In *Image-Music-Text* (Fontana, 1973).

James L. Baughman. *Henry R. Luce and the Rise of the American News Media* (Tawyne, 1987).

Bill Bishop. "A Warning from Smithville: Owning Your Own Weekly." *Washington Journalism Review* (May 10, 1988): 4, 25–32.

Leo Bogart. *Preserving the Press: How Daily Newspapers Mobilized to Keep Their Readers* (Columbia University Press, 1991).

Reginald Bragonier, Jr., and David J. Fisher. *The Mechanics of a Magazine* (Hearst, 1984).

Walter M. Brasch. *Forerunners of Revolution: Muckrakers and the American Social Conscience* (University of America Press, 1990).

Robert Brehl. "Conrad Black Takes on Toronto." *The Globe and Mail* (June 13, 1998).

Iain Calder. *The Untold Story: My 20 Years Running the National Enquirer* (Miramax, 2004).

Canada. Royal Commission on Newspapers, 1981.

Canada. Senate Special Committee on the Mass Media, *Report*. 3 vols. (Ottawa, 1970).

J. William Click and Russell N. Baird. *Magazine Editing and Production*, Fifth edition (Wm. C. Brown, 1990).

Ellis Cose. *The Press* (Morrow, 1989).

Jonathan Curiel. "Gay Newspapers." *Editor & Publisher* 224 (August 3, 1991): 32, 14–19.

Gregory Curtis. "The End of the Trail." *Brill's Content* (November 2000): 76–80.

Keith Damsell. "Magazine Numbers Unravelled." *The Globe and Mail* (July 6, 2001).

Francis X. Dealy. *The Power and the Money: Inside* The Wall Street Journal (Birch Lane Press, 1993).

Peter Desbarats. *Guide to the Canadian News Media* (Harcourt, Brace, Jovanovich, 1990).

Edwin Diamond. *Behind the Times: Inside* The New York Times (Villard Books, 1994).

Robert Draper. *Rolling Stone Magazine: The Uncensored History* (Doubleday, 1990).

Elizabeth L. Eisenstein. *The Printing Press as an Agent of Change: Communications and Cultural Transformation in Early-Modern Europe*, 2 vols. (Cambridge University Press, 1980).

Bob Ferguson. "Critics Crank Up Pressure over Black's Newspaper Play." *Toronto Star* (May 23, 1998).

Douglas Fetherling. *The Rise of the Canadian Newspaper* (Oxford University Press, 1990).

Otto Friedrich. *Decline and Fall* (Harper & Row, 1969).

John Geddes. "The Izzy and Leonard Show." *Maclean's* (August 14, 2000).

Douglas H. George. *The Smart Magazines: 50 Years of Literary Revelry and High Jinks at* Vanity Fair, The New Yorker, Life, Esquire *and* The Smart Set (Archon Books, 1991).

The Globe and Mail: 150 Years in Canada (1994).

Dennis Holder, Robert Love, Bill Meyers, and Roger Piantadosi, contributors. "Magazines in the 1980s." *Washington Journalism Review* 3 (November 1981): 3, 28–41.

Ernest C. Hynds. *American Newspapers in the 1980s* (Hastings House, 1980).

M. Thomas Inge, ed. *Handbook of American Popular Culture*, Second edition (Greenwood, 1989).

Amy Janello and Brennon Jones. *The American Magazine* (Harry N. Abrams, 1991).

Sammye Johnson and Patricia Projatel. *Magazine Publishing* (NTC, 2000).

Lauren Kessler. *Against the Grain: The Dissident Press in America* (Sage, 1984).

Wilfred Kesterton. *A History of Journalism in Canada* (McClelland and Stewart, 1967).

Wilfred Kesterton. "The Growth of the Newspaper in Canada, 1981." In *Communications in Canadian Society*, edited by Benjamin Singer (Addison-Wesley, 1983).

Michael Leapman. *Arrogant Aussie: The Rupert Murdoch Story* (Lyle Stuart, 1985).

Kent MacDougall. *The Press: A Critical Look from the Inside* (Dow Jones Books, 1972).

Magazines Canada. *Fast Facts 2006*.

Ted Magder. "Franchising the Candy Store." *Canadian American Public Policy Centre* (April 1998).

Casey Mahood. "Black Daily Marks Sector's Boom." *The Globe and Mail* (April 9, 1998).

Barbara Matusow. "Allen H. Neuharth Today." *Washington Journalism Review* 8 (August 1986): 8, 18–24.

Richmond M. McClure. *To the End of Time: The Seduction and Conquest of a Media Empire* (Simon & Schuster, 1992).

Marshall McLuhan. *The Gutenberg Galaxy* (University of Toronto Press, 1962).

Minister of Supply and Services Canada. *A Question of Balance: Report of the Task Force on the Canadian Magazine Industry* (1994).

Al Neuharth. *Confessions of an S.O.B.* (Doubleday, 1989).

Alan and Barbara Nourie. *American Mass-Market Magazines* (Greenwood, 1990).

D. M. Osborne. "Paying Respects." *Brill's Content* (October 1998): 93–95.

Andrew M. Osler. "From Vincent Massey to Thomas Kent: The Evolution of National Press Policy in Canada, 1981." In *Communications in Canadian Society*, edited by Benjamin Singer (Addison-Wesley, 1983).

Theodore Peterson. *Magazines in the Twentieth Century* (University of Illinois Press, 1964).

Sam G. Riley, eds. *Corporate Magazines in the United States* (Greenwood Press, 1992).

Sam G. Riley and Gary W. Selnow, eds. *Regional Interest Magazines of the United States* (Greenwood Press, 1991).

Katherine Rosman. "The Secret of Her Success." *Brill's Content* (November 1998): 102–111.

Edward E. Scharfe. *Worldly Power: The Making of* The Wall Street Journal (Beaufort, 1986).

William Shawcross. *Murdoch* (Simon & Schuster, 1993).

Ted Curtis Smythe. "Special Interest Magazines: Wave of the Future or Undertow." In *Readings in Mass Communication*, 6th ed., edited by Michael Emery and Smythe (Wm. C. Brown, 1986).

James D. Squires. *Read All About It! The Corporate Takeover of America's Newspapers* (Times Books, 1993).

Jim Strader. "Black on Black." *Washington Journalism Review* 14 (March 1992): 2, 33–36.

W. A. Swanberg. *Luce and His Empire* (Scribners, 1972).

William H. Taft. *American Magazines for the 1980s* (Hastings House, 1982).

John Tebbel. *A History of Book Publishing in the United States*, Vols. 1–3 (R. R. Bowker, 1972–1977).

John Tebbel and Mary Ellen Zuckerman. *The Magazine in America, 1741–1990* (Oxford University Press, 1991).

Hunter S. Thompson. *Fear and Loathing in America: The Brutal Odyssey of an Outlaw Journalism 1968–1976* (Simon & Schuster, 2000).

Times Mirror Center for the People and the Press. *The Age of Indifference* (Times Mirror Company, 1990).

Eric Utne. "Tina's New Yorker." *Columbia Journalism Review* 31 (March/April 1993): 6, 31–37.

Jeannette Walls. *Dish: The Inside Story of World Gossip* (Avon/Spike, 2000).

Jennifer Wells. "Assessing Black's Toronto Plan." *Maclean's* (October 13, 1997).

Anthony Wilson-Smith. "The Scoop on Black." *Maclean's* (March 30, 1998).

Mary Ellen Zuckerman. *History of Popular Women's Magazines in the United States, 1792–1995* (Greenwood, 1999).

Do the Math Once considered an icon in the Canadian music industry, Sam the Record Man closed the doors on its flagship store in Toronto in 2007. Owners cited competition from music downloading as the primary reason.

Sound Recording

Media in Theory

Analysis of Canadian Content

Since 1971, the Canadian Radio-television and Telecommunications Commission (CRTC) has required that Canadian radio stations play a certain amount of Canadian content (known as **Cancon**) between the hours of 6 a.m. and midnight. While some good Canadian singers and groups emerged in the early 1970s, Canadian music was difficult to find at the time. As a result, some Canadian recordings were seen as inferior to American recordings. In his autobiography, *Taking Care of Business,* Randy Bachman of The Guess Who and Bachman Turner Overdrive said that quite often Canadian radio wouldn't play a Canadian song until it became a "hit" in the United States. That's why the group called itself "The Guess Who": to eliminate any anti-Canadian bias from radio. Hard to believe, but according to Nicholas Jennings in *Before the Goldrush,* when debate began in the late 1960s on the issue of Canadian content on radio, radio stations were against it. Jennings explains that the Canadian Association of Broadcasters claimed that imposing Canadian content regulations on radio would "lower the attractiveness of stations to the listener."

Adding to this negative myth about Canadian music, certain broadcasters played little Canadian content during the day, instead choosing to "bury" it after 10 p.m. on weeknights and early in the morning on weekends, when fewer people listened to the radio. This practice was also reported in 1994, following a two-year study of FM radio stations sponsored by SOCAN (Society of Composers, Authors and Music Publishers of Canada) and CIRPA (Canadian Independent Record Production Association). In its report, the task force found that only 18 percent of music was Canadian during morning drive times, while Canadian music accounted for 26 percent of the music played during the corresponding afternoon period. Nancy Lanthier, in *Music Scene* magazine, has referred to this as the "Cancon Ghetto." Since 1998, English language Canadian radio stations must play 35 percent Cancon equally throughout the day. Stations in Quebec must play 65 percent Cancon.

Cancon ■ Short form for Canadian content.

RECORD INDUSTRY

1877 Thomas Edison introduced a recording-playback device, the Phonograph.

1887 Montreal's Emile Berliner introduced technology to record discs simultaneously

1920s Joseph Maxwell introduced electrical microphones and recording system.

1948 Peter Goldmark introduced long-play microgroove vinyl 33 1/3-rpm records.

1950s Rock 'n' roll, a new musical genre, shook up the record industry.

1960 Stereo recordings and playback equipment were introduced.

1970 CRTC introduced Canadian content (Cancon) to radio.

1983 Digital recording on CDs was introduced.

1998 Streaming technology made downloading from the web possible.

2001 Apple introduced handheld iPod MP3-playing device coupled with its online iTunes Music Store, a new model for music retailing.

2004 The Supreme Court of Canada claimed music downloading is legal. The Canadian Recording Industry Association (CRIA) launched an immediate appeal of the ruling.

2004 PureTracks, Napster 2.0, legal music downloading services introduced in Canada.

2005 Recording industry won U.S. Supreme Court case against online music-swapping facilitators, like Grokster, slowing a drain on sales.

2005 DualDiscs introduced. They are part CD, part DVD.

What Is Canadian about Canadian Content?

From a semiotic perspective, if music and lyrics (as signs) signify something other than themselves, one might ask, "What does the lyrical and musical content of Cancon say about Canadian culture?"

A statistical analysis of all the songs that reached number one on the CHUM chart for a 13-year period before and a 13-year period after the implementation of Cancon regulations might help answer these questions. CHUM was a Top 40 powerhouse in Toronto from May 1957 to 1986. The survey reveals that 13 Canadian songs reached number one between 1957 and 1969, while between 1970 and 1982 there were 19 number-one Canadian songs. On the surface, this seems to show that the regulations were successful in promoting Canadian talent and the music industry, as six more Canadian songs reached number one. But a closer analysis shows that these songs had few Canadian signifiers in their lyrics.

During the period before the regulations, 1957 to 1969, at least four of the Canadian songs that reached number one were written by Canadians but recorded by Americans. They included "It Doesn't Matter Anymore" by Buddy Holly, "Love Child" by The Supremes, "Aquarius/Let the Sun Shine In" by the Fifth Dimension, and "Sugar, Sugar" by the Archies. From an economic standpoint, these songs undoubtedly helped the Canadian music industry, but their lyrics say little, if anything, about Canada. In essence they are American songs, written for the U.S. market. In addition, two of the number-one Canadian songs were included on American movie soundtracks. For example, "Born to Be Wild" by Steppenwolf was featured in the film *Easy Rider*, while "One Tin Soldier" by The Original Caste was used in the movie *Billy Jack*. The only Canadian song to reach number one that was explicitly about Canada was the novelty song "Clear the Track, Here Comes Shack" by Douglas Rankine & the Secrets. The song was a tribute to Eddie Shack, a hockey player with the Toronto Maple Leafs.

After the Canadian content regulations came into effect in 1970, the number of Canadian number-one singles on the CHUM charts in a 13-year period increased from 13 to 19. However, the same patterns that existed before the Cancon regulations were still evident: American artists continued to record songs written by Canadians. For example, "Puppy Love," recorded by Donny Osmond, and "She's a Lady," sung by Tom Jones, were written by Paul Anka. "Woodstock," about the mythic American music festival, was written by Joni Mitchell and recorded by Crosby, Stills, Nash & Young. Perhaps only two number-one Canadian singles in Canada during this period were openly nationalistic. The first was "American Woman" (which also reached number one in the United States) by The Guess Who. The song's lyrics made clear distinctions between Canadian and American culture. The other uniquely Canadian number-one single was "Take Off" by Bob and Doug McKenzie (SCTV comics Rick Moranis and Dave Thomas). However, like "Clear the Track, Here Comes Shack," this brand of nationalism was humorous in nature and perhaps reached number one due to its novelty.

Influence of Sound Recordings

studypreview Recorded music has become a pervasive element in our lives. It is everywhere almost all the time. The companies that dominate the music industry, despite revenue leakage to online music-swapping, are a major force in the global music business.

PERVASIVENESS OF MUSIC

When urban sophisticates in earlier eras wanted music, they arranged to attend a concert. Many middle-class people went to the parlour and sat at the piano. Rural folks had their music too—a fiddle on the front porch in the evening, a harmonica at the campfire. Music was a special event, a social gathering that had to be arranged. To those people, life today would seem like one big party—music everywhere all the time. Yes, we arrange for concerts and major musical events, but we also wake to music, shop to music and drive to music. Many of us work to music and study to music. In fact, the recording industry has products in so many parts of our lives that many people take most of them for granted.

SCOPE OF THE RECORDING INDUSTRY

The recording industry that brings music to mass audiences, both the flashy stuff and everything else, is gigantic. Global sales in 2004 were estimated at $33.6 billion. In 2005, the Ministry of Canadian Heritage reported that music sales were worth $902 million. These totals don't include symbiotic industries like fan magazines, music television and radio. That's worth billions more. Then there are concerts, performers' merchandise, sponsorships and a miscellany of related enterprises.

Even in leaner times, with major losses to online music swapping, recordings from Canadian acts continue to sell well. Canadian artists sold 6.8 million albums in 2001; that rose to 8.5 million by 2004. That's an increase of 25 percent during the heyday of free music downloading.

Recording Industry

studypreview Four major players dominate the global music-recording industry, all with big-name acts. Most of the industry's musical innovations, however, originate with independent recording companies. The indies gave rock 'n' roll its start—rap too.

MAJORS

The recording industry is concentrated in four major companies known as the Big Four, which have 75 percent of the global market. Each of these companies, in turn, is part of a larger media conglomerate.

The file-sharing crisis in the early 2000s shook up the industry's corporate landscape. Sony and Bertelsmann merged their music units. Bertelsmann, the German company that is the world's fifth largest media company, runs the combined Sony BMG. Alarmed at declining sales in the new file-swapping era, Time Warner sold its Warner Music in 2004 to Edgar Bronfman Jr. and fellow investors. Bronfman, heir to the Seagram liquor fortune in Canada, earlier had run the Universal movie and recording empire but had sold it to the French media conglomerate Vivendi. Although Vivendi, financially overextended, sold off many holdings to solve its own crisis in 2003, it decided to stay the course with Universal Music. There were no buyers anyway. Times were tough in the industry, and prospects for a recovery were cloudy at best.

INDIES

For decades a secondary tier of independent recording companies, **indies**, as they were known in industry jargon, struggled against the majors and occasionally produced a hit. When an indy amassed enough successes, it invariably was bought out by a major. The Ministry of Canadian Heritage says that more than 250 independent labels are responsible for roughly 90 percent of Cancon produced here at home. Most of the companies are based in Ontario, but Quebec and British Columbia are also responsible for much of our independent music. Some major Canadian independent labels include Nettwerk, Aquarius, and Quebec's Tacca Musique.

media DATABANK

Recording Companies

Four companies dominate the recording industry, although nonmajors, called *indies,* typically claim about 15 percent of U.S. sales—even more globally. This is the global picture, with major acts on the companies' labels:

Universal Music (French) 25.5%
Guns N' Roses (Universal), Jay-Z (Def Jam), Nelly Furtado (Dreamworks), George Strait (MCA Nashville), Snoop Dogg (Geffen), Gwen Stefani (Interscope), The Killers (Island)

Sony BMG (German) 21.5%
Bruce Springsteen (Columbia), Jennifer Lopez (Epic), Santana (Legacy), Travis Tritt (Sony Nashville), Sloan (Yep Rok)

EMI (Anglo-Dutch) 13.1%
Beastie Boys (Capitol), Janet Jackson (Virgin), Tina Turner (Capitol)

Warner Music 11.3%
Doors (Elektra), Rush (Atlantic), Green Day (Reprise), Madonna (Maverick)

Streaming: Suicide or Success?

Wilco Guitarist Jeff Tweedy Wilco demonstrated that musicians can succeed without major labels. The band took its album *Yankee Hotel Foxtrot* back after the Warner label Reprise declined to market it aggressively. Wilco posted the album online for free downloading, which spurred sales and led to a profitable tour. Still, there is evidence aplenty that downloading can undermine the economics of the record music industry. The Wilco experience may not be the right business model.

"What if there was a movement to shut down libraries because book publishers and authors were up in arms over the idea that people are reading books for free?" asks Jeff Tweedy, leader of the band Wilco.

Wilco is a success story, and its success came from the internet. Tweedy says that we live in a connected world, and the web is taking the place of radio, MTV and retail stores. The web is where kids are learning about new music.

When the group's label, Warner's Reprise, decided in 2001 that Wilco's fourth album, *Yankee Hotel Foxtrot,* was no good, Wilco got out of its contract by purchasing the album back for $50 000. The band then released the album on its website. That was followed by a sold-out 30-city tour, filled with fans who had found the band on the internet. Then Nonesuch Records, another Warner label, bought the rights to *Yankee Hotel Foxtrot,* reportedly at three times the original price.

Nonesuch wasn't worried that hundreds of thousands of fans had downloaded the band's next release, *A Ghost Is Born,* before the disc came out. Tweedy says when the album started showing up on the internet, the band was contacted by fans who were excited that they had found the album on peer-to-peer (P2P) networks and wanted to give something back in good faith. "We couldn't take the money ourselves, so we pointed them to Doctors Without Borders." The charity ended up receiving about $11 000. And *A Ghost Is Born* picked up two Grammys.

Other bands found similar success when they partnered with the web. Nine Inch Nails and Jupiter Sunrise joined a community website called MySpace.com, which had 240 000 band members and 14 million listener members in mid-2005. The president of MySpace.com describes the experience as being similar to going to a friend's house and hearing music that is new to you. Even music industry reps search sites like MySpace for talent.

Recording artists have many different opinions about using the internet. Some see the web as a potential source for hooking new fans, but others think the free downloading is bad for their business. As one DJ says, "I don't work for free, do you?" CD sales in Canada are down. According to the CRIA (The Canadian Recording Industry Association), the 10 best-selling albums in Canada in 1999 sold 5.9 million units. By 2003, the top 10 albums sold only 3.4 million copies. Although many factors may have contributed to this loss—including pricing and competition from DVDs and games, the ever-shrinking playlists on commercial radio, the declining popularity of replacing vinyl with CDs and limited title availability at retail—some artists connect the music industry's troubles to the internet.

As you will see later in the chapter, Canadian Terry McBride, the CEO of Nettwerk Records, sees peer-to-peer sharing (P2P) as the future. He claims that "kids aren't formatted. They just like music." He agrees with Wilco. The traditional "top-down" method of music popularity, with radio and MuchMusic telling teenagers what's popular, doesn't work anymore. It's word of mouth and sharing of songs that now determines popularity.

Artists who have found success through the internet say that it gives them the power to direct their own futures. Bands can create a buzz in the music world by releasing their work on the web. In 2007, Radiohead released *In Rainbows* online, allowing downloaders to pay whatever they could. Is this a glimpse into the future of music distribution? Time will tell.

WHAT DO YOU THINK?

1. Will file sharing become a regular part of music promotion?

2. The sound quality of an MP3 is lower than that of the original CD or vinyl record. Do you think that should make a difference in how the record industry views P2P networks?

3. Do you think the Recording Industry Association of America's (RIAA) lawsuits against individual file sharers will slow the streaming of music?

Thomas Edison ■ Built the first audio recorder-playback machine.

Phonograph ■ Trade name for the first recorder-playback machine.

acoustic recording ■ Vibration-sensitive recording technology.

Emile Berliner ■ His machine played discs that could be mass-produced.

Joseph Maxwell ■ Introduced electrical recording in the 1920s.

digital recording ■ Recording and playback system using on-off binary code for sound.

compact disc ■ Digital record format; now dominant.

CD ■ Short for "compact disc."

◰ Transforming Innovations

study<u>preview</u> **Technology created the recorded music industry, which goes back to Thomas Edison and Emile Berliner. Later innovations reshaped recorded products, mostly through playback discs and digital delivery. Also pivotal in shaping the industry in Canada have been the Cancon regulations.**

SOUND TECHNOLOGY

For years, scientific journals had speculated on ways to reproduce sound, but not until 1877 did anyone build a machine that could do it. That was when U.S. inventor **Thomas Edison** applied for a patent for a talking machine. He used the trade name **Phonograph**, which was taken from Greek words meaning "to write sound."

Acoustic Recording The heart of Edison's invention was a cylinder wrapped in tin foil. The cylinder was rotated as a singer shouted into a large metal funnel. The funnel channeled the voice against a diaphragm, which fluttered to the vibrations. A stylus, which most people called a "needle," was connected to the diaphragm and cut a groove in the foil, the depth of the groove reflecting the vibrations. To listen to a recording, you put the cylinder on a player and set a needle in the groove that had been created in the recording process. Then you placed your ear to a megaphonelike horn and rotated the cylinder. The needle tracked the groove, and the vibrations created by the varying depths of the groove were fed through the horn. This process was called **acoustic recording**.

Edison's system contained a major impediment to commercial success: a recording could not be duplicated. In 1887, Montreal's **Emile Berliner** introduced a breakthrough. Rather than recording on a cylinder covered with flimsy foil, as Edison did, Berliner used a sturdy metal disc. From the metal disc Berliner made a mould and then poured a thermoplastic material into the mould. When the material hardened, Berliner had a near-perfect copy of the original disc—and he could make hundreds of them. Berliner's system, called the Gramophone, led to mass production.

Electrical Recording In the 1920s the Columbia and Victor record companies introduced records based on an electrical system perfected by **Joseph Maxwell** of Bell Laboratories. Metal funnels were replaced by microphones, which had superior sensitivity. For listening, it was no longer a matter of putting an ear to a mechanical amplifying horn that had only a narrow frequency response. Instead, loudspeakers amplified the sound electromagnetically.

Digital Recording Record-makers developed a technological revolution in 1978: the **digital recording**. No longer were continuous sound waves inscribed physically on a disc. Instead, sound waves were sampled at millisecond intervals, and each sample was logged in computer language as an isolated on-off binary number. When discs were played back, the digits were

What Edison Wrought The prolific inventor Thomas Edison devised a machine that took sound waves and etched them into grooves on a foil drum. Although technologically a breakthrough, the sound was primitive. Only the most obvious tones could be picked up. Whatever few tonal subtleties and soft trills were recorded got lost in playback scratchiness. Firm horns and percussions did well.

translated back to the sound at the same millisecond intervals at which they were recorded. The intervals would be replayed so fast that the sound would seem continuous, just as the individual frames in a motion picture become a moving blur that is perceived by the eye as continuous motion.

By 1983 digital recordings were available to consumers in the form of **compact discs**, silvery 4.7-inch platters. The binary numbers were tiny pits on the disc that were read by a laser light in the latest version of the phonograph: the **CD** player. The player itself converted the numbers to sound.

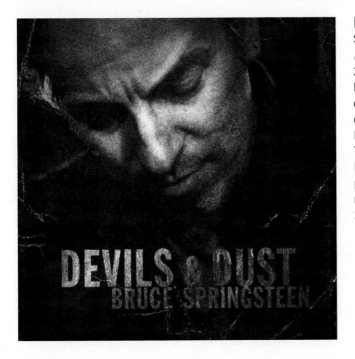

DualDisc When Bruce Springsteen's 19th album, *Devils & Dust,* was released in 2005, it was on **DualDisc**—a hybrid format with music on one side, like a CD, and video content on the other, like a DVD. Springsteen was the first Top List performer to go with DualDisc, the first major new physical format for recorded music since the compact disc 20 years earlier.

DualDisc ■ Hybrid CD-DVD format introduced in 2005.

PERFORMER INFLUENCES

The recording industry's main product, pop music, has been shaped by changing public tastes. This has been especially true since the end of World War II.

Rockabilly After World War II, major record labels groomed singers in the sentimental croon-swoon style, typified by Frank Sinatra and Rosemary Clooney in the United States and The Four Lads in Canada. Cavalierly, the majors figured that they could manipulate public tastes to their products. So confident were major labels in their strategy that they were blindsided by the sudden grassroots enthusiasm in the 1950s for Elvis Presley, "the white boy who sang coloured," as he was called at the time. In Memphis an independent

media ONLINE

Elvis Presley He ain't nothin' but a hound dog. Get all shook up at the official site.
www.elvis.com

Beatles A multimedia look at the band that started the British Invasion.
www.beatles.com

Rap Dictionary Decodes the lingo, identifies the artists, and locates the places they talk about.
www.rapdict.org

All Music An excellent website that covers all genres and artists.
www.allmusic.com

Elvis Presley Rock 'n' roll, a new hybrid musical form epitomized by Elvis Presley, took root with independent recording companies. To their peril, major labels tried to ignore the phenomenon, figuring it soon would pass. It didn't. Just when some indies, like Sun, were on the brink of becoming larger players in the recording industry landscape, the majors swept into rock 'n' roll and maintained their dominance in the industry.

label, Sun Records, had assembled a lineup consisting of Carl Perkins, Roy Orbison, Johnny Cash and Presley. The music was called **rockabilly**, a linkage of black and hillbilly music.

After months of inroads from rockabilly acts, the major labels scrambled to catch the wave. The major label RCA signed Presley. Other majors absorbed rockabilly indies. In the nick of time the majors saved themselves from the course they had been following and embraced the new genre, which was coming to be called **rock 'n' roll**.

British Invasion The U.S. record industry was rocked again in the early 1960s, this time by music from Britain. The Beatles caught the ear of a new generation, not only on radio but also with a series of platinum singles and albums. The **British Invasion** was a new wake-up call for U.S. record-makers. The industry's largely insular concept of itself was no longer viable. International licensing agreements to market music became a new way of doing business and introduced a new view of the global potential for U.S. record-makers. All the major North American record companies were parts of larger media corporations, like RCA and Columbia Broadcasting, and thus had far more financial muscle than their foreign competitors.

Rap As transforming as rock was, so too, 40 years later, was **rap**. Born in the impoverished Bronx section of New York City, this new style of music had an intense bass line for dancing and rhyming riffs, often attitude-strong and rapid-fire, overlaid on the music. Slowly, rap spread to other black urban areas. Indie-produced *Run-D.M.C.* and *King of Rock* were the first black rap albums to break into the U.S. music mainstream. Major record companies soon were signing up rap acts. Controversial groups Public Enemy and N.W.A., using violence and racism as themes, made rap a public issue in the 1990s, which only fanned die-hard enthusiasm.

GOVERNMENT INFLUENCE ON CANADIAN MUSIC

Historically, the radio and record industries have always been intimately connected. This was the main reason for instituting Canadian content regulations for radio in 1970. But what makes a song "Canadian"? In 1970, **Stan Klees** of *RPM* magazine developed the "Cancon MAPL" to help the industry define Canadian content. To be categorized as Cancon, a song must generally fulfill two of the following four conditions:

● **M (music):** The music must be written by a Canadian (citizen or landed immigrant).
● **A (artist):** The music or lyrics must be principally performed by a Canadian artist.
● **P (produced/performed):** The recording must have been either produced in Canada or performed and broadcast live in Canada.
● **L (lyrics):** The lyrics must be written by a Canadian.

Since its introduction in 1970, Canadian content has been a hotly debated topic in Canadian radio circles. Since then, the **CRTC** regulations have required radio stations in Canada to play a certain level of Canadian content. One of the reasons for this policy was to help strengthen the Canadian music industry by encouraging radio to support Canadian singers, songwriters, performers and others involved in the production of Canadian music. Prior to the 1970 regulations, it's estimated that Canadian music made up about 4 percent of all music heard on Canadian radio.

While the system seems to favour Canadian artists, it can also discriminate against Canadian singers. A controversy involving Bryan Adams is a good example of discrimination against Canadian singers. His song from *Robin Hood: Prince of Thieves,* "I Do It for You (Everything I Do)," and other songs on his album *Waking Up the Neighbours* were not originally considered Canadian content because he co-wrote them with a British songwriter. Due to the controversy that ensued from this classification, the CRTC amended the MAPL formula (the criteria of music, artist, produced/performed, lyrics) to allow for Canadian songwriters who collaborate with foreigners.

Have the Canadian content regulations worked? The regulations had two general objectives: to promote Canadian culture and to help strengthen the Canadian music industry. One could easily argue that the music industry is stronger today than it was in 1970. Canadian music certainly doesn't have the same negative connotation it did in

Best of the Cancon Crop

Since the early days of rock 'n' roll, Canadians have been successful in the United States. According to *Billboard* magazine, here are the top 10 Canadian songs of all time in the United States.

Some would argue that the reason these Canadian artists have been able to be successful abroad is due to Cancon regulations here in Canada.

1. "How You Remind Me," Nickelback (2001)
2. "You're Still the One," Shania Twain (1998)
3. "Because You Loved Me," Celine Dion (1996)
4. "Theme from a Summer Place," Percy Faith (1960)
5. "Informer," Snow (1993)
6. "Nobody's Supposed to Be Here," Deborah Cox (1998)
7. "The Power of Love," Celine Dion (1994)
8. "It's All Coming Back to Me Now," Celine Dion (1996)
9. "I Do It for You (Everything I Do)," Bryan Adams (1991)
10. "Have You Ever Really Loved a Woman?" Bryan Adams (1995)

Source: Fred Bronson, "Billboard's Hottest Hot 100 Hits."

the 1970s and 1980s. A 2005 Decima Research study claims that 93 percent of Canadians consider Canadian music to be as good as or better than music by foreign artists. The study also suggested that over 90 percent of Canadians listen to Canadian music. Cancon is a success.

Social Issues and Music

study<u>preview</u> **Campaigns to ban recorded music are nothing new. In the Roaring Twenties some people saw jazz as morally loose. White racists of the 1950s called Bill Haley's rock "nigger music." War protest songs of the Vietnam period angered many Americans.**

RECORD LABELING

In the 1980s, complaints about lyrics narrowed to drugs and sexual promiscuity. In the United States, **Parents' Music Resource Center**, a group led by Tipper Gore and wives of several other influential members of Congress, claimed there were links between explicit rock music and teen suicide, teen pregnancy, abusive parents, broken homes, and other social ills. The group objected to lyrics such as those in Def Leppard's "High and Dry," which extols drug and alcohol use; Mötley Crüe's "Bastard," with its violent overtones; and Cyndi Lauper's "She Bop," which was a thinly veiled song about masturbation.

The Parents' Music Resource Center argued that consumer protection laws should be invoked to require that records with offensive lyrics be labeled as dangerous, similar to cigarette warning labels or the movie industry's rating system. Record companies began labeling potentially offensive records: "Explicit Lyrics—Parental Advisory." In some cases, the companies printed lyrics on album covers as a warning. Online retailers, including iTunes, put a label of "explicit" on songs that might raise the prudish eyebrows.

Parents' Music Resource Center ■ Crusaded for labels on "objectionable" music.

▇. ■ Artistic Autonomy

study<u>preview</u> Major labels once dominated the nation's music with expensive talent and recording operations that neither indies nor individual performers could match. Digital recording equipment in the 1980s loosened the majors' artistic control.

A&R STRUCTURE

A&R (artist and repertoire) ■
Units of recording company responsible for talent.

The heart of the recording industry once was the powerful **A&R** units, short for **artist and repertoire**, at major labels. In an arrogant tyranny over artists, A&R executives manufactured countless performers. They groomed artists for stardom, chose their music, ordered the arrangements, controlled recording sessions and even chose their wardrobes for public performances.

In his book *Solid Gold,* Serge Denisoff quotes a Capitol executive from the 1950s explaining how the A&R system worked: "The company would pick out 12 songs for Peggy Lee and tell her to be at the studio Wednesday at 8, and she'd show up and sing what you told her. And she'd leave three hours later and Capitol'd take her songs and do anything it wanted with them. That was a time when the artist was supposed to shut up and put up with anything the almighty recording company wanted."

The muscle of the major record companies, aiming for mass market sales, contributed to a homogenizing of culture. Coast to coast, everybody was humming the same new tunes from Peggy Lee and other pop singers, who served a robotlike role for A&R managers. The A&R structure was a top-down system for creating pop culture. A relatively small number of powerful A&R executives decided what would be recorded and marketed. It was the opposite of grassroots artistry.

MUSIC DEMASSIFICATION

garage bands ■ Coined term for upstart performers without a studio contract.

In the 1980s, sophisticated low-cost recording and mixing equipment gave individual artists and **garage bands** a means to control their art. The million-dollar sound studio, controlled by major labels and their A&R people, became less important. As little as $15 000 could buy digital recorders and 24-channel mixing boards, plus remodeling of the garage, to do what only a major studio could have done a few years earlier. Artists suddenly had an independence that big recording companies were forced to learn to accommodate. Linda Ronstadt, for example, shifted her recording to a home studio in her basement. Some artists, like LL Cool J, went so far as to create their own labels.

Another result has been greater diversity. A rap fan might never have heard the Dixie Chicks. The music of Barry Manilow is obscure to most young fans of My Chemical Romance. In this sense, recorded music has become less of a unifying element in the whole society. The unification, rather, is in subsets of the mass audience.

TOURING

touring ■ Live performances in highly promoted road trips; increasingly important revenue source for big-name performers.

Big-name performers have found a significant income stream outside of the recording industry by taking their music directly to fans on a new scale. On tour, U2 commands ticket prices from $50 to $170. Prices for the 2005 tours of Paul McCartney and the Rolling Stones were higher. On-tour performances and recorded-music sales fuel each other symbiotically. Also significant, **touring** is controlled not by recording companies but by concert promotion companies. The largest in North America are Clear Channel and the House of Blues. To varying degrees the growth of the touring industry has lessened performers' reliance on the recording industry as their main revenue source. This too has contributed to less recording company control and greater artist autonomy.

When music industry analysts assess the revenue streams of performers today, they consider three major factors.

Retail The traditional outlet for recorded music, once mostly free-standing record shops, has shifted to giant retailers like Future Shop and Costco. In the post-Napster era, traditional retail sales have slipped.

Media PEOPLE

Alan Cross

Alan Cross

Since his days as a political science student, **Alan Cross** has had a passion for music and radio. His first show was on the University of Winnipeg's closed-circuit radio station, CKUW, in 1980. He turned that passion into a radio career that has seen him become somewhat of a music "guru" in Canada.

The radio program "Ongoing History of New Music" has been a staple of the Canadian alternative music scene since its debut in 1993. The show began as a way of educating listeners about the grunge revolution that was happening at the time. According to Cross, "It was obvious that there was a change happening in the world of rock and a new generation was about to take over and displace the hair metal bands that had been around since the 1980s. Our radio station jumped on the new music bandwagon. It was also decided that in order to put this new music into the appropriate context, it was necessary to have a documentary program that would help everybody

understand where this music came from, why it's important, where it's going, and where its heritage was."

The music industry has undergone some seismic changes in the last 10 years. "Back in the 1960s, 1970s and 1980s, bands were allowed to develop over time. REM really didn't have a hit until album number six. U2 had to wait until album number three until they had their breakthrough. The major record labels had patience for talent development. Those luxuries don't exist anymore. Although sales of digital downloads continue to climb, they have yet to offset the decline in the sales of physical CDs. Meanwhile, small, nimble independent record companies are able to pounce on trends more quickly—plus they're able to service niche music markets more effectively. In fact, most of the truly groundbreaking new music today is coming from the small independent labels—just like back in the 1950s and 1960s—and is once again becoming more and more prevalent. Small Canadian labels like Sonic Unyon, Arts&Crafts and Maple Music are becoming more important in developing new music."

In regards to Canadian content, Cross also has an interesting point of view: "When the regulations were first introduced more than 35 years ago, Cancon was a necessary cultural and industrial strategy. The country was being completely overrun by international interests. Most record companies were simply branch offices of their American parents and they, naturally, were interested in marketing their American artists. Homegrown performers were squeezed out and not given a chance to develop in any way. It was a vicious circle. You couldn't get on the radio

because you weren't good enough, and you couldn't get good enough because you couldn't get on the radio. It was tough, but the imposition of Cancon quotas has been a very successful strategy. It helped create an industry where we actually have vibrant, profitable, and relevant record labels, not to mention some world-class musicians. Canada probably exports more than its fair share of music, given our population."

That being said, Cross feels that since Cancon has made Canadian music successful, we have to ask ourselves, "At what point are the quotas no longer necessary? People will point to the cultural imperialism of the United States and say that the only way to maintain Canadian cultural sovereignty is to maintain or even raise these quotas. They feel the Cancon rules have accomplished their mission and now it's time for Canadian artists to stand on their own. After a few years, the question became 'Should Cancon quotas be raised, lowered or eliminated altogether?' During the CRTC's review of radio in 2006, some groups lobbied for Cancon to be increased from 35% to 40, 45 and even beyond 50% while others argued that with the increasingly popular and borderless world of the Internet, traditional broadcasters shouldn't be hobbled with additional regulation and quotas. When the dust cleared, though, the Commission left levels at 35%. Still, the subject of Cancon levels remains a very politically charged debate amongst broadcasters, record companies, artists, songwriters, music publishers, music collectives, the Heritage Ministry, and the CRTC."

Alan Cross ■ New music historian

Downloading The new retailing is through download sites like iTunes Music Store and Puretracks. This is a growing revenue source.

Touring Concerts are big business for performers who can attract sell-out crowds for their shows, especially the techno-spectaculars.

iTunes For a fee, Apple makes music singles available for the iPod and other players.
www.apple.com/ca/itunes

Puretracks A Canadian equivalent to iTunes.
www.puretracks.ca

MySpace.com The music section of this community website includes featured artists, online prerelease songs and music videos.
www.myspace.com

Shawn Fanning

The courts found his 1998 Napster music-downloading software violated the copyrights of the music owners. Nonetheless, Napster paved the way for other systems that facilitated free and inexpensive public access to music that transformed the music industry at the start of the 21st century.

Shawn Fanning ■ Inventor of Napster.

Napster ■ First online music-swapping software.

Recording Industry Association of America (RIAA) ■ Trade association of music recording companies.

Canadian Recording Industry Association (CRIA) ■ Canadian trade association of music recording companies.

peer-to-peer sharing (P2P) ■ Music-swapping software without a central server.

iPod ■ Brand name for Apple's handheld digital music device.

Steve Jobs ■ Driving force behind Apple Computer revival, iPod, and iTunes.

iTunes ■ Online music store.

■ Streaming Crisis

study<u>preview</u> **Napster and other file-sharing technology that facilitates music swapping seriously eroded music sales and record industry viability.**

FILE SHARING

Shawn Fanning's **Napster** technology ushered in a frenzy of free music-swapping on the internet in 2000. Suddenly, record stores found themselves unable to move inventory. The free fall continued. For the first time in its history the record industry was not in control of new technology—unlike the earlier adjustments, when companies exploited developments to goose sales, such as switches to high fidelity and stereo and the introduction of eight tracks, cassettes and CDs.

The **Recording Industry Association of America (RIAA)**, which represents recorded music companies, went to court against Napster. A federal judge bought the argument that Napster was participating in copyright infringement by facilitating illicit copying of protected intellectual property. Napster was toast. But other file-swapping mechanisms remained, some harder to tackle. Kazaa, for example, kept moving its operations from one offshore site to another, where legal actions were impossible. In a surreal initiative in 2003, RIAA began legal action against individuals who downloaded music without paying. The association's goal was a few hundred highly publicized lawsuits, perhaps some showcase trials, to discourage download piracy. In one respect, the strategy backfired, only engendering hard feelings among music consumers. By 2006, consumers began suing the RIAA.

In Canada, the CRIA (The **Canadian Recording Industry Association**) also went to court. From a legal standpoint, in early 2004, CRIA's hopes of having the law on its side were dealt a severe blow. CRIA was hoping the Supreme Court of Canada would force internet service providers (ISPs) to identify people who shared files using P2P file-sharing programs. The Supreme Court decreed that simply placing files in a shared P2P folder does not constitute copyright infringement.

There's no doubt that file sharing has impacted music sales. Data from the Department of Canadian Heritage claims that one-third of Canadians download music for free. Teenagers, not surprisingly, are the worst offenders with 68 percent of them claiming they prefer to download music for free. For example, in 2005, Gwen Stefani's "Hollaback Girl" was the first song to reach one million (legal) digital downloads in America. In Canada, it was downloaded a mere 20 000 times.

Jeff Rose-Martland, host of VOCM-Radio Labrador, claims that the decline in music sales has little to do with peer-to-peer (P2P) file sharing. Rather, it has to do with the quality of music today. According to Rose-Martland, "CRIA suggests that sales of all albums are down. Not true. Sales of the currently hyped albums are down. Sales of good-quality standards are up, as downloaders discover *The White Album, Ziggy Stardust,* and *Nevermind.*" In fact, two of the RIAA's top 100 albums of all time are by Canadian artists: Shania Twain's *Come on Over* and Alanis Morissette's *Jagged Little Pill.*

IPOD

Another favourable development for the industry was already easing the doomsayers' gloomy scenario: the **iPod**. In 2002 the innovator behind Apple Computer, **Steve Jobs**, introduced a handheld music playback device that he called the iPod, which he quickly followed with the online **iTunes** Music Store. From the iTunes site people could sample a song with a single click and then download with another click for 99 cents. In comparison to P2P file sharing, Apple's

Steve Jobs

sound quality was exceptional and virus free. In iTunes' first week, more than 1 million songs were downloaded, juicing a 27 percent spike in Apple stock.

A casualty of file sharing might be the record album itself. The introduction of the iPod has given new importance to the single song as an art form and as a commercial product. In 1948, when music was recorded and sold on discs, **Peter Goldmark**, the chief engineer at Columbia Records, had introduced slow-spinning, **long-play** records, LPs for short. An LP could carry 20 to 30 minutes of music per side. Many artists regarded their work not as songs but as coherent bodies of music packaged in albums. In the past, consumers had no choice but to buy the entire album. File sharing and iPods have changed that. Terry McBride, of Canada's Nettwerk Music Group, believes that P2P is the key to the success of the music industry in the future. Just because album sales are down, that doesn't mean people aren't listening to music. Nettwerk found great success using P2P to help them promote Sarah McLachlan's *Wintersong* CD in 2006. They allowed fans to download a vocal track of one of the songs on the album and remix it themselves. McBride says the results were incredible. "There's now hundreds of thousands of Sarah mixes, all over the place, getting played, and it cost us nothing."

Peter Goldmark ■ Inventor of long-play records.

long-play (LP) ■ 33 1/3-rpm microgroove discs that turned the recorded music industry into conceiving of its products as albums.

Evaluating Recording Companies

study<u>preview</u> Sales and profits are quantitative measures of a record company's success. How about its artistic success? Qualitative measures are harder to come by. Elitists give high marks to companies that have a commitment to music that breaks new ground artistically.

POPULIST MEASURES

People vote with their pocketbooks, which means that popularity is an important measure of success for record company products. Measuring success, however, is problematic. Different gauges don't necessarily correlate. A dominant market share, for example, doesn't always translate into profits.

Market Share One measure of a record company's success is reflected in market share. In recent years, Universal has led, but rankings can change overnight. A super-selling soundtrack, like *Titanic,* or a runaway hit album, like Coldplay's *X&Y,* can mean a near-instant reshuffling.

Sales Another measure is the **gold record.** Once a single sells 1 million copies or an album sells 500 000 copies, the RIAA confers a gold-record award. A **platinum record** is awarded for 2 million singles or 1 million albums. In Canada, The Canadian Recording

gold record ■ Award for sales of 1 million singles, 500 000 albums.

platinum record ■ Award for sales of 2 million singles, 1 million albums.

The "Sopranos Bounce" In the days after the 2007 series finale of HBO's *Sopranos,* sales of Journey's 1981 song "Don't Stop Believin'" spiked on both iTunes and Amazon.com. This "bounce" effect is usually attributed to the Grammy Awards. The Grammy Bounce is a perennial phenomenon. In 2003 Norah Jones's "Come Away with Me" zoomed to number one within a week. In 2005, sales of Ray Charles's "Genius Loves Company" rose 875 percent in the days after the Grammy tribute to the musical legend.

gold seal ■ Award for sales of 50 000 units in Canada.

platinum seal ■ Award for sales of 100 000 units in Canada.

diamond seal ■ Award for sales of 1 million units in Canada

Industry Association (CRIA) awards a **gold seal** for sales of 50 000, a **platinum seal** for sales of 100 000, and a **diamond seal** for recordings that sell 1 million copies in Canada.

Profit Because many conglomerates don't release profit figures for the record company subsidiaries, measuring profitability isn't easy. Aggregate data compiled by the RIAA indicates market share, but numerous variables can render market share an imperfect signal about profitability. One indicator, although usually vague, can be the annual reports to conglomerate shareholders, which sometimes contain hints like "disappointing sales in the music unit."

Another indicator for assessing record company performance is industry insiders who are quoted in the trade journals and in fan magazines like *Rolling Stone.* Another indicator, also reported in the trade journals, is the promotion and firing of record company executives.

QUALITY MEASURES

Media elitists, who argue that the media should lead public taste, not be mere panderers, are not swayed by commercial and popular measures of success. Elitists look to the media, including record companies, to incubate cultural innovation even when it means taking risks. However, most record companies don't take many risks. Have you ever heard pop rock lyrics without the word "baby"? Although there are exceptions galore, redundant and even tiresome themes seem to work in the marketplace. Many people take comfort in familiar lyrics, instrumentation and even performance styles. But this popularity is hardly satisfying to elitist critics who say the media have a responsibility to push the society's cultural explorations to new levels. To these critics, regurgitation, no matter how pleasant, doesn't count for much. In short, a record company that encourages artistic risk-taking will score well among elitists.

Grammy ■ Award for excellence in music in the United States.

Juno ■ Award for excellence in music in Canada.

Nelly Furtado at the Juno Awards

The Junos have signified excellence in the Canadian music industry since 1971.

Two awards that honour the best in contemporary music are the Grammys and the Junos. The **Grammy** award has been the symbol of music success in the United States since 1957. Winners are determined by members of the National Academy of Recording Arts and Sciences (NARAS) (also known as The Recording Academy). The **Junos** were named after Pierre Juneau, who was head of the CRTC when the Canadian content regulations were implemented. The idea of honouring the Canadian music industry came from Walt Grealis and Stan Klees, who published *RPM,* a music industry trade journal. Like the Grammys, it's a peer award. Members of the CARAS (Canadian Academy of Recording Arts and Sciences) vote on nominees and winners.

The impact on the music industry of Shawn Fanning's Napster, which at one point threatened to force a fundamental restructuring, is a reminder that the mass media are technology-driven. But just as digital internet technology bedeviled the recording industry, technology has come to its rescue. The Apple iTunes online store that coordinates the mind-meld between personal computers and iPods has reshaped music retailing. The iPod also has allowed the music-recording industry to survive in its traditional form with a few dominant major companies.

Questions for Review

1. How is the music industry integrated into our daily lives?
2. What are major developments in sound recording from Thomas Edison on?
3. What effects are economic pressures having on the corporate structure of the music-recording industry?
4. How have technological innovations in sound recording affected musical styles?
5. How have innovations in music genres and styles threatened the corporate structure of the recording industry?
6. How has the recording industry answered threats of government control on objectionable lyrics?
7. What has happened to the A&R units at major record companies?
8. How was the recording industry threatened by Napster and other software that facilitates online music-swapping?
9. What are examples of populist measures for evaluating record companies? What are some elitist measures?
10. What are the Juno Awards? Grammy Awards?

Questions for Critical Thinking

1. In recent months, how has new recorded music shaped significant human events? Consider music that is inspiring human actions. This might be war music. It might be music that's flowing from a generation or subculture and giving it an identity. It might be a new love song that has become a standard at weddings.
2. What has been the effect of global conglomeration in the record industry on the music you like?
3. Look into your crystal ball to assess how technological changes in the record business will play out in the future.
4. How has the relationship between artists and recording companies changed since World War II? Why has the change occurred?
5. How are measures of commercial and artistic success different in the recorded music business?
6. Why is airplay important to a recording's becoming a commercial success? Explain the exceptions.

7. What do you see as a solution to the revenue drain created by MP3 technology on the record industry? If there is no solution, what will happen?
8. Discuss the effect of moralists and others who would like to change the content of some recorded music. How do these people go about trying to accomplish their goals? What common threads have there been to their criticism throughout the 20th century?
9. Is Alan Cross right? Given the success of Canadian music in recent years, do we still need Cancon regulations for radio?

Deepening Your media LITERACY

Does popular music reflect our personal identity?

STEP 1 Write down the lyrics of your favourite song. Conduct a semiotic analysis of this song.

Dig Deeper

STEP 2 Consider the following:

1. Why do you like these lyrics and this kind of music?
2. What does your preference in music say about you?
3. What do you think this song's fans have in common?
4. Would your parents like this song? Why or why not?
5. Who would find it objectionable?

What Do You Think?

STEP 3 Answer these questions: Does this song or music reflect your life? Does it reflect the lives of its fans? Does it reflect the life of the artist? Do you like this song because you identify with it? Do you think your preference in music reflects your place in society?

Keeping Up to Date

The weekly *Billboard* is the recording industry's leading trade journal.

Consumer magazines that track popular music and report on the record industry include *Canadian Musician, Rolling Stone,* and *Spin*.

Entertainment Weekly and Maclean's both have regular sections on music, as do many daily papers, such as The Globe and Mail and the National Post.

For Further Learning

Jason Scott Alexander. "Record Labels Got Hip to the Download Culture: Now It's Radio's Turn." *Broadcast Dialogue Magazine* (March 2004).

Paul Audley. *Canada's Cultural Industries* (Lorimer and Company, 1983).

Randy Bachman and John Einarson. *Taking Care of Business* (McArthur and Company, 2000).

Karen Bliss. "25 Years of Canadian Artists." *Canadian Musician* (March/April 2004).

Robert Brehl. "CRTC Causes Static among Radio Bosses." *The Globe and Mail* (June 9, 1998).

Ethan Brown. *Queens Reigns Supreme* (Anchor, 2005).

Iain Chambers. *Urban Rhythms: Pop Music and Popular Culture* (St. Martin's, 1985).

Steve Chapple and Reebee Garofalo. *Rock 'n' Roll Is Here to Pay: The History and Politics of the Music Industry* (Nelson-Hall, 1977).

Stan Cornyn, with Paul Scanlon. *Exploding: The Highs, Hits, Hype, Heroes and Hustler of the Warner Music Group* (Harper, 2002).

R. Serge Denisoff, with William Schurk. *Tarnished Gold: The Record Industry Revisited* (Transaction Books, 1986).

Colin Escort, with Martin Hawkins. *Good Rockin' Tonight: Sun Records and the Birth of Rock 'n' Roll* (St. Martin's, 1991).

Peter Fornatale and Joshua E. Mills. *Radio in the Television Age* (Overlook Press, 1980).

Roland Gelatt. *The Fabulous Phonograph: From Tin Foil to High Fidelity* (J. B. Lippincott, 1955).

Peter Goddard and Phillip Kamin, eds. *Shakin' All Over: The Rock and Roll Years in Canada* (McGraw-Hill Ryerson, 1989).

Hugh Graham. "Rule Changes May See Rebirth of Top 40 Radio." *The Globe and Mail* (July 19, 1997).

Steven Hagar. *Hip Hop: The Illustrated History of Break Dancing, Rap Music, and Graffiti* (St. Martin's Press, 1984).

Ron Hall. *The CHUM Chart Book* (Stardust Publications, 1984).

Dick Hebdige. *Cut 'N' Mix: Culture, Identity and Caribbean Music* (Methuen, 1987).

David N. Howard. *Sonic Alchemy: Visionary Music Producers and Their Maverick Recordings* (Hal Leonard, 2004).

Laurel Hyatt. "Back in the Black." *Broadcaster* (February, 1998).

Nicholas Jennings. *Before the Gold Rush: Flashbacks to the Dawn of the Canadian Sound* (Viking, 1997).

Nicholas Jennings. "Canadian Rock Explodes." *Maclean's* (March 27, 1995).

Jill Jonnes. *Empires of Light: Edison, Tesla, Westinghouse, and the Race to Electrify the World* (Random House, 2003).

Ted Kennedy. *Oh! Canada Cuts* (Canadian Chart Research, 1989).

Nancy Lathier. "The CanCon Ghetto." *Music Scene* (May/June 1989).

Daphne Lavers. "The Canadian Music Industry." *Broadcast Dialogue* (April 2000).

Daphne Lavers. "Canadian Music Week: 2004." *Broadcast Dialogue* (April 2004).

Daphne Lavers. "Canadian Music Week: 2006: That Was Then, This Is Now." *Broadcast Dialogue* (May 2006).

Elianna Lev. "Music Mogul Wants to Change How Music Is Sold." *Canadian Press* (November 30, 2006).

Nanda Lwin. *Canada's Top Hits of the Year, 1975–1996* (Music Data Canada, 1998).

Katherine Macklem. "Turn Up the Music." *Maclean's* (July 30, 2001).

Greil Marcus. *Mystery Train: Images of America in Rock 'n' Roll Music* (Penguin Usapaper Plume, 1997).

Michael McCabe. "CANCON Not the Only Measure of Radio's Contribution." *Broadcaster* (February 1998).

Darryl McDaniels with Bruce Haring. *King of Rock: Respect, Responsibility and My Life with Run-DMC* (St. Martin's, 2001).

Steve McLean. "HMV Analysis Reveals 23% Canadian Sales." *The Record* (May 25, 1998).

Martin Melhuish. *Heart of Gold: 30 Years of Canadian Pop Music* (CBC Enterprises, 1983).

James Miller. *Flowers in the Dustbin: The Rise of Rock 'n' Roll, 1947–1977* (Simon & Schuster, 1999).

Angela Pacienza. "Court Rejects Music Copyright Suit." *Toronto Star* (March 31, 2004).

Mike Roberts. "Finger on the Pulse: MuchMusic Still Strong after 10 Years." *Gazette* (Montreal) (January 22, 1995).

Jeff Rose-Martland. "Takin' Care of Business: Is Suing Your Clientele a Sound Idea?" *Broadcast Dialogue Magazine* (May 2004).

Heather Schoffield and Robert Brehl. "Radio Stations Told to Turn Up the Volume" and "CRTC Opens Radio Markets." *The Globe and Mail* (May 1, 1998).

Barry L. Sherman and Joseph R. Dominick. "Violence and Sex in Music Videos: TV and Rock 'n' Roll." *Journal of Communication* 36 (Winter 1986):1, 79–93.

Stephen Singular. *The Rise and Rise of David Geffen* (Birch Lane, 1997).

Justin Smallbridge. "Think Global: Act Local." *Canadian Business* (June 1996).

Nancy Smith. "Morality in the Media." *Broadcast Dialogue Magazine* (May 2006).

Dick Weissman. *The Music Business: Career Opportunities and Self-Defense* (Crown Publishers, 1979).

Howard Stern By taking shock jock Howard Stern's show to satellite radio, Sirius aimed to siphon more listeners from traditional stations. In a case study later in this chapter, you will have a chance to discuss the effect Stern has had on radio.

Radio

Media in Theory

What Makes Radio Different?

What makes radio different from other media? **Andrew Crisell**, a cultural theorist, refers to radio as a blind medium: You can't see it with your eyes, like you can television, a movie or a newspaper. You can only see the pictures in your mind. Radio broadcasters use time, not space, as their canvas to communicate their messages. Building on the ideas of Barthes, radio uses four signs to create its imagery: words, sounds, music and silence. As Canada's Radio Marketing Bureau puts it, radio lets you "imagine the possibilities." Even Marshall McLuhan referred to radio as a visual medium.

> **Andrew Crisell** ■ Uses the ideas of semiotician Roland Barthes to analyze how radio meaning is created.

As discussed earlier, words can be symbolic in that they represent something other than themselves: The phrase *maple leaf* isn't a real maple leaf; it is only a label that our culture attaches to the physical object of a maple leaf. This naming process is entirely arbitrary. However, words in radio differ from words in print. Why? Because they are spoken. It's not so much what you say, but how you say it. The way in which an announcer or radio performer speaks also communicates meaning. Words end up working on two levels; not only do the words themselves stand for something else, but the way in which they are spoken signifies something as well. For example, an announcer can say "great!" and mean it in two different ways—one positive, one negative.

Sounds or sound effects are indexical signs. The sound of a creaking door is an index of a creaking door. To someone listening to Jerry Howarth broadcast a Blue Jays game, the loud crack of a bat and the cheering of a crowd signify that a home run has been hit. Sounds anchor the meaning or image created by radio; this is important due to the invisible nature of radio. Sounds let us know where we are and what's going on.

The third sign of radio, music, works on several levels. The music you hear on a radio station helps you identify the station. When you hear Paul Brandt or Terri Clark, you know you're listening to a country station; if you hear The New Pornographers or Broken Social Scene, you know the station is not country. Music can also act as a bridge between segments of a radio show, newsmagazine, or play, or it can be used to create a mood in a radio play.

An absence of any of these three signs signifies something in itself. As a sign, silence works to communicate meaning in two ways. First, it can be symbolic. A minute of silence on Remembrance Day symbolizes respect and honour for soldiers who died in war. But silence can also be an index that something's wrong with the broadcast—a power outage, a faulty microphone, or radio transmitter problems can all cause what is known as "dead air."

media TIMELINE

RADIO TECHNOLOGY AND REGULATION

1901   Guglielmo Marconi received a message from Cornwall, England, by radio in Signal Hill, Newfoundland.

1906   Reginald Fessenden broadcast to ships at sea on Christmas Eve.

1906   Lee de Forest created the audion tube that allowed voice transmission.

1912   David Sarnoff used radio to learn news of the *Titanic* disaster, putting radio in the public eye.

1920   XWA in Montreal began broadcasting in Canada.

1927   Canada's Diamond Jubilee was broadcast.

1929   Aird Commission released its report on radio broadcasting in Canada.

1936   CBC began broadcasting.

1939   Edwin Armstrong put the first FM station on air.

1998   CRTC relaxed regulations on radio ownership.

1999   Digital audio broadcasting (DAB) began in Canada.

2005   CRTC reviewed Canada's radio policy.

▪ Influence of Radio

study preview   **Radio has become a ubiquitous mass medium, available everywhere, anytime. As an industry, however, there are troubling signs. Radio's primary programming—music—has become available through other devices, many with no advertising. A key radio audience, the segment aged 12 to 34, has fallen off in recent years.**

UBIQUITY

Radio is everywhere. The signals are carried on the electromagnetic spectrum to almost every nook and cranny. Hardly a place in the world is beyond the reach of radio. At no time in recent Canadian history was this more evident than during the massive east coast blackout in August 2003. At that time, people turned to their portable radios for the latest information. This is a wonderful example of radio doing what it does best. **Howard Christensen**, publisher of *Broadcast Dialogue*, says that that blackout illustrated "just how dependent we can be on local radio stations—and on our ownership of battery powered radios. On August 14 at 4:11 EST, more than 50 million people would have been left in a news dissemination void were it not for this century old, voices in the ether technology. It was radio's community involvement, its caring and, indeed, its sharing. The medium was—gadzooks—rediscovered."

But why would radio need to be rediscovered, given its ubiquity? Statistics abound about radio's importance. Consider the following data from the CRTC's *Broadcast Policy Monitoring Report 2007*:

- Canada has 1238 radio stations; 919 of these are English, 286 are French, 33 are Third Language. We are also home to satellite radio.
- The average Canadian listens to about 18.6 hours of radio each week, while 91 percent of Canadians listen to the radio at some point during the week.
- Radio is accessible anytime and anywhere; 99 percent of homes have radios and 90 percent of cars do, too.

Howard Christenson ▪
Publishes *Broadcast Dialogue* magazine.

Who's Listening?

Although radio is a ubiquitous medium, listenership is slipping. Here's a look at the changes in radio tuning habits for different age groups between the years of 1999 and 2006 from the CRTC's *Broadcast Policy Monitoring Report 2007*.

Age Group	1999	2006	Difference
12–17	11.3 hours	7.6 hours	–3.7%
18–24	17.3 hours	14.1 hours	–3.2%
25–34	21.3 hours	18.3 hours	–3.0%
35–49	21.6 hours	20.6 hours	–1.0%
50–54	21.6 hours	21.0 hours	–0.6%
55–64	23.2 hours	21.1 hours	–2.1%
65 +	22.7 hours	21.3 hours	–1.4%

Source: CRTC, Broadcast Policy Monitoring Report 2007.

Canada's **Radio Marketing Bureau** sums up the power of radio in its 2007 Foundation Research Study when it says, "Radio is a perfect fit for modern life; it's effortless, easy to listen to during other activities; entertains and informs throughout the day; is compatible with other media and provides a soundtrack for life."

Although radio is important, cracks are developing in the medium's reach. The audience is slipping from the traditional stations to iPods, direct-to-listener satellite services, webcasts and cell phones. Plus, the audience is shifting. Canadians 12 to 34 years old are listening to less radio than in the past. This has serious implications for its future.

SCOPE OF RADIO INDUSTRY IN CANADA

Of the 1238 radio stations in Canada, more than 700 of them are commercial AM or FM stations. Most of these are owned by large corporations. Corus Entertainment, Standard Broadcasting, Rogers Communications, Astral Media and CHUM Limited are the five largest radio companies in Canada. In total, they combine for over half the radio listening in Canada.

Although radio as a business was 54 percent more profitable in 2006 than it was in 1997, the profits are due less to audience and advertising growth than to the chains' economies of scale and radical cost-cutting. This is an effect of conglomeration within the industry.

Radio Technology

study<u>preview</u> **Human mastery of the electromagnetic spectrum, through which radio is possible, is only a century old. In 1895 an Italian physicist and inventor, Guglielmo Marconi, was the first to transmit a message through the air. Later came Canadian Reginald Fessenden and voice transmissions.**

ELECTROMAGNETIC SPECTRUM

Radio waves are part of the physical universe. They have existed forever, moving through the air and the ether. Like light waves, they are silent—a part of a continuing spectrum

Radio Marketing Bureau ■
Claims radio is a perfect fit for modern life.

of energies: the **electromagnetic spectrum**. As early as 1873, physicists speculated that the electromagnetic spectrum existed, but it was an Italian nobleman, **Guglielmo Marconi**, who made practical application of the physicists' theories while living in Canada.

Young Marconi became obsessed with the possibilities of the electromagnetic spectrum and built equipment that could ring a bell by remote control—no strings, no wires, just turning an electromagnetic charge on and off. In 1895, when he was 21, Marconi used his wireless method to transmit codes for more than a mile on his father's Bologna estate. Then, on December 12, 1901, Marconi stood on Signal Hill, Newfoundland, and received the Morse code signal for the letter "S" from Cornwall, England. Marconi patented his invention in England, and his mother, a well-connected Irish woman, arranged British financing to set up the Marconi Wireless Telegraph Company. Soon oceangoing ships were equipped with Marconi radiotelegraphy equipment to communicate at sea, even when they were beyond the horizon—something never possible before. Marconi made a fortune. Many feel that Marconi is the father of telegraphy, while a Canadian, Reginald Fessenden, is the father of radio.

TRANSMITTING VOICES

Breakthroughs came quickly. In 1906 a message was sent across the Atlantic. In 1906 **Lee de Forest**, a promoter who fancied himself an inventor, created what he called the **audion tube** to make voice transmission possible. Some say he stole the underlying technology from Canadian inventor **Reginald Aubrey Fessenden**, who was born in Knowlton, Quebec. Whatever the truth of the matter, it was Fessenden who broadcast the first radio program, also in 1906. From Brant Rock, Massachusetts, where he had a laboratory, Fessenden played the violin, sang the Christmas Carol "O Holy Night" and played an Ediphone recording of Handel's

Who Invented Radio? Numerous theorists conceived of wireless transmission ahead of the Irish-Italian inventor Guglielmo Marconi. A dentist, Mahlon Loomis, detected signals between two mountains in Virginia in 1866 and won a patent for wireless telegraphy in 1872. Scottish mathematician James Maxwell and German physicist Heinrich Hertz did important theorizing. Who, then, invented radio? Admirers of a reclusive but brilliant scientist, Nikola Tesla, have mounted a campaign for him to be recognized as the inventor of radio. Among their evidence is a 1943 U.S. Supreme Court decision recognizing that Tesla transmitted on the electromagnetic spectrum before Marconi.

Largo. This shocked wireless operators on ships at sea. Instead of the dots and dashes of Morse code, suddenly there was music. Len Arminio, a journalism professor at Ontario's Loyalist College, refers to Fessenden as "broadcasting's overlooked genius." De Forest, however, took the limelight with show-off broadcasts from the Eiffel Tower and other stunts. In 1910 de Forest clearly demonstrated radio's potential as an entertainment medium with a magnificent performance by the tenor Enrico Caruso from the New York Metropolitan Opera House. But it was Fessenden who realized the dream of broadcasting voices through the air.

WHICH CAME FIRST: XWA OR KDKA?

A Pittsburgh engineer, **Frank Conrad**, fiddled with radiotelegraphy in his home garage, playing music as he experimented. People with homemade receivers liked what they heard from Conrad's transmitter, and soon he had a following. When Conrad's Westinghouse bosses learned that he had become a local celebrity, they saw profit in building receivers that consumers could buy at $10 a set and take home to listen to. To encourage sales of the receivers, Westinghouse built a station to provide regular programming of news, sports and music—mostly music. That station, **KDKA** in Pittsburgh, became America's first licensed commercial station in 1920.

The licensing of KDKA was important because it demonstrated the United States' commitment to placing radio in the private sector. In Europe, broadcasting was a government monopoly. In Canada, there was, and continues to be, a mix of public and private broadcasting.

In 1918, the Montreal-based radio station **XWA** (now 940 News, CINW, owned by Corus), owned by the Marconi Wireless Telegraph Company, was the first station to get a broadcasting licence, under the Radiotelegraph Act of 1913, from the federal government. Its first broadcast took place in May 1920, under Marconi's supervision. XWA was the first station to have regularly scheduled programs, the first of which was a musical program, a Dorothy Lutton concert to the Royal Society of Canada in Montreal. This was the first radio broadcast not only in Canada but also in North America, contrary to what Pittsburgh's KDKA claims. The first broadcast licence for radio was issued to CJCG in Winnipeg in May 1922. This station was on the air for only one year. All in all, 33 radio licences were issued in 1922. Some of those stations are still on the air today, including CKOC in Hamilton and CKCK in Regina.

FM RADIO

Static-free transmission was developed by **Edwin Armstrong**, a Columbia University researcher. In 1939 Armstrong built an experimental station in New Jersey using a new system called **frequency modulation**, FM for short. FM's system, piggybacking sound on airwaves, was different from the older **amplitude modulation**, or AM method. In time, Armstrong developed FM stereo with two soundtracks, one for each ear, duplicating the sensation of hearing a performance live. FM radio wasn't fully used as a medium until the 1950s and 1960s in North America. **CHFI** in Toronto, owned by Rogers, was Canada's first FM station. It began broadcasting in 1961. The CBC developed its network of FM stations in the early 1960s.

NEW TECHNOLOGIES

In the early 2000s, other technologies were working against the radio industry's traditional infrastructure.

Satellite Radio Two **satellite radio** operations went on the air in the United States in 2001; by 2005, satellite radio had arrived in Canada. Satellite radio provides digital-quality sound, much of it commercial-free, for a monthly fee ranging between $10 and $13. The companies tried to build an immediate audience by lining up automobile manufacturers to install receivers into new vehicles—about 12 million a year. Both Sirius and XM offered at least a hundred channels—pop, country, news, sports and talk—but also specialized programming like chamber music, Broadway hits, CBC Radio, NHL hockey, Major League Baseball, audio books and gardening tips.

Frank Conrad ■ Pioneer whose work led to KDKA.

KDKA ■ First licensed commercial radio station in the United States.

XWA ■ Canada's first radio station.

Edwin Armstrong ■ Invented FM as an alternative transmission method.

frequency modulation ■ FM

amplitude modulation ■ AM

CHFI ■ Canada's first FM radio station.

satellite radio ■ Delivery method of programming from a single source beamed to an orbiting satellite for transmission directly to individual end-users.

shock jock ■ Announcer whose style includes vulgarities, taboos.

Howard Stern and Satellite Radio

Howard Stern began his career at Boston University, where he volunteered at the college radio station. His show was cancelled after one broadcast. He had spoofed a game show with contestants confessing their worst sins. It was a precursor of Stern's unorthodoxy: a mix of phone chat, much of it inane; music, a lot of it offbeat; and crude, sophomoric shock-talk. His on-air antics earned him the label "shock jock," a new radio programming genre in the 1980s.

No matter how tasteless, Stern amassed a following. He soon had star status and big bucks—and critics who pushed for federal fines against his on-air vulgarities. At one point, the accumulated unpaid fines totaled $1.7 million. The corporate owner of his flagship New York station had no problem paying the fines from the profits Stern was bringing in.

People kept listening to his bathroom-wall jokes and his topless female studio guests. He even arrived on Canadian airwaves in 1997. During his first Canadian broadcast, he thanked CHOM-FM for "opening up the sewer gate for me to pollute yet another country." During his first few shows, he referred to French Canadians as "peckerheads" and "jack offs." To those Canadians who don't like his approach to morning radio, Stern replied that the show was "just entertainment. Jokes, laughter and whatever's on our minds." By 1998 CHOM-FM had dropped Howard Stern. Q-107 dropped Stern in 2001.

Still the fines kept coming. A $495 000 fine in 2004 brought Stern's career total to $2.5 million. Analysts say the giant Clear Channel chain, which acquired Stern in its buy-up of stations, earned $25 million a year in advertising revenue from Stern's show, which played in 40 cities. That was after $70 million in production costs and Stern's $30 million salary. Clear Channel could afford the fines, but concerned that the government might revoke its stations' licences, the corporate executives became uneasy. In 2004 they tried putting a lid on Stern.

Refusing to be bridled, Stern announced that he wouldn't renew with Clear Channel when his contract expired in 2006. Instead, he would leave so-called terrestrial radio and go to the unregulated airwaves of the fledgling Sirius satellite radio service. With Sirius, Stern's program would go directly to subscribers, bypassing the traditional delivery mechanism through federally licensed local stations that send their signals from land-based towers. His shows, *Howard 100* and *Howard 101*, are also available on satellite radio in Canada.

Typical of his egocentric confidence, Stern declared the death of terrestrial radio with stations licensed to broadcast to local audiences. The future, he said, was in national stations that transmitted directly to individuals, not relaying through local stations. Howard Stern is not alone in seeing problems for the radio industry as everyone had come to know it since the 1920s. Radio has had to withstand the challenges of iPods, the internet and satellite radio.

Depending on who you talk to, Howard Stern represents the best in radio, meeting the interests and needs of a mass audience, or the worst, pandering to the lowest instincts in society and getting rich in the process.

WHAT DO YOU THINK?

1. Would you pay to hear shock jocks like Howard Stern on satellite radio? Why or why not?

2. Is the fact that XM and Sirius merged in 2007 evidence that people simply won't pay for radio, something that has been "free" for almost a century?

3. How does Howard Stern epitomize the crisis in contemporary radio?

4. Is Howard Stern right: is terrestrial radio dead? Does the future of radio lie in national stations that transmit directly to individuals either via satellite radio or the internet?

Terrestrial Listeners to over-the-air or **terrestrial radio** hope their new competitors lose the bet. When the CRTC approved satellite radio, local stations told advertisers that satellite stations wouldn't have radio's traditional local thrust. However, many local stations save money by piping in—usually via satellite—programming from far away sources that serve hundreds of stations simultaneously with the same all-music, all-talk or all-sports content. In reality, many local stations are mere conduits for national programming, although technology allows them to insert local weather forecasts and, of course, advertising. Other than that local factor, some stations' programming could be mistaken for that on Sirius and XM.

iPod Handheld MP3 players, epitomized by the Apple iPod, siphoned listeners from over-the-air local radio. With these devices and music downloaded from the internet or ripped from their own CDs, people are able to create their own playlists—no inane disc-jockey patter, no commercials, no waiting through less-than-favourite tunes for the good stuff.

Podcasting Almost anybody who wanted to create a show could prerecord a batch of favourite music, complete with narration, as an audio file on a personal computer. Then, by adding a hyperlink on a web server, they could let the world download the show for playback on a computer or MP3 player. Whenever the listener links to the server again, a new show from the same source is downloaded automatically. Podcasting has the potential to make everybody a disc jockey. This too cuts into the audience of traditional radio.

Webcasting Most Canadian radio stations stream their signals on the web. In these days of convergence, the web and radio may be perfect partners, says John Harding of the Canadian Radio Marketing Bureau: "As radio content evolves onto the internet, radio will excel in its ability to attract and maintain ears and eyes, that being radio's forte. Radio knows how to hold an audience. The skill sets are transferable from terrestrial radio to internet radio to build and maintain audience loyalty." However, radio does have competition on the web with online music channels such as Canada's Iceberg Radio.

Satellite Radio
A driver's face is reflected in the curved dash of his car as he adjusts the control panel of his satellite radio receiver. A conventional radio is above the XM panel.

Corporate Radio

studypreview A few corporations dominate the Canadian and American radio industries, using mostly programming geared to mass tastes. The approach, however, has earned the disapproving moniker "corporate radio" for its bland sameness. The chains have taken steps to win back listeners who have left for alternative sources of music, news and information.

CHAIN OWNERSHIP

In a drive to cut costs to maximize profits, the big radio chains consolidated their new properties in the post-1996 era and centralized not only **playlists** but also disc jockeys. Through a system called **voice tracking**, a handful of announcers can be heard on several radio stations, owned by the same company, in different markets. This robo-programming was efficient. Canadian radio followed suit, many stations voice tracking during evenings, overnights and weekends.

Some stations with robo-programming shifted gears in 2005 with **Jack**, a format developed by Rogers Media of Canada that had a decidedly more eclectic mix of music. Jack playlists typically include 1200 songs. Unlike robo-formulas, few songs get played even once a day in Jack's unlikely patterns, with none of the segues that slide from one tune seamlessly into another. Eight U.S. stations licensed Jack from Rogers in 2005. Others are imitating it. At KSJK in Kansas City, which calls itself 105.1 Jack FM, program director Mike Reilly prides himself on "train wrecks," a collision of unlikely music in sequence: "If you hear MC Hammer go into the Steve Miller Band, I've done my job." It's the kind of programming excitement that people can create on an iPod.

terrestrial radio ■ Traditional name for over-the-air radio stations.

corporate radio ■ A disapproving term for programming engineered by radio chains for use in multiple markets.

playlist ■ A list of songs that a radio station plays.

voice tracking ■ A few announcers who prerecord music intros and outros for multiple stations to create a single personality for stations.

Jack ■ An eclectic, somewhat unpredictable musical radio format.

Top Five Radio Chains by Hours Tuned, 2006

For years the government restricted a radio company to owning no more than two radio stations in any Canadian city. In 1998, the CRTC relaxed ownership limits. Now a company could own up to three radio stations in markets of less than 8 stations; 4 in markets over 8 stations. The only stipulation was that no one company could own more than 2 AM or 2 FM stations in any one city. Here are the biggest radio chains in Canada, by total hours tuned:

Corporation	Total Listening Hours
Corus	87 258 000
Standard	61 653 000
Rogers Communications	46 772 000
Astral	37 681 000
CHUM Limited	34 004 000

Note: In 2007, Astral Media purchased Standard Broadcasting, while CTVglobemedia purchased CHUM Limited.

Source: CRTC, Broadcast Policy Monitoring Report 2007.

Jack, say critics, is less than it seems. The playlists don't venture beyond what is familiar to listeners. A Jack consultant, Mike Henry, put it this way in an interview in *The Wall Street Journal*: "You're only challenging them on a stylistic level. You're not challenging them on a familiar/unfamiliar level." Nirvana grunge may butt up against Village People disco, but both are proven pop.

Canadian media writer and director Doug Thompson argues that Jack, or any of its clones, such as Dave or Bob, isn't really radio, it's a jukebox and "that's not what radio was meant to be. I didn't grow up listening to radio for a bunch of songs played back to back. There is no substitute for a live person talking one on one with a listener." In short, corporate radio needs to look to developing new personalities for radio, not just new formats. Thompson adds that right now, the creative, personality radio DJ is an endangered species.

Some stations set themselves apart with local and distinctive content. These channels tend to be owned by small companies or corporations who are more likely to take a chance on something different. "Radio Newfoundland" features nothing but east coast artists. Country stations in the west continue to serve their largely agricultural listeners well, while CHWO in Oakville calls itself "Prime Time Radio," with an emphasis on older listeners. In Ottawa, Live 88.5 embraced the podcast generation by merging the online music subculture with an alternative music format.

■ Radio Content

studypreview **Radio programming falls mostly into three categories: entertainment, mostly music; news; and talk.**

RADIO ENTERTAINMENT

During the 1920s, radios became an integral part of Canadians' living rooms. These were big radios, some as large as today's home entertainment units. People listened to the radio then in much the same way we watch television today: after supper, with or without the family. A radio was considered a status symbol, and much of the programming reflected this: broadcasts included concerts, political commentary, dramas and comedies. Broadcasts of hockey games, sponsored by General Motors, were the most popular radio programs of the early days of the medium, beginning in 1923. Within 10 years, hockey broadcasts were heard on 20 Canadian radio stations from coast to coast. This sponsorship also marked the beginning of "commercial" radio in Canada.

The comedies, dramas, variety shows and quiz shows that dominated network-provided radio programming in the 1930s and 1940s moved to television in the 1950s. So did the huge audience that radio had cultivated. The radio networks, losing advertisers to television, scaled back what they offered to affiliates. As the number of listeners dropped, local stations switched to more recorded music, which was far cheaper than producing concerts, dramas and comedies. Thus, radio reinvented itself, survived and prospered.

The industry found itself shaken again in the 1970s when the listeners flocked to new FM stations. Because FM technology offered superior sound fidelity, these became the stations of choice for music. AM listenership seemed destined to tank until, in another reinvention, most AM stations converted to nonmusic formats. From roots in 1961 with programming genius Gordon McLendon, who beamed the first 24/7 news into southern California from XTRA across the border in Tijuana, all-news took off as a format in major cities. So did listener call-in shows with colourful hosts.

RADIO NEWS

Radio news today has diverse forms, some based on the notion of drawing listeners to reports on breaking events as they happen, some more focused on depth and understanding. Mostly, though, radio news is known for being on top of events as they happen.

Media PEOPLE

Gordon McLendon

Gordon McLendon

A crisis hit the U.S. radio history in the 1950s. As comedies, dramas and quiz shows moved to television, so did the huge audience that radio had cultivated. The radio networks, losing advertisers to television, scaled back what they offered to stations.

As the number of listeners dropped, local stations switched more to recorded music, which was far cheaper than producing programs.

To the rescue came Gordon McLendon, who perfected a new format, the Top 40, which repeated the day's most popular new music in rotation. McLendon developed the format at KLIF in Dallas, Texas, by mixing the music with fast-paced newscasts, disc jockey chatter, lively commercials and promotional jingles and hype. It was catchy, almost hypnotizing—and widely imitated.

With the portable transistor radios that were coming onto the market and a growing number of automobiles outfitted with radios, Top 40 was right for the times. People could tune in and tune out on the go. Most tunes lasted only three minutes or so. It was not

programming designed for half-hour blocks. It reshaped radio as a medium that began a recovery in a new incarnation even as some observers were writing the medium's epitaph.

McLendon was no one-shot wonder. He also designed so-called beautiful music as a format at KABL, San Francisco, in 1959; all-news at XTRA, Tijuana, Mexico, aimed at southern California, in 1961; and all-classified ads at KADS, Los Angeles, in 1967. In all of his innovations, McLendon was firm about a strict structure. In Top 40, for example, there were no deviations from music in rotation, news every 20 minutes, naming the station by call letters twice between songs, upbeat jingles and no deadpan commercials. McLendon's classified-ad format bombed, but the others have survived. For better or worse, McLendon is the father of format radio.

Breaking News Radio news came into its own in World War II, when the networks sent correspondents abroad. Americans, eager for news from Europe, developed the habit of listening to the likes of Edward R. Murrow and other giants of mid-20th-century journalism, including Walter Cronkite. As a medium of instantaneous reporting, radio offered news on breakthrough events even before newspapers could issue special extra editions. The term **breaking news** emerged as something to which radio was uniquely suited.

Headline Service In the relatively tranquil period after World War II, with people less intent on news, the radio industry recognized that listeners tuned away from lengthy stories. News formats shifted to shorter stories, making radio a **headline service**. Details and depth were left to newspapers. Gordon McLendon's influential rock 'n' roll format in the 1960s epitomized the headline service, generally with 3-minute newscasts dropped every 20 minutes amid 3-minute songs, with no story more than 20 seconds, most only two sentences.

All News As contradictory as it may seem, Gordon McLendon also invented **all-news radio**, also in the 1960s. For the Los Angeles market, McLendon set up a skeletal staff at XTRA across the border in Tijuana to read wire copy nonstop. When XTRA turned profitable, McLendon took over a Chicago station, renamed it WNUS, and converted it to all-news. This was a dramatic departure from the idea of radio as a mass medium with each station trying for the largest possible audience. McLendon's WNUS and later all-news stations sought niche listenerships, finding early profitability in demassification—a narrow part of the larger mosaic of the whole radio market. Today all-news stations are available in almost every Canadian market.

TALK RADIO

Call-in formats were greeted enthusiastically at first because of their potential as forums for discussion of public issues, but there was a downside. Many stations with music-based formats used the advent of news and talk stations to reduce their news programming. In effect, many music stations were saying, "Let those guys do news and talk, and we'll do music." While some might lament the lack of news on all-music stations, in these days of demassification and diversification, people who tune in to a music station are tuning in for music; they don't want much in the way of news and information programming.

Talk radio may offer access to the "commoners," or so it would seem; Paul Rutherford, a communication professor at the University of Toronto, says that talk radio is "providing a voice for people who otherwise wouldn't have one." Today, many Canadians feel a sense of alienation; they believe that politicians simply aren't listening to them. To vent their frustrations, many turn to talk radio. This gives listeners a sense that they are finally being heard. Sometimes politicians listen; sometimes they don't.

How is Canadian talk radio different from American talk radio? Many differences exist, according to those who claim that Canadians are "kindler, gentler" talk show participants. Rutherford claims that there are two types of talk show hosts: warriors and father figures. The warrior is clearly American: confrontational and in your face. Male Canadian talk show hosts tend to be father figures and offer more thought-provoking and well-researched fare and content.

Perhaps one of the reasons talk radio is different in Canada is the regional or local nature of talk shows. Compared to the United States, which boasts numerous national talk show hosts, Canadian talk show hosts are generally local or regional. Gary Slaight of Standard Broadcasting says there's only one real issue in the United States, "and that's whether you're left wing or right wing. Whether you're in New York or Seattle, it's the same question. Not in Canada, where we're defined so many ways: English/French, east/west."

MUSIC RADIO

Most radio today is based on music programming. Below are terms used to distinguish radio's major music formats for private radio in Canada. Due to demassification, many formats have become fragmented.

Adult Contemporary (A/C) Many advertisers like the A/C format because so many people in the big-spending 25-to-40 age group listen to it. Variations of this format include "soft rock," such as the EZ-Rock brand across Canada.

Top 40 Top 40, also called CHR (short for Contemporary Hits Radio), emphasizes current rock but not as strictly as McLendon insisted. These stations target teenagers. Some variations within this format include Rhythmic Top 40 and Adult Top 40.

Country Once called country and western, or CW for short, this format goes back to WSM's *Grand Ole Opry* program in Nashville. The music varies significantly from twangy western ballads to what's called "urban country." In Canada, "young country" and "new country" have become two popular music formats. By abandoning Loretta Lynn and George Jones in favour of Shania Twain and Terri Clark, new country radio stations have been able to attract younger listeners.

Album-Oriented Rock (AOR) AOR formats offer songs from the 100 best-selling albums. A casual listener might confuse AOR with Top 40, but album stations go back a couple of years for wider variety. Audiences tend to be aged 18 to 24. This is one of the most diversified formats, with classic rock available on CIRK-FM (Edmonton), mainstream rock on The Goat (Lloydminster), and new music on CFNY (Toronto).

Oldies Oldies stations play music that the 45- to 64-year-old demographic grew up with, mostly music of the 1960s and 1970s. It's sometimes called "classic hits."

Ethnic More than 9 million Canadians belong to ethnic groups other than First Nations, French or British. These people represent more than 70 different cultures. Given this fact and Canada's official status as a multicultural country, it's not surprising that full-time ethnic radio stations have taken root in many of Canada's urban centres. Toronto has six ethnic stations, Vancouver has three, Montreal has two, and Edmonton, Calgary, Ottawa and Winnipeg each have one. Many other radio stations feature ethnic programming on a part-time basis, during the evenings and on weekends.

Classical This format offers the basic repertoire of enduring music since the Baroque era, although some classical stations also play experimental symphonies, operas and contemporary composers. Because highbrow music has a limited following, most classical stations are supported not by advertising but by listener donations, universities and government funding. CBC Radio Two broadcasts classical music on a national basis. CFMX, located in Cobourg, Ontario, has achieved significant ratings in the Toronto area.

Religious Inspirational music is the programming core of religious stations. The music is interspersed with sermons from evangelists who buy time for their programs, seeking both to proselytize and to raise funds to support ministries.

Other Formats The CRTC has recently issued licences for some new formats in Canada. These include "smooth jazz" in Calgary and Hamilton, "urban" in Vancouver, Calgary and Toronto, and **AVR** (Aboriginal Voices Radio) across Canada.

Codi Jeffries, an "80s Chick"
Jeffries hosts *That 80s Show* on Majic 100 in Ottawa. The show features everything 1980s from new wave to hair bands. Shows like this are an example of demassified programming in radio. Jeffries is also the music director for Majic 100.

A CANADIAN ALTERNATIVE: CBC

As Canada's public broadcaster, CBC Radio brought Canadian programming home to Canadians. Today, CBC Radio is known as either Radio One or Radio Two. Radio One features a mix of information, talk and Canadian music, while Radio Two's programming is more highbrow, with an emphasis on classical music and opera. CBC Radio is commercial-free, funded through taxpayer money. Much of its programming, as mandated by the Broadcasting Act, is regional. More than 85 percent of CBC English Radio is produced at the local level, with much of that broadcast nationally. CBC Radio also spotlights Canadian talent. More than 60 hours of performance programming on both networks focuses on Canadian performers. The listenership for CBC Radio has remained fairly steady in recent years, as 3.5 million Canadians tune in each week to either CBC Radio One or Radio Two.

OTHER ALTERNATIVES: CAMPUS AND COMMUNITY RADIO

Campus and Community radio stations in Canada, geared to neighborhood service with low-power transmitters, have made possible a level of interactivity with their

Campus Radio Campus and Community radio stations in Canada allow members of the public access to the airwaves. There are currently almost 100 Community radio stations in Canada, mostly in Quebec. There are an additional 53 campus stations across Canada. You probably have one on your campus.

ONLINE

Canadian Campus Stations A link to a listing of all campus stations in Canada.
www.umfm.com/campus_stations.shtml

National Campus and Community Radio Association Read about the alternative radio programming available.
www.ncra.ca

audiences not possible for traditional stations that seek large audiences to draw advertising and pay the bills. These low-power stations, many staffed with volunteers, are alternative voices in the radio universe. Under CRTC conditions of licence, programming on these stations must "differ in style and substance from the services provided by conventional broadcasters." These stations are usually funded through grants, student fees and some advertising. They also support social causes. Every year since 2003, CKUT at McGill University in Montreal has been the host station for something called "The Homelessness Marathon," to raise awareness of the growing problem in Canada. Campus and Community radio stations from across the country simulcast the event, with each station contributing local reports and commentary.

Quality on the Air

studypreview With deregulation, radio programming has become more populist, formulaic and bland. Many stations are devoid of local identity. Even so, some stations set themselves apart with local and distinctive content.

QUALITY ON THE AIR

Quality is in the beholder's eye—or ear. If wall-to-wall music is a measure of quality, then a lot of superb stations are on the air. Recorded music, though, is a low-overhead format that's so formulaic that stations have a hard time distinguishing themselves from each other. There are, however, other quality measures.

The CRTC states that Canadian radio should reflect a Canadian way of life. The idea was for radio to play the local community back to itself. How well do stations do this? By this standard, a station would get high marks for programming indigenous culture: performances by local musicians, coverage of local news, discussion of local issues and play-by-plays of local athletic events. Radio can have a role in creating a distinctive local culture. Two Ontario radio stations were reprimanded by the CRTC for not serving their local communities. CKDK-FM (The Hawk) in Woodstock and CING-FM (Country 95.3) in Hamilton were licensed to broadcast in their respective communities. However, both stations were targeting larger markets within their radius. Woodstock targeted listeners in London, while Hamilton targeted the Toronto market. They did this with news, weather and traffic reports from those communities rather than their own.

MARKETPLACE VALUES

Audience measures come mostly from the ratings service Bureau of Broadcast Measurement, or BBM for short. Because the surveys are paid for by stations that want numbers to persuade advertisers to buy time, BBM does not release its findings to the public. The results usually surface, however, when station sales reps pass them out to potential advertisers, although the information is often recast to make particular selling points. BBM data are broken down by day parts, like morning drive time, and by audience demographics, like gender and age groupings.

CHAPTER 4 Wrap-Up

While radio will still continue to be a presence in the life of Canadians for many years to come, the medium faces challenging times. Suddenly, at the dawn of the 21st century, new technologies have shaken the structure of the radio industry as listeners opt for cutting-edge alternatives including satellite direct-to-listener radio, iPods, podcasts and webcasts, or online music stations. To stem listener losses, mainstream companies have eased their drive for centralized programming and cost cutting, some trying the new format Jack and copycats.

Questions for Review

1. What is happening to the number of people who listen to traditional radio?
2. How has radio technology evolved since the pioneering work of Guglielmo Marconi and Reginald Fessenden?
3. Who "invented" radio: Tesla, Fessenden or Marconi?
4. How does radio move invisibly through the air on electromagnetic waves?
5. What is the dominant programming of corporate radio? Has it run its course?
6. How has the mix of entertainment and information changed through the course of radio's history?
7. What are measures of excellence in radio?

Questions for Critical Thinking

1. Guglielmo Marconi introduced radio wireless telegraphy, while Fessenden was responsible for the first radio broadcast. What was the difference?

2. Lee de Forest was a technical and programming innovator. Explain the significance of his audion tube.
3. A new way of transmitting radio was developed by Edwin Armstrong in the 1930s, and by the 1980s it had left the original AM broadcast system in economic peril. Discuss Armstrong's invention and how it has reshaped radio.
4. Radio was reshaped by the advent of television in the 1950s. Explain these influences, and be sure to cite radio's transition from literal broadcasting toward demassification. What about the influence of Gordon McLendon? What of the future?
5. Radio listenership seems to be on the decline. Review the Media Databank on listening trends in this chapter. Does the data reflect your own radio listening? That of your parents? Grandparents? What must radio do to stop the slide?
6. Many radio stations have webcams set up in the studio so people can watch announcers/DJs while they perform on air. Given the fact that radio is a "blind medium," is it still radio if you can see the announcers?

Deepening Your
media LITERACY

What must radio do to survive into the new millennium? Which concept of ownership of the airwaves is more in the public interest?

STEP 1 The radio industry in Canada is mostly privately owned. In some countries the airwaves are controlled by the government.

1. Think of the Canadian system, which is more and more controlled by chains and corporations.
2. Consider government-controlled radio such as the BBC, the British broadcasting system that is accountable to Parliament and to household licence payers and that is often cited as one of the world's most independent news sources, and a station in a country that is notorious for censoring media content.
3. Also consider Campus and Community stations.

Dig Deeper

STEP 2 Each of these models of airwave ownership has pluses and minuses. Make a list of the pros and cons of privately owned airwaves. Make a second list of the pros and cons of government-owned airwaves. Make a third list of the pros and cons of low-power radio.

What Do You Think?

STEP 3 Which model do you think best serves the public interest? Is there some other model, a new one, or a combination of the ones you just analyzed, that would do a better job?

Keeping Up to Date

The trade journals *Broadcaster* and *Broadcast Dialogue* keep abreast of news and issues.

Other news coverage can be found in the *National Post, The Globe and Mail,* and other major daily newspapers.

Scholarly articles can be found in the *Canadian Journal of Communication, Journal of Broadcasting, Electronic Media, Journal of Communication,* and *Journalism Quarterly.*

R&R, a weekly trade journal published by Radio & Records, carries charts and playlists that not only reflect what music is getting airtime but also shape what will be getting airtime.

For Further Learning

Jason Scott Alexander. "Newcap's Latest Arrival is Bringing iPod Listeners Back to Ottawa Radio." *Broadcast Dialogue* (April 2006).

Len Arminio. "Broadcasting's Overlooked Genius." *Broadcast Dialogue* (October 2006).

Erik Barnouw. *A Tower in Babel, A History of Broadcasting in the United States to 1933* (Oxford, 1966).

Erik Barnouw. *The Golden Web, A History of Broadcasting in the United States, 1933–1953* (Oxford, 1968).

Erik Barnouw. *The Image Empire, A History of Broadcasting in the United States, 1953–On* (Oxford, 1970).

John R. Bittner. *Broadcast Law and Regulation* (Prentice Hall, 1982).

Robert Brehl. "CRTC Causes Static among Radio Bosses." *The Globe and Mail* (June 9, 1998).

John Bugailiskis. "Stern's Show Slim on Canadian Content." *Broadcaster* (September 1997).

"CAB Fires Back at Music Industry Radio Content Claims." *Broadcaster Industry News* (April 1996).

Canadian Association of Broadcasters. *A Broadcaster's Guide to Canada's Cultural Mosaic, 1988.*

Gerald Carson. *The Roguish World of Dr. Brinkley* (Holt, Rinehart & Winston, 1960).

CBC Enterprises. *Fifty Years of Radio: A Celebration of CBC Radio 1936–1986.*

Howard Christensen. "Blackout: Radio to the Rescue." *Broadcast Dialogue* (October 2003).

Ray Conlogue. "Radio Shock Jock Strikes a Nerve." *The Globe and Mail* (September 3, 1997).

Andrew Coyne. "Cracking Down on Howard." *St. Catharines Standard* (September 20, 1997).

Andrew Crisell. *Understanding Radio* (Methuen, 1990).

CRTC. *Broadcast Policy Monitoring Report 2007.*

Guy Dixon. "Out of Tune?" *The Globe and Mail* (March 14, 2006).

Thomas Doherty. "Return with Us Now to Those Thrilling Days of Yesteryear: Radio Studies Rise Again." *Chronicle of Higher Education* (May 21, 2004): B12–B13.

Philip Fine. "Radio Stations Ponder Fate of Stern's Show." *The Globe and Mail* (November 22, 1997).

Marc Fisher. "Resurgent Radio." *American Journalism Review* (December 2000): 32–37.

James C. Foust. *Big Voices of the Air: The Battle over Clear Channel Radio* (Iowa State University Press, 2000).

"The Fowler Years: A Chairman Who Marches to His Own Drummer." *Broadcasting* 112 (March 23, 1987): 12, 51–54.

Peter Goddard. "It's Talk, Talk, Talk All over the Radio." *Toronto Star* (October 29, 1995).

Lynne Schafer Gross. *Telecommunications: An Introduction to Radio, Television and Other Electronic Media,* Second edition (Wm. C. Brown, 1986).

John Harding. "Radio—The Momentum Continues." *Broadcast Dialogue* (January 2001).

Susanne Hiller. "That You Bas? After 40 Years on Air, Bas Jamieson's Not Allowed to Retire." *Newfoundlanders Abroad, 2002.*

Laurel Hyatt. "Back in the Black." *Broadcaster* (February 1998).

Laurel Hyatt. "Radio's Recipe for Success." *Broadcaster* (April 1996): 12–15.

Donald Jack. *Sinc, Betty and the Morning Man* (Macmillan, 1977).

Daphne Lavers. "DAB Launch." *Broadcast Dialogue* (August 1999).

Murray B. Levin. *Talk Radio and the American Dream* (D.C. Heath, 1987).

Kirk Makin. "Brrrrring . . . brrrrring: You're on the Air." *The Globe and Mail* (July 16, 1994).

Michael McCabe. "CANCON Not the Only Measure of Radio's Contribution." *Broadcaster* (February 1998).

Doug Saunders. "AM Listeners Tuning Out." *The Globe and Mail* (October 20, 1997).

Heather Schoffield and Robert Brehl. "Radio Stations Told to Turn Up the Volume" and "CRTC Opens Radio Markets." *The Globe and Mail* (May 1, 1998).

Philip M. Seib. *Going Live: Getting the News Right in a Real-Time, Online World* (Rowman & Littlefield, 2000).

Sandy Stewart. *A Pictorial History of Radio in Canada* (Gage, 1975).

Doug Thompson. "Ode to the Disc Jockey." *Broadcast Dialogue* (May 2006).

Kevin G. Wilson. *Deregulating Telecommunications: U.S. and Canadian Telecommunications, 1840–1997* (Rowman & Littlefield, 2000).

Erik Zorn. "The Specialized Signals of Radio News." *Washington Journalism Review* 8 (June 1986): 6, 31–33.

The Sweet Hereafter Canadian directors, such as Atom Egoyan, have achieved critical success both here and abroad. Sarah Polley, one of the stars of *The Sweet Hereafter*, is now a director. Her film *Away from Her* debuted at the 2006 Toronto Film Festival. Egoyan was the executive producer on the project.

5

Movies

Media in Theory

American versus Canadian Movies: What's the Difference?

Why are Canadian movies different from American movies? Notice that the question doesn't imply that Canadian movies are "worse" than American movies, although for many Canadians, that seems to be the common belief. For students of communication, the questions really should be: "What makes Canadian movies different from American movies?" and "What do our films say about our culture?"

While funding, marketplace economics, and distribution have certainly all played a role in the development of the Canadian film industry and the "look" of Canadian films, particularly in the early days, there may be other differences as well. **Peter Harcourt**, in his 1976 essay "Introduction," argues that Canadian movie scripts symbolically reflect "our own social uncertainties—both our uncertainty of action as a nation and our own present lack of security in dealing with ethnic and cultural problems which, throughout our vast nation, we are trying to define ourselves."

This uncertainty is clearly evident in the films of one of Canada's best-known filmmakers, **Atom Egoyan**. Harcourt, in the journal *Film Quarterly,* described Egoyan's work as "expressing the classic Canadian dilemma as formulated by Northrop Frye . . . Egoyan devises films that register the personal uncertainties of people who are striving to find a place of rest within a culture not their own." **David Cronenberg**'s films also feature these themes, and don't always feature the happy endings of Hollywood cinema. According to Cronenberg, both he and Egoyan "have a horror of the cheap emotional affect of Hollywood movies."

Meanwhile, in Quebec, French-Canadian cinema has developed a strong following in Quebec and around the world. Directors such as **Denys Arcand** are among the best in the world. His works include *The Decline of the American Empire, Jesus of Montreal*

Peter Harcourt ■ Writes that Canadian movies reflect our own uncertainty.

Atom Egoyan ■ Directs movies about personal uncertainty.

David Cronenberg ■ His films are the antithesis to Hollywood endings.

Denys Arcand ■ Award-winning French-Canadian film director.

and *Les Invasions barbares.* When asked if there were any similarities between French- and English-Canadian movies, Arcand says "there might be something we share in our constant resistance to American genre film." Even the Canadian cult classic film *Ginger Snaps* encourages us to "forget the Hollywood rules."

In her history of Canadian film, *Weird Sex and Snowshoes,* **Katherine Monk** offers a "Canadian checklist" of themes in Canadian movies. These include the following variations of "uncertainty" that Harcourt introduced in 1976: identity issues, being an outsider, empty landscapes, internal demons, personal alienation, language barriers, being on a road to nowhere, questions of faith, survivor guilt and ambiguous endings.

Perhaps our nation's preoccupation with developing a national identity is reflected in the uncertainties of Canadian movies. Many factors are at work here. First, since Canada is officially bilingual and multicultural, how can we have a truly "national cinema" as other countries do? Second, funding has always been an issue for Canadian filmmakers. We simply don't have the economic resources of Hollywood. Finally, finding an audience for Canadian movies has always been a struggle. However, despite all these factors, there have been success stories. Recently, the works of directors Bruce McDonald, Deepa Mehta, Don McKellar and István Szabó have all become successful here at home.

media TIMELINE

MOVIES

1826 French scientist Joseph Niépce found chemicals to capture and preserve an image on a light-sensitive metal.

1888 William Dickson devised a camera to capture sequential motion.

1891 George Eastman devised flexible celluloid for film that could be run through projectors.

1895 Auguste and Louis Lumière opened a movie house in Paris.

1896 The Vitascope was demonstrated in Montreal.

1906 Canada's first movie theatre, the Ouimetoscope, opened in Montreal.

1922 Fox used sound in newsreels.

1927 Warner distributed the first talkie, *The Jazz Singer.*

1932 Disney issued the first full-colour movie, *Flowers and Trees.*

1948 Canadian Nat Taylor opened the first multiplex theatre, The Elgin, in Ottawa.

1970s Multiscreen movie houses, many in the suburbs, became the norm.

1999 George Lucas offered a version of *Star Wars Episode I: The Phantom Menace* for digital projection.

2005 Movie studios agreed to finance a major part of converting theatres for digital movies.

2007 Cineplex Odeon began converting its Canadian cinemas to digital.

■ Importance of Movies

study preview The experience of watching a movie uninterrupted in a darkened auditorium has entranced people since the medium's earliest days. It is an all-encompassing experience, which has given movies a special power in shaping cultural values.

OVERWHELMING EXPERIENCE

Movies have a more intense hold on people, at least while they are watching one, than does any other medium. It is not unusual for a movie reviewer to recommend taking a handkerchief. Never will you hear such advice from a record reviewer and seldom from a book reviewer. Why do movies have such powerful effects? It is not movies themselves. Remember what Canadian Marshall McLuhan said about the medium being the message. Nowhere is this truer than when watching a movie in a darkened theatre. The viewer sits in a darkened auditorium in front of a giant screen, with nothing to interrupt the experience. The rest of the world is excluded. Movies, of course, can be shown outdoors at drive-in theatres and on television, but the experience is strongest in the darkened cocoon of a movie house.

HOLLYWOOD'S CULTURAL INFLUENCE

When Clark Gable took off his shirt in the 1934 movie *It Happened One Night* and revealed that he was not wearing anything underneath, American men in great numbers decided that they too would go without undershirts. Nationwide, undershirt sales plummeted. Whether men prefer wearing underwear is trivial compared with some of the following concerns about how Hollywood portrays U.S. life and its influence:

● Sociologist Norman Denzin says that the treatment of drinking in U.S. movies has contributed to a misleading bittersweet romanticism about alcoholism in the public consciousness.

● Scholars using content analysis have found that exponential increases in movie violence far outpace violence in real life and contribute to perceptions that violence is a growing social problem in modern life.

● Political leaders express concern from time to time that movies corrupt the morals of young people and glamorize deviant behaviour.

Movies are part of our everyday lives in more ways than we realize. Even the way we talk is loaded with movie metaphors. *The New Yorker* magazine noted this while introducing an issue on Hollywood: "Our personal scenarios uncoil in a sequence of flashbacks, voice-overs and cameos. We zoom in, cut to the chase, fade to black."

Because of the perceived influences of movies, some real and some not, it is important to know about the industry that creates them. This is especially true now that television entertainment programming has been largely subsumed by Hollywood and that the book, magazine and sound recording industries are closely tied into it.

persistence of vision ■ Retina's capability to retain an image briefly, allowing brain to fill in gaps between successive images.

William Dickson ■ Developed the first movie camera.

George Eastman ■ Devised celluloid film.

Lumière brothers ■ Opened the first movie exhibition hall.

Movie Technology

studypreview Motion picture technology is based on the same chemical process as photography. The medium developed in the 1880s and 1890s. By the 1930s, movie houses everywhere were showing "talkies." Today, chemical-free digital shooting and editing are beginning to transform production, distribution and exhibition.

ADAPTATION FROM PHOTOGRAPHY

The technical heritage of motion pictures is photography. The 1727 discovery that light causes silver nitrate to darken was basic to the development of motion picture technology. So was a human phenomenon called **persistence of vision**. The human eye retains an image for a fraction of a second. If a series of photographs capture something in motion and if those photographs are flipped quickly, the human eye will perceive continuous motion.

All that was needed was the right kind of camera and film to capture about 16 images per second. Those appeared in 1888. **William Dickson** of Thomas Edison's laboratory developed a workable motion picture camera. Dickson and Edison used celluloid film perfected by **George Eastman**, who had just introduced his Kodak camera. By 1891 Edison had begun producing movies.

Edison movies were viewed by looking into a box. In France, the **Lumière brothers**, Auguste and Louis, brought projection to motion pictures. By running the film in front of a specially aimed powerful light bulb, the Lumières projected movie images on a wall. In 1895 they opened an exhibition hall in Paris—the first movie house. Edison recognized the commercial advantage of projection and himself patented the Vitascope projector, which he put on the market in 1896.

Movies came to Canada in June of 1896 when a private demonstration of the Vitascope was held in Montreal. The report in Montreal's *La Presse* explained what viewers saw and how they reacted to the imagery of a cavalry charge: "You see each and every man in all his glory. There are thousands of them. They are coming right onto the stage. You are going to be crushed—but no, at the crucial moment everything vanishes and you remain gaping. All that was needed to complete the illusion was colour and a phonograph to reproduce sounds. That is soon to come." And it didn't take long to come. Canada's first movie house, the **Ouimetoscope**, opened in Montreal in 1906.

D-CINEMA

Digital technology seems destined to replace film that is "pulled through the (chemical) soup" (described in Chapter 1). The pace of the transition is hard to forecast. There remain technical and financial impediments to big-screen digital projection, but the economic advantages of digital are driving a transition. Cameras and editing equipment are handier than massive celluloid filming equipment. Also, shipping the finished product on optical discs is far more efficient than using the back-breaking film canisters that now are carted from movie house to movie house by truck. Even in the projection rooms, reels of film are awkward. Theoretically, the day will arrive when digital movies can be transmitted by satellite to movie-house projectors, even with central projection control.

Digital Transition George Lucas, producer of the Star Wars series, pioneered digital work through his Industrial Light and Magic production house. For his 1999 Star Wars instalment, *The Phantom Menace*, Lucas shot several scenes with digital equipment, which facilitated their integration into digitally created special effects scenes. For exhibition, there were two masters: one on film, which is what most moviegoers saw, and one in digital form, which was shown in a few theatres. Thus, *The Phantom Menace* became the first major motion picture to be seen in digital form, albeit only at the few theatres equipped with digital projectors.

Relatively few films have been released in digital form because the conversion of movie houses to show them has been slow. Of 36 485 screens nationwide in 2005, only 92 had digital servers and projectors. From 1999 through 2004, a period with almost 3000 Hollywood releases, only 86 titles were digital.

Champions of **d-cinema**, as the new technology is called, expect a sudden upsurge in digital releases. Only one major director, Steven Spielberg, still edits on celluloid. As well, the studios are keen to cut the cost of making hundreds of celluloid prints that are shipped from theatre to theatre. Hollywood's distribution costs are roughly $630 million a year for the United States and Canada, $1 billion worldwide. Distributing d-cinema via the internet or optical disks could cut costs 90 percent.

There are purists who prefer traditional over d-cinema technology, but their number is ebbing. Canadian James Cameron, best known for *Titanic*, says he will never shoot on film again. The next stage in three-dimensional (3-D) movies, stereoscopic 3-D, can be done only digitally.

Technical Standards The studios seem on the verge of making the plunge. In 2002, Disney, Fox, MGM, Paramount, Sony, Universal and Warner combined forces to develop an industry-wide technical standard for d-cinema. The joint venture, **Digital Cinema Initiatives**, has narrowed the quest to two competing technologies, known as 2K and 4K.

One company, Texas Instruments, has devised a 2K-chip imaging device that displays 2048 pixels across. JVC and Sony are pushing 4K, which displays 4096 pixels on a wider canvas. The early d-cinema films used 4K with the Barco D-Cine DP100 projector, but critics say that 4K is a bandwidth hog that offers a resolution far finer than the human eye can detect—so why bother? For practical purposes, say 2K advocates, the two look equally sharp. Too, it's not just a pixel race. The millisecond rate at which images are updated is more important than the number of pixels to meet the upper limits of human persistence of vision. Cineplex Odeon began converting some of their theatres to d-cinema in 2007 using 2K projectors.

The big remaining issue is the financing of movie-house conversion. At $100 000 a theatre for new equipment, the big exhibition chains, always wary about the consequences of increasing ticket prices, are hesitant to make the investment. In 2005, the studios proposed a $1000 incentive to theatres, called a **virtual print fee**, to offset the cost of the new equipment. The mathematics were promising. Studios would save about $1000 without making and shipping film prints. Theatres, assuming a film runs three weeks, would average about $17 000 a year in new fees, which would pay for the new equipment in six years.

Movie-house chains were cautious, noting that digital projection equipment has a notoriously short life span, about three years compared to decades for older equipment. But exhibitors may have no choice as people become enamoured of digital images on computer screens and the growing trend to digital transmission in television.

James Cameron

Stereoscopic 3-D Forget those silly, tinted, throw-away glasses required for early-generation 3-D movies. A new technique, possible through digital shooting and which brings the action to the tip of your nose, has caught the fancy of directors, including Canadian-born James Cameron for *Aliens of the Deep* in 2005 and *Battle Angel* in 2007.

◼ Movie Industry Structure

study<u>preview</u> The movie industry has three major components: production, distribution and exhibition.

STUDIOS AND PRODUCTION

production ◼ Content-creation component of the movie industry.

The flashy corporate names in the movie business are the big studios that are the heart of the **production** component.

Major Studios Some studios are brand names. About 90 percent of the U.S. box office revenue comes from the so-called Big Six: Columbia, Paramount, 20th Century Fox, Universal, Disney and Warner. These companies are called **studios** because each once maintained acres of stage sets—*studios*, if you will. In their heyday, the studios dominated the whole movie industry. Not only did they conceive and nurture movies into existence, but they also controlled the distribution of their products and owned many movie houses. The scope of the studios was trimmed in a landmark 1948 U.S. Supreme Court antimonopoly decision, the **Paramount Decision** (also known as the Paramount Case or the Hollywood Antitrust Case of 1948), but the studios' high-visibility role in producing Hollywood products continued. For decades, studio publicity machines made idols of scriptwriters, directors and actors and simultaneously promoted themselves with glitz.

studio ◼ A company that produces movies, sometimes also involved in distribution.

Paramount Decision ◼ The landmark 1948 U.S. Supreme Court anti-monopoly decision which broke the major studios' hold on the U.S. movie industry.

Even in the uncertain post-1948 period, the studios maintained a reputation for glamour—and with justification. No other country had such a highly developed movie industry.

Hollywood was such a valued homegrown industry that the nation was rattled when Sony, the Japanese electronics company, bought venerable Columbia in 1989. The public generally doesn't have much interest in the owners behind brand names, but there had been modest curiosity a few years earlier when Coca-Cola bought the Columbia studio. It seemed a novel thing for a soda-pop company to do. But now Sony, a company from a distinctly different culture, suddenly had a foothold in the U.S. movie industry. What did it mean? Newsmagazines and pundits had a field day in speculating.

As it turned out, Sony had no alien political, social or ideological agenda. Sony was as profit-driven as corporate parents of the other major studios. There was no magic. Columbia under Sony had as many flops—successes too—as the other studios. Over the next few years, 20th Century Fox became part of Rupert Murdoch's Australian media empire. Universal went into Canadian, then French hands. Now Universal is back in U.S. ownership under General Electric and merged with NBC. One lesson from these transactions is that, whatever the nationality of their headquarters, movie studios are attractive as acquisitions because of either perceived profit potential or synergetic opportunities.

Besides the major studios, all with roots in Hollywood's earliest days, there is United Artists.

United Artists Concerned that the studios were disproportionately focused on profits and infringing creativity, director D.W. Griffith and box-office darlings Charlie Chaplin, Douglas Fairbanks and Mary Pickford (born Gladys Louise Smith in 1892 in Toronto) created **United Artists** in 1919. With full creative control, they produced movies that scored well among critics and attracted huge audiences. United was among the few insurgent movie companies to make a long-term mark on Hollywood after the giants had established themselves. United Artists' history, however, was rocky. It almost was done in by Michael Cimino's out-of-control spending to make *Heaven's Gate* in 1980. A year later the insurance company that had acquired United Artists, Transamerica, unloaded the studio on MGM. But the amalgamated MGM/UA produced one disaster after another until the early 2000s, when it had money-makers including *Legally Blonde* and *Die Another Day*. Whether MGM/UA can break into the Big Six is an open question.

DreamWorks For 21 years the new kid on the Hollywood block was **DreamWorks**, created by retired record executive David Geffen, former Disney executive Jeff Katzenberg and superdirector Steven Spielberg. It was a dream team of exceptionally able, well-connected and seasoned Hollywood people who, each with a fortune from successful entertainment industry careers, could bankroll major projects. Spielberg's *Saving Private Ryan* in

ONLINE

Sony Pictures The parent company of the American icon, Columbia Pictures.
www.sonypictures.com

Paramount News About Paramount movies and home videos. You can also link to Paramount's television or entertainment arms.
www.paramount.com

Fox Movies View the trailers for movies in theatres and online, and take a look at what's coming.
www.foxmovies.com

Universal Pictures Learn about current Universal films. You can also hit links to projects still in production, as well as some surprises.
www.universalpictures.com

Disney Links to the corporate side of Disney, including corporate news, attractions, entertainment media magazines, television, interactive features, movies, music and more.
http://disney.go.com

Warner More than just "What's up, Doc?"
www2.warnerbros.com

United Artists See what the company founded by Charlie Chaplin, Douglas Fairbanks and "Canada's Sweetheart" Mary Pickford is up to now.
www.unitedartists.com

United Artists ▪ Upstart artist-directed movie studio, started in 1919.

DreamWorks ▪ Upstart movie studio, created in 1994 by David Geffen, Jeff Katzenberg and Steven Spielberg.

media DATABANK

Major Movie Studios

In the high-risk movie business, with drastic revenue swings every weekend of new releases, a ranking of the major studios based on revenue is impossible. A single mega-success can catapult one studio to the top instantly, and a series of flops can push a studio toward insolvency. These, though, are the enduring giants of the industry:

	Corporate Parent	Parent Nationality
Columbia	Sony	Japan
Paramount	Viacom	United States
20th Century Fox	News Corporation	Australia
Universal	General Electric	United States
Walt Disney	Disney	United States
Warner Brothers	Time Warner	United States

Alliance Atlantis ■ Canadian movie distributor.

exhibition ■ What movie houses do.

box office ■ Fanciful term for revenue that a movie earns in exhibition.

Cineplex Entertainment LP ■ Canada's largest theatre chain.

nut ■ Upfront distribution payment to exhibitor.

1998 established an early DreamWorks benchmark for filmic excellence that resonated with audiences. *Gladiator* was 2000's best picture at the Academy Awards. Sixty films later, in 2005, the founding threesome sold DreamWorks to Viacom's Paramount for $1.6 billion. It was yet another incidence of a successful media start-up being absorbed by a larger, more established media company.

DISTRIBUTION

For moviegoers, the least visible part of the movie industry is distribution. The major studios are largely responsible for this task. They schedule the bookings for movie releases at the theatres, perform the marketing activities to promote the release and then supply the actual film to the movie houses for showing the movie. Also, the big studios provide distribution services. Independent producers often contract out the distribution function to the major studios because the cost of building up the network of contacts with the large theatre chains is too steep for small producers.

The major film distributor in Canada is **Alliance Atlantis**. It indirectly owns a majority interest in Motion Picture Distribution LP. In addition to distributing Canadian movies, such as *Trailer Park Boys: The Movie*, it distributes films and DVDs for New Line Cinema, Dimension Films, Miramax Films, The Weinstein Company and others.

How does Canada fit into the distribution and exhibition plans of Hollywood? We're simply "America Junior." James Adams of *The Globe and Mail* says that "when the U.S. movie industry gathers statistics on how its films are faring at the box office, Canada isn't considered a sovereign nation: It's part of the American domestic market, right alongside Guam, Puerto Rico, the Virgin Islands and various other U.S. unincorporated territories."

EXHIBITION

The motion picture industry once derived all its revenue from **exhibition**—at movie houses, where customers pay to see a movie. The receipts, called the **box office**, are split between the exhibitor and the distributor, and the distributor uses its share to pay the studio for distribution rights. As of 2007, **Cineplex Entertainment LP** was the largest movie exhibitor in Canada, controlling 128 theatres and almost 1300 screens. Movie houses under their corporate umbrella include Cineplex Odeon, Galaxy and Famous Players. Atlantic Canada's Empire Theatres is the second largest movie exhibitor with some 59 theatres with over 400 screens across Canada. Movie theatres aren't just for movies anymore. NHL hockey, WWE events and even the high-brow Metropolitan Opera are now also available at many theatre locations in Canada.

Exhibitors get an upfront payment, called the **nut**, to help cover their costs. After the nut, distributors take the lion's share of box-office revenue, often 90 percent for the first week. Deals vary, but eventually, if a movie runs long enough, the split ends up being 50–50. For movie houses, the concession stand is an important revenue source. Concessions are so profitable that exhibitors sometimes agree to give up their nut entirely for a blockbuster and rely on popcorn and candy to make money. Movie-house markups on confections are typically 60 percent, more on popcorn.

■ Economics of Movies

study<u>preview</u> **The movie industry is dominated by six companies, all of them subsidiaries of larger companies. Major studios have also found economic advantages in picking up projects from independent producers and capitalizing on auxiliary enterprises. Canadian filmmakers are also eligible for government subsidies.**

STUDIO FINANCING

Just as in D.W. Griffith's time, movies are expensive to make—about $43 million on average. Then there are the big-budget movies. Depending on how the expenses are tallied, the 2005 movie *Chronicles of Narnia: The Lion, the Witch and the Wardrobe* cost more than $200 million to make. Some estimates peg *Titanic* (1997) costs as high as $240 million. Where does the money come from?

media DATABANK

Big-Budget Movies

Movie Title	Year	Amount Spent ($)
Titanic	1997	240 million
Chronicles of Narnia	2005	200 million
Terminator 3: Rise of the Machines	2003	175 million
Spider-Man	2002	170 million
Matrix Reloaded	2003	170 million
The Hulk	2003	150 million
Pearl Harbor	2001	140 million
Charlie's Angels: Full Throttle	2003	135 million
Bad Boys II	2003	130 million
Harry Potter and the Sorcerer's Stone	2001	120 million
Harry Potter and the Chamber of Secrets	2002	100 million

Major Studios Major studios finance many movies with profits from earlier movies. Most movies, however, do not originate with major studios but with independent producers. These producers are autonomous in many ways, but most rely on major studios for financing. The studios hedge their risks by distributing the movies themselves, a profitable enterprise involving rentals to movie houses and TV, home video sales and merchandise licensing.

The studios, and other financial backers, do more than write cheques. To protect their investments, some get directly involved in film projects. They examine budgets and schedules in considering a loan request. Often, they send representatives to shooting sites to guard against budget overruns.

Major studios that are part of conglomerates can draw on the resources of their corporate parents. In 1952, giant MCA (Music Corporation of America) acquired the ailing Universal studio and plowed its recording business profits into the studio. Universal turned profitable and MCA became even stronger by having another profitable subsidiary.

major studios ■ Include Warner Brothers, Columbia, Universal, 20th Century Fox, Paramount, Disney, MGM.

media ONLINE

D.W. Griffith Learn more about this early film pioneer from this PBS American Masters website.
www.pbs.org/wnet/americanmasters/database/griffith_d.html

Newmarket Films Film distribution company with only one criterion—quality.
www.newmarketfilms.com

Criterion Collection Find out about the most important movies of all time, all on DVD.
www.criterionco.com

media DATABANK

Global Box-Office Sales

Movie Title	Year	Amount Earned ($)
Titanic	1997	1.8 billion
Harry Potter and the Sorcerer's Stone	2001	980 million
Harry Potter and the Chamber of Secrets	2002	880 million
Spider-Man	2002	820 million
Matrix Reloaded	2003	740 million
Pearl Harbor	2001	450 million
Terminator 3: Rise of the Machines	2003	435 million
Bad Boys II	2003	270 million
Charlie's Angels: Full Throttle	2003	260 million
The Hulk	2003	250 million

The Gulf and Western conglomerate later did the same with Paramount. Coca-Cola acquired Columbia in 1982 with a promise to help Columbia through the rough times that had beset the movie company.

In the 1980s several studios acquired new corporate parents, which made it easier to finance movies. The Japanese electronics giant Sony bought Columbia in 1989. At $3.4 billion, it was the biggest Japanese takeover of an American corporation in history. The size of the deal was a sign of the new resources Columbia could tap to make movies. By the early 1990s three of the largest U.S. studios were owned by giant foreign companies with the ability to generate cash from other enterprises to strengthen their new U.S. movie subsidiaries.

Investor Groups Special investment groups sometimes are put together to fund movies for major studios. Less proven producers, or those whose track records are marred by budget overruns and loose production schedules, often seek financing from **risk investors**, who include venture capitalists, tax-shelter organizers and foreign distributors. Risk investors often take a bigger share of revenue in exchange for their bigger risk.

Banks To meet front-end production expenses, studios go to banks for loans against their assets, which include their production facilities and warehouses of vintage films awaiting re-release. By bankrolling movies early in Hollywood's history, California-based Bank of America grew into one of the nation's biggest banks.

INDEPENDENT PRODUCERS

Before the U.S. Supreme Court's Paramount Decision in 1948, which broke the major studios' hold on the U.S. movie industry, there was not much opportunity for **independent producers** to get their movies into the distribution and exhibition network. The Big Six controlled almost the entire system. That has changed drastically. Today the big studios scout for independent producers to pick up movies without the development costs.

Mel Gibson's personal take from *The Passion of the Christ* will not be known for years. The money is still coming in. But experts in Hollywood finance wouldn't be surprised if the total exceeded $350 million, perhaps overtaking the record of George Lucas, who spurned the studio system and financed and controlled every aspect, with no studio interference, of his Star Wars movie *The Phantom Menace* in 1999. Both Gibson and Lucas functioned as independent producers. In Gibson's case, he had no choice. He couldn't interest any studio in doing *The Passion of the Christ.*

Gibson is in an elite group of $25 million-a-film actors who have amassed sufficient fortunes from the studios that they can afford to bankroll their own movies. For *Passion*, Gibson paid the $30 million in production costs. He farmed out exhibition to Newmarket Films, which signed up theatres to exhibit the film for a share of the revenue. Capitalizing on controversy about Gibson's portrayal of Jews to increase publicity, Newmarket more than doubled its projection for the initial box office. In the first five days, *Passion* grossed $125 million. Newmarket's projection was $45 million.

Unlike Gibson and Spielberg, many independent producers are unknowns. *The Blair Witch Project,* for example, cost $35 000 in 1998. Within a year it was a commercial smash, with box-office receipts of $141 million. It even spawned a sequel.

Studios bankroll projects from independent producers, whose overhead costs are relatively low. This doesn't mean that studio financing is easy to come by, as attested by Spike Lee, the legendary director of black-themed movies, including *Malcolm X*. Even so, Lee has had studio backing for numerous films. Some actors have succeeded in directing and producing on their own, with studio backing, including Clint Eastwood, Tom Hanks and Ron Howard. Then there are independent producers who come from nowhere, it seems, and hit a chord that resonates with the public, like Michael Moore with his bleak 1989 documentary on General Motors, *Roger and Me*, his equally bleak *Bowling for Columbine* in 2002 and his politically charged *Fahrenheit 9/11* in 2004.

The independent producers demonstrate that the major studios have a monopoly on neither originality nor creativity. But as they will tell you, they are outsiders.

risk investors ■ Individuals and companies willing to put capital into ventures shunned by conservative financial institutions.

independent producers ■ Movie production enterprises outside of the major studios.

GOVERNMENT FUNDING

Financing for Canadian movies can also come from the public sector. Founded in 1967, Telefilm Canada is a crown corporation that provides funding for Canadian filmmakers to help them produce Canadian movies and television programs. According to Telefilm, their "role is to foster the production of films, television programs and cultural products that reflect Canadian society, with its linguistic duality and cultural diversity, and to encourage their dissemination at home and abroad." In 2007, the 40th anniversary of Telefilm, their budget was $390 million.

AFTERMARKETS

When moviemakers plan films today, they build budgets around anticipated revenues that go beyond first runs in movie houses. Unlike the old days, when movies either made it or didn't at the box office, today moviemakers earn more than 5.7 percent of their revenue from pay television services like HBO and TMN after the movie has played itself out in the movie houses. Another 31.4 percent comes from selling videotapes and DVDs.

AUXILIARY ENTERPRISES

Movie studios have found auxiliary revenue sources to wring additional income, besides the box office, from their product. Hollywood has hundreds of lawyers in various specialties, including copyright law, who negotiate deals with other companies to use characters, themes, outtakes and music from movies. Then too there are the television spinoffs, Burger King toys, comic books and school lunch boxes.

Merchandise Tie-Ins Fortunes can be made by licensing other companies to use characters and signature items from a movie. In one of the most successful **merchandise tie-ins**, 20th Century Fox and George Lucas licensed Ewok dolls, R2D2 posters and even *Star Wars* bedsheets and pillowcases. By 1985, seven years after the movie's release, tie-ins had racked up sales of $2 billion. The licensing fee typically is 10 percent of the retail price of the merchandise. *Batman* tie-ins rang up $500 million in sales in 1989, within six months of the movie's release, and Warner Brothers was earning 20 percent of the retail revenue on some products.

merchandise tie-ins ■ Studio deals to profit from merchandise carrying movie names and logos.

Toys For the 1995 film *Batman Forever*, Warner Brothers let the Hasbro toy company dress the Riddler. Hasbro wanted tight pants, not the baggy ones in the script, so the Riddler action toy would look better. The result? The Riddler wore tight pants on screen. A recurrent report from *Pocahontas* animators is that their bosses ordered them to have the raccoon Meeko braid the Indian maiden's hair so that Mattel could market Braided Beauty Pocahontas dolls.

Some moviemakers deny that the cart is ahead of the horse. Disney officials, for example, say that Mattel had no hand in the script for *Pocahontas*; the script came first, the toys second. Whatever the truth, moviemakers have huge financial incentives to do whatever it takes to ensure success. Toymakers pay licensing fees, typically 10 percent of a toy's retail price. Disney earned $16 million, the record, for the 1994 movie *The Lion King*. In 1995, *Batman Forever* paraphernalia generated $13 million, *Pocahontas* $10 million. Power Ranger gear, tied into both the movie and the television series, has totaled $300 million, of which an estimated $30 million went back to Fox—a significant revenue source requiring hardly any studio expense.

Is this kind of commercialism undermining the artistic autonomy that normally is associated with creative enterprises like moviemaking? This is the same elitist–populist issue that is at the heart of the ongoing debate about media content. At one extreme is the pristine elitist preference for creative forces to drive content oblivious to commercial considerations. At the other extreme is the laissez-faire populist belief that nothing is wrong with marketplace forces. Populists say that if a movie's box office suffers because toymakers have had too much sway on script decisions, moviemakers will make future adjustments— and an appropriate balance will result eventually. Some elitists accept that argument but worry nonetheless about the commercial contamination that occurs in the meantime.

Music Tie-ins are not new. Music, for example, was a revenue source for moviemakers even before talkies. Just about every early movie house had a piano player who kept one eye on the screen and hammered out supportive mood music, and sheet-music publishers bought the rights to print and sell the music to musicians who wanted to perform it on their own. This was no small enterprise. D.W. Griffith's *The Birth of a Nation* of 1915 had an accompanying score for a 70-piece symphony. Today, music has assumed importance beyond supporting the screen drama. It has become a moviemaking profit centre—just count the number of songs in the credits at the end of today's movies.

Product Placement Moviemakers also have begun building commercial products into story lines in a subtle form of advertising. It was no coincidence that Tom Cruise downed Pepsi in *Top Gun*. Some movie producers work brand names into their movies for a fee. When the alien E.T. was coaxed out of hiding with a handful of candy, it was with Reese's Pieces. The Hershey company, which makes Reese's, paid to have its candy used. Sales soared in the next few months. Producers had first offered the Mars company a chance for the candy to be M&Ms, but Mars executives were squeamish about their candy being associated with anything as ugly as E.T. They did not realize that moviegoers would fall in love with the little alien.

After *E.T.* the product placement business boomed. Miller beer paid to have 21 references in *Bull Durham*. The same movie also included seven references for Budweiser, four for Pepsi, three for Jim Beam and two for Oscar Mayer. A simple shot of a product in the foreground typically goes for $25 000 to $50 000. Some advertisers have paid $350 000 for multiple onscreen plugs.

Critics claim that **product placements** are sneaky. Some want them banned. Others say the word "advertisement" should be flashed on the screen when the products appear. Movie people, on the other hand, argue that using real products adds credibility. In the old days, directors assiduously avoided implicit endorsements. In a bar scene the players would drink from cans marked "beer"—no brand name. Today, says Marvin Cohen, whose agency matches advertisers and movies, "A can that says 'Beer' isn't going to make it anymore." The unanswered question is how much product-placement deals affect artistic decisions.

Canadian Film Industry

study preview While Hollywood's focus tends to be on blockbuster movies, the Canadian film industry pursued another direction. The National Film Board of Canada has won innumerable awards for its documentaries and animation. Feature films in Canada have also followed in the documentary tradition.

Jeannette Sloniowski, in *Canadian Communications: Issues in Contemporary Media and Culture*, sums up the plight of Canadian movies like this: "Canadian Movies: Not Coming to a Cinema near You." Due to economic and distribution issues, Canadian movies account for less than 11 percent of all screen time at movie houses in Canada. Because of this, television is often the only outlet for Canadian films. Canadian channels, both conventional channels like the CBC and specialty, are the primary outlet for Canadian movies to be seen by Canadians. As a result of exposure on television, the Canadian Film and Television Production Association (CFTPA) announced that more than 40 percent of revenue earned by Canadian movies came from pay television.

Canadian movies have always lived in the shadow of American fare. As a result, they have had to struggle to mature and gain acceptance in this country. In his article "American Domination of the Motion Picture Industry," **Garth Jowett** points out that Canada has always been dependent on Hollywood for movies. Jowett writes, "From the outset, Canada because of its geographic situation was considered to be merely one of the many marketing areas designated by the American film industry." Jowett also claims that most Canadians have always preferred Hollywood movies to British or Canadian films. However, this does not mean that filmmaking traditions do not exist in this country.

From the earliest days of the medium, movies were shot and produced in Canada. Douglas Fetherling says that the first film shot in Canada was in Manitoba in 1897.

product placement ■ When a manufacturer pays for its products to be used as props.

Garth Jowett ■ Believes Canada has always been dependent on Hollywood movies.

Many other short films followed; however, the first Canadian feature film wasn't made until 1913. *Evangeline* was a five-reel film produced by the Canadian Bioscope Company of Halifax. Based on a poem by Longfellow about the flight of the Acadians, it was shot on location in the Annapolis Valley. It featured an American cast and turned a profit. The Canadian Biograph Company was never able to match the success of *Evangeline*. The same was true of other early Canadian filmmakers; it's estimated that only about 70 Canadian feature films were produced during the first half of the 20th century.

American movie mogul D.W. Griffith, whose narrative style was influential in the development of Hollywood movies, visited Toronto in 1925. During that visit, he told Canadian officials that Canada should make Hollywood-type movies to trade with the United States. Almost 15 years later, a British filmmaker disagreed with him and the Canadian film industry went in another direction. That man was John Grierson, and the National Film Board of Canada was born.

The **National Film Board (NFB)** was formed by an act of Parliament in 1939 to "interpret Canada to Canadians." The board's first commissioner was **John Grierson**, a British documentary filmmaker. Grierson advocated a strong national film industry. He wanted to make movies that celebrated Canada's geographic and social diversity. In a statement about government film policy, Grierson said that while Canada could never compete with the glamour of Hollywood, it should not abandon the idea of a national film industry. Grierson felt that making short, inexpensive films about Canadians and their experiences could complement more expensive Hollywood fare, while still giving Canadians a cinematic voice. Grierson also believed that films should tackle social issues and that filmmakers should try to produce films that make a difference.

During World War II, the NFB produced several propaganda films in support of the war effort. After the war, Grierson returned to England, but the NFB continued to make successful documentary films. During this time, it became known for a style called **cinéma vérité**, which roughly translated means "truth in cinema." For the NFB, cinéma vérité has meant documentaries by Canadians about Canadians.

The NFB is also known for its animation. The board's animation roots can be traced back to the arrival of **Norman McLaren** in 1941. Although he made 59 films for the NFB, including the propaganda movies *V for Victory* (1941) and *Keep Your Mouth Shut* (1944), animation was McLaren's first love. While his films have won more than 200 international awards, his best-known work is the 1953 Oscar-winning short *Neighbours*. The eight-minute antiwar film is about two neighbours fighting over a flower. The dispute escalates into tribal warfare. The film used live actors, but they were animated with the same techniques used to animate puppets and drawings.

In 1950, Parliament passed the National Film Act, which changed the NFB's mandate to include producing, promoting and distributing films in the national interest. In the NFB's early days, it would send projectionists from city to city and town to town to show its latest offerings in arenas, community centres, and even fields. These films were also shown in movie houses and eventually on television. NFB films were (and still are) distributed by public libraries, schools, universities and colleges.

Some classic NFB films include *The Corporation* (2003), *A Place Called Chiapas* (1998), *The Champagne Safari* (1996), *Bob's Birthday* (1995), *Manufacturing Consent* (1992), and the controversial *The Boys of St. Vincent* (1992). NFB's women's division, called Studio D, produced 1981's *Not a Love Story* and the controversial *If You Love This Planet* in 1982.

FEATURE FILMS IN CANADA

Despite its success in the documentary and animated areas, Canada, with the exception of Quebec, has left the bulk of dramas and literary

NFB ■ Canada's award-winning National Film Board.

John Grierson ■ Founder of the NFB.

cinéma vérité ■ Truth or realism in movies. The basis for the documentary tradition.

Norman McLaren ■ Canadian innovator in animation.

ONLINE

Telefilm Canada Government agency dedicated to developing and promoting Canadian film, television, video and multimedia industries.
www.telefilm.gc.ca

NFB The National Film Board of Canada.
www.nfb.ca

NFB Classic Richard Condie's Genie Award–winning *The Big Snit* (1985) is just one of many NFB animated shorts to receive plaudits worldwide. The NFB continues to trailblaze in the spirit of Norman McLaren.

adaptations to the Americans. The feature film industry in Canada remained largely dormant until the 1960s. In 1964, two films marked the unofficial start of the feature film industry in Canada: Don Owen's *Nobody Waved Goodbye* and Gilles Groulx's *Le Chat dans le sac*. Both of these films were NFB productions, but they were feature films shot in the documentary tradition that featured regional themes without the glamour of Hollywood movies. The better-known Canadian films from this era include *Goin' down the Road* (1970), *Mon Oncle Antoine* (1971), *Paperback Hero* (1973), *Between Friends* (1973) and the classic *The Apprenticeship of Duddy Kravitz* (1974).

By the late 1970s, government incentives, such as those of the Canadian Film Development Corporation (now known as Telefilm) for producers investing in Canadian feature films, created a glut of product—some good, but mostly bad. It's this time period that gave Canadian movies a bad name. Many people invested money in movies simply as a tax break. The quality of the script, actors and movie were not always factors. *Why Shoot the Teacher?* (1978), *Atlantic City* (1980), *Scanners* (1981), and the largest-grossing Canadian movie of all time, the less than classy *Porky's* (1982), were all produced during this period.

Through the 1990s, Canadian films matured, particularly in English language cinema with movies such as *Margaret's Museum* (1995), *Hard Core Logo* (1996), *The Hanging Garden* (1997) and *Last Night* (1999). This trend continued into the 21st century with such eclectic films as *Ginger Snaps* (2000), *Fubar* (2002), *Men with Brooms* (2002) and *My Big Fat Greek Wedding* (2002).

Issues of ethnicity and multiculturalism continued to be explored in recent Canadian movies. Mina Shum's *Double Happiness* (1994), Davor Marjanovic's *My Father's Angel* (2000), and Deepa Mehta's *Water* (2001) are all excellent examples of Canadian films exploring these themes.

However, despite the increase in the quality of Canadian movies that are being produced, English Canadians don't usually see these films at their local movie theatre. Television, particularly specialty channels, is where most English Canadians watch their national cinema. Brian D. Johnson, the film critic for *Maclean's*, in his article "The Lost Picture Show," says, "welcome to the Byzantine world of English Canadian film financing—a surreal maze of auteur dreams, bureaucratic nightmares and ritualized failure. It's a world where distributors routinely snap up publicly funded movies, flip the TV rights to broadcasters for an easy profit, then dump the films into a few theatres for a token release."

Media DATABANK

Movie Revenue: Canadian Style

Financially, Canadian films are stronger than ever, but the majority of profits don't come from the box office. On average, only 11 percent of movies shown in Canadian theatres are Canadian, so Canadian film and videomakers must look to other sources of revenue. Data from Statistics Canada illustrates how movies made money in Canada in 2004/2005:

Box office	$446 million
Conventional TV	$404 million
DVD sales	$247 million
Pay television	$135 million

Source: Adapted from Statistics Canada publication "Film, video and audio-visual distribution, 2004/2005," *The Daily,* Catalogue 11-001, August 28, 2006, http://www.statcan.ca/Daily/English/060828/d060828a.htm.

The Best of Canadian Films

The United States has the Oscars; Canada has the **Genie Awards**, which are awarded annually to the best in Canadian movies by the Academy of Canadian Cinema and Television. Here's a list of recent Genie award winners for best picture in Canada. Any of these films would be a good place to test Harcourt's theory about Canadian movies and the theme of "uncertainty":

Genie Awards ■ Canada's Oscars.

1990:	*Jésus de Montréal/Jesus of Montreal*
1991:	*Black Robe*
1992:	*Naked Lunch*
1993:	*Thirty-Two Short Films about Glenn Gould*
1994:	*Exotica*
1995:	*Le Confessional*
1996:	*Lilies*
1997:	*The Sweet Hereafter*
1998:	*The Red Violin*
1999:	*Sunshine*
2000:	*Maelström*
2001:	*Atanarjuat, The Fast Runner*
2002:	*Ararat*
2003:	*Les invasions barbares/The Barbarian Invasions*
2004:	*Les Triplettes de Belleville/The Triplets of Belleville*
2005:	*C.R.A.Z.Y.*
2006:	*Bon Cop, Bad Cop*

Source: www.genieawards.ca. Reprinted with the permission of the Academy of Canadian Cinema & Television.

Movie Issues and Trends

study**preview** Hollywood's initial response to television was to combat the new medium with technical innovations. Then came movies with edgy content. Today, movies and TV are financially and technologically intertwined. But censorship remains an issue.

TELEVISION'S CHALLENGE

Movies caught on big early on. There was nothing like them. By the 1920s, opulent theatres had been built, surpassing even the best opera houses in elegant decorations and architectural flourishes. Movies were a unique form of diversion and entertainment. Ticket sales topped $90 million a week in 1946. Then came television.

To buy a television set, many families piggybanked what they had been spending on movies—50 cents for adults, 25 or 35 cents for the kids. Movie attendance plummeted to 46 million by 1955. Was the end of Hollywood at hand?

The movie industry flailed wildly to stem the audience loss. High-budget spectaculars that network television couldn't afford were tried. In 1951 MGM hired 5500 extras for its three-hour *Quo Vadis*. Although such spectaculars drew audiences, the investment was risky. 20th Century Fox almost bankrupted itself by spending an unprecedented $44 million on *Cleopatra* in 1963.

To differentiate itself from television, the movie industry tried technical innovations. Some were immediately forgettable, like Smell-o-Vision. Odours were wafted through movie houses with appropriate scenes to enhance the audience's sensual involvement.

media
ONLINE

Canadian Films and Actors We have a long history of filmmaking in Canada. Find out more at this site.
www.northernstars.ca

I Dream of Genies All about the award for Canadian movie excellence.
www.genieawards.ca

Other gimmicks included 3-D, complete with free eyeglasses for the audience, one lens blue, one red. Some movie houses were remodeled with wraparound screens—Cinerama, it was called—to occupy the audience's peripheral vision.

More enduring was the almost total shift to colour. Although colour had been introduced in the 1930s, black and white had remained dominant. In the 1950s colour became the standard—something that early television couldn't match. Also, a less costly alternative to Cinerama, which had required multiple cameras and projectors, was the horizontal CinemaScope screen. The screens, two times wider than they were high, offered more realistic images than the old squarish screens. CinemaScope also differentiated movies from television, which had squarish screens.

CONTENT INNOVATION

Despite the innovations, ticket sales ebbed to 19 million a week. By the 1970s, exhibitors had shuttered many of the grand movie palaces and adjusted to the reality that it was sharing its audience with television. Although only a quarter of its former self, there remained a large audience for movies. At 19 million tickets a week, 52 weeks a year, movies still have a significant financial base.

Hollywood found genres that network television, timid in its infancy, wouldn't touch. There were films on disturbing social issues. MGM released *Blackboard Jungle* in 1955, examining disruptive classroom behaviour in a way that was inconceivable for the television sitcom *Our Miss Brooks*. That same year Warner issued *Rebel Without a Cause*, the James Dean classic about a bad boy from a good family. If television had dared to adapt Tennessee Williams's steamy play *Cat on a Hot Tin Roof*, with its implied homosexuality and marital intimacy, it wouldn't have been recognizable. In 1958 MGM made the movie.

Riding high on an intensive growth period, television executives saw no need to match Hollywood's edginess. Hollywood, meanwhile, continued to test new waters. Columbia and United Artists explored social inequity and injustice, including interracial issues, in a trilogy starring Sidney Poitier: *Guess Who's Coming to Dinner, To Sir with Love* and *In the Heat of the Night*. In *The Wild Bunch* in 1969, director Sam Peckinpah brought new blood-spurting violence to the screen, in slow motion for additional impact. Similar effects in Arthur Penn's 1967 classic *Bonnie and Clyde* left audiences awed in sickened silence. Nevertheless, people kept coming back to movies that showed graphic violence. Sex was taboo on television but not at the movies. It was the theme in *Bob & Carol & Ted & Alice* (1969), *Carnal Knowledge* (1971) and *I Am Curious (Yellow)* (1969). Sex went about as far as it could with the hard-core *Deep Throat* of 1973, which was produced for porno houses but achieved crossover commercial success in regular movie houses.

Movies came to be made for a younger crowd. By 1985, regular moviegoers fell into a relatively narrow age group: from teenagers through college age. Fifty-nine percent of the tickets were purchased by people between the ages of 12 and 24. Even so, the industry did not produce exclusively for a young audience. Moviemakers recognized that the highest profits came from movies with a crossover audience. These were movies that attracted not only the regular box-office crowd but also infrequent moviegoers. Essential, however, was the youth audience. Without it a movie could not achieve extraordinary success. The immensely profitable *E.T.* was an example. It appealed to the youth audience, to parents who took their small children and to film aficionados who were fascinated by the special effects.

ONLINE

Documentary Films.net
Comprehensive source of information for documentary viewers and makers.
www.documentaryfilms.net

documentary ■ A video examination of a historical or current event or a natural or social phenomenon.

DOCUMENTARIES

Documentaries are nothing new. Canada's NFB has been producing them since 1939. However, the new millennium has seen a dramatic increase in mainstream documentaries coming from the United States. Morgan Spurlock went on a fast-food diet, eating only Big Macs and other McDonald's fare. It wreaked havoc on Spurlock's body, as anybody can see in his movie *Super Size Me*. We learned about the delicate nature of freedom of speech for the Dixie Chicks in 2006's *Shut Up & Sing*. Al Gore's 2006 Oscar winner *An Inconvenient Truth* set the agenda for discussions on global warming. These are among a growing number of point-of-view documentaries that mainstream movie houses have been booking in recent years.

Relatively inexpensive digital filmmaking equipment has driven the new documentaries. Morgan Spurlock could never have persuaded a major studio to provide the budget, several million dollars upfront, for a documentary attacking an American icon like McDonald's. Not even Spurlock's record as an MTV producer would have done it. But with a $3000 digital camera, $5000 in software and an Apple computer, he created his personal statement on fast food. So compelling was *Super Size Me* that 200 theatres showed it, and it grossed $7.5 million in a month. In all Spurlock had spent $65 000 to create the movie.

More typical is $250 000 to plan, shoot and edit a documentary with the production quality of a studio movie—easily within the budgets of small distribution companies and the art-house divisions of major studios. In 2004 Michael Moore's *Fahrenheit 9/11*, which cost $6 million, most of it for archival footage that had to be purchased, grossed $119.2 million. Despite potentially huge profit margins, major studios have been skittish about new-breed documentaries. Miramax, for example, was ready to distribute *Fahrenheit 9/11* when executives at its parent company, Disney, fretting at the movie's anti-Bush and antiwar message, said: "Absolutely not." Disney unloaded the movie, which found its way into theatres through other channels.

Michael Moore His record of activist journalism included a stint at *Mother Jones* magazine, but Michael Moore's reputation for raw-fisted antiestablishment slants was cemented with his *Roger & Me* documentary assault on General Motors. Some thought his unfriendly assessment of the first George W. Bush administration, *Fahrenheit 9/11*, might affect the outcome of the 2004 election. It didn't.

MOVIE CENSORSHIP

When things seem wrong in society, people look for a cause. It's easy, although hardly logical, to blame something new for worsening social ills. The mass media, especially when delivering content with new technology, is historically a handy whipping boy. Movies are no exception, not only at their outset but through their history.

Morality as an Issue It was no wonder in Victorian 1896 that a movie called *Dolorita in the Passion Dance* caused an uproar. There were demands that it be banned—the first but hardly last such call against a movie. In 1907 Chicago passed a law restricting objectionable motion pictures. State legislators across the land were insisting that something be done. To clean up movies, worried moviemakers created in 1922 the **Motion Picture Producers and Distributors of America (MPPDA)**, now known as the Motion Picture Association of America (MPAA). **Will Hays**, a prominent Republican who was an elder in his Presbyterian church, was put in charge. Despite his efforts, movies with titillating titles continued to be produced. A lot of people shuddered at titles such as *Sinners in Silk* and *Red Hot Romance*. Hollywood scandals were no help. Actor William Wallace Reid died from drugs. Fatty Arbuckle was tried for the drunken slaying of a young actress. When the Depression struck, many people linked the nation's economic failure with "moral bankruptcy." Movies were a target.

Under pressure, the movie industry adopted the **Motion Picture Production Code** in 1930 (also known as the Hays Code), which codified the kind of thing that Will Hays had been doing. There was to be no naughty language, nothing sexually suggestive and no bad guys going unpunished.

Church people led intensified efforts to clean up movies. The 1930 code was largely the product of Father **Daniel Lord**, a Roman Catholic priest, and **Martin Quigley**, a Catholic layperson. In 1934, after an apostolic delegate from the Vatican berated movies in an address to a New York church convention, U.S. bishops organized the **Legion of Decency**, which worked closely with the movie industry's code administrators.

The legion, which was endorsed by religious leaders of many faiths, moved on several fronts. Chapters sprouted in major cities. Some chapters boycotted theatres

Motion Picture Producers and Distributors of America (MPPDA) ■ 1922 Hollywood attempt to establish moral code for movies.

Will Hays ■ Led MPPDA.

Motion Picture Production Code ■ 1930 Hollywood attempt to quiet critical moralists.

Daniel Lord ■ Priest who led a morality crusade against Hollywood.

Martin Quigley ■ Partner of Father Daniel Lord.

Legion of Decency ■ Church listing of acceptable movies.

Robert Flaherty

Explorer Robert Flaherty, who attended Upper Canada College, took a camera to the Arctic in 1921 to record the life of an Eskimo family. The result was a new kind of movie: the documentary. While other movies of the time were theatrical productions with scripts, sets and actors, Flaherty tried something different: recording reality.

His 57-minute *Nanook of the North* was compelling on its own merits when it started on the movie-house circuit in 1922, but the film received an unexpected macabre boost a few days later when Nanook, the father of the Eskimo family, died of hunger on

Robert Flaherty

Nanook of the North The documentary became a film genre with explorer Robert Flaherty's *Nanook of the North* in 1922. This film was an attempt to record reality—no actors, no props. The film was especially potent, not only because it was a new approach and on a fascinating subject but also because, coincidentally, Nanook died of starvation on the ice around the time that the film was released.

the ice. News stories of Nanook's death stirred public interest—and also attendance at the movie, which helped to establish the documentary as an important new film genre.

Flaherty's innovative approach took a new twist in the 1930s when propagandists saw reality-based movies as a tool to promote their causes. In Germany the Nazi government produced propaganda films, and other countries followed. **Frank Capra** directed the vigorous five-film series

Why We Fight for the U.S. War Office in 1942.

After World War II there was a revival of documentaries in Flaherty's style—a neutral recording of natural history. Walt Disney produced a variety of such documentaries, including the popular *Living Desert* in the 1950s.

The CBS television network gained a reputation in the 1950s and 1960s for picking up on the documentary tradition with *Harvest of Shame,* about migrant workers, and *Hunger in America*. In the same period the National Geographic Society established a documentary unit, and French explorer Jacques Cousteau went into the television documentary business.

Such full-length documentaries are now mostly relegated to the CBC in Canada and PBS in the United States. The Documentary Channel is also an excellent outlet for these types of films. The major networks, meanwhile, have shifted most documentaries away from full-length treatments. Typical is CBS's *60 Minutes*, a twice-weekly one-hour program of three minidocumentaries. These new network projects combine reality programming and entertainment in slick packages that attract larger audiences than do traditional documentaries.

Frank Capra ■ Hollywood movie director who produced powerful propaganda movies for U.S. war effort in World War II.

for six weeks if they showed condemned films. Members slapped stickers marked "We Demand Clean Movies" on car bumpers. Many theatre owners responded, vowing to show only approved movies. Meanwhile, the industry itself added teeth to its own code. Any members of the MPPDA who released movies without approval were fined $25 000.

Movies and Changing Mores In the late 1940s the influence of the policing agencies began to wane. The 1948 Supreme Court's Paramount Decision was one factor. It took major studios out of the exhibition business. As a result, many movie houses could rent films from independent producers, many of which never subscribed to the code. A second factor was the movie *The Miracle*, which became a First Amendment issue in 1952. The movie was about a simple woman who was sure Saint Joseph had seduced her. Her baby, she believed, was Christ. Critics wanted the movie banned as sacrilege, but in *The Miracle* **case**, the Supreme Court sided with exhibitors on grounds of free expression. Filmmakers became a bit more venturesome.

***The Miracle* case** ■ U.S. Supreme Court ruled that the First Amendment protected movies from censorship.

The New Documentaries

This is a sampler of documentaries with a 21st-century point of view that have found their way into the movie-house circuit, with their directors:

Bowling for Columbine (2002) Michael Moore

Tries to relate U.S. gun laws with corporate greed, social dysfunction and political short-sightedness and pandering.

The Corporation (2003) Mark Achbar, Jennifer Abbott and Joel Bakan

Examines how media content and pop culture is controlled by only a few large corporations.

Spellbound (2003) Jeffrey Blitz

Follows eight contenders and their families through regional heats to the three-day national spelling bee final.

Tupac: Resurrection (2003) Lauren Lazin

Tries to explain the life of murdered rapper Tupac Shakur through his own interviews and public appearances.

Control Room (2004) Jehane Noujaim

Demystifies Al Jazeera by eavesdropping on the Arab television network's gatekeepers.

Fahrenheit 9/11 (2004) Michael Moore

Presents the 2003 Iraq war as a non sequitur to the September 11 terrorism attacks.

Super Size Me (2004) Morgan Spurlock

Too many Big Macs make too much you.

March of the Penguins (2005) Luc Jacquet

Traces the courtship of Antarctic penguins on a ritual journey of hundreds of miles.

Shut Up & Sing (2006) Barbara Kopple and Cecilia Peck

Chronicles the freedom-of-speech fallout of lead singer Natalie Maines's comments about the war in Iraq and George Bush.

An Inconvenient Truth (2006) Davis Guggenheim

A look at the causes of, effects of and solutions to global warming. Hosted by Al Gore.

At the same time, with mores changing in the wake of World War II, the influence of the Legion of Decency was slipping. In 1953 the legion condemned *The Moon Is Blue*, which had failed to receive code approval for being a bit racy. Despite the legion's condemnation, the movie was a box-office smash. The legion contributed to its own undoing with a series of incomprehensible recommendations. It condemned significant movies such as Ingmar Bergman's *The Silence* and Michelangelo Antonioni's *Blowup* in 1966 while endorsing the likes of *Godzilla vs. the Thing*.

Current Movie Code Moviemakers sensed the change in public attitudes in the 1950s but realized that audiences still wanted guidance that they could trust on movies. Also, there remained some moralist critics. In 1968 several industry organizations established a new rating system. No movies were banned. Fines were out. Instead, a board representing movie producers, distributors, importers and exhibitors, the **Classification and Rating Administration Board**, placed movies in categories to help parents determine what movies their children should see. Here are the categories, as modified through the years:

media ONLINE

Motion Picture Association of America (MPAA) They rate the movies we all see.
www.mpaa.org

Movie Ratings A history of how the ratings evolved.
www.mpaa.org/Ratings_history1. asp

Classification and Rating Administration Board ■ Rates movies on G, PG, PG-13, R, NC-17 scale.

- **G:** Suitable for general audiences and all ages.
- **PG:** Parental guidance suggested because some content may be considered unsuitable for preteens.
- **PG-13:** Parental guidance especially suggested for children younger than 13 because of partial nudity, swearing or violence.
- **R:** Restricted for anyone younger than 17 unless accompanied by an adult.
- **NC-17:** No children under age 17 should be admitted.

Whether the rating system is widely used by parents is questionable. One survey found that two out of three parents couldn't name a movie their teenagers had seen in recent weeks.

■ Media Literacy and Movies

study<u>preview</u> Populist measures of a movie's success are in box office, aftermarket and merchandise revenue. Critical success is harder to measure. Knowledgeable, sophisticated reviewers are helpful.

BOX OFFICE AND GROSSES

Weekends are when Hollywood studio executives bite their fingernails. The success or disappointment of their latest offerings is in the weekend box-office tabulations, the week-to-week tallies of how many customers the latest movies attracted. The numbers, gathered at the turnstile, are accurate in and of themselves. Not much can be inferred from them, though. A great new movie could be hurt if it was opening against strong rivals. Inversely, a weak movie may look better in a single weekend's books than it really should. Also, a single weekend's success is only part of the complex formula for a movie to break even financially. Many strong weeks might be needed to offset the costs of an expensive movie. But a single good weekend could bring a low-budget movie into black ink right away.

An advance indicator of commercial success, though not entirely reliable, is the number of screens nationwide that a movie shows on. Movie houses choose movies according to what they anticipate will be their popularity. Although exhibitors are savvy about what will play well, they make occasional wrong calls.

The least reliable precursor of a movie's success is the predictable marketing hoopla accompanying a release. Actors and directors who make the talk show rounds are enthusiastic. How could they be otherwise with their own careers in the balance? Trailers can be misleading. Some previews draw on scenes that don't even make the final cut.

The best check on a movie's popularity is the long-term box-office record. The all-time leader easily is James Cameron's 1997 *Titanic*. Even with long-term, revenue-based data, look at the criteria on which a ranking is based. Some lists are true box office, the revenue from movie-house showings. Others include aftermarket revenue, like video rentals. Some include merchandise income. Some are domestic, some worldwide. Also, with ticket prices approaching $12 in many cities, currency inflation gives newer movies an edge over classics. Has *Titanic* really been more popular than 1939's *Gone with the Wind*?

MOVIE CRITICISM

Commercial success doesn't always equate with critical success, which is a subjective rating. Some critics applauded *Titanic*. The technical effects, for example, drew rave comments. The praise, however, wasn't universal. Some critics saw the storyline as trite—a bodice-buster cliché that manipulated unsophisticated audiences.

How, then, can a serious media consumer go beyond the box office and the bottom line to assess a movie? Many critics produce immensely helpful reviews and commentary that cut through hype and dazzle to bring a critical, cultivated eye to their reviews. The best reviewers know movies as a medium, including the techniques of the craft. They understand the commercial and artistic dynamics that go into a movie. They know the history of a movie's production, from its seminal moment in a book or whatever the conceptual source.

Where do you find such reviewers? The best sources over the years have included *The New Yorker* magazine and *The New York Times*. Even then, you need to come to know reviewers and their strengths and blind spots. In the end, it is you as a media consumer who makes a critical judgment. This comes from your own increasing sophistication, informed by the dialogue in which the best critics are engaging.

CHAPTER 5 Wrap-Up

Movies passed their 100th birthday in the 1980s as an entertainment medium with an especially strong following among young adults and teenagers. From the beginning, movies were a glamorous medium, but beneath the glitz were dramatic struggles between competing businesspeople whose success depended on catching the public's fancy. The most dramatic period came at mid-century. Fanatic anticommunists in Congress intimidated moviemakers into backing away from cutting-edge explorations of social and political issues, and then a government antitrust action forced the major studios to break up their operations. Meanwhile, television was siphoning people away from the box office. Movie attendance fell from 90 million to 16 million per week. It took a few years, but the movie industry regrouped. More than ever, political activism and social inquiry have become themes in American movies. Moviemakers met the threat from television by becoming a primary supplier of television programming.

Questions for Review

1. Why do movies have such a strong impact on people?
2. What is the role of movie studios in the production and exhibition?
3. What are the major Hollywood studios?
4. What are the advantages of digital technology for the movie industry?
5. How has Hollywood responded to the threat of television?

Questions for Critical Thinking

1. How would you describe the success of these innovations—Cinerama, CinemaScope, 3-D and Smell-o-Vision—in the movie industry's competition against television? What are the prospects for d-cinema?
2. Epic spectaculars marked one period of moviemaking, social causes another, and sex and violence another. Have these genres had lasting effect?
3. What were the contributions of William Dickson, George Eastman and the Lumière brothers to early moviemaking?

4. What is meant by the National Film Board's mandate to "explain Canada to Canadians?"
5. Describe what makes American movies different from Canadian movies.

Deepening Your media LITERACY

Are the most popular films the best films?

STEP 1 Choose a popular Hollywood movie and either a Canadian, independent or foreign film to compare.

Dig Deeper

STEP 2

1. Read several critical reviews of these movies.
2. Look up the box-office receipts of the two movies.
3. Find out how many awards each of these films won.

What Do You Think?

STEP 3 Answer these questions:

1. Do critical acclaim, popularity and film awards go hand in hand?

2. Do you think critical acclaim or winning awards is a good way to measure a film's quality? Why or why not?
3. Are box office receipts the best measure of its success? Why or why not?
4. If your movie was Canadian, test Harcourt's idea of uncertainty. Was it evident in the Canadian film you watched? Use Monk's "Canadian checklist" to uncover themes.

Keeping Up to Date

People serious about movies as art will find *American Film* and *Film Comment* valuable sources of information.

Among consumer magazines with significant movie coverage are *Premiere*, *Entertainment Weekly*, *Maclean's* and *Rolling Stone*.

Trade journals include *Variety* and *Hollywood Reporter*.

Canadian newspapers that cover movies include the *Toronto Star*, the *National Post, The Globe and Mail*.

For Further Learning

James Adams. "Our Box Office Not So Boffo." *The Globe and Mail* (February 3, 2007).

Sid Adilman. "Nat Taylor, 98: Canada's First Movie Mogul." *Toronto Star* (March 2, 2004).

Peter Biskind. *Down and Dirty Pictures: Miramax, Sundance and the Rise of Independent Film* (Simon & Schuster, 2004).

Paul Buhle and Dave Wagner. *A Very Dangerous Citizen: Abraham Lincoln Polonsky and the Hollywood Left* (University of California Press, 2001).

Steven DeRosa. *Writing with Hitchcock: The Collaboration of Alfred Hitchcock and John Michael Hayes* (Faber & Faber, 2001).

Bernard F. Dick. *Engulfed: Paramount Pictures and the Birth of Corporate Hollywood* (University Press of Kentucky, 2001).

Harvey Enchin. "Film Industry Has Its Critics." *The Globe and Mail* (September 8, 1997).

Gary Evans. "Canadian Film" in *Mediascapes: New Patterns in Canadian Communication* (Thomson, 2002).

Seth Feldman and Joyce Nelson. *Canadian Film Reader* (Peter Martin and Associates, 1977).

Douglas Fetherling. *Documents in Canadian Film* (Broadview Press, 1988).

Richard E. Foglesong. *Married to the House: Walt Disney World and Orlando* (Yale University Press, 2001).

Louis Giannetti and Jim Leach. *Understanding Movies*, Third Canadian edition (Prentice Hall, 2005).

Dade Hayes and Jonathan Bing. *Open Wide: How Hollywood Box Office Became a National Obsession* (Miramax, 2004).

Nicholas Jarecki. *Breaking In: How 20 Film Directors Got Their Start* (Broadway, 2002).

Brian D. Johnson. "The Lost Picture Show." *Maclean's* (April 17, 2006).

Garth Jowett. "American Domination of the Motion Picture Industry." In *Movies as Mass Communication*, edited by Garth Jowett and James M. Linton (Sage, 1980).

Jim Leach. *Film in Canada* (Oxford University Press, 2006).

Spike Lee, as told to Kaleem Aftab. *Spike Lee: That's My Story and I'm Sticking to It* (Norton, 2005).

Peter Lefcourt and Laura J. Shapiro, editors. *The First Time I Got Paid for It: Writers' Tales from the Hollywood Trenches* (Public Affairs, 2000).

Emmanuel Levy. *Oscar Fever: The History and Politics of the Academy Awards* (Continuum, 2001).

Jon Lewis. *Hollywood v. Hardcore: How the Struggle over Censorship Created the Modern Film Industry* (New York University Press, 2001).

Gayle Macdonald. "The Vast Picture Show." *The Globe and Mail* (January 17, 1998).

Katherine Monk. *Weird Sex and Snowshoes and Other Canadian Film Phenomena* (Raincoast Books, 2001).

David L. Robb. *Operation Hollywood: How the Pentagon Shapes and Censors Movies* (Prometheus, 2004).

Kazi Stastna. "The Golden Age of the Silver Screen." *Montreal Gazette* (January 13, 2006).

Bohdan Szuchewycz and Jeannette Sloniowski. *Canadian Communications: Issues in Contemporary Media and Culture* (Prentice Hall, 2001).

First Telecast A production still from the CBC's first *Hockey Night in Canada* telecast. The program has been a staple of Canadian television programming for more than 40 years. In 2003, *Hockey Night in Canada* broadcast its first game in HDTV: The Heritage Classic between Montreal and Edmonton.

Television

chapter

6

Media in Theory

Cultural Impact of Television

There's no doubt that television is a big part of our lives. Many of us have two or more television sets and each of us watches about 28 hours of TV per week. We even watch TV on our iPods, laptops and other portable devices.

Scholars and broadcasters may have different views on the potency of television's effect on society, but they all agree that there is some degree of influence. The role of television in riveting attention on serious matters was demonstrated in the fall of 2001 after terrorists launched attacks on the World Trade Center and the Pentagon. For months, people were tuned to CTV Newsnet or CBC Newsworld to hear about the latest developments in the war on terrorism from a Canadian point of view.

Fictional television characters can capture the imagination of the public. Perry Mason did wonders for the reputation of the law profession. Mary Tyler Moore's role as a television news writer showed that women could succeed in male-dominated industries. *The Cosby Show* changed the image of prime-time fatherhood in the 1980s. *Friends* became a ritual on Thursday nights on NBC during the 1990s.

Although television can be effective in creating short-term impressions, there also are long-term effects. A whole generation of children grew up with *Teenage Mutant Ninja Turtles* as part of their generational identity. Later came *Pokémon* and *Beyblade*. The long-term effects exist at both a superficial level, as with *Teenage Mutant Ninja Turtles,* and a serious level. Social critic **Michael Novak** puts the effect of television in broad terms: "Television is a molder of the soul's geography. It builds up incrementally a psychic structure of expectations. It does so in much the same way that school lessons slowly, over the years, tutor the unformed mind and teach it how to think."

What are the lessons to which Novak refers? Scholars **Linda and Robert Lichter** and **Stanley Rothman**, who have surveyed the television creative community, make a case that the creators of television programs are social reformers who build their political ideas into

Michael Novak ■ Believes TV is broad shaper of issues.

Linda and Robert Lichter and Stanley Rothman ■ Scholars who claim TV is reformist.

their scripts. The Lichters and Rothman identify the television creative community as largely secular and politically liberal.

Media scholar **George Comstock**, in his book *Television in America,* wrote, "Television has become an unavoidable and unremitting factor in shaping what we are and what we will become." But what of this American influence on English-Canadian culture? Canadian broadcaster **Moses Znaimer** claims that "as transmitter of information and entertainment, television is the acknowledged king. It's also very effective as a reflector of values and teacher of ideals, often in ways you don't notice." If Comstock, Novak, and Znaimer are correct, the need for Canadian television is obvious.

media TIMELINE

TELEVISION

1927 Philo Farnsworth devised a tube that picks up moving images for transmission.	**1958** Fowler Commission set first levels for Canadian content on television.	**2001** First wave of digital specialty channels was launched in Canada.
1939 Television was demonstrated at the New York World's Fair and at the Canadian National Exhibition.	**1961** CTV began broadcasting as a private network.	**2005** Canadian channels began broadcasting in HDTV.
1952 Television arrived in Canada; CBFT (Montreal) and CBLT (Toronto) began broadcasting.	**1975** Gerald Levin put HBO on satellite for cable systems.	**2009** All American channels will broadcast in HDTV.
1952 Standard was adopted for compatible black-and-white and colour transmission.	**1976** Ted Turner put WTBS (Atlanta) on satellite for cable systems.	**2011** Canadian television stations must broadcast in HDTV.
	1998 Networks began occasional digital transmissions.	

■■ Influence of Television

study<u>preview</u> **Television's huge audiences have made it a medium with not only profound effects on people and on culture but also on other media. Today television is the dominant mass medium for entertainment and news.**

TELEVISION'S ECONOMIC IMPACT

Although audiences for major networks that provide programming to local affiliate stations have dwindled, the Canadian television industry has continued to grow. Advertising revenue topped $3.2 billion in 2006 percent of the total for all advertising-based media. Newspapers were a distant second at $1.7 billion.

MASS-MEDIA SHAKE-UP

Since television's introduction in the early 1950s, its presence has reshaped the other media. Consider the following.

Books The discretionary time people spend on television today is time that once went to other activities, including reading for diversion and information. To stem the decline in reading, book publishers have responded with more extravagant promotions to draw attention to their products. A major consideration in evaluating fiction manuscripts at publishing houses is their potential as screenplays, many of which end up on television. Also, in deciding which manuscripts to accept, some publishers even consider how well an author will come across in television interviews when the book is published.

Newspapers Evening television newscasts and 24-hour news channels have been a major factor in the near disappearance of afternoon newspapers. Most have either ceased publication or switched to mornings. Also, hometown newspapers have lost almost all of

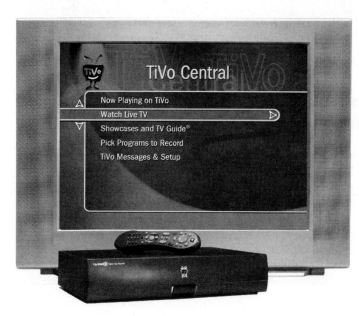

Digital Video Recorder A hot consumer technology introduced in 1999 was DVR, short for "digital video recorder," or PVR, short for "personal video recorder," marketed under names such as TiVo and ReplayTV. DVRs record programs digitally so that people can play back programs when they want to, on their own schedule rather than on the networks' schedule.

their national advertisers, primarily to television. Most newspaper redesigns today attempt to be visually stimulating in ways that newspapers never were before television.

Magazines Television took advertisers from the big mass-circulation magazines such as *Life,* forcing magazine companies to shift to magazines that catered to smaller segments of the mass audience that television could not serve.

Recordings The success of recorded music today hinges in many cases on the airplay that music videos receive on television on MuchMusic.

Movies Just as magazines demassified after television took away many of their advertisers, Hollywood demassified after television stole the bulk of its audience. Today, savvy movie-makers plan their projects both for the big screen and for reissuing, to be shown on television via the networks and for home video rental. These aftermarkets, in fact, have come to account for far more revenue to major studios than movie-house exhibition.

Radio Radio demassified with the arrival of television. The television networks first took radio's most successful programs and moved them to the screen. Having lost its traditional programming strengths, radio then lost both the mass audience and the advertisers it had built up since the 1920s. For survival, individual radio stations shifted almost entirely to recorded music and geared the music to narrower and narrower audience segments.

■ Technology of Television

studypreview Television is based on electronic technology. In the still-dominant analog technology, light-sensitive cameras scan a scene with incredibly fast sweeps across several hundred horizontally stacked lines. The resulting electronic blips are transmitted to receivers, which re-create the original image by sending electrons across horizontally stacked lines on a screen. Today a shift has begun from analog to digital technology.

ELECTRONIC SCANNING

In the 1920s an Idaho farm boy, **Philo Farnsworth**, came up with the idea for using a vacuum tube to pick up moving images and then display them electronically on a screen. Farnsworth found financial backers to build a lab, and in 1927 the first live moving image was transmitted. At age 21 Philo Farnsworth had invented television. Farnsworth's tube,

ONLINE

Philo T. Farnsworth The Farnsworth archives.
http://philotfarnsworth.com

Vladimir Zworykin Exposition about the work of Zworykin.
www.museum.tv/archives/etv/Z/htmlZ/zworykinvla/zworykinvla.htm

Persistence of Vision Experiments that help in understanding of persistence of vision.
www.exploratorium.edu/snacks/persistence_of_vision.html

Philo Farnsworth ■ Invented technology that uses electrons to transmit moving images live.

Farm Boy Invention While harvesting an Idaho potato field in 1921, the 13-year-old Philo Farnsworth came up with the idea to transmit moving pictures live on a magnetically deflected electron beam. Crafting his own materials, including hand-blown tubes, Farnsworth completed his first image dissector while barely in his twenties. Later, RCA used the technology for its flamboyant public introduction of television.

image dissector ■ Farnsworth's television vacuum tube.

Vladimir Zworykin ■ RCA engineer who claimed to have invented television.

iconoscope ■ Zworykin's television vacuum tube.

David Sarnoff ■ Head of RCA.

persistence of vision ■ Retina's capability to retain an image briefly, allowing brain to fill in gaps between successive images.

CBFT ■ First Canadian TV channel.

CBLT ■ Second Canadian TV channel.

ONLINE
The History of Canadian Broadcasting
Trace the history of television in your province, courtesy of the Canadian Communications Foundation.
www.broadcasting-history.ca/

Watching TV A look at a previous exhibition examining the past, present and future of television at the Canadian Museum of Civilization.
www.civilization.ca/hist/tv/ tv00eng.html

which he called the **image dissector**, was an incredible feat, considering that some of the world's great corporate research labs, including RCA's, were trying to accomplish the same thing.

Not wanting to be upstaged, RCA claimed that its **Vladimir Zworykin** had invented a tube, the **iconoscope**, and deserved the credit for television. That would have meant, of course, that RCA would reap a fortune from patent rights. In a patent trial, however, it was learned that both Zworykin and his boss, RCA chief **David Sarnoff**, had visited Farnsworth's lab and had the opportunity to pirate his invention. Zworykin claimed that he had the idea for the iconoscope as early as 1923, but his evidence was not forthcoming. RCA ended up paying Farnsworth a licence fee to use his technology.

In retrospect the technology seems simple. A camera picks up light reflected off a moving subject and converts the light to electrons. The electrons are zapped one at a time across stacked horizontal lines on a screen. The electrons follow each other back and forth so fast that they seem to show the movement picked up by the camera. As with the motion picture, the system freezes movement at fraction-of-a-second intervals and then replays it to create an illusion of movement—the **persistence of vision** phenomenon.

THE EARLY DAYS OF CANADIAN TV

While there were several experimental television broadcasts in Canada through the 1930s and 1940s, Canadians were first exposed to American television signals. The first television broadcast signal received in Canada was in 1947. Engineers at General Electric in Windsor picked up the transmission of WWDT from Detroit. This set the trend for television viewing in the early years of television in Canada. If you lived close enough to the border and had access to a television, you probably watched some American programming.

Television officially arrived in Canada in 1952. As had been the case with the first radio station 30 years earlier, the first television station was in Montreal. **CBFT**, a public station, began broadcasting on September 6, 1952, with **CBLT** Toronto broadcasting two days later. In 1953, stations began broadcasting in Vancouver, Sudbury and Ottawa; by 1954, Winnipeg and Halifax had television stations. At first, programming was a mix of Canadian and American fare. Early Canadian programming also reflected its roots in radio. *Wayne and Shuster* was a staple of Canadian television during the 1960s and 1970s, while *Hockey Night in Canada,* which began on radio in the 1920s, continues to draw a huge audience for the CBC on Saturday nights. A microwave link between Buffalo and Toronto made it possible to carry American programs live. There was no doubt about it: Television was a hit in Canada. A million television sets had been purchased in Canada by 1954. By 1958, the CBC network stretched from Victoria to Halifax. In 1961, CTV began as Canada's first private broadcaster.

Don Ferguson and the *Royal Canadian Air Farce*

Don Ferguson

Canadian content has never been funnier.

For more than a dozen years, Canadians have tuned in to the *Royal Canadian Air Farce* to watch the comedy troupe's take on popular culture and life in Canada. Some of their most memorable characters include Colonel Stacey and his Chicken Cannon, Gilbert Smythe-Bite Me, Melissa the Fast Food Worker, and Jimmy and Seamus from down east.

The *Royal Canadian Air Farce* has been telling Canadian stories and making us laugh at ourselves since 1973. Originally on CBC radio, the *Air Farce* made the transition to television in 1992 and hasn't looked back since. Don Ferguson has been with the troupe since its inception. He attributes the success of the *Air Farce* to two reasons: "We have been as funny as anything viewers can get anywhere on TV. The great plus is that it's funny about us."

The fact that the *Air Farce* is "funny about us" is an excellent example of what Barthes refers to as myth in the mass communication process. What the *Air Farce* does is proof that Canadian culture doesn't have to be about beavers, Mounties, and maple syrup. In its simplest form, Canadian culture is simply talking about Canadian people, places, things and ideas. The *Air Farce* has taken aim at our prime ministers, other broadcasters (for example, George Stroumboulopoulos and Don Cherry), and our cultural institutions, such as Tim Hortons and the CBC. For the *Air Farce,* it's simply a way of connecting with its audience and getting viewers thinking about Canada. Ferguson says the *Air Farce* never set out to promote Canadian culture, but it makes a point of *being Canadian* on the show. As a result, it has become part of Canadian culture itself: "We've always felt that we reflect our environment. The sum total of everything we do over the years *becomes* Canadian culture.

This becomes part of a Canadian's imaginative life."

Despite competition from American networks and programming, this emphasis on comedy from a Canadian perspective attracts almost 1.3 million Canadian *Air Farce* viewers each week. The reason for big ratings is simple, according to Ferguson: "The one feature that you can't get on American TV is references to our politicians, to hockey, or to our way of life. I think it's extremely important that Canadians see and hear Canadian stories done by the best Canadians possible to help nurture our sense of Canadianness."

Ferguson is a strong believer in government support for Canadian media. He sees the impact television can have as an agent of socialization. "What really amazes me is that the politicians don't really seem to get it. The real danger in not having Canadian stuff on television and being bombarded by American programming is that sooner or later Canadians will wonder why we bother with Ottawa, because it's not important, is it? The really important politicians we have to convince are in Washington. Once people start thinking like that, then the end of Canada is at hand."

DIGITAL TELEVISION FINALLY ARRIVES

In comparison to other countries, federal regulators (FCC in the United States, CRTC in Canada) moved slowly on technology to improve onscreen picture quality. The Europeans have had sharper images since television was introduced, and in the 1980s the Japanese developed high-definition television. Both the European and Japanese systems were refinements of traditional **analog** technology that sends images as pulsing, continuous signals.

Both the CRTC and FCC spent years in exhaustive evaluations of new possibilities. Digitizing makes for super-sharp screen images—but at a cost. More broadband space was needed per channel, which necessitated a reshuffling of bandwidth and channels. Plus there's the expense to convert to **digital** for broadcasters. By 2005, most channels were broadcasting in HDTV in major cities across Canada. Because the transition from traditional to digital transmission was costly, the CRTC bent to industry pressure to extend the deadline for compliance. Now the deadline is 2009 for all transmission to be digital in the United States; 2011 in Canada.

Don Ferguson ■ Says Canadians need to see themselves reflected on Canadian TV.

analog ■ Broadcast transmission that uses a continuous, pulsing signal.

digital ■ Broadcast transmission that sends signals in on-off data bits.

Digital Channels: Demassification in Action

Since their introduction in 2001, digital channels have had to compete for subscribers. Here are the top digital channels in Canada, each with a subscriber base of at least one million Canadians, as of August 2005:

Channel	Subscribers
Showcase Action	1 262 000
Animal Planet	1 204 000
Showcase Diva	1 159 000
IFC (Independent Film Channel)	1 111 000
Court TV	1 083 000
Scream	1 070 000

Source: CRTC, Broadcast Policy Monitoring Report 2006.

Television Delivery Systems

study preview **The corporate structure of television parallels three waves of technology, beginning with stations licensed by the federal government to serve particular cities.**

OVER-THE-AIR STATIONS

radio with pictures ■ Simplistic definition of TV.

The engineers and corporate leaders who conceived television really thought in terms of **radio with pictures**. That's not surprising. They were radio people. The television systems they built used towers, just like radio, to send signals via the electromagnetic spectrum to homes, just like radio.

Early American and Canadian television networks thwarted localism and diversity to a great extent by creating popular national programs for local stations. As with radio, this created a two-tier national television system. Stations were local and offered local programs, but the most popular shows came from the national networks. The networks really came into their own, with strong advertising revenue, when **coaxial cable** linked the east and west coasts in 1951. Pioneer broadcast newsman Edward R. Murrow opened his *See It Now* with live pictures from cameras on the Atlantic and Pacific oceans. People marveled at this new technology.

coaxial cable ■ Heavy-duty landline for video signals.

SATELLITE-DIRECT

Stanley Hubbard ■ Satellite TV pioneer.

direct-broadcast satellite ■ Transmission from orbit to receiver; no TV station or cable system intermediary.

Stanley Hubbard believed his KSTP-TV in Minnesota, although incredibly profitable, might become a dinosaur. In the age of satellite communication, why should people tune into local stations, which picked up network signals from satellite for local retransmission, when technology had been devised so they could tune in directly to a satellite? Skeptics scoffed, but in 1994 Hubbard joined General Motors to offer a **direct-broadcast satellite** service. People could pick up signals from over the world with home dishes the size of a large pizza.

Rupert Murdoch ■ Media mogul who created Fox network.

The biggest global satellite service was put together by media mogul **Rupert Murdoch** with BSkyB in Britain, STAR TV in Asia, SKY Italia in Italy and FOXTEL in Australia. The crown jewel for the Murdoch network, DIRECTV in the United States, was acquired in 2003. Integration of the systems faced government and other hurdles, but Murdoch proceeded to upgrade the systems with shared technology that, among other things, included TiVo-like personal recording devices and the capability of downloading Hollywood movies on demand. Canada's first two direct-broadcast satellite providers, sometimes known as DTH for direct-to-home, were Bell ExpressVu and Star Choice.

■ Over-the-Air Networks

study<u>preview</u> **Three American national television networks, first NBC and CBS, then also ABC, dominated programming to local over-the-air stations until the 1980s, when Fox grew into a formidable competitor. Later, the UPN and WB networks came into existence in the Fox model, but the audience and advertising base were insufficient and the new CW was born. In Canada we have three national networks: CBC, CTV and CanWest Global.**

THE NETWORKS

NBC Television The U.S. government licensed the first television stations in 1941, on the eve of U.S. entry into World War II. But when factories converted to war production, no more television sets were manufactured until after peace arrived in 1945. By 1948 the coaxial cables that were necessary to carry television signals had been laid to the Midwest, and **NBC** began feeding programs to affiliates. The coaxial link-up, with some stretches linked by **microwave relays**, connected the east and west coasts in 1951.

NBC innovations included two brainstorms by **Pat Weaver**, an ad executive recruited to the network as a vice-president. In 1951 Weaver created a late-night comedy–variety talk show, precursor to the venerable *Tonight Show*. Weaver also created an early-morning entry, the still-viable *Today*. With those shows, NBC owned the early morning and insomniac audiences for years.

In 1985 **General Electric** bought NBC. During a three-year period, 1982 to 1985, all of the **Big Three** networks (ABC, CBS, NBC) moved out of the hands of the broadcast executives, such as NBC's David Sarnoff, who grew up in the business and nurtured these giant influential entities. As it turned out, the Big Three's heyday was over with new competitive pressures from cable and other quarters. The new owners, with their focus on the bottom line and their cost-cutting instincts, fundamentally changed network television for a new era. General Electric bought the Universal movie studio in 2004 and merged it into a new unit, NBC Universal.

CBS Television CBS was outmanoeuvred by NBC in lining up affiliates after World War II, but soon caught up. By 1953 CBS had edged out NBC in audience size by acquiring affiliates and creating popular programs. By 1953 the *I Love Lucy* sitcom series, which eventually included 140 episodes, was a major draw.

CBS established its legacy in television public affairs programming when **Edward R. Murrow**, famous for his live radio reporting from Europe, started *See It Now*, a weekly investigative program. Three years later, when Senator Joseph McCarthy was using his office to smear people as communists when they weren't, it was Murrow on *See It Now* who exposed the senator's dubious tactics. Many scholars credit Murrow with undoing McCarthy and easing the Red Scare that McCarthy was promoting.

The CBS television network was shepherded in its early years by **William Paley**, who had earlier created the CBS radio network. Paley retired in 1982, and Laurence Tisch, a hotel mogul, came into control of CBS. Today, Viacom owns the network.

ABC Television ABC established its television network in 1948 but ran a poor third. Things began changing in 1953 when ABC merged with **United Paramount Theaters**, whose properties included several television stations. The new company went into fast production schedules of programs that were aimed at Hollywood-like mass audiences. Live programming, the hallmark of early network television, was not part of ABC's recipe.

NBC ■ National Broadcast Company. Built from NBC radio network under David Sarnoff. One of the Big Three over-the-air networks.

microwave relays ■ Towers re-angle over-the-air signals to match the earth's curvature.

Pat Weaver ■ Created NBC's *Tonight Show* and *Today*.

General Electric ■ Current NBC owner.

Big Three ■ ABC, CBS, NBC.

CBS ■ Columbia Broadcasting System. Built from CBS radio network under William Paley. One of the Big Three over-the-air networks.

Edward R. Murrow ■ Reporter who criticized Joseph McCarthy.

William Paley ■ Long-time CBS boss.

ABC ■ American Broadcasting Company. Built from ABC radio network. One of the Big Three over-the-air networks.

United Paramount Theaters ■ Strengthened ABC in 1953 merger.

By 1969 more than 90 percent of the network's programs were on film, tightly edited and with no live gaffes.

ABC's growth was pegged largely to two Disney programs: *Disneyland* in 1954 and *The Mickey Mouse Club* in 1955. Another audience builder was ABC's decision not to carry gavel-to-gavel coverage of the national political conventions. That brought criticism that ABC was abdicating its public responsibility, but by leaving the conventions mostly to CBS and NBC, ABC cleaned up in the ratings with entertainment alternatives. ABC picked up more steam in 1961 with its *Wide World of Sports,* a weekend anthology with appeal that extended beyond sports fans. **Roone Arledge**, the network sports chief, created *Monday Night Football* in 1969. Network television was a three-way race again, and in 1975 ABC was leading by a hair.

CapCities Communications (also known as Capital Cities Communications), a profitable Kansas City–based television station chain, bought ABC in 1985. The network's parent company operated as ABC/CapCities until Disney bought the operation in 1996. Today it is variously called ABC Disney or Disney ABC.

Fox Conventional wisdom through most of television history was that the dominance of NBC, CBS and ABC precluded a fourth network. The only significant attempt at the fourth network, by television-set manufacturer **Allen DuMont**, fizzled in the mid-1950s. Even though the **DuMont network** transmitted 21 hours of prime-time shows to 160 stations at its peak, the other networks had more affiliates. Also, DuMont stations had smaller local audiences, which made the network less attractive to national advertisers.

Then came **Fox**. In 1986 the Australian media mogul Rupert Murdoch made a strategic decision to become a major media player in the United States. He bought seven non-network stations in major cities and also the 20th Century Fox movie studio. The stations gave Murdoch the nucleus for a fourth over-the-air network, and 20th Century Fox gave him production facilities and a huge movie library. Murdoch recruited **Barry Diller**, whose track record included impressive programming successes at ABC, to head the proposed television network.

When Fox went on the air, the signal went to Murdoch's stations and to other independent stations that weren't affiliated with the Big Three. There were doubts whether Fox would make it, but Diller kept costs low. First there was only a late-night talk show. Then Sunday night shows were added, then Saturday night. There was no costly news operation, just relatively low-cost programming. The programs, however, drew a following. Shows like *Married . . . with Children,* featuring the crude, dysfunctional Bundys, and the cartoon series *The Simpsons* attracted mostly young people in their free-spending years, as did new programs like *Beverly Hills 90210* and *Melrose Place.* The young audience made Fox popular with advertisers.

CW Seeing the success of Fox, Time Warner launched the WB Television Network in 1995 to create an outlet for its Warner Brothers production unit. A week later Viacom announced it was creating UPN, short for United Paramount Network, for basically the same reasons. Time Warner and Viacom ended up wishing they hadn't. Not only were both networks slow in getting a prime-time schedule running, the audiences just weren't there in the fragmenting media market. Nor were advertisers, at least not in the quantity or with the enthusiasm networks had traditionally commanded.

Not seeing black ink in their future, Viacom and Time Warner folded the UPN and WB into a new broadcast television network, called the **CW network**, for September 2006. The new network, the *C* for *CBS* and the *W* for *Warner,* drew on programming from its predecessors with the target still being the profitable 18–34 age group. Programs included *America's Next Top Model, Veronica Mars, Smallville,* and *Friday Night SmackDown.* The goal was to attract viewers from the four established networks.

CANADIAN NETWORKS

At present, there are three national networks in Canada. Two of them are privately owned, while one, the CBC, is Canada's national public broadcaster.

CBC The CBC was created by an act of Parliament in 1936 as a radio network. CBC television began in 1952. Today, despite cutbacks in funding, the CBC has developed a loyal following for its programming on several media platforms. CBC television programming outlets include CBC TV in English and French, CBC Newsworld, and Galaxie, a pay audio service available through digital cable and DTH. Over the last few years, some of CBC television's best-known shows include *Hockey Night in Canada, This Hour Has 22 Minutes, Royal Canadian Air Farce,* and *Little Mosque on the Prairie.*

CBCtelevision

In *Canada's Cultural Industries,* Paul Audley sums up the history of television in Canada well. He writes, "The general pattern from the beginning of television in 1952 until the present has been one of a rapidly expanding private television broadcasting system and an underfinanced public system." Given the changes in the late 20th and early 21st centuries, this still appears to be true. Writing in *Maclean's,* Peter C. Newman argues that Canadians need the CBC to become important again. Says Newman, "With our kids watching 900 hours or more of TV a year—and at least 80 percent of it spreading the gospel of the American way of life—we must maintain a vibrant indigenous alternative." Private broadcasters, such as Global and CTV, would disagree with Newman, claiming that the Canadian identity can be preserved by the private sector.

CTV While the CBC is Canada's public network, CTV was Canada's first privately owned national network. In 1960, the Board of Broadcast Governors or BBG (the forerunner of today's CRTC) held hearings for privately owned television stations. One of the victors was **John Bassett's** CFTO, Channel 9, in Toronto. His background in media included part ownership of both the *Sherbrooke Daily Record* and the *Toronto Telegram;* he founded Baton Broadcasting in 1960 and began broadcasting on CFTO, Channel 9, in Toronto. **Spence Caldwell** wasn't as lucky. His application for a TV channel had been denied, but he didn't let that stop him from becoming a Canadian TV pioneer. He approached several of the new television channels, including Bassett's CFTO, with the idea of forming a network. He eventually was able to convince eight channels to form CTN in 1961 with CFTO as its flagship station. CTN changed its name to CTV in 1962. Today, CTV stations reach more than 99 percent of English Canada with their programming. In addition to airing American programming, CTV stations promote Canadian television with shows such as *Canadian Idol, Robson Arms, Corner Gas* and *W-FIVE.*

Global As far back as 1960, Ontario broadcasters **Ken Soble and Al Bruner** had an idea for a Canadian superstation. Although Soble passed away in 1966, Bruner formed Global Communications Limited in 1970. By 1974, CKGN-TV began broadcasting in Ontario. It wasn't a success and lost money from the outset. By 1975 it had been restructured and refinanced. One of its saviours was the late lawyer and journalist **Izzy Asper.** Through a series of buyouts and takeovers that began in the mid-1970s, CanWest Global became Canada's third national network and second private national network in 2000. Its 11 stations in 8 provinces reach more than 94 percent of Canadian viewers. CanWest has interests in both conventional television and specialty channels. Channels under the CanWest banner include TVtropolis, Mystery, and Lonestar. Some of the more notable Canadian productions aired by CanWest are *Blue Murder, Are You Smarter Than a Canadian Fifth Grader?* and *Deal or No Deal Canada.*

Global®

French- vs. English-Canadian TV

In 1971, Canadian writer Hugh MacLennan used the term *two solitudes* to describe the differences between French and English Canada. Nowhere is this more evident than in a comparison of what francophones and anglophones watch on television.

The TV viewing experience in Quebec is significantly different from that in English Canada. For example, according to the CRTC's 2007 *Broadcasting Policy Monitoring Report,* while Canadian programming accounts for 48 percent of total viewing in English Canada, it accounts for 66 percent of total viewing in Quebec. In *Building on Success: A Policy Framework for Canadian Television,* the CRTC wonders why Canadian programming is such a success in Quebec, but not in English Canada. The report says: "French-language programming in particular is extremely successful. Canadian programs regularly achieve some of the highest program ratings; in some years, as many as 19 of the 20 highest-rated programs in the Québec market have been Canadian-produced."

The easy answer, of course, is the language barrier. English-language Canadian shows have to compete with American shows while French-language Canadian shows don't. That's too simple an explanation, according to Patricia Bailey. Writing in the *Winnipeg Free Press,* Bailey argues that the real reason is cultural:

> One fundamental reason for the success of Quebec TV lies in the province's history. Television came on the scene at the right time in this province, and blossomed. Its presence in living-rooms coincided with the start of a major cultural revolution. In the early 1950s, Quebec's artists and intellectuals were frustrated with the repression of both the Duplessis government and the Catholic Church. They needed an outlet, and television provided it. This "revolutionary" class used television as a way to communicate a radical message: Quebec had to change and enter the modern world. Because their vision of a new Quebec was a populist one, their goal from the start was mass appeal. And their preferred tool was drama. At the same time as Quebecers were developing their own unique form of television drama, English-Canadians were being seduced by Ed Sullivan and Jackie Gleason. When the CBC first went to air, thousands of English Canadians had already been setting their aerials to receive signals from the American networks. English CBC decided to focus on news and current affairs rather than drama.

What else accounts for the difference? The CRTC says that the success of French television in Canada is "due in no small part to the well-developed and effective 'star system' in Québec that showcases Canadian actors and programs." The CRTC is encouraging English-Canadian TV to build a star system of its own. It says "audiences for English-language Canadian entertainment programs are lower than those for either foreign programs or Canadian French-language programs, in part because viewers are unfamiliar with the programs and their stars. In French Canada, a well-developed 'star system' promotes new programs and acting talent through all media. In contrast, the pervasive

Why are ratings for Canadian shows higher in Quebec than in the rest of the country? *Star Académie*, a reality show, airs on TVA in Quebec.

promotion of U.S. television shows and stars through foreign and Canadian media often means that English-speaking audiences are more familiar with programs and stars from Hollywood and New York than those from their own country. Audiences might be more attracted to Canadian entertainment programs if they were better informed through television programs about the Canadian entertainment industry and its performers. Canadian entertainment magazine programs will be considered as priority programs." Shows like Global's *Entertainment Tonight Canada* and the specialty channels Star! and E! attempt to showcase Canadian talent and help foster an English-Canadian star system. Whether this model for promoting Canadian television programming will work remains to be seen.

WHAT DO YOU THINK?

1. Log onto www.bbm.ca and compare the weekly TV ratings for French- and English-speaking Canada. How many of the Top 20 shows in Quebec are Canadian? How many of the Top 20 shows in English Canada are Canadian?

2. What do you feel accounts for any differences in viewing patterns between English and French Canada?

3. How can English-language television in Canada develop a "star system" similar to that in Quebec? Would demassification help?

EDUCATIONAL TV

In addition to commercial broadcasting, North America is also home to many educational broadcasters. With federal funding in 1967, the Public Broadcasting Service began providing programs to noncommercial stations. While PBS has offered some popular programs, such as *Sesame Street,* the biography show *American Masters* and the news-magazine *Frontline,* commercial stations do not see it as much of a threat. In fact, with its emphasis on informational programming and high-quality drama and arts, PBS relieved public pressure on commercial stations for less profitable highbrow programming. Like PBS in America, noncommercial broadcasting, including provincial broadcasters such as British Columbia's Knowledge Network, Saskatchewan's SCN, and Ontario's TVO, rely heavily on viewer contributions and provincial funding.

NETWORK ADVERTISING

The big television networks have become an enigma. While cable networks and other media choices have nibbled steadily at the audience once commanded by the networks, these major networks still have been able to continue raising their advertising rates. Strange as it seems, advertisers are paying the networks more money than ever to reach fewer viewers.

Upfront Drama prevails every spring when the networks ask big advertisers to commit themselves upfront to spots in the future year's programming. The networks list shows that they plan to continue, as well as a sample of new programs, and announce their asking price per 30-second spot based on audience projections. Then begins jockeying and bidding between the networks and the agencies that represent advertisers. The **upfront**, as the process is called, locks sponsors into specific shows three to five months ahead of the new season, although contracts generally have options that allow an advertiser to bail out.

upfront ■ Advance advertiser commitments to buy network advertising time.

Law & Order NBC and CTV found an upscale audience that many advertisers sought with the upscale characters in the long-running prime-time series *Law & Order.* The perps in murders may be seedy, but they're wearing button-down shirts with silk ties. Audiences related.

Eighty percent of a year's commercial time typically gets spoken for in the upfront process. If a show misses its projection, advertisers are given **make-goods**, the industry's term for additional spots to compensate for the financial commitment. If a show turns into a smash hit and exceeds audience forecasts, the price per spot gets jacked higher, or in some cases, if there is no escalation clause, the advertisers end up with a real deal.

Until recently, under CRTC regulations, Canadian TV stations could air only 12 minutes of advertising. In 2008, that limit was increased to **15 minutes** per hour to reflect a more American economic model. This was in response to the television industry's call for ways of making more revenue to help offset the cost of transition to digital.

make-goods ■ Additional time that networks offer advertisers when ratings fall short of projections.

15 minutes ■ CRTC limit on TV advertising per hour.

Quality Audience The major television networks once based advertising rates entirely on audience size, but by the 2005–2006 prime-time season the concept of "quality audience" had moved to the fore. That translates into "upscale." To attract big-budget advertisers, the networks pitched programs that were expected to draw well-heeled viewers. Their hope was to charge premium rates to advertisers seeking the hard-to-reach high-income audience niche with messages for five-star hotels and luxury automobiles, not home hair-colouring kits and muffler shops. For delivering upscale viewers, networks charge advertisers 5 to 20 percent extra.

What attracts a quality audience? A consensus has emerged that the characters need to be upscale, even the criminals. NBC improved the posture of its venerable *Law & Order* by introducing upper-class perpetrators to whom upscale viewers could relate. Upscale viewers also value high production values, sophisticated dialogue, and less formulaic storylines.

ONLINE

CATV ■ Short for community antenna television. An early name for cable systems.

■ Cable Television

study<u>preview</u> The cable television industry has grown from independent small-town community antenna systems into a well-heeled, consolidated industry. Today cable is a major threat to the traditional networks and their over-the-air affiliates.

ROOTS OF CABLE

In the early 1950s, television networks and their local affiliates reached only major cities. Television signals, like FM radio, do not follow the curvature of the earth, so communities 40 to 50 miles away were pretty much out of range. Rough terrain kept even nearer towns from receiving television. One by one, small-town entrepreneurs hoisted antennas on nearby hilltops to catch television signals from the nearest cities with over-the-air stations. These local cable television systems, called **CATV**, for *community antenna television,* ran a cable down into town and stretched wire on telephone poles to deliver

Media DATABANK

Canadian Cable and Satellite Operators

Convergence means that cable and satellite companies, known as BDUs (broadcast distribution undertakings) can own cable channels and also provide content for their channels. The following list shows the leading cable and satellite companies in Canada, with their number of subscribers:

Company	Subscribers
Rogers	2 300 000
Shaw	2 200 000
Bell ExpressVu	1 700 000
Vidéotron (Quebecor)	1 500 000
Star Choice	862 000
Cogeco	836 000

Source: CRTC, Broadcast Policy Monitoring Report 2006.

pictures to houses from the hilltop antenna. Everybody was happy. Small towns got big-city television, local entrepreneurs made money, and the networks and their stations gained viewers they couldn't otherwise reach. With this larger, cable-enhanced audience, the networks and stations were able to hike advertising rates.

Interestingly, cable TV arrived in Canada before the first Canadian television station, perhaps reflecting our desire for American programming. An experiment with redistributing U.S. antenna signals in 1952 in London, Ontario, marked the start of cable TV in Canada. Later that year, cable companies were also established in Vancouver and Montreal. The CRTC refers to cable companies as **broadcast distribution undertakings**, or **BDUs**.

GERALD LEVIN AND HBO

Television entered a new era in 1975 when **Gerald Levin** took over **HBO**, a Time Life subsidiary. HBO had been offering movies and special events, such as championship boxing, to local cable systems, which sold the programs to subscribers willing to pay an extra fee. It was a **pay-per-view** service. Levin wanted to expand HBO to a pay-per-month service with 24-hour programming, mostly movies. If it worked, this would give local cable systems a premium channel from which to derive extra revenue.

For an expanded HBO to succeed, Levin needed to cut the tremendous expense of relaying HBO transmission across the country from microwave tower to microwave tower. Then it occurred to Levin: Why not bypass microwaving and instead send the HBO signal to an orbiting satellite, which could then send it back to earth in one relay to every local cable system in the country? Levin put up $7.5 million to use the Satcom 1 satellite. That allowed him to cut microwave costs while expanding programming and making HBO available to more of the country.

Lost ABC and CTV found a prime-time audience for *Lost* with strong cinematic qualities, tight scripting and multi-layered storylines. Plus, fans could also download episodes to their iPods featuring their favourite "losties," including Canadian Evangeline Lilly and her co-star Matthew Fox.

■■ Television Entertainment

studypreview **Early national television networks patterned their programs on their successful radio experience, even adapting specific radio programs to the screen. Until *I Love Lucy* in 1951, programs were aired live. Today, most entertainment programming is taped and then polished by editing.**

EARLY PROGRAMMING

In the early days of television, the networks provided their affiliate stations with video versions of popular radio programs, mostly comedy and variety shows. Like the radio programs, the TV programs originated in New York. With videotape still to be invented, almost everything was broadcast live. Early television drama had a live theatrical onstage quality that has been lost with today's multiple taping of scenes and slick postproduction polishing. Comedy shows like Milton Berle's and variety shows like Ed Sullivan's, also live, had a spontaneity that typified early television. Canada had variety shows like *Juliette* and *Don Messer's Jubilee* and comedy with *Wayne and Shuster* during that time period.

Desi Arnaz and Lucille Ball's *I Love Lucy* situation comedy, introduced in 1951, was significant not just because it was such a hit but because it was not transmitted live. Rather, multiple cameras filmed several takes. Film editors then chose the best shots, the best lines and the best facial expressions for the final production. Just as in movie production, sequences could be rearranged in the cutting room. Even comedic pacing and

BDU ■ Broadcast distribution undertakings. Technical name for cable companies and satellite providers.

Gerald Levin ■ Offered exclusive HBO programming to cable systems.

HBO ■ Short for Home Box Office. First cable programming via satellite.

pay-per-view ■ Cable companies charge subscribers for each program they watch.

timing could be improved. Final responsibility for what went on the air shifted from actors to editors. Taping also made possible the libraries of programs that are reissued by syndicates for rerunning.

I Love Lucy also marked the start of television's shift to Hollywood. Because Arnaz and Ball, who were married to one another at the time, wanted to continue to live in California, they refused to commute to New York to produce the show. Thus, *Lucy* became television's first Los Angeles show. Gradually, most of television's entertainment production went west.

Entertainment programming has gone through phases. Cowboy programs became popular in the 1950s, later supplemented by quiz shows. The cowboy genre was replaced successively by doctor shows, spy shows and cop shows in the 1960s. Through the changes, sitcoms have remained popular, although they have changed with the times, from *Father Knows Best* in the 1950s through *All in the Family* in the 1970s to *Friends* in the 1990s. Reality shows, led by *Survivor* on CBS, began a ride in 2000.

PRODUCING ENTERTAINMENT PROGRAMS

Until 1995 the networks produced some entertainment programs but relied on independent companies for the majority of their shows. The independent companies create prototype episodes called **pilots** to entice the networks to buy the whole series, usually a season in advance. When a network buys a series, the show's producers work closely with network programming people on details.

Like the networks, stations buy independently produced entertainment programs. To do this, stations go to distributors, called **syndicators**, which package programs specifically for sale to individual stations, usually for one-time use. Syndicators also sell programs that previously appeared on the networks. Local stations, like the networks, buy old movies from motion picture companies for one-time showing.

CANADIAN PROGRAMMING

Getting Canadians to watch Canadian TV has been a struggle for English-language broadcasters. Although viewership levels have increased, the fact remains that 52 percent of the time, Canadians watch American programming. It's worse for Canadian comedies and dramas; 77 percent of the time, we prefer American programming to homegrown. Meanwhile, in Quebec, the opposite is true: 66 percent of all viewing in Quebec is Canadian. The question for the industry and academics is how to get English Canadians to watch more Canadian programming.

According to Canadian writer, actor and producer of Canadian television programs **Steve Smith** ("Red Green" to many), Canadian television has an important role as a vehicle for Canadian culture. Smith claims that with "Canadians being constantly exposed to and bombarded with American culture, there's a natural tendency to assimilate and, with Canadians, if all they're exposed to is American media, they will become more and more like Americans and less and less like Canadians. We'd be more like North Dakota with more interesting currency. For some people, that doesn't bother them. For me I think that would be a terrible tragedy."

Smith feels very passionately about Canadian television. He says it's unfair to categorize all American TV shows as better than all Canadian shows. "There are some great Canadian shows. If you look at the ratings book, people would be surprised that a lot of Canadian shows outrate a lot of the American shows." Smith says that Canadian sports broadcasts are among the best.

The real problem for English-Canadian TV is "the philosophy behind some of the broadcast outlets in that they really aren't in the business of making Canadian television good or popular. They are really in the business of importing American shows. That bothers me. Canadian broadcasters should be judged on the Canadian shows that they offer to the public, not on how many American shows they run. If Canadian networks lived or died by the success of their Canadian programming, they would find a way to make them great." For many broadcasters in Canada, the production and scheduling of Canadian programming is an afterthought.

It's this last point about Canadian TV becoming an afterthought for Canadian networks that has many upset. As Atallah and Shade argue in *Mediascapes,* the 60 percent

Cancon may actually be hurting English-Canadian television. "Content quotas set aside certain hours that *must* be filled with Canadian content. Since that content must be shown, it hardly matters whether it is very popular or very good. Indeed, it may be more rational to satisfy quota requirements as inexpensively as possible."

In 1998, the CRTC's TV Policy hoped to address this issue. The changes offered broadcasters some flexibility in acquiring and scheduling Canadian programs, notably:

- Canadian stations need to schedule **60 percent Canadian content** overall, with at least 50 percent during the "**Peak Viewing Period**" of 7 p.m. until 11 p.m., seven days a week.
- Included in this 50 percent of Canadian content during this time period are "priority programs." These aren't just entertainment programs, such as comedies and dramas, but Canadian-produced entertainment magazines, documentaries, regionally produced programs, dramas and comedies.
- The CRTC also offers a **drama credit** of up to 150 percent for new Canadian dramas. This means that a new, one-hour Canadian drama would count as 90 minutes toward the channel's Cancon requirements for that week.
- The Commission also encouraged English-Canadian broadcasters to learn from the experience and success of French broadcasters, including developing a Canadian "**star system**."

This policy moved Canadian TV to a more American model of producing television shows. Canadian networks don't have to produce their own Cancon; that's done by independent production houses. Canada has many successful independent television producers, including Alliance Atlantis, Nelvana, S&S Productions Inc. and Salter Street. These companies have an eye for producing television that is not only (as the CRTC requires) "Canadian in content and character" but also exportable to the United States. In other words, quality of the program becomes a factor.

The goal for Canadian networks, according to **Michael McCabe**, former president of the Canadian Association of Broadcasters, is viewing. Says McCabe, "Viewing is what really counts. Not just how many hours we have or how many dollars we spend. These are just proxies for what should be the real goal—more Canadians watching, being informed by and, most importantly, enjoying Canadian television."

Television News

studypreview The television networks began newscasts with anchors reading stories into cameras, embellished only with occasional newsreel clips. Networks expanded their staffs and programming over the years. Unlike Canadian entertainment programming, Canadian news does well. Given a choice, 92 percent of Canadians will watch Canadian news and information programming over American news.

TALKING HEADS AND NEWSREELS

The U.S. networks began news programs in 1947, CBS with *Douglas Edwards with the News* and NBC with **John Cameron Swayze**'s *Camel News Caravan.* In Canada, news pioneers such as Lloyd Robertson, Knowlton Nash, Peter Desbarats and Harvey Kirck cut their teeth as reporters for this new medium. The evening programs rehashed AP and CP dispatches and ran film clips from movie newsreel companies. The networks eventually built up their own reporting staffs and abandoned the photogenic but predictable newsreel coverage of events like beauty contests and ship launchings. With on-scene reporters, network news focused more on public issues.

Television's potential as a serious news medium was demonstrated in 1951 when producer **Fred W. Friendly** and reporter Edward R. Murrow created *See It Now,* mentioned previously. Television gained new respect when Friendly and Murrow exposed the false, hysterical charges of Senator Joseph McCarthy about communist infiltration of federal agencies. In 1963 the U.S. evening newscasts expanded to 30 minutes with NBC's **Chet Huntley–David Brinkley** team and CBS's **Walter Cronkite** in nightly competition for serious yet interesting accounts of what was happening.

60 percent Canadian content ■ Level of Canadian content required by the CRTC.

Peak Viewing Period ■ 7–11 p.m., seven days a week.

drama credit ■ CRTC incentive for production sector and Canadian channels.

star system ■ Helps raise the awareness of Canadian shows and stars.

Michael McCabe ■ Former head of Canadian Association of Broadcasters.

media ONLINE

Building on Success Read more about the CRTC's 1998 TV policy. www.crtc.gc.ca/Archive/ENG/Notices/1999/PB99-97.htm

TV News Arrives in Canada View one of the very first news stories aired on the CBC. http://archives.cbc.ca/IDC-1-69-543-2729/life_society/boyd_gang/

Douglas Edwards ■ Pioneer anchor.

John Cameron Swayze ■ Pioneer anchor.

Fred W. Friendly ■ Partner of Edward R. Murrow; showed power of TV news through *See It Now* and other programs.

Chet Huntley and David Brinkley ■ Headed first 30-minute network newscast.

Walter Cronkite ■ Best-known television news anchor, now retired.

The arrival of television also added an element to Canadian journalism. In *A Guide to Canadian News Media,* Peter Desbarats reports that by the late 1950s, Canadian news programs were becoming in-depth and analytical. René Lévesque's *Point de mire* and Pierre Berton's *Close-Up* were popular newsmagazine-style shows. Probably the best-known newsmagazine in the 1960s was *This Hour Has Seven Days,* hosted by Laurier LaPierre and Patrick Watson. It debuted in the fall of 1964. The program became known for its controversial style and was taken off the air in 1966 after only 50 episodes. *W-5* (now called *W-FIVE*) began broadcasting in 1966 on CTV and is now the longest running newsmagazine in North America. CBC's *Fifth Estate* is also known for hard-hitting, take-no-prisoners journalism. CBC's *The Hour* with George Stroumboulopoulos continues this tradition with a millennial attitude.

CTV aired its first nightly newscast in 1961 with Harvey Kirck as the anchor. Today, people tune in to the trustworthy images of Lloyd Robertson and the *CTV National News,* Peter Mansbridge on CBC's *The National* or Kevin Newman on *Global National.*

SHIFT IN NETWORK NEWS

Some say television news was at its best during the Murrow period. It is a fact that the networks have scaled down their global news-gathering systems since the mid-1980s. New, bottom-line-oriented owners and budget problems forced the changes. Newscasts have suffered most, losing a lot of original coverage from abroad.

Prime-time **magazine programs** like *60 Minutes* and *W-FIVE* once were a sideline of network news divisions. Today, those programs have become so popular with viewers that network news divisions have shifted resources to produce more of them. NBC's *Dateline,* for example, aired four nights a week one season. The proliferation of magazine programs has further reduced the talent and budget for the newscasts that once were the main identity of the network's news. Critics point out that some network magazine projects are of the tabloid mould—flashy but not much substance. Edward R. Murrow set a higher standard.

24-HOUR TELEVISION NEWS

When Ted Turner launched Cable News Network as an around-the-clock news service in 1980, critics belittled the shoestring operation as "Chicken Noodle News." Gradually, CNN built up its resources and an audience and advertiser base. CNN proved its mettle in the 1991 Persian Gulf War, routinely outdoing the Big Three networks in coverage from the Gulf and being wholly competitive from Washington and other world centres. In 1982, Turner launched Headline News, which offered a quick overview of the latest news, weather and sports. By the late 1990s other players had joined the 24-hour news competition.

Fox News Channel When Rupert Murdoch decided that CNN needed competition, he hired one-time Richard Nixon confidante Roger Ailes to build **Fox News Channel**. Ailes hired a corps of respected Washington reporters and bright young anchors who trumpeted a "we report, you decide" slogan. However, Ailes's conservative bent rubbed off on the product. Extreme conservative Bill O'Reilly added to the Fox News right-wing image in prime time.

MSNBC A third all-news cable network, **MSNBC**, was created by a Microsoft–NBC alliance. The network drew on NBC's depth of news-gathering and on-air talent, including Tom Brokaw's successor, Brian Williams.

CBC Newsworld To offer Canadians a Canadian perspective on the news, *Newsworld* began broadcasting from Halifax, Toronto, Winnipeg and Calgary in 1989. It offers what CBC news has always done well: news with insight and analysis. *Newsworld* is not funded by the government. It relies on advertising revenue and its rather large subscriber base of 10 million viewers.

CTV Newsnet In 1997, CTV launched an all-news channel. At first, it featured a prerecorded 15-minute "headline news" style of format. Eventually, it developed into a full-service news channel that features *Mike Duffy Live* and *CTV National News.* It boasts 7.5 million subscribers.

News Shows

These are the most common types of television nonfiction shows:

Evening Newscasts The major networks have evening newscasts built on reporting the day's main events. These are anchored by seasoned newspeople. Almost all network affiliates carry their flagship local newscast with the network program. Evening newscasts run 30 to 60 minutes.

Sunday Interviews *Meet the Press* on NBC is the longest running show on television. It and similar shows like *Face the Nation* on CBS, *This Week* on ABC and *Question Period* on CTV feature interviews, mostly with government leaders.

Newsmagazines The CBS program *60 Minutes,* which celebrated its 40th anniversary in 2003, comprises several segments on subjects that don't lend themselves to coverage on daily programs. Many segments are investigative. Other newsmagazines include *Dateline* on NBC and *20/20* on ABC, CTV's *W-FIVE* and CBC's *The Fifth Estate.*

Documentaries Sometimes called long-form news, documentaries are lengthy examinations, usually an hour, of a social or political issue. They have been largely displaced in over-the-air network programming by newsmagazines, but they remain a staple at CNN in programs like *CNN Presents,* on PBS with *Frontline* and on CBC Newsworld's *The Passionate Eye.* These shows give producers and correspondents an hour, sometimes longer, to develop an issue.

Morning Shows *Today* on NBC was first a mix of news and softer, but still mostly informational, content. Latter-day morning shows include *Good Morning America* on ABC and *The Early Show* on CBS. CTV's *Canada AM* and *CBC News: Morning* are Canadian versions.

Talk Shows These mostly are independent productions that local stations buy and choose to run at times to build audiences or to fill times during which the networks aren't supplying programming. Some like *Jerry Springer* have been called "trash television," dealing as they do with interpersonal strife of the guests. The two most successful over the years, *Phil Donahue* and *Oprah Winfrey,* cover a broad range of subjects and issues, but rarely breaking news.

Tabloid News Sometimes called *reality shows,* tabloid news programs deal with celebrity news, like the supermarket tabloids, often dwelling on gossipy personal life details. *Entertainment Tonight Canada* and *e-Talk Daily* are among the most widely featured of these programs.

▪ Whither Goes Television?

study<u>preview</u>   **More than in other traditional mass media, the corporate and social structures that have been built around television are well suited to become the hub of tomorrow's mass communication.**

TIME SHIFTS

The centrepiece of television in people's lives in the evening is already waning, even prime time. With TiVo-like playback devices, people don't need to tune in at 8 p.m. for a favourite sitcom. To be sure, events like the Stanley Cup playoffs, elections and the *American Idol* finale will draw huge prime-time audiences. But the end may be in sight for prime-time scheduling for ongoing network series, the historic foundation of network programming.

**media
ONLINE**

CNN This is CNN.
www.cnn.com

Fox News All the latest headlines.
www.foxnews.com

CBC Newsworld News from a Canadian perspective.
www.cbc.ca/newsworld

BBC News News network competition from across the pond.
http://news.bbc.co.uk

Corner Gas Christmas Don't tell us there's not a lot going on. Besides being a hit with both critics and fans, *Corner Gas* employed product placement of the Sears catalogue during its "Merry Gasmas" episode.

SPACE SHIFTS

People still call television receivers *sets*—but less so. The idea of television as a piece of furniture or even a stationary appliance is giving way as miniaturization, possible with digital technology, makes reception possible on palm-size screens that are so light they can be taken anywhere as easily as, say, a wallet. Television is less a bulky appliance around which people cluster and more a portable device that is often incorporated with other functions like telephone, on-demand music, real-time email communication, web access and personal data storage. Plus, fans can now download **podcasts**, which are often sponsored, of their favourite shows and watch them on their portable devices. What does this technological transformation mean for television as we know it?

ADVERTISING SHIFTS

Once the darling of almost every national brand for marketing, 30-second spots on network television are losing some of their luster. The change reflects partly the declining audience for over-the-air stations served by the traditional networks, partly the continuing network push for higher rates. Also a factor is concern that record-replay devices like TiVo mean more viewers are skipping ads.

Webisodes One brand-name advertiser that's shifted away from 30-second spots is American Express. In the mid-1990s, Amex put 80 percent of its advertising budget into network spots. By 2005, however, the amount was down to 35 percent. Where have Amex and other brand-name advertisers diverted their dollars? Some Amex dollars have stayed with the networks through product mention in scripts, which addresses TiVo leakage. But much has gone into web initiatives, concert sponsorships and promotional experiments, such as stocking trendy health clubs with blue-labeled bottled water to hype Amex's blue card. There have been blue popcorn bags at movie houses and Amex-sponsored museum exhibits. Amex has been a leader in **webisodes**, those four-minute mini-movies on the web. Blue card logos were everywhere for an Amex-sponsored concert with Elvis Costello, Stevie Wonder and Counting Crows at the House of Blues in Los Angeles, which was renamed the House of Blue for the event.

Product Placement Mindful that advertisers are scouting for alternative media, television networks have gone to selling paid plugs for products and services in scripts. It's not unlike early radio and 1950s television, when hosts for sponsored programs touted products. For Arthur Godfrey, no tea was as good as Lipton's—and viewers never knew when to expect a plug. This was a leftover from an era when radio advertisers produced their own programs. As the networks took over programs, selling commercial slots to the highest bidder, a purist distinction between creative control of programming content and advertising became a given.

In the 1980s, Hollywood began selling product mentions in movie scripts. The result was a continuing boiling controversy. The controversy now is back in television, with networks—facing the drain of TiVo viewers who watch programs but skip the ads—weaving product names into scripts. CTV's *Corner Gas* was one of the first Canadian shows to include product placement in their Christmas episode entitled "Merry Gasmas." The storyline included mentions of the Sears catalogue. *Rock Star: Supernova* integrated Virgin Mobile phones. Despite protests from some producers, the practice seems destined to stay. As of 2007, the CRTC had no plans to regulate the practice.

North American television patterned itself after radio. From the beginning, television was a dual national system of locally owned commercial stations and national networks. Companies that were heavily involved in radio were also the television heavyweights. Even television's programming mimicked radio's. The networks—NBC, CBS and ABC in America and CBC, CTV and Global in Canada—were the most powerful shapers of television, leading in entertainment programming and news. Gerald Levin and then Ted Turner led a restructuring when they realized that they could deliver programs to local cable companies via orbiting satellite. Levin's HBO and Turner's WTBS, both movie services, became unique features of cable companies in the 1970s. Now satellite and digital technology is contributing to major changes. Also changing the face of television is conglomeration and the emergence of large, multi-platform media companies.

Questions for Review

1. How does television influence people in the short term and the long term?
2. Describe the development of television technology.
3. What technologies deliver television signals to viewers?
4. How has government regulation shaped programming on Canadian TV?
5. How was radio the role model for early television programming?
6. How do owners of local stations, cable systems and satellite-delivery systems view each other?
7. What are Don Ferguson's views on Canadian television?
8. How is television suited to become the hub medium of tomorrow's mass communication?

Questions for Critical Thinking

1. What did social critic Michael Novak mean when he described television as "a molder of the soul's geography"?
2. How did Philo Farnsworth use electronics to pick up moving images and relay them live to faraway screens? How was his invention different from movie technology?
3. How will the competition for television viewers shake out among satellite delivery systems, cable delivery systems and locally licensed stations?
4. Did the two-tier television system, with locally licensed stations and national networks, make sense when it was put into effect? Does it make sense now? For the future?
5. Affiliate stations of the television networks once shared a monopoly on local television audiences, but their dominance has been chipped away. How can these affiliates adapt? Can they survive in a changing mass media environment?

6. Should product placement be regulated by the CRTC?
7. Television once was a place-based medium. To watch, people gathered at television sets, usually at home in a living room, and scheduled their daily routines around favourite programs. How has technology changed viewing habits? What effects have these changes had on programming?

Deepening Your media LITERACY

Is television news on the decline?

STEP 1 The big networks have scaled down their global news-gathering systems, creating opportunities for other sources of news. What does this mean for the news-watching public?

Dig Deeper

STEP 2 Interview three or four of your friends about where they like to get their local news, their global news, their breaking news, their sports news, their entertainment news. How much of it is from the traditional television networks, how much from all-news networks, how much from television newsmagazines and how much from talk shows? How much do they get from sources other than television? If another war were declared tomorrow, where would they turn to get the news about it?

What Do You Think?

STEP 3 Answer these questions:

1. What can you conclude about the state of television news based on your small sample?
2. Do you see any possible trends for the future of television news? Do they match what the experts predict?

Keeping Up to Date

Playback, Broadcaster, and *Broadcast Dialogue* are broadcasting trade journals. *Television/Radio Age* is another trade journal.

Journal of Broadcasting and Electronic Media and the *Canadian Journal of Communication* are quarterly scholarly journals published by the Broadcast Education Association.

Consumer magazines that deal extensively with television programming include *Entertainment* and *People.*

Newsmagazines that report on television issues more or less regularly include *Newsweek, Maclean's* and *Time.*

Major newspapers with strong television coverage include the *National Post,* the *Toronto Star,* and *The Globe and Mail.*

For Further Learning

Paul Atallah and Leslie Regan Shade. *Mediascapes: New Patterns in Canadian Communication* (Thomson Nelson, 2002).

Paul Audley. *Canada's Cultural Industries* (Lorimer and Company, 1983).

Patricia Bailey. "Why Canuck TV Sucks—And Quebec Shows Thrive." *Winnipeg Free Press* (July 6, 2003).

Erik Barnouw. *Tube of Plenty: The Evolution of American Television* (Oxford, 1975).

Warren Bennis and Ian Mitroff. *The Unreality Industry* (Carol Publishing, 1989).

Roger Bird. *Documents in Canadian Broadcasting* (Carleton University Press, 1988).

Donald Bogle. *Primetime Blues: African Americans on Network Television* (Straus & Giroux, 2001).

Robert Brehl. "Specialty Channels Change TV Patterns." *The Globe and Mail* (March 21, 1998).

Jennings Bryant and J. Alison Bryant, eds. *Television and the American Family,* Second edition (Erlbaum, 2001).

John Bugailiskis. "TV Finally Gets Interactive." *Broadcaster* (April 2000).

CanWest Global Communications. *2006 Annual Report.*

Mary Lu Carnevale. "Untangling the Debate over Cable Television." *Wall Street Journal* (March 19, 1990): 107, B1, B5, B6.

CBC. *2005–2006 Annual Report.*

Mark Christensen and Cameron Stauth. *The Sweeps* (Morrow, 1984).

CRTC. *Broadcasting Policy Monitoring Report 2007.*

CRTC. "Dramatic Choices: A Report on English Language Drama." 2003.

CRTC. "The New Policy on Canadian Television: More Flexibility, Diversity and Programming Choice."

CTV. *2006 Annual Report.*

Peter Desbarats. *Guide to the Canadian News Media* (Harcourt Brace, 1990).

Ian Edwards. "Specs Enjoy Stellar Growth." *Playback* (March 2004).

Danylo Hawaleshka, "Converging on Your Living Room." *Maclean's* (August 6, 2001).

Helen Holmes and David Tara. *Seeing Ourselves: Media Power and Policy in Canada* (Harcourt Brace, 1996).

Laurel Hyatt. "Canadian Content Key to New Television Policy." *Broadcaster* (July 1999).

Ed Joyce. *Prime Times, Bad Times* (Doubleday, 1988).

J. D. Lasica. *Darknet: Hollywood's War against the Digital Generation* (Wiley, 2005).

John McGrath. "The Smart Road to HDTV in Canada." *Broadcaster* (July 2000).

Joshua Meyrowitz. *No Sense of Place: The Impact of the Electronic Media on Social Behavior* (Oxford, 1985).

Peter C. Newman. "Save the Country by Salvaging the CBC." *Maclean's* (February 19, 1996).

Peter B. Orlik. *Electronic Media Criticism: Applied Perspectives,* Second Edition. (Erlbaum, 2000).

Lucas A. Powe, Jr. *American Broadcasting and the First Amendment* (University of California Press, 1987).

John P. Robinson and Mark R. Levy. *The Main Source* (Sage, 1986).

Reese Schonfeld. *Me and Ted Against the World: The Unauthorized Story of the Founding of CNN* (HarperCollins, 2001).

Roger P. Smith. *The Other Face of Public Television: Censoring the American Dream* (Algora, 2002).

Duncan Stewart. "Video on Demand." *National Post* (September 29, 2003).

Bohdan Szuchewycz and Jeannette Sloniowski. *Canadian Communications: Issues in Contemporary Media and Culture* (Prentice Hall, 2001).

Mary Vipond. *The Mass Media in Canada* (James Lorimer and Company, 1992).

Jennifer Wells. "Izzy's Dream." *Maclean's* (February 19, 1996).

Hank Whittemore. *CNN: The Inside Story* (Little, Brown, 1990).

Browser Genius At 21, Marc Andreessen and a geek buddy created Mosaic, which facilitated web access. Then they trumped themselves by creating Netscape.

The Internet

Media in Theory

Push-Pull Model

Web communication shifts much of the control of the communication through the mass media to the recipient, turning the traditional process of mass communication on its head. Receivers are no longer hobbled to sequential presentation of messages, as on a network television newscast. Receivers can switch almost instantly to dozens, hundreds even, of alternatives through a weblike network that, at least theoretically, can interconnect every recipient and sender on the planet. This is the basic idea behind the **push-pull model**.

The communication revolution requires a new model to understand new ways that the media are working. One new model classifies some media as passive. These are **pull media**, which you steer. Examples are the traditional media, like radio and television, over which you have control to pull in a message. You can turn them on or off. You can pick up a book and put it down. You can go to a movie or not.

Push media, on the other hand, propel messages at you whether invited to or not. A simple, low-tech example is a recorded voice in a grocery store aisle that encourages you to buy a certain brand of cornflakes as you pass by the cereal display. Push media are taking sophisticated forms with the World Wide Web and new technologies that are making the media more pervasive than ever. They're always on.

Some push media you can program include:

● Signing up for an online newsletter on your favourite topic. Ipsos Reid claims that 8 out of 10 Canadians sign up for various internet newsletters.
● Your cell phone that updates the score on a hockey game you can't watch while you're doing something else.
● News and travel updates from Egypt you ask for after booking airline tickets for a vacation to the pyramids.

push-pull model ■ Some of the control in the communication process shifts to the receiver.

pull media ■ Messages requested by the receiver.

push media ■ Messages sent to the receiver with or without prior consent.

Other push media intrude gently or are in your face without your doing any programming:

- A heads-up automobile windshield display, like OnStar, that flashes directions to nearby repair shops when sensors detect your engine is overheating.
- Banners across your computer screen that advertise products that your past online purchases indicate you're likely to want.
- Wall screens that push items at you based on assumptions about your interests—like music video samplers for a performing star who is popular on a radio station you listen to.

The editors of *Wired* magazine, describing push media, give this example: You are in your study, answering email from the office when you notice something happening on the walls. Ordinarily, the large expanse in front of you features a montage generated by Sci-Viz (meaning *scientific visualization*)—a global news feed of scientific discoveries, plus classic movie scenes and 30-second comedy routines. You picked this service because it doesn't show you the usual disaster junk, yet the content is very lively, a sort of huge screen saver, which you usually ignore. But just now you notice a scene from your hometown, something about an archaeological find. You ask for the full video. This is always-on, mildly in-your-face networked media.

No model is perfect, which means push media and pull media are extremes that rarely exist in reality. Most media messages are push-pull hybrids. The "media wall" in the Wired magazine example intrudes without a specific invitation, but it also leaves it to you to choose what to pull in when you want more detail. Most emerging new media have such hybrid capabilities.

Influence of the Internet

study<u>preview</u> The internet has emerged as the eighth major mass medium with a range of content, especially through web coding, that exceeds that of traditional media in many ways.

NEW MASS MEDIUM

From a dizzying array of new technologies, the internet emerged in the mid-1990s as a powerful new mass medium. What is the internet? It's a jury-rigged network of telephone and cable lines and satellite links that connect computers. Almost anybody on the planet with a computer can tap into the network. A few clicks of a mouse button will bring in vast quantities of information and entertainment that originate all over the world.

media TIMELINE

INTERNET

1945 Vannevar Bush proposed a memex machine for associative links among all human knowledge.

1962 Ted Nelson introduced the term *hypertext*.

1969 U.S. military created ARPANET to link contractors and researchers.

1989 Tim Berners-Lee devised coding that made the web possible.

1993 Marc Andreessen created predecessor to Netscape browser.

1997 Rob Malda, a college student, created Slashdot, "news for news," one of the first blogs.

1999 CRTC decided "not to govern the internet at this time."

2001 Dot-com bubble burst.

2003 Amazon.com demonstrated a new speed of search engines with "Search Inside a Book."

2007 Apple introduced the iPhone.

Although in some ways the internet resembles a traditional mass medium that sends messages from a central transmission point, it is much more interactive and participatory. Message recipients are able to click almost instantly from one source to another—from ordering online from the Sears catalogue to listening to their favourite music genre from Iceberg Radio to reading their local newspaper online. Users of the internet are also creators of content, from blogs to Wikipedia to Facebook or MySpace. The role of individuals in shaping the internet swayed *Time* magazine to name "You" as their Person of the Year in 2006.

TECHNOLOGICAL CONVERGENCE

Today, the traditional primary media are in various stages of transition to digital form. Old distinctions are blurring. This **technological convergence** is fueled by accelerated miniaturization of equipment and the ability to compress data into tiny digital bits for storage and transmission. And all the media companies, whether their products traditionally relied on print, electronic or photographic technology, are involved in the convergence.

As the magazine *The Economist* noted, once-discrete media industries "are being whirled into an extraordinary whole." Anticipating the arrival of phone companies becoming satellite providers and cable companies offering VoIP (voice over internet protocol) phone technology, *USA Today*'s Kevin Maney put it this way in *Quill* magazine: "All the devices people use for communicating and all the kinds of communication have started crashing together into one massive megamedia industry. The result is that telephone lines will soon carry TV shows. Cable TV will carry telephone calls. Desktop computers will be used to watch and edit movies. Cellular phone-computers the size of a notepad will dial into interactive magazines that combine text, sound and video to tell stories."

SCOPE OF THE INTERNET

Every major mass media company has put products on the internet. Thousands of start-up companies are establishing themselves on the ground floor. The technology is so straightforward and access is so inexpensive that millions of individuals have set up their own sites.

How significant is the internet as a mass medium? Statistics Canada estimates that the number of internet users in Canada in 2006 was about 17 million—68 percent of the population, with 81 percent of Canadians using broadband. In only a few years the internet has become a major medium for advertising. In 2006 advertisers spent $519 million for space on the internet.

The significance of the internet is measurable in other ways too. There are people who have given up reading the print edition of newspapers and instead browse through the internet edition. Some of the news sites are updated constantly. Almost every U.S. magazine and newspaper has an **internet site**, from the venerable but tech-savvy *Globe and Mail* to local papers in the hinterlands.

NEW TERMINOLOGY

The terms *internet* and *web* are often tossed around loosely, leading to lots of confusion. The fundamental network that carries messages is the internet. It dates to a military communication system created in 1969. The early internet carried mostly text.

The web is a structure of codes that permits the exchange not only of text but also of graphics, video and audio. Web codes are elegantly simple for users, who don't even need to know them to tap into the web's content. The underlying web codes are accepted universally, which makes it possible for anyone with a computer, a modem and an internet connection to tap into anything introduced from anywhere on the global web. The term *web* comes from the spidery links among millions of computers that tap into the system—an ever-changing maze that not even a spider could visualize and that becomes more complex all the time.

The prefix **cyber-** is affixed almost casually to anything involving communication via computer. *Cyberspace* is the intangible place where the communication occurs. *Cyberporn* is sexual naughtiness delivered on-screen. A *cyberpunk* is a kid obsessed with computer protocols and coding.

media DATABANK

Canadians and the Internet

Ipsos Reid claims that almost 7 in 10 Canadians have internet access at home. What do Canadians do online?

Here are some of the reasons that we go online at home, according to Statistics Canada:

Activity	Percentage of Canadians Engaging in Activity from Home
Email	91%
General Browsing	84%
Weather or Road Conditions	67%
Travel Arrangements	63%
News or Sports	62%
Medical or Health Information	58%
Online Banking	58%
Play Games	39%
Chat	38%
Downloading Music (free or paid)	37%

Source: Adapted from Statistics Canada publication "Canadian Internet Use Survey, 2005," *The Daily,* Catalogue 11-001, August 15, 2006, http://www.statcan.ca/Daily/English/060815/d060815b.htm.

William Gibson ■ Sci-fi writer who coined the term *cyberspace.*

The term *cyberspace* was introduced by science-fiction novelist **William Gibson** in his book *Neuromancer.* At that point, in 1984, he saw a kind of integration of computers and human beings. Paraphrasing a bit, here is Gibson's definition of *cyberspace:* "A consensual hallucination experienced daily by billions of people in every nation. A graphic representation of data abstracted from the banks of every computer in the human system. Unthinkable complexity. Lines of light ranged in the nonspace of the mind. Clusters and constellations of data." Gibson got it right.

media ONLINE

The *Time* 100: William Shockley Profile of William Shockley as part of the *Time* 100 (The Most Important People of the Century).
www.time.com/time/time100/scientist/profile/shockley.html

■ Internet Technology

study<u>preview</u> **The 1947 invention of the semiconductor led to digitization and compression that became building blocks for technology that made the internet possible. Web coding and the Netscape browser widened access.**

UNDERLYING TECHNOLOGIES

Researchers Walter Brattain, John Bardeen and William Shockley at AT&T's Bell Labs knew they were on to something important for telephone communication in 1947. They had devised glasslike silicon chips—piece of sand, really—that could be used to respond to a negative or positive electrical charge.

semiconductor ■ Silicon chips that are used in digitization.

Digitization The tiny chips, called **semiconductors**, functioned very rapidly as on-off switches. With the chips, the human voice could be reduced to a stream of digits—1 for on, 0 for off—and then transmitted as rapid-fire pulses and reconstructed so fast at the other end that they sounded like the real thing. Digitization dramatically expanded the capacity of telephone systems and revolutionized telephone communication. Brattain, Bardeen and Shockley won a Nobel Prize. Little did they realize, however, that they had laid the groundwork for revolutionizing not just telephonic communication but all human communication.

compression ■ Technology that makes a message more compact by deleting nonessential underlying code.

Compression Bell Labs took semiconductors to a new level with **compression** technology in 1965. The on-off digital technology had so compacted messages for transmission that,

Semiconductor Inventors A semiconductor switch can be likened to a tiny triple-decker sandwich. The sandwich, made of silicon, responds to slight variations in electrical current that allow incredibly fast processing of data that have been converted into on-off signals. In addition to speed, the semiconductor ushered in miniaturization of data-processing equipment and storage devices. Since 1947, when Bell Labs engineers devised the semiconductor, it has become possible to store thousands of pages of text on a device as small as a pinhead and to transmit them almost instantly to other devices, like your home computer. The 1956 Nobel Prize went to Bell Labs' Walter Brattain, John Bardeen and William Shockley for inventing the semiconductor.

suddenly, it was possible to break calls into spurts and transmit them simultaneously on a single line, each spurt like a railroad car joining a train on a track and then leaving the train to go to its own destination. People marveled that 51 calls could be carried at the same time on a single wire.

Miniaturization Semiconductors gradually replaced electrical tubes in broadcast equipment. The idea of a radio as a piece of furniture disappeared with semiconductor-equipped portable radios in the 1950s. But that was only the beginning of miniaturization of all kinds of electrical and mechanical functions. In the emerging field of computers, early models used electrical tubes and were housed in entire buildings. Now the movement is toward central units with footprints of less than four square feet. Laptops are a marvel of miniaturization. The Marquardt Corporation estimates that all the information recorded in the past 10 000 years can be stored in a cube six feet by six feet by six feet.

CREATING THE INTERNET

The internet had its origins in a 1969 U.S. Department of Defense computer network called **ARPANET**, which stood for Advanced Research Projects Agency Network. The Pentagon built the network for military contractors and universities doing military research to exchange information. In 1983 the **National Science Foundation (NSF)**, whose mandate is to promote science, took over.

This new National Science Foundation network attracted more and more institutional users, many of which had their own internal networks. For example, most universities that joined the NSF network had intracampus computer networks. The NSF network then became a connector for thousands of other networks. As a backbone system that interconnects networks, **internet** was a name that fit.

By 1996 the internet had become clogged with exponential growth in traffic. University network engineers designed a new high-speed backbone to connect research networks. Called **Internet2**, the new backbone was up and running by 1999, carrying data as fast as 2.4 gigabits per second—four times faster than its predecessors. In 2003 it was upgraded to 10 gigabits per second.

One solution, an even faster Internet3, may not be financially possible. An interim possibility is to lease **dark fibre**, the unused fibre optic capacity that commercial telecommunications companies overbuilt in the late 1990s. Already Internet2 is too costly for many colleges. Basic connection and membership fees range from $160 000 to $450 000 a year. Internet3 would cost even more.

WORLD WIDE WEB

The early internet created access to lots of data at speeds that were unprecedented. But it was an uninviting place visually. Text and data were in black-and-white and image-free—something only a researcher could love. Even so, there were possibilities to take the new medium in commercial directions.

ARPANET ■ Military network that preceded internet.

National Science Foundation ■ Developed current internet to give scholars access to supercomputers.

internet ■ A network of computer networks.

Internet2 ■ A network consortium owned by research institutions for fast data transfer.

dark fibre ■ Excess telecommunication capacity available for data transfer.

media ONLINE

LexisNexis Subscribe to this online database service or use the à la carte option and pay as you go.
www.lexisnexis.com

The Eyeball as a Screen A Seattle company, Microvision, is hoping to market a device that projects images directly onto the human eyeball. This VRD, short for *virtual retinal display,* is not much more cumbersome to wear than a pair of glasses, and it gives a sharper image than a 70-millimetre IMAX screen. With VRD, people would not need television or computer screens. Microvision says this device can be made for less than $100.

The *Time* **100: Tim Berners-Lee** Profile of Tim Berners-Lee as part of the *Time* 100 (The Most Important People of the Century).
www.time.com/time/time100/ scientist/profile/bernerslee.html

Canadian ISPs Looking to change your ISP? Here's a list of 350 Canadian ISPs.
www.canadianisp.com

internet service provider (ISP) ■ Company that charges a fee for online service.

Tim Berners-Lee ■ Devised protocols, codes for the World Wide Web.

World Wide Web ■ System that allows global linking of information modules in user-determined sequences.

universal resource locator (URL) ■ Address assigned to a page on the internet. Now known as a uniform resource locator.

hypertext transfer protocol (HTTP) ■ Coding that allows computers to talk with each other to read web pages.

hypertext markup language (HTML) ■ Language that is used to code for web pages.

hypertext ■ System for nonsequential reading.

bandwidth ■ Space available in a medium, such as cable or the electromagnetic spectrum, to carry messages.

Internet Service Providers A new kind of company, **internet service providers (ISPs)**, went into business in the 1980s to give ordinary folks a portal to the internet and help in navigating the internet's inherent complexity and disorganization. Compuserv was first to provide online service to consumers. These companies charged subscription fees for a combination of services— internet access, email and, most important, a mapping structure to help users get to where they wanted to go among the seemingly infinite number of places to go on the internet.

Tim Berners-Lee A major breakthrough came from English engineer **Tim Berners-Lee**, who in 1991 devised an addressing system that could connect every computer in the world. The name that Berners-Lee came up with for his system sounded audacious, the **World Wide Web**, but it was accurate—a decentralized global network with the potential, theoretically, for everyone at a computer to communicate with everyone else at a computer anywhere on the planet.

Berners-Lee's invention was built on three components:

● **Universal resource locators (URL)**. Now known as uniform resource locators, this addressing system was devised by Berners-Lee to give every computer a unique identifier, much like a postal address that enables mail to be delivered to the right place. The identifiers, URLs, allowed computers connected in a network to exchange messages. Being "universal," it was a comprehensive and standardized system that became the foundation for the World Wide Web.

● **Hypertext transfer protocol (HTTP)**. This is a protocol that allows computers to connect to read internet files.

● **Hypertext markup language (HTML)**. This was a relatively simple computer language that permitted someone creating an internet message to insert so-called hot spots or links that, if clicked, would instantly switch the onscreen image to something else. For example, a research article could include visible indicators, usually the underlining of a term, that when clicked on with a mouse would cause the browser to move to another article on the subject.

The term **hypertext** was devised by technologist Ted Nelson in his 1962 book *Literary Machines* for a system that would allow people to interrupt themselves while reading through material in the traditional linear way, from beginning to end, and transport themselves nonlinearly to related material. Nelson also called it *nonsequential writing,* but the term *hypertext* stuck.

It was a quarter century later when Berners-Lee devised the HTML coding that made nonsequential reading possible.

BANDWIDTH

An impediment to the web's realizing its potential was the capacity available on traditional telephone systems for transmitting data. Text was no problem, but as graphics joined the mix, this capacity, called **bandwidth**, became packed and transmissions slowed, sometimes to a crawl. Superdetailed photos required several minutes to traverse from point A to point B. The more

Tim Berners-Lee

Tim Berners-Lee

Single-handedly, Tim Berners-Lee invented the World Wide Web. Then, unlike many entrepreneurs who have used the internet to amass quick fortunes, Berners-Lee devoted his life to refining the web as a medium of communication open to everyone for free.

Berners-Lee, an Oxford engineer, came up with the web concept because he couldn't keep track of all his notes on various computers in various places. It was 1989. Working at CERN, a physics lab in Switzerland, he proposed a system to facilitate scientific research by letting scientists' computers tap into each other. In a way, the software worked like the brain. In fact, Berners-Lee said that the idea was to keep "track of all the random associations one comes across in real life and brains are supposed to be so good at remembering, but sometimes mine wouldn't."

Working with three software engineers, Berners-Lee had a demonstration up and running within three months. As Berners-Lee traveled the globe to introduce the web at scientific conferences, the potential of what he had devised became clear. The web was a system that could connect all information with all other information.

The key was a relatively simple computer language known as HTML, short for hypertext markup language, which, although it has evolved over the years, remains the core of the web. Berners-Lee also developed the addressing system that allows computers to find each other. Every web-connected computer has a unique address, a universal (or uniform) resource locator (URL). For it all to work, Berners-Lee also created a protocol that actually links computers: HTTP, short for hypertext transfer protocol.

In 1992, leading research organizations in the Netherlands, Germany and the United States committed to the web. As enthusiasm grew in the scientific research community, word spread to other quarters. In one eight-month period in 1993, web use multiplied 414 times. Soon "the web" was a household word.

As you would expect, Berners-Lee had offers galore from investors and computer companies to build new ways to derive profits from the web. He said no. Instead, he chose the academic life. At the Massachusetts Institute of Technology he works out of spartan facilities as head of the W3 consortium, which sets the protocol and coding standards that are helping the World Wide Web realize its potential.

It's hard to overrate Berners-Lee's accomplishment. The internet is the information infrastructure that likely will, given time, eclipse other media. Some liken Berners-Lee to Johannes Gutenberg, who 400 years earlier had launched the age of mass communication with the movable type that made mass production of the written word possible.

---

complex a visual, the more data are needed to make it blossom at the other end. Theoretically, music could be sent on the internet, but it was a bandwidth hog. Video was worse.

A combination of technologies is being used to address the bandwidth issues. Some are eliminating choke points in the pipelines. Others are squeezing more data to consume less space.

Fibre Optic Cable While AT&T was building on its off-on digital technology to improve telephone service in the 1960s, **Corning Glass** developed a cable that was capable of carrying light at incredible speeds—theoretically 186 000 miles per second. It was apparent immediately that this new **fibre optic cable** could carry far more digitized messages than could the copper wire used for telephones. The messages were encoded as light pulses rather than as the traditional electrical pulses for transmission.

By the 1980s, new equipment to convert data to light pulses for transmission was in place, and long-distance telephone companies were replacing their copper lines with fibre optics, as were local cable television systems. With fibre optic cable and other improvements, a single line could carry 60 000 telephone calls simultaneously.

Multiplexing One innovation that expanded bandwidth was **multiplexing**, a process through which a message is broken into bits for transmission through whichever cables have capacity

Corning Glass ■ Company that developed fibre optic cable.

fibre optic cable ■ Glass strands capable of carrying data as light.

multiplexing ■ Technology to transmit numerous messages simultaneously.

Global Fibre Optics

The Fiber Optic Link Around the Globe, "FLAG" for short, is the longest engineering project in human history—a 17 400-mile communication link of England and Japan. Many of the lines shown are undersea fibre optic routes that are planned or in place. The world is being wired for faster World Wide Web communication.

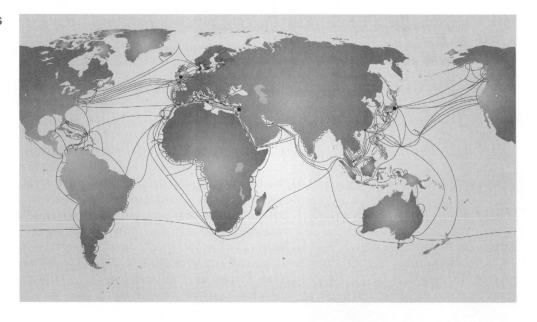

ONLINE

Timeline of Fibre Optic Cable
Beginning with Albert Einstein and ending with the Fiber Optic Link Around the Globe, the National Academy of Engineering developed this timeline.
www.greatachievements. org/?id = 3706

streaming ■ Technology that allows playback of a message to begin before all the components have arrived.

media
ONLINE

Looking for Free Wi-Fi? A website that lists free Wi-Fi hot spots not only in Canada, but the United States and Europe.
www.wififreespot.com

Wi-Fi ■ Wireless fidelity technology.

digital divide ■ The economic distinction between impoverished groups and societal groups with the means to maintain and improve their economic well-being through computer access.

at the moment. Then the bits are reassembled at the delivery point. So instead of a message getting clogged in a pipeline that's already crammed, tiny bits of the message, called packets, find alternative paths through whichever pipeline has room. All of this happens in fractions of a second, with the message ending up at its destination faster.

Compression Technology has been devised that screens out nonessential parts of messages so that they need less bandwidth. This is especially important for graphics, video and audio, which are incredibly code-heavy. Coding for blue sky in a photo, for example, need not be repeated for every dot of colour. Even without redundant coding, the sky still appears blue. Unless compressed, audio too is loaded with redundant coding.

Some compression technology further streamlines a message by eliminating details that the human eye or ear will not miss. For example, compression drops sound on a CD that would start dogs howling but that humans cannot hear.

Streaming When a message is massive with coding, such as audio and video, the message can be segmented with the segments stored in a receiving computer's hard drive for replay even before all segments of the message have been received. This is called **streaming**. Most audio and video today is transmitted this way, which means some downloading delay—often only seconds. The more complex the coding, the longer it takes.

▛▖ Reshaping the Internet

study<u>preview</u> Wireless internet connections, called *Wi-Fi*, have added to the portability of the internet. Further untethering from a wired infrastructure is possible through ultrawideband and mesh network technology.

WI-FI

Another development in interactive media is wireless fidelity technology, better known as **Wi-Fi**. It untethers laptops and allows internet access anywhere through radio waves. The coffee chain Starbucks made a splash with Wi-Fi, encouraging people to linger. Hotels and airports were naturals for Wi-Fi. Many Canadian cities from Chilliwack to St. John's have free Wi-Fi "hot spots" in their downtown areas.

One justification for municipal Wi-Fi is to bridge the **digital divide**, the socioeconomic distinction between people that can afford internet access and those that can't.

ULTRAWIDEBAND

Short-range Wi-Fi networks, which become sluggish as more people tap in, may pick up capacity with UWB technology, short for **ultrawideband**, unless opponents prevail. The technology uses existing frequencies, including commercial broadcast channels, but with such low power that the primary signals seem to be unaffected. The aviation industry is concerned that frequencies used by on-board collision-avoidance systems could be compromised by crowding.

ultrawideband (UWB) ■ Low-power Wi-Fi system that rides on existing frequencies licensed for other uses.

MESH NETWORKS

After Wi-Fi, what? The most anticipated next technology is **dynamic routing**, in which every wireless gadget serves also as a receiver and transmitter to every other wireless device within its range. Messages would just keep moving, hop-skipping invisibly from device to device until each reaches its intended destination. There is no formal network; messages go to whatever device has capacity at the moment—or, rather, at the nanosecond. Every wireless device outfitted for dynamic routing would be on call as a stepping stone for however many messages come its way. Engineers say that **mesh networking**, as it is called, using high-speed protocols, will be 15 times faster than currently touted DSL services.

dynamic routing ■ Technology that makes every wireless device a vehicle for furthering a message along to its destination, rather than moving in a structured network.

mesh networking ■ The ad hoc network created for each single message to reach its destination; also called *dynamic routing*.

■ Commerce and the Internet

study<u>preview</u> The internet has emerged as a commercial medium. Some sites are built around products. Others, in a more traditional vein, are designed to attract an audience with content, such as news. The sites sell access to that audience to advertisers.

ADVERTISING-FREE ORIGINS

Before the web, the internet was a pristine, commerce-free medium. If somebody put out a message that had even a hint of "filthy lucre," purists by the dozens, even hundreds, deluged the offender with harsh reminders that commerce was not allowed. By and large, this self-policing worked.

When the web was introduced as an advanced internet protocol, its potential for commerce was clear almost right away. The World Wide Web Consortium, which sets standards for web protocols, created the dot-com suffix to identify sites that existed to do business. That decision transformed the internet and our lives.

DOT-COM BUBBLE

By 1996, internet traffic was doubling every three months. On an annual basis that was 800 percent growth. Billions of investment dollars flowed in to finance additional fibre optic infrastructures. The investment frenzy generated more than $1 trillion to wire the world with extraordinary new capacity.

Meanwhile, seeing no end to the exponential growth in **dot-com** companies, investors poured billions of dollars into ventures for exploiting the internet's commercial potential. Much of the investment, it turned out, was reckless. The so-called **dot-com bubble** burst in 2001 and 2002 with bankruptcies and a massive scaling down that caught thousands of internet careers in the downward spiral. Investment portfolios withered with profound implications for pension plans that resulted in many people delaying their retirement.

But there was good news. A vast fibre optic system was in place, with far more capacity than was needed. Nobody was going to dig it up. As telecommunications companies went belly up, banks acquired the assets in bankruptcy sales and then sold the fibre optic networks at 10 cents on the dollar. The new owners operated the networks profitably, having bought them at fire-sale prices. The new owners also installed new transmitter and receiver switches to increase the volume and speed of data moving through the networks.

Thomas Friedman of *The New York Times,* who studied the dot-com phenomenon, described what happened this way: "So as the switches keep improving, the capacity of all of the already installed fibre cables just keeps growing, making it cheaper and easier

dot-coms ■ Commercial websites, so named because their web address ended with the suffix ".com."

dot-com bubble ■ Frenzied overinvestment in the telephone and internet infrastructure and also internet commerce in late 1990s.

to transmit voices and data every year. . . . It's as though we laid down a national highway system where people were first allowed to drive 50 mph, then 60 mph, then 70 mph, then 80 mph, then eventually 150 mph on the same highways without any fear of accidents."

INTERNET ADVERTISING

When the bubble burst for so many dot-coms, most remaining sites looked to advertising rather than venture capitalists to sustain them economically. With more than 217 million people with web access in the United States and Canada by 2005, and the number growing, the potential for dot-coms to be advertising-supported was clear. The Interactive Advertising Bureau of Canada claims that many Canadians use the internet as a research tool when making purchases. Also, in 2006, 52 percent of Canadians with internet access had made purchases online. Meanwhile, in its *Broadcast Policy Monitoring Report 2006,* the CRTC claims that internet advertising increased 5090 percent, from $10 million in 1997 to $519 million in 2006.

TRACKING INTERNET TRAFFIC

An impediment to attracting advertisers to the internet was the difficulty of measuring the audience. Advertisers want solid numbers on which to base decisions on placing their ads. Gradually, the Interactive Advertising Bureau and the Advertising Research Foundation developed uniform measurement guidelines. Nielsen, known mostly for surveys on network television audiences, has established monitoring mechanisms.

hit ■ Tallied every time someone goes to a web page.

The most-cited measure of web audiences is the **hit**. Every time someone browsing the web clicks an onscreen icon or onscreen highlighted section, the computer server that offers the web page records a hit. Some companies that operate websites tout hits as a measure of audience, but savvy advertisers know hits are a misleading indicator of audience size. The online edition of *Wired* magazine, *HotWired,* for example, records an average of 100 hits from everybody who taps in. *HotWired*'s 600 000 hits on a heavy day come from a mere 6000 people.

visit ■ Tallied for every person who visits a website.

Another measure of web usage is the **visit**, a count of the people who visit a site. But visits too are misleading. At *Playboy* magazine's website, 200 000 visits are scored on a typical day, but that doesn't mean that *Playboy* cyber-ads are seen by 200 000 different people. Many of the same people visit again and again on a given day.

clickthrough ■ A registered visit to an advertising site from a gateway elsewhere on the internet.

The **clickthrough** has emerged as a measure. When someone clicks a link to an advertising site, the click is registered and a fee is paid to the site from which the ad visitor came, called the gateway site. The gateway site is the internet equivalent of a newspaper, which charges advertisers for space, or a television station, which charges for airtime.

Some electronic publications charge advertisers by the day, others by the month, others by the hit. But because of the vagaries of audience measurements, there is no standard pricing. Knowing that the web cannot mature as an advertising medium until advertisers can be given better audience data, electronic publications have asked several companies, including Nielsen, to devise tracking mechanisms. But no one expects data as accurate as press runs and broadcast ratings any time soon. In the meantime, advertisers are making seat-of-the-pants assessments as to which websites are hot.

▛▖ Evaluating the Internet

studypreview Traditional gatekeeping processes that filter media content for quality are less present in the internet. Users need to take special care in assessing material they find.

STRENGTHS OF INTERNET SITES

Several organizations issue awards to excellent internet sites. The most prestigious are the **Webby** awards, a term contrived from the nickname for the somewhat parallel Emmy awards of television. Many web awards, though, are for design and graphics, not content, although there are many measures of a site's excellence.

Webby ■ A major award of excellence for websites.

Content The heart of all mass media messages is the value of the content. For this, traditional measures of excellence in communication apply, such as accuracy, clarity and coherence.

Navigability   Does the site have internal links so that users can move easily from page to page and among various points on the site? Among the mass media, navigability is a quality unique to the internet.

External Links   Does the site connect to related sites on the internet? The most distinctive feature of the internet as a mass medium is interconnectivity with other sites on the global network. Good sites exploit this advantage.

Intuitive to Use   The best sites have navigational aids for moving around a site seamlessly and efficiently. These include road signs of many sorts, including clearly labeled links.

Loading Times   Well-designed sites take advantage of the internet as a visual medium with images. At the same time, pages should load quickly so users don't have to wait and wait and wait for a page to write itself to their screens. This means the site needs a balance. Overdoing images, which require lots of bandwidth, works against rapid downloads. Absence of images makes for dull pages.

ACCURACY

The internet has been called a democratized mass medium because so many people create internet content. Almost anybody can put up a site. A downside of so much input from so many people is that the traditional media gatekeepers (see Chapter 1) aren't necessarily present to ensure accuracy. To be sure, there are many reliable sites with traditional gatekeeping, but the internet is also littered with junk.

To guard against bad information, internet users should pay special heed to the old admonition: Consider the source. Is the organization or person behind a site reliable? If you have confidence in the *National Post* as a newspaper, you can have the same confidence in its website. Another news site, no matter how glitzy and slick, may be nothing more than a person working alone in a dank basement somewhere recasting the news from their perspective. Lobby groups and political parties also publish content on the internet on sites that appear to be neutral. Norman Spector, who was Chief of Staff to Brian Mulroney in the 1980s, says "there's so much concern on the part of the public now as to whether they're getting the straight goods and people are going to the internet, they say, because their confidence in the mainstream media has been shaken. So I think this on the web is problematic."

In research reports, footnotes or endnotes need to be specific on internet sources, including URL addresses. This allows people who read a report to go to the source to make their own assessment—just as traditional footnotes allow a reader to go to the library and check a source.

Even with notations, a report that cites internet sources can be problematic. Unlike a book, which is permanent once it's in print, internet content can be in continuing flux. What's there today can be changed in a minute—or disappear entirely. To address this problem at least in part, notation systems specify that the date and time of the researcher's internet visit be included.

In serious research, you can check whether an online journal is refereed. A mission statement will be on the site with a list of editors and their credentials and a statement about the journal's editorial process. Look to see whether articles are screened through a **peer review** process.

peer review ■ A screening mechanism in which scholarly material is reviewed by leaders in a discipline for its merits, generally with neither the author nor the reviewers knowing each other's identity.

THE INTERNET: GOOD, BAD OR UGLY?

Steve Maich, writing in *Maclean's* magazine in October of 2006, had some issues about the internet. The entire title of his article was "Pornography, Gambling, Lies, Theft and Terrorism: The Internet Sucks (Where Did We Go Wrong?)" His issue wasn't only with the internet itself, but the discourse surrounding it. Maich writes that "right from the beginning, experts competed with one another to see who could come up with the most outrageous superlative to the nascent technology. It was the most important breakthrough since the personal computer, no, since the telephone— or rather the telegraph, or maybe the printing press." Even in 2006 when Google bought out YouTube, creating a "titan of new media," Maich claims the rhetoric hadn't changed.

Steve Maich ■ *Maclean's* columnist with issues about the impact of the internet and the rhetoric surrounding it.

Maich doesn't believe the internet has lived up to its hype. He says "after 15 years and a trillion dollars of investment, just about everything we've been told about the internet and what the information age would mean has come up short." Instead of Tim Berners-Lee's dream of the internet becoming "an interactive sea of shared knowledge," the internet became a place that "the public at large saw as an invitation to indulge vice on an unimaginable scale."

Despite the issues with the internet, Maich does admit that there's nothing that can be done.

"There's no going back. It is now so deeply entrenched in our culture—in the way we speak and work and create and think—that the only thing to do is try and make it better and hope that maybe we might somehow realize some of the dreams the idealists had when they invented the thing."

▛ Public Policy and the Internet

study<u>preview</u> **The ability of almost anyone to post content on the internet poses new public policy questions and issues. This whole new media world is illustrated by the free-wheeling nature of blogs. Media issues of privacy, decency and access are posed in newly critical ways.**

BLOGS

In an era when the price of entry to media ownership precludes most mortals, the internet, although young as a mass medium, is already democratizing mass communication. The rules are new. The most powerful member of the U.S. Senate, Trent Lott, never figured that his career would end under pressure created by a pipsqueak citizen in the hinterlands. It happened.

Joshua Marshall, creator of his own website (talkingpointsmemo.com), picked up on a speech by Lott that, depending on your view, was either racist or racially insensitive. Lott uttered his comment at the 100th birthday party of Senator Strom Thurmond, once a strong segregationist.

Mainstream news media missed how Lott's comments could be interpreted. Not Joshua Marshall. In his **blog** (at http://talkingpointsmemo.com) he hammered away at Lott day after day. Other bloggers, also outraged, joined in. Three days later the story hit NBC. Four days later Lott apologized. Two weeks later his Senate colleagues voted him out as majority leader.

As a blogger who made a difference, Joshua Marshall is hardly alone. Best known is Matt Drudge, whose revelations propelled the Bill Clinton–Monica Lewinsky dalliances in the Oval Office into a national scandal. Another blogger, college student Russ Kick, at his computer in Arizona, looked for information on government refusals to release photographs of caskets of fallen U.S. soldiers in Iraq and Afghanistan, which he regarded as documents to which the public, himself included, had legal access. Kick filed a request for the documents under the Freedom of Information Act, then on his website (thememoryhole.org), he posted the photographs of the flag-draped coffins and also of the astronauts who had died in the *Columbia* disaster. The photos became front-page news. At one point Kick's blog was receiving 4 million hits a day—almost twice the circulation of *USA Today*.

Both the beauty and bane of blogs is their free-for-all nature. On the upside, the web gives ordinary citizens access to mass audiences. It can be a loud and effective megaphone that is outside the traditional news media that have resulted from institutionalized practices and traditions.

Joshua Marshall's work on Trent Lott is an example of outside-the-box news reporting. Most bloggers are amateurs at news, and their lack of experience with journalistic traditions has a downside.

blog ▪ An amateur website, generally personal in nature, often focused on a narrow subject, such as politics. Short for "web log."

PRIVACY AND THE INTERNET

The genius of Tim Berners-Lee's original web concept was its openness. Information could be shared easily by anyone and everyone. Therein was a problem. During the web's commercialization in the late 1990s, some companies tracked where people ventured on the internet. The tracking was going on silently, hidden in the background, as people coursed their way around the internet. Companies gathering information were selling it to other companies. There was fear that insurance companies, health-care providers, lenders and others had a new secret tool for profiling applicants.

Government agencies began hinting at controls. Late in 1999, Berners-Lee and the web protocol-authoring consortium he runs came up with a new architecture, **P3P**, short for *Platform for Privacy Preferences Project,* to address the problem. With P3P, people could choose the level of privacy they wanted for their web activities. Microsoft, Netscape and other browser operators agreed to screen sites that were not P3P-compliant. In effect, P3P automatically bypassed websites that didn't meet a level of privacy expectations specified by individual web users.

CYBERPORNOGRAPHY

Moralists, many in elected offices, are trying to eradicate indecency from cyberspace, especially if children have access. How serious is the problem? No one is certain how much **cyberpornography** is out there. Although a lot of internet traffic is to porn sites, Vanderbilt University business professors Donna Hoffman and Thomas Novak estimate that only one-half of 1 percent of the files available on the internet could be described as pornographic. How often kids visit those sites is impossible to measure. Some people would argue that even a single child's exposure to pornography is too much and justifies sanctions.

Still, policing the internet, including websites, presents unique challenges. The nature of the internet is that it is unstructured and unregulated, and the available material is in ongoing flux. The anarchy of the internet is its inherent virtue. The immensity of cyberspace is another problem for would-be regulators. The web system that Tim Berners-Lee and his associates devised has infinite capacity.

Among alternatives to protect children are desktop programs that have come on the market to identify objectionable internet bulletin boards and websites. **SurfWatch**, for example, blocks access to such sites as soon as they are discovered. Bill Duvall of Los Altos, California, who created SurfWatch, hires college students to monitor cyberspace for sexual explicitness and updates SurfWatch regularly. He identifies five to 10 new smut sites a day.

UNIVERSAL ACCESS

Although internet use is growing dramatically, the fact is that not everybody has access. Those who can afford computers and access fees will benefit tremendously. What about everybody else? This is a profound public policy question, especially in a democracy that prides itself on ensuring equality for every citizen on basic matters like access to information. One line of reasoning is that the government should not have to guarantee **universal access**. This rationale draws on the highway system as an analogy. The government builds the roads, but individuals have to provide the vehicles to drive around on the system.

The counter-argument is that access to information will become so essential to everyone's well-being that we could end up with a stratified society of info-rich and info-poor people. Such a knowledge gap hardly is the democratic ideal.

However, it's not simply a case of access. Limiting individuals' access to the internet also limits their ability to create content for the internet. **Michael Geist**, the Canada Research Chair in Internet and E-Commerce Law at the University of Ottawa, says, "an obvious starting point for connectivity is the role that the federal, provincial and municipal governments can play to ensure that all Canadians have access to the high-speed networks that are the price of admission to the participatory Internet."

GLOBAL INEQUITIES

The exchange of information facilitated by the internet boosted North America into unprecedented prosperity going into the 21st century. One measure of efficiency, **diffusion of innovation**, improved dramatically. The time that innovations take to be widely used, which was once

P3P ■ A web protocol that allows users to choose a level of privacy. Short for *Platform for Privacy Preferences Project.*

cyberpornography ■ Indecency delivered by computer.

SurfWatch ■ Software that intercepts indecent material.

universal access ■ Giving everyone the means to use the internet.

Michael Geist ■ Canadian expert on how new technology is affecting Canadian law.

diffusion of innovation ■ Process through which news, ideas, values and information spread.

10 years, dropped to 1 year. The Giga Information Group projected that by 2002, businesses would be saving $1.3 trillion because of internet commerce—an incredible 765 percent gain over five years.

A problem, though, is that much of the world isn't well plugged in. All of the Middle East and Africa have only 7.5 million web users in total.

In short, the economic advantages of the internet may be creating new international inequities. If maximum prosperity depends on free trade in a global economy, as many economists argue, then all of the world must be folded fully into the internet.

As the technological breakthroughs leapfrog each other, we will see the traditional media shift increasingly to the internet. Don't expect to wake up one morning, though, and find that the world is paperless and that local television stations have vanished. Just as horses and buggies and the automobile coexisted for 40 years, so will e-books (digital books) and p-books (print books). Television will still be television as we know it today, with many people satisfied with living room sets pretty much as now—although with bigger screens, sharper pictures and movie-house sound quality.

In short, media companies will need to use two redundant modes to maximize their audience. Already we see this with over-the-air radio stations that stream online; magazines and newspapers on paper and on the internet; and recordings available at the record store and also downloadable.

Could the internet lose its diversity? Media mogul Barry Diller, well regarded for his crystal-ball–like view on media trends, sees ownership consolidation ahead for the internet, just like the other media. Citing cable giant Comcast, he said in a *Newsweek* interview: "You can already see at Comcast and others the beginning of efforts to control the home pages that their consumers plug into. It's for one reason: To control a toll bridge or turnstile through which others must pay to go. The inevitable result will be eventual control by media giants of the Internet in terms of independence and strangulation. This is a situation where history is absolutely destined to repeat itself." Most internet users hope Diller is wrong.

THE INTERNET AND THE CRTC

The CRTC was the first broadcast regulator in the world to address the issue of controlling the internet. In 1999, Canada's broadcast regulator announced it would not regulate the internet at that time, as the internet doesn't fall under the authority of Canada's Broadcasting Act. Following are among the reasons they cited for their conclusion:

- The internet is not, by definition, broadcasting. Its messages are largely communicated using alphanumeric text.
- The internet does not replace broadcasting; it simply complements it.
- Web material can be customized by the user, its messages are broadcast for a mass audience in the same way a radio or television broadcast is. The web is a "push" medium.
- There is already a large Canadian presence on the internet.
- The CRTC felt that the Criminal Code of Canada and the use of content-filtering software by users would be the best way to deal with offensive content on the internet.

CHAPTER 7 Wrap-Up

The World Wide Web utilizes the global internet, so computers anywhere can exchange digitized data—including text, visuals and audio. Many media companies are investing heavily in cyberspace, and the expansion of high-capacity fibre optic cable networks will increase capacity tremendously so that audio and moving visuals are on tap live on any computer screen connected to the internet. Two-way communication via the internet already is standard fare. With every passing day, more mass communication is occurring on the internet.

Questions for Review

1. How can the internet be defined as a new and distinctive mass medium?
2. What technological breakthroughs made the internet possible?
3. What are the new directions in which technology is taking the internet?
4. What has been the role of advertising in driving internet development?
5. How is gatekeeping different on the internet than in other major mass media?
6. How is the internet contributing to a melding of the mass media?
7. What public policy questions has the internet raised?

Questions for Critical Thinking

1. What makes books, magazines, newspapers, sound recordings, movies, radio and television different from one another? What will become of these distinctions in coming years?
2. Trace the development of the technology that has made the web possible.
3. What innovations did Tim Berners-Lee introduce that are revolutionizing mass communication?
4. How does hypertext depart from traditional human communication? And does hypertext have a future as a literary form?
5. What obstacles would you have in designing public policy to assure access to the internet for every citizen?
6. Some people say there is no point in trying to regulate the internet. Do you agree? Disagree? Why?
7. Is Steve Maich correct: Does the internet suck? List examples to illustrate your point of view.

Deepening Your media LITERACY

Can you trust what you read and see on the internet?
STEP 1 Choose two or three different websites that a student might access for information for a paper, such as Google or Wikipedia.

Dig Deeper
STEP 2 Write evaluations of the sites you chose based on the following criteria:

1. How is the site funded? What is the intended purpose of the site? And of the information on the site? Is it user-driven or owner/product-driven?

2. Does the site appeal to your emotions? If so, how? What other techniques are used to engage the viewer?
3. All media contain ideological and value messages. What are the messages of the site? Are any of them unintended? Are they positive or negative? Are they obvious or intentionally hidden?
4. Does the site use traditional gatekeepers?
5. Does it use a peer review process?

What Do You Think?
STEP 3 Answer these questions: What are the potential drawbacks of using a user-driven site for research? Is the emotional appeal of a site important to a user seeking research information? Are traditional gatekeepers the best way to ensure accuracy on a website? Why or why not? Is how a site is paid for a fair way to measure its trustworthiness? Why or why not? How could the value messages of a site affect its informational worth?

Keeping Up to Date

Industry Standard is the main trade journal of e-commerce.

The magazines *Wired* and *Infoworld* offer coverage of cyberdevelopments, issues and people.

Trade journals *Editor & Publisher, Advertising Age, Playback, Broadcaster* magazine and *Broadcast Dialogue* have excellent ongoing coverage of their fields.

Widely available news media that explore cyberissues include *Time, Maclean's, Toronto Star, National Post* and *The Globe and Mail.*

Don't overlook surfing the web for sites that track internet developments.

For Further Learning

Alan B. Albarran and David H. Goff, editors. *Understanding the Web: Social, Political and Economic Dimensions of the Internet* (Iowa State University Press, 2000).

Ken Auletta. *World War 3.0* (Random House, 2001).

Tim Berners-Lee, with Mark Fischetti. *Weaving the Web: The Original Design and the Ultimate Destiny of the World Wide Web by Its Inventor* (Harper San Francisco, 1999).

Robert Brehl. "Brave New World." *Toronto Star* (March 30, 1996).

Vannevar Bush. "As We May Think." *Atlantic Monthly* (July 1945).

Bruce Cheadle. "Beware: There's Bad News Behind Internet Headlines." *Hamilton Spectator* (January 15, 2007).

Adam Cohen. "A Wired Village." *Time Digital* (December 2000): 58–62.

"Crime in Cyberspace." *Maclean's* (May 22, 1995): 50–58.

CRTC. *Broadcast Policy Monitoring Report 2006* (CRTC, 2006).

CRTC. "CRTC Won't Regulate the Internet." CRTC (May 19, 1999).

Ben Elgin, with Steve Hamm. "The Last Days of Net Mania." *Business Week* (April 16, 2001): 110–118.

Martha FitzSimons, editor. *Media, Democracy and the Information Highway* (Freedom Forum Media Studies Center, 1993).

Urs E. Gattiker. *The Internet as a Diverse Community: Cultural, Organizational and Political Issues* (Erlbaum, 2001).

Michael Geist. "Time's Choice Could Prove Inspired." *Toronto Star* (January 8, 2007).

George Gilder. *Telecosm: How Infinite Bandwidth Will Revolutionize Our World* (Free Press, 2000).

John Heilemann. *Pride Before the Fall: The Trials of Bill Gates and the End of the Microsoft Era* (HarperCollins, 2001).

Industry Canada. "An Anti Spam Plan for Canada" (May 2004).

Ipsos Reid Canada. "The Canadian Inter@ctive Reid Report: Fact Guide."

Ipsos Reid Canada. "Digital Divide Remains Wide: Only 6 in 10 Canadians Aged 55 + Have Access to the Internet" (February 15, 2007).

Robert Lucky. *Silicon Dreams* (St. Martin's, 1989).

Steve Maich. "'Pornography, Gambling, Lies, Theft, and Terrorism: The Internet Sucks (Where Did We Go Wrong?" *Maclean's* (October 30, 2006): 44–49.

Kevin Maney. "Will the Techno Tsunami Wash Us Out?" *Quill* (March 1994): 16–18.

Gordon Moore. "Solid State Physicist: William Shockley." *Time* (March 29, 1999): 193–195.

JoAnn Napier. "Online Advertising Rise 96 % in a Year." *Ottawa Citizen* (March 20, 2000).

John V. Pavlik. *New Media Technology: Cultural and Commercial Perspectives* (Allyn & Bacon, 1995).

Mark Slouka. *War of the Worlds* (Basic Books, 1996).

Statistics Canada. "Canadian Internet Use Survey." *The Daily* (August 15, 2006).

Statistics Canada. "Internet Service Providers." *The Daily* (December 18, 2006).

Neal Stephenson. "Mother Earth, Motherboard." *Wired* (December 1996): 97–160.

Robert Wright. "The Man Who Invented the Web." *Time* (May 19, 1997): 160–164.

Global National After spending
a few years with ABC, Kevin Newman
returned to Canada to anchor
Global National.

News

chapter

8

Media in Theory

Gatekeeping

This just in . . . Canadians love news. A 2004 survey conducted by the Canadian Media Research Consortium (CMRC) found that 90 percent of Canadians are "interested" or "somewhat interested" in news and follow it on a daily basis. Although Canadians have a hunger for news, few ask the question: What is news? It's not an easy question to answer in practice or in theory. There is no one single definition of news. In *Canadian Broadcast News: The Basics,* journalism professor **Brian Green** says that news is "the significant, the unusual, that which affects us." However, the definition of what is "significant" is open to personal interpretation. Journalists know they have a high level of responsibility in deciding what to report as news. While most reporters will agree on the newsworthiness of some events and issues, such as a catastrophic storm or a tax proposal, their judgments will result in stories that take different slants and angles. This is the role of a journalist as a **gatekeeper**.

Although individual reporters have independence in determining what to report and how, news work is a team effort. News dispatches and photographs are subject to changes at many points in the communication chain. At these points, called *gates,* gatekeepers delete, trim, embellish and otherwise try to improve messages. You will remember gatekeepers were part of the **concentric circle model** introduced in Chapter 1.

A reporter exercises judgment in deciding what to report and how to report it. Hardly any message, except live reporting, reaches its audience in its original form. Along the path from its originator to the eventual audience, a message is subject to all kinds of deletions, additions and changes of emphasis. With large news organizations, this process may involve dozens of editors and other persons.

The gatekeeping process affects all news. A public relations practitioner who doesn't tell the whole story is a gatekeeper. A reporter who emphasizes one aspect of an event and neglects others is a gatekeeper. Even live, on-scene television coverage

Brian Green ■ Canadian journalism professor who defines news as "the significant, the unusual, that which affects us."

gatekeeper ■ Media people who influence messages en route.

concentric circle model ■ Useful radiating model of the mass communication process.

involves gatekeeping because it's a gatekeeper who decides where to point the camera, and that's a decision that affects the type of information that reaches viewers.

Gatekeeping can be a creative force. Trimming a news story can add potency. A news producer can enhance a reporter's field report with specific file footage. An editor can call a public relations person for additional detail to illuminate a point in a reporter's story. A newsmagazine's editor can consolidate related stories and add context that makes an important interpretive point.

Most gatekeepers are invisible to the news audience, working behind the scenes and making crucial decisions in near anonymity on how the world will be portrayed in the evening newscast and the next morning's newspaper.

media TIMELINE

ROOTS OF JOURNALISTIC PRACTICES

1690	Benjamin Harris published the first newspaper, *Publick Occurrences,* in Boston.	**1835**	Joseph Howe was acquitted of publishing "seditious libel" in the *Novascotian.*	**1980**	CNN introduced 24-hour television news.
1735	Colonial jury exonerated John Peter Zenger of "seditious libel for publishing articles about the governor's incompetence."	**1844**	Samuel Morse devised the telegraph, hastening delivery of faraway news in the United States and Canada.	**2001**	CRTC warned conglomerates to keep newsroom management separate to ensure a diversity of voices in Canadian news.
1752	John Bushnell began publishing *The Halifax Gazette,* the first newspaper in Canada.	**1880s**	Joseph Pulitzer and William Randolph Hearst's circulation war led to yellow press excesses.	**2001**	A wave of digital cable news channels was unleashed in Canada.
1833	Ben Day founded *The New York Sun,* the first penny newspaper.	**1917**	The Canadian Press was founded.		

▛▖ Journalism Traditions

study<u>preview</u> U.S. journalism has evolved through four distinctive eras: the colonial, partisan, penny press and yellow periods. Each of these periods made distinctive contributions to contemporary news media practices in both the United States and Canada.

COLONIAL PERIOD

colonial period ■ From the founding of the colonies to the American Revolution.

Benjamin Harris ■ Published *Publick Occurrences.*

Publick Occurrences ■ First colonial newspaper, Boston, 1690.

John Peter Zenger ■ Defied authorities in *New-York Weekly Journal.*

Andrew Hamilton ■ Urged truth as defence for libel.

In the American **colonial period**, **Benjamin Harris** published the first newspaper, *Publick Occurrences*, in Boston in 1690. He was in hot water right away. Harris scandalized Puritan sensitivities by alleging that the king of France had dallied with his son's wife. In the colonies, just as in England, a newspaper needed royal consent. The governor had not consented, and Harris was put out of business after one issue.

Even so, Harris's daring was a precursor for emerging press defiance against authority. In 1733 **John Peter Zenger** started a paper in New York in competition with the existing Crown-supported newspaper. Zenger's was backed by merchants and lawyers who disliked the royal governor. From the beginning, the newspaper antagonized the governor with items challenging his competence. Finally, the governor arrested Zenger. The trial made history. Zenger's attorney, **Andrew Hamilton**, argued that there should be no punishment for printing articles that are true. The argument was a dramatic departure from the legal practice of the day, which allowed royal governors to prosecute for articles that might undermine their authority regardless of whether the information in the articles was true. Hamilton's argument prevailed, and Zenger, who had become a hero for standing up to the Crown, was freed.

These traditions from the colonial period remain today:

- The news media, both print and broadcast, relish their independence from government censorship and control.
- The news media, especially newspapers and magazines, actively try to mould government policy and mobilize public sentiment. Today this is done primarily on the editorial page.
- Journalists are committed to seeking truth, which was articulated as a social value in Zenger's "truth defence."
- In a capitalistic system the news media are economic entities that sometimes react in their own self-interest when their profit-making ability is threatened.

PARTISAN PERIOD

After the Revolution, newspapers divided along partisan lines. What is called the Federalist period in U.S. history is also referred to as the **partisan period** among newspaper historians. Intense partisanship characterized newspapers of the period, which spanned roughly 50 years to the 1830s.

Initially, the issue was over a constitution. Should the nation have a strong central government or remain a loose coalition of states? James Madison, Alexander Hamilton, Thomas Jefferson, John Jay and other leading thinkers exchanged ideas through articles and essays in newspapers. The *Federalist Papers*, a series of essays printed and reprinted in newspapers throughout the nation, were part of the debate.

After the Constitution was drafted, partisanship intensified, finally culminating lopsidedly when the Federalist party both controlled the Congress and had the party leader, **John Adams**, in the presidency. In firm control and bent on silencing their detractors, the Federalists ramrodded a series of laws through Congress in 1798. One of the things the **Alien and Sedition Acts** prohibited was "false, scandalous, malicious" statements about government. Using these laws, the Federalists made 25 indictments, which culminated in 10 convictions. Among those indicted was **David Brown**, a Revolutionary War veteran who felt strongly about free expression. He put up a sign in Dedham, Massachusetts: "No stamp tax. No sedition. No alien bills. No land tax. Downfall to the tyrants of America. Peace and retirement to the president [the Federalist John Adams]. Long live the vice-president [the anti-Federalist **Thomas Jefferson**] and the minority [the anti-Federalists]. May moral virtues be the basis of civil government." If only criticisms of recent presidents were so mild! But the Federalists were not of a tolerant mind. Brown was fined $400 and sentenced to 18 months in prison.

Here are traditions from the partisan period that continue today:

- Government should keep its hands off the press.
- The news media are a forum for discussion and debate, as newspapers were in the *Federalist Papers* dialogue on what form the Constitution should take.
- The news media should comment vigorously on public issues.
- Government transgressions against the news media will ultimately be met by public rejection of those committing the excesses, which has happened periodically throughout history.

PENNY PRESS PERIOD

In 1833, when he was 22, the enterprising **Benjamin Day** started a newspaper that changed journalism: *The New York Sun*. At a penny a copy, the *Sun* was within reach of just about everybody. Other papers were expensive, an annual subscription costing as much as a full week's wages. Unlike other papers, which were distributed mostly by mail, the *Sun* was hawked every day on the streets. The *Sun*'s content was different too. It avoided the political and economic thrust of the traditional papers, concentrating instead on items of interest to common folk. The writing was simple, straightforward and easy to follow. As a motto for the *Sun*, Day came up with "It Shines for All," his pun fully intended.

Day's *Sun* was an immediate success. Naturally, it was quickly imitated, and the **penny press period** began. Partisan papers that characterized the partisan period continued, but the mainstream of American newspapers came to be in the mould of the *Sun*.

Zenger Trial Printer John Peter Zenger, in the dock, won his 1735 trial for criticizing New York's royal governor. The victory fed a colonial exuberance that culminated 46 years later in winning the revolution against British rule.

partisan period ■ From the American Revolution at least to the 1830s.

Federalist Papers ■ Essays with diverse views on the form the new nation should take.

John Adams ■ Federalist president.

Alien and Sedition Acts ■ Discouraged criticism of government.

David Brown ■ Punished for criticizing the majority party.

Thomas Jefferson ■ Anti-Federalist president.

Benjamin Day ■ Published *The New York Sun*.

The New York Sun ■ First penny newspaper, 1833.

penny press period ■ One-cent newspapers geared to mass audience and mass advertising.

penny papers ■ Affordable by almost everyone.

Mass Media Pioneer When Benjamin Day launched *The New York Sun* in 1833 and sold it for one cent a copy, he ushered in an era of cheap newspapers that common people could afford. Years later his successors pushed circulation past 1 million a week.

Samuel Morse ■ Invented the telegraph.

lightning news ■ Delivered by telegraph.

inverted pyramid ■ Most important information first.

Merchants saw the unprecedented circulation of the **penny papers** as a way to reach great numbers of potential customers. Advertising revenue meant bigger papers, which attracted more readers, which attracted more advertisers. A snowballing momentum began that continues today with more and more advertising being carried by the mass media. A significant result was a shift in newspaper revenues from subscriptions to advertisers. Day, as a matter of fact, did not meet expenses by selling the *Sun* for a penny a copy. He counted on advertisers to pick up a good part of his production cost. In effect, advertisers subsidized readers, just as they do today.

Several social and economic factors, all resulting from the Industrial Revolution, made the penny press possible:

● **Industrialization.** With new steam-powered presses, hundreds of copies an hour could be printed. Earlier presses had been hand-operated.
● **Urbanization.** Workers flocked to the cities to work in new factories, creating a great pool of potential newspaper readers within delivery range. Until the urbanization of the 1820s and 1830s, the U.S. population had been almost wholly agricultural and scattered across the countryside. Even the most populous cities had been relatively small.
● **Immigration.** Waves of immigrants arrived from impoverished parts of Europe. Most were eager to learn English and found that penny papers, with their simple style, were good tutors.
● **Literacy.** As immigrants learned English, they hungered for reading material within their economic means. Also, literacy in general was increasing, which contributed to the rise of mass-circulation newspapers and magazines.

In 1844, late in the penny press period, **Samuel Morse** invented the telegraph. Within months, the nation was being wired. When the Civil War came in 1861, correspondents used the telegraph to get battle news to eager readers. It was called **lightning news**, delivered electrically and quickly. The Civil War also gave rise to a new convention in writing news, the **inverted pyramid**. Editors instructed their war correspondents to tell the most important information first in case telegraph lines failed—or were snipped by the enemy—as a story was being transmitted. That way, when a story was interrupted, editors would have at least a few usable sentences. The inverted pyramid, it turned out, was popular with readers because it allowed them to learn what was most important at a glance. They did not have to wade through a whole story if they were in a hurry. Also, the inverted pyramid helped editors to fit stories into the limited confines of a page—a story could be cut off at any paragraph and the most important parts remained intact. The inverted pyramid remains a standard expository form for telling event-based stories in newspapers, radio and television.

Several New York newspaper publishers, concerned about the escalating expense of sending reporters to gather faraway news, got together in 1848 to share stories. By sending only one reporter to represent all the newspapers, publishers cut costs dramatically. They called their co-operative venture the **Associated Press (AP)**, a predecessor of today's giant global news service. The AP introduced a new tone in news reporting. So that AP stories could be used by member newspapers of different political persuasions, reporters were told to write from a nonpartisan point of view. The result was a fact-oriented kind of news writing often called **objective reporting**. It was widely imitated and is still the dominant reporting style for event-based news stories in the U.S. news media.

Associated Press (AP) ■ Co-op for gathering and distributing news.

objective reporting ■ Telling news without bias.

There are traditions of today's news media, both print and electronic, that can be traced to the penny press period:

● Inverted pyramid story structures.
● Coverage and writing that appeal to a general audience, sometimes by trying to be entertaining or even sensationalistic.
● A strong orientation to covering events, including the aggressive ferreting out of news.
● A commitment to social improvement, which included a willingness to crusade against corruption.
● Being on top of unfolding events and providing information to readers quickly, something made possible by the telegraph but that also came to be valued in local reporting.
● A detached, neutral perspective in reporting events.

YELLOW PERIOD

The quest to sell more copies led to excesses that are illustrated by the Pulitzer-Hearst circulation war in New York in the 1890s, in what came to be known as the **yellow period**.

yellow period ■ Late 1800s; marked by sensationalism.

Joseph Pulitzer, a poor immigrant, made the *St. Louis Post-Dispatch* into a financial success. In 1883 Pulitzer decided to try a bigger city. He bought the *New York World* and applied his St. Louis formula. He emphasized human interest, crusaded for worthy causes and ran lots of promotional hoopla. Pulitzer's *World* also featured solid journalism. His star reporter, **Nellie Bly**, epitomized the two faces of the Pulitzer formula for journalistic success. For one story Bly feigned mental illness, entered an insane asylum and emerged with scandalous tales about how patients were treated. It was enterprising journalism of great significance. Reforms resulted. Later, showing the less serious, show-biz side of Pulitzer's formula, Nellie Bly was sent out to circle the globe in 80 days, like Jules Verne's fictitious Phileas Fogg. Her journalism stunt took 72 days.

Joseph Pulitzer ■ Emphasized human interest in newspapers; later sensationalized.

Nellie Bly ■ Stunt reporter.

In San Francisco, Pulitzer had a young admirer, **William Randolph Hearst**. With his father's Nevada mining fortune and mimicking Pulitzer's New York formula, Hearst made the San Francisco *Examiner* a great success. In 1895 Hearst decided to go to New York and take on the master. He bought the *New York Journal* and vowed to "out-Pulitzer" Pulitzer. The inevitable resulted. To outdo each other, Pulitzer and Hearst launched crazier and crazier stunts. Not even the comic pages escaped the competitive frenzy. Pulitzer ran the *Yellow Kid,* and then Hearst hired the cartoonist away. Pulitzer hired a new one, and both papers ran the yellow character and plastered the city with yellow promotional posters. The circulation war was nicknamed "yellow journalism," and the term came to be a derisive reference to sensational excesses in news coverage.

William Randolph Hearst ■ Built circulation with sensationalism.

The yellow excesses reached a feverish peak as Hearst and Pulitzer covered the growing tensions between Spain and the United States. Fueled by hyped stories of atrocities, the tension eventually exploded in war. One story, perhaps apocryphal, epitomizes the no-holds-barred competition between Pulitzer and Hearst. Although Spain had consented to all demands by the United States, Hearst sent the artist **Frederic Remington**

Frederic Remington ■ Illustrator sent by Hearst to find atrocities in Cuba.

Joseph Pulitzer

William Randolph Hearst

ONLINE

The R.F. Outcault Society's Yellow Kid Site Read about the creator of the Yellow Kid, America's first "comic character superstar."
www.neponset.com/yellowkid/index.htm

to Cuba to cover the situation. Remington cabled back: "Everything is quiet. There is no trouble here. There will be no war. Wish to return." Hearst replied: "Please remain. You furnish the pictures. I'll furnish the war."

The yellow tradition, however, still lives. The New York *Daily News,* founded in 1919 and almost an immediate hit, ushered in a period that some historians characterize as **jazz journalism**. It was just Hearst and Pulitzer updated in tabloid form with an emphasis on photography. Today, newspapers like the commercially successful *National Enquirer* are in the yellow tradition. This tradition is obvious too in tabloid television interview programs like *The Jerry Springer Show,* which pander to public taste for the offbeat, tawdry and sensational.

HISTORY OF JOURNALISM IN CANADA

In his *Guide to the Canadian News Media,* **Peter Desbarats** comments that journalism in Canada "has been closer to Main Street USA than to Fleet Street." By this he means that Canadian news traditions followed the U.S. model and not the British model. A comparison of the press periods in Canada and the United States seems to indicate that similar ideals developed, albeit at different times. **Wilfred Kesterton**'s research on the history and growth of journalism in Canada is regarded as the definitive work in this area. Kesterton observes that Canadian journalists were fueled by ideals similar to those that characterized the partisan and colonial periods in U.S. history. He breaks down journalism in Canada into four periods.

The Transplant Period (1752–1807) Kesterton refers to this press period as the **transplant period** because Canada's first newspapers were literally British or American newspapers or publishers that transplanted, or resettled, in Canada. *The Halifax Gazette,* Canada's first newspaper, was published by John Bushnell, who moved from Boston in 1752. The oldest newspaper in existence, the *Quebec Gazette*, was started by two printers from Philadelphia in 1764. *The Halifax Gazette* appeared every two weeks and had about 70 subscribers, while the *Quebec Gazette* had about 150 subscribers when it began publishing. As conditions improved and immigrants began moving down the St. Lawrence River and into Upper Canada, other newspapers began publishing.

As with their early American counterparts, most of the first papers in Canada were organs for the fledgling governments of British North America. Most of the content of

DATABANK

Canadian Television News: Demassified

Like other media, news has itself demassified. Sports and entertainment news channels are also included. The number of subscribers indicated is as of August 31, 2005.

Channel	Subscribers
CBC Newsworld	9.7 million
TSN	8.1 million
Rogers Sportsnet	7.6 million
CTV Newsnet	7.5 million
The Score	5.7 million
Business News Network (BNN)	4.8 million
Star! TV	4.4 million
Pulse24 (CP24)	3.0 million

Source: CRTC, Broadcast Policy Monitoring Report 2006.

these three- or four-page newsletter-type sheets was government information with a sprinkling of news from "back home." It was felt that for the settlements in the New World to be successful, the government needed this voice to inform and educate settlers. These newspapers were also a primitive advertising tool for early Canadian merchants. The first ads in Canadian newspapers appeared in 1752 when *The Halifax Gazette* printed three ads: for a lawyer, a clerical service and butter. While some ads appeared in these publications, the main source of income for most early newspapers was printing government information. Therefore, the success of newspapers during this time was contingent on government support, both financial and ideological. As a result, most of these papers didn't "rock the boat." In 1766, *The Halifax Gazette* dared to question the government on the new stamp tax. As a result, the government suspended the publication.

The Growth Period (1807–1858)
Following the War of 1812, immigration in Canada flourished, particularly in Upper Canada, where the population doubled by the mid-1820s. Combine this population surge with the effects of the Industrial Revolution and you will begin to understand the changing social climate in Canada. People stopped working at home or in the fields and began to work in factories. These factors contributed to the growth of newspapers, and thus to what Kesterton refers to as the **growth period** of Canadian journalism. At the end of the War of 1812, Canada had only a handful of newspapers; by the mid-1820s, that number had risen to almost 300. Canada's first daily newspaper arrived in 1833 with Montreal's *Daily Advertiser*.

As during the penny press period in the United States, growth in immigration and urbanization created markets for Canadian newspapers. As a result, newspapers were less dependent on government revenue for their economic success. This, in turn, created a kind of "partisan" press period in Canada, as newspapers began to take sides along political lines.

The most significant event in this period in Canadian journalism history involved **Joseph Howe**. On New Year's Day, 1835, Howe published "the letter" signed by "the people" in his *Novascotian*. In the letter, he accused the local police and the lieutenant-governor of corruption. In his defence, he asked the jury "to leave an unshackled press as a legacy to your children." Despite the fact that Howe was charged with seditious libel under the criminal code of the day, and the presiding judge instructed the jurors to bring back a verdict of guilty, a jury acquitted him of libel in only 10 minutes. The jury felt that publishing something that is true shouldn't be illegal. As with the earlier American example of Zenger's *New York Journal,* the message to Canadian journalists was clear: Freedom of the press and intellectual freedom were important principles.

Third Canadian Press Period: Westward Growth (1858–1900)
During the latter half of the 1800s, immigration and migration became two important factors in the growth of Canadian newspapers. As the Canadian population increased, it moved west and north and newspapers soon followed. Kesterton calls this the **westward growth** period of Canadian journalism. The gold rushes in the west made Victoria, British Columbia, a centre for commerce and transportation. In 1858, *The Victoria Gazette and Anglo-American* began publishing. New papers also began publishing in central and eastern Canada: the *Montreal Star* in 1869, the *Toronto Telegram* in 1876, and the *Ottawa Journal* in 1885. By the turn of the century, more than 1200 newspapers served Canada's population, which at that time stood at close to 5.5 million.

This period was also a sort of "partisan period" for Canadian journalism. The debate over Confederation, the Riel rebellion, and the completion of the Canadian National Railway were the subjects of many an article. Thomas D'Arcy McGee, George Brown, and Joseph Howe were among the country's most opinionated journalists.

Fourth Canadian Press Period: The Twentieth Century Onward
In the 1900s, journalism came of age in Canada. Although immigration levels and migration patterns were

Early to Print A snapshot of the Monday, March 23, 1752, edition of *The Halifax Gazette*—Canada's first newspaper.

growth period ■ Second period in Canadian journalism; marked by expansion due to immigration following the War of 1812.

Joseph Howe ■ Advocate of an unshackled press.

westward growth ■ Third period in Canadian journalism: As Canadians moved west, so did the press.

inconsistent due to the world wars and the Great Depression during the first half of the 20th century, improvements in technology helped the newspaper grow to new heights. This technology included better printing presses and better-quality newsprint, which helped improve the form of the newspaper. Improvements in communication and transportation helped distribution. As a result of these changes and the continuing growth of cities, the large metropolitan daily as a business enterprise became the norm for many newspapers.

News agencies arrived in Canada during this period. The Canadian Press (**CP**) was founded in 1917. A statute of Parliament officially made the Canadian Press a corporation in 1923. Today, more than 250 journalists write stories for CP, which supplies news for print and broadcast outlets.

CP ■ The Canadian Press.

media ONLINE

Joseph Howe Read about this Canadian and his fight for freedom of the press.
www.collectionscanada.ca/confederation/023001-2350-e.html

Thomas D'Arcy McGee One of Canada's most opinionated journalists and a Father of Confederation.
http://www.collectionscanada.ca/confederation/023001-2370-e.html

George Brown The founder of *The Globe*.
www.collectionscanada.ca/confederation/023001-2309-e.html

The Canadian Press Home page for the co-operatively owned national news agency. There's also a link for Broadcast News.
www.cp.org

objectivity ■ A concept in journalism that news should be gathered and told value-free.

■ Concepts of News

studypreview The contemporary notion that news media content should be objective is relatively recent. Also, it is a notion not shared in all modern democracies. The word "objectivity" is overused and not very useful. Better is to think of journalism as the process of pursuing truth to tell truth.

U.S. MODEL

Two phenomena in the mid-1800s, both rooted in the economics of the newspaper industry, introduced the notion of value-free news—or **objectivity**.

Associated Press As mentioned earlier in this chapter, several cost-conscious New York newspaper publishers agreed in 1848 to a joint venture to cover distant news. The Associated Press, as they called the venture, saved a lot of money. Inherent in the AP concept was that its stories needed to be nonpartisan to be usable by all of its member newspapers, whose political persuasions spanned the spectrum. The result was an emphasis on fact-driven journalism devoid of even a hint of partisanship. The same is generally true about CP (The Canadian Press) style. In *The Canadian Press Stylebook*, 12th Edition, CP claims that "everything we do must be honest, unbiased and unflinchingly fair."

Newspaper Economics A second fundamental shift cemented the AP style, often called an objective style: News became profitable—highly so. The fortune that Benjamin Day made with *The New York Sun* in the mid-1830s was puny compared with the Pulitzer, Hearst and other news empires that came within 50 years. These superpublishers saw their newspapers as money machines as much as political tools. The bottom line gradually and inevitably gained more weight. There was money to be made in presenting news in as neutral a tone as possible. By the early 20th century, when news practices became institutionalized in the first journalism textbooks and in the formation of professional organizations, the notion of a detached, neutral presentation was firmly ensconced. Ethics codes, new at the time, dismissed other approaches as unacceptable and unethical, even though they had been dominant only three generations earlier. The word "objectivity" became a newsroom mantra.

Media Conglomeration By the late 20th century, the value-free approach to news was more entrenched than ever. Most news organizations had become parts of vast media empires that included government-regulated broadcast outlets. A detached, neutral tone in news content was the least apt to upset political leaders and government agencies from whom the media needed favours—like broadcast licence renewals, broadcast spectrum access, and consent for more mergers and consolidations that reduced competition and could invite scrutiny by government. As a result, the CRTC had to deal with the issue of convergence and editorial control. TVA, CTV, and CanWest Global were asked how they were planning to handle issues of newsroom policy and editorial decision making. Leonard Asper, president and CEO of CanWest Global Communications, had this vision of journalists in a converged media world: "In the future, journalists will wake up, write a story for the web, write a column, take their cameras, cover an event and do a report for TV and file a video clip for the web. What we have really acquired is a quantum leap in the product we offer advertisers and a massive, creative content-generation machine."

Quebec media giant TVA, on the other hand, wanted to keep the broadcast and print newsrooms separate, saying that "information professionals working in the newsrooms of TVA, LCN and LCN affiliates shall at no time transmit, receive, exchange or discuss information by phone, fax, Internet or other technology with information professionals working in the newsroom of Quebecor newspapers."

According to the Broadcasting Act, radio and television stations in Canada must provide varied and comprehensive coverage of significant issues. While the CRTC has no control over what happens in print newsrooms, they do have a say in what goes on in broadcast newsrooms. In its 2001 decisions concerning TVA, Global, and CTV, the CRTC's viewpoint is clear: Keep editorial decisions between multimedia platforms within conglomerates separate. To the CRTC, its favoured approach adds to objectivity and the diversity of voices within the Canadian broadcasting system.

media
ONLINE

Columbia Journalism Review Motto: America's premier media monitor.
www.cjr.org

CAJ Canadian Association of Journalists' Code of Ethics is described under the "Advocacy – Education – Truth" link.
www.caj.ca

EUROPEAN MODEL

The notion that news could be conveyed neutrally, devoid of perspective or values, was peculiarly American. In Europe, newspapers traditionally have flaunted their partisanship to attract like-minded readers. The result is flavourful, interesting reporting that flows from a point of view—and, say its defenders, is more truthful than the U.S. model. Leonard Doyle, foreign editor at *The Independent* in London, claims the European model encourages journalists to tell about events as they see them, rather than through the eyes of government officialdom, which can have its own agendas. The U.S. model, by contrast, tends merely to chronicle claims as provided by supposedly credible albeit partisan sources. There is too little attention in the U.S. model, say critics, to sorting through the claims with journalistic analysis.

In a forum sponsored by *Columbia Journalism Review*, Doyle offered striking examples of failures of the U.S. model. One was during the 2002 Afghan war. CNN quoted Pentagon authorities who said that B-52 bombers had dropped dozens of precision-targeted bombs in the Tora Bora area in an attempt to flush out terrorist mastermind Osama bin Laden. That, in itself, was accurate, but CNN missed what the Pentagon had not released: that the bombs had killed 115 people in the village of Kama Ado. The British press, less inclined to merely echo official views, told about the Kama Ado carnage—the whole story.

Doyle says that U.S. journalists' quest for "objectivity" has led to the tying of every fact to a source that can be named. This is a kind of timidity that Doyle says leaves journalists vulnerable to being duped: "The loudest demands for objectivity are made by groups or lobbies who want to ensure that they get equal time." The loudest and most persistent groups make the news. The U.S. approach, as Doyle sees it, is largely clerical and lacks the probing that would serve the audience better by coming closer to truth.

British journalists gloat that their U.S. counterparts uncritically reported the repeated but erroneous claim of President George W. Bush, in pushing for war, that Iraq possessed weapons of mass destruction. The redundancy of the message over many months fueled the early U.S. public support for the war, even though it turned out that no such weapons existed. To U.S. journalists, Doyle says: "Ask why the God of Objectivity so failed you in your hour of need." The British government had advanced the same claims about weapons of mass destruction, but many British newspapers, openly unfriendly to the government, kept casting doubt on the claim, which tempered British public enthusiasm for the Iraq war. Europeans argue that their model, which places an emphasis on judgment and analysis, yields reporting that comes nearer to truth.

truth ■ A broad and accurate understanding.

Michael Getler The fact orientation (or, some say, obsession) of U.S. news has a defender in Michael Getler of *The Washington Post*. Getler says the perspective-oriented British model, dominant in much of the world, gets in the way of telling news and leaves readers suspicious about whether they're getting good information.

EVOLVING NEWS MODELS

How did the British and North American press end up so different? The newspaper industry in Britain, and the rest of Europe too, never consolidated on the scale of U.S. or Canadian newspapers. Historically, European papers have found profits by pandering to the political preferences of segments in the mass audience. In contrast, U.S. newspaper ownership consolidated to the point that the United States is a nation of mostly one-paper towns. Now media conglomerates have their feet also in broadcast news. The financial might of conglomerates, far greater than that of any European news organization, perpetuates itself more easily with blander news coverage. The thrust is to tell news as safely as possible, which means to seek to avoid alienating anybody—readers, advertisers and, increasingly, government.

Europeans will argue that their newspapers, characterized by reporting that reflects values, are not only livelier but also more effective. Thirty million Brits, out of a population of 58 million, read a morning newspaper—a far higher percentage than in the United States. Too, everyone agrees that British and other European audiences are better informed about public issues and more engaged.

DEFINING OBJECTIVITY

In North American journalism, the concept of objectivity is often extolled, but journalists back off the term when pressed. Considering that all human beings, journalists included, have personal values that influence all that they do, objectivity, being value-free, is an impossible ideal. Only someone who is totally amoral can be objective. That means that journalists can do nothing more than work at appearing to be free of any values, which requires playing word games to conceal their values. That, say critics, is a fraud perpetrated on the news audience. It also works against journalists' asking tough questions that might hint at personal values. This all suggests that the word "objective" and the concept of objectivity are so problematic that they have limited usefulness.

A more useful concept, one on which North Americans and Europeans can agree, is that journalists do their best work when they pursue news with the goal of telling truth. What is truth? **Truth** is a broad and accurate understanding, which the Europeans note is far more important than the factual detail about which American journalism obsesses. With truth as the goal, journalists can be honest about the personal values they bring to their work. When the goal is to find truth, values become secondary. In fact, journalists with different values can all have the same goal: truth.

Both North American and European models of news are fact-driven and committed to accuracy. The Europeans argue, however, that facts yield truth only when sorted through and subjected to analysis. *Truth,* a word for broad understanding, does not result automatically from an array of facts or quotes from shouting partisans. In short, the Europeans caution, don't confuse facts and factual accuracy with *truth,* which is broader and more important.

▊ Journalists' Personal Values and Biases

study<u>preview</u> **As gatekeepers, journalists make important decisions on which events, phenomena and issues are reported and which are not. The personal values that journalists bring to their work and that therefore determine which stories are told—and also how they are told—generally coincide with mainstream values.**

The journalistic ideal, an unbiased seeking of truth and an unvarnished telling of it, dictates that the work be done without partisanship. Yet, as human beings, journalists have personal values that influence all that they do, including their work. Because the news judgment decisions that journalists make are so important to an informed citizenry, we need to know what makes these people tick.

When asked whether biases exist in journalism, **David Rooney**, author of *Reporting and Writing for Canadian Journalists* and a teacher at Calgary's Mount Royal College, says, "Of course they do. No one gets through life without acquiring political attitudes and prejudices and journalists are no different in that regard. But, for the most part, conscientious reporters keep their biases out of their copy. They leave it to fellow journalists—the columnists and editorial writers—to openly advocate particular policies or ideologies."

A sociologist who studied stories in the American news media for 20 years, **Herbert Gans** concluded that journalists have a typical North American value system. Gans identified primary values, all in the North American mainstream, that journalists use in making news judgments:

- *Ethnocentrism.* **Ethnocentrism** means journalists see things through their culture's eyes, which affects news coverage.
- *Commitment to democracy and capitalism.* Coverage of other governmental forms dwells on corruption, conflict, protest and bureaucratic malfunction. Gans also found that when they report corruption and misbehaviour in business, journalists treat these events as aberrations.
- *Small-town pastoralism.* Like most of their fellow citizens, journalists romanticize rural life. Given similar stories from metropolitan Vancouver and tiny Estevan, Saskatchewan, editors usually opt for the small town. This helps explain the success of Wayne Rostad's long-running *On the Road Again* series on CBC.
- *Individualism tempered by moderation.* Gans found that journalists love stories about rugged individuals who overcome adversity and defeat powerful forces. This is a value that contributes to a negative coverage of technology as something to be feared because it can stifle individuality.
- *Social order.* Journalists cover disorder—earthquakes, catastrophes, protest marches, the disintegrating nuclear family and transgressions of laws and mores. This coverage, noted Gans, is concerned not with glamorizing disorder but with finding ways to restore order.

In the final analysis, news is the result of journalists' scanning their environment and making decisions, first on whether to cover certain events and then on how to cover them. The decisions are made against a backdrop of countless variables, many of them changing during the reporting, writing and editing processes.

■ Variables Affecting News

study<u>preview</u> The variables that determine what is reported include things beyond a journalist's control, such as how much space or time is available to tell stories. Also, a story that might receive top billing on a slow news day might not even appear on a day when an overwhelming number of major stories are breaking.

NEWS HOLE

A variable affecting what ends up being reported as news is called the **news hole**. In newspapers the news hole is the space left after the advertising department has placed in the paper all the ads it has sold. The volume of advertising determines the number of total pages, and generally, the bigger the issue, the more room for news. Newspaper editors can squeeze more stories into a fat Wednesday issue than a thin Monday issue.

In broadcasting, the news hole tends to be more consistent. A 30-minute television newscast may have room for only 22 minutes of news, but the format doesn't vary. When the advertising department doesn't sell all the seven minutes available for advertising, it usually is public-service announcements, promotional messages and program notes—not news—that pick up the slack.

NEWS FLOW AND NEWS STAFFING

flow ■ Variation from day to day in significance of events worth covering.

Besides the news hole, the **flow** varies from day to day. A story that might be played prominently on a slow news day can be passed over entirely in the competition for space on a heavy news day.

On one of the heaviest news days of all time—June 4, 1989—death claimed Iran's Ayatollah Khomeini, a central figure in U.S. foreign policy; Chinese young people and the government were locked in a showdown in Tiananmen Square; the Polish people were voting to reject their one-party communist political system; and a revolt was under way in the Soviet republic of Uzbekistan. That was a heavy news day, and the flow of major nation-rattling events pre-empted many stories that otherwise would have been considered news, like the grand opening that weekend of the SkyDome (now the Rogers Centre) in Toronto.

staffing ■ Available staff resources to cover news.

Staffing affects news coverage, for example, whether reporters are in the right place at the right time. A newsworthy event in Nigeria will receive short shrift on television if the network correspondents for Africa are occupied with a natural disaster in next-door Cameroon. A radio station's city government coverage will slip when the city hall reporter is on vacation or if the station can't afford a regular reporter at city hall.

PERCEPTIONS ABOUT AUDIENCE

How a news organization perceives its audience affects news coverage. The *National Enquirer* lavishes attention on unproven cancer cures that *The Globe and Mail* treats briefly if at all. Canada's BNN (Business News Network) sees its purpose as news for viewers who have special interests in finance, the economy and business.

AVAILABILITY OF MATERIAL

The availability of photographs and video is also a factor in what ends up being news. Television is often faulted for overplaying visually titillating stories, such as fires, and underplaying or ignoring more significant stories that are not photogenic. The media are partial to stories with strong accompanying visuals, as shown with images of the Red River flooding in Manitoba, guns and gangs violence in Toronto, and the pomp and ceremony of the funeral of former prime minister Pierre Trudeau.

COMPETITION

One trigger of adrenaline for journalists is landing a scoop and, conversely, being scooped. Journalism is a competitive business, and the drive to outdo other news organizations keeps news publications and newscasts fresh with new material.

consensible nature of news ■ News organization second-guessing competition in deciding coverage.

Competition has an unglamorous side. Journalists constantly monitor each other to identify events that they missed and that they need to catch up on to be competitive. This catch-up aspect of the news business contributes to similarities in coverage, which scholar Leon Sigal calls the **consensible nature of news**. It also is called "pack" or "herd" journalism.

▛▪ Influences on News

study<u>preview</u> **The subtlety of most attempts outside the newsroom to control news coverage makes them difficult to count. Even one is too many. External influence undermines journalists as honest brokers of news and information.**

ADVERTISER INFLUENCE

Special interests sometimes try to squelch stories or insist on self-serving angles. Usually, these attempts are made quietly, even tacitly, among executives—country-club decision making. Sometimes the pressure is exerted on media advertising people, who quietly exert influence on the newsroom.

When a Wyoming grocery store was concerned over a warning from a state agency that Bon Vivant vichyssoise was possibly tainted with botulism, the advertising manager at the *Laramie Boomerang,* the only newspaper in town, kept the story out of the paper. A Laramie radio station that aired the story lost the grocery store's advertising.

To their credit, most news organizations place allegiance to their audiences ahead of pleasing advertisers, as Terry Berger, president of an advertising agency representing the Brazilian airline Varig, found out from the *Condé Nast Traveler,* a travel magazine. After an article on air pollution in Rio de Janeiro, Berger wrote this to the magazine: "Is your editorial policy then to see how quickly you can alienate present and potential advertisers and at the same time convince your readers to stick closer to home? I really think that if you continue with this kind of editorial information, you are doing both your readers and your advertisers a disservice. For this kind of information, people read *The New York Times.* I therefore find it necessary to remove the *Condé Nast Traveler* from Varig's media schedule." Unintimidated, the magazine's editor, Harold Evans, did not recant. Not only did Evans print the letter, but he followed with this comment: "Mrs. Berger is, of course, entitled to use her judgment about where she advertises Brazil's national airline. I write not about that narrow commercial issue, but about her assertion that it is a disservice to readers and advertisers for us to print true but unattractive facts when they are relevant. This goes to the heart of the editorial policy of this magazine. . . . We rejoice in the enrichments of travel, but our aim is to give readers the fullest information, frankly and fairly, so they can make their own judgments."

David Rooney explains the strained relationship between advertiser and journalist like this: "Once an advertiser understands that news stories are about placing people, events, and comments in a broadly understood context and not about taking one side or another in a dispute, the less likely it is that he or she will feel abandoned or beleaguered by the local media."

CORPORATE POLICY

No matter how committed journalists may be to truth seeking and truth telling, the people in charge have the final word on matters big and small. It is owners, publishers, general managers and their immediate lieutenants who are in charge. Their corporate responsibilities dictate that they are business executives before all else, even if once they were journalists. Executives sometimes make self-serving decisions on coverage that gall the journalists who work for them, but that is how chains of command work.

Lowell Bergman, former executive producer at *60 Minutes,* recalls his days at CBS: "You could not do a story about a supplier or major advertiser. You could try to do it, but you were taking a lot of risks getting close to the limit." At both ABC and CBS, Bergman said, he was told that the networks would not initiate a critical story about the business practices and histories of National Football League team owners. The networks, of course, stood to derive handsome revenue from airing NFL games if they were awarded contracts for play-by-play coverage.

Admonitions not to go near certain stories are not in written policy, although they are real. ABC newspeople got an unusual overt reminder when Michael Eisner, then chair of Disney, which owns ABC, said in an interview on the NPR program *Fresh Air,* "I would prefer ABC not to cover Disney. I think it's inappropriate." Eisner went on to say that *ABC News* knew of his preference.

In fairness it must be said that media owners generally are sensitive to their truth-seeking and truth-telling journalistic responsibilities and assiduously avoid calling the shots on news coverage. Those who answer to a call other than journalistic soundness are within their court-recognized First Amendment rights, which allow media people to exercise their freedom responsibly as well as irresponsibly. Journalists who are bothered by wrong-headed news decisions have three choices: persuade wayward owners of the error of their ways, comply with directives, or quit and go to work for a more respectable journalistic organization.

SOURCE PRESSURE

Journalists sometimes feel external pressure directly. At the courthouse, valuable sources turn cold after a story appears that they don't like. A tearful husband begs an editor not to use his wife's name in a story that points to her as a bank embezzler. A bottle

media ONLINE
Condé Nast Traveler Find out what kind of news the audience of this magazine gets.
www.concierge.com/cntraveler

of Canadian Club arrives at Christmas from a sports publicist who says she appreciates the excellent coverage over the past year. Most journalists will tell you that their commitment to truth overrides external assaults on their autonomy. Even so, external pressures exist.

The relationship between journalists and publicists can be troublesome. In general, the relationship works well. Publicists want news coverage for their clients and therefore provide information and help reporters to line up interviews. Some publicists, however, are more committed to advancing their clients' interests than to advancing truth, and they work to manipulate journalists into providing coverage that unduly glorifies their clients.

Staging events is a publicity tactic to gain news coverage that a cause would not otherwise attract. Some staged events are obvious hucksterism, such as flagpole-sitting stunts by celebrity disc jockeys. Covering such events is usually part of the softer side of news and, in the spirit of fun and games and diversion, is relatively harmless.

Of more serious concern are staged events about which publicists create a mirage of significance to suck journalists and the public into giving more attention than the event deserves. For example, consider the following:

- The false impression created when hundreds of federal workers are released from work for an hour to see an incumbent's campaign speech outside a government office building.
- The contrived photo opportunity at which people, props and lighting are carefully, even meticulously, arranged to create an image on television.
- Stunts that bring attention to a new product and give it an undeserved boost in the marketplace.

Staged events distort a balanced journalistic portrayal of the world. Worse, they divert attention from truly significant events.

media ONLINE

You Be the Producer This game from CNN shows you that news producing is not a job for the decision-impaired. **www.cnn.com/EVENTS/1996/ anniversary/how.things.work/ producer.game**

Canadians and the News Media Read all about Canadians and the love . . . and perception . . . of news online. **www.cmrcccrm.ca/english/ reportcard2004/01.html**

media DATABANK

Where Do Canadians Go for News and How Do They Define Trust?

Here is a summary of findings of the *Report Card on Canadian News Media*, according to a 2004 Canadian Media Research Consortium telephone survey of 3012 Canadians. The research was conducted by researchers from the University of British Columbia Graduate School of Journalism, The York/Ryerson Joint Graduate Program in Communication and Culture, and the Communications Program at Laval University.

Media used for news and information:

TV	67%
Newspapers	42%
Radio	57%
Internet	33%

The survey also found that the most important factors influencing the perception of trust included:

Accuracy	33%
Impartiality	32%
Credibility	16%
Ownership	15%

Source: Canadian Media Research Consortium, Report Card on Canadian News Media, 2004.

Diversity: Women Are Still Missing as News Sources

Authority Figure A United Nations representative, unusual in being a woman, addresses a refugee crisis in Jordan. Study after study of media coverage find women represented much less in the news than in their growing presence in political, research and academic leadership.

Women make up slightly more than half of the population, but you would never know it if your news comes from television, the internet or newspapers.

Women are particularly absent in coverage of politics, the military, and foreign policy, according to a study released in 2005 by the Project for Excellence in Journalism, a Washington-based think tank affiliated with the Columbia University Graduate School of Journalism. Women are most likely to be included in feature stories about children, celebrities and homemaking.

The study examined nearly 17 000 news reports by 45 different news outlets during 20 randomly selected days over 9 months in 2004. Three-quarters of all stories studied contained at least one male source. Just one-third contained a female source. The sourcing gap widened as the number of sources in a story increased. Reporters were more than three times as likely to cite two or more men within a news story as to cite at least two women. "Finding a male as the best first source does not apparently lead a journalist to look for a female as the second or third source," the report said. The worst offenders were cable television and PBS, and newspapers gave women the most exposure.

The dismal trend of using few women as sources in news stories hasn't changed much since it was first studied in 1989. A series of studies beginning that year found that women were mentioned less than 25 percent of the time on the front pages of newspapers, and those who were mentioned were often of a lower socioeconomic status than male sources. A 2000 study of news coverage of the military found that civilian experts and politicians commenting on military stories almost never are women. Research by Canadians Gertrude Robinson and Armande Saint Jean for the International Federation of Journalists echoes the findings of these studies. Their 2001 investigation found that only 28 percent of print journalists and 37 percent of broadcast journalists are female.

The London-based Media Diversity Institute says that women are further discriminated against when they are members of minority ethnic communities: "When individuals are mentioned in stories less than 3 percent of them are women, which is three and half times less than men at 35 percent. The majority of women appear in roles that comply with the dominant patriarchal pattern—women are mostly victims and witnesses of events."

WHAT DO YOU THINK?

1. Should women be quoted as authorities in stories about the military? Why or why not?

2. Does the media's lack of female sources in news stories reflect and/or reinforce existing cultural beliefs and values? If so, how?

3. Could the media, as agenda-setters, change the way women are regarded in society?

Are you up to the challenge? See how well you can diversify a newsroom by playing the interactive game at www.maynardije.org/resources/game.

nonstop coverage ■ News reporting geared to ever-present deadlines, as 24/7 formats.

■ Journalism Trends

study<u>preview</u> The explosion of 24/7 news on television and the internet is transforming news gathering and redefining news practices and audience expectations. Traditional avenues for news, sometimes called mainstream media, were shaken in the 2004 political campaign by individuals, mostly without journalistic training, generally operating alone, who created hundreds of blog sites. Bloggers offer an interconnected web of fascinating reading. Sometimes they score scoops.

NONSTOP COVERAGE

Reporters for news agencies were a breed apart through most of the 20th century. In contrast to most newspaper reporters, who had one deadline a day, agency reporters sent dispatches to hundreds of news organizations, each with its own deadlines. Agency reporters literally had a deadline every minute.

The advent of all-news radio and then all the demassified 24/7 news channels expanded **nonstop coverage** beyond the news agencies. This is no better illustrated than on Parliament Hill where reporters race from an event or interview to a camera for a live stand-up report, often ad-libbing from notes scribbled on the run, and then, adrenaline surging, run back to sources for a new angle or event. This is event-based reporting, which emphasizes timely reports but which has a downside. Going on air a dozen times a day, perhaps more when the news flow is heavy or especially significant, stand-up reporters have scant time to think through implications and context. Theirs is a race to cover events more than to provide understanding. This too was a classic criticism of the news agencies.

In short, nonstop coverage, whatever the advantage of keeping people on top of breaking events, has shortcomings. The pressure for new angles tends to elevate the trivial. Also, context and understanding are sacrificed.

LIVE NEWS

Over the past 150 years, the news media have evolved standard and accepted practices. These practices, taught in journalism schools and institutionalized in codes of ethics, guide reporters and editors in preparing their summaries and wrap-ups. In general, the traditional practices worked well when newspapers were the dominant news medium, and they worked well in broadcasting too—until the advent of highly portable, lightweight equipment that enabled broadcasters to carry news events live, bypassing the traditional editing process.

With television cameras focused on the towers of the World Trade Center as they turned into infernos in the 2001 terrorist attack, trapped people began jumping from windows hundreds of feet above ground. The plunges were desperate and fatal, and audiences viewing the scene live were shocked and horrified. Neither the video nor still photographs were included in some later newscasts or newspapers.

UNEDITED BLOGS

When the *Columbia Journalism Review* created a website for commentary on reporting of the 2004 presidential campaign, the magazine went out of its way to distance the new site from the thousands of web log sites, called **blogs**, on which amateurs post whatever is on their minds. No, said *CJR*, its website (http://campaigndesk.org) would be held to the highest journalistic standards. Their concern was that a lot of irresponsible content gets posted on the web by people without any journalistic training or sense of journalistic standards. The web has made it possible for anyone to create a blog that is as easily accessible as are sites from news organizations that consciously seek to go about journalism right.

No gnashing of teeth, however, will make blogs go away—and their impact is substantial. Blog rumours, gossip and speculation, even when untrue, gain such currency that the mainstream media cannot ignore them. It's become a cliché, drawn from the tail-wags-dog metaphor, that blogs can wag the media.

blog ■ An amateur website, generally personal in nature, often focused on a narrow subject, such as politics. Short for "web log."

Greg Oliver

Greg Oliver (left)

Quebecor Media's Canoe is an excellent example of the recent emergence of online journalism. Canoe is a web portal for all kinds of online news and information. The "Sports" link from www.canoe.ca will take you to SLAM! Sports, which in turn will take you to the place **Greg Oliver** has called home since 1996: the SLAM! Wrestling page.

Oliver's been writing about pro wrestling since 1985 when, as a high-school student, he created *The Canadian Wrestling Report,* a monthly newsletter that he published and marketed out of his basement for five years. Then, after graduating from Toronto's Ryerson University, Oliver went to work for the *Toronto Sun.* He has also written three books for ECW Press: *The Pro Wrestling Hall of Fame: The Canadians, The Pro Wrestling Hall of Fame: The Tag Teams* and *The Pro Wrestling Hall of Fame: The Heels.*

But is this legitimate journalism? Greg Oliver thinks so. "SLAM! Wrestling is proof that pro wrestling journalism doesn't need to be an oxymoron. We're legitimate journalists. We just happen to write about wrestling. Wrestlers are fascinating people with fascinating tales. Isn't that what journalism is all about? Journalism is about telling stories. Sure, it's a worked sport, but how is it any different than an actor trying to get his or her break or the young baseball player trying to break into the majors? It's human interest in the end, and that's what any good story should be. We're not rumour mongers. Our strength is talking to people and telling their stories."

Oliver will always remember the biggest story he broke: "Nothing has ever compared to the night Owen Hart died. I called the *Calgary Sun* within seconds to get the ball rolling.

I penned a column that night on my own personal experiences with Owen, then led the site to its biggest numbers ever—the only time wrestling was ever the top sport on the SLAM! Sports site, dislodging the perennial number one: hockey."

Writing for SLAM! Wrestling has offered Oliver the chance to apply his love of wrestling in many different ways. He's not only a writer, but also an editor and mentor to other aspiring wrestling journalists. "I'm the guy assigning stories, shepherding new writers, offering editing advice, or setting up interviews for other people. I enjoy that as much as I do writing. But every now and then I get a real urge to write."

Oliver's advice to would-be wrestling writers? "Wrestling journalism is about more than your opinion. It takes real skill to interview somebody and to check your sources and facts and create some good writing. You need to be able to develop suggestions and ideas for stories."

Is SLAM! Wrestling true journalism? While many critics and mainstream journalists may not appreciate it, fans certainly do. SLAM! Wrestling gets approximately 50 000 page views a day.

EXPLORATORY NEWS

Although in-depth reporting has deep roots, the thrust of U.S. journalism until the 1960s was a chronicling of events: meetings, speeches, crimes, deaths and catastrophes. That changed dramatically in 1972. Two persistent *Washington Post* reporters, **Bob Woodward** and **Carl Bernstein**, not only covered a break-in at the Democratic national headquarters, at a building called the Watergate, but also linked the crime to the White House of Republican President Richard Nixon. The morality questions inherent in the reporting forced Nixon to resign. Twenty-five aides went to jail. The **Watergate** scandal created an enthusiasm for **investigative reporting** and in-depth approaches to news that went far beyond mere chronicling, which is relatively easy to do and, alas, relatively superficial.

SOFT NEWS

In contrast to hard investigative reporting came a simultaneous trend toward **soft news**. This included consumer-help stories, lifestyle tips, entertainment news and offbeat gee-whiz items often of a sensational sort. The celebrity-oriented *National Enquirer,* whose circulation skyrocketed in the 1960s, was the progenitor of the trend. Time Life launched *People* magazine. The staid *New York Times* created *Us.* Newspaper research found that

Greg Oliver Wrestling journalist.

Bob Woodward ■ Bernstein's colleague in the Watergate revelations.

Carl Bernstein ■ *Washington Post* reporter who dug up Watergate.

Watergate ■ Reporting of the Nixon administration scandal.

investigative reporting ■ Enterprise reporting that reveals new information, often startling; most often these are stories that official sources would rather not have told.

soft news ■ Geared to satisfying audience's information wants, not needs.

readers liked soft stuff. Soon many dailies added "People" columns. The television show *Entertainment Tonight Canada* focuses on glamour and glitz, usually as a follow-up to the evening news on many Global stations.

War Zones: Combat Reporting

study<u>preview</u> The need in a democracy for people to be informed doesn't square easily with military necessity in time of war. The United States has tried a wide range of policies for war coverage. The latest—embedded reporters in the 2003 Iraq war—generally worked well from the military, media and public perspectives. All the historic media–government arrangements for war coverage, however, raise the looming question of how global media serving international audiences can be faithful both to truth and to competing national causes.

War is a danger zone for journalists. The Committee to Protect Journalists, which tracks reporters in peril, tallied 54 reporters killed doing their work in 2004—23 in Iraq alone—compared to 13 in 2003. In addition, 22 journalists were kidnapped in Iraq.

media ONLINE

War Stories An interactive exhibition from the Newseum.
www.newseum.org/warstories

South Asian Journalists Association. Tips on War Reporting.
www.saja.org/tipsreportingwar. html

EARLY LESSONS

The struggle to find ways for journalists to report from the battlefield without getting in the way or jeopardizing operations is not recent.

In World War II, correspondents wore uniforms with the rank of captain and usually had a driver and a Jeep. The reporters generated lots of field coverage, but the reporting, reflecting the highly patriotic spirit of the times, as evidenced by the reporters' actually wearing military uniforms, was hardly dispassionate and sometimes propagandist.

VIETNAM REPORTING

Reporters had great freedom in reporting the Vietnam War in the 1960s and 1970s. Almost at will, reporters could link up with South Vietnamese or U.S. units and go on patrols. The result, dubbed **rice-roots reporting**, included lots of negative stories on what was, in fact, an unsuccessful military campaign that was unpopular among many troops and a growing majority at home. For the first time the reporting was filmed for television, with gruesome footage being pumped by the networks into living rooms across the nation on the evening news, deepening opposition to the war.

rice-roots reporting ■ Uncensored field reporting from the Vietnam War.

Commanders didn't like negative reports, which some blamed for losing the public's support for the war. In the end, demoralized, the United States withdrew in defeat—the first war the nation had lost in its history. For the next wars, relatively quick incursions, the Pentagon had new rules. In 1983, when the United States took over the Caribbean nation of Grenada, a naval blockade kept reporters out. The war, secretly planned, surprised the news media. Scrambling to get on top of the story but barred from the action, enterprising reporters hired small boats to run the blockade but were intercepted.

POOL SYSTEM

Major newspapers, the networks and news agencies protested loudly at being excluded. Acknowledging that the policy had ridden roughshod over the democratic principles on which the nation was founded, with an informed electorate essential for the system to work, the Pentagon agreed to sit down with news media leaders to devise new ground rules. The result was a **pool system**, in which a corps of reporters would be on call on a rotating basis to be shuttled to combat areas on short notice for the next quick war.

pool system ■ Reporters chosen on a rotating basis to cover an event to which access is limited.

In 1989, when U.S. forces invaded Panama to capture dictator Manuel Noriega on drug charges, the Pentagon activated the pool system and took reporters along. Top military commanders, however, still smarting from their Vietnam experience and blaming the news media, carefully controlled the reporters and their access to information. Army drivers took reporters only to secure areas. For a while reporters were locked in a window-less building and had only information the Army fed them. When the military had accomplished its mission, news organizations again protested. Plainly, the Pentagon had failed again to find a system that met both military necessity and democratic principles.

EMBEDDED REPORTERS

The 2003 Iraq war was covered by journalists like no other. The U.S. government, after flip-flopping on rules for war correspondents for 50 years, seemed to recognize the futility of trying to manipulate information in the digital age. Months before the invasion, the Pentagon chief for media relations, Victoria Clarke, invited news organizations to send reporters to special combat mini-courses to get up to speed—and also into physical shape—to go to war with combat units. These reporters would be embedded in the units to cover combat for the duration of hostilities. The reporters, called **embeds**, would need to supply their own equipment, including vehicles, but would be free to tell the story of the war as they saw it. Commanders were told to let the cameras roll whenever the journalists wanted.

embeds ■ A 2003 Iraq war term for reporters accompanying, or embedded with, U.S. military combat units.

Ground rules were few. Among them was not to disclose unit positions, lest the enemy be tipped to locations. Also, the Pentagon warned that it might need to black out reports for "operational security, success of the mission, and the safety of the people involved."

News organizations sent hundreds of reporters to Pentagon boot camps. Time Warner set aside $30 million to cover the war and dispatched Eason Jordan, CNN's chief news executive, to the Middle East to buy a fleet of Humvees to haul crews and their equipment, including satellite uplink dishes, into combat.

How well did the embedded reporter system work?

The Pentagon was pleased. Yes, the embeds showed the ugliness of war, as well as gaffes. But the invasion went well for the United States and its allies, and the Pentagon concluded that the coverage, perceived by the public as honest and independent, contributed to public enthusiasm for the war during the initial combat phase. The news media were pleased, too, remembering that only 10 years earlier, in the Kuwait war, reporters were kept away from combat and had access only to information fed to them at headquarters briefings.

Critics said the embeds were too limited in their perspective, lacking an overview, and that, losing objectivity, they picked up the gung-ho spirit of the units they were assigned to. The criticism, however, missed the fact that reporters were in regular contact with editors and producers in their home newsrooms, as well as in field newsrooms, who fed them information from other sources. Also, reports from the embeds were integrated into newscasts and stories that presented the broad picture.

Could the embedded system work better? Walter Cronkite, whose war reporting experience went back to World War II, noted that embeds, almost all with frontline units, missed details in the haste of moving forward. He suggested that reporters be assigned to follow up to verify information and ask questions that frontline embeds didn't have time to pursue.

Whatever the critics say, embedded journalism in times of war is likely here to stay. While CBC News did not allow its journalists to embed, Tony Burman, editor-in-chief of CBC News, said, "The introduction of technology, the video phone, the satellite phone, the incredible ease to satellite feeds, pictures, sound reports and obviously the whole embedding experience, the whole notion that you can, in fact, get live pictures from the front, is quite unprecedented." The president of CTV News, Robert G. Hurst, says that in the future, we may see battles live on TV and journalists embedded on both sides of a conflict. Bill Schiller, formerly the foreign editor for the *Toronto Star,* says that would not be in the best interests of journalism. He says that embedded journalists do no more than serve the interests of the status quo—in the case of the 2003 Iraq war, the Pentagon: "Editorial independence is everything. It's fundamental to what we do, no matter how good the pictures are."

CHAPTER 8 **Wrap-Up**

Journalism is an art, not a science. Judgments, rather than formulas, determine which events and issues are reported and how—and no two journalists approach any story exactly the same way. This leaves the whole process of gathering and telling news subject to second-guessing and criticism. Journalists ask themselves all the time whether there are ways to do a better job. All journalists can do is try to find truth and to relate it accurately. Even then, the complexity of modern news-gathering—which involves many people, each with an opportunity to change or even kill a story—includes dozens of points at which inaccuracy and imprecision can creep into a story that started out well.

Questions for Review

1. What contemporary news practices are rooted in the various press periods in U.S. and Canadian history?
2. What is the core difference between the U.S. and European concepts of news?
3. What variables beyond journalists' control affect news?
4. What pressures from outside the media affect news reporting?
5. What responsibilities do journalists have as gate-keepers?
6. Is there a contradiction between the two contemporary journalistic trends of exploratory reporting and soft news?
7. How has convergence affected journalism in Canada?

Questions for Critical Thinking

1. The 19-year-old son of the premier of a troubled Central American country in which the CIA has deep involvement died, perhaps of a drug overdose, aboard a Northwest Airlines plane en route from Tokyo to Singapore. On the plane was a young female country-western singer, his frequent companion in recent weeks. The plane was a Boeing 747 manufactured in Washington state. Northwest's corporate headquarters is in Minnesota. The death occurred at 4 a.m. Eastern time. Consider the six elements of news—proximity, prominence, timeliness, consequence, currency and drama—and discuss how this event might be

reported on morning television newscasts in Miami, Minneapolis, Nashville, Seattle and the District of Columbia. How about in Managua? Singapore? Tokyo? Rome? Istanbul? Johannesburg? What if the victim were an ordinary college student? What if the death occurred a week ago?

2. Explain news judgment.

3. How do the news hole and news flow affect what is reported in the news media?

4. *Time* and *Maclean's* carry cover stories on the same subject one week. Does this indicate that executives of the magazine have conspired, or is it more likely to be caused by what Leon Sigal calls *the consensible nature of news*?

5. How does the nature of news provide ammunition to conservatives to criticize the news media as left-ist promoters of change?

6. Discuss whether the news media reflect mainstream North American values. Do you see evidence in your news media of an underlying belief that democracy, capitalism, rural small-town life, individualism and moderation are virtues?

7. Do you feel that the mass media revel in disorder? Consider Herbert Gans's view that the media cover disorder from the perspective of identifying ways to restore order.

8. If a college president calls a news conference and makes a major announcement, who are the gate-keepers who determine how the announcement is covered in the campus newspaper?

Deepening Your
media LITERACY

How important is freedom of the press to you?
STEP 1 Write down your definition of freedom of the press.

Dig Deeper
STEP 2 Imagine that you are a blogger covering Parliament Hill and you have uncovered a scandal. Compare how you would cover it with freedom of the press and how that would change without freedom of the press.

What Do You think?
STEP 3 Answer these questions:

1. If you exercise freedom of the press irresponsibly, should your right be revoked?

2. How important is editorial independence to freedom of the press?

3. Do you think freedom of the press and the *Canadian Charter of Rights and Freedoms* are important to you and your life as a Canadian? Are they more important

to a student, to a parent, to a businessperson, to a journalist, to a politician, to a religious person, to a person who belongs to a minority?

4. How would your life change without freedom of the press?

Keeping Up to Date

Among publications that keep current on journalistic issues are *Columbia Journalism Review, Quill, American Journalism Review,* and *Editor & Publisher.*

Bridging the gap between scholarly and professional work is *Newspaper Research Journal.*

For Further Learning

Angus Reid Group. *Canadians and the News Media* (Canadian Corporate News, 1998).

Jim Bawden. "Taking Care of Business." *Starweek Magazine* (May 17, 1997).

L. Brent Bozell III and Brent H. Baker, editors. *And That's the Way It Isn't: A Reference Guide to Media Bias* (Media Research Center, 1990).

Ben Bradlee. *A Good Life: Newspapering and Other Stories* (Simon & Schuster, 1996).

"Brits vs. Yanks: Who Does Journalism Right?" *Columbia Journalism Review* (May/June 2004): 44–49.

Canada. *Kent Commission on Newspapers, Canadian News Services,* Volume 6 (Ottawa: Supply and Services, 1981).

Canada. *Kent Commission on Newspapers, The Journalists,* Volume 2 (Ottawa: Supply and Services, 1981).

Canadian Media Research Consortium. *Report Card on Canadian News Media* (CMRC, 2004). Available online at http://www.cmrcccrm.ca/english/reportcard2004/01.html.

Robert Cribb. "Iraqi War Reshaped Reporting." *Toronto Star* (April 16, 2003).

James L. Crouthamel. *Bennett's New York Herald and the Rise of the Popular Press* (Syracuse University Press, 1989).

Daniel J. Czitrom. *Media and the American Mind: From Morse to McLuhan* (University of North Carolina Press, 1982).

Peter Desbarats. *Guide to the Canadian News Media* (Harcourt Brace, 1990).

Hazel Dicken-Garcia. *Journalistic Standards in the Nineteenth Century* (University of Wisconsin Press, 1989).

Rosie DiManno. "Too Many Critics Shooting the Messenger in Iraq." *Toronto Star* (March 26, 2004).

Edwin and Michael Emery. *The Press and America,* Fourth edition (Prentice Hall, 1984).

Kathleen L. Endress. "Help-Wanted Finale: *Editor & Publisher* Frames Civil Rights Issue." *Journalism and Mass Communication Quarterly* (Spring 2004): 7–21.

Mark Fishman. *Manufacturing the News* (University of Texas Press, 1980).

Thomas L. Friedman. *From Beirut to Jerusalem* (Farrar, Straus & Giroux, 1989).

Herbert J. Gans. *Deciding What's News: A Study of* CBS Evening News, NBC Nightly News, Newsweek *and* Time (Pantheon, 1979).

Brian Green. *Canadian Broadcast News: The Basics* (Harcourt Canada, 2001).

Jane T. Harrigan. *Read All About It! A Day in the Life of a Metropolitan Newspaper* (Globe Pequot Press, 1987).

Michael Higgins. "Vigilant, Honest Media Imperative in a War." *The Record,* Kitchener-Waterloo (March 25, 2003).

Norman E. Isaacs. *Untended Gates: The Mismanaged Press* (Columbia University Press, 1986).

Ryszard Kapuscinski. *The Soccer War* (Alfred A. Knopf, 1991).

H.G. Kariel and L.A. Rosenvall. *Places in the News: A Study of News Flows* (Carleton University Press, 1995).

Wilfred Kesterton. *A History of Journalism in Canada* (McClelland and Stewart, 1967).

Anne Kingston. "Pamela Wallin's Wild Kingdom." *Saturday Night* (June 1997).

Brooke Kroeger. *Nellie Bly: Daredevil, Reporter, Feminist* (Random House, 1994).

Molly Moore. *A Woman at War: Storming Kuwait with the U.S. Marines* (Scribner's, 1993).

Michael Parenti. *Inventing Reality: The Politics of the Mass Media* (St. Martin's, 1988).

Nancy Roberts. *The Press and America: An Interpretive History of the Mass Media,* Eighth edition (Allyn & Bacon, 1997).

David F. Rooney. *Reporting and Writing for Canadian Journalists* (Prentice Hall, 2001).

Karenna Gore Schiff. *Lighting the Way: Nine Women Who Changed Modern America* (Miramax, 2006).

Michael Schudson. *Discovering the News: A Social History of American Newspapers* (Basic Books, 1978).

Pamela J. Shoemaker with Elizabeth Kay Mayfield. *Building a Theory of News Content: A Synthesis of Current Approaches.* Journalism Monographs, No. 103 (June 1987.

David Walkis, editor. *Killed: Great Journalism Too Hot to Print* (Nation, 2004).

David H. Weaver and G. Cleveland Wilhoit. *The American Journalist: A Portrait of U.S. News People and Their Work,* 2nd edition (Indiana University Press, 1991).

Anthony Wilson-Smith. "Wall to Wall News." *Maclean's* (March 2, 1998).

Bob Woodward and Carl Bernstein. *All the President's Men* (Simon & Schuster, 1974).

Antonia Zerbisias. "The News about TV News." *Toronto Star* (July 20, 1997).

Sam Walton He was a contrarian to the dominant thinking today that public relations needs to be a major component in corporate management. Was he on to something? Or was Wal-Mart's meteoric rise in U.S. retailing despite Walton's disdain for public relations?

Public Relations

Media in Theory

Public Relations as "Sleaze"?

Public relations operates in the realm of what Canadian **Joyce Nelson** calls the "legitimacy gap" in her book *The Sultans of Sleaze: Public Relations and the Media*. The term *legitimacy gap* was coined by business professor Prakash Sethi to describe the difference between a corporate image and the corporate reality. Nelson applies Jungian psychology to the term in her analysis of public relations. She argues that a corporation has two sides: a persona and a shadow. The persona is its corporate image, the positive image that is promoted via **advertising**; the shadow is its dark side, which is not usually seen in the news media and certainly not in advertising. According to Nelson, the shadow may include "the ways in which [the corporation's] activities infringe upon our health and safety, our environment, [and contribute] to our oppression or to that of others, despite what all their persona-related activity would like us to believe." When something happens that threatens the persona and reveals the shadow of a corporation, public relations professionals are called to fix the problem.

Nelson provides an interesting example. In a two-week period during the summer of 1981, Ontario Hydro was involved in two environmental accidents. First, it dumped heavy water containing 3500 curies of radiation into the Ottawa River. The event received front-page coverage in *The Globe and Mail* and was reported on television news. A week later, almost 4000 gallons (18 000 litres) of radioactive water were accidentally spilled at Ontario Hydro's Bruce nuclear power plant. More than twice as much tritium—about 8000 curies—was released in the accident. These incidents created a problem for Ontario Hydro. The nuclear power industry's persona centres on concern for public safety and the environment. But Nelson argues that these spills raised questions about the safety of nuclear power, thus revealing Hydro's shadow.

The second incident received less coverage in both *The Globe and Mail* and the *Toronto Star*. One of the reasons for this may have been "information overload"; perhaps

Joyce Nelson ■ Says public relations has two sides: the shadow and the persona.

advertising ■ Unlike public relations, advertising seeks to sell a product or service.

the news media were simply tired of writing about problems at nuclear power plants. According to Nelson, another reason the second accident received less negative coverage had to do with the well-crafted press release that ended up as a news story in the *Toronto Star*. Consider the lead of the news story: "Armed with mops, pails and pumps, an Ontario Hydro crew has recovered 3400 gallons of radioactive heavy water at the Bruce Nuclear Power Plant." This passage succeeds in diverting attention from the accident by focusing instead on the cleanup. Any suspicions the reader may have about the corporation's shadow are discarded. The story goes on to outline the cost of the cleanup in detail, which underlines Hydro's commitment to protecting the environment, whatever the cost, and thus reinforces its corporate image, or persona. The story makes no mention of damage to the surrounding area.

The Canadian Public Relations Society would agree—and disagree—with Nelson's ideas. In the article "Truth Pays Dividends with Public," **Jean Valin** argues that up to 50 percent of the public will not believe most media messages due to a lack of trust of the media. However, Valin discounts Nelson's idea that public relations is "smoke and mirrors." She says that, in the end, "organizations will always be well served by telling the truth. It takes a long time to build your credibility and an even longer time to rebuild it . . . this provides all the more reason to practice good public relations and avoid the pitfalls of manipulation and disinformation—honesty pays."

Jean Valin ■ Believes organizations are served best when they tell the truth.

media TIMELINE

PUBLIC RELATIONS

1859 Charles Darwin advanced survival-of-the-fittest theory, which led to social Darwinism.

1880s Public became dissatisfied with unconscionable business practices justified with social Darwinism.

1906 Ivy Lee began the first public relations agency.

1917 George Creel headed a federal agency that generated support for World War I.

1927 Arthur W. Page became the first corporate public relations vice-president.

1930s Paul Garrett created the term *enlightened self-interest* at General Motors.

1942 Elmer Davis headed a federal agency that generated support for World War II.

1947 Public Relations Society of America was formed.

1951 PRSA adopted "Professional Standards for the Practice of Public Relations," a forerunner to the current Code of Ethics.

1953 The Canadian Public Relations Society was formed.

1965 PRSA created an accreditation system.

1969 The Canadian Public Relations Society introduced a voluntary accreditation program.

1970s Herb Schmertz pioneered adversarial public relations at Mobil Oil.

2000 PRSA revised its Code of Ethics.

▀▄ Importance of Public Relations

study preview Public relations is a persuasive communication tool that people can use to motivate other people and institutions to help them achieve their goals.

DEFINING PUBLIC RELATIONS

public relations ■ A management tool to establish beneficial relationships.

Edward Bernays, the public relations pioneer, lamented how loosely the term **public relations** is used. To illustrate his concern, Bernays told about a young woman who approached him for career advice. He asked her what she did for a living. "I'm in public relations," she said. He pressed her for details, and she explained that she handed out circulars in Harvard Square. Bernays was dismayed at how casually people regard the work of public relations. The Canadian Public Relations Society says that public relations is "the management function which evaluates public attitudes, identifies the policies of an individual or organization with the public interest, and plans and executes a program of action to earn public understanding and acceptance." An Ipsos Reid poll, released in 2000, claimed that 96 percent of Canadian CEOs felt that good public relations is essential for businesses today.

Four steps are necessary for public relations to accomplish its goals:

Identify Existing Relationships In modern society, institutions have many relationships. A college, for example, has relationships with its students, its faculty, its staff, its alumni, its benefactors, the neighbourhood, the community, the legislature, other colleges, accreditors of its programs, perhaps unions. The list could go on and on. Each of these constituencies is called a public—hence the term *public relations*.

Evaluate the Relationships Through research, the public relations practitioner studies these relationships to determine how well they are working. This evaluation is an ongoing process. A college may have excellent relations with the legislature one year and win major appropriations, but after a scandal related to the president's budget the next year, legislators may be downright unfriendly.

Design Policies to Improve the Relationships The job of public relations people is to recommend policies to top management to make these relationships work better, not only for the organization but also for the partners in each relationship. **Paul Garrett**, a pioneer in corporate relations, found that General Motors (GM) was seen in unfriendly terms during the Great Depression, which put the giant auto maker at risk with many publics, including its own employees. GM, he advised, needed new policies to seem neighbourly—rather than as a far-removed, impersonal, monolithic industrial giant.

Paul Garrett ■ Devised the notion of enlightened self-interest.

Implement the Policies Garrett used the term **enlightened self-interest** for his series of policies intended to downsize GM in the eyes of many of the company's publics. Garrett set up municipal programs in towns with GM plants and grants for schools and scholarships for employees' children. General Motors benefited from a revised image, and in the spirit of enlightened self-interest, so did GM employees, their children and their communities.

enlightened self-interest ■ Mutually beneficial public relations.

Public relations is not a mass medium itself, but PR often uses the media as tools to accomplish its goals. To announce GM's initiatives to change its image in the 1930s, Paul Garrett issued news releases that he hoped newspapers, magazines and radio stations would pick up. The number of people in most of the publics with which public relations practitioners need to communicate is so large that it can be reached only through the mass media. The influence of public relations on the news media is extensive. Half of the news in many newspapers originates with formal statements or news releases from organizations that want something in the paper. It is the same with radio and television.

PUBLIC RELATIONS IN A DEMOCRACY

Misconceptions about public relations include the idea that it is a one-way street for institutions and individuals to communicate to the public. Actually, the good practice of public relations seeks two-way communication between and among all the people and institutions concerned with an issue.

A task force established by the **Public Relations Society of America** (PRSA) to explore the stature and role of the profession concluded that public relations has the potential to improve the functioning of democracy by encouraging the exchange of information and ideas on public issues. The task force made these points:

Public Relations Society of America ■ Professional public relations association.

- Public relations is a means for the public to have its desires and interests felt by the institutions in our society. It interprets and speaks for the public to organizations that otherwise might be unresponsive, and it speaks for those organizations to the public.
- Public relations is a means to achieve mutual adjustments between institutions and groups, establishing smoother relationships that benefit the public.

- Public relations is a safety valve for freedom. By providing means of working out accommodations, it makes arbitrary action or coercion less likely.
- Public relations is an essential element in the communication system that enables individuals to be informed on many aspects of subjects that affect their lives.
- Public relations people can help to activate the social conscience of the organizations for which they work.

◼ Origins of Public Relations

study<u>preview</u> **Many big companies found themselves in disfavour in the late 1800s for ignoring the public good to make profits. Feeling misunderstood, some moguls of industry turned to Ivy Lee, the founder of modern public relations, for counsel on gaining public support.**

MOGULS IN TROUBLE

William Henry Vanderbilt ◼ Embodied the bad corporate images of the 1880s, 1890s with "The public be damned."

Nobody would be tempted to think of **William Henry Vanderbilt** as being very good at public relations. In 1882 it was Vanderbilt, president of the New York Central Railroad, who said, "The public be damned," when asked about the effect of changing train schedules. Vanderbilt's utterance so infuriated people that it became a banner in the populist crusade against robber barons and tycoons in the late 1800s. Under populist pressure, state governments set up agencies to regulate railroads. Then the federal government established the Interstate Commerce Commission to control freight and passenger rates. Government began insisting on safety standards. Labour unions formed in the industries with the worst working conditions, safety records and pay. Journalists added pressure with muckraking exposés on excesses in the railroad, coal and oil trusts; on meat-packing industry frauds; and on patent medicines.

social Darwinism ◼ Application of Darwin's survival-of-the-fittest theory to society.

Charles Darwin ◼ Devised survival-of-the-fittest theory.

The leaders of industry were slow to recognize the effect of populist objections on their practices. They were comfortable with **social Darwinism**, an adaptation of **Charles Darwin**'s survival-of-the-fittest theory. In fact, they thought themselves forward-thinking in applying Darwin's theory to business and social issues. It had been only a few decades earlier, in 1859, that Darwin had laid out his biological theory in *On the Origin of Species by Means of Natural Selection*. To cushion the harshness of social Darwinism, many tycoons espoused paternalism toward those whose "fitness" had not brought them fortune and power. No matter how carefully put, paternalism seemed arrogant to the "less fit."

George Baer ◼ Epitomized offensive corporate paternalism in the 1890s.

George Baer, a railroad president, epitomized both social Darwinism and paternalism in commenting on a labour strike: "The rights and interests of the laboring man will be protected and cared for not by labor agitators but by the Christian men to whom God in His infinite wisdom has given the control of the property interests of the country." Baer was quoted widely, further fueling sentiment against big business. Baer may have been sincere, but his position was read as a cover for excessive business practices by barons who assumed superiority to everyone else.

Meanwhile, social Darwinism came under attack as circuitous reasoning: Economic success accomplished by abusive practices could be used to justify further abusive practices, which would lead to further success. Social Darwinism was a dog-eat-dog outlook that hardly jibed with democratic ideals, especially not as described in the preamble to the U.S. Constitution, which sought to "promote the general welfare, and secure the blessings of liberty" for everyone—not for only the chosen "fittest." Into these tensions at the turn of the century came public relations pioneer Ivy Lee.

THE IDEAS OF IVY LEE

Coal mine operators, like railroad magnates, were held in the public's contempt at the start of the 20th century. Obsessed with profits, caring little about public sentiment or even the well-being of their employees, mine operators were vulnerable in the new populist wave. Mine workers organized, and 150 000 in Pennsylvania went out on strike in 1902, shutting down the anthracite industry and disrupting coal-dependent industries, including the railroads. The mine operators snubbed reporters, which probably contributed to a pro-union slant in many news stories and worsened the operators' public image. Not until six months into the strike, when President Theodore Roosevelt threatened to take over the mines with Army troops, did the operators settle.

Shaken finally by Roosevelt's threat and recognizing Roosevelt's responsiveness to public opinion, the mine operators began reconsidering how they went about their business. In 1906, with another strike looming, one operator heard about **Ivy Lee**, a young publicist in New York who had new ideas about winning public support. He was hired. In a turnabout in press relations, Lee issued a news release that announced: "The anthracite coal operators, realizing the general public interest in conditions in the mining regions, have arranged to supply the press with all possible information." Then followed a series of releases with information attributed to the mine operators by name—the same people who earlier had preferred anonymity and refused all interview requests. There were no more secret strike-strategy meetings. When operators planned a meeting, reporters covering the impending strike were informed. Although reporters were not admitted into the meetings, summaries of the proceedings were given to them immediately afterward. This relative openness eased long-standing hostility toward the operators, and a strike was averted.

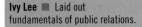

Ivy Lee ■ Laid out fundamentals of public relations.

Lee's success with the mine operators began a career that rewrote the rules on how corporations deal with their various publics. The following are among his accomplishments.

Converting Industry toward Openness Railroads had notoriously secretive policies, not only about their business practices but even about accidents. When the Pennsylvania Railroad sought Ivy Lee's counsel, he advised against suppressing news—especially on things that inevitably would leak out anyway. When a train jumped the rails near Gap, Pennsylvania, Lee arranged for a special car to take reporters to the scene and even take pictures. The Pennsylvania line was applauded in the press for the openness, and coverage of the railroad, which had been negative for years, began changing. A "bad press" continued plaguing other railroads that persisted in their secretive tradition.

Turning Negative News into Positive News When the U.S. Senate proposed investigating International Harvester for monopolistic practices, Lee advised the giant farm implement manufacturer against reflexive obstructionism and silence. A statement went out announcing that the company, confident in its business practices, not only welcomed but also would facilitate an investigation. Then began a campaign that pointed out International Harvester's beneficence toward its employees. The campaign also emphasized other upbeat information about the company.

Ivy Lee

Ludlow Massacre Colorado militiamen, called in to augment company guards, opened fire during a 1914 mine labour dispute and killed women and children. Overnight, John D. Rockefeller Jr. became the object of public hatred. It was a Rockefeller company that owned the mine, and even in New York, where Rockefeller lived, there were rallies demanding his head. Public relations pioneer Ivy Lee advised Rockefeller to tour the Ludlow area as soon as tempers cooled to show his sincere concern and to begin work on a labour contract to meet the concerns of miners. Rockefeller ended up a popular character in the Colorado mining camps.

Putting Corporate Executives on Display In 1914, when workers at a Colorado mine went on strike, company guards fired machine guns and killed several men. More battling followed, during which 2 women and 11 children were killed. It was called the Ludlow Massacre, and **John D. Rockefeller Jr.**, the chief mine owner, was pilloried for what had happened. Rockefeller was an easy target. Like his father, widely despised for the earlier Standard Oil monopolistic practices, John Jr. tried to keep himself out of the spotlight, but suddenly mobs were protesting at his mansion in New York and calling out, "Shoot him down like a dog." Rockefeller asked Ivy Lee what he should do. Lee began whipping up articles about Rockefeller's human side, his family and his generosity. Then, on Lee's advice, Rockefeller announced that he would visit Colorado to see conditions himself. He spent two weeks talking with miners at work and in their homes and meeting their families. It was a news story that reporters could not resist, and it unveiled Rockefeller as a human being, not a far-removed, callous captain of industry. A myth-shattering episode occurred one evening when Rockefeller, after a brief address to miners and their wives, suggested that the floor be cleared for a dance. Before it was all over, John D. Rockefeller Jr. had danced with almost every miner's wife, and the news stories about the evening did a great deal to mitigate antagonism and distrust toward Rockefeller.

Avoiding Puffery and Fluff Ivy Lee came on the scene at a time when many organizations were making extravagant claims about themselves and their products. Circus promoter **P.T. Barnum** made this kind of **puffery** a fine art in the late 1800s, and he had many imitators. It was an age of puffed-up advertising claims and fluffy rhetoric. Lee noted, however, that people soon saw through hyperbolic boasts and lost faith in those who made them. In launching his public relations agency in 1906, Lee vowed to be accurate in everything he said and to provide whatever verification anyone requested. This became part of the creed of good practice in public relations, and it remains so today.

■ Public Relations Services

studypreview Public relations deals with publicity and promotion, but it also involves less visible activities. These include lobbying, fundraising and crisis management. Public relations is distinct from advertising.

HOW PUBLIC RELATIONS IS ORGANIZED

No two institutions are organized in precisely the same way. At General Motors, 200 people work in public relations. In smaller organizations, PR may be one of several hats worn by a single person. Except in the smallest operations, the public relations department usually has three functional areas of responsibility:

External Relations External public relations involves communication with groups and people outside the organization, including customers, dealers, suppliers and community leaders. The external relations unit is usually responsible for encouraging employees to participate in civic activities. Other responsibilities include arranging promotional activities like exhibits, trade shows, conferences and tours.

Public relations people also lobby government agencies and legislators on behalf of their organization, keep the organization abreast of government regulations and legislation, and coordinate relations with political candidates. This may include fundraising for candidates and coordinating political action committees.

In hospitals and nonprofit organizations, a public relations function may include recruiting and scheduling volunteer workers.

Internal Relations Internal public relations involves developing optimal relations with employees, managers, unions, shareholders and other internal groups. In-house newsletters, magazines and brochures are important media for communicating with organizations' internal audiences.

Media Relations Communication with large groups of people outside an organization is practicable only through the mass media. An organization's coordinator of **media relations** responds to news media queries, arranges news conferences and issues news releases. These coordinators coach executives for news interviews and sometimes serve as their organization's spokesperson.

PUBLIC RELATIONS AGENCIES

Even though many organizations have their own public relations staff, they may go to **public relations agencies** for help on specific projects or problems. In the United States today, hundreds of companies specialize in public relations counsel and related services.

The biggest agencies offer a full range of services on a global scale. Hill & Knowlton has offices in Cleveland, its original home; Toronto; Dallas; Frankfurt; Geneva; London; Los Angeles; New York, now its headquarters; Paris; Rome; Seattle; and Washington, D.C. The agency will take on projects anywhere in the world, either on its own or by working with local agencies.

Besides full-service agencies, there are specialized public relations companies, which focus on a narrow range of services. For example, clipping services cut out and provide newspaper and magazine articles and radio and television items of interest to clients. Among specialized agencies are those that focus exclusively on political campaigns. Others coach corporate executives for news interviews. Others coordinate trade shows.

Some agencies bill clients only for services rendered. Others charge clients just to be on call. Agency expenses for specific projects are billed in addition. Staff time usually is charged at an hourly rate that covers the agency's overhead and allows a profit margin. Other expenses are usually billed with a 15 to 17 percent markup.

ACTIVITIES BEYOND PUBLICITY

Full-service public relations agencies provide a wide range of services built on two of the cornerstones of the business: **publicity** and **promotion**. These agencies are ready to conduct media campaigns to rally support for a cause, create an image or turn a problem into an asset. Publicity and promotion, however, are only the most visible services offered by public relations agencies. Others include the following.

Lobbying Every province has hundreds of public relations practitioners whose specialty is representing their clients to legislative bodies and government agencies. In one sense, **lobbyists** are expediters. They know local traditions and customs, and they know who is in

media relations ◼ Using mass media to convey messages.

public relations agencies ◼ Companies that provide public relations services.

publicity ◼ Brings public attention to something.

promotion ◼ Promoting a cause, idea.

lobbyists ◼ Influence public policy, usually legislation or regulations.

media DATABANK

Top Public Relations Firms in Canada

The following are the largest public relations firms in Canada, according to a survey conducted by *Marketing*

Magazine. The list was compiled based on companies that provided financial information.

Company	Gross Revenues, 2003 (in Canadian Dollars)
Thornley Fallis Group	$3.2 million
Torchia Communications	$2.8 million
Allard Johnson Communications	$2.5 million
Marketing Communication Group	$1.5 million
PALM Publicite Marketing	$359 000

Source: Marketing Magazine, June 21, 2004. Reprinted with permission.

a position to affect policy. Lobbyists advise their clients, which include trade associations, corporations, public interest groups and regulated utilities and industries, on how to achieve their goals by working with legislators and government regulators. Many lobbyists call themselves "government relations specialists."

Political Communication Every provincial capital has political consultants whose work is mostly advising candidates for public office in **political communication**. Services include campaign management, survey research, publicity, media relations and image consulting. Political consultants also work on elections, referendums, recalls and other public policy issues.

Image Consulting **Image consulting** has been a growing specialized branch of public relations since the 1970s. Jacqueline Thompson, author of *Directory of Personal Image Consultants*, listed 53 entries in 1981 and has been adding up to 157 new entries a year since then. About these consultants, said Thompson: "They will lower the pitch of your voice, remove your accent, correct your 'body language,' modify your unacceptable behavior, eliminate your negative self-perception, select your wardrobe, restyle your hair, and teach you how to speak off the cuff or read a speech without putting your audience to sleep."

Financial Public Relations Financial public relations dates to the 1920s and 1930s, when the U.S. Securities and Exchange Commission cracked down on abuses in the financial industry. Regulations on promoting sales of securities are complex. It is the job of people in financial PR to know not only the principles of public relations but also the complex regulations governing the promotion of securities in corporate mergers, acquisitions, new issues and stock splits.

Fundraising Some public relations people specialize in fundraising and membership drives. Many colleges, for example, have their own staffs to perform these functions. Others look to fundraising firms to manage capital drives. Such an agency employs a variety of techniques, from mass mailings to telephone soliciting, and charges a percentage of the amount raised.

Contingency Planning Many organizations rely on public relations people to design programs to address problems that can be expected to occur, known as **contingency planning**. Airlines, for example, need detailed plans for handling inevitable plane crashes—situations requiring quick, appropriate responses under tremendous pressure. When a crisis occurs, an organization can turn to public relations people for advice on dealing with it. Some agencies specialize in **crisis management**, which involves picking up the pieces either when a contingency plan fails or when there was no plan to deal with a crisis.

Polling Public-opinion sampling is essential in many public relations projects. Full-service agencies can either conduct surveys themselves or contract with companies that specialize in surveying.

Events Coordination Many public relations people are involved in coordinating a broad range of events, including product announcements, news conferences and convention planning. Some in-house public relations departments and agencies have their own artistic and audiovisual production talent to produce brochures, tapes and other promotional materials. Other agencies contract for these services.

PUBLIC RELATIONS AND ADVERTISING
Both public relations and advertising involve persuasion through the mass media, but most of the similarities end there.

Management Function Public relations people help to shape an organization's policy. This is a management activity, ideally with the organization's chief public relations person offering counsel to other key policymakers at the vice-presidential level. Advertising, in contrast, is not a management function. The work of advertising is much narrower. It focuses on developing persuasive messages, mostly to sell products or services, after all the management decisions have been made.

political communication Advising candidates, groups on public policy issues, usually in elections.

image consulting Coaching individuals for media contacts.

contingency planning Developing programs in advance of an unscheduled but anticipated event.

crisis management Helping a client through an emergency.

Measuring Success Public relations "sells" points of view and images. These are intangibles and therefore are hard to measure. In advertising, success is measurable with tangibles, such as sales, that can be calculated from the bottom line.

Control of Messages When an organization decides that it needs a persuasive campaign, there is a choice between public relations and advertising. One advantage of advertising is that the organization controls the message. By buying space or time in the mass media, an organization has the final say on the content of its advertising messages. In public relations, by contrast, an organization tries to influence the media to tell its story a certain way, but the message that actually goes out is up to the media. For example, a news reporter may lean heavily on a public relations person for information about an organization, but the reporter also may gather information from other sources. In the end, it is the reporter who writes the story. The upside of this is that the message, coming from a journalist, has a credibility with the mass audience that advertisements don't. Advertisements are patently self-serving. The downside of leaving it to the media to create the messages that reach the audience is surrendering control over the messages that go to the public.

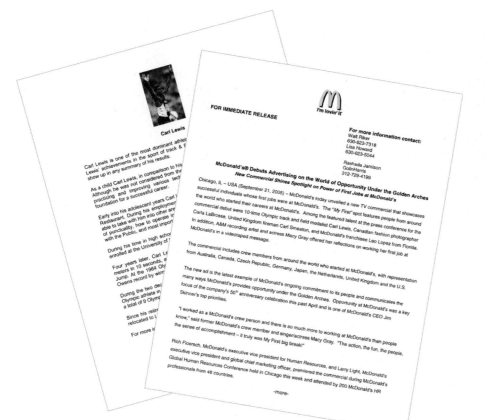

News Release The workhorse of media relations is the news release, issued to newspapers, broadcast stations and other media to stir reporter interest in covering an event or developing a story or in hope of getting a point of view included in news stories. Studies have found that as many as 90 percent of news stories rely to some extent on information in news releases. Some releases even are reported verbatim, particularly in small-market, low-budget newsrooms.

INTEGRATED MARKETING

For many persuasive campaigns, organizations use both public relations and advertising. Increasingly, public relations and advertising people find themselves working together. This is especially true in corporations that have adopted **integrated marketing communication** (IMC), which attempts to coordinate advertising as a marketing tool with promotion and publicity of the sort that public relations experts can provide. Several major advertising agencies, aware of their clients' shift to integrated marketing, have acquired or established public relations subsidiaries to provide a wider range of services under their roof.

It is this overlap that has prompted some advertising agencies to move more into public relations. The WWP Group of London, a global advertising agency, has acquired both Hill & Knowlton, the third-largest public relations company in the United States, and the Ogilvy PR Worldwide, the ninth largest. The Young & Rubicam advertising agency has three public

integrated marketing communication ■
Comprehensive program that links public relations, advertising.

relations subsidiaries: Burson-Marsteller, the largest; Cohn & Wolf, the 13th largest; and Creswell, Munsell, Fultz & Zirbel, the 50th largest. These are giant enterprises that reflect the conglomeration and globalization of both advertising and public relations.

To describe IMC, media critic James Ledbetter suggests thinking of the old Charlie the Tuna ads, in which a cartoon fish made you chuckle and identify with the product—and established a brand name. That's not good enough for IMC. "By contrast," Ledbetter says, "IMC encourages tuna buyers to think about all aspects of the product. If polls find that consumers are worried about dolphins caught in tuna nets, then you might stick a big 'Dolphin Safe' label on the tins and set up a website featuring interviews with tuna fishermen." The new wave of IMC, according to one of its primary texts, is "respectful, not patronizing; dialogue-seeking, not monologuic; responsive, not formula-driven. It speaks to the highest point of common interest—not the lowest common denominator."

Public relations and advertising crossovers are hardly new. One area of traditional overlap is **institutional advertising**, which involves producing ads to promote an image rather than a product. The fuzzy, feel-good ads of agricultural conglomerate Archer Daniels Midland, which pepper Sunday morning network television, are typical.

institutional advertising ■ Paid space and time to promote an institution's image, position.

■ Media Relations

study<u>preview</u> **Public relations people generally favour candor in working with the news media. Even so, some organizations opt to stonewall journalistic inquiries. An emerging school of thought in public relations is to challenge negative news coverage aggressively and publicly.**

OPEN MEDIA RELATIONS

The common wisdom among public relations people today is to be open and candid with the mass media. It is a principle that dates to Ivy Lee, and case studies abound to confirm its effectiveness. A classic case study on this point is the Tylenol crisis.

Johnson & Johnson had spent many years and millions of dollars to inspire public confidence in its painkiller Tylenol. By 1982 the product was the leader in a crowded field of headache remedies with 36 percent of the market. Then disaster struck. Seven people in Chicago died after taking Tylenol capsules laced with cyanide. James Burke, president of Johnson & Johnson, and Lawrence Foster, vice-president for public relations, moved quickly. Within hours, Johnson & Johnson had accomplished the following:

- Halted the manufacture and distribution of Tylenol.
- Removed Tylenol products from retailers' shelves.
- Launched a massive advertising campaign requesting people to exchange Tylenol capsules for a safe replacement.
- Summoned 50 public relations employees from Johnson & Johnson and its subsidiary companies to staff a press centre to answer media and consumer questions forthrightly.
- Ordered an internal company investigation of the Tylenol manufacturing and distribution process.
- Promised full co-operation with government investigators.
- Ordered the development of tamper-proof packaging for the reintroduction of Tylenol products after the contamination problem was resolved.

Investigators determined within days that an urban terrorist had poisoned the capsules. Although the news media exonerated Johnson & Johnson of negligence, the company nonetheless had a tremendous problem: how to restore public confidence in Tylenol. Many former Tylenol users were reluctant to take a chance, and the Tylenol share of the analgesic market dropped to 6 percent.

To address the problem, Johnson & Johnson called in the Burson-Marsteller public relations agency. Burson-Marsteller recommended a media campaign to capitalize on the high marks the news media had given the company for openness during the crisis. Mailgrams went out inviting journalists to a 30-city video teleconference to hear James

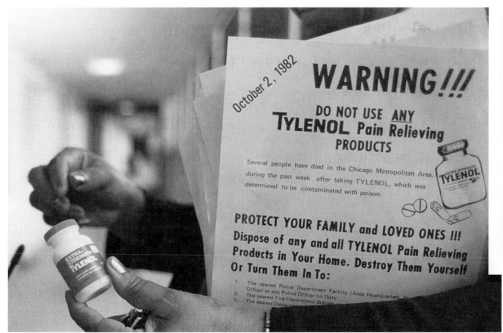

James Burke

Product-Tampering Crisis When cyanide-laced Tylenol capsules killed seven people in Chicago, the manufacturer, Johnson & Johnson, responded quickly. Company President James Burke immediately pulled the product off retailers' shelves and ordered company publicists to set up a press centre to answer news media inquiries as fully as possible. Burke's action and candor helped to restore the public's shaken confidence in Tylenol, and the product resumed its significant market share after the crisis ended. It turned out that it probably was somebody outside Johnson & Johnson's production and distributing system who had contaminated the capsules rather than a manufacturing lapse.

Burke announce the reintroduction of the product. Six hundred reporters turned out, and Johnson & Johnson officials took their questions live.

To stir even wider attention, 7500 **media kits** had been sent to newsrooms the day before the teleconference. The kits included a news release and a bevy of supporting materials: photographs, charts and background information.

The resulting news coverage was extensive. On average, newspapers carried 32 column inches of copy on the announcement. Network television and radio as well as local stations also afforded heavy coverage. Meanwhile, Johnson & Johnson executives, who had attended a workshop on how to make favourable television appearances, made themselves available as guests on the network morning shows and talk shows. At the same time, Johnson & Johnson distributed 80 million free coupons to encourage people to buy Tylenol again.

Sarah Evans of the Canadian Public Relations Society says that "this is the classic example in public relations annals of how to deal with a situation. You take immediate action, you worry about people first, you provide as much information as you can as fast as you've got it. Did Johnson & Johnson stock suffer? No. Did Tylenol suffer? No."

> **media kit** ■ A packet provided to news reporters to tell the story in an advantageous way.

PROACTIVE MEDIA RELATIONS

Although public relations campaigns cannot control what the media say, public relations people can help to shape how news media report issues by taking the initiative. In the Tylenol crisis, for example, Johnson & Johnson reacted quickly and decisively and took control of disseminating information, which, coupled with full disclosure, headed off false rumours that could have caused further damage. This is a good example of **proactive media relations**.

> **proactive media relations** ■ Taking initiative to release information.

Proactive Crisis Responses A principle in crisis management is to seize leadership on the story. This involves anticipating what journalists will want to know and providing it to them before they even have time to formulate their questions. Ivy Lee did this time and again, and Johnson & Johnson did it in 1982.

For successful crisis management, public relations people need strong ongoing relationships with an organization's top officials. Otherwise, when a crisis strikes, they likely will have difficulty rounding up the kind of breaking information they need to deal effectively with the news media. During the 1991 Persian Gulf War, Pentagon spokesperson **Pete Williams** received high marks as a public relations person for shaping news coverage of the conflict. Williams did this by tapping his close working relationships with Secretary of Defense Dick Cheney and the Joint Chiefs of Staff for information favourable to the war effort. At regular news briefings, sometimes several a day, Williams provided so much grist for the journalistic mill that reporters were overwhelmed at putting it together for stories, which reduced the time available for them to go after stories on their own. The war was reported largely as the Pentagon wanted.

Ongoing Media Relationships

Good media relations cannot be forged in the fire of a crisis. Organizations that survive a crisis generally have a history of solid media relations. Their public relations staff people know reporters, editors and news directors on a first-name basis. They avoid hyping news releases on routine matters, and they work hard at earning the trust of journalists.

Many public relations people, in fact, are seasoned journalists themselves, and they understand how journalists go about their work. It is their journalistic background that made them attractive candidates for their PR jobs. Pete Williams, for example, was a television news reporter before making a midcareer shift to join Dick Cheney's staff in Washington when Cheney was first elected to Congress from Wyoming.

Sound Operating Principles

An underlying strength that helped to see Johnson & Johnson through the Tylenol crisis was the company's credo. The credo was a written vow that Johnson & Johnson's first responsibility was to "those who use our products and services." The credo, which had been promoted in-house for years, said, "Every time a business hires, builds, sells or buys, it is acting *for the people* as well as *for itself,* and it must be prepared to accept full responsibility." With such a sound operating principle, Johnson & Johnson's crisis response was, in some respects, almost reflexive. Going silent, for example, would have run counter to the principles that Johnson & Johnson people had accepted as part of their corporate culture for years.

AMBIVALENCE IN MEDIA RELATIONS

Despite the advantages of open media relations, there are companies that choose not to embrace that approach.

Some corporations take a middle ground, currying media coverage selectively. This is an example of **ambivalent media relations**. Giant IBM, which receives 30 000 media queries a year, frets that news coverage would underscore its sheer size and invite federal antitrust scrutiny. IBM has long turned away journalists' questions on many issues, including the company's long-term planning. The corporation's PR chief, Seth McCormick, explicitly spurned Ivy Lee's maxim that corporate executives should be "on display." In an interview, McCormick told *Fortune:* "We control what is said about the company through the sparsity of heads for the outside world to talk to. We like it that way."

Public relations never figured much in Sam Walton's thinking as he built the world's largest retail chain, Wal-Mart. To Walton, PR was a frill. It didn't fit his keep-costs-minimal concept. Even after Walton died, his legacy lingered. By 2005 his company had only a 17-member public relations staff—minuscule in business. How minuscule? Wal-Mart sales exceeded $285 billion, yet the company had but one public relations staffer per $216 billion in earnings. Put another way, the company had one public relations person per 76 000 employees.

Realizing that inattentiveness to image would no longer work, Wal-Mart had begun to dabble in traditional public relations techniques in 2004 by sending its chief executive out for a few broadcast interviews. The company also invested in feel-good, paid television messages depicting happy employees and suppliers. In 2005 the company invited reporters to its spartan corporate headquarters in Bentonville, Arkansas, for the first time.

This was all new for Wal-Mart. At the media open house in Bentonville, a Wal-Mart senior executive mounted a stage seeming to expect reporters to jump to their feet in cheering enthusiasm, as adoring Wal-Mart employees always do. Discombobulated by the news reporters' cool, journalistically detached demeanour, the executive blew a basketball joke that was intended as an icebreaker. Realizing that the joke had bombed, he started to elaborate on how he thought it was funny. Finally a reporter shouted, "Blah, blah, blah."

Not only was the executive unprepared for the meeting, he was clueless about how journalists approach their work. These are fundamental errors in public relations that must be anticipated and resolved before executives put themselves on display. A major component of public relations is to be on the same wavelength as the news media.

Rescuing the executive from disaster, somebody shouted out an on-the-spot lesson about news reporters: "They don't applaud. They don't play basketball." The executive laughed, acknowledging a lesson learned the hard way. Everyone else laughed too, easing the tension of the first moments of what Wal-Mart had hoped would be a grand excursion into open public relations.

Herb Schmertz

Mobil Advertorial
Many public relations practitioners seek to avoid confrontation, but Herb Schmertz of Mobil bought space in newspapers and magazines beginning in the 1970s to lay out his company's positions on controversial issues and even to be confrontational. Schmertz tackled the news media when he felt Mobil had not received a fair shake in coverage. These position statements are called "advertorials" because they are in space purchased as advertising and their content is like an editorial.

ADVERSARIAL PUBLIC RELATIONS
Public relations took on aggressive, even feisty tactics when Mobil Oil decided in the 1970s not to take media criticism lightly any more. **Herb Schmertz**, vice-president for Mobil's public affairs, charted a new course by:

- Filing formal complaints with news organizations when coverage was unfair in the company's view.
- Taking Mobil's case directly to the general public with paid advertising, called **advertorials**—a splicing of the words "advertising" and "editorial"—that explained the company's views.
- Sending corporate representatives on media tours to spread Mobil's side to as many constituencies as possible.

Schmertz's energetic counterattacks, an example of **adversarial public relations**, were a departure from conventional wisdom in public relations, which was to let criticism go unanswered or, at most, to complain privately to executives of news organizations that negative coverage is unwarranted. The conventional wisdom was that a public response would only bring more attention to the negative coverage.

In abandoning passivity, Mobil was adapting what sports fans call the Red Auerbach technique. Auerbach, the legendary coach of the Boston Celtics, was known for criticizing

Herb Schmertz ■ Pioneered advertorials.

advertorials ■ Paid advertisements that state an editorial position.

adversarial public relations ■ Attacking critics openly.

referees. He realized he would never get a ref to change a call, but he believed that refs would be less inclined to make questionable calls against the Celtics in the future if they knew that Auerbach would jump all over them. Mobil President Rawleigh Warner Jr. explained the new Mobil policy this way: "People know that if they take a swipe at us, we will fight back."

Schmertz employed the full range of PR tools in 1974 when ABC aired a television documentary that raised critical questions about the U.S. oil industry. Mobil objected first to ABC and then fired off a formal complaint to the National News Council, a volunteer media watchdog group. Mobil claimed 32 inaccuracies and instances of unfairness and requested that the council investigate. Mobil also issued an unusually lengthy news release, quoting from the documentary and offering point-by-point rebuttals.

Advertorials were part of Mobil's initiatives. Under Schmertz, as much as $6 million a year went into newspaper and magazine ads explaining the company's position. Mobil also began producing its own television programs on energy issues and providing them free to stations. The programs had a journalistic tone, and many stations ran them as if they were actual documentaries rather than part of Mobil's media campaign.

The jury is still out on whether Schmertz's aggressive sparring is good policy. Most organizations continue to follow the traditional thinking that taking on the media only generates more attention on the original bad news. On the other hand, Schmertz's approach has been tried by some major corporations. Bechtel, Illinois Power and Kaiser Aluminum all have called for independent investigations of stories that reflected badly on them.

Another adversarial approach, though not recommended by most public relations people, is for an offended organization to sever relations with the source of unfavourable news—an **information boycott**. In 1954, in a spectacular pout, General Motors cut off contact with *Wall Street Journal* reporters and withdrew advertising from the newspaper. This approach carries great risks:

- By going silent, an organization loses avenues for conveying its message to mass audiences.
- An organization that yanks advertising to punish detractors is perceived negatively for coercively wielding its economic might.
- An organization that quits advertising in an effective advertising medium will lose sales.

A boycott differs from Schmertz's adversarial approach in an important respect. Schmertz responded to negative news by contributing to the exchange of information and ideas, which is positive in a democratic society. An information boycott, on the other hand, restricts the flow of information. Today, GM's policy has returned to the conventional wisdom of not arguing with anyone who buys paper by the ton and ink by the barrel—with the exception of its suit against NBC for faking the explosion of a GMC truck.

information boycott ■ Severing ties with news media.

■ **Professionalization**

study preview Public relations has a tarnished image that stems from short-sighted promotion and whitewashing techniques of the late 1800s. Although some dubious practices continue, PR leaders are working to improve standards.

A TARNISHED IMAGE

Unsavoury elements in the heritage of public relations remain a heavy burden. P.T. Barnum, whose name became synonymous with hype, attracted crowds to his stunts and shows in the late 1800s with extravagant promises. Sad to say, some promoters still use Barnum's tactics. The claims for snake oils and elixirs from Barnum's era live on in commercials for pain relievers and cold remedies. The early response of tycoons to muckraking attacks, before Ivy Lee came along, was **whitewashing**—covering up the abuses but not correcting them. It is no wonder that the term *PR* is sometimes used derisively. To say something is "all PR" means that it lacks substance. Of people whose apparent positive qualities are a mere façade, it may be said that they have "good PR."

whitewashing ■ Covering up.

Media PEOPLE

Edward Bernays

Edward Bernays

Integrity was important to public relations pioneer Edward Bernays. When he was asked by agents of fascist dictators Francisco Franco and Adolf Hitler to improve their images in the United States, he said no. "I wouldn't do for money what I wouldn't do without money," Bernays said.

After graduation from college in 1912, Edward Bernays tried press agentry. He was good at it, landing free publicity for whoever would hire him. Soon his bosses included famous tenor Enrico Caruso and actor Otis Skinner. Bernays felt, however, that his success was tainted by the disdain in which press agents were held in general. He also saw far greater potential for affecting public opinion than his fellow press agents did. From Bernays's discomfort and vision was born the concept of modern public relations. His 1923 book *Crystallizing Public Opinion* outlined a new craft he called public relations.

Bernays saw good public relations as counsel to clients. He called the public relations practitioner a "special pleader." The concept was modeled partly on the long-established lawyer–client relationship in which the lawyer, or counsellor, suggests courses of action. Because of his seminal role in defining what public relations is, Bernays sometimes is called the "Father of PR," although some people say the honour should be shared with Ivy Lee.

No matter, there is no question of Bernays's ongoing contributions. He taught the first course in public relations in 1923 at New York University. Bernays encouraged firm methodology in public relations, a notion that was captured in the title of a book he edited in 1955: *The Engineering of Consent*. He long advocated the professionalization of the field, which laid the groundwork for the accreditation of the sort the Public Relations Society of America has developed.

Throughout his career, Bernays stressed that public relations people need a strong sense of responsibility. In one reflective essay, he wrote, "Public relations practiced as a profession is an art applied to a science in which the public interest and not pecuniary motivation is the primary consideration. The engineering of consent in this sense assumes a constructive social role. Regrettably, public relations, like other professions, can be abused and used for anti-social purposes. I have tried to make the profession socially responsible as well as economically viable."

Bernays became the Grand Old Man of public relations, still attending PRSA and other professional meetings past his 100th birthday. He died in 1993 at age 102.

Although journalists rely heavily on public relations people for information, many journalists look at PR practitioners with suspicion. Not uncommon among seasoned journalists are utterances such as "I've never met a PR person I couldn't distrust." Such cynicism flows partly from the journalists' self-image as unfettered truth-seekers whose only obligation is serving their audience's needs. PR people, on the other hand, are seen as obligated to their employers, whose interests do not always dovetail with the public good. Behind their backs, PR people are called "flaks," a takeoff on the World War II slang for anti-aircraft fire intended to stop enemy bombers. PR **flacks**, as journalists use the term, interfere with journalistic truth-seeking by putting forth slanted, self-serving information that is not necessarily the whole story.

flacks ■ Derisive word for public relations people.

The journalism–PR tension is exacerbated by a common newsroom view that PR people try to get free news-hole space for their messages rather than buying airtime and column inches. This view might seem strange, considering that 50 to 90 percent of all news stories either originate with, or contain information supplied by, PR people. It is also strange considering that many PR people are former news reporters and editors. No matter how uncomfortable PR people and journalists are as bedfellows, they are bedfellows nonetheless.

Some public relations people have tried to leapfrog the negative baggage attached to the term *PR* by abandoning it. The U.S. military shucked *PR* and tried **public information**, but it found itself still dogged by the same distrust that surrounded "public relations." The military then tried *public affairs,* but that was no solution either. Many organizations have tried

public information ■ One alternative word for public relations; others are public affairs, corporate communication.

communication as a way around the problem. Common labels today include the military's current *public affairs* offices and businesses' *corporate communication* departments.

STANDARDS AND CERTIFICATION

In 1948, two public relations groups, one in Montreal and the other in Toronto, merged. By 1953, they became the **Canadian Public Relations Society** (CPRS); in 1957, they became recognized as a national society. Today, CPRS has 16 member societies in major cities across Canada. The association adopted the following code of professional standards. Although CPRS is a Canadian association, its codes clearly reflect lessons learned in both the United States and Canada.

Canadian Public Relations Society Code of Professional Standards

Members of the Canadian Public Relations Society feel strongly about standards within the profession and abide by the following codes of ethics:

- A member shall practice public relations according to the highest professional standards.
- A member shall deal fairly and honestly with the communications media and the public.
- A member shall practice the highest standards of honesty, accuracy, integrity and truth, and shall not knowingly disseminate false or misleading information.
- A member shall deal fairly with past or present employers/clients, with fellow practitioners, and with members of other professions.
- A member shall be prepared to disclose the name of their employer or client for whom public communications are made and refrain from associating themselves with anyone that would not respect such policy.
- A member shall protect the confidences of present, former and prospective employers/clients.
- A member shall not represent conflicting or competing interests without the express consent of those concerned, given after a full disclosure of the facts.
- A member shall not guarantee specified results beyond the member's capacity to achieve.
- Members shall personally accept no fees, commissions, gifts or any other considerations for professional services from anyone except employers or clients for whom the services were specifically performed.

(Reprinted by permission of the CPRS.)

In a further professionalization step, the CPRS established a certification process. Those who meet the criteria and pass exams are allowed to place **APR**, which stands for *accredited public relations professional,* after their names. Canadian public relations professionals can apply for accreditation only after they've worked in the business for at least five years. Exams are held once a year.

CHAPTER 9 **Wrap-Up**

When Ivy Lee hung up a shingle in New York for a new publicity agency in 1906, he wanted to distance himself from the huckstering that marked most publicity at the time. To do that, Lee promised to deal only in legitimate news about the agency's clients and no fluff. He invited journalists to pursue more information about the agency's clients. He also vowed to be honest and accurate. Those principles remain the bulwark of good public relations practice today.

Questions for Review

1. What is public relations? How is public relations connected to the mass media?
2. Why did big business become interested in the techniques and principles of public relations beginning in the late 1800s?
3. How is public relations a management tool?
4. What is the range of activities in which public relations people are involved?
5. What kind of relationship do most people strive to have with the mass media?
6. Why does public relations have a bad image? What are public relations professionals doing about it?

Questions for Critical Thinking

1. When Ivy Lee accepted the Pennsylvania Railroad as a client in 1906, he saw the job as "interpreting the Pennsylvania Railroad to the public and interpreting the public to the Pennsylvania Railroad."
2. How are public relations practitioners trying to overcome the complaints from journalists that they are flacks interfering with an unfettered pursuit of truth?
3. Defend or rebuke Canadian Joyce Nelson's idea that public relations creates a persona for a corporation in an attempt to hide its shadow.
4. How do public relations agencies turn profits?
5. When does an institution with its own in-house public relations operation need to hire a PR agency?
6. Explain the concept of enlightened self-interest.
7. How did the concept of social Darwinism contribute to the emergence of modern public relations?
8. Showman P.T. Barnum epitomized 19th-century press agentry with extravagant claims, such as promoting the midget Tom Thumb as a Civil War general. To attract crowds to a tour by an unknown European soprano, Jenny Lind, Barnum labeled her "the Swedish Nightingale." Would such promotional methods work today? Keep in mind that Barnum, explaining his methods, once said, "There's a sucker born every minute."

Deepening Your media LITERACY

Do press releases serve the public?
STEP 1   Get a copy of a newspaper that you can mark up.

Dig Deeper
STEP 2   Mark all the stories that you think came from press releases, in whole or in part. Choose one of them—it can be on any subject, for example, an upcoming concert or event, an award ceremony or an announcement from a local business.

What Do You Think?
STEP 3   Answer these questions in relation to the press release you chose:

1. How does this story benefit the public? Which public? Who else does it benefit?
2. Is this story, or the part of it that came from a press release, socially responsible?
3. Is the press release proactive?

If all the press releases were taken out of the newspaper, how much news would you miss?

Keeping Up to Date

PRWeek is the industry trade journal.

The trade journal *O'Dwyer's PR Services* tracks the industry on a monthly basis.

Other sources of ongoing information are *Public Relations Journal, Public Relations Quarterly* and *Public Relations Review.*

For Further Learning

Scott M. Cutlip, Allen H. Center, and Glen M. Broom. *Effective Public Relations,* 6th edition (Prentice Hall, 1985).

Stewart Ewen. *PR! A Social History of Spin* (Basic Books, 1996).

Rene A. Henry. *Marketing Public Relations* (Iowa State University Press, 2000).

Ray Eldon Hiebert. *Courtier to the Crowd: The Story of Ivy Lee and the Development of Public Relations* (Iowa State University Press, 1966).

Robert Jackall and Janice M. Hirota. *Image Makers: Advertising, Public Relations and the Ethos of Advocacy* (University of Chicago Press, 2000).

Bruce Livesey. "PR Wars: How the PR Industry Flacks for Big Business." *Canadian Dimension* (November–December 1996).

George S. McGovern and Leonard F. Guttridge. *The Great Coalfield War* (Houghton Mifflin, 1972).

Kevin McManus. "Video Coaches." *Forbes* 129 (June 7, 1982).

Lael M. Moynihan. "Horrendous PR Crises: What They Did When the Unthinkable Happened." *Media History Digest* 8 (Spring–Summer 1988): 1, 19–25.

Joyce Nelson. *The Sultans of Sleaze: Public Relations and the Media* (Between the Lines, 1989).

Barbara Pollock. "A Profession for Tomorrow." Canadian Public Relations Society. Available online at www.cprs.ca/cprsprof_tom.html (July 9, 1998).

"The Rankings." *Marketing Magazine* (June 21, 2004).

Sally J. Ray. *Strategic Communication in Crisis Management: Lessons from the Airline Industry* (Quorum, 1999).

Herbert Schmertz and William Novak. *Good-bye to the Low Profile: The Art of Creative Confrontation* (Little, Brown, 1986).

Michael S. Sweeney. *Secrets of Victory: The Office of Censorship and the American Press and Radio in World War II* (University of North Carolina Press, 2001).

Ray Truchansky. "In Today's Business World, Good PR is Priceless." *Edmonton Journal* (April 7, 2001).

Larry Tye. *The Father of Spin: Edward L. Bernays and the Birth of Public Relations* (Crown, 1998).

Jean Valin. "Truth Pays Dividends with Public." Canadian Public Relations Society. Available online at www.cprs.ca/cprstruth.htm (July 9, 1998).

Perry Dean Young. *God's Bullies: Power Politics and Religious Tyranny* (Henry Holt, 1982).

Sex in the Clams? Author Wilson Bryan Key is convinced that Madison Avenue hides sex in advertisements to attract attention and sell products. To demonstrate his point, he outlines the human figures that he saw in an orgy in a photograph of clam strips on a restaurant menu. Most advertising people dismiss his claims. It's a good example of what communication theorists call connotation.

Advertising

chapter

10

Media in Theory

Subliminal Advertising

Jim Vicary claimed in 1957 that he had studied the effect of inserting into movies messages such as "Drink Coca-Cola" and "Eat popcorn." The messages, although flashed too fast to be recognized by the human eye, still registered in the brain and, said Vicary, prompted moviegoers to rush to the snack bar. In experiments at a New Jersey movie house, he said, Coke sales increased 18 percent and popcorn sales almost 60 percent. Vicary's report stirred great interest, and also alarm, but researchers who tried to replicate his study found no evidence to support his claim.

Despite Vicary's dubious claims, psychologists have identified a phenomenon they call **subception**, in which certain behaviour sometimes seems to be triggered by messages perceived subliminally. Whether the effect works outside of laboratory experiments and whether the effect is strong enough to prod a consumer to buy something is uncertain. Nevertheless, there remains a widespread belief among the general population that **subliminal advertising** works, and fortunes are being made by people who peddle various devices and systems with extravagant claims that they can control human behaviour. Among these are the "hidden" messages in stores' sound systems that say shoplifting is not nice.

This idea that advertising is loaded with hidden messages has been taken to extremes by **Wilson Bryan Key**, who spins out books alleging that plugs are hidden in all kinds of places for devil worship, homosexuality, and a variety of libertine activities. He has accused Nabisco of baking the word *sex* into Ritz crackers. At Howard Johnson restaurants, he has charged, placemat pictures of plates heaped with clams portray orgies and bestiality. Though widely read, Key offers no evidence beyond his own observations and interpretations. In advertising circles, his views are dismissed as amusing but wacky. The views of Nabisco and Howard Johnson are less charitable.

Jim Vicary ■ Made dubious subliminal advertising claims.

subception ■ Receiving subconscious messages that trigger behaviour.

subliminal advertising ■ Ads that cannot be consciously perceived.

Wilson Bryan Key ■ Believes he sees subliminal advertising widely used.

Wilson Bryan Key

In 1990, Wilson Bryan Key's views suffered a serious setback. He was a primary witness in a highly publicized Nevada trial on whether the Judas Priest heavy metal album *Stained Glass* had triggered the suicide of an 18-year-old and the attempted suicide of his 20-year-old friend. The families said that the pair had obsessed about a Judas Priest album that dealt with suicide and that one song was subliminally embedded with the words "Do it" over and over. The families' attorneys hired Key as an expert witness to help make their point. From Key's perspective, the case did not go well. Millions of television viewers who followed the trial strained to make out the supposed words "Do it," but even when isolated from the rest of the music, they were almost impossible to decipher. It turned out the sounds were neither lyrics nor even vocals but rather instrumental effects. Members of Judas Priest testified that they had not equated the sound to any words at all and had inserted it for artistic effect, hardly to encourage suicide. The jury sided with Judas Priest, and Key left town with his wobbly ideas about subliminal messages having taken a serious blow under a jury's scrutiny.

David Ogilvy, founder of the Ogilvy & Mather agency, once made fun of claims like Key's, pointing out the absurdity of "millions of suggestible consumers getting up from their armchairs and rushing like zombies through the traffic on their way to buy the product at the nearest store." The danger of "Vote Bolshevik" being flashed during the *NBC Nightly News* is remote, and whether it would have any effect is questionable.

media TIMELINE

DEVELOPMENT OF ADVERTISING

1468	William Caxton promoted a book with the first printed advertisement.	**1890s**	Brand names emerged as an advertising technique.	**1963**	Canadian Code of Advertising Standards was established.
1704	Joseph Campbell included advertisements in *The Boston News-Letter.*	**1899**	Anson McKim opened the first Canadian advertising agency.	**1980s**	Conglomeration hit the advertising world through mergers and acquisitions.
1833	Benjamin Day created *The New York Sun* as a combination news and advertising vehicle.	**1950s**	David Ogilvy devised brand imaging technique.	**2003**	Store brands emerged as a major challenge to brand names.
		1950s	Jack Trout devised positioning technique.		
1869	F. Wayland Ayer opened the first advertising agency, in Philadelphia.	**1957**	James Vicary claimed success for subliminal advertising.	**2004**	Thirty-second spot during the Super Bowl cost US$2.5 million.
		1960s	Rosser Reeves devised unique selling proposition technique.		

■ Importance of Advertising

study**preview** Advertising is vital in a consumer economy. Without it, people would have a hard time even knowing what products and services were available. Advertising also is the financial basis of important contemporary mass media.

CONSUMER ECONOMIES

The essential role of advertising in a modern consumer economy is obvious if you think about how people decide what to buy. If a shoe manufacturer were unable to tout the virtues of its footwear by advertising in the mass media, people would have a hard time learning about the product, let alone knowing whether it is what they want.

In *Canadian Advertising in Action,* Keith Tuckwell estimates that Canadian companies spend more than $8 billion a year on advertising. General Motors of Canada alone spends about $130 million on advertising each year. When production of goods and services is up, so is advertising spending. When production falters, as it did in the early 1990s, many manufacturers, distributors and retailers reduce their advertising expenditures.

ADVERTISING AND PROSPERITY

Advertising's phenomenal continuing growth has been a product of a plentiful society. In a poor society with a shortage of goods, people line up for necessities like food and clothing. Advertising has no role and serves no purpose when survival is the question. With prosperity, however, people have not only discretionary income but also a choice of ways to spend it. Advertising is the vehicle that provides information and rationales to help them decide how to enjoy their prosperity.

Besides being a product of economic prosperity, advertising contributes to prosperity. By dangling desirable commodities and services before mass audiences, advertising can inspire people to greater individual productivity so that they can have more income to buy the things that are advertised.

Advertising also can introduce efficiency into the economy by allowing comparison shopping without in-person inspections of all the alternatives. Efficiencies also can result when advertising alerts consumers to superior and less costly products and services, which displace outdated, outmoded and inefficient offerings.

On the other hand, Canadian economist **John Kenneth Galbraith**, in his classic book *The Affluent Society,* argued that advertising did more than just satisfy our *needs.* It actually created *wants.* By creating wants, those in power could sell products that made people live beyond their means and buy more than they needed. Andrew Potter, writing in *Maclean's,* refutes Galbraith's ideas. Potter claims each of us has free will (or at least self-restraint) and isn't easily duped by every ad campaign we see. "That is not to say that advertising isn't harmless, but that it's more like seduction than brainwashing. Just as you can't seduce someone who is not interested in sex, you can't sell teeth whitener to someone who is not concerned about their appearance."

John Kenneth Galbraith ■ Advertising isn't about needs, it's about wants.

ADVERTISING AND DEMOCRACY

Advertising first took off as a modern phenomenon in the United States and Canada more than elsewhere, which has given rise to a theory that advertising and democracy are connected. This theory notes that North Americans, early in their history as a democracy, were required by their political system to hold individual opinions. They looked for information so that they could evaluate their leaders and vote on public policy. This emphasis on individuality and reason paved the way for advertising: Just as Americans looked to the mass media for information on political matters, they also came to look to the media for information on buying decisions.

Advertising has another important role in democratic societies in generating most of the operating revenue for newspapers, magazines, television and radio. Without advertising, many of the media on which people rely for information, for entertainment and for the exchange of ideas on public issues would not exist as we know them.

■. Origins of Advertising

study<u>preview</u> **Advertising is the product of great forces that have shaped modern society, beginning with Gutenberg's movable type, which made mass-produced messages possible.**

STEPCHILD OF TECHNOLOGY

Advertising is not a mass medium, but it relies on media to carry its messages. **Johannes Gutenberg**'s movable type, which permitted mass production of the printed word, made mass-produced advertising possible. First came flyers. Then advertisements in newspapers and magazines were introduced. In the 1800s, when technology created high-speed presses that could produce enough copies for larger audiences, advertisers used them

Johannes Gutenberg ■ Inventor of printing press which, in turn, made mass media and advertising possible.

to expand markets. With the introduction of radio, advertisers learned how to use electronic communication. Then came television and the internet.

Flyers were the first form of printed advertising. The British printer **William Caxton** issued the first printed advertisement in 1468 to promote one of his books. In America, publisher **John Campbell** of *The Boston News-Letter* ran the first advertisement in 1704, a notice from somebody wanting to sell an estate on Long Island. Colonial newspapers listed cargo arriving from Europe and invited readers to come, look and buy.

INDUSTRIAL REVOLUTION

The genius of **Benjamin Day**'s *New York Sun,* in 1833 the first penny newspaper (see Chapter 8), was that it recognized and exploited so many changes spawned by the Industrial Revolution. Steam-powered presses made large press runs possible. Factories drew great numbers of people to jobs within geographically small areas to which newspapers could be distributed quickly. The jobs also drew immigrants who were eager to learn—from newspapers as well as other sources—about their adopted country. Industrialization, coupled with the labour union movement, created unprecedented wealth, with labourers gaining a share of the new prosperity. A consumer economy was emerging, although it was primitive by today's standards.

A key to the success of Day's *Sun* was that, at a penny a copy, it was affordable for almost everyone. Of course, Day's production expenses exceeded a penny a copy. Just as the commercial media do today, Day looked to advertisers to pick up the slack. As Day wrote in his first issue, "The object of this paper is to lay before the public, at a price within the means of everyone, all the news of the day, and at the same time afford an advantageous medium for advertising." Day and imitator penny press publishers sought larger and larger circulations, knowing that merchants would see the value in buying space to reach so much purchasing power.

National advertising took root in the 1840s as railroads, another creation of the Industrial Revolution, spawned new networks for mass distribution of manufactured goods. National brands developed, and their producers looked to magazines, also delivered by rail, to promote sales. By 1869 the rail network linked the Atlantic and Pacific coasts.

PIONEER AGENCIES

By 1869 most merchants recognized the value of advertising, but they grumbled about the time it took away from their other work. In that grumbling, a young Philadelphia man sensed opportunity. **F. Wayland Ayer**, aged 20, speculated that merchants, and even national manufacturers, would welcome a service company to help them create advertisements and place them in publications. Ayer feared, however, that his idea might not be taken seriously by potential clients because of his youth and inexperience. So when Ayer opened a shop, he borrowed his father's name, N.W. Ayer, for the shingle. The Ayer agency not only created ads but also offered the array of services that agencies still offer clients today:

- Counsel on selling products and services.
- Design services, that is, actually creating advertisements and campaigns.
- Expertise on placing advertisements in advantageous media.

In 1872, Toronto newspapers began selling advertising space to clients outside their geographic area when the *Toronto Mail* sent a young man to Montreal to sell advertising space. **Anson McKim** saw this as a great opportunity and he began to act as a broker for other publications in south-central Ontario. By 1889, McKim opened Canada's first ad agency in Montreal, A. McKim and Company. McKim also published the first directory of media in Canada, *The Canadian Newspaper Directory,* in 1892.

▛■ Advertising Agencies

study**preview** Central in modern advertising are the agencies that create and place ads on behalf of their clients. These agencies are generally funded by the media in which they place ads. In effect, this makes agency services free to advertisers.

AGENCY STRUCTURE

Full-service advertising agencies conduct market research for their clients, design and produce advertisements and choose the media in which the advertisement will run. The 500 leading U.S. agencies employ 120 000 people worldwide. The responsibilities of people who work at advertising agencies fall into these broad categories:

Creativity This category includes copywriters, graphics experts and layout people. These creative people generally report to **creative directors**, art directors and copy supervisors.

Liaison Most of these people are **account executives**, who work with clients. Account executives are responsible for understanding clients' needs, communicating those needs to the creative staff and going back to clients with the creative staff's ideas.

Buying Agency employees called **media buyers** determine the most effective media in which to place ads, and then place them.

Research Agency research staffs generate information on target consumer groups, data that can guide the creative and media staffs.

Many agencies also employ technicians and producers who turn ideas into camera-ready proofs, colour plates, videotape, audio clips and web-based ads, although a lot of production work is contracted to specialty companies. Besides full-service agencies there are creative boutiques, which specialize in preparing messages; media buying houses, which recommend strategy on placing ads; and other narrowly focused agencies.

creative director ■ Key person in ad campaigns.

account executives ■ Agency reps to clients.

media buyers ■ Decide where to place ads.

media DATABANK

Advertising Agencies

These are the largest worldwide advertising organizations, all operating numerous subsidiaries, ranked by worldwide revenue:

	Headquarters	Worldwide Revenues ($)
Omnicom	New York	7.5 billion
Interpublic	New York	6.2 billion
WPP	London	5.8 billion
Publicis	Paris	2.7 billion
Dentsu	Tokyo	2.1 billion

Here are the largest marketing communication service agencies in Canada, according to a survey done by *Marketing* magazine. These are "full-service" companies that not only provide traditional advertising services but also offer direct and digital marketing, market research, and media planning and buying.

Firm	Headquarters	Gross Revenues*
Cossette Communication Group	Quebec City	$143 403 000
MDC Partners	Toronto	$61 635 000
Maritz Canada	Mississauga	$51 882 000
Carlson Marketing Group Canada	Toronto	$48 011 000
Nurun	Montreal	$33 200 000

* All figures are in Canadian dollars and represent domestic business.

Source: Marketing, June 19, 2006.

AGENCY COMPENSATION

Advertising agencies once earned their money in a standard way—15 percent of the client advertiser's total outlay for space or time. On huge accounts, like Procter & Gamble, agencies made killings.

commission contract ■ An advertising agency earns an agreed-upon percentage of what the advertising client spends for time and space, traditionally 15 percent.

Commissions The 15 percent **commission contract** system broke down in the 1990s when businesses scrambled to cut costs to become more competitive. Today, according to a guesstimate by the trade journal *Advertising Age,* only 10 to 12 percent of agency contracts use a standard percentage. Agency compensation generally is negotiated. Big advertisers, like P&G, are thought to be paying 13 percent on average, but different agencies handle the company's brands, each in a separate contract. For competitive reasons, all parties tend to be secretive about actual terms.

performance contract ■ An advertising agency earns expenses and an agreed-upon markup for the advertising client, plus bonuses for exceeding minimal expectations.

Performance Commission contracts have been replaced largely with **performance contracts.** The advertiser pays an agency's costs plus a negotiated profit. In addition, if a campaign works spectacularly, agencies land bonuses.

equity contract ■ An advertising agency is compensated with shares of stock in an advertising client.

Equity In the 1990s dot-com boom, a performance contract variation was to pay agencies with shares in the company. **Equity contracts** are chancy for agencies because an advertiser's success hinges on many variables, not just the advertising, but the return for an agency with a soaring client can be stratospheric.

ADVERTISER'S ROLE IN ADVERTISING

advertising director ■ Coordinates marketing and advertising.

brand manager ■ Coordinates marketing and advertising for a specific brand.

Most companies, although they hire agencies for advertising services, have their own advertising expertise among the in-house people who develop marketing strategies. These companies look to ad agencies to develop the advertising campaigns that will help them meet their marketing goals. For some companies the **advertising director** is the liaison between the company's marketing strategists and the ad agency's tacticians. Large companies with many products have in-house **brand managers** for this liaison. Although it is not the usual pattern, some companies have in-house advertising departments and rely hardly at all on agencies.

Global Marketing
Knowing the following that Houston Rockets star Yao Ming has in his China homeland, the distributor for the Chinese beer Yanjing paid $6 million for Chinese-language billboards at the Rockets' arena.

▉ Placing Advertisements

study<u>preview</u> The placement of advertisements is a sophisticated business. Not only do different media have inherent advantages and disadvantages in reaching potential customers, but so do individual publications and broadcast outlets.

MEDIA PLANS

Agencies create **media plans** to ensure that advertisements reach the right target audience. Developing a media plan is no small task. Consider the number of media outlets available: daily or weekly newspapers, magazines, radio stations and television stations. Other possibilities include direct mail, banners on websites, billboards, blimps, skywriting and even printing the company's name on T-shirts.

Media buyers use formulas, some very complex, to decide which media are best for reaching potential customers. Most of these formulas begin with a factor called **CPM,** short for cost per thousand readers, listeners or viewers. If airtime for a radio advertisement costs 7.2 cents per thousand listeners, it's probably a better deal than a magazine with a 7.3-cent CPM, assuming that both reach the same audience. CPM by itself is just a starting point in choosing media. Other variables that media buyers consider include whether a message will work in a particular medium. For example, radio wouldn't work for a product that lends itself to a visual pitch and sight gags.

Media buyers have numerous sources of data to help them decide where advertisements can be placed for the best results. The **Audit Bureau of Circulations**, created by the newspaper industry in 1914, provides reliable information based on independent audits of the circulation of most newspapers. Survey organizations like Nielsen Media Research and BBM conduct surveys on television and radio audiences. *Canadian Advertising Rates and Data* (*CARD*) publishes volumes of information on media audiences, circulations and advertising rates.

MEDIA CHOICES

Here are the pluses and minuses of major media as advertising vehicles.

Newspapers The hot relationship that media theorist Marshall McLuhan described between newspapers and their readers attracts advertisers. Newspaper readers are predisposed to consider information in advertisements seriously. Studies show that people, when ready to buy, look more to newspapers than to other media. Because newspapers are tangible, readers can refer back to advertisements just by picking up the paper a second time, which is not possible with ephemeral media like television and radio. Coupons are possible in newspapers. Newspaper readers tend to be older, better educated and higher earning than television and radio audiences. Space for newspaper ads usually can be reserved as late as 48 hours ahead, and 11th-hour changes are possible. Newspapers account for 20 percent of all advertising revenue spent in Canada.

However, newspapers are becoming less valuable for reaching young adults. To the consternation of newspaper publishers, there has been an alarming drop in readership among these people in recent years, and it appears that, unlike their parents, young adults are not picking up the newspaper habit as they mature.

Another drawback to newspapers is printing on newsprint, a relatively cheap paper that absorbs ink like a slow blotter. The result is that ads do not look as good as they do in slick magazines. Slick, stand-alone inserts offset the newsprint drawback somewhat, but many readers pull the inserts out and discard them as soon as they open the paper.

Magazines As another print medium, magazines have many of the advantages of newspapers plus longer **shelf life**, an advertising term for the amount of time that an advertisement remains available to readers. Magazines remain in the home for weeks, sometimes months, which offers greater exposure to advertisements. People share magazines, which gives them high **pass-along circulation**. Magazines are more prestigious,

media DATABANK

Advertising Spending by Medium

According to the CRTC, this is how the 2005 advertising pie was divided among Canadian media. Notice how each medium has experienced significant growth in revenue since 1997, particularly the internet:

Medium	Advertising Revenues	% Change from 1997 to 2005
Television	$3.01 billion	43
Daily newspapers	$1.8 billion	15
Radio	$1.3 billion	54
Magazines	$1.03 billion	59
Weekly newspapers	$883 million	39
Internet	$519 million	5090
Billboards	$404 million	84

Source: CRTC, Broadcast Policy Monitoring Report 2006.

ad clutter ■ So many competing ads that all lose impact.

online advertising ■ Provide messages to computers.

sponsored link ■ Onscreen hot spot to move to an online advertisement.

clickthrough fee ■ A charge to advertisers when an online link to their ads is activated; also a fee paid to websites that host the links.

with slick paper and splashier graphics. With precise colour separations and enameled papers, magazine advertisements can be beautiful in ways that newspaper advertisements cannot. Magazines, specializing as they do, offer more narrowly defined audiences than do newspapers. Twelve percent of all advertising revenue is spent on magazines.

On the downside, magazines require reservations for advertising space up to three months in advance. Opportunities for last-minute changes are limited, often impossible.

Radio Radio stations with narrow formats offer easily identified target audiences. Time can be bought on short notice, with changes possible almost until airtime. Comparatively inexpensive, radio lends itself to repeated play of advertisements to drive home a message introduced in more expensive media like television. Radio lends itself to jingles that can contribute to a lasting image.

However, radio offers no opportunity for a visual display, although the images that listeners create in their minds from audio suggestions can be more potent than those set out visually on television. Radio is a mobile medium that people carry with them. The extensive availability of radio is offset, however, by the fact that people tune in and out. Another negative is that many listeners are inattentive. Also, there is no shelf life. Still, radio accounts for 14 percent of all advertising in Canada.

Television As a moving and visual medium, television can offer unmatched impact, and the rapid growth of both network and local television advertising, far outpacing other media, indicates its effectiveness in reaching a diverse mass audience. It's the king of all media with 34 percent of the advertising pie.

Drawbacks include the fact that production costs can be high. So are rates. The expense of television time has forced advertisers to go to shorter and shorter advertisements. A result is **ad clutter**, a phenomenon in which advertisements compete against each other and reduce the impact of all of them. Placing advertisements on television is a problem because demand outstrips the supply of slots, especially during prime hours. Slots for some hours are locked up months, even whole seasons, in advance. Because of the audience's diversity and size, targeting potential customers with any precision is difficult with television—with the exception of emerging narrowly focused cable services.

Online Services One advantage of **online advertising** is that readers can click to deeper and deeper levels of information about advertised products. A lot more information can be packed into a layered online message than within the space and time confines of a print or broadcast ad. High-resolution colour is standard, and the technology is available for moving pictures and audio.

Advertisers are not abandoning traditional media, but they are experimenting with online possibilities. For mail-order products, orders can be placed over the internet right from the ad. For some groups of potential customers, online advertising has major advantages. To reach college students, almost all of whom have computer access, online advertising makes sense.

Google Ads The internet search engine Google, capitalizing on its superfast hunt technology, has elbowed into the traditional placement service provided by advertising agencies. Google arranges for advertising space on thousands of websites, many of them narrowly focused, like blogs, and places ads for its clients on the sites. Every blog visitor who clicks a **sponsored link** placed by Google will go to a fuller advertisement. Google charges the advertiser a **clickthrough fee**. Google pays the site for every clickthrough. Google matches sites and advertisers, so a search for new Cadillacs doesn't display ads for muffler shops.

Google also places what it calls "advertiser links" on search screens. *The New York Times,* for example, has a licence to use Google technology for readers who enter search terms for searches on the *Times* site. The licence allows Google to display ads of likely interest whenever a *Times* site reader conducts an internal site search. A search for *Times* coverage of news about Jamaica, for example, will produce links to *Times* stories on Jamaica as well as to advertisements for Caribbean travel elsewhere on the internet. If a *Times* reader clicks on an ad link, Google pays the *Times* a clickthrough fee—from the revenue the advertiser paid to Google to place its ads.

Google has quickly become a major player in internet advertising. Of an estimated $10 billion spent by advertisers for online messages in 2004, Google had $1.9 billion. Nobody was earning more advertising revenue from the internet.

■ Pitching Messages

studypreview When the age of mass production and mass markets arrived, common wisdom in advertising favoured aiming at the largest possible audience of potential customers. These are called lowest-common-denominator approaches, and such advertisements tend to be heavy-handed so that no one can possibly miss the point. Narrower pitches, aimed at segments of the mass audience, permit more deftness, subtlety and imagination.

IMPORTANCE OF BRANDS

A challenge for advertising people is the modern-day reality that mass-produced products intended for large markets are essentially alike: Toothpaste is toothpaste is toothpaste. When a product is virtually identical to the competition, how can one toothpaste maker move more tubes?

Brand Names By trial and error, tactics were devised in the late 1800s to set similar products apart. One tactic, promoting a product as a **brand** name, aims to make a product a household word. When it is successful, a brand name becomes almost the generic identifier, like Coke for cola and Kleenex for facial tissue.

Techniques of successful brand-name advertising came together in the 1890s for an English product, Pears' soap. A key element in the campaign was multimedia saturation. Advertisements for Pears' were everywhere—in newspapers and magazines and on posters, vacant walls, fences, buses and lampposts. Redundancy hammered home the brand name. "Good morning. Have you used Pears' today?" became a good-natured greeting among Britons that was still being repeated 50 years later. Each repetition reinforced the brand name.

Brand Image David Ogilvy, who headed the Ogilvy & Mather agency, developed the **brand image** in the 1950s. Ogilvy's advice: "Give your product a first-class ticket through life."

Explaining the importance of image, Ogilvy once said: "Take whisky. Why do some people choose Jack Daniel's, while others choose Grand Dad or Taylor? Have they tried all three and compared the taste? Don't make me laugh. The reality is that these three brands have different images which appeal to different kinds of people. It isn't the whisky they choose, it's the image. The brand image is 90 percent of what the distiller has to sell. Give people a taste of Old Crow, and tell them it's Old Crow. Then give them another taste of Old Crow, but tell them it's Jack Daniel's. Ask them which they prefer. They'll think the two drinks are quite different. They are tasting images."

Using Ogilvy's assumptions, do Canadians taste coffee or image? Consider this: Many Canadians don't go for coffee any more. For some, the brand "Tim Hortons" has become synonymous with coffee. They go to "Hortons" or to "Timmy's." It's no wonder that in Interbrand's list of the Best Canadian Brands of 2006, Tim Hortons was among the top brands. Why is Tim Hortons successful? Interbrand claims that Canadians view Tim Hortons as their "fourth place, after home, work and the hockey/curling rink." Meanwhile, John Gray, writing in *Canadian Business,* says, "The brand has become a part of Canadian culture. That happened by design and not by accident. The company measures just about everything it does against its list of brand characteristics: unpretentious, friendly, dependable, caring—characteristics you might use to describe an ideal Canadian."

brand ■ A nongeneric product name designed to set the product apart from the competition.

David Ogilvy ■ Championed brand imaging.

brand image ■ Spin put on a brand name.

ONLINE

Ogilvy One of the largest marketing communications firms in the world. **www.ogilvy.com**

Leo Burnett Worldwide Check out this colourful site and see what campaigns Leo Burnett is creating. **www.leoburnett.com**

What Brand Are You? Enter your name, choose your values and your goals, and they will tell you your brand name. **www.thedesignconspiracy.com/whatbrandareyou/index.html**

Best Canadian Brands Look at Interbrand's entire 2006 study of Canadian brands. **www.interbrand.ca**

media DATABANK

Best Brands in Canada

According to Interbrand and *Report on Business Magazine,* the following were the top-ranking brands by brand value in 2006:

RBC Financial Group
TD Canada Trust
Petro Canada
Bell
Shoppers Drug Mart
Tim Hortons

Source: www.interbrand.ca, Best Canadian Brands 2006, July 2006.

LOWEST COMMON DENOMINATOR

Early brand-name campaigns were geared to the largest possible audience, sometimes called an LCD, or **lowest-common-denominator**, approach. The term *LCD* is adapted from mathematics. To reach an audience that includes members with IQs of 100, the pitch cannot exceed their level of understanding, even if some people in the audience have IQs of 150. The opportunity for deft touches and even cleverness is limited by the fact they might be lost on some potential customers.

LCD advertising is best epitomized in contemporary advertising by USP, short for **unique selling proposition**, a term coined by **Rosser Reeves** of the giant Ted Bates agency in the 1960s. Reeves's prescription was simple: Create a benefit of the product, even if from thin air, and then tout the benefit authoritatively and repeatedly as if the competition doesn't have it. One early USP campaign boasted that Schlitz beer bottles were "washed with live steam." The claim sounded good—who would want to drink from dirty bottles? However, the fact was that every brewery used steam to clean reusable bottles before filling them again. Furthermore, what is "live steam"? Although the implication of a competitive edge was hollow, it was done dramatically and pounded home with emphasis, and it sold beer. Just as hollow as a competitive advantage was the USP claim for Colgate toothpaste: "Cleans Your Breath While It Cleans Your Teeth."

Perhaps to compensate for a lack of substance, many USP ads are heavy-handed. A unique selling proposition need be neither hollow nor insulting, however. **Leo Burnett**, founder of the agency bearing his name, refined the USP concept by insisting that the unique point be real. For Maytag, Burnett took the company's slight advantage in reliability and dramatized it with the lonely Maytag repairman.

MARKET SEGMENTS

Rather than pitching to the lowest common denominator, advertising executive **Jack Trout** developed the idea of **positioning**. Trout worked to establish product identities that appealed not to the whole audience but to a specific audience. The cowboy image for Marlboro cigarettes, for example, established a macho attraction beginning in 1958. Later, something similar was done with Virginia Slims, aimed at women.

Positioning helps to distinguish products from all the LCD clamour and noise. Advocates of positioning note that there are more and more advertisements and that they are becoming noisier and noisier. Ad clutter, as discussed earlier in this chapter, drowns out individual advertisements. With positioning, the appeal is focused and caters to audience segments, and it need not be done in such broad strokes. Campaigns based on positioning have included Johnson & Johnson's baby oil and baby shampoo, which

lowest common denominator ■ Messages for broadest audience possible.

unique selling proposition (USP) ■ Emphasizing a single feature.

Rosser Reeves ■ Devised unique selling proposition.

Leo Burnett ■ Unique selling proposition doesn't need to be insulting.

Jack Trout ■ Devised positioning.

positioning ■ Targeting ads for specific consumer groups.

were positioned as adult products by advertisements featuring athletes; and Alka-Seltzer, once a hangover and headache remedy, which was positioned as an upscale product for stress relief among health-conscious, success-driven people.

REDUNDANCY TECHNIQUES

As we learned in Chapter 1, a redundant message is one that's easy to decode. Advertising people learned the importance of **redundancy** early on. To be effective, an advertising message must be repeated, perhaps thousands of times. Redundancy is expensive, however. To increase effectiveness at less cost, advertisers use several techniques:

- **Barrages**. Scheduling advertisements in intensive bursts called **flights** or **waves**.
- **Bunching**. Promoting a product in a limited period, such as running advertisements for school supplies in late August and September.
- **Trailing**. Running condensed versions of advertisements after the original has been introduced, as auto makers do when they introduce new models with multipage magazine spreads, following with single-page placements.
- **Multimedia trailing.** Using less expensive media to reinforce expensive advertisements. Relatively cheap drive-time radio in major markets is a favourite follow-through to expensive television advertisements created for major events like the Super Bowl.

Marshall McLuhan, the media theorist prominent in the 1960s, is still quoted as saying that advertising is important after the sale to confirm for purchasers that they made a wise choice. McLuhan's observation has not been lost on advertisers that seek repeat customers.

UNDER-THE-RADAR ADVERTISING

Inundated with advertisements, 6000 a week on network television, double since 1983, many people tune out. Some do it literally with their remotes. Ad people are concerned that traditional modes are losing effectiveness. People are overwhelmed. Consider, for example, that a major grocery store carries 30 000 items, each with packaging that screams "buy me." More commercial messages are put there than a human being can handle. The problem is ad clutter. Advertisers are trying to address the clutter in numerous ways, including stealth ads, new-site ads and alternative media. Although not hidden or subliminal, stealth ads are subtle—even covert. You might not

redundancy ■ Repetition of media messages

barrages ■ Intensive repetition of ads.

flights ■ Intensive repetition of ads.

waves ■ Intensive repetition of ads.

bunching ■ Short-term ad campaign.

trailing ■ Running shorter, smaller ads after campaign is introduced.

ONLINE

Prop Star An agency that specializes in placing products and brand names in movies and on TV.
www.propstar.com

Omnipresent Ads

Bamboo Lingerie's stenciled sidewalk messages may have been unsettling to some folks, but they sold underwear. Like many advertisers worried that their messages are lost in ad-crammed traditional media, Bamboo has struck out for nontraditional territory to be noticed. Regina Kelley, director of strategic planning for the Saatchi & Saatchi agency in New York, said: "Any space you can take in visually, anything you can hear, in the future will be branded."

Air Canada Centre New site ads, like corporate sponsorship of sports arenas such as the Air Canada Centre in Toronto, offer a new revenue stream for owners but may also add to the problem of "ad clutter."

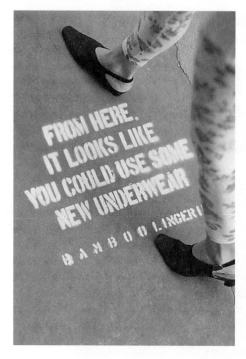

know you're being pitched unless you're attentive, really attentive.

Stealth Ads So neatly can **stealth ads** fit into the landscape that people may not recognize they're being pitched. Consider the Bamboo lingerie company, which stenciled messages on a Manhattan sidewalk: "From here it looks like you could use some new underwear." Sports arenas like Rexall Place in Edmonton work their way into sportscasts and everyday dialogue, subtly reinforcing product identity. In 2007, movie theatres began being sponsored when the Paramount Theatre in Toronto was renamed the Scotiabank Theatre.

Product Placement In the 1980s, advertisers began wriggling brand-name products into movie scripts, creating an additional although minor revenue stream for moviemakers. The practice, **product placement**, stirred criticism about artistic integrity, but it gained momentum. Fees zoomed upward. For the 2005 release of *The Green Hornet,* Miramax was seeking an automaker willing to pay at least $35 million for its products to be written into the script, topping the $15 million that Ford paid for its 2003 Thunderbird, Jaguar and Aston Martin lines to be in the James Bond movie *Die Another Day.*

Later, placing products into television scenes gained importance with the advent of **TiVo** and DVRs that allow people to record shows and replay them commercial-free at their convenience. Their growing popularity worried the television industry, whose business model was dependent on revenue from advertisers to which it guaranteed an audience for ads. With TiVo and DVRs, audiences no longer were trapped into watching commercials. Was the 30-second spot commercial doomed? The television and advertising industries struck product placement deals that went beyond anything seen before. For a fee, products are being built into scripts not only as props but also for both implicit and explicit endorsement.

Infomercials Less subtle is the **infomercial**, a program-length television commercial dolled up to look like either a newscast, a live-audience participation show or a chatty talk show. With the proliferation of 24-hour television service and of cable channels, airtime is so cheap at certain hours that advertisers of even offbeat products can afford it.

'Zine A print media variation is the **'zine**, a magazine published by a manufacturer to plug a single line of products with varying degrees of subtlety. 'Zine publishers, including such stalwarts as IBM and Sony, have even been so brazen as to sell these wall-to-wall advertising vehicles at newsstands. In 1996, if you bought a splashy new magazine called *Colors,* you paid $4.50 for it. Once inside, you probably would realize it was a thinly veiled ad for Benetton casual clothes. *Guess Journal* may look like a magazine, but guess who puts it out as a 'zine? It's the makers of the Guess fashion brand.

An under-the-radar advertisement tries "to morph into the very entertainment it sponsors," wrote Mary Kuntz, Joseph Weber and Heidi Dawley in *Business Week*. The goal, they said, is "to create messages so entertaining, so compelling—and maybe so disguised—that rapt audiences will swallow them whole, oblivious to the sales component."

POST-BRAND-NAME ERA

Perhaps prematurely, perhaps not, obituaries are being written for brand names—and brand-name advertising. Retailers are pushing **store brands**, on which they typically score 10 percent higher profits. Every time somebody buys Wal-Mart's Ol' Roy dog chow, Purina and other brand-name manufacturers lose a sale. Wal-Mart spends virtually nothing other than packaging costs for in-store displays to advertise Ol' Roy, which has knocked off Purina as top-seller. The store-brand assault has struck at a whole range of venerable brand names: Kellogg's, Kraft, Procter & Gamble and Unilever. Forrester Research, which tracks consumer trends, said in a 2002 report: "Wal-Mart will become the new P&G." In Canada, popular store brands include President's Choice (Loblaws), Master Choice (A&P) and Compliments (Sobeys).

Before the mega-retailers, brand names gave products an edge—with network television and national magazines carrying the messages. In those days the major networks—ABC, CBS and NBC—delivered messages to millions of consumers with greater effect than could small retailers. Not only are small retailers disappearing, but also the networks can't deliver what they used to. Television systems with 500 channels and the highly diverse web have divided and subdivided the audience into fragments. In a 2003 newsletter to clients, the ad agency Doremus noted, despairingly, that "it's almost impossible to get your name in enough channels to build substantial awareness." Willard Bishop Consulting came to a similar conclusion from a study on network television, noting that three commercials could reach 80 percent of one target audience, 18- to 49-year-old women, in 1995. That penetration level required 97 ads in 2000. In an analysis of the phenomenon, *Fortune* magazine writer Michael Boyle said the big superstores are displacing brand-name advertising as the new direct connection to consumers. The new mass channel, he said, is the superstore.

TiVo ■ A television recording and playback device that allows viewers to edit out commercials. Also called a digital video recorder (DVR) or personal video recorder (PVR).

infomercial ■ Program-length broadcast commercial.

'zine ■ Magazine whose entire content—articles and ads—pitches a single product or product line.

store brands ■ Products sold with a store brand, often manufactured by the retailer. Also called *house brands* and *private labels.*

Dave Nichol ■ Canadian who was a store brand pioneer.

Media PEOPLE

Dave Nichol

Dave Nichol

Dave Nichol didn't invent store brands, but he was the wizard of the phenomenon that is rewriting the rules of consumer marketing. When he was an executive at the Canadian grocery chain Loblaws, he introduced knock-off products under the brand No Name in 1978. Nichol's emphasis was quality on par with that of brand names at lower cost. After all, he had no advertising expenses, which can add 25 cents to the cost of a tube of toothpaste.

Nichol then created a coffee blend, President's Choice, modeled on the coffee in a top Toronto restaurant. Then came Decadent cookies, with 39 percent chocolate chips, compared to 19 percent in Chips Ahoy. When Kellogg's proclaimed two scoops of raisins in its bran flakes, Nichol's Loblaws brand put in four scoops.

Nichol, with a law degree from Harvard, regards himself as a food connoisseur and has his own vineyard. His contribution to marketing consumer products has been packaging higher quality into products than is in brand-name products and selling them for less. He also expanded the Loblaws store brands by selling them to U.S. chains. President's Choice coffee picked up a quick following—without advertising—in 15 chains in 36 states.

In 1990, Wal-Mart founder Sam Walton hired Nichol to devise a store brand plan for Wal-Mart. A year later, Sam's Choice, modeled on Loblaws' President's Choice, was on Wal-Mart shelves. Next came a value brand of Wal-Mart coffee, Great Value. Then came vitamins, batteries, toilet paper, and even tuna. By 2000, 40 percent of Wal-Mart's sales were store brands, and that share is growing.

Product Placement A financial linchpin for the CBS adventure series *Survivor* was integrating identifiable brand-name products into the storylines for a price. Advertisers have gravitated to product placement to counter viewership that's lost to fast-growing use of DVRs.

◼ Advertising Regulation

study<u>preview</u> The "buyer beware" underpinning of much of 19th-century advertising has given way to "seller beware." Today, advertising is regulated on many fronts: by the media that carry advertisements, by the advertising industry itself and by government agencies.

MEDIA GATEKEEPING

A dramatic reversal in thinking about advertising has occurred in the 20th century. The earlier *caveat emptor* ("let the buyer beware") mindset tolerated extravagant claims. Anybody who believed that the same elixir could cure dandruff, halitosis and cancer deserved to be conned, or so went the thinking. Over the years, owing partly to the growing consumer movement, the thinking changed to *caveat venditor* ("let the seller beware"), placing the onus on the advertiser to avoid misleading claims and to demonstrate the truth of claims.

In advertising's early days, newspapers and magazines skirted the ethics question posed by false advertisements by saying that their pages were open to all advertisers. Under growing pressure, publications sometimes criticized dubious advertisements editorially, but most did not ban them. **Edward Bok**, who made *Ladies' Home Journal* a runaway success in the 1890s, crusaded against dishonest advertising. In one exposé on Lydia E. Pinkham's remedies for "female maladies," Bok reported that Lydia, to whom women readers were invited in advertisements to write for advice, had been dead for 22 years. Yet the advertisements continued.

ADVERTISING REGULATION AND SELF-REGULATION

The advertising industry in Canada must adhere to a variety of laws and regulations, most notably the **Competition Act**. This is a federal statute that covers many different aspects of advertising in Canada. According to the Act, any representation (flyer, brochure, in-store display, newspaper ad, or material on the internet, radio or television) that offers a product or service for sale must adhere to specific guidelines. Some specific aspects covered by the act include false and misleading advertising, bait-and-switch advertising, selling at a higher than advertised price and testimonials. Fines levied under the Competition Act can be steep.

The advertising industry itself has numerous organizations that try, through ethics codes and moral suasion, to eradicate falsity and deception. Besides the explicit purposes of these self-policing mechanisms, their existence can be cited by advertising people to argue that their industry is able to deal with misdeeds itself with a minimum of government regulation. Advertising Standards Canada (**ASC**) is the self-regulatory body that oversees advertising in Canada. The ASC administers many industry codes. The Canadian Code of Advertising Standards, which has been in place since 1963 but most recently updated in 2005, includes 14 clauses with an emphasis on the following themes:

caveat emptor ◼ Buyer beware.

caveat venditor ◼ Seller beware.

Edward Bok ◼ Set media standards for ads.

Competition Act ◼ Federal regulator of advertising in Canada.

ASC ◼ Advertising Standards Canada, the self-regulatory body for advertising.

- Clear and accurate information on the price, availability, and performance of goods or services.
- No deceptive price claims.
- Warranties and guarantees must be fully explained.
- Products cannot be shown encouraging use that may be dangerous.
- Children's advertising should not exploit their naïveté, nor should it harm them physically, morally or emotionally.
- If the good or service is prohibited to minors, for instance tobacco or alcohol, its advertising cannot appeal to underage people.
- Advertising cannot exploit violence, gender or sexuality. It should always be in good taste.

◤◾ Problems and Issues

study<u>preview</u> **People are exposed to such a blur of ads that advertisers worry that their messages are being lost in the clutter. Some advertising people see more creativity as the answer so that people will want to see and read ads, but there is evidence that creativity can work against an ad's effectiveness.**

ADVERTISING CLUTTER

Leo Bogart of the Newspaper Advertising Bureau noted that the number of advertising messages doubled through the 1960s and 1970s and, except for the recession at the start of the 1990s, the trend continues. This proliferation of advertising creates a problem: too many ads. The problem has been exacerbated by the shortening of ads from 60 seconds in the early days of television to today's widely used 15-second format. At one time the CRTC limited the amount of TV commercials a station could air to 12 minutes. In 2008, that limit was raised to 15 minutes. While this may make it easier for TV stations to make money, it will only contribute to ad clutter.

Ad clutter is less of an issue in the print media. Many people buy magazines and newspapers to look at ads as part of the comparative shopping process. Even so, some advertisers, concerned that their ads are overlooked in massive editions, such as a 7-pound metro Sunday newspaper or a 700-page bridal magazine, are looking to alternative means to reach potential customers in a less cluttered environment.

The clutter that marks much of commercial television and radio today may be alleviated as the media fragment further. Not only will demassification create more specialized outlets, such as narrowly focused cable television services, but there will be new media. The result will be advertising aimed at narrower audiences.

Advertisers are reviewing whether creativity is as effective an approach as hard sell. **Harry McMahan** studied **Clio Awards** for creativity in advertising and discovered that 36 agencies that produced 81 winners of the prestigious awards for advertisements had either lost the winning account or gone out of business.

Predicted advertising commentator E.B. Weiss: "Extravagant license for creative people will be curtailed." The future may hold more heavy-handed pitches, perhaps with over-the-counter regimens not only promising fast-fast-fast relief but also spelling it out in all caps and boldface with exclamation marks: **F-A-S-T! F-A-S-T!! F-A-S-T!!!**

ADVERTISING EFFECTIVENESS

Long-held assumptions about the effectiveness of advertising itself are being questioned. **Gerald Tellis**, a University of Iowa researcher, put together a sophisticated statistical model that found that people are relatively unmoved by television advertisements in making brand choices, especially on mundane everyday products like toilet paper and laundry detergents. Tellis's conclusions began with consumer purchasing studies in Eau Claire, Wisconsin. Not surprisingly, considering its self-interest, the advertising industry has challenged the Tellis studies.

Harry McMahan ◾ Dubious about ad creativity.

Clio Award ◾ Award for advertising creativity.

Gerald Tellis ◾ Dubious about TV ads.

Nice Smile Actress Nicollette Sheridan, known most recently as a serial divorcee who kept the neighbourhood buzzing on television's *Desperate Housewives,* opens an old-fashioned photo booth to promote Crest Whitestrips at a Central Park skating rink in New York. The promotional stunt for the Procter & Gamble Crest product was typical of a new wave of alternatives to traditional media for advertising.

MEASURING CREATIVITY

Consumer-products giant Procter & Gamble has adopted a computerized tool to measure the creativity of advertising agencies competing for its accounts. By quantifying creativity, the company hopes to identify agencies that can bring new ideas and imagination to promoting P&G products.

Former P&G executives who formed Cincinnati Consulting Consortium devised the system. Although the system is cloaked in secrecy, it's known that the system assigns points for prizes that agencies win for creativity contests. Awards are weighed according to their prestige. Plugged in, too, are other numbers, including the number of awards for advertising per every dollar that's spent.

Procter & Gamble began applying the tool in 2005 not only to advertising agencies already holding P&G accounts but also to competing agencies. Agencies can expect new pressure to show external confirmation for their creativity.

CHAPTER 10 **Wrap-Up**

The role of advertising in North American mass media cannot be overstated. In one sense, advertisers subsidize readers, viewers and listeners who pay only a fraction of the cost of producing publications and broadcasts. The bulk of the cost is paid by advertisers, who are willing to do so to make their pitches to potential customers who, coincidentally, are media consumers.

Besides underwriting the mass media, advertising is vital for a prosperous, growing consumer economy. It triggers demand for goods and services, and it enables people to make wise choices by providing information on competing products. The result is efficiency in the marketplace, which frees more capital for expansion. This all speaks to an intimate interrelationship involving advertising in a democratic and capitalistic society.

Questions for Review

1. Why is advertising essential in a capitalistic society?
2. Trace the development of advertising since the time of Johannes Gutenberg.
3. What is the role of advertising agencies?
4. Why do some advertisements appear in some media and not others?
5. What are the major tactics used in advertising? Who devised each one?
6. How do advertising people use psychology and research to shape their messages?
7. What are the advantages and the problems of the globalization of the advertising industry?
8. Does advertising still follow the dictum "let the buyer beware"?
9. What are some problems and unanswered issues in advertising?

Questions for Critical Thinking

1. How does the development of modern advertising relate to Johannes Gutenberg's technological innovation? To the Industrial Revolution? To long-distance mass transportation? To mass marketing?
2. Why does advertising flourish more in democratic than in autocratic societies? In a capitalistic more than in a controlled economy? In a prosperous society?
3. What were the contributions to advertising of F. Wayland Ayer, Anson McKim, Rosser Reeves, Jack Trout, Wilson Bryan Key and David Ogilvy?
4. What are the responsibilities of advertising account executives, copywriters, media buyers, researchers, brand managers, ad reps and brokers?
5. What are the advantages of the commission system for advertising agency revenue? Of the fee system? The disadvantages of both?
6. Describe these advertising tactics: brand-name promotion, unique selling proposition, lowest-common-denominator approach, positioning and redundancy.
7. How is ad clutter a problem? What can be done about it?
8. How has Advertising Standards Canada improved the image of companies that advertise, agencies that create advertisements and media that carry advertisements? Give examples.

Deepening Your media LITERACY

How does advertising affect the consumer?

STEP 1 Find a newspaper or magazine with a lot of ads.

Dig Deeper

STEP 2 Make a list of the persuasion techniques used in advertising. Find ads in your publication that best exhibit each technique.

What Do You Think?

STEP 3 Answer these questions:

1. Which ad do you like best? Why?
2. Which ad do you like least? Why?
3. Which ad do you think is most persuasive? Why?
4. Are any of the ads unfair? In what way?

Keeping Up to Date

Weekly trade journals are *Marketing* magazine, *Advertising Age* and *AdWeek*.

Scholarly publications include *Journal of Marketing Research* and *Journal of Advertising*. *The Globe and Mail* regularly reports on the industry.

The *Journal of Consumer Psychology* includes analysis, reviews, reports and other scholarship on the role of advertising in consumer psychology.

For Further Learning

Mary Billard. "Heavy Metal Goes on Trial." *Rolling Stone* 582–583 double issue (July 12–26, 1990): 83–88, 132.

Competition Bureau. "Law and Litigation: About the Acts." Available online at www.competitionbureau.gc.ca.

CRTC. *Broadcast Policy Monitoring Report, 2006*.

Bruce DeMara. "Now Playing: Corporate Sponsorship." *Toronto Star* (January 24, 2007).

Stephen Fox. *The Mirror Makers: A History of American Advertising and Its Creators* (Morrow, 1984).

John Kenneth Galbraith. *The Affluent Society* (Mariner Books, 1998).

Interbrand. *Interbrand's Best Canadian Brands, 2006*. Available at www.interbrand.ca.

Wilson Bryan Key. *Subliminal Seduction: Ad Media's Manipulation of a Not So Innocent America* (New American Library, 1972).

Otto Kleppner, Thomas Russell, and Glenn Verrill. *Advertising Procedure,* 8th edition (Prentice Hall, 1990).

Bob Levenson. *Bill Bernbach's Book: A History of the Advertising That Changed the History of Advertising* (Random House, 1987).

Jay Conrad Levinson and Charles Rubin. *Guerrilla Advertising* (Mariner Books, 1998).

Nancy Millman. *Emperors of Adland: Inside the Advertising Revolution* (Warner Books, 1988).

David Ogilvy. *Confessions of an Advertising Man* (Atheneum, 1963).

David Ogilvy. *Ogilvy on Advertising* (Vintage, 1985).

Andrew Potter. "Galbraith's Theory of Advertising Had Us All Fooled." *Maclean's* (May 15, 2006).

Anthony Pratkanis and Elliot Aronson. *Age of Propaganda: The Everyday Use and Abuse of Persuasion* (W. H. Freeman, 1992).

Brenda Pritchard and Susan Vogt. *Advertising and Marketing Law in Canada,* Second Edition (Butterworth's, 2006).

Ronald H. Rotenberg. *Advertising: A Canadian Perspective* (Allyn and Bacon, 1986)

Paul Rutherford. *The New Icons? The Art of Television Advertising* (University of Toronto Press, 1994).

Michael Schudson. *Advertising: The Uneasy Persuasion: Its Dubious Impact on American Society* (Basic Books, 1984).

Alan Shanoff. *Advertising and Law* (Hallion Press, 1995).

Keith J. Tuckwell. *Canadian Advertising in Action* (Prentice Hall, 2000).

Robbin Lee Zeff and Brad Aronson. *Advertising on the Internet,* Second edition (John Wiley, 1999).

Jerry Bruckheimer The signature cinematic feature of his movies and television shows, including *CSI,* is the pace. Because of Bruckheimer, editing has become faster—shots average 2 to 3 seconds, compared to 8 to 11 seconds only 20 years earlier.

Entertainment

Media in Theory

The Bruckheimer Effect

There's no doubt that the mass media are a source of entertainment for most North Americans. One of the architects of a good deal of content is Jerry Bruckheimer, who has produced fast-paced films like *The Rock, Con Air, Pearl Harbor, Pirates of the Caribbean, National Treasure* and *Black Hawk Down* and films about people who made a difference like *Remember the Titans* and *Veronica Guerin.*

Before 1980, the average shot in a mainstream film lasted 8 to 11 seconds, according to film scholar David Bordwell. In Bruckheimer's *Top Gun,* made in 1986, the shots shrank to 3 to 4 seconds. In 1998's *Armageddon* they were 2 to 3 seconds. Jeanine Basinger, historian and chair of film studies at Wesleyan University, says Bruckheimer may have been the first filmmaker to understand how quickly audiences can assimilate images and their meaning. "Bruckheimer movies are the opposite of what his critics say. They're not mindless—they engage a different part of the mind."

Not many people can make the leap from movies to television, but Bruckheimer brought his action-packed brand to shows like *CSI* and its spinoffs, the *Amazing Race* reality shows, and *Without a Trace.* Bruckheimer says he just wants to keep the story moving, and to do that he "takes the air out," just as in his movies, although he likes being able to develop a character through a season of shows.

He came to Hollywood in 1972 with a degree in psychology and a successful career as an advertising art director. In 2003 his films earned $12.5 billion in worldwide box-office receipts. Bruckheimer is "able to make the world's best B movies without condescending to the audience," *Time*'s Joel Stein stays. "His instinct for what excites audiences is eerily perfect." "We are in the transportation business," says Bruckheimer. "We transport audiences from one place to another." And he does it at high speed.

Through the mass media, including Bruckheimer's works, people can escape everyday drudgery, immersing themselves in a soap opera, a murder mystery or pop music.

The pervasiveness of all these entertainment choices is not always a good thing, according to some theorists who say a plethora of information and access to ideas and entertainment can induce information anxiety. Even a relatively slender weekday edition of *The New York Times* contains more information than the average person in the 17th century was likely to come across in a lifetime, according to Richard Saul Wurman in his book *Information Anxiety.*

While educated people traditionally have thirsted for information, the quantity has become such that many people feel overwhelmed by what is called **information pollution**. We are awash in it and drowning, and the mass media are a factor in this.

Another effect of the mass media is embodied in the stereotypical couch potato, whose greatest physical and mental exercise is heading to the refrigerator during commercials. Studies indicate that television is on seven hours a day on average in U.S. homes and that the typical American spends four to six hours a day with the mass media, mostly with television. The experience is primarily passive, and such **media-induced passivity** has been blamed, along with greater mobility and access to more leisure activities, for major changes in how people live their lives:

- **Worship services.** In 1955 Gallup found that 49 percent attended worship services weekly. Today, it is less than 40 percent.
- **Churches and lodges.** The role of church auxiliaries and lodges, once central in community social life with weekly activities, has diminished.
- **Neighbourhood taverns.** Taverns at busy neighbourhood corners and rural crossroads once were the centre of political discussion in many areas, but this is less true today.
- **Participatory sports.** Despite the fitness and wellness craze, more people than ever are overweight and out of shape, which can be partly attributed to physical passivity induced by television and media-based homebound activities.

information pollution ■ Media deluge people with information and no sense of order, priority.

media-induced passivity ■ Media entice people away from social involvement.

■ Entertainment in History

study<u>preview</u> **The mass media, during their 550-year existence, have magnified the audience for entertainment. Technology has wrought many refinements, but the core categories of media entertainment remain storytelling and music.**

PRE–MASS MEDIA ROOTS

Entertainment predates the written history of the human species. Around the prehistoric campfire there was music. We know this from Neolithic animal-hide drums that archaeologists have unearthed. Certainly, the cave dwellers must have told stories. Who knows when the visual arts began? The record goes back to paintings on cave walls. Through the eons, entertainment became higher and higher art. Archaeologists know that the elites of ancient civilizations enjoyed lavish banquets that included performing entertainers—acrobats, musicians and dancers. Sports and athletics became institutionalized entertainment by the time of ancient Greece with the Olympic games and large stadiums. Then came ancient Rome with athletics and competition on an even larger scale. Circus Maximus in Rome could hold 170 000 spectators for chariot races and gladiator games.

Entertainment that has survived the ages includes music, literature, sports and sex. Other breakdowns can be made, like performing arts and visual arts. Some people distinguish entertainment from art, relegating entertainment to a somehow less worthy category. On close examination these distinctions blur, however. Art is in the eye of the beholder, a highly personal and subjective issue.

TECHNOLOGY-DRIVEN ENTERTAINMENT

What distinguished the Age of Mass Communication, which began with Gutenberg's movable type in the 1440s, was that messages, including entertainment, could be mass produced to reach audiences of unprecedented size. The post-Gutenberg press gave literature wider and wider audiences. But even 200 years after Gutenberg, the audience for John Milton's *Paradise Lost,* to take one example, was remarkable for the time but minuscule compared to the audience for every book now on *The New York Times* weekly list of leading titles. Too, literature has taken on diverse forms today, from academic tomes in the Milton tradition to pulp romances and westerns—and it's not all in printed form.

As media technology leapfrogged into photographic and electronic forms, literature adapted to the new media. Movies extended the reach and the artistic form of books. So did radio and then television. Music, a rare treat in people's lives before audio recording was invented, is everywhere today. Indeed, the impact of the entertainment content of today's mass media is hard to measure. With television turned on seven hours a day in U.S. homes on average—most of it tuned to entertainment content—it's obvious that people are being entertained more than ever before in history.

ENTERTAINMENT GENRES

To make sense of the gigantic and growing landscape of entertainment in the mass media, people have devised **genres** that are, in effect, subdivisions of the major categories of storytelling and music.

Storytelling Whether novels, short stories, television drama or movies, literature can be divided into genres. Popular genres include suspense, romance, horror, westerns, fantasy, history and biography. Some genres are short-lived. In the early 1970s a movie genre dubbed *blaxploitation* emerged, for better or worse, with a black racist appeal to black audiences. The genre culminated in the Shaft series, which, although updated in 2003, had been eclipsed by the ongoing racial integration of society.

Music A lot of crossover makes for genre confusion in music. Wanting to define their tastes, aficionados keep reinventing thematic trends. The array of subgenres is dizzying. How is acid rock different from hard rock, from solid rock, from progressive rock, from alternative rock, from power rock, from metal rock? Don't ask. Categorizing is not a neat, clinical task.

media ONLINE

Main Film Genres A primer on the main genres, subgenres and nongenre categories of film.
www.filmsite.org/genres.html

Music Genres Indiana University offers this list of types of music.
www.music.indiana.edu/
music_resources/genres.html

genres ■ Broad thematic categories of media content.

media DATABANK

Record Sales by Genre

Rock music has dominated North American culture since the 1950s. Following are the current broadly defined genres, but music—like all entertainment—isn't easily pigeonholed. Rock, for example, has subspecies galore that defy any clinical description. Lots of music straddles more than one genre, which has led the radio industry to try to make sense of it all with subcategories like country rock and adult contemporary.

Rock	25.7 percent
Country	14.1 percent
Rhythm and blues	12.8 percent
Rap	10.0 percent
Pop	9.7 percent
Gospel	6.3 percent
Classical	3.3 percent
Jazz	1.9 percent
Movie music	1.7 percent

From the Fringes Rap music, with its intense bass and rhyming riffs, often attitude-strong, grew into mainstream pop despite critics who doubted the artistic content. Rapper Nelly and Christina Aguilera perform at the MTV Music Video Awards, representing the integration of rap into the repertoire of pop.

Sports Genres are clearest in sports because the rules, although not set in granite, have been agreed on, as have the procedures for revising the rules. Nobody confuses baseball with hockey or lacrosse with NASCAR. Attempts at crossover genres, like the wrestling-inspired XFL football experiment, don't do well.

■. Performance as Media Entertainment

studypreview The mass media's entertainment content is performance, but it's not pure performer-to-audience. The media change the performance. Authentic performance is live and eyeball-to-eyeball with the audience. Mediated performance is adapted to meet an unseen and distant audience.

AUTHENTIC PERFORMANCE

When American liberal commentator Al Franken does a routine before a live audience, it's uproariously funny unless his bite hits a raw ideological nerve. That's why conservatives avoid his shows. But in 2004, when Franken took his humour to radio in a talk show on the new Air America network, his humour and bite didn't translate well. On radio he was flat. As Canadian Marshall McLuhan would argue, "the medium was the message." There are many reasons for this.

Audience At a play, whether on Broadway or in a high-school auditorium, the audience is assembled for one purpose. It's **authentic performance**, live with the audience on-site. Everyone is attentive to the performance. Nuances are less likely to be missed.

Feedback Performers on stage are in tune with their audience's reactions. There can be reaction and interplay. For the same performance through a mass medium, performers guess—some better than others—at how they are coming across. The fact is, taking television as an example, what resonates in one living room does not resonate in another. Some performers are more gifted at maximizing their impact, but to reach the massive, scattered, heterogeneous mass audience requires pandering to some extent to common denominators. There is less edge.

MEDIATED PERFORMANCE

In ways we don't always realize, media technology affects and sometimes shapes the messages the media disseminate. The changes to make a **mediated message** work are a function of the technology that makes it possible to reach a mass audience.

Technology The equipment that makes mass communication possible is what sets it apart from interpersonal and group communication. Technology imposes its own requirements on performance. Media transform a performance. In ways large and small, it becomes a mediated performance.

authentic performance ■ Live with on-site audience.

ONLINE
Playbill Online version of the well-recognized theatre bill that's been around since 1884.
www.playbill.com

mediated message ■ Adjusted to be effective when carried by the mass media.

Music Edison's mechanical recording technology, which captured acoustic waves in a huge horn, picked up no subtleties. Brass bands and loud voices recorded best. Scratchy background noise drowned out soft sounds. It's no wonder that the late 1800s and early 1900s were marked by popularity of martial music and marching bands. High-pitched voices came through best, which also shaped the popular music of the period.

When Joseph Maxwell's electrical technology was refined in the 1920s, subtle sounds that now could survive the recording and playback processes came into vogue. Rudy Vallee and Bing Crosby were in, John Philip Sousa was out. Improvements in fidelity beginning in the 1950s meant that music could be played louder and louder without unsettling dissonance—and many rockers took to louder renditions.

Movies Media technology profoundly affects art. When audio and film technology were merged to create talkies, moviemakers suddenly had all kinds of new creative options for their storytelling. Directors had more new possibilities when wide screens replaced squarish screens in movie houses. When technology changes the experience for the moviemaker, it also changes the experience for moviegoers.

Sports Technology has dazzled sports fans. Instant replays on television, tried first during an Army–Navy football game in the early 1960s, added a dimension that in-stadium fans could not see. Then came miniature cameras that allowed viewers to see what referees see on the field. Putting microphones on referees, coaches and players let the mass audience eavesdrop on the sounds of the playing field that no one in the stands or sidelines could pick up.

Some digital cable channels allow viewers to select various static camera angles during a game. Viewers, in effect, can participate in creating the media coverage they see. This is a profound development. Watching television, once a largely passive activity, now can involve the viewer at least to some degree.

Storytelling as Media Entertainment

study<u>preview</u> **The media are powerful vehicles for exponentially extending the reach of literature. The most enduring include romances and mysteries, but variations and hybrids come and go in popularity.**

GENRES OF LITERATURE

Some of literature's storytelling genres have been enduring through the centuries. Shakespeare was neither the first to do romances and mysteries, nor the last. Genres help us make sense of literature, giving us a basis for comparison and contrast. Literature can be categorized in many ways, one as basic as fiction and nonfiction, another being prose and poetry. Bookstores use thematic genres to sort their inventory, including mysteries, romances, sports, biographies and hobbies.

TRENDS AND FADS

Genres rise and fall in popularity. Early television was dominated by variety shows, which featured a range of comedy, song and dance, and other acts. Then came the wave of 1950s quiz shows, then westerns, then police shows. Going into the 21st century, the television programming fads were talk shows in the style pioneered by Phil Donahue and sustained by Oprah Winfrey, reality shows epitomized by the unending CBS *Survivor* series, and yet another rush of who-done-it police shows.

Some categories are short-lived. A wave of buddy movies was ushered in by *Butch Cassidy and the Sundance Kid* in 1969. Later *Thelma and Louise* spawned girlfriend movies.

media ONLINE

Triple Crown Publications The company started in 2001 by self-publishing author Vickie Stringer.
http://writers.aalbc.com/ triple_crown_publications.htm

Paradoxa Publishes articles on genre literature. Check out this month's genre.
http://paradoxa.com

History of the Mystery A timeline of mystery stories, detailing the major genres and authors.
www.mysterynet.com/timeline

Television Episodes

The western *Gunsmoke* ran 20 seasons, a record in U.S. television, but the record for the number of prime-time episodes for a series is held by the sitcom *Ozzie and Harriet.* Here are the leaders by episode:

Ozzie and Harriet	435	Sitcom
The Simpsons	400	Cartoon sitcom
My Three Sons	380	Sitcom
Dallas	357	Prime-time soap opera

Genre trends are audience-driven. People flock to a particular book, song, film or television show and then to the thematic sequels until they tire of it all. Although a lot of genre content is derivative rather than original art, new twists and refinements can reflect artistic fine tuning by authors, scriptwriters and other creators. People may quibble about whether Francis Ford Coppola's *The Godfather* or *The Godfather, Part II,* was the better, but almost everyone, including the critics, concur that both were filmic masterpieces. At the same time, nobody serious about creative media content is looking forward to Jason Voorhees to return in *Friday the 13th XXXXIII.*

▄▖ Music as Media Entertainment

studypreview Audio technology accelerated the effect of music as a social unifier. This is nowhere better illustrated than in the integration of traditional black music and white hillbilly music into rock 'n' roll, a precursor to the racial integration of society. The potency of music has been enhanced by its growing role in other media forms, including movies and television.

AMERICAN FOLK MUSIC

Most music historians trace contemporary popular music to roots in two distinctive types of American folk music, both of which emerged in the South.

Black Music Africans who were brought to the colonies as slaves used music to soothe their difficult lives. Much of the music reflected their oppression and hopeless poverty. Known as **black music**, it was distinctive in that it carried strains of slaves' African roots and at the same time reflected the black American experience. This music also included strong religious themes, expressing the slaves' indefatigable faith in a glorious afterlife. Flowing from the heart and the soul, this was folk music of the most authentic sort.

After the Civil War, black musicians found a white audience on riverboats and in saloons and pleasure palaces of various sorts. That introduced a commercial component into black music and fueled numerous variations, including jazz. Even with the growing white following, the creation of these latter-day forms of black music remained almost entirely with African-American musicians. White musicians who picked up on the growing popularity of

black music ■ Folk genre from American black slave experience.

black music drew heavily on black songwriters. Much of Benny Goodman's swing music, for example, came from black arranger Fletcher Henderson.

In the 1930s and 1940s a distinctive new form of black music, **rhythm and blues**, emerged. The people who enjoyed this music were all over the country, and these fans included both blacks and whites. Mainstream American music had come to include a firm African-American presence.

Hillbilly Music Another authentic American folk music form, **hillbilly music**, flowed from the lives of Appalachian and Southern whites. Early hillbilly music had a strong colonial heritage in English ballads and ditties, but over time hillbilly music evolved into a genre in its own right. Fiddle playing and twangy lyrics reflected the poverty and hopelessness of rural folk, "hillbillies" as they called themselves. Also like black music, hillbilly music reflected the joys, frustrations and sorrows of love and family. However, hillbilly music failed to develop more than a regional following—that is, until the 1950s, when a great confluence of the black and hillbilly traditions occurred. This distinctive new form of American music, called **rockabilly** early on, became rock 'n' roll.

EARLY ROCK 'N' ROLL

Music aficionados quibble about who invented the term *rock 'n' roll*. There is no doubt, though, that Memphis disc jockey **Sam Phillips** was a key figure in the development of the genre. From his job at WREC, Phillips found an extra $75 a month to rent a 20-foot-by-35-foot storefront, the paint peeling from the ceiling, to go into business recording, as he put it, "anything, anywhere, anytime." His first jobs, in 1949, were weddings and bar mitzvahs, but in 1951 Phillips put out his first record, "Gotta Let You Go," by blues singer Joe Hill Louis, who played his own guitar, harmonica and drums for accompaniment. In 1951 Phillips recorded B.B. King and then **Jackie Brenston**'s "Rocket 88," which many musicologists call the first rock 'n' roll record. Phillips sold his early recordings, all by black musicians, mostly in the blues tradition, to other labels.

In 1952 Phillips began his own Sun Records label and a quest to broaden the appeal of the black music he loved to a wide audience. "If I could find a white man who had the Negro sound and the Negro feel, I could make a billion dollars," he said. In a group he recorded in 1954, the Starlight Wranglers, Sam Phillips found Elvis Presley.

Presley's first Sun recording, "That's All Right," with Scotty Moore and Bill Black, found only moderate success on country radio stations, but Sam Phillips knew that he was onto something. It wasn't quite country or quite blues, but it was a sound that could move both white country fans and black blues fans. Elvis moved on to RCA, a major label. By 1956 he had two of the nation's best-selling records, the flip-side hits "Don't Be Cruel" and "Hound Dog," plus three others among the year's top 16. Meanwhile, Sam Phillips was recording Carl Perkins, Roy Orbison, Johnny Cash and Jerry Lee Lewis, adding to the distinctively American country-blues hybrid: wild, thrashing, sometimes reckless rock 'n' roll.

The new music found a following on radio stations that picked up on the music mix that Cleveland disc jockey Alan Freed had referred to as "rock 'n' roll" as early as 1951— occasional rhythm and blues amid the mainstream Frank Sinatra and Peggy Lee. By 1955 Freed was in New York and clearly on a roll. Freed helped propel Bill Haley and the Comets' "Rock Around the Clock" to number one. Rock's future was cemented when "Rock Around the Clock" was the musical bed under the credits for the 1955 movie *Blackboard Jungle*. Young people flocked to the movie not only for its theme of teen disenchantment and rebellion but also for the music.

ROCK 'N' ROLL IN CANADA

While rock 'n' roll is an American musical genre, many Canadians have been successful rock 'n' rollers. Paul Anka is the most obvious Canadian success story. His good looks, combined with his singing and songwriting abilities, brought him success—not only at home, but in the United States.

rhythm and blues ■ Distinctive style of black music that took form in the 1930s.

hillbilly music ■ Folk genre from rural Appalachian, Southern white experience.

rockabilly ■ Black–hillbilly hybrid that emerged in the 1950s.

ONLINE

Sam Phillips Tribute page from the Rockabilly Hall of Fame.
www.rockabillyhall.com/
SamPhillips.html

Elvis Presley He ain't nothin' but a hound dog. The official site.
www.elvis.com

Alan Freed Disc jockey credited with coining the term "rock 'n' roll."
www.alanfreed.com

Sam Phillips ■ Pioneered rockabilly, rock 'n' roll; discovered Elvis Presley.

Jackie Brenston ■ Recorded "Rocket 88," first rock 'n' roll record, in 1951.

Anka wasn't alone in having success south of the border. Randy Bachman reached the top of the charts in both countries with "These Eyes," "Undun" and, of course, "American Woman." Bachman's success in the United States continued when he left The Guess Who and formed Bachman Turner Overdrive, which reached number one with "You Ain't Seen Nothin' Yet." Throughout the 1960s, 1970s, 1980s, and 1990s, Canadians like Anne Murray, Gordon Lightfoot, Rush, Neil Young, Bryan Adams, Shania Twain, Céline Dion, and others became pop music stars in the United States. This trend continues in the 21st century with Avril Lavigne, Nelly Furtado, and Nickelback carrying the Cancon torch into America. More recently, bands like The Tragically Hip, Sloan, Finger Eleven, and Sum 41 developed loyal followings in Canada, but had limited success in the United States.

MUSIC AS MULTIMEDIA CONTENT

Although music often is studied as the content issued by the recording industry, music is hardly a one-dimensional form of media message. Even in pre–mass media eras, going back to prehistoric times, music was integrated with dance and theatre. When movies were establishing themselves, music was an important component. Even before movie soundtracks were introduced with the "talkies," many movie houses hired a piano player who kept one eye on the screen and hammered out supportive music. D.W. Griffith's *The Birth of a Nation* of 1915 had an accompanying score for a 70-piece symphony.

Sports as Media Entertainment

study<u>preview</u> **Early on, mass media people sensed the potential of sports to build their audiences, first through newspapers, then through magazines, radio and television. The media feed what seems an insatiable demand for more sports. Why the huge public intrigue with sports? One expert suggests it's the mix of suspense, heroes, villains, pageantry and ritual.**

MASS AUDIENCES FOR SPORTS

The brilliant newspaper publisher **James Gordon Bennett** sensed how a public interest in sports could build circulation for his *New York Herald* in the 1830s. Bennett assigned reporters to cover sports regularly. Fifty years later, with growing interest in horse racing, prize fighting, yacht racing and baseball, **Joseph Pulitzer** organized the first separate sports department at his *New York World*. Sportswriters began specializing in different sports.

Audience appetite for sports was insatiable. For the 1897 Corbett–Fitzsimmons heavyweight title fight in remote Nevada, dozens of writers showed up. *The New York Times* introduced celebrity coverage in 1910 when it hired retired prizefighter John L. Sullivan to cover the Jeffries–Johnson title bout in Reno.

Sports historians call the 1920s the Golden Era of Sports, with newspapers glorifying athletes. Heroes, some with enduring fame, included Jack Dempsey in boxing, Knute Rockne and Jim Thorpe in football, and Babe Ruth in baseball. The 1920s also marked radio as a medium for sports. In 1921 **KDKA** of Pittsburgh carried the first play-by-play baseball game, the Davis Cup tennis matches and the blow-by-blow Johnny Ray versus Johnny Dundee fight. Sportswriter Grantland Rice, the pre-eminent sportswriter of the time, covered the entire World Series live from New York for KDKA, also in 1921. In 1923, Hockey Night in Canada began broadcasting on Canadian radio with the legendary **Foster Hewitt** as play-by-play announcer. Within a decade, Saturday night hockey games became a staple for Canadian hockey fans.

Sports magazines have their roots in *American Turf Register*, which began a 15-year run in Baltimore in 1829. The *American Bicycling Journal* rode a bicycling

ONLINE

Movie Music Links to reviews, official and unofficial sites, places to buy soundtracks and more.
www.moviemusic.com/directory

MusicIP Mixer Show it a song, and it will find others that you're sure to love.
www.musicip.com

MoodLogic Download the Mix Maker and see what it can do for your MP3s.
www.moodlogic.com

James Gordon Bennett ■ New York newspaper publisher in 1830s; first to assign reporters to sports regularly.

Joseph Pulitzer ■ New York newspaper publisher in 1880s; organized the first newspaper sports department.

KDKA ■ Pittsburgh radio station that pioneered sports broadcasting in 1920s.

Foster Hewitt ■ First play-by-play announcer for Hockey Night in Canada.

craze from 1877 to 1879. Nothing matched the breadth and scope of *Sports Illustrated,* founded in 1954 by magazine magnate **Henry Luce**. The magazine, launched with 350 000 charter subscribers, now boasts a circulation of 3.3 million a week.

Although television dabbled in sports from its early days, the introduction of *Wide World of Sports* in 1961 established that television was made for sports and, conversely, that sports was made for television. The show, the brainchild of ABC programming wizard **Roone Arledge**, covered an unpredictable diversity of sports, from ping-pong to skiing. In this period, professional athletic leagues agreed to modify their rules to accommodate television for commercial breaks and, eventually, to make the games more exciting for television audiences.

Television commentator Les Brown explains sports as the perfect program form for television: "At once topical and entertaining, performed live and suspensefully without a script, peopled with heroes and villains, full of action and human interest and laced with pageantry and ritual."

The launching of ESPN as an all-sports network for cable television systems prompted millions of households to subscribe to cable. By 1984, TSN began broadcasting in Canada. Since then, Sportsnet and The Score offer Canadians their daily dose of sports.

Arledge and Cosell
Hands-on ABC Sports executive Roone Arledge's innovations included *Monday Night Football* with the edgy and abrasive Howard Cosell, putting the network on the prime-time map.

AUDIENCE AND ADVERTISER CONFLUENCE

The television networks and national advertisers found a happy confluence of interest in the huge audience for televised sports. This goes back at least to *Friday Night Fights,* sponsored by Gillette, and *Wednesday Night Fights,* sponsored by Pabst beer, in the 1950s. Today, sports and television are almost synonymous. Not only do the Stanley Cup finals pack fans into arenas, but hockey fans tune in to CBC to watch the games. The World Cup soccer tournament held every four years draws the largest worldwide television audiences.

In part to keep their names on screen, some firms have bought the rights to put their name on sports stadiums. The value of brand-name exposure at places like the Air Canada Centre, the Bell Centre or Rexall Place is impossible to measure.

SPORTS AND THE WEB

Media sports coverage technology keeps evolving. At one time, not enough broadcast channels existed in a community to air all the games that interested people. Now audio and video coverage can be web-delivered. Some colleges have arranged for their games to be carried on the web so that faraway alumni can track the touchdowns live.

■ Sex as Media Entertainment

study preview **Despite the risk of offending some people's sensitivities, the media have long trafficked in sexual content. Undeniably, there is a market. The media have fought for their right to carry sexually explicit content and for the right of adults to have access to it.**

Henry Luce ■ Magazine publisher known for *Time, Life, Sports Illustrated* and others.

Roone Arledge ■ ABC television executive responsible for *Wide World of Sports* in 1961.

media ONLINE
SI The online presence of *Sports Illustrated.*
http://sportsillustrated.cnn.com

Roone Arledge Thorough and well-linked biography of the man who changed TV sports forever.
www.museum.tv/archives/etv/A/htmlA/arledgeroon/arledgeroon.htm

Take your pick: TSN, Sportsnet and The Score All sports, all the time, online.
www.tsn.ca
www.sportsnet.ca
www.thescore.ca

media ONLINE
World Wrestling Entertainment Formerly known as the World Wrestling Federation.
www.wwe.com

ADULT CONTENT

Sexually oriented content has bedeviled the mass media for longer than anyone can remember. Clearly, there is a demand. Sales of banned books soared as soon as the courts overruled government restrictions, as was no better illustrated than with the Irish classic *Ulysses* by James Joyce in 1930. Firm data on the profitability of sexual content are hard to come by, partly because definitions are elusive. *Ulysses,* as an example, is hardly a sex book for most people, yet its sexual content is what once prompted a federal import ban. The definition difficulty gives partisans the opportunity to issue exaggerated estimates of the scope of the sexual media content.

It was no sleazy outfit that first imported *Ulysses* but the venerable publisher Random House. Today the major purveyors of adult content include Astral Media's TMN who pipes late-night adult content to subscribers. Satellite providers Star Choice and Bell ExpressVu offer porn to their subscribers. Big-name hotel chains pipe adult movies into rooms.

PORNOGRAPHY VERSUS OBSCENITY IN CANADA

The Broadcasting Act states that Canadian broadcasters cannot broadcast anything "obscene," so why are sexually explicit movies available through all cable companies and satellite providers? The reason is simple: there is a difference between **pornography** and **obscenity** in Canada. This availability is due in large part to the 1992 **Butler ruling** by the Supreme Court of Canada. It has been the basis for the definition of obscenity in Canada. It ruled that any material that mixed sex with violence, included depictions of children having sex, or any sex that is degrading or dehumanizing was obscene. Any other sexually explicit material would not seem to be considered obscene because, as the decision ruled, under Canada's Charter of Rights and Freedoms, laws can't "inhibit the celebration of human sexuality."

■ Evaluating Media Content

study<u>preview</u> **By definition, media content is creative, but the quality of the creativity is a matter for debate. Mass-production techniques, pioneered in factories, have been applied in the mass media to supply the incessant commercial demand for content, which is one of many factors working against consistent creative innovation and excellence.**

MEDIA CONTENT AS ART

Mass media messages can be art of a high order, as was perhaps no better illustrated than by early filmmaker D.W. Griffith. In the 1910s, Griffith proved himself a filmmaking author whose contribution to the culture, for better or worse, was original in scale, content and style. Griffith had something to say, and the new mass medium of film was the vehicle for his message.

In the 1950s, when French New Wave directors were offering distinctive stories and messages, film critic **André Bazin** devised the term **auteur** to denote their significant and original cinematic contributions. Bazin's auteurs included Jean-Luc Godard, who made *Breathless,* and François Truffaut, who made *The 400 Blows.* Their work was marked by distinctive cinematic techniques—freeze-frames, handheld cameras and novel angles, many of them common in movies now. Perhaps the most famous of these highbrow filmmakers who developed a global following was the Swedish director Ingmar Bergman, with *The Seventh Seal* and other dark, moody and autobiographical works.

American filmmakers have also contributed to the auteur movement. Among them was Stanley Kubrick, who directed *2001: A Space Odyssey.* Other notable contemporary American film auteurs include Martin Scorsese, whose films include *Taxi Driver;* David Lynch, who made *Blue Velvet;* and Spike Lee, who focuses on African-American life. In Canadian cinema, both David Cronenberg and Atom Egoyan are noted auteurs.

Spike Lee

Spike Lee (far right)

Spike Lee, a bright, innovative young film director, was in deep trouble in 1992. He had persuaded Warner Brothers, the big Hollywood studio, to put up $20 million for a film biography of controversial black leader Malcolm X, one of Lee's heroes. He insisted on expensive foreign shooting in Cairo and Soweto, and now, not only was the $20 million from Warner gone but so was $8 million from other

investors. To finish the movie, Lee put up his own $3 million upfront salary to pay, he hoped, all the production bills.

The crisis was not the first for Lee, whose experience as a moviemaker illustrates several realities about the U.S. movie industry, not all of them flattering:

- Hollywood is the heart of the U.S. movie industry, and it is difficult, if not impossible, for feature filmmakers to succeed outside of the Hollywood establishment.
- Hollywood, with rare exceptions, favours movies that follow themes that already have proven successful rather than taking risks on innovative, controversial themes.
- Fortunes come and go in Hollywood, even studio fortunes. Although Warner is a major studio and often flush with money, it was on an austerity binge when Spike Lee came back for more money in 1992.

- The U.S. movie industry has been taken over by conglomerates, which, as in the case of Warner Brothers, at the time a subsidiary of Time Warner, was being pressured in 1992 to maximize profits to see the parent company through a difficult economic period.

To hear Spike Lee tell it, his problem also was symptomatic of racism in the movie industry. Addressing the Los Angeles Advertising Club during the *Malcolm X* crisis, Lee, who is black, was blunt: "I think there's a ceiling on how much money Hollywood's going to spend on black films or films with a black theme."

Although studio executives would deny Lee's charge, his perceptions were born of experience in making five movies, all critically acclaimed and all profitable but all filmed on shoestring budgets and with little or no studio promotion.

Culturally significant media content is hardly limited to movies. Older media forms, including novels and short stories, have long been home for creative people whose work adds insight to our lives and deepens our understandings and appreciations. The impact of great composers from eras before the mass media has been exponentially extended through recording, film and television. The printing press greatly expanded the audience for religious scriptures whose messages went back to prehistoric times.

PRODUCTION-LINE ENTERTAINMENT

To be sure, not all media content is high art. A television soap opera, whatever its entertainment value, lacks the creative genius of Shakespeare's enduring *Romeo and Juliet.* Why can't all media content rank high on an artistic scale? Besides the obvious explanation that not everyone is born a Shakespeare, the modern mass media are commercial enterprises that must produce vast quantities of material. In the 1920s, for example, an insatiable public demand for movies led to the creation of the Hollywood **studio system**, in effect turning moviemaking into a factory process. Production quotas drove movie production. The studios, loaded with money, hired leading authors of the day, including F. Scott Fitzgerald and William Faulkner, for creative storylines and scripts, but inexorable demands for material drained them. It has been said that Hollywood had some of the most gifted writers of the time doing their weakest work.

The factory model, a product of the Industrial Age, extends throughout the media. The Canadian book publisher **Harlequin**, owned by Torstar, grinds out romance novels with their bodice-busting covers. Nobody confuses them with high art. Imagine, also, filling a television network's prime-time obligation, 42 half-hour slots a week. It can't all be great stuff, despite the promotional claims in pre-season ramp-ups. Also, many in the mass audience don't want great art anyway.

studio system ■ A production-line movie production system devised by Hollywood in the 1920s.

Harlequin ■ Canadian publisher known for romances with cliché characters, settings and themes; the term is applied generically to pulp romances.

COPYCAT CONTENT

Significant amounts of media content are imitative. Copycat sounds abound in material from the recording industry. In network television a sudden success, like Fox's *American Idol,* spawned other talent-based reality shows, including *Canadian Idol.* Alas, even *American Idol* was hardly original. The concept was licensed from *Pop Idol,* a British show. In 2007, Global aired *Deal or No Deal Canada* as a way of cashing in the success of the Howie Mandel show in the United States.

CROSS-MEDIA ADAPTATIONS

The demand for content creates a vacuum that sucks up material from other media. Movie studios draw heavily on written literature, from best-selling novels to comic books like *Spider-Man* and *The X-Men.* Conversely, fresh movies sometimes are adapted into book form.

Cross-media adaptations don't always work well. Movie versions of books often disappoint readers. Scenes change. So do characters. Inevitably, a lot is left out. Some of the criticism is unfair because it fails to recognize that movies are a distinct medium. How, for example, could a screenwriter pack everything from a 100 000-word novel into a 100-minute script? These are different media. Passages that work brilliantly in a word-driven medium, like a magazine short story, can fall flat in a medium with visual enhancements. Conversely, the nuances compactly portrayed by a master actor, like Meryl Streep or Jack Nicholson, could take pages and pages in a book and not work as well. Also, movie studio producers, almost always needing to appeal to the widest possible audience, will alter plots, scenes and characters and sometimes even reverse a storyline's climactic events.

Some cross-media adaptations are commercial disasters. With limited success, movie studios have tried to cash in on the popularity of video games. Despite high expectations, *Super Mario Bros.* flopped in 1993. The explanation? Some critics cite the same difficulties as occur in transferring messages from books to movies. With video games the audience member plays an active role by exercising some control over the storyline. Watching a movie, however, is relatively passive.

media DATABANK

Cross-Media Exploitation

Harvard symbology professor Dan Brown found surprise success with his novel *The Da Vinci Code,* a whodunit that drew on religion and art history.

With follow-up, spinoff and subsidiary deals, it was expected to spawn almost $1 billion in sales. The projected revenue:

The Da Vinci Code sales	$210 million
Sequel	220 million
Paperback	75 million
Movie with DVD, VHS and TV rebroadcast	450 million
New sales of early Dan Brown books	60 million
Audio books	10 million
Spinoff books, like *De-Coding Da Vinci*	10 million
New sales of books on general subject	10 million

Dan Brown On his way to a reading from *The Da Vinci Code* in his hometown of Exeter, New Hampshire, Dan Brown stops for a photographer. The fast-paced thriller, his fourth book, mixed code-breaking, art history, secret societies, religion and love in a fast-paced thriller that unravels in a 24-hour period.

UNPRETENTIOUS MEDIA CONTENT

Although critics pan a lot of media content as unworthy, the fact is that lowbrow art and middlebrow art find audiences, sometimes large audiences, and have a firm place in the mix that the mass media offer. There is nothing artistically pretentious in **pulp fiction**, including the Harlequin romances, nor their soap-opera equivalents on television.

pulp fiction ■ Quickly and inexpensively produced easy-to-read short novels.

CHAPTER 11 **Wrap-Up**

Entertainment content of the mass media draws huge audiences and drives the economics of most media companies. The drama inherent in good storytelling is a major component that dates to prehistoric tribal gatherings around the campfire. The modern-day campfire is books, movies and television. The emotive power of music, which also has prehistoric roots, is another major component of today's mass media entertainment content. So is sports, which has all the fascination of compelling literature to keep people in tune until the outcome reveals itself. Sometimes overlooked as a genre in media content is sex—probably best explained by the great mystery of sexuality and insuppressible curiosity.

Mass media are not mere conduits for entertainment. The media themselves shape entertainment. Changes in media technology have thrust musical styles into popularity. Marches lent themselves to early acoustic recording, which couldn't handle subtleties. Crooners had their heyday when electric recording was introduced.

The huge audiences that mass media can attract also shape entertainment content. A regional drama that might go over in an isolated community with a unique culture and local issues might not interest a larger audience. The powerhouse media companies seek content that will attract national and even global audiences, which places a premium on entertainment that travels easily and widely.

Questions for Review

1. What categories of entertainment have endured from prehistoric times and now reach people through mass media?
2. How does the use of genres both clarify and cloud a serious discussion of the literary content of the mass media?
3. How has recorded music radically changed the social complexion of the United States?
4. How do you explain the obsession that many people have with mass media coverage of sports?
5. How is it that the Canadian Charter of Rights and Freedoms protects pornography but not obscenity?
6. What changes in mass media technology have reshaped entertainment?
7. Why are creativity and artistry often sacrificed in producing mass media entertainment?

Questions for Critical Thinking

1. Pigeonholing media content into genres involves judgment calls about which informed, clear-thinking people can disagree. Can you make a case for reassigning an example of at least one media product to multiple genres?
2. When do you expect public enthusiasm over *Harry Potter* to fade? *Star Wars? Lord of the Rings?*
3. Do you see any difficulty in defining hip-hop and rap as distinct music genres?
4. Are extreme sports faddish or do you see them as an enduring media genre?
5. Would further miniaturization of electronic media devices serve any purpose for media consumers?

Deepening Your media LITERACY

Is Spike Lee right?

STEP 1 Film director Spike Lee claims that racism is rampant in the movie industry. He asserts that black films or films with black themes get smaller budgets and little or no promotion. Write down what you think makes a black film "black." Is it the theme, the actors, the director?

Dig Deeper

STEP 2

1. The 2000 census estimated that 35.5 million African-Americans live in the United States. This is approximately 13 percent of the total population. That number could rise to 47.1 million in 2025 or 14 percent. On the basis of these figures, what percentage of films made in the United States would you expect to be black films? If your definition of a black film changes, does the percentage also change?

2. Get several copies of the entertainment section of the newspaper or an entertainment weekly or magazine with more than four ads from the film industry for current movies. Count the total number of ads for movies. How many of them fit your definition of a black film? Does the percentage of ads for black films match the percentage of the black population in the United States?

What Do You Think?

STEP 3 Answer these questions:

1. Do you think that homogenization is a factor in how Spike Lee says the movie industry treats black filmmakers and films? What about globalization of the mass media?

2. Do you think that audience fragmentation could be a factor in the future for black films?

3. Do you think Spike Lee's claim of racism in the film industry is true?

Keeping Up to Date

Rolling Stone carries serious articles on music and movies.

Entertainment Weekly is among an array of fan magazines, many of which are more ga-ga over celebrities than concerned with media issues.

Because the mass media are a major industry, you can find regular coverage of media entertainment issues in *The Globe and Mail, National Post, Toronto Star, Maclean's* and other publications.

For Further Learning

Glenn C. Altschuler. *All Shook Up: How Rock 'n' Roll Changed America* (Oxford University Press, 2004).

Barry Diller. "Don't Repackage, Redefine!" *Wired* (February 1995): 82–85.

Stuart Evey. *ESPN: Creating an Empire* (Triumph, 2004).

Elliot Gorn and Warren Goldstein. *A Brief History of American Sports* (Hill and Wang, 1993).

Kathleen Krull. *The Book of Rock Stars: 24 Musical Icons That Shine Through History* (Hyperion, 2004).

Robert L. Hilliard and Michael C. Keith. *Dirty Discourse: Sex and Indecency in American Radio* (Iowa State Press, 2003).

James A. Michener. *Sports in America* (Random House, 1976).

Guthrie P. Ramsey Jr. *Race Music: Black Culture from Bebop to Hip-Hop* (University of California Press, 2003).

Eric Schlosser. "Empire of the Obscene." *The New Yorker* (March 10, 2003): 60–71.

Ronald A. Smith. *Radio, Television, and Big-Time College Sport* (Johns Hopkins University Press, 2001).

Richard Saul Wurman. *Information Anxiety* (Bantom, 1990).

Dolf Zillmann and Peter Voderer. *Media Entertainment: The Psychology of Its Appeal* (Erlbaum, 2000).

Billboard Meter To measure the number of people who pass electronically tagged billboards, Nielsen Media Research issues palm-size devices that tell when participants pass an electronically coded billboard. Data are uploaded from the device to a satellite, then down to Nielsen data keepers who keep score.

Media Research

Media in Theory

Applied and Theoretical Research

MEDIA-SPONSORED RESEARCH

Studies sponsored by mass media companies seek information that can be put to use. This is called **applied research**. When broadcasters pay someone to conduct research on media consumption, they do it because the information will help them make programming decisions. It's called *applied research* because the audience measures and analysis are used to enhance profits.

Mass media research ranges from developing new technology to seeking historical lessons from previous practices. Here are some fields of applied media research:

Technological Research Mass media companies and their suppliers finance **technological research** to take economic advantage of new opportunities. Early radio in Canada, for example, was spearheaded by the CNR who saw it as a business opportunity.

Policy Analysis The media have intense interests in how changes in public policy will affect their business. The importance of good **policy analysis** was illustrated by the decision of the government 30 years ago to allow people to install backyard satellite dishes to pick up television signals. Analysts had anticipated correctly that the television networks would go to satellites to send programs to their affiliates.

Opinion Surveys When anchor Dan Rather began wearing a sweater on the *CBS Evening News,* ratings improved. The network learned about the "sweater factor" from audience **opinion surveys**. Survey research also helps media executives make content decisions—whether to expand sports coverage, to hire a disc jockey away from the competition or to axe a dubious sitcom. Advertisers and public relations practitioners also look to public-opinion surveys.

applied research ■ Usefulness, usually economic, is apparent.

technological research ■ To improve technology and find new technology.

policy analysis ■ Seeks implications of public policy, future effects.

opinion surveys ■ Seek audience reaction, views.

MASS COMMUNICATION SCHOLARSHIP

theoretical research ■ Goal is to advance knowledge.

In contrast to applied research, **theoretical research** looks for truths regardless of practical application. Scholars consider most theoretical research to be on a higher level than applied research, partly because the force that drives it is the seeking of truths for their own sake rather than for any economic goal. Here are some of the kinds of studies and analyses that are the subject of theoretical research:

Effects Studies The greatest ferment in mass communication scholarship has involved questions about effects. In the 1920s, as mass communication theory took form, scholars began exploring the effects of mass communication and of the mass media themselves on society and individuals. Conversely, scholars are also interested in how ongoing changes and adjustments in society influence the mass media and their content. The research is known as **effects studies**.

effects studies ■ Impact of media on society, of society on media.

Process Studies A continuing interest among scholars is the mystery of how the process of mass communication works. Just as human beings have developed theories to explain other great mysteries, such as whether thunder is caused by unhappy gods thrashing about in the heavens, mass communication scholars have developed, in **process studies**, a great many explanations to help us understand mass communication.

process studies ■ To understand the mass communication process.

Uses and Gratifications Studies Beginning in the 1940s, studies about how and why individuals use the mass media attracted scholarly interest. These today are called **uses and gratifications studies** (see also the discussion in Chapter 14).

uses and gratifications studies ■ Theory that people choose media that meet their needs, interests.

Content Analysis George Gerbner, a scholar of media violence, studied the 8 p.m. hour of network television over a period of 19 years and found an average of 168 violent acts a week. Gerbner arrived at his disturbing statistic through **content analysis**, a research method involving the systematic counting of media content. Gerbner's tallying became a basic reference point for important further studies that correlated media-depicted violence with changes in incidents of violence in society at large.

content analysis ■ Measuring media content to establish a database for analysis.

It is also content analysis when a researcher tallies the column inches of sports in a newspaper to determine what percentage of available space goes to sports. While interesting for its own sake, such information can become a significant indicator of the changing role of sports in contemporary life.

media TIMELINE

MEDIA RESEARCH

1914 Advertisers, publications created the Audit Bureau of Circulations to verify circulation claims.

1929 Archibald Crossley conducted the first listenership survey.

1932 George Gallup used quota sampling in an Iowa election.

1936 Gallup used quota sampling in a presidential election.

1940s A.C. Nielsen conducted a demographic listenership survey.

1948 Gallup used probability sampling in a presidential election.

1970s SRI introduced VALS psychographics.

1974 Jonathan Robbin introduced PRIZM geodemographics.

2000 Portable People Meters were introduced to track listenership for radio and television, including cable.

■■ Public-Opinion Sampling

study<u>preview</u> **The effectiveness of mass media messages is measured through research techniques that are widely recognized in the social sciences and in business.**

THE SURVEYING INDUSTRY

Public-opinion surveying is a multi-billion-dollar-a-year business whose clients include major corporations, political candidates and the mass media. Hundreds of companies are in the survey business in the United States and in Canada, most of them performing advertising- and product-related opinion research for private clients. During election campaigns, political candidates become major clients. There are dozens of other survey companies that do confidential research for and about the media. Their findings are important because they determine what kind of advertising will run and where, what programs will be developed and broadcast, and which ones will be cancelled. Some television stations even use such research to choose anchors for major newscasts.

PROBABILITY SAMPLING

Although polling has become a high-profile business, many people do not understand how questions to a few hundred individuals can tell the mood of 350 million North Americans. In the **probability sampling** method pioneered by **George Gallup** in the 1940s, four factors figure into accurate surveying:

Sample Size To learn how students from a certain college or university feel about abortion on demand, you start by asking one student. Because you can hardly generalize from one student to the whole student body of 10 000, you ask a second student. If both agree, you start developing a tentative sense of how students feel, but because you cannot have much confidence in such a tiny sample, you ask a third student and a fourth and a fifth. At some point between interviewing just one and all 10 000 students, you can draw a reasonable conclusion.

How do you choose a **sample size**? Statisticians have found that **384** is a magic number for many surveys. Put simply, no matter how large the **population** being sampled, if every member has an equal opportunity to be polled, you need ask only 384 people to be 95 percent confident that you are within 5 percentage points of a precise reading. For a lot of surveys, that is close enough.

Here is a breakdown, from Philip Meyer's *Precision Journalism,* a book for journalists on surveying, on necessary sample sizes for 95 percent confidence and being within 5 percentage points:

Population Size	Sample Size
Infinity	384
500 000	384
100 000	383
50 000	381
10 000	370
5 000	357
3 000	341
2 000	322
1 000	278

At a college or university with a total enrollment of 10 000, the sample size would need to be 370 students.

Sample Selection The process of choosing whom to interview is known as **sample selection**. Essential in probability sampling is giving every member of the population being sampled an equal chance to be interviewed. If, for example, you want to know how people in Winnipeg intend to vote, you cannot merely go to the corner of Portage and Main and survey the first 384 people who pass by. You would need to check a list of the province's registered voters (450 000) and then divide by the magic number, 384.

$$\frac{450\ 000}{384} = 1172$$

You would need to talk with every 1172nd person on the list.

media ONLINE

Nielsen Nielsen Media Research, the famous TV ratings company.
www.nielsenmedia.ca

BBM Bureau of Measurement measures TV and radio audiences in Canada,
www.bbm.ca

Gallup See results of current and past Gallup polls.
www.gallup.com

Ipsos Canada Canadian research company.
www.ipsos.ca

George Gallup ■ Introduced probability sampling.

probability sampling ■ Everyone in population being surveyed has an equal chance to be sampled.

sample size ■ Number of people surveyed.

384 ■ Number of people in a properly selected sample for results to provide 95 percent confidence that results have less than 5 percent margin of error.

population ■ Group of people being studied.

media ONLINE

Polls The Gallup Poll people explain how they conduct polls.
http://media.gallup.com/PDF/FAQ/HowArePolls.pdf

American Association for Public Opinion Research Individuals who share an interest in public opinion and survey research.
www.aapor.org

sample selection ■ Process for drawing individuals to be interviewed.

Probability Sampling Data collection has become more sophisticated since George Gallup began polling in the 1930s. Polls today track changes in public attitudes over the several decades that data have been accumulated.

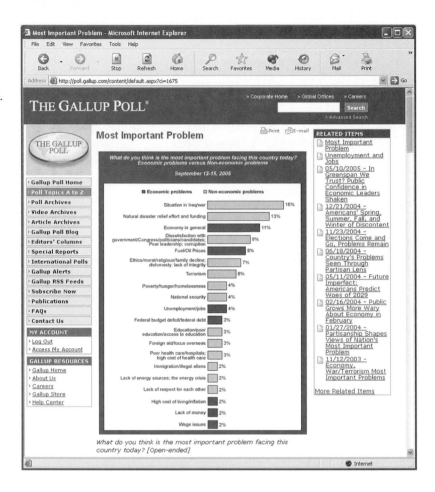

Besides the right sample size and proper interval selection, two other significant variables affect survey accuracy: margin of error and confidence level.

Margin of Error For absolute precision, every person in the population must be interviewed, but such precision is hardly ever needed, and the process would be prohibitively expensive and impracticable. Pollsters must therefore decide what is an acceptable **margin of error** for every survey they conduct. This is a complex matter, but in simple terms, you can have a fairly high level of confidence that a properly designed survey with 384 respondents can yield results within 5 percentage points, either way, of being correct. If the survey finds that two candidates for provincial office are running 51 to 49 percent, for example, the race is too close to call with a sample of 384. If the survey says that the candidates are running 56 to 44 percent, however, you can be reasonably confident who is ahead in the race because, even if the survey is 5 points off on the high side for the leader, the candidate at the very least has 51 percent support (56 percent minus a maximum 5 percentage points for possible error). At best, the trailing candidate has 49 percent (44 percent plus a maximum 5 percentage points for possible error).

Increasing the sample size will reduce the margin of error. Meyer gives this breakdown:

Population Size	Sample Size	Margin of Error
Infinity	384	5 percentage points
Infinity	600	4 percentage points
Infinity	1067	3 percentage points
Infinity	2401	2 percentage points
Infinity	9605	1 percentage point

Professional polling organizations that sample U.S. voters typically use sample sizes between 1500 and 3000 to increase accuracy. Also, measuring subgroups within the population being sampled requires that each subgroup, such as men and women, Catholics and non-Catholics or Northerners and Southerners, be represented by 384 properly selected people.

margin of error ■ Percentage that a survey may be off the mark.

Media PEOPLE

George Gallup

George Gallup

George Gallup was excited. His mother-in-law, Ola Babcock Miller, had decided to run for secretary of state. If elected, she would become not only Iowa's first Democrat but also the first woman to hold the statewide office. Gallup's excitement, however, went beyond the novelty of his mother-in-law's candidacy. The campaign gave him an opportunity to pull together his three primary intellectual interests: survey research, public opinion and politics. In that 1932 campaign, George Gallup conducted the first serious poll in history for a political candidate. Gallup's surveying provided important barometers of public sentiment that helped Miller to gear her campaign to the issues that were most on voters' minds. She won and was re-elected twice by large margins.

Four years after that first 1932 election campaign, Gallup tried his polling techniques in the presidential race and correctly predicted that Franklin Roosevelt would beat Alf Landon. Having called Roosevelt's victory accurately, his Gallup Poll organization had clients knocking at his door.

Gallup devoted himself to accuracy. Even though he predicted Roosevelt's 1936 victory, Gallup was bothered that his reliability was not better. His method, quota sampling, could not call a two-way race within four percentage points. With quota sampling, a representative percentage of women and men was surveyed, as was a representative percentage of Democrats and Republicans, Westerners and Easterners, Christians and Jews and other constituencies.

In 1948 Gallup correctly concluded that Thomas Dewey was not a shoo-in for president. Nonetheless, his pre-election poll was 5.3 percentage points off. So he decided to switch to a tighter method, probability sampling, which theoretically gave everyone in the population being sampled an equal chance to be surveyed. With probability sampling, there was no need for quotas because, as Gallup explained in his folksy Midwestern way, it was like a cook making soup: "When a housewife wants to test the quality of the soup she is making, she tastes only a teaspoonful or two. She knows that if the soup is thoroughly stirred, one teaspoonful is enough to tell her whether she has the right mixture of ingredients." With the new method, Gallup's **statistical extrapolation** narrowed his error rate to less than 2 percentage points.

Even with improvements pioneered by Gallup, public opinion surveying has detractors. Some critics say that polls influence undecided voters toward the front-runner—a bandwagon effect. Other critics say that polls make elected officials too responsive to the momentary whims of the electorate, discouraging courageous leadership. George Gallup, who died in 1984, tirelessly defended polling, arguing that good surveys give voice to the "inarticulate minority" that legislators otherwise might not hear. Gallup was convinced that public-opinion surveys help to make democracy work.

Confidence Level With a sample of 384, pollsters can claim a relatively high 95 percent **confidence level**, that is, that they are within 5 percentage points of being on the mark. For many surveys, this is sufficient statistical validity. If the confidence level needs to be higher, or if the margin of error needs to be decreased, the number of people surveyed will need to be increased. In short, the level of confidence and margin of error are inversely related. A larger sample can improve confidence, just as it also can reduce the margin of error.

QUOTA SAMPLING

Besides probability sampling, pollsters survey cross-sections of the whole population. With **quota sampling**, a pollster checking an election campaign interviews a sample of people that includes a quota of men and women that corresponds to the number of male and female registered voters. The sample might also include an appropriate quota of Liberals, Conversatives and New Democrats; of poor, middle-income and wealthy people; of Catholics, Jews and Protestants; of the employed and unemployed; and other breakdowns significant to the pollster.

Both quota sampling and probability sampling are valid if done correctly, but Gallup abandoned quota sampling because he could not pinpoint public opinion more closely

statistical extrapolation ■ Drawing conclusions from a segment of the whole.

confidence level ■ Degree of certainty that a survey is accurate.

quota sampling ■ Demographics of the sample coincide with those of the whole population.

than four percentage points on average. With probability sampling, he regularly came within two percentage points.

EVALUATING SURVEYS

Sidewalk interviews cannot be expected to reflect the views of the population. The people who respond to such polls are self-selected by virtue of being at a given place at a given time. Just as unreliable are phone-in polls with 1-800 or 1-900 telephone numbers. These polls test the views only of people who are aware of the poll and who have sufficiently strong opinions to go to the trouble of calling in.

Journalists run the risk of being duped when special-interest groups suggest that news stories be written based on their privately conducted surveys. Some organizations selectively release self-serving conclusions.

To guard against being duped, the Canadian Press insists on knowing methodology details before running poll stories. In *The Canadian Press StyleBook,* CP tells reporters to ask:

- **How many people were interviewed and how were they selected?** Any survey of fewer than 384 people selected randomly from the population group has a greater margin for error than is usually tolerated.
- **When was the poll taken?** Reporters should make note of the date the survey was taken. Opinions shift over time. During election campaigns, shifts can be quick, even overnight.
- **Who paid for the poll?** A sponsored poll may be biased; therefore reporters should be skeptical, asking whether the results being released constitute everything learned in the survey. The timing of the release of political polls to be politically advantageous is not uncommon.
- **How was the sample selected?** Reporters should ensure that respondents were selected via random selection. Margins of error exist in all surveys unless everyone in the sample had an equal chance of being surveyed.
- **How was the poll conducted?** Whether a survey was conducted over the telephone or face-to-face in homes is important. Polls conducted on street corners or in shopping malls are not worth much statistically. Mail surveys are flawed unless surveyors follow up on people who do not answer the original questionnaires.
- **How were questions worded and in what order were they asked?** Drafting questions is an art. Sloppily worded questions yield sloppy conclusions. Leading questions and loaded questions can skew results. So can question sequencing.

It is with great risk that a polling company's client misrepresents survey results. Most polling companies, concerned about protecting their reputations, include a clause in their contracts with clients that gives the pollster the right to approve the release of findings. The clause usually reads: "When misinterpretation appears, we shall publicly disclose what is required to correct it, notwithstanding our obligation for client confidentiality in all other respects."

LATTER-DAY STRAW POLLS

Many media outlets dabble, some say irresponsibly, with phone-in polling on public issues. The vehicle is the **1-900 telephone number**, which listeners dial at 50 cents a call to register yea or nay on a question. These **straw polls** are conducted on the internet too. While they can be fun, statistically they are meaningless.

Just as dubious are the candid camera features, popular in weekly newspapers, in which a question is put to people on the street. The photos of half a dozen individuals and their comments are then published, often on the editorial page. These features are circulation builders for small publications whose financial success depends on how many local names and mug shots can be crammed into an issue, but it is only coincidental when the views expressed are representative of the population as a whole.

These **roving photographer** features are at their worst when people are not given time to formulate an intelligent response. The result too often is a contribution to the public babble, not public understanding. The result is irresponsible pseudojournalism.

1-900 telephone numbers
Used for phone-in surveys; respondents select themselves to participate and they pay for the call.

straw poll Respondents select themselves to be polled; unreliable indicator of public opinion.

roving photographer
Statistically unsound way to tap public opinion.

Measuring Audience Size

ONLINE
Audit Bureau of Circulations
Measuring print circulation.
www.accessabc.com

Print Measurement Bureau Measuring
the reading habits of Canadians.
www.pmb.ca

studypreview To attract advertisers, the mass media need to know the number and kinds of people they reach. This is done for the print media by audits and for the broadcast media by surveys. Some approaches are more reliable than others.

NEWSPAPER AND MAGAZINE AUDITS

The number of copies a newspaper or magazine puts out, called **circulation**, is fairly easy to calculate. It is simple arithmetic involving data like press runs, subscription sales and unsold copies returned from newsracks. Many publishers follow strict procedures, which are checked by independent audit organizations, like the **Audit Bureau of Circulations** (ABC), to assure advertisers that the system is honest and circulation claims are comparable.

> **circulation** ■ Number of readers of a publication.
>
> **Audit Bureau of Circulations** ■ Checks newspaper circulation claims.

The Audit Bureau of Circulations was formed in 1914 to remove the temptation for publishers to inflate their claims to attract advertisers and hike ad rates. Inflated claims, contagious in some cities, were working to the disadvantage of honest publishers. Today, most newspapers and magazines belong to ABC, which means that they follow the bureau's standards for reporting circulation and are subject to the bureau's audits.

The **Print Measurement Bureau** (PMB) tracks magazine sales in Canada. In 2001, they introduced a new method to measure readership in Canada. The "recent reading" method doesn't measure how many magazines have been sold, but rather how many have been read. A survey asks respondents when they last read an issue of *Maclean's* or *Reader's Digest*. PMB feels that this helps paint a truer picture of how successful Canadian magazines are. This method is also used worldwide to measure magazine readership.

> **Print Measurement Bureau** ■ Checks magazine circulation claims.

BROADCAST RATINGS

Radio and television audiences are difficult to measure, but advertisers still need counts to help them decide where to place ads and what is a fair price. To keep track of broadcast audiences, a whole **ratings** industry, now with about 200 companies worldwide, has developed. Today in Canada, the Bureau of Measurement (BBM) and Nielsen Media Research both provide useful data for Canadian advertisers by measuring radio, television and web audiences. In 2006, the two companies entered into a joint venture and formed **BBM Nielsen Media Research.**

> **ratings** ■ Measurements of broadcast audience size.
>
> **BBM Nielsen Media Research** ■ Surveys TV and radio in Canada.

Radio ratings began in 1929 when advertisers asked pollster Archibald Crossley to determine how many people were listening to network programs. Crossley checked a small sample of households and then extrapolated the data into national ratings, the same process that radio and television audience tracking companies still use, though there have been refinements.

In the 1940s Nielsen began telling advertisers which radio programs were especially popular among men, women and children. Nielsen also divided listenership into age brackets: 18 to 34, 35 to 49 and 50 plus. These were called **demographic** breakdowns. When Nielsen moved into television monitoring in 1950, it expanded audience data into more breakdowns. Today breakdowns include income, education, religion, occupation, neighbourhood and even which products the viewers of certain programs use frequently.

> **demographics** ■ Characteristics of groups within a population being sampled, including age, gender, affiliations.

AUDIENCE MEASUREMENT TECHNIQUES

The primary techniques, sometimes used in combination, for measuring broadcast audiences are interview, diaries and meters.

Interviews In his pioneer 1929 listenership polling, Archibald Crossley placed telephone calls to randomly selected households. Although many polling companies use telephone **interviews** exclusively, they're not used much in broadcasting anymore. Also rare in

> **interviews** ■ Face-to-face, mail or telephone survey technique.

broadcasting are face-to-face interviews. Although eyeball-to-eyeball interviewing can elicit fuller information, it is labour-intensive and relatively expensive.

Diaries Nielsen began using **diaries** in the 1950s. Instead of interviews, Nielsen mailed forms to selected families in major markets to list program titles, times, channels and who was watching. This was done in major sweep periods: February, May, July and November. Although diaries were cost-efficient, viewers would forget their duty and then try to remember days later what they had watched. The resulting data were better than no data but were rather muddy.

Meters Meters were introduced in the 1970s as a supplement to diaries to improve accuracy. Some Nielsen families had their sets wired to track what channel was on. Some were issued meters that household members could click so that Nielsen could determine for whom programs have their appeal—men, women or children.

People Meters In 1987 Nielsen introduced **people meters**. These were two-function units, one on the television set to scan the channels being watched every 2.7 seconds and a handheld remote that monitored who was watching. With data flowing in nightly to Nielsen's central computers, the company generates next-day reports, called **overnights**, for the networks and advertisers.

Portable Meters In 2001 Nielsen and **Arbitron**, which focuses on radio audiences, jointly tested portable meters for people to carry around. The pager-size meters, weighing about 70 grams, were set to pick up inaudible signals transmitted with programs. The goal: to track away-from-home audiences at sports bars, offices and airports and, in the case of radio, cars. Tracking those "lost listeners" could affect ratings. The "walking meters," as they are called, also track commuter radio habits for the first time.

INTERNET AUDIENCE MEASURES

The leading internet audience measuring company, **Media Metrix**, uses a two-track system to determine how many people view websites. Media Metrix gathers data from 40 000 individual computers whose owners have agreed to be monitored. Some of these computers are programmed to track internet usage and report data back by email. In addition, Media Metrix has lined up other computer users to mail in a tracking disc periodically. In 1998 the Nielsen television ratings company set up a similar methodology. Other companies also are in the internet ratings business.

How accurate are internet ratings? Some major content providers, including CNN, ESPN and Time Warner, claim that the ratings undercount their users. Such claims go beyond self-serving comments because, in fact, different rating companies come up with widely divergent ratings. The question is: Why can't the ratings companies get it right? The answer, in part, is that divergent data flow from divergent methodologies. Data need to be viewed in terms of the methodology that was used. Also, the infant internet ratings business undoubtedly is hobbled by methodology flaws that have yet to be identified and corrected.

BILLBOARD MEASURES

Nielsen has devised devices to gauge billboard readership. In the United States, $5 billion a year is spent on outdoor advertising, but until the Nielsen device was introduced in 2004, the effectiveness had always been by guess and hunch. The Nielsen system, first tested in South Africa, went into operation in Chicago with 700 palm-size devices carried by volunteers. A global-positioning satellite tracks a device's movements every 10 seconds to determine how many times it passes GPS-coded billboards. That information is relayed to a Nielsen database in Tampa, Florida, where it is overlaid with a map of billboard sites. The system doesn't measure whether the participants see the billboards, only whether they travel near them. But for billboard companies, including Nielsen clients JCDecaux and Viacom Outdoor, the data figure into pitches for clients.

diaries ■ Sampling technique in which respondents keep their own records.

people meters ■ Devices that track individual viewers.

overnights ■ Next-morning reports on network viewership.

Arbitron ■ International media and marketing research company.

ONLINE

comScore Media Metrix Leading internet audience measurement company. **www.comscore.com/metrix**

Media Metrix ■ A service measuring internet audience size.

CRITICISM OF RATINGS

However sophisticated the ratings services have become, they have critics. Many fans question the accuracy of ratings when their favourite television program is cancelled because the network finds the ratings inadequate. Something is wrong, they say, when the viewing preferences of a few thousand households determine network programming for the entire nation. Ratings have problems, some inherent in differing methodologies and some attributable to human error and fudging.

Discrepancies When different ratings services come up with widely divergent findings in the same market, advertisers become suspicious. Minor discrepancies can be explained by different sampling methods, but significant discrepancies point to flawed methodology or execution.

Slanted Results Sales reps of some local stations, eager to demonstrate to advertisers that their stations have large audiences, extract only the favourable data from survey results. It takes a sophisticated local advertiser to reconcile slanted and fudged claims.

Sample Selection Some ratings services select their samples meticulously, giving every household in a market a statistically equal opportunity to be sampled. Some sample selections are seriously flawed. How reliable, for example, are the listenership claims of a rock 'n' roll station that puts a disc jockey's face on billboards all over town and then sends the disc jockey to a high school to ask about listening preferences?

Hyping Ratings-hungry stations have learned how to build audiences during **sweeps** weeks in February, May and November when major local television ratings are done. Consider these examples of **hyping**:

- Radio giveaways often coincide with ratings periods.
- Many news departments promote sensationalistic series for the sweeps and then retreat to routine coverage when the ratings period is over. Just ahead of a Minneapolis sweeps, one station mailed out thousands of questionnaires, asking people to watch its programs and mail back the form. Accused of trickery to look good in the ratings, the station responded with a straight face that it merely was trying a new technique to strengthen viewership. The timing, it argued, was mere coincidence.
- Besides sweeps weeks, there are **black weeks** when no ratings are conducted. In these periods some stations run all kinds of odd and dull serve-the-public programs that they would never consider during a sweeps period.

Respondent Accuracy Respondents don't always answer truthfully. People may tell interviewers or diaries that they watched *Masterpiece Theatre* on PBS when they really watched *Trailer Park Boys* on Showcase. For the same reason, shock radio and trash television may have more audience than the ratings show.

Zipping, Zapping and Flushing Ratings services measure audiences for programs and for different times of day, but they do not measure whether commercials are watched. Advertisers are interested, of course, in whether the programs in which their ads are sandwiched are popular, but more important to them is whether people are watching the ads.

This vacuum in audience measurements was documented in the 1960s when somebody with a sense of humour correlated a major drop in Chicago water pressure with the Super Bowl halftime, in what became known as the **flush factor**. Football fans were getting off the couch by the thousands at halftime to go to the bathroom. Advertisers were missing many people because although viewers were watching the program, many were not watching the ads.

This problem has been exacerbated with the advent of handheld television remote controls and DVR systems. Viewers can **zip** from station to station to avoid commercials, and when they record programs for later viewing, they can **zap** out the commercials.

sweeps ■ When broadcast ratings are conducted.

hyping ■ Intensive promotion to attract an audience during ratings periods.

black weeks ■ Periods when ratings are not conducted.

flush factor ■ Viewers leave during commercials to go to refrigerator, bathroom, etc.

zipping ■ Viewers change television channels to avoid commercials.

zapping ■ Viewers record programs and eliminate commercial breaks.

New Tracking Technology

As Ron Kolessar was developing the Portable People Meter, he knew it could shape the future of media and advertising. Kolessar, the chief engineer at Arbitron, began work on the PPM in early 1992 when his bosses asked him to find a less expensive way to monitor television and radio audiences at the same time.

At first, research companies collected data by asking people to fill out a diary. Then Nielsen began using its electronic People Meter, which automatically recorded what channel a television set was tuned to. But Kolessar realized that to get the complete story, they needed to "monitor the person." His PPM records what the wearer is hearing at all times—not just at home, but also at the sports bar, at work, in the supermarket, in hotel rooms. After 13 years and $80 million in development, tests were run in Philadelphia and Houston in which people wore the pager-size device all day, docking it at night so that it could send information back to its mother computer.

The device works through a process known as psycho-acoustic masking. Arbitron has asked radio and television stations around the country to run their broadcasts through an encoding device that embeds a signal that is inaudible to humans but that can be picked up by the PPM.

The object is to track audience fragmentation, the emerging phenomenon in which members of a family no longer sit on the couch together to watch a television program. Today's family views different television, radio and internet fare at the same time. As time becomes more precious, people seek content in whatever way works best for them—broadband, digital satellite, terrestrial. As the audience fragments, the economic model for advertisers changes—and bigger samples are needed. BBM Nielsen Media Research began using PPM in 2002 on a trial basis in Quebec markets. The rest of Canada will soon follow.

Once feared by advertisers, audience fragmentation now is seen as a great opportunity. Advertisers will be able to target small niche audiences, and media

70 Gram Walking Meter

Outside-the-Home Television Measuring television audiences has become a greater challenge with the proliferation of sets in airports, bars and even luxury SUVs. Here, students at Minnesota State University, Mankato, jog on treadmills while watching television and surfing the net. The Nielsen audience measurement company is working on devices that volunteers wear with them and that will allow Nielsen to check even on exposure to billboards. The walking meters, as they're called, pick up an inaudible code embedded in the audio of television, radio and streamed programs—and signals sent out by billboards as the volunteers pass by. When people get home, they put the meters in a dock that transmits accumulated data to survey-company computers for aggregation.

producers will be able to judge audience reactions down to the second of a broadcast. To take advantage of this opportunity, new ways are needed to track these increasingly sought-after audiences. The future may see voice- and face-recognition meters and systems that can measure what media people absorb and then what they buy—an advertiser's dream.

WHAT DO YOU THINK?

1. Will consumers benefit as much as providers will when the technology enabling providers to target smaller niche groups develops?

2. As ways to measure our culture's reaction to the media become more sophisticated, some people fear that Big Brother, the leader of a totalitarian government that censored everyone's behaviour, even their thoughts, in George Orwell's classic novel *1984,* is coming. What do you think?

3. A major concern about the PPM is that initial tests showed that people listen to twice as many radio stations as was previously thought, and critics say that it records even when the listener doesn't actively choose the station. Could it be that the system simply picks up too much?

Measuring Audience Reaction

study<u>preview</u> The television ratings business has moved beyond measuring audience size to measuring audience reaction. Researchers measure audience reaction with numerous methods, including focus groups, galvanic skin checks and prototypes.

FOCUS GROUPS

Television consulting companies measure audience reaction with **focus groups**. Typically, an interview crew goes to a shopping centre, chooses a dozen individuals by gender and age, and offers them cookies, soft drinks and $25 each to sit down and watch a taped local newscast. A moderator then asks their reactions, sometimes with loaded and leading questions to open them up. It is a tricky research method that depends highly on the skill of the moderator. In one court case an anchor who had lost her job as a result of responses to a focus group complained that the moderator had contaminated the process with prejudicial assertions and questions:

- "This is your chance to get rid of the things you don't like to see on the news."
- "Come on, unload on those sons of bitches who make $100 000 a year."
- "This is your chance to do more than just yell at the TV. You can speak up and say I really hate that guy or I really like that broad."
- "Let's spend 30 seconds destroying this anchor. Is she a mutt? Be honest about this."

Even when conducted skilfully, focus groups have the disadvantage of reflecting the opinion of the loudest respondent.

GALVANIC SKIN CHECKS

Consulting companies hired by television stations run a great variety of studies to determine audience reaction. Local stations, which originate news programs and not much else, look to these consultants for advice on news sets, story selection and even which anchors and reporters are most popular. Besides surveys, these consultants sometimes use **galvanic skin checks**. Wires are attached to individuals in a sample group of viewers to measure pulse and skin reactions, such as perspiration. Advocates of these tests claim that they reveal how much interest a newscast evokes and whether the interest is positive or negative.

These tests were first used to check audience reaction to advertisements, but today some stations look to them in deciding whether to remodel a studio. A dubious use, from a journalistic perspective, is using galvanic skin checks to determine what kinds of stories to cover and whether to find new anchors and reporters. The skin checks reward short, photogenic stories like fires and accidents rather than significant stories, which tend to be longer and don't lend themselves to flashy video. The checks also favour good-looking, smooth anchors and reporters, regardless of their journalistic competence. One wag was literally correct when he called this "a heartthrob approach to journalism."

PROTOTYPE RESEARCH

Before making major investments, media executives need to obtain as much information as they can to determine how to enhance a project's chances for success or whether it has a chance at all. This is known as **prototype research**. The **American Research Institute** of Los

focus groups ■ Small groups interviewed in loosely structured ways for opinion, reactions.

galvanic skin checks ■ Monitor pulse, skin responses to stimuli.

If It Bleeds, It Leads Audience researchers have found newscast ratings go up for stations that consistently deliver graphic video. This has prompted many stations to favour fire stories, for example, if graphic video is available—even if the fire wasn't consequential. The ratings quest also prompts these stations to favour crimes and accidents over more substantive stories, like government budgets, that don't lend themselves to gripping graphics.

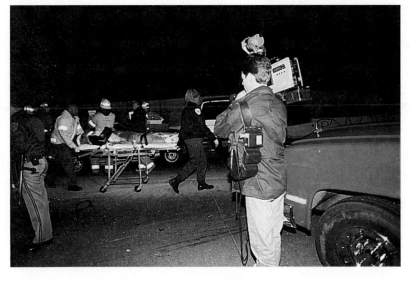

prototype research ■ Checks response to product still in development.

American Research Institute ■ Conducts movie prototype research.

Angeles specializes in showing previews of television programs and even promotional ads to sample audiences. It is a method originated by movie studios, which invite people to advance showings and watch their reaction to decide how to advertise a new film most effectively, how to time the film's release and even whether to re-edit the film.

■ Audience Analysis

studypreview Traditional demographic polling methods divided people by gender, age and other easily identifiable population characteristics. Today, media people use sophisticated lifestyle breakdowns such as geodemographics and psychographics to match the content of their publications, broadcast programs and advertising to the audiences they seek.

DEMOGRAPHICS

Early in the development of public-opinion surveying, pollsters learned that broad breakdowns had limited usefulness. Archibald Crossley's pioneering radio surveys, for example, revealed the number of people who were listening to network programs, which was valuable to the networks and their advertisers, but Crossley's figures did not tell how many listeners were men or women, urban or rural, old or young. Such breakdowns of overall survey data, called demographics, were developed in the 1930s as Crossley, Gallup and other early pollsters refined their work.

Today, if demographic data indicate a prime ministerial candidate is weak in the Maritimes, campaign strategists can gear the candidate's message to Maritime concerns. Through demographics, advertisers keen on reaching young women can identify magazines that will carry their ads to that audience. If advertisers seek an older audience, they can use demographic data to determine where to place their television ads.

While demographics remains valuable today, newer methods can break the population into categories that have even greater usefulness. These newer methods, which include cohort analysis, geodemography and psychographics, provide lifestyle breakdowns.

COHORT ANALYSIS

cohort analysis ■ Demographic tool to identify marketing targets by common characteristics.

Millennials ■ Today's 20-something generation. Sometimes referred to as Generation Y.

Generation X ■ Today's 30-something generation.

Baby Boomers ■ Today's 40-something and 50-something generations.

Postwar Generation ■ Today's 60-something generation.

World War II Veterans ■ Today's 70-something and 80-something generations.

Marketing people have developed **cohort analysis**, a specialized form of demographics, to identify generations and then design and produce products with generational appeal. Advertising people then gear media messages with the images, music, humour and other generational variables that appeal to the target cohort. The major cohorts are dubbed:

- **Millennials**, who came of age in the 1990s and early 21st century.
- **Generation X**, who came of age in the 1980s.
- **Baby Boomers**, who came of age in the late 1960s and 1970s.
- **Postwar Generation**, who came of age in the 1950s.
- **World War II Veterans**, who came of age in the 1940s.
- **Depression Survivors**, who came of age during the economic depression of the 1930s.

Cohort analysis has jarred traditional thinking that people, as they get older, simply adopt their parents' values. The new 50-plus generation, for example, grew up on Coke and Pepsi drinks and, to the dismay of coffee growers, may prefer to start the day with cola—not the coffee their parents drank.

The Chrysler automobile company was early to recognize that Baby Boomers aren't interested in buying Cadillac-type luxury cars even when they have amassed the money to afford them. In 1996 Chrysler scrapped plans for a new luxury car to compete with Cadillac and instead introduced the $35 000 open-top 1997 Plymouth Prowler that gave Baby Boomers a nostalgic feel for the hot rods of their youth. Chrysler also determined that graying Baby Boomers preferred upscale Jeeps to the luxo-barge cars that appealed to the Postwar Generation.

Advertising people who use cohort analysis know that Baby Boomers, although now in their 50s, are still turned on by pizzas and the Rolling Stones. In short, the habits of youth stick with a generation as it gets older. And what appealed to the 30-somethings a decade ago won't necessarily sail with today's 30-something set. David Bostwick, Chrysler's marketing research director, puts it this way: "Nobody wants to become their parents."

GEODEMOGRAPHICS

While demographics, including cohort analysis, remains valuable today, new methods can break the population into categories that have even greater usefulness. These newer methods, which include geodemography, provide lifestyle breakdowns.

Computer whiz **Jonathan Robbin** provided the basis for more sophisticated breakdowns in 1974 when he began developing his **PRIZM** system for **geodemography**. From census data, Robbin grouped every zip code by ethnicity, family life cycle, housing style, mobility and social rank. Then he identified 34 factors that statistically distinguished neighbourhoods from each other. All this information was cranked through a computer programmed by Robbin to plug every zip code into 1 of 40 clusters. Here are the most frequent clusters created through PRIZM, which stands for Potential Rating Index for Zip Markets, with the labels Robbin put on them:

- **Blue-Chip Blues.** These are the wealthiest blue-collar suburbs. These Blue-Chip Blues, as Robbin calls them, make up about 6 percent of households. About 13 percent of these people are college graduates.
- **Young Suburbia.** Child-rearing outlying suburbs, 5.3 percent of population; 24 percent are college grads.
- **Golden Ponds.** Rustic mountain, seashore or lakeside cottage communities, 5.2 percent of population; 13 percent are college grads.
- **Blue-Blood Estates.** Wealthiest neighbourhoods; 51 percent are college grads.
- **Money and Brains.** Posh big-city enclaves of townhouses, condos and apartments; 46 percent are college grads.

Geodemographic breakdowns are used not only for magazine advertising but also for editorial content. At Time Warner magazines, geodemographic analysis permits issues to be edited for special audiences. *Time,* for example, has a 600 000 circulation edition for company owners, directors, board chairs, presidents, other titled officers and department heads. Among others are editions for physicians and college students.

PSYCHOGRAPHICS

A refined lifestyle breakdown introduced in the late 1970s, **psychographics**, divides the population into lifestyle segments. One leading psychographics approach, the Values and Life-Styles program, known as **VALS** for short, uses an 85-page survey to identify broad categories of people:

- **Belongers.** Comprising about 38 percent of the U.S. population, these people are conformists who are satisfied with mainstream values and are reluctant to change brands once they're satisfied. Belongers are not very venturesome and fit the stereotype of Middle America. They tend to be churchgoers and television watchers.
- **Achievers.** Comprising about 20 percent of the population, these are prosperous people who fit into a broader category of inner-directed consumers. Achievers pride themselves on making their own decisions. They're an upscale audience to which a lot of advertising is directed. As a group, achievers aren't heavy television watchers.
- **Societally Conscious.** Comprising 11 percent of the population, these people are aware of social issues and tend to be politically active. The societally conscious also are upscale and inner-directed, and they tend to prefer reading to watching television.
- **Emulators.** Comprising 10 percent of the population, these people aspire to a better life but, not quite understanding how to do it, go for the trappings of prosperity. Emulators are status seekers, prone to suggestions on what makes the good life.
- **Experientials.** Comprising 5 percent of the population, these people are venturesome, willing to try new things in an attempt to experience life fully. They are a promising upscale audience for many advertisers.

Depression Survivors ■ Today's 80-something and 90-something generations.

Jonathan Robbin ■ Devised PRIZM geodemography system.

PRIZM ■ Identifies population characteristics by zip code.

geodemography ■ Demographic characteristics by geographic area.

psychographics ■ Breaking down a population by lifestyle characteristics.

VALS ■ Psychographic analysis by values, lifestyle, life stage.

ONLINE

VALS Take a survey to find out where you fit into the VALS categories. **www.sric-bi.com/VALS/ presurvey.shtml**

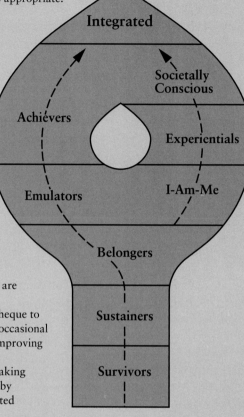

INTEGRATED PEOPLE
These people have "put it all together," as the VALS theorists describe it. These people see many sides of an issue and are capable of assuming leadership if appropriate or a secondary role if that is appropriate.

OUTER-DIRECTED PEOPLE
These people are motivated by external things, like making money, keeping up with the neighbours, and fitting in.
Achievers. These people are success-oriented, hard-working, and materialistic.
Emulators. These people are status-seekers. Having the symbols of success is important to them.
Belongers. These people are conforming and tend to be conservative and conventional. They lean toward nostalgic sentimentalism with a puritanical streak.

NEED-DRIVEN PEOPLE
Basic human needs like food and shelter are central issues for need-driven people.
Sustainers. These people live from paycheque to paycheque. Although they engage in an occasional extravagance, they have little hope for improving their lot in life.
Survivors. These people worry about making ends meet. As a group, they are marked by poverty, low education, old age and limited access to upper mobility.

INNER-DIRECTED PEOPLE
These people are self-motivated in much that they do. They are oriented to personal growth.
Societally Conscious. These people feel obliged to improve the world and tend to be active on political and social issues.
Experientials. These people want new experiences and tend to be venturesome. They seek personal growth.
I-Am-Me's. These people work very hard at setting themselves apart. Sometimes they are obnoxious in trying to attract attention to how they are different.

Figure 12.1 VALS Hierarchy Developmental psychologists have long told us that people change their values as they mature. Today, to identify potential consumers and to design effective messages, many advertisers rely on the Values and Life-Styles model, VALS for short, which was derived from developmental psychology. Relatively few advertising messages are aimed at survivors and sustainers, who have little discretionary income. However, belongers and people on the divergent outer-directed or inner-directed paths are lucrative advertising targets for many products and services.

- **I-Am-Me's.** Comprising 3 percent of the population, these people work hard to set themselves apart and are susceptible to advertising pitches that offer ways to differentiate themselves, which gives them a kind of subculture conformity. SRI International, which developed the VALS technique, characterized I-Am-Me's as "a guitar-playing punk rocker who goes around in shades and sports an earring." Rebellious youth, angry and maladjusted, fit this category.
- **Survivors.** This is a small downscale category that includes pensioners who worry about making ends meet.
- **Sustainers.** These people live from paycheque to paycheque. Although they indulge in an occasional extravagance, they have slight hope for improving their lot in life. Sustainers are a downscale category and aren't frequent advertising targets.
- **Integrateds.** Comprising only 2 percent of the population, integrateds are both creative and prosperous—willing to try different products and ways of doing things, and they have the wherewithal to do it.

Applying psychographics is not without hazard. The categories are in flux as society and lifestyles change. SRI researchers who chart growth in the percentage of I-Am-Me's, experientials and the societally conscious project that they total one-third of the population. Belongers are declining.

Another complication is that no person fits absolutely the mould of any one category. Even for individuals who fit one category better than another, there is no single mass medium to reach them. VALS research may show that achievers constitute the biggest market for antihistamines, but belongers also head to the medicine cabinet when they're congested.

Theoretical research, which mostly takes place in the academic realm, and applied research, which the media eagerly fund, use many of the same tools. A unifying tool of these disparate research approaches is public-opinion sampling. It is used to track public opinion, which is essential in public relations work; to learn which television programs are the most watched, which is essential in programming and advertising decisions; and to determine the effects of media and how people use the media, which are scholarly endeavours.

Questions for Review

1. What do surveys tell the mass media about their audiences?
2. How is the size of mass media audiences measured?
3. How is the reaction of people to the mass media measured?
4. What are techniques of audience analysis?
5. Why are mass media organizations more interested in applied than theoretical research?

Questions for Critical Thinking

1. Street-corner polls are based on weak methodology. Explain how quota sampling and probability sampling are improvements.
2. What is the basis for arguments that public-opinion surveys subvert democracy? What is the counter-argument?
3. The Audit Bureau of Circulations and broadcast ratings services like BBM Nielsen Media Research are essential media services to advertisers. How are these services similar? How different?
4. How can local television and radio stations manipulate their ratings?
5. Explain how applied research and theoretical research differ.

Deepening Your
media LITERACY

How reliable are "person-in-the-street" interviews?

STEP 1 Some news organizations conduct straw polls where they interview people on the street or in the mall on a variety of issues. Have you ever participated in such an interview? If so, did you tell the truth?

Dig Deeper

STEP 2 Critics say that these types of straw polls are irresponsible journalism. They claim it's not a representative sample of people. Write a list of reasons why you think they believe this. Write another list of reasons why you think straw polls might play a useful role in the democratic process.

What Do You Think?

STEP 3 Evaluate your lists. Do the possible pros for straw polling outweigh the possible problems? Do these types of "person-in-the-street" interviews affect the political process?

Keeping Up to Date

Public Opinion Quarterly is a scholarly publication. *American Demographics* and *Public Opinion* have a lot of general-interest content for media observers.

Online, BBM Canada publishes *In Sync* on a quarterly basis. It highlights trends in audience measurement.

For Further Learning

James Atlas. "Beyond Demographics: How Madison Avenue Knows Who You Are and What You Want." *Atlantic* 254 (October 1984): 4, 49–58.

Charles O. Bennett. *Facts without Opinion: First Fifty Years of the Audit Bureau of Circulations* (Audit Bureau of Circulations, 1965).

Keith Damsell. "Magazine Numbers Unravelled." *The Globe and Mail* (July 6, 2001).

Tom Dickson. *Mass Media Education in Transition: Preparing for the 21st Century* (Erlbaum, 2000).

Dan Fleming, editor. *Formations: 21st Century Media Studies* (Manchester University Press, 2001).

George Gallup. *The Sophisticated Poll Watcher's Guide* (Princeton Opinion Press, 1972).

Michelle Gaulin. "Measuring Readership." *Ryerson Review of Journalism* (Spring 2004).

Shearson A. Lowery and Melvin L. DeFleur. *Milestones in Mass Communication Research: Media Effects* (Longman, 1983).

Philip Meyer. *Precision Journalism,* Second edition (Indiana University Press, 1979).

David W. Moore. *The Superpollsters: How They Measure and Manipulate Public Opinion in America* (Four Walls Eight Windows, 1992).

Paula M. Poindexter and Maxwell E. McCombs. *Research in Mass Communication: A Practical Guide* (St. Martin's, 2000).

Alan Prendergast. "Wendy Bergin's Exclusive Hoax." *Washington Journalism Review* 13 (October 1991): 8, 30–34.

Philip Preville. "Do We Have a Sweeps Week?" *Saturday Night* (March 10, 2001).

William S. Rubens. "A Personal History of TV Ratings, 1929 to 1989 and Beyond." *Feedback* 30 (Fall 1989): 4, 3–15.

Robert Strauss. "The Man without a Dog in the Fight." *Trust* 1 (2) (Fall 1998): 2–7.

Kenneth F. Warren. *In Defense of Public Opinion Polling* (Westview, 2001).

James G. Webster, Patricia F. Phalen and Lawrence W. Lichty. *Ratings Analysis: The Theory and Practice of Audience Research,* Second edition (Erlbaum, 2000).

Michael J. Weiss. *The Clustering of America* (Harper & Row, 1988).

Roger D. Wimmer and Joseph R. Dominick. *Mass Media Research: An Introduction,* Fifth edition (Wadsworth, 1997).

Richard Saul Wurman. *Information Anxiety* (Doubleday, 1989).

Mass Media

chapter

Law and Ethics

13

Media in Theory

Digital Technology and Media Law

John Perry Barlow ■ Believes copyright laws are archaic.

As former lyricist for the Grateful Dead **John Perry Barlow** envisions the future, giant media companies will shrivel. The internet makes it possible for people to acquire mass messages, like pop music, directly from artists.

Such direct transactions between artists and consumers undermine the profitable role that media companies have been playing in the dissemination of messages.

To make his point, Barlow, cofounder of the Electronic Frontier Foundation, points to Napster file-sharing technology that burst onto the scene in 1999. Until the courts stopped the practice in 2001, music fans used Napster to bypass media companies and traditional record-sales channels. Record companies were cut out. What's happened with records, Barlow says, inevitably will happen with other kinds of mass messages.

No wonder media executives were watching closely when the record industry went to court to shut Napster down and later to sue individual downloaders. The issue was copyright law, which guarantees that people who create intellectual property, like music, hold the right to benefit financially from their work. According to conventional wisdom, the financial incentive inspires creative people to keep producing and thus enriches society.

Until the internet, creative people almost always turned over the ownership of their work to media companies because those companies owned the only means to disseminate messages to mass audiences. In exchange, media companies gave a percentage of their revenue to the creative people.

In court against Napster, the record companies argued that composers, lyricists and performers were in danger of losing their share of the revenue generated by the record companies. Without that financial incentive, according to these anti-Napster forces, creativity would suffer, perhaps dry up.

To that, Barlow said balderdash. He argues that creative people hardly need copyright protection, either legal or ethical, to do their thing. Rhetorically, he asks, how about Shakespeare? Da Vinci? Homer? His point is that creativity is inherent in human nature and occurs independently of financial incentives. Further, Barlow says, technology makes it possible for the first time in modern history for creative people to reach mass audiences on their own. In short, as he sees it, the underlying premise for copyright is an archaic relic from the pre-internet era. Equally archaic, he says, is the need for creative people to rely on media companies to disseminate their creative work and, in return, take a lion's share of the revenue. In short, Napster and similar technologies undermine the entire financial foundation on which media companies have been built.

In this chapter you will explore copyright to help you assess the merits of Barlow's argument, as well as that of the media companies. You also will learn about other aspects of mass media law and ethics.

ONLINE

Electronic Frontier Foundation
Defending freedom in a digital world.
www.eff.org

Canadian Charter of Rights and Freedoms Everything you want and more regarding your rights under Canadian law.
http://laws.justice.gc.ca/en/ charter/index.html

media
TIMELINE

LANDMARKS IN CANADIAN MEDIA LAW AND ETHICS

1923 First code of ethics was adopted as the Canons of Journalism of the American Society of Newspaper Editors.

1926 Canadian Association of Broadcasters was formed.

1928 Canada's first royal commission into broadcasting began looking at the role radio plays in the daily lives of Canadians.

1932 Canadian Radio Broadcasting Act was passed.

1936 CBC was formed; it was Canada's first public broadcaster and its first broadcast regulator.

1957 Fowler Report was released, and the Board of Broadcast Governors (BBG) was formed to regulate broadcasters in Canada. It also introduced the idea of Canadian content for television.

1982 *Canadian Charter of Rights and Freedoms* was passed into law, guaranteeing media freedom.

1990s CRTC began the slow process of deregulating radio and television.

1990 SOCAN was formed in Canada.

1990 Canadian Broadcast Standards Council (CBSC) was formed by the Canadian Association of Broadcasters.

1992 Butler ruling on pornography.

2004 For the first time in history, the CRTC revoked the licence of a radio station: CHOI in Quebec

■■ The *Canadian Charter of Rights and Freedoms*

study<u>preview</u> Since 1982, the *Canadian Charter of Rights and Freedoms* bars the government from limiting freedom of expression, including expression in the mass media, or so it seems. There are limits to freedoms.

Canadian Charter of Rights and Freedoms ■ Basis for all laws, including media laws, in Canada.

The *Canadian Charter of Rights and Freedoms* is the basis for both media law and ethics codes. Interestingly, in the United States, "freedom of the press" has been a First Amendment Right since 1791. While the phrase "freedom of the press" was included in Canada's Bill of Rights in 1961, it only covered federal statutes and still wasn't a protected constitutional right. Officially, the media in Canada have only held these press freedoms since Queen Elizabeth II signed the Constitution Act on April 17, 1982. In his *Pocket Guide to Media Law,* Stuart Robertson states that three specific parts of the Charter affect the Canadian media:

- *Section 1.* The Charter "guarantees the rights and freedoms set out in it subject only to such reasonable limits prescribed by law as can be demonstrably justified in a free and democratic society."
- *Section 2.* All Canadians have "freedom of thought, belief, opinion and expression, including freedom of the press and other media of communication."
- *Section 52(1).* "The Constitution of Canada is the supreme law of Canada, and any law that is inconsistent with the provisions of the Constitution is, to the extent of the inconsistency, of no force or effect."

Robertson goes on to argue that the Charter has affected the media in at least two ways. First, it has granted all Canadians the same basic rights and freedoms. Second, it protects everyone, including those who work in the media, from unfair limitations on expression.

However, although freedom of the media is listed in the Charter, it isn't guaranteed. That is made explicit in Section 1 of the Charter. The rights in the Charter are guaranteed only "to such reasonable limits prescribed by law as can be demonstrably justified in a free and democratic society." In simpler terms, this means that while there is media freedom, the media must also take responsibility for their actions and there may be times when the media's right to free speech may be limited.

PUBLICATION BANS

For many years, the courts tended to put an individual's right to a fair trial above the rights of the media. Although the media are granted freedom of speech under the Charter, **publication bans** were often issued limiting what could be reported by the media. That changed in 1994 when the Supreme Court of Canada issued its **Dagenais ruling**. It all began with the CBC scheduled to air the NFB's movie *The Boys of St. Vincent* about atrocities at a Maritime orphanage. The movie was based on actual events at the Mount Cashel orphanage in Newfoundland and the movie was set to air nationally during the actual trial. Lawyers for the defence argued that the movie might affect their right to a fair trial. The judge agreed and, based on legal precedence, ordered the CBC not to show the movie. The CBC appealed the ban and, in a landmark ruling, the Supreme Court of Canada quashed the publication ban. Dean Jobb, writing in *Media Law for Canadian Journalists,* explains Chief Justice Lamer's rationale for the outcome: "the Charter entrenches the right of accused persons to a fair trial . . . the publication ban imposed on *The Boys of St. Vincent* however had a profound impact on the right of the film director to express himself, the CBC's interest in broadcasting the film, the public's interest in viewing it and society's interest in having an important issue—child abuse—publicly exposed and debated." Since Dagenais, judges need to weigh the individual's right to a fair trial against the media's freedom of speech before making a decision to issue a publication ban.

There are times when the judge has no choice but to issue a publication ban. For example, under Canada's new **Youth Criminal Justice Act**, it is illegal to print or broadcast the name(s) of anyone under 18 who has been charged with or convicted of a crime, unless that person received an adult sentence. It also prohibits the naming of parents or siblings of those who have been charged, underage witnesses, or victims of crimes unless parental consent is given.

PORNOGRAPHY VERSUS OBSCENITY

One other limit on freedom of the press deals with obscenity. Why are sexually explicit movies available on Viewer's Choice Canada or on Showcase? The reason, as discussed in Chapter 11, is that there is a difference between pornography and obscenity in Canada, based on the **Butler ruling** of 1992. Obscenity can be controlled by the government, but pornography cannot.

publication bans ■ Limitations on media freedom of speech.

Dagenais ruling ■ Rights need to be balanced.

Youth Criminal Justice Act ■ Prohibits reporting on trials involving minors.

Butler ruling ■ Supreme Court ruling that defined legal differences between obscenity and pornography.

defamation ■ False comments that harm a reputation.

libel ■ A written defamation.

slander ■ A spoken defamation.

defences for defamation ■ Consent, truth, privilege, fair comment.

Cherry Sisters ■ Complainants in a case that barred performers from suing critics.

▼■ Defamation

study<u>preview</u> When the mass media carry disparaging descriptions and comments, they risk being sued for defamation, which is a serious matter. Not only are reputations at stake when defamation occurs, but also losing a suit can be so costly that it can put a publication or broadcast organization out of business.

THE CONCEPT OF DEFAMATION

A civil limitation on media freedom of speech is the issue of defamation. If someone punched you in the face for no good reason, knocking out several teeth, breaking your nose and causing permanent disfigurement, most courts would rule that your attacker should pay your medical bills. If your disfigurement or psychological upset causes you to lose your job, to be ridiculed or shunned by friends and family or perhaps to retreat from social interaction, the court would probably order your attacker to pay additional amounts. Like fists, words can cause damage. Freedom of speech and the press is not a licence to say absolutely anything about anybody.

Defamation is sometimes referred to as **libel** or **slander**. Canadian lawyer Michael G. Crawford, who has worked for both the CBC and CTV, defines defamation in *The Journalist's Legal Guide* as the publication or broadcast of a statement that harms someone's reputation. If someone can prove the following three things, that person may be able to sue for defamation under Canadian law:

● The words or pictures were defamatory.
● The words or pictures were published or broadcast.
● The words or pictures refer to a specific, living person.

If a defamatory statement is false, the utterer may be liable for millions of dollars in damages. When *Toronto Life* magazine published an article about the Reichmann family, the Reichmanns sued for $102 million. After four years in the courts, the case was settled out of court. *Toronto Life* issued a statement that it made "serious mistakes" in the research and writing of the story. In 1999, the *Red Deer Advocate* published a letter from Stockwell Day, then a member of the Alberta Legislature. In the letter, Day made defamatory remarks comparing a lawyer to a pedophile. Day tried to use the fair comment defence but lost. The letter cost Day $792 000 in damages and legal costs.

These types of awards and cases are the foundation of what has become known as "libel chill." Many journalists, editors and others in the media are deciding to play it safe and not publish controversial material that may result in a lawsuit. While this may make economic sense, one needs to question the role libel chill plays in a democratic country that relies on information to educate its people.

DEFENCES FOR DEFAMATION

It is up to the media, in its defence, to prove any of the following as **defences for defamation** to avoid conviction:

● The person mentioned in the story or picture consented to its broadcast or publication.
● The words or pictures are true.
● The words or pictures were published under privilege. This means reporting and commenting fairly and accurately any comments made on public record. For example, quoting something that was said during a town council meeting or in a courtroom, or contained in a media release would constitute privilege.
● The words or pictures were fair comments.

What is fair comment? For the answer to this question, we look to the Cherry Sisters. People flocked to see the **Cherry Sisters'** act. Effie, Addie, Jessie, Lizzie and Ella toured the country with a song and dance act that drew big crowds. They were just awful. They could neither sing nor dance, but people turned out because the sisters were so funny. Sad to say, the Cherry Sisters took themselves seriously. In 1901, desperate for respect, the sisters decided to sue the next newspaper reviewer who gave them a bad notice. That reviewer, it turned out, was Billy Hamilton, who included a lot of equine metaphors in his piece for the *Des Moines Leader:* "Effie is an old jade of 50 summers, Jessie a frisky filly of 40, and Addie, the flower of the family, a capering monstrosity of 35. Their long skinny arms, equipped with talons at the extremities, swung mechanically, and anon waved frantically at the suffering audience. The mouths of their rancid features opened like caverns, and sounds like the wailings of damned souls issued therefrom. They pranced around the stage with a motion that suggested a cross between the *danse du ventre* and the fox trot—strange creatures with painted faces and hideous mien. Effie is spavined, Addie is stringhalt, and Jessie, the only one who showed her stockings, has legs with calves as classic in their outlines as the curves of a broom handle."

Fair Comment and Criticism Upset with what an Iowa reviewer had written about their show, the Cherry Sisters sued. The important 1901 court decision that resulted said that journalists, critics and anybody else can say whatever they want about a public performance. The rationale was that someone who puts on a performance for public acceptance has to take a risk also of public rejection.

The outcome of the suit was another setback for the Cherrys. They lost in a case that established that actors or others who perform for the public must be willing to accept both positive and negative comments about their performance. This right of fair comment and criticism, however, does not make it open season on performers in aspects of their lives that do not relate to public performance. The *National Enquirer* could not defend itself when entertainer Carol Burnett sued for a story that described her as obnoxiously drunk at a restaurant. Not only was the description false (Carol Burnett abstains from alcohol), but Burnett was in no public or performing role at the restaurant. This distinction between an individual's public and private life also has been recognized in cases involving public officials and candidates.

DEFAMATION AND THE INTERNET

Although this is new territory for the law, with no case law to look to for precedents, it appears that defamation laws will extend to the internet. On several occasions Canadian bloggers have found themselves guilty of defamation. University of Ottawa law professor Michael Geist says that defamation laws "apply online as well as offline. Just because bloggers have the ability to write whatever they want doesn't give them the licence to defame anyone." Geist also says we're likely to see more defamation lawsuits aimed at bloggers in the future, as "people are increasingly realizing that blogs have an impact and that more people are reading them."

Still, the issue of defamation on the internet isn't clear at this point. Lawyers David Potts and Sally Harris list several legal issues that will need to be defined before laws in this area are clear. One of the most difficult factors is jurisdiction. Where does the plaintiff live? Where does the defendant live? Where should litigation take place? How can decisions be enforced?

ONLINE

Michael Geist Online University of Ottawa professor Michael Geist's blog on media law.
www.michaelgeist.ca

Defamation on the Internet Read the original article by Potts and Harris online.
www.cyberlibel.com/defnet.html

▪ The CRTC and Broadcast Regulation in Canada

study<u>preview</u> **The Canadian Radio-television and Telecommunications Commission has regulated broadcasting in Canada since the early days of radio in the 1930s. With the advent of television and the internet, regulations have been updated.**

YOU'RE "ON THE AIRD": CANADA'S FIRST ROYAL COMMISSION ON BROADCASTING

The idea that radio could help build a country was one of the factors behind the first Royal Commission on Broadcasting. The fact that Canadians were listening to more American than Canadian programming worried Ottawa, especially combined with the fact that there were 400 000 radios in Canada. For the first time (and certainly not the last time) in Canadian media history, politicians began to worry about the domination of Canada by American mass media. To solve this problem, they set up the first of many royal commissions on broadcasting in Canada. The **Aird Commission** (named after Sir John Aird) was created to examine the danger that American programming posed to Canadian culture. The verdict it reached in 1929 wasn't surprising: American networks were a threat to our airwaves and our culture.

> **Aird Commission** ■ First royal commission into Canadian broadcasting.

The commission recommended that Canada set up and fund a public broadcasting network similar to the BBC in England. This network would produce and broadcast Canadian programs for and by Canadians. This recommendation caused quite a conflict between the owners of private radio stations, who were making a tidy profit, and those who preferred the public system. By 1932, Prime Minister Bennett laid out the government's official position on radio broadcasting in Canada: Canada would have both public and private radio stations. The government's proposal regarding public broadcasting revolved around three issues, which still form the basis of CRTC policy today:

- National sovereignty was to be preserved.
- Broadcasting services were to be made available to anyone in Canada, no matter where they lived.
- Broadcasting was not to be exploited by private interests.

> **Canadian Radio Broadcasting Act** ■ First statute governing broadcasting in Canada.

In 1932, the **Canadian Radio Broadcasting Act** was passed, resulting in the creation of the Canadian Radio Broadcasting Commission, which began broadcasting in 1933. The CRBC was a direct product of the Aird Commission. Initially, it broadcast for only one hour a day. By the time it was replaced by the CBC in 1936, it was reaching just under half of the Canadian population. By 1936, the Canadian Broadcasting Corporation (CBC) was formed. In addition to being a national radio network, it was responsible for granting licences to private radio broadcasters, even though the government did not officially recognize private broadcasting—an ideal position for the government to be in.

THE EVOLUTION OF CANADA'S BROADCASTING ACT

The evolution of television in Canada paralleled the growth of radio, a system with both public and private broadcasting. Initially, private television broadcasters had to apply to the CBC for broadcast licences. Private television broadcasters were not happy; they felt a conflict of interest existed. During this time, even private broadcasters had to carry 10 hours of CBC programming each week. How could the CBC, a broadcaster itself, also be responsible for overseeing private broadcasting?

> **Fowler Commission** ■ Royal commission into television broadcasting in Canada.

In 1955 a royal commission into broadcasting was formed. The **Fowler Commission**, headed by Robert Fowler, analyzed Canadian broadcasting from the points of view of culture and regulations. Its report, tabled in 1957, formed the basis of the Broadcasting Act of 1958:

> **Board of Broadcast Governors (BBG)** ■ Forefather of the current CRTC.

- The forming of the **Board of Broadcast Governors (BBG)**, which would oversee the granting of broadcasting licences.
- Official government recognition of private broadcasters in Canada. This allowed stations to affiliate themselves with a body other than the CBC. This would lead to the formation of Canada's first private television network, CTV.
- Programming on radio and TV that was as Canadian in "content and character" as possible.

THE 1968 BROADCASTING ACT

In March of 1968 another broadcasting act further defined the broadcast system and the function it should serve in Canada. This act resulted in the formation of the Canadian Radio-television Commission (CRTC), the precursor to the Canadian Radio-television and Telecommunications Commission. The changes to television were as follows:

- The CRTC replaced the BBG and had the power to regulate brodcasting in Canada.
- The CBC was given its mandate to provide a national broadcasting service in both official languages and to provide Canadian programming that helped develop national unity and allowed for Canadian cultural expression.
- Canadian broadcasting should be owned and operated by Canadians.

THE 1991 BROADCASTING ACT

In 1975 the CRTC became the Canadian Radio-television and Telecommunications Commission when it assumed responsibility for regulating the telephone industry. In 1991 a new broadcasting act was issued to help further define broadcasting and cultural issues in Canada. The new act:

- Stressed the importance of radio and television programming that was Canadian in content and character.
- Redefined the CBC's role as the national broadcaster, which was to help create a "Canadian consciousness." However, no attempt to define the term "Canadian consciousness" was made, nor was the issue of funding addressed.

THE CRTC AND THE BROADCASTING ACT

The **CRTC** is the federal regulator in charge of regulating and supervising the broadcast media in Canada. It's an independent authority, whose mandate is "to maintain a delicate balance, in the public interest, between the cultural, social and economic goals of the legislation on broadcasting and telecommunications." Its roots and traditions echo the findings of the Aird Commission in 1929. The CRTC has power over 3300 broadcasters in this country. It is the lawmaking authority for all television, radio and direct-to-home (DTH) systems in Canada. The CRTC reports to the prime minister through the Minister of Canadian Heritage.

The CRTC is the political apparatus through which the spirit of the **Broadcasting Act** is made manifest. According to the CRTC, the main objective of the Broadcasting Act is "to ensure that all Canadians have access to a wide variety of high-quality Canadian programming." While specifics regarding the Broadcasting Act and its effect on radio and television content were discussed earlier in the text, the main thrust of the act today is as follows:

- Canadian radio and television stations should be "effectively owned and operated by Canadians."
- The Canadian system has two parts: a public system and a private system.
- Canadian broadcasters should "safeguard, enrich and strengthen" life in Canada.
- Anyone who is involved in broadcasting in Canada is responsible for what he or she broadcasts.
- Adding another limitation to "freedom of the press" here in Canada, the Broadcasting Act specifically states that broadcasts should not include anything "in contravention of the law," nor should they contain obscenities, profanities or false news.

ONLINE

On the "Aird" Again Revisit the highlights of government media regulation.
www.crtc.gc.ca/eng/BACKGRND/ Brochures/B19903.htm

CRTC Canadian Radio-television and Telecommunications Commission. It ensures that Canadians are seen and heard on Canadian media.
www.crtc.gc.ca

CRTC ■ Canadian broadcast regulator.

Broadcasting Act ■ Governs the CRTC and all broadcasters in Canada.

CHOI-FM

The *Canadian Charter of Rights and Freedoms* gives everyone in Canada, including those that work in the media, "freedom of thought, belief and expression." In short, we are given the right to think, believe and say what we want. However, as the chapter has outlined, there are limitations to "freedom of speech."

The CRTC strives to work with Canadian radio and television stations to ensure that they operate within a profitable environment. However, in 2004, the CRTC showed how far-reaching their powers were when they did not renew the licence of radio station CHOI-FM, owned by Genex, in Quebec City. Some saw it as censorship. Genex felt that they were only exercising their right to free speech and that certain comments were not taken in context. The CRTC saw it as a radio station consistently not adhering to the objectives of the Broadcasting Act and flaunting their right to freedom of speech. This action was not a knee-jerk reaction by the Commission. It was a long time coming, as CHOI-FM had a history of questionable content:

- Allegedly making defamatory comments about former Quebec Premier Daniel Johnson.
- Referring to a rival talk show host on another radio station as a "conceited asshole," a "worthless piece of trash," a "piece of vomit," a "shit disturber" and a "tree with rotten roots."
- Calling anyone who worked for Radio Énergie, a competitor in the Quebec City market, "a bunch of faggots."
- Suggesting that there be an "Indian hunting season" and that severely mentally disturbed patients at a local psychiatric hospital be gassed just like during the Holocaust.

In its decision, the CRTC noted that these complaints "did not reflect isolated incidents, but appeared to be part of a pattern of behaviour by the licensee that continued and even grew worse, over the course of two consecutive licence terms, despite clear unequivocal warnings from the Commission." The CRTC cited the following section of the Canadian Radio Broadcasting Act as the basis for its decision: "A licensee shall not broadcast any abusive comment that, when taken in context, tends to or is likely to expose an individual or a group or class of individuals to hatred or contempt on the basis of race, national or ethnic origin, colour, religion, sex, sexual orientation, age or mental or physical disability."

As a result of this history, the CRTC decided not to renew CHOI-FM's licence in August 2004. It also immediately issued a call for applications to take over the licence for Quebec City.

CHOI-FM immediately appealed the ruling and was able to continue broadcasting during the appeal

Freedom of speech or censorship? CHOI-FM tested the boundaries of free speech . . . and lost.

process, but, in 2005, the Supreme Court of Canada agreed with the CRTC. In its decision, it stated that "freedom of expression, freedom of opinion and freedom of speech do not mean freedom of defamation, freedom of oppression and freedom of opprobrium." Again, CHOI-FM appealed the ruling. On June 14, 2007, the Supreme Court said it would not hear the appeal. Genex, owners of CHOI-FM, sold the station to Radio Nord, which runs the station today as a rock station.

WHAT DO YOU THINK?

1. Was the case of CHOI-FM a simple matter of freedom of speech or censorship?

2. What role did the CRTC play? The *Charter of Rights and Freedoms?*

3. Review the CRTC's decision on CHOI-FM at www.crtc.gc.ca/archive/ENG/Decisions/2004/db2004–271.pdf. Could any of the comments made by some of CHOI-FM's announcers be protected as "fair comment"? Why or why not?

◼ Copyright

study<u>preview</u> Mass media people are vulnerable to thievery. Because it is so easy for someone to copy someone else's creative work, copyright laws prohibit the unauthorized re-creation of intellectual property, including books, music, movies and other creative production.

COPYRIGHT IN CANADA

Canada has had a copyright law on the books since 1924. The Canadian Copyright Act, governed by Canadian Heritage and Industry Canada, covers all forms of communication: books, pamphlets, newspapers, magazines, maps, sheet music, movies, videos and music. The Act defines **copyright** as "the sole right to produce or reproduce the work of any substantial part thereof in any material form whatever or to perform the work or any substantial portion thereof in public." Basically, all original works in Canada are protected by copyright for the life of the creator, plus 50 years. In the United States, copyright laws protect a creative work for the lifetime of the author plus 70 years. After this time, either in Canada or the United States, the work enters what is called the **public domain** and anyone may use it without permission. The creator of the "act" of communication has the sole right to copy it or have it performed in public. That right may be granted to others.

The works of Canadians are also protected internationally under the copyright protection of the Berne Convention and the Universal Copyright Convention. These also protect the works of international artists in Canada. Several Canadian organizations exist to ensure that creators of communication content are compensated for their efforts and that copyright laws do not get broken.

COPYRIGHT AND THE WEB

The technological convergence of the traditional mass media is creating some new issues for copyright. The term *digital media* refers to any information that is stored in binary form (1s and 0s). This includes material stored in "fixed form" on the internet, on CD, CD-ROM, DVD, floppy disk, hard drives, and so on. The list is almost endless. The material can include text, music, and images.

While the full influence of the web on copyright is still being debated in the courts, and will be for some time, some of the legal issues remain the same for material stored in "traditional" or "digital" forms. For example, it must be original and in a fixed form. That being said, digital technology is stretching what was covered (or at the very least implied) under older copyright laws. Some legal issues that are currently being debated include:

- File sharing (mostly music and video) on the internet.
- Duration of copyright. It's life of the creator plus 50 years in Canada, but in the United States it's life plus 70 years.
- Radio stations streaming their signals over the internet.
- "Netcasting" of television programming over the internet.
- The role of ISPs in identifying customers who upload music.
- Newspapers not reprinting articles written by freelance journalists or "stringers," as freelancers are compensated for only one printing of their article.

MUSIC LICENSING IN CANADA

SOCAN, the Society of Composers, Authors and Music Publishers of Canada, licenses the public performance of music. It was formed in 1990, when two other performing rights organizations, PROCAN (Performing Rights Organization of Canada) and CAPAC (Composers, Authors and Publishers Association of Canada) combined to form a new, nonprofit organization. Its jurisdiction includes the playing of music, not only on radio and television, but also in restaurants, by mobile disc jockeys, in parades, at sporting events, and at the movies. Almost anywhere you hear music, SOCAN is there to ensure that the writers of the song get paid.

copyright ◼ Protects intellectual property from theft.

public domain ◼ Intellectual property that may be used without permission of the creator or owner.

SOCAN ◼ Society of Composers, Authors and Music Publishers of Canada; music licensing organization.

SOCAN collects tariffs from anyone who uses music and passes them along to the songwriters. No one, other than the songwriter, has the right in Canada to use a song's material in any way, shape or form without permission. SOCAN recognizes several types of rights held by the songwriters pertaining to music:

- *Performance rights.* These cover songwriters when their material is performed publicly. This can include a song on the radio, on television, or performed by a band at the local bar. These tariffs are collected by SOCAN.
- *Reproduction rights.* There are two types of reproduction rights. Mechanical rights are the rights to copy the music onto a tape or CD, while synchronization rights refer to using the music in a film or video.
- *Moral rights.* A creator can claim violation of moral rights if, after selling performance and/or reproduction rights, he or she feels that the original vision is altered. For example, members of the Canadian pop group The Parachute Club claimed that their moral rights were violated first when their 1983 hit "Rise Up" was used in a commercial for frozen pizza, and then when the song was used to promote a political event in 1999. They felt that their song, with its spiritual and self-empowering message, was morally diminished when it began to be associated with pizza and politicians.

SOCAN has several methods to assist in the collection of royalties for its members. Media outlets are surveyed several times each year for a listing of all music used. TV stations pay 1.8 percent of their gross revenue, while radio stations pay between 1.4 percent and 3.2 percent of their gross revenue, depending on the amount of music played.

Three other organizations license the use of music in Canada. AVLA (the Audio-Visual Licensing Agency) overlooks the exhibition of music videos, while SODRAC (the Society for Reproduction Rights of Authors, Composers and Publishers in Canada Incorporated) and CMRRA (the Canadian Musical Reproduction Rights Agency Limited) authorize the reproduction of music (onto tapes and CDs) and the use of music in videos and film.

Besides SOCAN, there are other large licensing organizations worldwide. They are known in the trade by their abbreviations: **ASCAP** (The American Society of Composers, Authors and Publishers) and **BMI** (Broadcast Music, Inc.).

media ONLINE

SOCAN This site provides information on performing rights, copyright, licensing, and distribution.
www.socan.ca

ASCAP The American Society of Composers, Authors and Publishers is influential in copyright issues.
www.ascap.com/index.html

BMI Provides musicians with information about copyright and licensing concerns.
www.bmi.com/licensing

ASCAP ■ Music licensing organization.

BMI ■ Music licensing organization.

The Difficulty of Ethics

study<u>preview</u> **Mass media organizations have put together codes of ethics that prescribe how practitioners should go about their work. Although useful in many ways, these codes neither sort through the bedeviling problems that result from conflicting prescriptions nor help much when the only available options are negative.**

PRESCRIPTIVE ETHICS CODES

The mass media abound with codes of ethics. The earliest was adopted in 1923, the **Canons of Journalism of the American Society of Newspaper Editors**. Many newcomers to the mass media make an erroneous assumption that the answers to all the moral choices in their work exist in the prescriptions of these codes, a stance known as **prescriptive ethics**. While the codes can be helpful, ethics is not so easy. Attitudes toward codes of ethics vary, but most Canadian media organizations have a code, as do public relations and advertising associations. These codes go far beyond the question of "freebies" and at least try to address issues of social equality, controversy, offensive content, and fairness in handling complex stories.

Many media critics feel that ethics are not taken as seriously as they might be. According to journalism professor Brian Green, one news director's perspective on ethics was as follows: "It's hard to remember you're here to drain the swamp when you're up to your ass in alligators." Peter Desbarats argues that many media critics feel that while the media may talk a good line when it comes to ethics, it's more talk than walk. Other critics feel that codes of ethics are merely public relations tools the

Canons of Journalism of the American Society of Newspaper Editors ■ First media code, 1923.

prescriptive ethics ■ Follow the rules and your decision will be the correct one.

media use to perpetuate the myth that they are holier than thou. This may or may not be true. But the fact remains that most Canadian media organizations have a **code of ethics** that, if nothing else, serves as a guideline to follow should an alligator creep up on them. The same applies to the public relations and advertising industries. These codes are based in Canadian law but, as codes, violation of them may not necessarily result in legal problems.

The study of ethics manifests itself in the world of media in the form of codes of conduct. Among the many media organizations that have codes of conduct for their members are the Canadian Association of Broadcasters, the Canadian Newspaper Association, and the Radio-Television News Directors Association of Canada.

The Canadian Association of Broadcasters Self-proclaimed as the voice of Canada's private broadcasters, the Canadian Association of Broadcasters, or **CAB**, was founded by 13 broadcasters in 1926 as a voluntary organization that advocated self-rule for Canada's broadcasters with little, if any, government regulation. CAB was the lobby group for Canada's radio broadcasters prior to the findings of the Aird Commission in 1929. Currently, CAB represents 430 privately owned radio and television stations across Canada.

In 1990, CAB formed the **CBSC** (Canadian Broadcast Standards Council). This is a self-regulating council funded for and by private broadcasters in Canada. Its mandate is to promote high standards in radio and television broadcasting through self-regulation. If a viewer or listener has a complaint about programming in Canada, he or she writes to the CBSC. They administer several ethics codes, including the CAB Code of Ethics, the CAB Violence Code and the CAB Sex-Role Portrayal Code. All decisions are available online in over 30 languages.

Canadian Newspaper Association In 1919, the Canadian Daily Newspaper Association (CDNA) was formed. In 1996, it was renamed the Canadian Newspaper Association (CNA). The CNA represents 101 of Canada's English and French daily newspapers—99 percent of all newspapers sold in Canada on a daily basis. The CNA's statement of principles, which was originally adopted by the CDNA in 1977, was revised in 1995. This statement can be found at the CNA website. Some of the issues dealt with in the statement are freedom of the press, loyalty to the public good, accuracy, fairness and community responsibility.

Radio-Television News Directors Association of Canada The **Radio-Television News Directors Association (RTNDA)** was founded more than 50 years ago. It's an international organization with affiliations in Canada. Recognizing the importance to a democracy of an informed public, the members of the RTNDA of Canada believe that the broadcasting of factual, accurately reported, and timely news and public affairs is vital. To this end, RTNDA members in Canada pledge to observe a code of ethics, which can be found at the RTNDA website.

CONFLICT IN DUTIES

Media ethics codes are well-intended, usually helpful guides, but they are simplistic when it comes to knotty moral questions. When media ethicians Clifford Christians, Mark Fackler and Kim Rotzoll compiled a list of five duties of mass media practitioners in their book *Media Ethics,* some of these inherent problems became obvious.

Duty to Self Self-preservation is a basic human instinct, but is a photojournalist shirking a duty to subscribers by avoiding a dangerous combat zone?

Self-aggrandizement can be an issue too. Many newspaper editors are invited, all expenses paid, to Hollywood movie premieres. The duty-to-self principle favours going: The trip would be fun. In addition, it is a good story opportunity, and as a free favour, it would not cost the newspaper anything. However, what of an editor's responsibility to readers? Readers have a right to expect writers to provide honest accounts that are not coloured by favouritism. Can a reporter write fairly after being wined and dined and flown across the continent by movie producers who want a gung-ho story?

code of ethics ■ Statement that defines acceptable, unacceptable behaviour.

CAB ■ Canadian Association of Broadcasters.

CBSC ■ Canadian Broadcast Standards Council; self-regulatory body for Canadian radio and television broadcasters.

Radio-Television News Directors Association (RTNDA) ■ Organization that believes the broadcasting of factual, accurately reported, and timely news and public affairs is vital.

ONLINE

Radio-Television News Directors Association The association's current code of ethics is online.
www.rtndacanada.com

Canadian Association of Journalists Includes the CAJ Statement of Principles and Ethics Guidelines and links to *The Wire,* a quarterly newsletter about developments in journalism.
www.caj.ca

Canadian Broadcast Standards Council Link to the CAB Code of Ethics, Violence Code, Sex-Role Portrayal Code and the RTNDA Code of Ethics.
www.cbsc.ca

Canadian Newspaper Association Their statement of principles for the voice of Canada's newspaper industry.
www.cna-acj.ca

Center for the Study of Ethics in the Professions Links to codes of ethics for all kinds of organizations around the world.
http://ethics.iit.edu/codes

Duty to Audience Television programs that re-enact real cases of violence are popular with audiences, but do they do a disservice because they frighten many viewers into inferring that the streets are more dangerous than they really are?

Writing about real situations with humour may also do the audience a disservice. Tom Wicker of *The New York Times* tells a story about his early days as a reporter in Aberdeen, North Carolina. He was covering a divorce case involving one spouse chasing the other with an axe. Nobody was hurt physically, and everyone who heard the story in the courtroom, except the divorcing couple, had a good laugh. "It was human comedy at its most ribald, and the courtroom rocked with laughter," Wicker recalled years later. In writing his story, Wicker captured the darkly comedic details so skilfully that his editor put the story on the first page. Wicker was proud of the piece until the next day when the woman in the case called on him. Worn out, haggard, hurt and angry, she asked, "Mr. Wicker, why did you think you had a right to make fun of me in your paper?" The lesson stayed with Wicker for the rest of his career. He had unthinkingly hurt a fellow human being for no better reason than to evoke a chuckle, or perhaps a belly laugh, from his readers. To Wicker the duty-to-audience principle would never again transcend his moral duty to the dignity of the subjects of his stories.

Duty to Employer Does loyalty to an employer transcend the ideal of pursuing and telling the truth when a news reporter discovers dubious business deals involving the parent corporation? This is a growing issue as the mass media become consolidated into fewer gigantic companies owned by conglomerates. In 1989, for example, investigative reporter Peter Karl of Chicago television station WMAQ broke a story that General Electric had manufactured jet engines with untested and sometimes defective bolts. Although WMAQ is owned by NBC, which in turn is owned by General Electric, Karl's exclusive, documented and accurate story aired. However, when the story was passed on to the network itself, Marty Ryan, executive producer of the *Today* show, ordered that the references to General Electric be edited out.

Duty to the Profession At what point does an ethically motivated advertising-agency person blow the whistle on misleading claims by other advertising people?

Duty to Society Does duty to society ever transcend duty to self? To the audience? To the employer? To colleagues? Does ideology affect a media worker's sense of duty to society? Consider how Joseph Stalin, Adolf Hitler and Franklin Roosevelt would be covered by highly motivated communist, fascist and libertarian journalists.

▛▖ Media Ethics

study<u>preview</u> Media ethics is complicated by the different performance standards that mass media operations establish for themselves. This is further complicated by the range of expectations in the mass audience. One size does not fit all.

MEDIA COMMITMENT

A single ethics standard is impossible to apply to the mass media. Nobody holds a supermarket tabloid like *News of the World,* which specializes in celebrities being visited by aliens, to the same standard as *The New York Times.* Why the difference? Media ethics, in part, is a function of what a media operation promises to deliver to its audience and what the audience expects. The *News of the World* commitment is fun and games in a tongue-in-cheek news context. *The New York Times* considers itself a "Newspaper of Record." There is a big difference.

CNN touts accuracy in its promotional tagline: "News You Can Trust." Explicitly, the network promises to deliver truthful accounts of the day's events. CNN establishes its own standards. A lapse, like a misleading story, especially if intentional or the result of sloppiness, represents a broken promise and an ethics problem.

AUDIENCE EXPECTATION

The audience brings a range of ethics expectations to media relations, which further thwarts any attempt at one-size-fits-all media ethics. From a book publisher's fantasy science fiction imprint, readers have far different expectations than they do from NBC News, which, except for plainly labeled opinion, is expected to deliver unmitigated nonfiction.

A range in the type of messages purveyed by the mass media also bespeaks a variety of ethics expectations. Rarely is falsity excusable, but even the courts allow puffery in advertising. The news releases that public relations people produce are expected, by their nature, to be from a client's perspective, which doesn't always coincide with the perspective expected of a news reporter.

ETHICS AS AN INTELLECTUAL PROCESS

A set of rules, easily memorized and mindlessly employed, would be too easy. It doesn't work that way. Ethics, rather, needs to be an intellectual process of sorting through media commitments, audience expectations and broad principles. But even on broad principles there is more, as discussed in the next section.

Moral Principles

studypreview Concern about doing the right thing is part of human nature, and leading thinkers have developed a great number of enduring moral principles over the centuries.

THE GOLDEN MEAN

The Greek philosopher **Aristotle**, writing almost 2400 years ago, devised the **golden mean** as a basis for moral decision making. The golden mean sounds simple and straightforward: Avoid extremes and seek moderation. Modern journalistic balance and fairness are founded on this principle.

Aristotle ■ Advocate of the golden mean.

golden mean ■ Moderation is the best course.

The golden mean's dictate, however, is not as simple as it sounds. As with all moral principles, application of the golden mean can present difficulties. Consider the CRTC requirement that over-the-air broadcasters give equal opportunity to candidates at election time. On the surface this application of the golden mean, embodied in federal law, might seem to be reasonable, fair and morally right, but the issue is far more complex. The equality requirement, for example, gives an advantage to candidates who hold simplistic positions that can be expressed compactly. Good and able candidates whose positions require more time to explain are disadvantaged, and the society is damaged when inferior candidates win public office.

Although minute-for-minute equality in broadcasting can be a flawed application of the golden mean, Aristotle's principle is valuable to media people when making moral decisions, as long as they do not abdicate their power of reason to embrace formulaic tit-for-tat measurable equality. It takes the human mind, not a formula, to determine fairness. And therein lies the complexity of the golden mean. No two human beings think exactly alike, which means that applying the golden mean involves individuals' making judgment calls that are not necessarily the same. This element of judgment in moral decisions can make ethics intellectually exciting. It takes a sharp mind to sort through issues of balance and fairness.

Golden Mean The Greek thinker Aristotle told his students almost 2400 years ago that right courses of action avoid extremes. His recommendation: moderation.

"DO UNTO OTHERS"

The Judeo-Christian principle of "**Do unto others** as you would have them do unto you" appeals to most Americans. Not even the "do-unto-others" prescription is without problems, however. Consider the photojournalist who sees virtue in serving a mass audience with a truthful account

Universal Law

Immanuel Kant, an 18th-century German philosopher, urged people to find principles that they would be comfortable having applied in all situations. He called these principles *categorical imperatives.*

"Do unto others" ■ Judeo-Christian principle for ethical behaviour.

Immanuel Kant ■ Advocated the categorical imperative.

categorical imperative ■ Follow principles as if they had universal application.

ONLINE

Journal of Mass Media Ethics This journal addresses ethical situations in mass communication.
www.jmme.org

Media Watchdogs A collection of online media monitoring sources, from UBC's School of Journalism.
http://journalismethics.ca/ journalist_resources/ media_analysis.htm

John Stuart Mill ■ Advocated utilitarianism.

principle of utility ■ Best course bestows the most good for the most people.

John Dewey ■ Advocate of pragmatism.

pragmatic ethics ■ Judge acts by their results.

Utilitarianism

American journalists tend to like 19th-century British thinker John Stuart Mill's utilitarianism, which favours actions that result in the greatest good for the greatest number of people. This approach to ethics dovetails well with majority rule and modern democracy.

of the human condition. This might manifest itself in portrayals of great emotions, like grief. But would the photojournalist appreciate being photographed herself in a grieving moment after learning that her own infant son had died in an accident? If not, her pursuit of truth through photography for a mass audience would be contrary to the "do-unto-others" dictum.

CATEGORICAL IMPERATIVES

About 200 years ago, German philosopher **Immanuel Kant** wrote that moral decisions should flow from thoroughly considered principles. As he put it, "Act on the maxim that you would want to become universal law." He called his maxim the categorical imperative. A **categorical imperative**, well-thought-out, is a principle that the individual who devised it would be willing to apply in all moral questions of a similar sort.

Kant's categorical imperative does not dictate specifically what actions are morally right or wrong. Moral choices, says Kant, go deeper than the context of the immediate issue. He encourages a philosophical approach to moral questions, with people using their intellect to identify principles that they, as individuals, would find acceptable if applied universally.

Kant does not encourage the kind of standardized approach to ethics represented by professional codes. His emphasis, rather, is on hard thinking. Says philosopher Patricia Smith, of the University of Kentucky, writing in the *Journal of Mass Media Ethics,* "A philosophical approach to ethics embodies a commitment to consistency, clarity, the principled evaluation of arguments and unrelenting persistence to get to the bottom of things."

UTILITARIAN ETHICS

In the mid-1800s, British thinker **John Stuart Mill** declared that morally right decisions are those that result in "happiness for the greatest number." Mill called his idea the **principle of utility**. It sounds good to many of us because it parallels the democratic principle of majority rule, with its emphasis on the greatest good for the greatest number of people.

By and large, journalists embrace Mill's utilitarianism today, as evinced in notions like the *people's right to know,* a concept originally meant to support journalistic pursuit of information about government, putting the public's interests ahead of government's interests, but which has come to be almost reflexively invoked to defend pursuing very personal information about individuals, no matter what the human toll.

PRAGMATIC ETHICS

John Dewey, an American thinker who wrote in the late 1800s and early 1900s, argued that the virtue of moral decisions had to be judged by their results. Dewey's **pragmatic ethics**, like other ethics systems, has problems. One is that people do not have perfect crystal balls to tell them for sure whether their moral actions will have good consequences.

John Rawls He favoured putting a blind eye to all issues except rightness and wrongness.

John Dewey He saw decisions as ethical if the ascertainable outcomes were good.

EGALITARIAN ETHICS

In the 20th century, philosopher **John Rawls** introduced the **veil of ignorance** as an element in ethics decisions. Choosing a right course of action, said Rawls, requires blindness to social position or other discriminating factors. This is known as **egalitarianism**. An ethical decision requires that all people be given an equal hearing and the same fair consideration.

To Rawls a brutal slaying in an upscale suburb deserves the same journalistic attention as a similarly brutal slaying in a poor urban neighbourhood. All other things being equal, a $20 000 bank burglary is no more newsworthy than a $20 000 embezzlement.

John Rawls ■ Advocated egalitarianism.

veil of ignorance ■ Making decisions with a blind eye to extraneous factors that could affect the decision.

egalitarianism ■ Treat everyone the same.

media TIMELINE

DEVELOPMENT OF MEDIA ETHICS

400 B.C. Aristotle laid out the golden mean.

20s Jesus Christ articulated "Do unto others as you would have them do unto you."

1785 Immanuel Kant advanced the categorical imperative.

1865 John Stuart Mill proposed utilitarianism.

1903 John Dewey advanced pragmatism.

1919 Upton Sinclair exposed newsroom abuses in his book *The Brass Check.*

1923 American Society of Newspaper Editors adopted a media ethics code.

1947 Hutchins Commission urged the media to be socially responsible.

1971 John Rawls advanced the veil of ignorance theory.

Ralph Potter ■ Ethicist who devised the Potter's Box.

Potter's Box ■ Tool for sorting through the pros and cons of ethics questions.

▛▪ Potter's Box

study<u>preview</u> Moral problems in the mass media can be so complex that it may seem there is no solution. While ideal answers without any negative results may be impossible, a process exists for identifying a course of action that integrates an individual's personal values with moral principles and then tests conclusions against loyalties.

FOUR QUADRANTS

A Harvard Divinity School professor, **Ralph Potter**, devised a four-quadrant model for sorting through ethics problems. The quadrants of the square-like model, called **Potter's Box**, each pose a category of questions. Working through these categories helps to clarify the issues and leads to a morally justifiable position. These are the quadrants of Potter's Box:

Situation In Quadrant 1, the facts of the issue are decided. Consider a newsroom in which a series of articles on rape is being developed and the question arises whether to identify rape victims by name. Here is how the situation could be defined: The newspaper has access to a young mother who has been abducted and raped and who is willing to describe the assault in graphic detail and to discuss her experience as a witness at the assailant's trial. Also, the woman is willing to be identified in the story.

Values Moving to Quadrant 2 of Potter's Box, editors and reporters identify the values that underlie all the available choices. This process involves listing the positive and negative values that flow from conscience. One editor might argue that full, frank discussion on social issues is necessary to deal with them. Another might say that identifying the rape victim by name might discourage others from even reporting the crime. Other positions: Publishing the name is in poor taste. The newspaper has an obligation to protect the victim from her own possibly bad decision to allow her name to be used. The purpose of the rape series can be accomplished without using the name. Readers have a right to all the relevant information that the newspaper can gather. An editor who is torn between such contrary thoughts is making progress toward a decision by at least identifying all the values that can be posited.

Ralph Potter

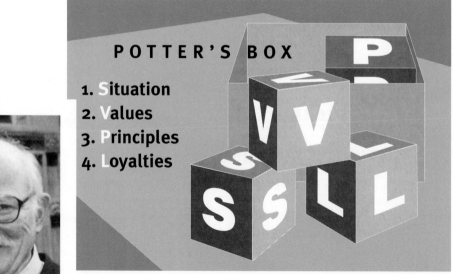

POTTER'S BOX

1. **S**ituation
2. **V**alues
3. **P**rinciples
4. **L**oyalties

Figure 13.1 **Clarifying Process** Potter's Box offers four categories of questions to help develop morally justifiable positions.

Principles In Potter's Quadrant 3, decision makers search for moral principles that uphold the values they identified in Quadrant 2. John Stuart Mill's principle of utility, which favours the majority over individuals, would support using the victim's name because it could add poignancy to the story, enhancing the chances of improved public sensitivity and perhaps even lead to improved public policy, all of which, Mill would say, outweigh the harm that might come to an individual. On the other hand, people who have used Immanuel Kant's ideas to develop inviolable operating principles—categorical imperatives—look to their rule book: We never publish information that might offend readers. One value of Potter's Quadrant 3 is that it gives people confidence in the values that emerged in their debates over Quadrant 2.

Loyalties In Quadrant 4 the decision maker folds in an additional layer of complexity that must be sorted through: loyalties. The challenge is to establish a hierarchy of loyalties. Is the first loyalty to a code of ethics, and if so, to which code? To readers, and if so, to which ones? To society? To the employer? To self? Out of duty to self, some reporters and editors might want to make the rape series as potent as possible, with as much detail as possible, to win awards and bring honour to themselves and perhaps a raise or promotion or better job with another newspaper. Others might be motivated by their duty to their employer: The more detail in the story, the more newspapers it will sell. For others their duty to society may be paramount: The newspaper has a social obligation to present issues in as powerful a way as possible to spur reforms in general attitudes and perhaps public policy.

LIMITATIONS OF POTTER'S BOX

Potter's Box does not provide answers. Rather, it offers a process through which the key elements in ethics questions can be sorted out.

Also, Potter's Box focuses on moral aspects of a problem, leaving it to the decision maker to examine practical considerations separately, such as whether prudence supports making the morally best decision. Moral decisions should not be made in a vacuum. For example, would it be wise to go ahead with the rape victim's name if 90 percent of the newspaper's subscribers would become so offended that they would quit buying the paper and, as a result, the paper would go out of business?

media ONLINE

Journalism Ethics Cases Online These cases address a variety of ethical problems faced by journalists, including privacy, conflict of interest, reporter–source relationships, and the role of journalists in their communities. **www.journalism.indiana.edu/ gallery/Ethics**

Silha Center for the Study of Media Ethics and Law This site of the University of Minnesota contains articles, news and links related to issues of both ethics and the law. **www.silha.umn.edu**

▪ Unsettled, Unsettling Issues

study<u>preview</u> **When mass media people discuss ethics, they talk about right and wrong behaviour, but creating policies on ethics issues is not easy.**

ACCEPTED PRACTICES

Just as there is not a reliable correlation between law and ethics, neither is there one between accepted media practices and ethics. What is acceptable at one advertising agency to make a product look good in photographs might be unacceptable at another. Even universally **accepted practices** should not go unexamined, for unless accepted practices are examined and reconsidered on a continuing basis, media practitioners can come to rely more on habit than on principles in their work.

accepted practices ■ What media do as a matter of routine, sometimes without considering ethics implications.

PRUDENCE AND ETHICS

Prudence is the application of wisdom in a practical situation. It can be a leveling factor in moral questions. Consider the case of Irvin Lieberman, who had built his *Main Line Chronicle* and several other weeklies in the Philadelphia suburbs into aggressive, journalistically excellent newspapers. After being hit with nine libel suits, all costly to defend, Lieberman abandoned the editorial thrust of his newspapers. "I decided not to do any investigative work," he said. "It was a matter of either feeding my family or spending

prudence ■ Applying wisdom, not principles, to an ethics situation.

my whole life in court." Out of prudence Lieberman decided to abandon his commitment to hard-hitting, effective journalism.

PLAGIARISM

Perhaps the most fiercely loyal media fans are those who read romance novels and swear by a favourite author. In an internet chatroom in 1997, romance writer Janet Dailey found herself boxed into an admission that she had plagiarized from rival writer Nora Roberts. There is no scorn like that of creative people for those who steal their work, and Roberts was "very, very upset." HarperCollins recalled *Notorious,* Dailey's book that contained the plagiarism, and Roberts's fans, many of them long-time Dailey detractors, began a hunt for other purloined passages.

What is **plagiarism**? Generally, it's considered passing off someone else's creative work as your own, without permission. It's still plagiarism if it's changed a bit, as was Dailey's loose paraphrasing.

The fact that Dailey's 93 books over 20 years had sold an average of more than 2 million each made the scandal all the juicier. In the end, Roberts proposed a financial settlement, and the proceeds went to promote literacy.

Everyone agrees that plagiarism, a form of thievery, is unethical, but the issue is not simple. The fact is that in many media, people draw heavily on other people's ideas and work. Think about sitcom storylines that mimic each other or the bandwagon of movies that follow an unexpected hit with an oddball theme that suddenly becomes mainstream. Journalists, most of whom consider themselves especially pristine compared to their media brethren, have standard practices that encourage a lot of "borrowing." Among factors that make journalists uncomfortable when pressed hard on plagiary questions are:

Swapping Stories Some creative work, like scholarship, requires that information and ideas be attributed to their sources. Journalists are not so strict, as shown by story swapping through the Canadian Press. CP picks up stories from its members and distributes them to other members, generally without any reference to the source. Some publications and broadcasters do not even acknowledge CP as the intermediary.

News Releases In many newsrooms the plagiarism question is clouded further by the practice of using news releases from public relations people word for word without citing the source. Even in newsrooms that rewrite releases to avoid the embarrassment of running a story that is exactly the same as the competition's, it is standard practice not to cite the source. Public relations people, who are paid for writing favourable stories on their clients, have no objections to being plagiarized, and news organizations find it an easy, inexpensive way to fill space. Despite the mutual convenience, the arrangement raises serious questions of ethics to which many in the media have not responded. Marie Dunn White, in the *Journal of Mass Media Ethics,* wrote: "In order for the reader to evaluate the information he or she is receiving correctly and completely, he or she must know which information came from a press release and, therefore, may be biased."

Monitoring the Competition Competitive pressure also contributes to fuzziness on the plagiarism issue. To avoid being skunked on stories, reporters monitor each other closely to pick up tips and ideas. Generally, reporters are not particular about where they pick up information as long as they are confident that it is accurate. For background, reporters tap newsroom libraries, databases, journals, books and other sources, and in the interest of not cluttering their stories, they do not use footnotes.

Subliminal Memory Covering breaking events has its own pressure that puts journalists at special risk. Almost every journalist who writes under the pressure of a deadline

plagiarism ■ Using someone else's work without permission or credit.

media ONLINE

Plagiarism This group is dedicated to fighting online plagiarism, especially in education.
www.plagiarism.org

has had the experience of writing a story and later discovering that phrases that came easily at the keyboard were actually somebody else's. In their voracious pursuit of information, reporters store phrases and perhaps whole passages subliminally in their memories. It's this concept of innocent recall that concerns the late Canadian columnist Don McGillivray, who argues that plagiarism is often a simple case of unintentionally borrowing from others. Journalists are like any other group of professionals: They like to "talk shop" when in the presence of other journalists. They discuss stories they've written and articles they've read. Later, while writing a story, a journalist may subconsciously remember a certain phrase from a conversation with a colleague and use it in a story. Is this plagiarism? McGillivray doesn't think so. It's simply the outcome of a psychological process.

The final word on plagiarism in journalism goes to Nick Russell, who, in *Morals and the Media,* writes, "Genuine plagiarism is theft and is indefensible; serious incidents of plagiarism happen rarely and there is a difference between plagiarism and lack of attribution . . . . Some media critics seem to think it's growing, but it may be more of a matter of perception. Partly because readers have a growing sense of empowerment and ownership so are now much more likely to blow the whistle and newsroom colleagues who might have tolerated such activities as hijinks in the past now see them as undermining everybody's credibility."

MISREPRESENTATION

Janet Cooke's meteoric rise at *The Washington Post* unraveled quickly the day after she received a Pulitzer Prize. Her editors had been so impressed with her story "Jimmy's World," about a child who was addicted to heroin, that they nominated it for a Pulitzer Prize. The gripping tale began: "Jimmy is 8 years old and a third-generation heroin addict, a precocious little boy with sandy hair, velvety brown eyes and needle marks freckling the baby-smooth skin of his thin brown arms." Janet Cooke claimed that she had won the confidence of Jimmy's mother and her live-in male friend, a drug dealer, to do the story. Cooke said she had promised not to reveal their identities as a condition for her access to Jimmy.

The story, which played on the front page, so shocked Washington that people demanded that Jimmy be taken away from his mother and placed in a foster home. *The Post* declined to help authorities, citing Cooke's promise of confidentiality to her sources. The mayor ordered the police to find Jimmy with or without the newspaper's help, and millions of dollars in police resources went into a door-to-door search. After 17 days the police gave up knocking on doors for tips on Jimmy. Some doubts emerged at *The Post* about the story, but the newspaper stood behind its reporter.

Janet Cooke, 25 when she was hired by *The Post,* had extraordinary credentials. Her résumé showed a baccalaureate degree, magna cum laude, from Vassar; study at the Sorbonne in Paris; a master's degree from the University of Toledo; abilities in several languages; and two years of journalistic experience with the Toledo *Blade.* Said Ben Bradlee, editor of the *Post:* "She had it all. She was bright. She was well spoken. She was pretty. She wrote well." She was black, which made her especially attractive to *The Post,* which was working to bring the percentage of black staff reporters nearer to the percentage of blacks in its circulation area.

"Jimmy's World" was published in September 1980. Six months later, the Pulitzer committee announced its decision and issued a biographical sheet on Janet Cooke. The Associated Press, trying to flesh out the biographical information, spotted discrepancies right away. Janet Cooke, it turned out, had attended Vassar for one year but had not graduated with the honours she claimed. The University of Toledo had no record of awarding her a master's degree. Suddenly, doubts that had surfaced in the days immediately after "Jimmy's World" was published took on a new intensity. The editors sat Cooke down and grilled her on the claims on which she was hired. No, she admitted, she was not multilingual. The Sorbonne claim was fuzzy. More important, they pressed her on whether there was really a Jimmy. The interrogation continued

Janet Cooke ■ Classic case of representing fiction as truth.

ONLINE
Museum of Hoaxes Offers a section on misrepresentative journalism, including stories on Janet Cooke and Jayson Blair.
www.museumofhoaxes.com

Jayson Blair

Jayson Blair

On one level, Jayson Blair's stories in *The New York Times* marked him as a rising star. Assigned in late 2002 to the team covering the Beltway Sniper story around Washington, D.C., Blair produced scoop after scoop that indicated a knack for ferreting out knowledgeable sources and charming information from them. Blair, age 27, exuded self-confidence. He even floated a prospectus for a book on the sniper case.

Then what to many had seemed a promising if not skyrocketing career imploded. Jayson Blair, it turned out, had fabricated sources, played fast and loose with the facts, concocted details that weren't true and purported to have conducted interviews that never took place. These transcended the kinds of forgivable errors that news reporters, being human, make from time to time. He was a serial liar. Time and again, Blair had sallied into fiction while pretending to be reporting the news of the day accurately. Confronted with his lies in May 2003, his career suddenly in shambles, Blair resigned.

His ethics transgressions shook *The Times,* the most prestigious newspaper in the nation, with more Pulitzer Prizes than any other paper—seven in 2002 alone. Said publisher Arthur Sulzberger Jr.: "It's a huge black eye."

In a self-flagellation, the editors assigned an eight-reporter team of reporters to investigate how Jayson Blair, at the paper six years, had attained the kind of trust that news organizations posit in their reporters. *The Times,* no supermarket tabloid, had a long reputation for truth-seeking and often aggressive reporting—and also for the confidence to back up its reporters when critics came down on them.

So what went wrong? For whatever reason, *Times* editors had fast-tracked Blair without putting his work through the rigours that other newsroom newcomers experienced. Factual errors in his work, an incredible 50 to 60 errors by some counts, had been gently excused. Although editors generally are leery about unnamed sources in stories, the anonymous sources who peppered Blair's stories went unchallenged. Surprisingly, none of the sources whom Blair did name in his stories complained about made up quotes and details.

It all began unraveling after a Blair story about details from interrogators of a Beltway Sniper suspect. The information, not true, rattled the investigators who were doing the interrogation. Statements attributed to the suspect in Blair's front-page story had never been made. People at *The Times* began watching Blair. They suddenly realized that he was turning out stories from faraway places without ever leaving town. Then the editor at the *San Antonio Express-News* called to complain that details in a Blair story purported to have been written in Texas had been lifted from his newspaper. Blair hadn't even been to Texas.

into the night, and finally Janet Cooke confessed all: There were no confidential sources, and there was no Jimmy. She had fabricated the story. She resigned, and *The Post,* terribly embarrassed, returned the Pulitzer.

In cases of outright fabrication, as in "Jimmy's World," it is easy to identify the lapses in ethics. When Janet Cooke emerged briefly from seclusion to explain herself, she said that she was responding to pressures in *The Post* newsroom to produce flashy, sensational copy. Most people found the explanation unsatisfying, considering the pattern of deception that went back to her falsified résumé.

There are **misrepresentations**, however, that are not as clearly unacceptable. Much debated are the following.

Staging News To attract favourable attention to their clients, public relations people organize media events, a practice known as **staging news**. These are designed to be irresistible to journalists. Rallies and demonstrations on topical issues, for example, find their way onto front pages, magazine covers and evening newscasts because their photogenic qualities give them an edge over less visual although sometimes more significant events. The ethics question is less important for publicists, who generally are upfront about what they are doing. The ethics question is more serious for journalists, who claim that their job is to present an accurate, balanced account of a day's events but who regularly overplay staged events that are designed by publicists to be photogenic and easy to cover.

Re-creations A wave of **reality programs** on television that began in the late 1980s featured **re-enactments** that were not always labeled as such. Philip Weiss, writing in *Columbia Journalism Review,* offered this litany: shadows on the wall of a woman taking a hammer to her husband, a faceless actor grabbing a tin of kerosene to blow up his son, a corpse in a wheelbarrow with a hand dangling, a detective opening the trunk of a car and reeling from the smell of a decomposing body. Although mixing re-creations with strictly news footage rankles many critics, others argue that it helps people understand the situation. The same question arises with docudramas, which mix actual events and dramatic re-creations.

reality programs ■ Broadcast shows with a nonfiction basis.

re-enactments ■ Re-creating real events.

Selective Editing The editing process, by its nature, requires journalists to make decisions on what is most worth emphasizing and what is least worth even including. In this sense, all editing is selective, but the term **selective editing** refers to making decisions with the goal of distorting. Selective editing can occur in drama too, when writers, editors and other media people take literary licence too far and intentionally misrepresent.

selective editing ■ Misrepresentation through omission and juxtaposition.

GIFTS, JUNKETS AND MEALS

In his 1919 book *The Brass Check*, a pioneer examination of newsroom ethics, **Upton Sinclair** told how newspeople took bribes to put stories in the paper. Today all media ethics codes condemn gifts and certainly bribes. Even so, there are still people who curry favour with the mass media through gifts, such as a college sports publicist who gives a fifth of whisky at Christmas to a sportswriter as a gesture of good will. Favours can take many forms: media-appreciation lunches; free trips abroad, known as **junkets**, especially for travel writers; season passes to cover the opera; discounts at certain stores.

The Brass Check ■ 1919 book that exposed newsroom corruption.

Upton Sinclair ■ Author of *The Brass Check.*

junket ■ Trip with expenses paid by someone who may expect favours in return.

Despite the consistent exhortation of the ethics codes against gifts, favours, free travel and special treatment and privileges, there is nothing inherently wrong in taking them if they do not influence coverage and if the journalist's benefactor understands that. The problem with favours is more a practical one than one of ethics. Taking a favour may or may not be bad, but it *looks* bad. Many ethics codes do not make this important distinction. One that does is the code of the Associated Press Managing Editors (APME), which states: "Journalists must avoid impropriety and *the appearance of impropriety* as well as any conflict of interest or *the appearance of conflict.* They should neither accept anything nor pursue any activity that might compromise or *seem to compromise* their integrity [italics added]." The APME's admonitions at least recognize the distinction between the inherent wrongness of impropriety, which is an ethics question, and the perception that something may be wrong, which is a perception that is unwise to encourage but is not necessarily unethical.

While ethics codes are uniform in prohibiting **freebies**, as gifts and favours are called, many news organizations accept free movie, drama, concert and other tickets, as well as recordings, books and other materials for review. The justification is usually that their budgets allow them to review only materials that arrive free and that their audiences would be denied reviews if the materials had to be purchased. A counter-argument is that a news organization that cannot afford to do business right should not be in business. Many news organizations insist on buying tickets for their reporters to beauty pageants, sports events and other things to which there is an admission fee. A frequent exception occurs when a press box or special media facility is available. With recordings, books and free samples, some media organizations return them or pass them on to charity to avoid any appearance that they have been bought off.

freebie ■ Gift for which the giver may expect favours in return.

The mass media enjoy great freedom under the *Canadian Charter of Rights and Freedoms,* which forbids the government from impinging on expression. Even so, the freedom has limits. Major restrictions on the mass media involve publication bans, censorship, commercial exploitation, invasion of privacy, libel, fair trials and obscenity.

Meanwhile, moral decision making is rooted in conscience, which makes it highly individual. Attempts to bring order to moral issues in journalism and the mass media have included codes of ethics. These codes identify behaviours that are recognized as ethically troublesome, but because they are generalized statements, the codes cannot anticipate all situations. There is no substitute for human reason and common sense.

Questions for Review

1. Why is the *Canadian Charter of Rights and Freedoms* important to the Canadian mass media?
2. In what situations may the government or legal system silence the media in Canada?
3. What constitutes defamation in Canada? What are the media's defences?
4. How is obscenity different from pornography?
5. How does copyright law protect intellectual property from being stolen from its owners?
6. What is the role of the CRTC and the Broadcasting Act in relation to broadcasting in Canada?

Questions for Critical Thinking

1. The *Canadian Charter of Rights and Freedoms* grants everyone in Canada, including the media, freedom of speech. Can this freedom of speech ever be absolute?
2. How useful is the Dagenais ruling in balancing the rights of the individual and the rights of the media?
3. Can you identify the ethics principle or system most associated with Aristotle? Immanuel Kant? John Stuart Mill? John Dewey? John Rawls? Ralph Potter?
4. How can codes of ethics help mass media people make the right decisions? Do codes always work? Why or why not? Review the various Canadian ethics codes in your answer.
5. A candidate for mayor tells a news reporter that the incumbent mayor is in cahoots with organized crime. What should the reporter do before going on the air with this bombshell accusation? Why?
6. Can media people ever defend breaking the law as ethical?
7. What do case studies such as Jayson Blair and Janet Cooke say about the values of contemporary journalism?

Deepening Your media LITERACY

Is objectivity a duty?

STEP 1 Write down your definition of an objective journalist. Be sure to include whose duty the objective journalist should serve: self, audience, employer, profession and/or society.

Dig Deeper

STEP 2

1. Describing Oprah Winfrey's influence, Gloria Steinem, feminist and founder of *Ms.* magazine, said: "Of course, her refusal to be uniformly negative—a frequent definition of objectivity—is exactly what keeps her influence from being taken seriously." How is the journalist who reports uniformly negative news serving his or her duty to the audience? To his or her employer? To society?
2. Media critic Benjamin Radford says that many journalists apply a form of agnostic objectivity, which is ultimately uninformative: "Amid all the finger pointing, contradicting experts, and dueling statistics, the journalist's role turns from claim analyzer to claim deliverer . . . a reporter's job is to help separate the wheat from the chaff; instead, they usually just present two different piles of chaff for the viewer to look at and choose from." Is it OK for a journalist to leave it to the audience to judge the truth of what he or she writes? Why? How is the journalist who reports two sides of an issue without telling the viewer that one of them is not based on fact serving the journalist's duty to himself or herself? To the journalist's employer? To the audience? To society?

Keeping Up to Date

Censorship News is published by the National Coalition Against Censorship.

Media Law Bulletin tracks developments in media law.

News Media and the Law is published by The Reporters Committee for Freedom of the Press.

Media Law Reporter is an annual collection of major court cases.

Student Press Law Reports, from the Student Press Law Center, follows events in the high-school and college press and broadcast media.

The *National Post, Toronto Star* and *The Globe and Mail* often have sections and articles on media law and ethics.

Ethicists sort through moral dilemmas involving mass communication in the scholarly *Journal of Mass Media.*

Many trade and professional journals also deal with media ethics, including the *Columbia Journalism Review, The Canadian Journal of Communication, Broadcast Dialogue* and *Broadcaster* magazine.

For Further Learning

Ellen Alderman and Caroline Kennedy. *The Right to Privacy* (Knopf, 1995).

Brian Bergman. "The Battle over Censorship." *Maclean's* (October 24, 1994).

Clifford G. Christians, Kim B. Rotzoll and Mark Fackler. *Media Ethics,* Sixth edition (Longman, 2002).

Roy Peter Clark. "The Original Sin: How Plagiarism Poisons the Press." *Washington Journalism Review* (March 1983): 43–47.

Ron Cohen. "Self-Regulation: A Canadian Success Story." *Broadcast Dialogue* (November 1999).

Michael G. Crawford. *The Journalist's Legal Guide* (Carswell, 1996).

Robert E. Denton Jr., editor. *Political Communication Ethics: An Oxymoron?* (Praeger, 2000).

Timothy Findlay. "Point–Counterpoint: Ethics in the Media." *Journal of Canadian Studies* 27(4).

Matthew Fraser. "Time to Change Channels." *National Post* (March 7, 2001).

Michael Gartner. "Fair Comment." *American Heritage* (October–November 1982): 28–31.

Bernard Goldberg. *Bias* (Regnery, 2002).

Brian Green. *Broadcast News Essentials* (Harcourt Brace, 2001).

Sally Harris and David Potts. "Important Elements of the Internet Applicable to Cyber Libel" (July 31, 2001). Available online at www.cyberlibel.com/elements.html.

Carl Hausman. *The Decision-Making Process in Journalism* (Nelson-Hall, 1990).

Matthew Ingram. "Media Stardom is Pricey." *The Globe and Mail* (June 15, 2007).

Walter B. Jaehnig. "Harrison Cochran—The Publisher with a Past." *Journal of Mass Media Ethics* 2 (Fall/Winter 1986–87): 1, 80–88.

Dean Jobb. *Media Law for Canadian Journalists* (Emond Montgomery Publications, 2006).

Paul Kaihla. "Sex and the Law." *Maclean's* (October 24, 1994).

Donna Soble Kaufman. *Broadcasting Law in Canada: Fairness in the Administrative Process* (Carswell, 1987).

Wilfred H. Kesterton. *The Law and the Press in Canada* (McClelland and Stewart, 1976).

Janet Malcolm. *The Journalist and the Murderer* (Knopf, 1990).

John C. Merrill. *The Dialectic in Journalism: Toward a Responsible Use of Press Freedom* (Louisiana State University Press, 1990).

Clark R. Mollenhoff. "25 Years of *Times* v. *Sullivan.*" *Quill* (March 1989): 27–31.

Ralph B. Potter. "The Structure of Certain American Christian Responses to the Nuclear Dilemma, 1958–1963" (Ph.D. Diss., Harvard University, 1965).

Lori Robertson. "Ethically Challenged." *American Journalism Review* (March 2001): 20–29.

Stuart Robertson. *The Media Law Handbook* (Self-Counsel Press, 1983).

Stuart Robertson. *Pocket Guide to Media Law* (Hallion Press, 1994).

Nick Russell. *Morals and the Media: Ethics in Canadian Journalism,* Second edition (University of British Columbia Press, 2006).

Ron F. Smith. *Groping for Ethics in Journalism,* Fourth edition (Iowa State University Press, 1999).

Colin Sparks and John Tulloch, editors. *Tabloid Tales: Global Debates over Media Standards* (Rowman & Littlefield, 2000).

Joe Strupp. "Policing Plagiarism." *Editor & Publisher* (August 7, 2000): 19–22.

Philip Weiss. "Bad Rap for TV Tabs." *Columbia Journalism Review* 28 (May/June 1989): 1, 39–42.

Marie Dunn White. "Plagiarism and the News Media." *Journal of Mass Media Ethics* 4 (1989): 2, 265–280.

Orson Welles Young Orson Welles scared the living daylights out of several million radio listeners with the 1938 radio drama *The War of the Worlds.* Most of the fright was short-lived, though. All but the most naïve listeners quickly realized that Martians, marching toward the Hudson River to destroy Manhattan, really had not devastated the New Jersey militia.

Media Effects

Media in Theory

The boy genius **Orson Welles** was on a roll. By 1938, at age 23, Welles's dramatic flair had landed him a network radio show, *Mercury Theater on the Air,* at prime time on CBS on Sunday nights. The program featured adaptations of well-known literature. For their October 30 program, Welles and his colleagues decided on a scary 1898 British novel, H.G. Wells's *The War of the Worlds*.

Orson Welles opened with the voice of a wizened chronicler from some future time, intoning an unsettling monologue. That was followed by an innocuous weather forecast, then hotel dance music. Then the music was interrupted by a news bulletin. An astronomer reported several explosions on Mars, propelling something at enormous velocity toward Earth. The bulletin over, listeners were transported back to the hotel orchestra. After applause the orchestra started up again, only to be interrupted by a special announcement: Seismologists had picked up an earthquake-like shock in New Jersey. Then it was one bulletin after another.

The storyline accelerated. Giant Martians moved across the countryside spewing fatal gas. One at a time, reporters at remote sites vanished off the air. The Martians decimated the Army and were wading across the Hudson River. Amid sirens and other sounds of emergency, a reporter on a Manhattan rooftop described the monsters advancing through the streets. From his vantage point he described the Martians felling people by the thousands and moving in on him, the gas crossing Sixth Avenue, then Fifth Avenue, then 100 yards away, then 50 feet. Then silence.

To the surprise of Orson Welles and his crew the drama triggered widespread mayhem. Neighbours gathered in streets all over the country, wet towels held to their faces to slow the gas. In Newark, New Jersey, people—many undressed—fled their apartments. Said a New York woman, "I never hugged my radio so closely . . . . I held a crucifix in my hand and prayed while looking out my open window to get a faint whiff of gas so that I would know when to close my window and hermetically seal my room with waterproof cement or anything else I could get a hold of. My plan was to stay in the room and hope that I would not suffocate before the gas blew away."

Orson Welles ■ His radio drama cast doubt on powerful effects theory.

The War of the Worlds ■ Novel that inspired a radio drama that became the test bed of the media's ability to instill panic.

Researchers estimate that one out of six people who heard the program, more than one million in all, suspended disbelief and braced for the worst.

The effects were especially amazing considering that:

- An announcer identified the program as fiction at four points.
- Almost 10 times as many people were tuned to a popular comedy show on another network.
- The program ran only one hour, an impossibly short time for the sequence that began with the blastoffs on Mars, included a major military battle in New Jersey and ended with New York's destruction.

Unwittingly, Orson Welles and his Mercury Theater crew had created an evening of infamy and raised questions about media effects to new intensity. Theoretically, how could this happen? In this chapter you will learn what scholars have found out about the effects of the mass media on individuals.

media ONLINE

War of the Worlds Information about every version of *The War of the Worlds* ever released, including books, performances, music, movies, television shows, models and games.
www.war-of-the-worlds.org

media TIMELINE

UNDERSTANDING MASS MEDIA EFFECTS

1922 Walter Lippmann attributed powerful effects to the mass media.

1938 Hadley Cantril concluded that "The War of the Worlds" panic was drastically overstated.

1940s Mass communication scholars shifted from studying effects to uses and gratification.

1948 Paul Lazarsfeld challenged powerful effects theory in voter studies.

1967 George Gerbner launched his television violence index.

1970s Mass communication scholars shifted to cumulative effects theory.

1972 Maxwell McCombs and Donald Shaw concluded that media create public agendas, not opinion.

1992 Virginie Larivière presented Prime Minister Brian Mulroney with a petition urging the government to do something about violence on TV.

1993 A new violence code was introduced by Canada's AGVOT.

▛▖ Effects Studies

study preview Early mass communication scholars assumed that the mass media were so powerful that ideas and even ballot-box instructions could be inserted as if by hypodermic needle into the body politic. Doubts arose in the 1940s about whether the media were really that powerful, and scholars began shaping their research questions and asking about long-term, cumulative media effects.

POWERFUL EFFECTS THEORY

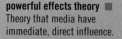

powerful effects theory ▆
Theory that media have immediate, direct influence.

Walter Lippmann ▆ His book *Public Opinion* assumed powerful media effects in 1920s.

The first generation of mass communication scholars thought the mass media had a profound, direct effect on people. Their idea, called **powerful effects theory**, drew heavily on social commentator **Walter Lippmann**'s influential 1922 book *Public Opinion*. Lippmann argued that we see the world not as it really is but as "pictures in our heads." The "pictures" of things we have not experienced personally, he said, are shaped by the mass media. The powerful impact that Lippmann ascribed to the media was a precursor of the powerful effects theory that evolved among scholars over the next few years.

Yale psychologist **Harold Lasswell**, who studied World War II propaganda, embodied the effects theory in his famous model of mass communication: *who, says what, in which channel, to whom, with what effect.* At their extreme, powerful effects theory devotees assumed that the media could inject information, ideas and even propaganda into the public. The theory was explained in terms of a hypodermic needle model or bullet model. Early powerful effects scholars would agree that newspaper coverage and endorsements of political candidates decided elections.

The early scholars did not see that the hypodermic metaphor was hopelessly simplistic. They assumed wrongly that individuals are passive and absorb uncritically and unconditionally whatever the media spew forth. The fact is that individuals read, hear and see the same things differently. Even if they did not, people are exposed to many, many media—hardly a single, monolithic voice. Also, there is a skepticism among media consumers that is manifested at its extreme in the saying "You can't believe a thing you read in the paper." People are not mindless, uncritical blotters.

MINIMALIST EFFECTS THEORY

Scholarly enthusiasm for the hypodermic needle model dwindled after two massive studies of voter behaviour, one in Erie County, Ohio, in 1940 and the other in Elmira, New York, in 1948. The studies, led by sociologist **Paul Lazarsfeld** of Columbia University, were the first rigorous tests of media effects on an election. Lazarsfeld's researchers went back to 600 people several times to discover how they developed their campaign opinions. Rather than citing particular newspapers, magazines or radio stations, as had been expected, these people generally mentioned friends and acquaintances. The media had hardly any direct effect. Clearly, the hypodermic needle model was off base, and the powerful effects theory needed rethinking. From that rethinking emerged the **minimalist effects theory**, which included:

Two-Step Flow Model Minimalist scholars devised the **two-step flow** model to show that voters are motivated less by the mass media than by people they know personally and respect. These people, called **opinion leaders**, include many clergy, teachers and neighbourhood merchants, although it is impossible to list categorically all those who are opinion leaders. Not all clergy, for example, are influential, and opinion leaders are not necessarily in an authority role. The minimalist scholars' point is that personal contact is more important than media contact. The two-step flow model, which replaced the hypodermic needle model, showed that whatever effect the media have on the majority of the population is through opinion leaders. Later, as mass communication research became more sophisticated, the two-step model was expanded into a **multistep flow** model to capture the complex web of social relationships that affects individuals.

Status Conferral Minimalist scholars acknowledge that the media create prominence for issues and people by giving them coverage. Conversely, neglect relegates issues and personalities to obscurity. Related to this **status conferral** phenomenon is **agenda setting** (see further discussion in the section entitled Media Agenda-Setting for Individuals, later in this chapter). Professors **Maxwell McCombs and Donald Shaw**, describing the agenda-setting phenomenon in 1972, said the media do not tell people *what to think* but tell them *what to think about.* This is a profound distinction. In covering a political campaign, explain McCombs and Shaw, the media choose which issues or topics to emphasize, thereby helping set the campaign's agenda. "This ability to affect cognitive change among individuals," say McCombs and Shaw, "is one of the most important aspects of the power of mass communication."

Narcoticizing Dysfunction Some minimalists claim that the media rarely energize people into action, such as getting them to go out to vote for a candidate. Rather, they say, the media lull people into passivity. This effect, called **narcoticizing dysfunction**, is supported by studies that find that many people are so overwhelmed by the volume of news and information available to them that they tend to withdraw from involvement in public issues. Narcoticizing dysfunction occurs also when people pick up a great deal of information from the media on a particular subject—poverty, for

Harold Lasswell ■ His mass communication model assumed powerful effects.

Paul Lazarsfeld ■ Found voters more influenced by other people than by mass media.

minimalist effects theory ■ Theory that media effects are mostly indirect.

two-step flow ■ Media effects on individuals are through opinion leaders.

opinion leaders ■ Influence friends, acquaintances.

multistep flow ■ Media effects on individuals come through complex interpersonal connections.

status conferral ■ Media attention enhances attention to people, subjects, issues.

agenda setting ■ Media tell people what to think about, not what to think.

Maxwell McCombs and Donald Shaw ■ Articulated agenda-setting theory.

narcoticizing dysfunction ■ People deceive themselves into believing they're involved when actually they're only informed.

ONLINE

Center for Research on the Effects of Television Based at Ithaca College in New York, the centre examines television content and its effect on viewers. www.ithaca.edu/cretv

Elisabeth Noelle-Neumann ■ Leading cumulative effects theorist.

cumulative effects theory ■ Theory that media influence is gradual over time.

spiral of silence ■ Vocal majority intimidates others into silence.

third-person effect ■ One person overestimating the effect of media messages on other people.

W.P. Davison ■ Scholar who devised third-person effect theory.

Melvin DeFleur ■ Scholar who concluded that mass communication theory has peaked.

example—and believe that they are doing something about a problem when they are really only smugly well informed. Intellectual involvement becomes a substitute for active involvement.

CUMULATIVE EFFECTS THEORY

In recent years, some mass communication scholars have parted from the minimalists and resurrected the powerful effects theory, although with a twist that avoids the simplistic hypodermic needle model. German scholar **Elisabeth Noelle-Neumann**, a leader of this school, concedes that the media do not have powerful immediate effects but argues that effects over time are profound. Her **cumulative effects theory** notes that nobody can escape either the media, which are ubiquitous, or the media's messages, which are driven home with redundancy. To support her point, Noelle-Neumann cites multimedia advertising campaigns that hammer away with the same message over and over. There's no missing the point. Even in news reports there is a redundancy, with the media all focusing on the same events.

Noelle-Neumann's cumulative effects theory has troubling implications. She says that the media, despite surface appearances, work against diverse, robust public consideration of issues. Noelle-Neumann bases her observation on human psychology, which she says encourages people who feel they hold majority viewpoints to speak out confidently. Those views gain credibility in their claim to be dominant when they are carried by the media, whether they are really dominant or not. Meanwhile, says Noelle-Neumann, people who perceive that they are in a minority are inclined to speak out less, perhaps not at all. The result is that dominant views can snowball through the media and become consensus views without being sufficiently challenged.

To demonstrate her intriguing theory, Noelle-Neumann has devised the ominously labeled **spiral of silence** model, in which minority views are intimidated into silence and obscurity. Noelle-Neumann's model raises doubts about the libertarian concept that the media provide a marketplace in which conflicting ideas fight it out fairly, all receiving a full hearing.

THIRD-PERSON EFFECT

A remnant of now-discredited perceptions that the media have powerful and immediate influence is called **third-person effect**. In short, the theory holds that people overestimate the impact of media messages on other people. Scholar **W.P. Davison**, who came up with the concept in 1983, told a story about a community film board that censored some movies because they might harm people who watch them—even though the board members would deny that they themselves were harmed by watching the movies. The theory can be reduced to this notion: "It's the other guy who can't handle it, not me."

FUTURE THEORIES

Scholar **Melvin DeFleur**, who has chronicled developments in mass communication theory, is pessimistic about what's happening now in mass communication studies. DeFleur, of Boston University, says recent years have lacked milestones, seminal studies on mass communication, after a rich history of significant studies from the 1930s to the early 1980s. Writing in the scholarly journal *Mass Communication and Society* in 1998, DeFleur said: "When asked by my publisher to revise a book summarizing the existing milestones and adding new ones, I could not identify even one that fit the same criteria as the earlier investigations."

The Golden Age of masscom research, as DeFleur calls it, yielded "important concepts, generalizations and theories that are now part of the accumulated knowledge of how the U.S. media function and the kinds of influence that they have on individuals and society."

Is mass communication theory dead in the water? DeFleur says that one factor has been a brain drain from universities, where such research took place in earlier times. Corporations now offer much higher salaries than universities—sometimes double and triple—to attract people with doctoral degrees who can do research for their marketing and other corporate pursuits and not purely academic reasons.

Uses and Gratifications Studies

study <u>preview</u> Beginning in the 1940s, many mass communication scholars shifted from studying the media to studying media audiences. These scholars assumed that individuals use the media to gratify needs. Their work, known as uses and gratifications studies, focused on how individuals use mass media—and why.

CHALLENGES TO AUDIENCE PASSIVITY

As disillusionment with the powerful effects theory set in after the Lazarsfeld studies of the 1940s, scholars re-evaluated many of their assumptions, including the idea that people are merely passive consumers of the mass media. From the re-evaluation came research questions about why individuals tap into the mass media. This research, called **uses and gratifications** studies (introduced in Chapter 12), explored how individuals choose certain media outlets. One vein of research said people seek certain media to gratify certain needs.

These scholars worked with social science theories about people being motivated to do certain things by human needs and wants, such as seeking water, food and shelter as necessities and wanting to be socially accepted and loved. These scholars identified dozens of reasons why people use the media, among them surveillance, socialization and diversion.

uses and gratifications ■
Theory that people choose media that meet their needs, interests.

SURVEILLANCE FUNCTION

With their acute sense of smell and hearing, deer scan their environment constantly for approaching danger. In modern human society, surveillance is provided for individuals by the mass media, which scan local and global environments for information that helps individuals make decisions to live better, even survive.

News coverage is the most evident form through which the mass media serve this **surveillance function**. From a weather report, people decide whether to wear a raincoat; from the Wall Street averages, whether to invest; from the news, whether the president will have their support. Although most people don't obsess about being on top of all that's happening in the world, there is a touch of the news junkie in everybody. All people need reliable information on their immediate environment. Besides wanting to know what the weather forecast is, most of us are curious about developments in politics, economics, science and other fields. The news media provide that information for us.

ONLINE
Media Awareness Network A rich media-literacy site from Canada. The section on media research provides many resources for further study.
www.media-awareness.ca

surveillance function ■ Media provide information on what's going on.

SOCIALIZATION FUNCTION

Except for recluses, people are always seeking information that helps them fit in with other people. This **socialization function**, a lifelong process, is greatly assisted by the mass media. Without paying attention to the media, for example, it is hard to participate in conversations about Tom Cruise's latest movie or the current political scandal in Ottawa. Jay Leno's monologues give late-night television watchers a common experience with their friends and associates the next day, as do the latest movie, the evening news and what happened last night on *Lost* or *American Idol*.

Less positive as a social function of the mass media is **parasocial interaction**. When a television anchor looks directly into the camera, as if talking with individual viewers, it is not a true social relationship that is being created. The communication is one-way without audience feedback. However, because many people enjoy the sense of interaction, no matter how false it is, many local stations encourage on-camera members of the news team to chat among themselves, which furthers the impression of an ongoing conversation with an extended peer group that includes the individual viewer.

socialization function ■ Media help people fit into society.

parasocial interaction ■ A false sense of participating in dialogue.

DIVERSION FUNCTION

Through the mass media, people can escape their everyday drudgery, immersing themselves in a soap opera, a murder mystery or pop music. This is the **diversion function**. The result can be stimulation, relaxation or emotional release.

diversion function ■ Media used as an entertainment source.

Stimulation Everybody is bored occasionally. When our senses—sight, hearing, smell, taste and touch—lack sufficient external stimuli, a sensory vacuum results. Following the physicist's law that a vacuum must be filled, we seek new stimuli to correct our sensory deprivation. In modern society, the mass media are almost always handy as boredom-offsetting stimulants.

Relaxation When someone's sensory abilities are overloaded, the media can be relaxing. Slower, softer music sometimes can help. Relaxation, in fact, can come through any change of pace. In some situations, a high-tension movie or a book can be as effective as a lullaby.

Release People can use the mass media to blow off steam. Somehow a Friday night horror movie dissipates the frustration pent up all week, as can a good cry during a "chick flick."

Using the mass media as a stimulant, relaxant or release is quick, healthy escapism. Escapism, however, can go further, as when soap-opera fans so enmesh themselves in the programs that they perceive themselves as characters in the storyline. Carried too far, escapism becomes withdrawal.

CONSISTENCY THEORY

Gratifications scholars learned that people generally are conservative and cautious in choosing media, looking for media that reinforce their personal views. Faced with messages that are consistent with their own views and ones that are radically different, people pay attention to the ones they're comfortable with and have slight recall of contrary views. These phenomena—selective exposure, selective perception, selective retention and selective recall—came to be called **consistency theory**.

Consistency theory does a lot to explain media habits. People read, watch and listen to media with messages that don't jar them. The theory raises serious questions about how well the media can meet the democratic ideal that they be a forum for the robust exchange of divergent ideas. The media can't fulfill their role as a forum if people hear only what they want to hear.

■ Individual Selectivity

studypreview Individuals choose to expose themselves to media whose perspective and approach reinforce their personal interests and values. These choices, called selective exposure, are consciously made. Similar selectivity phenomena are at work subconsciously in how individuals perceive and retain media content.

SELECTIVE EXPOSURE

People make deliberate decisions in choosing media. For example, outdoors enthusiasts choose *Field & Stream* at the newsrack. Academics subscribe to the *Canadian Journal of Communication*. Young rock fans watch MuchMusic. People expose themselves to media whose content relates to their interests. In this sense, individuals exercise control over the media's effects on them. Nobody forces these selections on anybody. This is called **selective exposure**.

SELECTIVE PERCEPTION

The selectivity that occurs in actually reading, watching and listening is less conscious than in selective exposure. No matter how clear a message is, people see and hear egocentrically. This phenomenon, known as **selective perception** or **autistic perception**, was demonstrated in the 1950s by researcher Roy Carter, who found that physicians concerned about socialized medicine at the time would hear "social aspects of medicine" as "socialized medicine." Rural folks in the U.S. Southeast, anxious for news about farming, thought they heard the words "farm news" on the radio when the announcer said "foreign news."

Scholars Eugene Webb and Jerry Salancik explain it this way: "Exposure to information is hedonistic." People pick up what they want to pick up. Webb and Salancik state that nonsmokers who read an article about smoking focus subconsciously on passages that link smoking with cancer, being secure and content, even joyful, in the information that reinforces the wisdom of their decision not to smoke. In contrast, smokers are more attentive to passages that hedge the smoking–cancer link. In using the mass media for information, people tend to perceive what they want. As social commentator Walter Lippmann put it: "For the most part we do not first see and then define, we define first and then see." Sometimes the human mind distorts facts to square with predispositions and preconceptions.

SELECTIVE RETENTION AND RECALL

Experts say that the brain records forever everything to which it is exposed. The problem is recall. Although people remember many things that were extremely pleasurable or that coincided with their beliefs, they have a harder time calling up the memory's file on other things.

Selective retention happens to mothers when they tend to deemphasize or even forget the illnesses or disturbances of pregnancy and the pain of birth. This phenomenon works the opposite way when individuals encounter things that reinforce their beliefs.

Nostalgia also can affect recall. For example, many mothers grossly pre-date when their children abandoned an undesirable behaviour like thumb sucking. Mothers tend also to suggest precocity about the age at which Suzy or José first walked or cut the first tooth. In the same way people often use rose-coloured lenses, not 20/20 vision, in recalling information and ideas from the media. This is known as **selective recall**.

In summary, individuals have a large degree of control over how the mass media affect them. Not only do individuals make conscious choices in exposing themselves to particular media, but also their beliefs and values subconsciously shape how their minds pick up and store information and ideas. The phenomena of selective exposure, selective perception and selective retention and recall are overlooked by people who portray the mass media as omnipotent and individuals as helpless and manipulated pawns.

The 1938 "War of the Worlds" scare demonstrates this point. The immediate response was to heap blame on the media, particularly Orson Welles and CBS, but panic-stricken listeners bore responsibility too. A Princeton University team led by psychologist **Hadley Cantril**, which studied the panic, noted that radio listeners brought to their radio sets predispositions and preconceptions that contributed to what happened. Among their subconscious baggage:

- A preconception, almost a reverence, about radio, especially CBS, as a reliable medium for major, breaking news.
- A predisposition to expect bad news, created by a decade of disastrous global economic developments and another war imminent in Europe.
- Selective perception, which caused them to miss announcements that the program was a dramatization. Although many listeners tuned in late and missed the initial announcement, others listened straight through the announcements without registering them.
- An awe about scientific discoveries, technological progress and new weapons, which contributed to gullibility.
- Memories from World War I about the horror of gas warfare.
- A failure to test the radio story against their own common sense. How, for example, could the Army mobilize for a battle against the Martians within 20 minutes of the invasion?

■ Socialization

study preview The mass media have a large role in initiating children into society. This socialization process is essential to perpetuating cultural values, but some people worry that it can be negative if the media report and portray undesirable behaviour and attitudes, such as violence and racism.

media ONLINE

Selective Perception An introduction to selective perception and how it's used in advertising.
www.ciadvertising.org/ student_account/fall_01/adv382j/ howardmo/selectiveperception. html

selective retention ■ Subconsciously, people retain some events and messages, not others.

selective recall ■ People recollect some events and messages for long term but not others.

Hadley Cantril ■ Concluded that there is less media effect than had been thought.

MEDIA'S INITIATING ROLE

Nobody is born knowing how to fit into society. This is learned through a process that begins at home. Children imitate their parents and brothers and sisters. From listening and observing, children learn values. Some behaviour is applauded, some is scolded. Gradually this culturization and **socialization** process expands to include friends, neighbours, school and at some point the mass media.

In earlier times the role of the mass media came late because books, magazines and newspapers required reading skills that were learned in school. The media were only a modest part of early childhood socialization. Today, however, television is omnipresent from the cradle. A young person turning 18 will have spent more time watching television than doing any other activity except sleeping. Television, which requires no special skills to use, has displaced much of the socializing influence that once came from parents. *Sesame Street* imparts more information on the value of nutrition than does Mom's admonition to eat spinach.

By definition, socialization is **pro-social** rather than anti-social, in that it teaches behaviour that will benefit others or society. Children learn that buddies frown on tattling; that honesty is virtuous; and that hard work is rewarded. The stability of a society is ensured through the transmission of such values to the next generation.

ROLE MODELS

The extent of media influence on individuals may never be sorted out with any precision, in part because every individual is a distinct person and because media exposure varies from person to person. Even so, some media influence is undeniable. This imitation, called **role modeling**, even includes popular quotes from whoever is hip at the moment—"You're Fired!" from *The Apprentice,* being "voted off the island" from *Survivor* and "yadda-yadda-yadda" from *Seinfeld.*

No matter how quirky, fashion fads are not terribly consequential, but serious questions can be raised about whether role modeling extends to behaviour. Many people who produce media messages recognize a responsibility for role modeling. Many newspapers have a policy to mention in accident stories whether seat belts were in use. In the

Asics Revival When Uma Thurman slashed her way through Quentin Tarantino's movie *Kill Bill,* the 1949-vintage Asics sneakers she wore, the Onitsuka Tiger model, were suddenly a hit again. In the first quarter after the movie, Asics's net profits outperformed $1.8 billion in expectations to $2.6 billion.

1980s, as concern about AIDS mounted, moviemakers went out of their way to show condoms as a precaution in social situations. For example, in the movie *Broadcast News,* the producer character slips a condom into her purse before leaving the house on the night of the awards dinner.

If role modeling can work for good purposes, such as promoting safety consciousness and disease prevention, it would seem that it could also have a negative effect. Some people linked the Columbine High School massacre in Littleton, Colorado, to a scene in the Leonardo DiCaprio movie, *The Basketball Diaries.* In one scene, a student in a black trench coat executes fellow classmates.

STEREOTYPING

Stereotyping is a kind of shorthand that can facilitate communication. Putting a cowboy in a black hat allows a movie director to sidestep complex character explanation and move quickly into a storyline because moviegoers hold a generalization about cowboys in black hats: They are the bad guys—a stereotype.

Newspaper editors pack lots of information into headlines by drawing on stereotypes held by the readers. Consider the extra meanings implicit in headlines that refer to a political "regime," a "Southern belle" or a "college jock." Stereotypes paint broad strokes that help create impact in media messages, but they are also a problem. A generalization, no matter how useful, is inaccurate. Not all Scots are tight-fisted, nor are all Wall Street brokers crooked, nor are all college jocks dumb—not even a majority.

By using stereotypes, the mass media perpetuate them. With benign stereotypes there is no problem, but the media can perpetuate social injustice with stereotypes. In the late 1970s the U.S. Civil Rights Commission found that blacks on network television were portrayed disproportionately in immature, demeaning or comic roles. By using a stereotype, television was not only perpetuating false generalizations but also being racist. Worse, network thoughtlessness was robbing black people of strong role models.

Feminists have leveled objections that women are both underrepresented and misrepresented in the media. One study by sociologist Eve Simson found that most female television parts were decorative, played by pretty California women in their 20s. Worse were the occupations represented by women, said Simson. Most frequent were prostitutes, at 16 percent. Traditional female occupations—secretaries, nurses, flight attendants and receptionists—represented 17 percent. Career women tended to be man-haters or domestic failures. Said Simson: "With nearly every family, regardless of socio-economic class, having at least one TV set and the average set being turned on seven hours per day, TV has emerged as an important source for promulgating attitudes, values and customs. For some viewers it is the only major contact with outside 'reality,' including how to relate to women. Thus, not only is TV's sexism insulting, but it is also detrimental to the status of women."

SOCIALIZATION VIA EAVESDROPPING

The mass media, especially television, have eroded the boundaries that people once respected between the generations, genders and other social institutions. Once adults whispered when they wanted to discuss certain subjects, like sex, when children were around. Today, children eavesdrop on all kinds of adult topics by seeing them depicted on television.

Joshua Meyrowitz, a communication scholar at the University of New Hampshire, brought the new socialization effects of intergenerational eavesdropping to wide attention with his 1985 book, *No Sense of Place.* In effect, the old socially recognized institution of childhood, which long had been protected from "grown-up issues" like money, divorce and sex, was disappearing. From television sitcoms, kids today learn that adults fight and goof up and sometimes are just plain silly. These are things kids may always have been aware of in a vague sense, but now they have front row seats.

Television also cracked other protected societal institutions, such as the "man's world." Through television many women entered the man's world of the locker room, the fishing trip and the workplace beyond the home. Older mass media, including books, had dealt with a diversity of topics and allowed people in on the "secrets" of other groups, but the ubiquity of television and the ease of access to it accelerated the breakdown of traditional institutional barriers.

stereotyping ■ Using broad strokes to facilitate storytelling.

media ONLINE

Media Stereotypes This educational introduction to media stereotyping details several categories of common stereotypes.
www.media-awareness.ca/english/issues/stereotyping/index.cfm

Young African-Americans Against Media Stereotypes Nonprofit organization working for equal and fair exposure of African-Americans in the media.
www.yaaams.org

media ONLINE

Media Action Network for Asian Americans Check out the memo from MANAA to Hollywood, regarding Asian American stereotypes in the media.
www.manaa.org/articles/stereo.html

Media Stereotypes of Young People Even children are stereotyped in the media.
www.headliners.org/storylibrary/stories/2006/stereotypes.htm?id=435805514099801882000606

Joshua Meyrowitz ■ Noted that media have reduced generational, gender barriers.

■ Media-Depicted Violence

studypreview Some individuals mimic aggressive behaviour they see in the media, but such incidents are exceptions. Some experts argue, in fact, that media-depicted violence actually reduces real-life aggressive behaviour.

LEARNING ABOUT VIOLENCE

Violence and its effect on children has been an important political issue for Canadians for many years. In 1990, a group of school-age children presented a petition with more than 150 000 names to the Federal Minister of Communications, urging the government to "enact rules to eliminate violent and war programming for children on television." The issue became more meaningful in 1992, when Virginie Larivière presented Prime Minister Brian Mulroney with a petition containing 1.3 million names, asking him to initiate legislation that would require broadcasters to reduce the level of violent programming on television, and asking Canadians to boycott violent TV shows. Larivière's sister, Marie-Eve, was robbed, sexually assaulted, and murdered. Virginie Larivière believed that violence on television was a factor that influenced her sister's murderer.

observational learning ■ Theory that people learn behaviour by seeing it in real life, in depictions.

The mass media help to bring young people into society's mainstream by demonstrating dominant behaviours and norms. This pro-social process, called **observational learning**, turns dark, however, when children learn deviant behaviours from the media. In Manteca, California, two teenagers, one only 13, lay in wait for a friend's father in his own house and attacked him. They beat him with a fireplace poker, kicked him and stabbed him, and choked him to death with a dog chain. Then they poured salt in his wounds. Why the final act of violence—the salt in the wounds? The 13-year-old explained that he had seen it on television. While there is no question that people can learn about violent behaviour from the media, a major issue of our time is whether the mass media are the cause of aberrant behaviour.

Individuals on trial for criminal acts occasionally plead that "the media made me do it." That was the defence in a 1974 California case in which two young girls playing on a beach were raped with a beer bottle by four teenagers. The rapists told police they had picked up the idea from a television movie they had seen four days earlier. In the movie a young woman was raped with a broom handle, and in court the youths' attorneys blamed the movie. Although the courts have never accepted transfer of responsibility as a legal defence, it is clear that violent behaviour can be imitated from the media. Some experts, however, say that the negative effect of media-depicted violence is too often overstated and that media violence actually has a positive side.

MEDIA VIOLENCE AS POSITIVE

cathartic effect ■ People release violent inclinations by seeing them portrayed.

Aristotle ■ Defended portrayals of violence.

People who downplay the negative effect of media portrayals of blood, guts and violence often refer to a **cathartic effect**. This theory, which dates to ancient Greece and the philosopher **Aristotle**, suggests that watching violence allows individuals vicariously to release pent-up everyday frustration that might otherwise explode dangerously. By seeing violence, so goes the theory, people let off steam. Most advocates of the cathartic effect claim that individuals who see violent activity are stimulated to fantasy violence, which drains off latent tendencies toward real-life violence.

Seymour Feshbach ■ Found evidence for media violence as a release.

In more recent times, scholar **Seymour Feshbach** has conducted studies that lend support to the cathartic effect theory. In one study, Feshbach lined up 625 junior high school boys at seven California boarding schools and showed half of them a steady diet of violent television programs for six weeks. The other half were shown nonviolent fare. Every day during the study, teachers and supervisors reported on each boy's behaviour in and out of class. Feshbach found no difference in aggressive behaviour between the two groups. Further, there was a decline in aggression among boys who were determined by personality tests to be more inclined toward aggressive behaviour.

PRODDING SOCIALLY POSITIVE ACTION

Besides the cathartic effect theory, an argument for portraying violence is that it prompts people to socially positive action. This happened after NBC aired *The Burning Bed,* a television movie about an abused woman who could not take any more and set fire to her

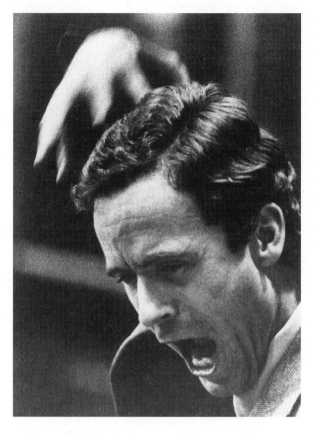

Scapegoating On the eve of his execution, serial killer Ted Bundy claimed that his violence had been sparked by pornographic magazines. Whatever the truth of Bundy's claim, scholars are divided about whether media depictions precipitate violent behaviour. At one extreme is the view that media violence is a safety valve for people inclined to violence. At the other extreme is the aggressive stimulation theory that media violence causes real-life violence. The most prevalent thinking, to paraphrase a pioneer 1961 study on television and children, is that *certain* depictions under *certain* conditions *may* prompt violence in *certain* people.

sleeping husband. The night the movie was shown, battered-spouse centres nationwide were overwhelmed by calls from women who had been putting off doing anything to extricate themselves from relationships with abusive mates. On the negative side, one man set his estranged wife afire and explained that he was inspired by *The Burning Bed*. Another man who beat his wife senseless gave the same explanation.

MEDIA VIOLENCE AS NEGATIVE

The preponderance of evidence is that media-depicted violence has the potential to cue real-life violence. However, the **aggressive stimulation** theory is often overstated. The fact is that few people act out media violence in their lives. For example, do you know anybody who saw a murder in a movie and went out afterward and murdered somebody? Yet you know many people who see murders in movies and *don't* kill anyone.

We need to be careful in talking about aggressive stimulation. Note how scholar Wayne Danielson, who participated in the 1995–1997 National Television Violence Study, carefully qualified one of the study's conclusions: "Viewing violence on TV *tends* to increase violent behavior in viewers, more *in some situations* and less in others. For whatever reason, *when the circumstances are right*, we *tend* to imitate what we see others doing. Our inner resistance to engage in violent behavior *weakens*."

The study concluded that children may be more susceptible than adults to media violence, but that too was far, far short of a universal causal statement.

Why, then, do many people believe that media violence begets real-life violence? Some early studies pointed to a causal link. These included the 1960 **Bobo doll studies** of **Albert Bandura**, who showed children a violent movie and then encouraged them to play with oversize, inflated dolls. Bandura concluded that kids who saw the film were more inclined to beat up the dolls than were other kids. Critics have challenged Bandura's methodology and said that he mistook childish playfulness for aggression. In short, Bandura and other aggressive stimulation scholars have failed to prove their theory to the full satisfaction of other scholars.

When pressed, people who hold the aggressive stimulation theory point to particular incidents they know about. A favourite is the claim by serial killer Ted Bundy that *Playboy* magazine led him to stalk and kill women. Was Bundy telling the truth? We will

aggressive stimulation ■ Theory that people are inspired to violence from media depictions.

Bobo doll studies ■ Kids seemed more violent after seeing violence in movies.

Albert Bandura ■ Found media violence stimulated aggression in children.

never know. He offered the scapegoat explanation on his way to the execution chamber, which suggests that there may have been other motives. The Bundy case is anecdotal, and anecdotes cannot be extrapolated into general validity.

CATALYTIC THEORY

An alternative to aggressive stimulation theory is a theory that people whose feelings and general view of the world tend toward aggressiveness and violence are attracted to violence in movies, television and other media depictions of violence. This alternative theory holds that people who are violent are predisposed to violence, which is far short of saying the media made them do it. This leads us to the **catalytic theory**, which sees media-depicted violence as having a contributing role in violent behaviour, not as triggering it.

Simplistic readings of both cathartic and aggressive stimulation effects research can yield extreme conclusions. A careful reading, however, points more to the media having a role in real-life violence but not necessarily triggering it and doing so only infrequently— and only if several nonmedia factors are also present. For example, evidence suggests that television and movie violence, even in cartoons, is arousing and can excite some children to violence, especially hyperactive and easily excitable children. These children, like unstable adults, become wrapped up psychologically with the portrayals and are stirred to the point of acting out. However, this happens only when a combination of other influences are also present. Among these other influences are:

- **Whether violence portrayed in the media is rewarded.** In 1984 David Phillips of the University of California at San Diego found that the murder rate increases after publicized prizefights, in which the victor is rewarded, and decreases after publicized murder trials and executions, in which, of course, violence is punished.
- **Whether media exposure is heavy.** Researcher Monroe Lefkowitz studied upstate New York third-graders who watched a lot of media-depicted violence. Ten years later, Lefkowitz found that these individuals were rated by their peers as violent. This suggests cumulative, long-term media effects.
- **Whether a violent person fits other profiles.** Studies have found correlations between aggressive behaviour and many variables besides violence viewing. These include income, education, intelligence and parental child-rearing practices. This is not to say that any of these third variables cause violent behaviour. The suggestion, rather, is that violence is far too complex to be explained by a single factor.

Most researchers note too that screen-triggered violence is increased if the aggression:

- Is realistic and exciting, like a chase or suspense sequence that sends adrenaline levels surging.
- Succeeds in righting a wrong, like helping an abused or ridiculed character get even.
- Includes situations or characters similar to those in the viewer's own experience.

All these things would prompt a scientist to call media violence a catalyst. Just as the presence of a certain element will allow other elements to react explosively but itself not be part of the explosion, the presence of media violence can be a factor in real-life violence but not a cause by itself. This catalytic theory was articulated by scholars **Wilbur Schramm**, Jack Lyle and Edwin Parker, who investigated the effects of television on children and came up with this statement in their 1961 book *Television in the Lives of Our Children,* which has become a classic on the effects of media-depicted violence on individuals: "For *some* children under *some* conditions, *some* television is harmful. For *other* children under the same conditions, or for the same children under *other* conditions, it *may* be beneficial. For *most* children, under *most* conditions, *most* television is *probably* neither particularly harmful nor particularly beneficial."

SOCIETALLY DEBILITATING EFFECTS

Media-depicted violence scares far more people than it inspires to violence, and this, according to **George Gerbner**, a leading researcher on screen violence, leads some people to believe the world is more dangerous than it really is. Gerbner calculates that 1 in 10 television characters is involved in violence in any given week. In real life the chances are only about 1 in 100 per *year*. People who watch a lot of television, Gerbner found, see their own chances of being involved in violence nearer the distorted television level

catalytic theory ■ Media violence is among factors that sometimes contribute to real-life violence.

Wilbur Schramm ■ Concluded that television has minimal effects on children.

George Gerbner ■ Speculated that democracy is endangered by media violence.

than their local crime statistics or even their own experience would suggest. It seems that television violence leads people to think they are in far greater real-life jeopardy than they really are.

The implications of Gerbner's findings go to the heart of a free and democratic society. With exaggerated fears about their safety, Gerbner says, people will demand greater police protection. They are also likelier, he says, to submit to established authority and even to accept police violence as a trade-off for their own security.

TOLERANCE OF VIOLENCE

An especially serious concern about media-depicted violence is that it has a numbing, callousing effect on people. This **desensitizing theory**, which is widely held, says not only that individuals are becoming hardened by media violence but also that society's tolerance for such anti-social behaviour is increasing.

Media critics say that the media are responsible for this desensitization, but many media people, particularly movie and television directors, respond that it is the desensitization that has forced them to make the violence in their shows even more graphic. They explain that they have run out of alternatives to get the point across when the storyline requires that the audience be repulsed.

desensitizing theory ◼
Tolerance of real-life violence grows because of media-depicted violence.

Desensitization Critics of media violence say movies like *The Exorcist* desensitize people, especially teenagers, to the horrors of violence. That concern extends to video games. In one, *Carmageddon,* kids are exhorted by the packaging blurb, "Don't slow down to avoid hitting that pedestrian crossing the street—aim, rev up and rack up those points." In one sequence in the *Mortal Kombat* video game, a crowd shouts encouragement for Kano to rip the heart out of Scorpion, his downed opponent. Kano waves the extracted heart at the crowd, which roars approvingly. Although scholars disagree about whether media violence begets real-life violence, most do agree that media violence leaves people more accepting of violence around them in their everyday lives.

Desensitization is apparent in news also. In 2004 *The New York Times,* traditionally cautious about gore, showed a photo of victims' corpses hanging from a bridge in Fallujah, Iraq. Only a few years earlier there was an almost universal ban on showing the bodies of crime, accident and war victims in newspapers and on television newscasts. Photos of U.S. troops torturing Iraqi prisoners, integral in telling a horrible but important story, pushed back the earlier limits. No mainstream media showed the entire execution of Saddam Hussein in 2006, but millions of people found longer versions of the gruesome sequence online. This desensitizing did not come suddenly with the 2003 Iraq war and its aftermath, but the war clearly established new ground rules.

Undeniable is that violence has had a growing presence in the mass media, which makes even more poignant the fact that we know far less about media violence than we need to. What do we know? Various theories explain some phenomena, but the theories themselves do not dovetail. The desensitizing theory, for example, explains audience acceptance of more violence, but it hardly explains research findings that people who watch a lot of television actually have heightened anxiety about their personal safety. People fretting about their own safety are hardly desensitized.

VIOLENCE STUDIES

The mass media, especially television and movies that deal in fiction, depict a lot of violence. Studies have found as many as six violent acts per hour on prime-time network television. In and of itself, that may seem a lot, but a study at the University of California, Los Angeles, operating on the premise that the issue should not be how much violence is depicted but the context in which it occurs, came to a less startling conclusion: Slapstick comedic violence shouldn't be lumped with graphic homicide in counting depictions of violence. Nor should a violent storm.

The UCLA research, called the **Television Violence Monitoring Project**, concluded in its first year that distressing human violence was much less prevalent than earlier studies counted. Of 121 prime-time episodes, only 10 had frequent violence and only 8 had occa-

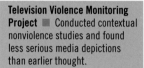

Television Violence Monitoring Project ■ Conducted contextual nonviolence studies and found less serious media depictions than earlier thought.

Media PEOPLE

George Gerbner

George Gerbner

George Gerbner worried a lot about media violence. And when he died in 2005, he had been doing this longer than just about anybody else. In 1967 Gerbner and colleagues at the University of Pennsylvania created a television violence index and began counting acts of violence. Today, more than three decades later, the numbers are startling. Gerbner

calculated the typical American 18-year-old has seen 32 000 murders and 40 000 attempted murders at home on television.

In a dubious sense, there may be good news for those who fear the effects of media violence. Gerbner's index found no significant change in the volume of violence since the mid-1970s. Maybe it maxed out.

Gerbner theorized that media violence has negative effects on society. It's what he called "the mean-world syndrome." As he saw it, people exposed to so much violence come to perceive the world as a far more dangerous place than it really is. One of his concerns is that people become overly concerned for their own safety and, in time, may become willing to accept a police state to ensure their personal security. That, he said, has dire consequences for the free and open society that has been a valued hallmark of the American lifestyle.

Are there answers? Gerbner pointed out that the global conglomeration of mass media companies works against any kind of media self-policing. These companies are seeking worldwide outlets for their

products, whether movies, television programs or music, and violence doesn't require any kind of costly translations. "Violence travels well," he said. Also, violence has low production costs.

Gerbner noted that violence is an easy fill for weak spots in a television storyline. Also, in television, violence is an effective cliff-hanger before a commercial break.

While Gerbner's statistics are unsettling, they have critics who say his numbers make the situation seem worse than it really is. The Gerbner index scores acts of violence without considering their context. That means when Bugs Bunny is bopped on the head, it counts the same as Rambo doing the same thing to a vile villain in a skull-crushing, blood-spurting scene. A poke in the eye on *The Three Stooges* also scores as a violent act.

Despite his critics, Gerbner provided a baseline for measuring changes in the quantity of television violence. Virtually every scholar cites him in the ongoing struggle to figure out whether media violence is something that should worry us all.

sional violence. This was after comedic violence and nonhuman violence, such as hurricanes, were screened out. The next year, 1996, found violence in only five prime-time shows—half the number of the year before. Also, most of the shows didn't survive the season. In 1998 the number was down to two series.

The UCLA study added sophistication to counting acts of media-depicted violence but still didn't assess whether the violence affected people. In 1986, scholar William McQuire reviewed the literature on mediated violence and found that hardly any of the studies' evidence was statistically reliable. The exception was controlled laboratory studies, for which the statistics were more meaningful but didn't indicate much causality.

VIOLENCE IN THE CANADIAN MEDIA

Canadian broadcasters have had a violence code since 1987. However, with the social and political developments brought about by the Larivière petition in 1992, the Canadian Association of Broadcasters and the CRTC took a hard look at the issue. In 1993, Larivière's petition was the subject of a Standing Committee on Communications and Culture. This, in combination with two conferences on the effects of media violence on children, led to the creation of **AGVOT**, the Action Group on Violence on Television. Members included the CAB, the CBC, the Canadian Cable Television Association, the Association of Canadian Advertisers, and the Canadian Film and Television Production Association.

A new violence code was introduced by AGVOT in late 1993. Some of the main elements of the code's rules for programming aimed at children less than 12 years of age involve the following criteria:

- Only violence essential to the plot is allowed.
- Violence cannot be the central theme in cartoons.
- Violence cannot be seen as the only way to resolve conflict.
- Realistic scenes of violence that downgrade the effects of violent behaviour are not allowed.
- Programming cannot invite imitation of violent or perilous acts.

For children over 12 years of age, 9 p.m. has become what AGVOT refers to as the "watershed" hour. In addition, a viewer advisory must accompany any program with violence, nudity, or strong language.

However, is it just the media that should be criticized for children's having access to violent imagery? What about parents? That was the one of the themes that emerged during a 2007 debate about the level of violence in the Canadian media—including music and video games. *Toronto Star* columnist Antonia Zerbisias says that "in the 1990s, the industry and the federal broadcast regulator spent millions on studies to raise awareness and to formulate codes of ethics. Still the problem exists. Which means the solution lies in one place alone. The power switch. You (parents) have the power. Use it."

■ Media Agenda-Setting for Individuals

study<u>preview</u> Media coverage helps to define the things people think about and worry about. This is called agenda setting. It occurs as the media create awareness of issues through their coverage, which lends importance to those issues. The media don't set agendas unilaterally but look to their audiences in deciding their priorities for coverage.

MEDIA SELECTION OF ISSUES

When the New York police wanted more subway patrols, their union public relations person, Morty Martz, asked officers to call him with every subway crime. Martz passed the accounts, all of them, on to newspapers and television and radio stations. Martz could not have been more pleased with his media blitz. News coverage of subway crime, he later boasted, increased several thousand percent, although there had been no appreciable change in the

William McQuire ■ Found most media violence research flawed.

 AGVOT ■ Action Group on Violence on Television; helped develop programming codes for Canadian television.

media ONLINE
Canadian Codes Administered by the Canadian Broadcast Standards Council, Canadian TV has a violence code.
www.cbsc.ca/english/codes/violence/violence.htm

Become More Aware Canada's Media Awareness Network offers some insight into the effects of violence in TV and video games.
www.education-medias.com/english/issues/violence/index.cfm

 media ONLINE
Canada Deals with Media Violence Read the code developed by Canadian broadcasters to deal with violence.
www.cbsc.ca/english/codes/violence/violence.htm

Approaches to Television Violence The CRTC's site about violence on Canadian television. Includes information about Canadian approaches to television, a bibliography, and source materials.
www.crtc.gc.ca/eng/social/tv.htm

Violence on Television The American Psychological Association provides this page with background on research into the effects of televised violence on children.
www.apa.org/releases/media_violence.html

crime rate itself. Suddenly, for no reason other than dramatically stepped-up coverage, people were alarmed. Their personal agendas of what to think about—and worry about—had changed. The sudden new concern, which made it easier for Martz's union to argue for more subway patrols, was an example of media agenda-setting at work. Martz lured news media decision makers into putting subway crime higher on their lists of issues to be covered. As a result, citizens moved subway crime up on their lists of personal concerns.

The agenda-setting phenomenon has been recognized for a long time. Sociologist **Robert Park**, writing in the 1920s, articulated the theory in rejecting the once-popular notion that the media tell people what to think (see earlier discussion in this chapter under Status Conferral). As Park saw it, the media create awareness of issues more than they create knowledge or attitudes. Agenda setting occurs at several levels:

Creating Awareness   Only if individuals are aware of an issue can they be concerned about it. Concern about parents who kill their children becomes a major issue with media coverage of spectacular cases. In 1994 Susan Smith, a South Carolina woman, attracted wide attention with her horrific report that her sons, ages 3 and 1, had been kidnapped. The story darkened later when the woman confessed to driving the family car into the lake and drowning the boys herself. Over several days of intense media attention the nation not only learned the morbid details of what happened, but also became better informed about a wide range of parental, family, mental health and legal issues that the coverage brought to the fore.

Establishing Priorities   People trust the news media to sort through the events of the day and make order of them. Lead-off stories on a newscast or on Page 1 are expected to be the most significant. Not only does how a story is played affect people's agendas, but so do the time and space afforded it. Lavish graphics can propel an item higher.

Perpetuating Issues   Continuing coverage lends importance to an issue. A single story on a bribed senator might soon be forgotten, but day-after-day follow-ups can fuel ethics reforms. Conversely, if gatekeepers are diverted to other stories, a hot issue can cool overnight—out of sight, out of mind.

INTRAMEDIA AGENDA-SETTING

Agenda setting also is a phenomenon that affects media people, who constantly monitor one another. Reporters and editors often are concerned more with how their peers are handling a story than with what their audience wants. Sometimes the media harp on one topic, making it seem more important than it really is, until it becomes tedious.

The media's agenda-setting role extends beyond news. Over time, lifestyles and values portrayed in the media can influence not just what people think about but what they do. Hugh Hefner's *Playboy* magazine of the 1950s helped to usher in the sexual revolution. Advertising has created a redefinition of American values by whetting an appetite for possessions and glamorizing immediate gratification.

Even so, individuals exercise a high degree of control in their personal agendas. For decades William Randolph Hearst campaigned with front-page editorials in all his newspapers against using animals in research, but animal rights did not become a pressing public issue. Even with the extensive media coverage of the Vietnam War, polls late in the 1960s found that many Americans still were unmoved. For the most part, these were people who chose to tune out the war coverage. The fact is that journalists and other creators of media messages cannot automatically impose their agendas on individuals. If people are not interested, an issue won't become part of their agendas. The individual values at work in the processes of selective exposure, perception and retention can thwart media leadership in agenda setting.

Also, media agendas are not decided in a vacuum. Dependent as they are on having mass audiences, the media take cues for their coverage from their audiences. Penny press editors in the 1830s looked over the shoulders of newspaper readers on the street to see what stories attracted them and then shaped their coverage accordingly. Today, news organizations tap the public pulse through scientific sampling to deliver what people want. The mass media both exert leadership in agenda setting and mirror the agendas of their audiences.

Agenda Setting A detailed discussion of the theory.
www.agendasetting.com

The mass media influence us, but scholars are divided about how much. There is agreement that the media help to initiate children into society by portraying social and cultural values. This is a serious responsibility because portrayals of aberrant behaviour such as violence have effects, although we are not sure about their extent. This is not to say that individuals are unwitting pawns of the mass media. People choose what they read and what they tune in to, and they generally filter the information and images to conform with their preconceived notions and personal values.

In other respects, too, the mass media are a stabilizing influence. The media try to fit into the lives of their audiences. An example is children's television programs on weekend mornings when kids are home from school but still on an early-rising schedule. The media not only react to audience lifestyles but also contribute to the patterns by which people live their lives, like going to bed after the late news. In short, the media have effects on individuals and on society, but it is a two-way street. Society is a shaper of media content, but individuals make the ultimate decisions about subscribing, listening and watching. The influence issue is a complex one that merits further research and thought.

Questions for Review

1. Why have most media scholars abandoned the powerful effects and minimalist effects theories for the cumulative theory?
2. What is the uses and gratifications approach to mass media studies?
3. Do individuals have any control over mass media effects on them?
4. What role do the mass media have in socializing children?
5. How do scholars differ on whether media-depicted violence triggers aggressive behaviour?
6. What is meant when someone says, "The mass media don't tell people what to think as much as tell them what to think about"?
7. Does being informed by mass media necessarily improve citizen involvement in political processes?

Questions for Critical Thinking

1. Although generally discredited by scholars now, the powerful effects theory once had many adherents. How do you explain the lingering popularity of this thinking among many people?
2. Name at least three opinion leaders who influence you on issues that you do not follow closely in the media. On what issues are you yourself an opinion leader?
3. Give specific examples of each of the eight primary mass media contributing to the lifelong socialization process. For starters, consider a current nonfiction best-selling book.
4. Discuss the human needs that the mass media help to satisfy in terms of the news and entertainment media.
5. Among the functions that the mass media serve for individuals are diversion and escape. Is this healthy?
6. Explain the pro-social potential of the mass media in culturization and socialization. What about the media as an anti-social force in observational learning?
7. Cite at least three contemporary role models who you can argue are positive. Explain how they might also be viewed as negative. Cite three role models who you can argue are negative.
8. How can serious scholars of mass communication hold such diverse ideas as the cathartic, aggressive stimulation and catalytic theories? Which camp is right?

Deepening Your media LITERACY

Reality shows: more than just entertainment?

STEP 1 From *Survivor* to *The Intern*, *The Bachelor* or *Canadian Idol*, reality shows have proliferated on North American television.

Dig Deeper

STEP 2 Think of your favourite reality show. Think about why you were first attracted to it. Think about why you kept watching it. Think about a reality show that doesn't appeal to you. Why doesn't it? To whom does it appeal?

What Do You Think?

STEP 3 Answer these questions:

1. Has your favourite reality show changed North American society, or does it just reflect society?
2. What needs does it gratify?
3. Does it tell you anything about the great human issues?
4. Does it reinforce your personal views? If so, which ones?
5. Do you want to emulate the people on the show? Do you think they are stereotyped?
6. Does the show help its viewers find their place in society?

Keeping Up to Date

The interdisciplinary scholarly journal *Media Psychology*, a quarterly, focuses on theory-based research on media uses, processes and effects.

For Further Learning

Jane D. Brown, Jeanne R. Steele and Kim Walsh-Childers, editors. *Sexual Teens, Sexual Media: Investigating Media's Influence of Adolescent Sexuality* (Erlbaum, 2001).

Donald Bogle. *Primetime Blues: African Americans on Network Television* (Straus & Giroux, 2001).

Carolyn Byerly and Karen Ross. *Women and Media: A Critical Introduction* (Blackwell, 2005).

Margaret Gallagher. *Gender Setting: New Media Agenda for Monitoring and Advocacy* (Palgrave, 2001).

Gabriele Griffin. *Representations of HIV and AIDS: Visibility Blues* (Manchester University Press, 2001).

Carolyn Kitch. *The Girl on the Magazine Cover* (University of North Carolina Press, 2002).

Lewis H. Lapham. *Gag Rule: On the Suppression of Dissent and the Stifling of Democracy* (Penguin, 2004).

Paul Lazarsfeld, Bernard Berelson and Hazel Gaudet. *The People's Choice: How the Voter Makes Up His Mind in a Presidential Campaign,* Second edition. Bureau of Applied Social Research, 1948.

Joshua Meyrowitz. *No Sense of Place: The Impact of Electronic Media on Social Behavior* (Oxford, 1985).

Elizabeth M. Perse. *Media Effects and Society* (Erlbaum, 2001).

Michael Pickering. *Stereotyping: The Politics of Representation* (Palgrave, 2001).

Antonia Zerbisias. "What You Can Restrict: Children" *Toronto Star* (January 18, 2007).

Marshall McLuhan The controversial Canadian theorist blamed Gutenberg for social alienation, but not all was lost. He also foresaw a transforming global village.

Mass Media and Society

Media in Theory

Canadian communication theorist **Marshall McLuhan** didn't invent the term *global village,* but he certainly cemented the notion in public dialogue. In numerous books and the scholarly journal *Explorations,* which he founded in 1954, McLuhan talked about the world shrinking, at least metaphorically. In a wired world, he said, television could present live information from anywhere to everyone. The result, as he saw it, could change human existence profoundly, reversing a trend that started with Gutenberg's mass-produced printed word in the 1400s.

As McLuhan saw it, Gutenberg's invention had a dark side. Reading, a skill necessary to partake of print media, is hardly a natural act. It requires so much concentration and focus that it squeezes out other sensory perceptions that a human being would normally sense and respond to. Reading requires you to block out the world around you. For example, if you are really into a book, you might miss a knock on the door.

Television would reverse this perversion of human nature, McLuhan said. With a wired world, people would respond spontaneously—or, as he saw it, naturally. Receiving the message would no longer be an isolated, insulated act. This global village, like pre-Gutenberg villages, could help human beings to return to a pristine form of existence, their senses in tune with their surroundings and their responses governed more by instinct than contrivances like reading, which, he said, had alienated human beings from their true nature.

HUMAN ALIENATION

An intriguing, contrarian assessment of the media's effects on human society was laid out by Canadian theorist **Marshall McLuhan** in the 1960s. McLuhan argued that the print media had **alienated** human beings from their natural state. In pre–mass media times, McLuhan said, people acquired their awareness about their world through their own observation and experience and through their fellow human beings, whom they saw face to face and with whom they communicated orally. As McLuhan saw it, this was a

Marshall McLuhan ■ Blamed human alienation on mass-produced written word.

alienation ■ Dissatisfaction with individual and cultural deviations from basic nature.

pristine communal existence—rich in that it involved all the senses—sight, sound, smell, taste and touch. This communal, tribal state was eroded by the written word, which involved the insular, meditative act of reading. The printing press, he said, compounded this alienation from humankind's tribal roots. The written word, by engaging the mind, not the senses, begat **detribalization**, and the printing press accelerated it.

detribalization ■ The removal of humankind from a natural, tribal state.

According to McLuhan, the printed word even changed human thought processes. In their tribal state, he said, human beings responded spontaneously to everything that was happening around them. The written word, in contrast, required people to concentrate on an author's relatively narrow, contrived set of data that led from Point A to Point B to Point C. Following the linear serial order of the written word was a lonely, cerebral activity, unlike participatory tribal communication, which had an undirected, helter-skelter spontaneity.

TELEVISION AND THE GLOBAL VILLAGE

McLuhan saw television bringing back tribalization. While books, magazines and newspapers engaged the mind, television engaged the senses. In fact, the television screen could be so loaded with data that it could approximate the high level of sensual stimuli that people found in their environments back in the tribal period of human existence. **Retribalization**, he said, was at hand because of the new, intensely sensual communication that television could facilitate. Because television could far exceed the reach of any previous interpersonal communication, McLuhan called the new tribal village a **global village**.

retribalization ■ Restoring humankind to a natural, tribal state.

global village ■ Instantaneous connection of every human being.

With retribalization, McLuhan said, people will abandon the print media's linear intrusions on human nature. Was McLuhan right? His disciples claim that certain earmarks of written communication—complex storylines, logical progression and causality—are less important to today's young people, who grew up with sense-intensive television. His disciples point to the music videos that excite the senses but make no linear sense. Many teachers say that children are having a harder time finding significance in the totality of a lesson. Instead, children fasten on to details.

McLuhan, whose works include bestselling theoretical books in the 1960s, was confusing in some of his writing, using concepts and terms in different ways over a long career of thinking about mass communication. Even so, his contributions to our understanding remain bulwarks in many advanced mass communication curriculums even 30 years after his death.

media TIMELINE

MASS COMMUNICATION AND CULTURE

1960s Marshall McLuhan theorized that television could end human alienation caused by print media.

1960s Dwight Macdonald equated pop art and kitsch.

1965 Susan Sontag saw pop art as emotive high art.

1976 Herbert Gans related cultural sensitivity to social and economic status.

■ Mass Media Role in Culture

studypreview The mass media are inextricably linked with culture because it is through the media that creative people have their strongest sway. Although the media have the potential to disseminate the best creative work of the human mind and soul, some critics say the media are obsessive about trendy, often silly subjects.

ELITIST VERSUS POPULIST VALUES

The mass media can enrich society by disseminating the best of human creativity, including great literature, music and art. The media also carry a lot of lesser things that reflect the culture and, for better or worse, contribute to it. Over time, a continuum has been devised that covers this vast range of artistic production. At one extreme is artistic material that requires sophisticated and cultivated tastes to appreciate it. This is called **high art**. At the other extreme is **low art**, which requires little sophistication to enjoy.

One strain of traditional media criticism has been that the media underplay great works and concentrate on low art. This **elitist** view argues that the mass media do society a disservice by pandering to low tastes. To describe low art, elitists sometimes use the German word **kitsch**, which translates roughly as "garish" or "trashy." The word captures their disdain. In contrast, the **populist** view is that there is nothing unbecoming in the mass media's catering to mass tastes in a democratic, capitalistic society.

In a 1960 essay still widely cited, "Masscult and Midcult," social commentator **Dwight Macdonald** made a virulent case that all popular art is kitsch. The mass media, which depend on finding large audiences for their economic base, can hardly ever come out at the higher reaches of Macdonald's spectrum.

This kind of elitist analysis was given a larger framework in 1976 when sociologist **Herbert Gans** categorized cultural work along socioeconomic and intellectual lines. Gans said that classical music, as an example, appealed by and large to people of academic and professional accomplishments and higher incomes. These were **high-culture audiences**, which enjoyed complexities and subtleties in their art and entertainment. Next came **middle-culture audiences**, which were less abstract in their interests and liked Norman Rockwell and prime-time television. **Low-culture audiences** were factory and service workers whose interests were more basic; whose educational accomplishments, incomes and social status were lower; and whose media tastes leaned toward kung fu movies, comic books and supermarket tabloids.

Gans was applying his contemporary observations to flesh out the distinctions that had been taking form in art criticism for centuries—the distinctions between high art and low art.

Highbrow

The high art favoured by elitists generally can be identified by its technical and thematic complexity and originality. High art is often highly individualistic because the creator, whether a novelist or a television producer, has explored issues in fresh ways, often with new and different methods. Even when it's a collaborative effort, a piece of high art is distinctive. High art requires a sophisticated audience to appreciate it fully. Often it has enduring value, surviving time's test as to its significance and worth.

The sophistication that permits an opera aficionado to appreciate the intricacies of a composer's score, the poetry of the lyricist and the excellence of the performance sometimes is called **highbrow**. The label has grim origins in the idea that a person must have great intelligence to have refined tastes, and a high brow is necessary to accommodate such a big brain. Generally, the term is used by people who disdain those who have not developed the sophistication to enjoy, for example, the abstractions of a Fellini film, a Matisse sculpture or a Picasso painting. Highbrows generally are people who, as Gans noted, are interested in issues by which society is defining itself and look to literature and drama for stories on conflicts inherent in the human condition and between the individual and society.

Middlebrow

Middlebrow tastes recognize some artistic merit but without a high level of sophistication. There is more interest in action than abstractions—in Captain Kirk aboard the starship Enterprise, for example, than in the childhood struggles of Ingmar Bergman that shaped his films. In socioeconomic terms, middlebrow appeals to people who take comfort in media portrayals that support their status quo orientation and values.

Lowbrow

Someone once made this often-repeated distinction: Highbrows talk about ideas, middlebrows talk about things and **lowbrows** talk about people. Judging from the circulation success of the *National Enquirer* and other celebrity tabloids, there must be

---

high art ■ Requires sophisticated taste to be appreciated.

low art ■ Can be appreciated by almost everybody.

elitism ■ Mass media should gear to sophisticated audiences.

kitsch ■ Pejorative word for trendy, trashy, low art.

populism ■ Mass media should seek largest possible audiences.

Dwight Macdonald ■ Said all pop art is kitsch.

Herbert Gans ■ Said social, economic and intellectual levels of audience coincide.

high-, middle- and low-culture audiences ■ Continuum identified by Herbert Gans.

McLuhan Global Research Network
The online hub for media research based on McLuhan.
www.mcluhan.ca

The Center for Media and Public Affairs The website's Media Monitor includes a political newswatch, economic studies, media factoids, TV studies, late-night comedy counts and more.
www.cmpa.com

Not Your Typical Post-Secondary Course about "Homer" Information about an honours literature course that uses *The Simpsons* as a starting point.
http://honors.rit.edu/amitraywiki/index.php/Honors_Literature:_Fall_2006

highbrow, middlebrow and lowbrow ■ Levels of media content sophistication that coincide with audience tastes.

Elitist Horror The National Book Foundation muddied the easy distinctions between elitists and populist literature with a 2003 National Book Award to horror novelist Stephen King. In his acceptance speech, King acknowledged the flap over his being chosen but called on authors and publishers to "build a bridge between the popular and the literary."

a lot of lowbrows in contemporary North America. Hardly any sophistication is needed to recognize the machismo of the WWE, the villainy of Darth Vader, the heroism of Superman or the sexiness of Lara Croft.

THE CASE AGAINST POP ART

Pop art is of the moment, including things like mood rings, hula-hoops and hip-hop garb—and trendy media fare. Even elitists may have fun with pop, but they traditionally have drawn the line at anyone who mistakes it as having serious artistic merit. Pop art is low art that has immense although generally short-lived popularity.

Elitists see pop art as contrived and artificial. In their view, the people who create **popular art** are masters at identifying what will succeed in the marketplace and then providing it. Pop art, according to this view, succeeds by conning people into liking it. When Nehru jackets were the fashion rage in the late 1960s, it was not because they were superior in comfort, utility or aesthetics, but because promoters sensed that profits could be made in touting them through the mass media as new and cashing in on easily manipulated mass tastes. It was the same with pet rocks, Tickle Me Elmo and countless other faddy products.

The mass media, according to the critics, are obsessed with pop art. This is partly because the media are the carriers of the promotional campaigns that create popular followings but also because competition within the media creates pressure to be first, to be ahead, to be on top of things. The result, say elitists, is that junk takes precedence over quality.

Much is to be said for this criticism of pop art. The promotion by CBS of the screwball 1960s sitcom *The Beverly Hillbillies,* as an example, created an eager audience that otherwise might have been reading Steinbeck's critically respected *Grapes of Wrath.* An elitist might chortle, even laugh, at the unbelievable antics and travails of the Beverly Hillbillies, who had their own charm and attractiveness, but an elitist would be concerned all the while that low art was displacing high art in the marketplace and that the society was the poorer for it.

popular art ■ Art that tries to succeed in the marketplace.

Gearing News to Audience The level of intellectual interest necessary to enjoy elitist news coverage, like that of *The New York Times,* is more sophisticated than that needed to enjoy popular tabloids edited for a broader audience, such as the *New York Post.*

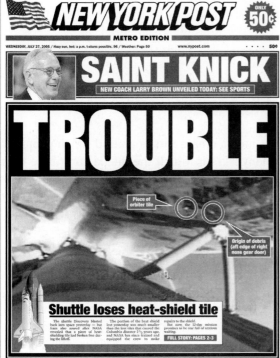

POP ART REVISIONISM

Pop art has always had a few champions among intellectuals, although the voices of **pop art revisionism** were usually drowned out in the din of elitist pooh-poohing.

In 1965, however, essayist **Susan Sontag** wrote an influential piece, "On Culture and the New Sensibility," which prompted many elitists to take a fresh look at pop art.

Pop Art as Evocative Sontag made the case that pop art could raise serious issues, just as high art could. She wrote: "The feeling given off by a Rauschenberg painting might be like that of a song by the Supremes." Sontag soon was being called the high priestess of pop intellectualism. More significantly, the Supremes were being taken more seriously, as were a great number of Sontag's avant-garde and obscure pop artist friends.

Pop Art as a Societal Unifier In effect, Sontag encouraged people not to look at art on the traditional divisive, class-conscious, elitist–populist continuum. Artistic value, she said, could be found almost anywhere. The word "camp" gained circulation among 1960s elitists who were influenced by Sontag. These highbrows began finding a perversely sophisticated appeal in pop art as diverse as Andy Warhol's banal soup cans and ABC's outrageous *Batman*. The mass media, through which most people experienced Warhol and all people experienced *Batman,* became recognized more broadly than ever as a societal unifier.

The Sontag-inspired revisionist look at pop art coincides with the view of many mass media historians that the media have helped bind the society rather than divide it. In the 1840s, these historians note, books and magazines with national distribution provided North Americans of diverse backgrounds and regions with common reference points. Radio did the same even more effectively in the 1940s. Later, so did network television. In short, the mass media are purveyors of cultural production that contributes to social cohesion, whether it be high art or low art.

High Art as Popular While kitsch may be prominent in media programming, it hardly elbows out all substantive content. In 1991, for example, Ken Burns's public television documentary *The Civil War* outdrew low art prime-time programs on ABC, CBS and NBC five nights in a row. It was a glaring example that high art can appeal to people across almost the whole range of socioeconomic levels and is not necessarily driven out by low art. Burns's documentary was hardly a lone example. Another, also from 1991, was Franco Zeffirelli's movie *Hamlet,* starring pop movie star Mel Gibson, which was marketed to a mass audience yet could hardly be dismissed by elitists as kitsch. In radio, public broadcasting stations, marked by highbrow programming, have become major players for ratings in some cities.

■ Social Stability

studypreview The mass media create rituals around which people structure their lives. This is one of many ways in which the media contribute to social stability. The media foster socialization throughout adulthood, contributing to social cohesion by affirming beliefs and values and helping reconcile inconsistent values and discrepancies between private behaviour and public morality.

MEDIA-INDUCED RITUAL

Northwest Airlines pilots, flying their Stratocruisers over the Dakotas in the 1950s, could tell when the late-night news ended on WCCO, the powerful Minneapolis radio station. They could see lights in ranches and towns all across the Dakotas going off as people, having heard the news, went to bed. The 10 o'clock WCCO news had become a ritual. Today, for people on the east and west coasts, where most television stations run their late news at 11 p.m., the commonest time to go to bed is 11:30, after the news. In the Midwest, where late newscasts are at 10 p.m., people tend to go to bed an hour earlier and to rise an hour earlier. Like other rituals that mark a society, media-induced rituals contribute order and structure to the lives of individuals.

The effect of media-induced rituals extends even further. Collectively, the lifestyles of individuals have a broad social effect. Consider just these two effects of evening newspapers, an 1878 media innovation:

Evening News E.W. Scripps changed people's habits with his evening newspapers, first in Cleveland in 1878, then elsewhere. Soon, evening papers outnumbered morning papers. The new habit, however, was not so much for evening newspapers as for evening news, as newspaper publishers discovered a hundred years later when television siphoned readers away with evening newscasts. The evening ritual persists, even though the medium is changing as evening papers go out of business or retreat to mornings.

Competitive Shopping In the era before refrigeration and packaged food, household shopping was a daily necessity. When evening newspapers appeared, housewives, who were the primary shoppers of the period, adjusted their routines to read the paper the evening before their morning trips to the market. The new ritual allowed time for more methodical bargain hunting, which sharpened retail competition.

Besides shaping routines, ritual contributes to the mass media's influence as a shaper of culture. People tune into morning radio for the latest weather and information as soon as they wake up. Think of the traditional *Hockey Night in Canada* ritual on Saturday nights or the pandemonium over voting for the likes of Kalan Porter or Brian Melo during broadcasts of *Canadian Idol.* Other rituals are going to Saturday movie matinees, reading a book at bedtime and watching Monday night football.

MEDIA AND THE STATUS QUO

In their quest for profits through large audiences, the mass media need to tap into their audience's common knowledge and widely felt feelings. Writers for network sitcoms avoid obscure, arcane language. Heroes and villains reflect current morals. Catering this

The Lichters and Stanley Rothman

Linda and Robert Lichter

Stanley Rothman

It was love over the statistics. Linda and Robert Lichter met while working on a massive study of major media decision-makers and married. Later, they formed The Center for Media and Public Affairs

in Washington, which today is a leading research organization on the mass media and social change. One of the most troubling findings of the Lichters and co-researcher Stanley Rothman is that the major U.S. media are out of touch with the American people. This conclusion comes out of massive studies of the people who run the entertainment media.

The Lichter-Rothman studies say that television executives and key creative people are overwhelmingly liberal on the great social issues of our time. More significantly, the studies have found that the programming these people produce reflects their political and social agenda. For example:

● Television scripts favour feminist positions in 71 percent of the shows, far more than public-opinion

surveys find among the general population.

● Three percent of television murders are committed by blacks, compared with half in real life.

● Two out of three people are portrayed in positive occupations on television, but only one out of three businesspeople is depicted in a positive role.

These examples, according to the Lichters and Rothman, indicate a bias toward feminism and minority people and against businesspeople. The Lichter-Rothman work documents a dramatic turnaround in television entertainment fare. Two generations ago, leading programs, ranging from sitcoms like *Leave It to Beaver* to dramatic programs like *Wagon Train,* extolled traditional values. In the 1970s came programs like *Mork and Mindy* and *All in the Family* that questioned some values. Today, network schedules make plenty of room for programs like *The Simpsons* and *The Sopranos* that examine nontraditional views and exhibit a dramatically different social orientation than, say, *Leave It to Beaver.*

way to a mass audience, the media reinforce existing cultural beliefs and values. People take comfort in learning through the media that they fit into their community and society, which furthers social cohesion. This is socialization continued beyond the formative years. It also is socialization in reverse, with the media taking cues from the society and playing them back.

The media's role in social cohesion has a negative side. Critics say that the media pander to the lowest common denominator by dealing only with things that fit the status quo easily. The result, the critics note, is a thwarting of artistic exploration beyond the mainstream. Critics are especially disparaging of predictable, wooden characters in movies and television and of predictability in many subjects chosen for the news.

A related negative aspect of the media's role as a contributor to social cohesion is that dominant values too often go unchallenged, which means that some wrong values and practices persist. Dudley Clendinen, a newspaper editor who grew up in the South, faults journalists for, in effect, defending racism by not covering it: "The news columns of Southern papers weren't very curious or deep or original in the late 1940s and 1950s. They followed sports and politics actively enough, but the whole rational thrust of Southern culture from the time of John C. Calhoun on had been self-defensive and maintaining. It had to be, to justify the unjustifiable in a society dedicated first to slavery and then to segregation and subservience. Tradition was everything, and the news pages were simply not in the habit of examining the traditions of the South."

Linda and Robert Lichter and Stanley Rothman ■ Colleagues whose research indicates a liberal agenda in entertainment programming.

The Center for Media and Public Affairs ■ Media research organization.

MEDIA AND COGNITIVE DISSONANCE

The media are not always complacent. Beginning in the late 1950s, after the period to which Clendinen was referring, media attention turned to racial segregation. News coverage, literary comment and dramatic and comedy portrayals began to point up flaws in the status quo. Consider the effect, through the mass media, of these individuals on North American racism:

- **John Howard Griffin.** In 1959 Griffin, a white journalist, dyed his skin black for a six-week odyssey through the South. His book *Black Like Me* was an inside look at being black in America. It had special credibility for the white majority because Griffin was white.
- **George Wallace.** The mass audience saw the issue of segregation personified in news coverage of Governor George Wallace physically blocking black students from attending the University of Alabama. The indelible impression was that segregation could be defended only by a clenched fist and not by reason.
- **Martin Luther King Jr.** News photographers captured the courage and conviction of Martin Luther King Jr. and other civil rights activists, black and white, taking great risks through civil disobedience to object to racist public policies.
- **Archie Bunker.** Archie Bunker, a television sitcom character, made a laughingstock of bigots.

To some people, the media coverage and portrayals seemed to exacerbate racial tensions. In the longer run, however, media attention contributed to a new consensus through a phenomenon that psychologists call **cognitive dissonance**. Imagine white racists as they saw George Wallace giving way to federal troops under orders from the White House. The situation pitted against each other the two values held by individual racists: segregation as a value, and an ordered society as symbolized by the presidency. Suddenly aware that their personal values were in terrible disharmony, or dissonance, many of these racists avoided the issue. Instead of continuing to express racism among family and friends, many tended to be silent. They may have been as racist as ever, but they were quiet or watched their words carefully. Gradually, their untenable view is fading into social unacceptability. This is not to say that racism does not persist. It does and continues to manifest itself in North American life, though, in many ways, in forms much muted since the media focused on the experiment of John Howard Griffin, the clenched fist of George Wallace and the crusade of Martin Luther King Jr.

When the media go beyond pap and the predictable, they are examining the cutting-edge issues by which the society defines its values. Newsmagazines, newspapers and television, using new printing, photography and video technology in the late 1960s, put war graphically into North American living rooms, pointing up all kinds of discrepancies between Pentagon claims and the Vietnam reality. The glamorized, heroic view of war, which had persisted through history, was countered by media depictions of the blood and death. Unable to resolve the discrepancies, some people withdrew into silence. Others reassessed their views and then, with changed positions or more confident in their original positions, they engaged in a dialogue from which a consensus emerged. And the United States, the mightiest power in history, began a militarily humiliating withdrawal. It was democracy at work, slowly and painfully, but at work.

During the 2003 Iraq war, cognitive dissonance set in between the Bush administration's premise for war—that the Saddam Hussein regime had a trigger finger on weapons of mass destruction—and growing evidence that there were no such weapons. The media attention to the issue forced the Bush administration to back away from its claim.

AGENDA SETTING AND STATUS CONFERRAL

Media attention lends a legitimacy to events, individuals and issues that does not extend to things that go uncovered. This conferring of status occurs through the media's role as agenda setters (see also Chapter 14). It puts everybody on the same wavelength, or at least a similar one, which contributes to social cohesion by focusing our collective attention on issues we can address together. Otherwise, each of us

cognitive dissonance ■ Occurs when people realize their values are inconsistent.

media ONLINE

Cognitive Dissonance A briefing on the psychological theory, from Wikipedia.
http://en.wikipedia.org/wiki/
Cognitive_dissonance

Cognitive Dissonance Many white Americans from racist backgrounds found themselves challenging their own values when the federal government adopted proactive civil rights policies in the 1950s and 1960s. This dissonance escalated as these people followed news coverage of the long-overdue demands of blacks for fair treatment, as in this 1963 march. Some white racists resolved the discrepancy by abandoning racism. Many others simply retreated from discussion on the issue.

could be going in separate directions, which would make collective action difficult if not impossible.

Examples abound of how media attention spotlights certain issues. An especially poignant case occurred in 1998 when a gay University of Wyoming student, Matthew Shepard, was savagely beaten, tied to a fence outside of town and left to die. It was tragic gay-bashing, and coverage of the event moved gay rights higher on the national agenda. Coverage of the gruesome death was an example of the media agenda-setting and of status conferral.

MEDIA AND MORALITY

A humourist once noted that people read the local newspaper not to find out what is going on, which everybody already knows, but to find out who got caught. The observation was profound. The mass media, by reporting deviant behaviour, help to enforce society's moral order. When someone is arrested for burglary and convicted, it reaffirms for everybody that human beings have property rights.

Beyond police blotter news, the mass media are agents for reconciling discrepancies between **private actions and public morality**. Individually, people tolerate minor infractions of public morality, such as taking pencils home from work. Some people even let life-threatening behaviour such as child abuse go unreported. When the deviant behaviour is publicly exposed, however, toleration ceases, and social processes come into action that reconcile the deviance with public morality. The reconciling process maintains public norms and values. Consider Douglas Ginsburg. In the 1970s Ginsburg, a young law professor, smoked marijuana at a few parties. It was a misdemeanour, but Ginsburg's friends tolerated it, and not a word was said publicly. In 1988, however, when President Reagan nominated Ginsburg to the U.S. Supreme Court, reporter Nina Totenberg of National Public Radio reported Ginsburg's transgressions. Exposed, he withdrew his name. There was no choice. His private action, publicly exposed, could not be tolerated, and his withdrawal maintained public norms and values, without which a society cannot exist.

media ONLINE

Morality in Media An organization established by a Catholic priest to combat obscenity and uphold decency standards in the media.
www.moralityinmedia.org

private actions versus public morality ■ Dichotomy that exposes discrepancies between behaviour and values.

Cindy Sheehan Even strident supporters of the Bush war on Iraq could relate at an emotional level to Cindy Sheehan, whose son Casey was killed in combat. This kind of cognitive dissonance can be pivotal in silencing people who otherwise might be vocal on an issue.

▉ Cultural Transmission

study<u>preview</u> The mass media transmit cultural values through history. Past generations talk to us through mass media, mostly books, just as we, often not realizing it, talk to future generations. The media also diffuse values and ideas contemporaneously.

HISTORICAL TRANSMISSION

Human beings have a compulsion to leave the wisdom they have accumulated for future generations. There is a compulsion, too, to learn from the past. In olden times, people gathered around fires and in temples to hear storytellers. It was a ritual through which people learned the values that governed their community. This is a form of **historical transmission**.

Five thousand years ago, the oral tradition was augmented when Middle Eastern traders devised an alphabet to keep track of inventories, transactions and rates of exchange. When paper was invented, clay tablets gave way to scrolls and eventually books, which became the primary vehicle for storytelling. Religious values were passed on in holy books. Military chronicles laid out the lessons of war. Literature provided lessons by exploring the nooks and crannies of the human condition.

Books remain the primary repository of our culture. For several centuries it has been between hard covers, in black ink on paper, that the experiences, lessons and wisdom of our forebears have been recorded for posterity. Other mass media today share in the preservation and transmission of our culture over time. Consider these archives:

● The Museum of Television and Radio in New York features 1200 hours of television documentaries; great performances, productions, debuts and series; and a sample of top-rated shows.

● The Canadian Science and Technology Museum in Ottawa features a look at the role of radio and television in Canadian society.

● For music fans, the Canadian Music Hall of Fame opened in Toronto in 2007. The Rock and Roll Hall of Fame in Cleveland and the Country Music Hall of Fame in Nashville offer a look at how each of those genres developed and influenced society over the years.

historical transmission ▉
Communication of cultural values to later generations.

What Role Do the Canadian Media Play?

Ian Morrison

Ian Morrison is patriotic about Canadian radio and television—so patriotic that in 1985 he helped create Friends of Canadian Broadcasting, a voluntary organization of 60 000 Canadian households whose main goal is to ensure that Canadians have access to high-quality Canadian media.

Friends of Canadian Broadcasting is a strong supporter of the CBC and the CRTC, and monitors private Canadian broadcasters, such as CTV and Global, to ensure that they invest money in Canadian productions. An Ipsos Reid poll, commissioned by Friends of Canadian Broadcasting, suggests that many Canadians share the same beliefs:

- 87 percent of Canadians agree that "as Canada's economic ties with the United States increase, it is becoming more important to strengthen Canadian culture and identity."
- 80 percent of Canadians agree that "we should build a new CBC capable of providing high-quality Canadian programming with strong regional content throughout Canada."
- 85 percent of Canadians believe that, to be in line with their own thinking, a political party should commit to maintain Canadian ownership and control of broadcasting and communications.

According to Morrison, "Patriotism and democracy are values that we care about. Telling Canadian stories establishes a sense of belonging as a distinct country on the northern half of the continent. Democracy is highly influenced by the diversity and integrity of programming." This need for Canadian programming to accurately portray who we are and where we came from was the theme of a series of successful public service announcements launched by Friends of Canadian Broadcasting in 2003 called "Let's Tell Our Own Stories." It featured a clueless American director, Buck Calder, played by Canadian comedian David Huband, who tried to interpret Canadian history through American eyes. Two of the PSAs, "Snow Gangsta" and "Sir John A. Macdonald," were shortlisted at the 2004 Cannes Lions Advertising Festival.

On a more serious note, Friends of Canadian Broadcasting has a clear agenda: to support a healthy Canadian media industry that will help in cultural transmission. Morrison believes that Canadian media provide excellent news and documentary-style programming. However, Morrison says that in a perfect world, English-Canadian TV would provide "good shelf space for Canadian nonfiction programming. At least two hours a night from Monday to Wednesday nights—as much as the French-language system now provides."

Friends of Canadian Broadcasting claims that "while it would have been easier to follow the movie theatre model—let the market rule—Canadian content laws have given great Canadian artists a chance to get their start in our market. Canadian content has delivered on so many fronts." Writing about Canadian musicians such as the Barenaked Ladies and The Tragically Hip, the organization says: "As a consequence to their art form, many of their songs remind us of our shared history."

WHAT DO YOU THINK?

1. With Canada becoming closer economically to America, should our media play a larger role in developing our identity?

2. Should the CBC be more regional in its focus as Morrison suggests?

3. Contrary to Morrison's views, should we as Canadians simply let the "marketplace" rule what we watch?

CONTEMPORARY TRANSMISSION

The mass media also transmit values among contemporary communities and societies, sometimes causing changes that otherwise would not occur. This is known as **contemporary transmission**. Anthropologists have documented that mass communication can change society. When Edmund Carpenter introduced movies in an isolated New Guinea village, the men adjusted their clothing toward the Western style and even remodeled their houses. This phenomenon, which scholars call **diffusion of innovation** (see also Chapter 7), occurs when ideas move through the mass media. Consider the following:

- **American Revolution.** Colonists up and down the Atlantic seaboard took cues on what to think and how to act from newspaper reports on radical activities, mostly in Boston, in the decade before the Declaration of Independence. These included inflammatory articles against the 1765 Stamp Act and accounts of the Boston Tea Party in 1773.
- **Music, fashion and pop culture.** In modern-day pop culture, the cues come through the media, mostly from New York, Hollywood and Nashville.
- **Third World innovation.** The United Nations creates instructional films and radio programs to promote agricultural reform in less developed parts of the world. Overpopulated areas have been targets of birth control campaigns.
- **Democracy in China.** As China opened itself to Western tourists, commerce and mass media in the 1980s, the people glimpsed Western democracy and prosperity, which precipitated pressure on the Communist government to Westernize and resulted in the 1989 Tiananmen Square confrontation. A similar phenomenon was a factor in the glasnost relaxations in the Soviet Union in the late 1980s.
- **Demise of Main Street.** Small-town businesses are boarding up as rural people succumb to advertisements from regional shopping malls, which are farther away but offer greater variety and lower prices than Main Street.

Scholars note that the mass media can be given too much credit for the diffusion of innovations. Diffusion almost always needs reinforcement through interpersonal communication. Also, the diffusion is hardly ever a one-shot hypodermic injection but a process that requires redundancy in messages over an extended period. The 1989 outburst for democracy in China did not happen because one Chinese person read Thomas Paine one afternoon, nor do rural people suddenly abandon their local Main Street for a Wal-Mart 40 miles away. The diffusion of innovations typically involves three initial steps in which the mass media can be pivotal:

- **Awareness.** Individuals and groups learn about alternatives, new options and possibilities.
- **Interest.** Once aware, people need to have their interest further whetted.
- **Evaluation.** By considering the experience of other people, as relayed by the mass media, individuals evaluate whether they wish to adopt an innovation.

The adoption process has two additional steps in which the media play a small role: the trial stage, in which an innovation is given a try, and the final stage, in which the innovation is either adopted or rejected.

CHAPTER 15 Wrap-Up

The media contribute both to social stability and to change. A lot of media content gives comfort to audiences by reinforcing existing social values. At the same time, media attention to nonmainstream ideas, in both news and fiction forms, requires people to reassess their values and, over time, contributes to social change.

Questions for Review

1. Why are mass media more interested in reaching large audiences than in contributing to cultural sensitivity?
2. How do the mass media contribute to stability in the society?
3. What are historical and cultural transmission?
4. How did scholar Marshall McLuhan foresee that television would ease the human alienation that he said was created by the mass-produced written word?

Questions for Critical Thinking

1. Why do the mass media find little room for great works that could elevate the cultural sensitivity of the society?
2. Explain essayist Susan Sontag's point that the mass media bring culturally significant works to mass audiences through the popularization process.
3. Give examples of how people shape their everyday lives around rituals created by the mass media. Also, give examples of how the mass media respond to social rituals in deciding what to present and how and when to present it.
4. Why would a radical social reformer object to most mass media content?
5. How has cognitive dissonance created through the mass media worked against racial separatism in North American society since the 1950s?
6. How do the mass media help to determine the issues that society sees as important?
7. How do the media contribute to social order and cohesion by reporting private acts that deviate from public morality? You might want to consider the case of President Bill Clinton and Monica Lewinsky.
8. Give examples of the mass media's allowing cultural values to be communicated through history to future societies. Also, give examples of contemporary cultural transmission.
9. Explain scholar Marshall McLuhan's theory that the mass-produced written word has contributed to an alienation of human beings from their true nature. How did McLuhan think television could reverse this alienation?

Deepening Your
media LITERACY

Are Christian fundamentalists savvy media users?

STEP 1   The fundamentalist Christian movement in the United States is often in the news, but its members often don't like the way the group is represented. They have

taken matters into their own hands and are creating their own media opportunities.

Dig Deeper

STEP 2   James Dobson, perhaps the most powerful figure in the Dominionist movement, is the founder and chairman of Focus on the Family. Dominionists take the beliefs of the Protestant Christian evangelical fundamentalists a bit further. They believe in more than political participation—they believe that it is their destiny to dominate the political process, to govern with a political and judicial system based on the Old Testament. While teaching at the University of Southern California, Dobson wrote *Dare to Discipline,* which encourages parents to spank their children and has sold over 3.5 million copies since its release in 1970. Dobson employs 1300 people, sends out 4 million pieces of mail each month, and is heard on radio broadcasts in 99 countries. His estimated listening audience is more than 200 million worldwide; in the United States alone he appears on 100 television stations each day. Not all fundamentalists endorse the Dominionist creed, but many on the Christian right believe that Christians are under attack. To counter that "problem," the National Religious Broadcasters association boasts 1600-plus members and claims to reach up to 141 million listeners and viewers. NRB President Dr. Frank Wright says that of 13 838 stations in the United States, 15 percent are religiously formatted. He puts it this way: "Does it strike you that we are the first generation in the history of the world that might see every nation, tongue, and tribe reached with the Gospel?"

What Do You Think?

STEP 3   Answer these questions:

1. In this chapter you learned that media attention lends legitimacy to events. How could this apply to the way the Christian right and the Dominionist movement are using the media they control?
2. Do you think the Dominionist movement is counting on cognitive dissonance to convert new followers? If so, how?
3. Christian fundamentalists often make fun of elitists and intellectuals. Why?
4. Have the Dominionists and the fundamental Christian movement benefited from their use of the media? What do you foresee for the movement, the media and society?

Keeping Up to Date

Recommended are *Journal of Popular Culture, Journal of American Culture* and *Journal of International Popular Culture,* all scholarly publications.

For Further Learning

Terence Corcoran. "Canadian Culture Safe with Canadians." *National Post* (June 12, 2004).

Richard Gruneau. "Why TVTV?" *Canadian Journal of Communication* (Winter 1996).

Howard Hampton. "Out of Our Heads." *Gannett Center Journal* 1: 133–147.

Leo W. Jeffres. *Mass Media Process and Effects,* Second edition (Waveland, 1994).

S. Robert Lichter, Linda S. Lichter and Stanley Rothman. *Watching America: What Television Tells Us about Our Lives* (Prentice Hall, 1991).

Robert M. Liebert, Joyce N. Spatkin and Emily S. Davidson. *The Early Window: Effects on Television on Children and Youth,* Third edition (Pergamon, 1988).

Marshall McLuhan. *The Gutenberg Galaxy: The Making of Typographic Man* (University of Toronto Press, 1967).

Joshua Meyrowitz. *No Sense of Place: The Impact of Electronic Media on Social Behavior* (Oxford, 1985).

Williard D. Rowland Jr. *The Politics of TV Violence: Uses of Communication Policy* (Sage, 1983).

Herbert Schiller. *Mass Communications and American Empire* (Kelley, 1969).

Wilbur Schramm, Jack Lyle and Edwin Parker. *Television in the Lives of Our Children* (Stanford University Press, 1961).

Susan Sontag. "One Culture and New Sensibility." In *Against Interpretation* (Farrar Straus & Giroux, 1966).

Michael Tracey. "The Poisoned Chalice: International Television and the Idea of Dominance." *Daedalus* 114 (Fall 1985): 4, 17–56.

Antonia Zerbisias. "The Campaign to Save Culture." *Toronto Star* (June 20, 2004).

Cultural Imperialism, CSI Style *CSI* and its spinoffs, like *CSI Miami*, aren't only popular in North America but around the world. The series runs in 70 countries. It's not just the show that's being exported, it's the franchise. Lithuanian TV has *CSI: Criminalistai*, while German audiences watch *CSI: Den Tätern auf der Spur.*

Global Mass Media

Media in Theory

Global Media Models

Models help us visualize different media systems. Models have different levels of sophistication, such as going from a bipolar model for political systems to a more complex continuum to an even more complex compass. Besides political systems, models can demonstrate media cultural environments, developmental states and other characterizing criteria.

BIPOLAR MODEL

To compare media systems, some scholars use a **bipolar model** with two extremes: authoritarianism at one end and libertarianism at the other. The model demonstrates opposites in an extreme way. Just as east is opposite from west, so is freedom opposite from control. Bipolar models are useful beginning points to separate political systems.

bipolar model ■ Portrays extremes as opposites, such as libertarian and authoritarian political systems.

CONTINUUM MODEL

More sophisticated than a simple bipolar model is a variation called the **continuum model**. The basics of the continuum political system model are bipolar, with the extremes being authoritarianism and libertarianism, but there is an added element of sophistication. The media system of each country is placed not at an extreme but at points along the line. Canada and the United States would be near the libertarian end, although not quite at the extreme because, indeed, North American media operate within limitations, like laws of treason, libel and intellectual property and also broadcast regulations.

The continuum model recognizes the uniqueness of media systems in different countries. By assessing variables, scholars can plant individual countries on the continuum, which facilitates grouping countries for comparison.

continuum model ■ A scale with authoritarianism at one end, libertarianism at the other and media systems at varying points in between.

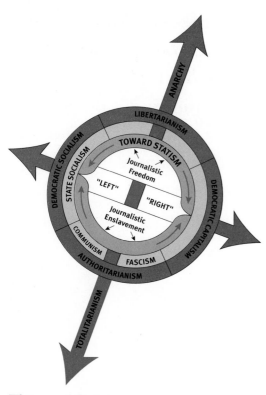

COMPASS MODEL

In his book *The Imperative of Freedom,* scholar **John Merrill** loops the libertarian–authoritarian continuum around so that its ends meet themselves. On the loop, Merrill marks the four major philosophical underpinnings as compass points that define the major media systems and their underlying political systems.

Among Merrill's points with the **compass model** is that a social responsibility system might not be just a variation on libertarianism but actually authoritarian. Merrill's compass addresses the troubling question about how to attain socially responsible media: Who ensures responsibility? If it's government, then we have introduced shades of authoritarianism. If not government, then who?

CHANGE MODEL

The effects of culture and geography on media systems are taken into account in the **change model**, which shows the interaction of many variables on media and systems and performance. One of the best of these models, introduced in 1974 by scholars Ray Hiebert, Donald Ungurait and Thomas Bohn, takes other variables into account:

- **Economics.** In impoverished parts of the world, such as Chad, few people can afford access to the mass media. There is no advertising. This lack of an economic base means a weak media system that is generally subservient to political leadership.
- **Culture.** A country's mass media reflect cultural values. Social norms, mores and values vary from country to country, all with an effect on the mass media. So do language and traditions.
- **Technology.** Outdated equipment can undermine the service that media provide. For print media, poor roads can limit distribution. In much of the Third World, presses are hand-me-downs from more developed countries, not only outdated but also prone to breakdowns.

Figure 16.1 **Compass Model** Scholar John Merrill rethought the libertarian–authoritarian continuum to develop this compass model. The result was a graphic representation showing that a responsible press, if responsibility is by government mandate, is frighteningly close to traditional authoritarianism.

John Merrill ■ Introduced the compass model, which showed that social responsibility and authoritarianism could be bedmates.

ONLINE

Freedom House Review Freedom House's annual survey of countries' freedom scores.
www.freedomhouse.org

compass model ■ A looped model that juxtaposes traditional authoritarian and social responsibility models.

change model ■ Shows the effect of mass media on numerous social variables and the effect of those variables on the media.

subsystem model ■ Examines media in terms of originator and intended audience.

- **Climate.** In tropical climates, where the kinds of trees used for pulp to make paper can't grow, the print media have extraordinary production expenses for importing paper. Mexico is an example.
- **Geography.** Broadcasters in a mountainous country like Nepal have a hard time getting signals to people living in narrow valleys shielded by steep terrain. This is a factor in the economics of broadcasting and also in a station's influence.
- **Literacy.** If people can't read, the print media are handicapped. In Cameroon, for example, compulsory education goes only to age 12. Even then, one-third of Cameroon's children don't attend school. The literacy rate is only 63 percent.
- **Media.** A country's media infrastructure can be an indicator of other realities. If the primary mass medium is radio, for example, it may be an indicator that low literacy has stunted the growth of the print media. A country wired well for the internet has a basis for sophisticated delivery of messages of all sorts.

SUBSYSTEM MODEL

The mass media have grown in complexity, especially in economically advanced countries. Some scholars are making a case that it doesn't make sense anymore to evaluate media in the traditional broad terms of major media, like television, magazines and newspapers. Instead, they advocate classifying media by subsystems to understand what's happening. The following are among the elements in a **subsystem model**:

- **Commercial media.** These are the profit-seeking media that have traditionally been the focus of comparative studies.
- **Government media.** Controlled by the government. May coexist with commercial media.

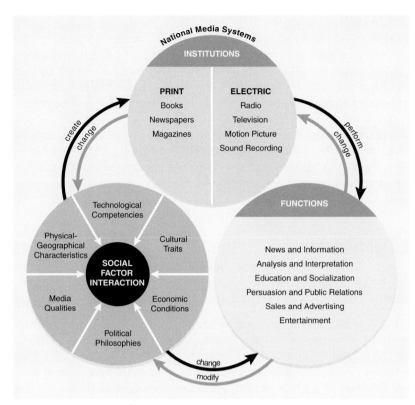

Figure 16.2 **Change Model** A 1974 model developed by scholars Ray Hiebert, Donald Ungurait and Thomas Bohn recognizes many factors in media systems.

- **Public media.** Financed by citizens and government money to further the public good, like PBS and NPR in the United States and CBC in Canada.
- **Organizational media.** Aimed at serving nongovernment bodies, such as professional groups, tribes, religions and corporations.
- **Individualized media.** Media customized to an individual's needs and interests, as is possible through the web.
- **Political media.** Used by political parties.

◤▪ Mass Media and Nation-States

study<u>preview</u> **The ability of national governments to control media content is diminishing with the technology that is allowing the globalization of the mass media.**

media TIMELINE

GLOBALIZATION OF MASS MEDIA

1974 Change model was developed by Ray Hiebert, Donald Ungurait, and Thomas Bohn.

1988 Associated Press bought Worldwide Television News.

1993 NBC bought European Super Channel.

1995 Disney bought ABC.

1998 The World Trade Organization adopted the Canadian model of media regulation.

GLOBAL COMMUNICATION

After the 2005 terrorist subway and bus bombings in London, the British news media flooded the streets and airwaves with stories about the suspects. Understandably, coverage was emotional. When the first arrests were made, the front page of the tabloid *Sun* blared: "Got the Bastards." Then the media went silent. British law forbids news coverage once a criminal charge has been filed. The rationale is not to prejudice potential jurors.

Hungry for news about the terrorism investigation and the people arrested, Britons needed to look no further than the internet. The internet's most-used coding structure is called the World Wide Web for a reason. And just down the street, newsstands stocked foreign newspapers and magazines full of ongoing revelations about the suspects. How could British law deal with the influx of information? The logistics would be overwhelming. The volume of internet communication bespeaks the futility of bans.

FRIEDMAN GLOBALIZATION MODEL

Globalization has been explained in a sweeping historical context by analyst Thomas Friedman of *The New York Times*. Friedman sees three great eras over the past 500 years. He casts these in computerese as Globalization 1.0, 2.0 and 3.0.

Globalization 1.0 The world shrank as governments projected power beyond their borders from the year 1492 to roughly 1800: "The key agent of change, the dynamic force driving the process of globalization was how much brawn—how much muscle, how much horsepower, wind power, or, later steam power—your country had and how creatively you could deploy it." In this period, Friedman says, the nation-state and commercial activities operating under national flags were supreme.

Globalization 2.0 After 1800, multinational companies used declining transportation costs to build global markets, particularly with railroads and steamships. This led industrialists to seek lower labour costs wherever they could be found on the planet because the cost of shipping kept falling and its efficiency kept increasing. In the late 1900s, telecommunication costs dropped dramatically with orbiting satellites, fibre optic cable and the internet. Multinational companies grew exponentially in reshaping human society, displacing some of the earlier power of the nation-states.

Globalization 3.0 In the 21st century, a kind of ultimate democratization is occurring. Technology, mostly through computer software, is empowering individuals to chart their own courses in wholly new ways. The new matrix, as Friedman sees it, is a global triad of nation-states, multinational corporations and individuals in dynamic relationships. Individuals, notably, are the new players with access to information that earlier was the province only of governments and corporations.

Thomas Friedman
This *New York Times* columnist had an epiphany while in India researching a Discovery documentary: Computer software has so empowered individuals that social, business and other infrastructures are in a fundamental transformation.

▛ Global Conglomeration

study<u>preview</u> **Media titan Rupert Murdoch has created the first global content creation and delivery system under a single corporate umbrella, but he's not alone in putting together a global media empire. Still developing are the ways in which global media companies adapt to the internet.**

MULTINATIONAL COMPANIES

The mass media have had international sales for centuries, going back to early book printers. Until the 20th century, however, media companies designed little specifically for export.

Rupert Murdoch

Rupert Murdoch

People love to hate media mogul Rupert Murdoch. Although his News Corp. is only one of many media companies gobbling up other media outlets, Murdoch's name has become synonymous with media power. Former CBS executive Howard Stringer has called him "the leader of a new Napoleonic era of communications." Now in his late 70s, Murdoch is training his children to take over for him.

Murdoch began by acquiring several British newspapers and then some in the United States. He bought the venerable U.S. book publisher Harper & Row, which he rechristened HarperCollins to fit with his British publishing interests. To qualify to own U.S. television stations, he became a U.S. citizen. That, in the 1980s, allowed him to create Fox as the fourth U.S. television network, which some said couldn't be done, and dovetail it with his recently acquired 20th Century Fox movie and television production studio. He bought the parent company of *TV Guide.* He created the Sky and Star satellite systems in Britain and Asia. Two-thirds of the world's population—3 billion people—watch Star! TV, which shows programming that Murdoch's company creates or buys. In 2003 he acquired DIRECTV, the major U.S. satellite television delivery service.

The expansion gave Murdoch the components to establish the first global system for content creation and delivery under a single corporate umbrella. This is the Murdochian significance—a grip on distribution that competitors don't have. Critic James Fallows cited how the Murdoch media empire synchronizes production, publicity and support: "They supply the content—Fox movies (*Titanic, The Full Monty, There's Something about Mary*), Fox TV shows (*The Simpsons, Ally McBeal, When Animals Attack*), Fox-controlled sports broadcasts, plus newspapers and books. They sell the content to the public and to advertisers—in newspapers, on the broadcast network, on cable channels. And they operate the physical distribution system through which the content reaches the customers." Murdoch's satellite systems distribute News Corporation content in Europe and Asia.

Critics fret that Murdoch media control too much of the world's media content and note that News Corp. entities have a politically conservative slant. Murdoch calls that balderdash. Using early 2004 data, he once pointed to U.S. talk radio, in which he has no part, and noted how lopsided it is, with 300-plus hours of nationally syndicated conservative talk a week versus five hours of liberal talk. The media, himself included, Murdoch says, merely offer what people want: "Apparently conservative talk is more popular."

Foreign Branches A new awareness of potential markets abroad came in the 1930s, typified by the *Reader's Digest*'s first foray overseas. The magazine, born in the United States in 1922, had obvious international potential. In 1938 publishers DeWitt and Lila Wallace established a British edition. It was largely the same as the U.S. edition, but British editors replaced some articles. Today, the magazine is published in 18 languages. Some editions are extensively edited for distinct audiences.

Acquisitions Another model for international media companies emerged in the 1980s. Media companies began buying up foreign media companies. Bertelsmann of Germany bought its way into many foreign markets. Acquisitions included the RCA and Arista record labels in the United States, then 14 women's magazines bought from *The New York Times,* then the venerable U.S. book company Random House.

Mergers Some media companies have found synergies in merging. A merger of Hachette of France and Filapacchi of Italy created cross-fertilization opportunities that generated more profits from existing products. The new company also exported concepts, such as the French fashion magazine *Elle* being adapted for additional markets, including the United States.

Alliances Most media companies rely on other companies for foreign distribution of their content. Viacom, for example, sells its television programs to existing networks and stations in other countries. Several magazine publishers have agreements with native companies to produce and distribute foreign editions.

Who Owns What List prepared by the *Columbia Journalism Review* to show how large media companies control many aspects of mass communication in the United States and around the world.
www.cjr.org/tools/owners

Reader's Digest *Reader's Digest* is now published in more than 20 countries.
www.rd.com

News Corporation Rupert Murdoch's global empire.
www.newscorp.com

Content-Distribution Model Media mogul **Rupert Murdoch**, known mostly for his 20th Century/Fox movie and Fox television empires, has moved media globalization into new directions by combining media content-creation companies and content-distribution companies under a super-corporate umbrella. Murdoch's orbiting satellite companies, including BSkyB, DIRECTV and Star! TV, beam signals directly to consumers, bypassing traditional delivery media. With 20th Century and Fox, he also generates content to supply his delivery system—no middlemen.

THE INTERNET AND GLOBALIZATION

New technologies are opening the way for more companies to seek global audiences directly, with no middlemen, at low cost. E-books, for example, don't require expensive presses to produce. Nor do they need massive warehouses or require expensive shipping. Producers of radio and television programs can use streaming instead of having to negotiate complex deals with networks or individual stations for distribution. In short, the internet can eliminate middlemen.

Easy access to the internet opens opportunities for upstarts to reach global audiences. Whether new companies can establish internet followings that compete with the majors, which also have created presences on the web, isn't clear. With the massiveness of their repertoires, the major players certainly have a leg up.

MediaChannel A nonprofit, public interest supersite dedicated to global media issues.
www.mediachannel.org

■ Effects of Globalization

study<u>preview</u> **Foreign ownership worries some media critics. At stake, as these critics see it, is control of the direction of cultural advancement—something they believe should not be farmed out.**

CULTURAL SUBVERSIVENESS

Experts disagree about the effect of globalization. Some critics, including respected media commentator Ben Bagdikian, fret that "anonymous superpowers" such as Bertelsmann are a potential threat to U.S. cultural autonomy and the free flow of information and ideas. In his book *The New Media Monopoly,* Bagdikian said: "The highest levels of world finance have become intertwined with the highest levels of mass media ownership, with the result of tighter control over the systems on which most of the public depends for its news and information."

Other observers, such as Toni Heinzl and Robert Stevenson at the University of North Carolina, note that many global media companies, including Bertelsmann, have learned to let their local operating companies adapt to local cultures: "Following a global strategy, it is the company's policy to respect the national characteristics and cultural traditions in each of the more than two dozen countries in which it operates. It is impossible to detect even hints of German culture from the product lineup of Bertelsmann's companies abroad. Targeting specific preference of a national public or audience, the company has custom-tailored its products for each country: French culture in France, Spanish culture in Spain, American culture in the United States, and so on." The target is growth.

CORPORATE IDEOLOGY

By and large the agenda of media conglomerates is profits and nothing more. They do not promote ideology. U.S. moviegoers did not see Japanese overtones in Columbia movies or CBS records after the Sony takeover or in MCA products after the Matsushita takeover. At the same time it cannot be ignored that Bertelsmann tried to transplant its successful German geographic magazine *Geo* in the United States in 1979, only to give it up two years and $50 million later when it realized that *National Geographic*'s following was unshakable. In the same vein Murdoch imported British tabloid editors to reshape some of the U.S. newspapers he bought. What can be said with certainty about media globalization is that it is occurring and that observers are divided about its consequences.

◾ Cultural Intrusion

study<u>preview</u> Some experts claim that the export of U.S. and other Western popular culture is latter-day imperialism motivated by profit and without concern for its effect on other societies. Other experts see charges of cultural imperialism as overblown.

LATTER-DAY IMPERIALISM

The great concern about media globalization has been about the flow of values not *among* developed countries but *to* developing countries. Critics use the term **cultural imperialism** for this dark side of international communication. Their view is that the media are like the 19th-century European colonial powers, exporting Western values, often uninvited, to other cultures. At stake, these critics say, is the cultural sovereignty of non-Western nations. These critics note the communication flow is one way from the powerful nations to the weak ones. The result, as they see it, is that Western values are imposed in an impossible-to-resist way.

Scholar **Herbert Schiller**, who wrote *Mass Communications and American Empire,* argued that the one-way communication flow is especially dangerous because the Western productions, especially movies and television, are so slick that they easily outdraw locally produced programs. As a result, says Schiller, the Western-controlled international mass media pre-empt native culture, a situation he sees as robbery, just like the earlier colonial tapping of natural resources to enrich the home countries.

India is a fascinating recent example of cultural intrusion, if not cultural imperialism. Until 1991 this nation had only one television network, which ran programs that originated in India almost exclusively. Then came Star! TV, Rupert Murdoch's satellite service from Hong Kong, which carried lots of U.S.-originated programming. Writing in *Media Studies Journal,* Shailaja Bajpai, India media critic and editor of an Indian television magazine, offered these observations:

- Many Indians were dressing like the Americans they saw on *Baywatch*.
- While Indian boys once wanted to grow up to be great cricket players, they now wanted to shoot baskets like Yao Ming.

Other anecdotal evidence of U.S. culture rubbing off elsewhere is in South Africa. According to Sebiletso Mokone-Matabane, an executive with the Independent Broadcast Authority there, robbers were shouting "freeze," a word that had no roots in Afrikaans or the indigenous languages, when they stormed into a bank. The robbers had been watching too much U.S. television.

Some media genres translate easily across cultures. Hoping to attract audiences with reality shows, which had been the rage in Europe, Canada and the United States in the early 2000s, Middle Eastern television producers tried a variety of adaptations. Some worked, toned down from their progenitors' risqué edginess. Sex was verboten. Swearing too. No kissing. In *Fear Factor* the female contestants in the swimming stunts wore full-body wet suits. There were no cameras in the showers. The bedrooms in *Big Brother* were off limits to the opposite sex.

THE CANADIAN EXPERIENCE WITH CULTURAL INTRUSION

The notion of latter-day imperialism is one of the reasons that the CRTC and the Canadian government have always had some form of content regulations for most Canadian-owned broadcast media. But this fear is not unique to Canada; other countries feel the same way. In fact, many countries look to the CRTC for guidance in how to deal with cultural intrusion. In 1998, the World Trade Organization adopted the so-called "Canadian model of regulation." What this means, according to the CRTC, is that other countries want to "understand how Canada meets public interest goals while encouraging the growth of the public sector."

NON-DOWNWARD MEDIA EXCHANGE

In some ways cultural imperialism is in the eyes of the beholder. Some Latin American countries, for example, scream "cultural imperialism" at the United States but don't object when Mexico exports soap operas to the rest of Latin America, as Brazil and Argentina

cultural imperialism ◾ One culture's dominance of another.

Herbert Schiller ◾ Saw Western cultures subsuming others.

ONLINE
Herbert Schiller Interview with Schiller in *Z Magazine,* from the British Columbia Library Association.
www.vcn.bc.ca/bcla-ip/ governments/schiller.html

U.S. Media Imperialism Herbert Schiller is one of many media theorists concerned about the influence of American culture on smaller nations.

do. Although they are exercising a form of cultural imperialism, nobody puts the label on them. Media observer Larry Lorenz, who has studied this phenomenon, explains it this way: "What is occurring is simply internationalism brought on by the ever more sophisticated media of mass communication."

The cultural imperialism theory has other doubters among scholars. The doubters note that the theory is a simplistic application of the now-discredited hypodermic needle model of mass communication. Media messages do not have immediate direct effects.

EMERGING GLOBAL MEDIA

Concern about Western cultural imperialism is slowly changing as two related things occur. First, the number of international media players, many in neither Europe nor the United States, is increasing. Second, rather than merely recycling domestic products abroad, U.S.-based media companies are creating new, local-oriented content in the countries where they do business.

Mideast Reality Show A Saudi Arabian and a Lebanese contestant sing during a live show of the *Star Academy,* one of the first reality shows to air in the Middle East. Other reality shows, many from Lebanon, are modeled on European and U.S. television and have attracted young viewers.

For generations, prime-time U.S. television shows have been prime-time fare throughout the world, either with subtitles or dubbed awkwardly into local languages. Today, local media people who have mastered Western production techniques are producing local media content. Although production quality in some countries isn't as slick as for U.S. programs, indigenous programs have their own attractions and are siphoning viewers and advertisers from imported fare. Their programs go over big, attracting viewers and advertisers better than imported programs.

Not only is indigenous local programming taking hold in other countries, especially those with a developing middle class, but also many of these emerging media are exporting their material. Throughout Latin America, for example, people watch soap operas

Movie Power

In ranking the most powerful countries for *Newsweek* magazine in 2003, analyst John Spark used movies as one measure.

"Hollywood and Bollywood fantasies of the good life shape the desires of billions," he said in offering these data.

Movie Tickets Sold per Year	
India	2.9 billion
United States	1.4 billion
Canada	113 million
Film Investment	
United States	$14.7 billion
Japan	1.3 billion
India	192 million
Canada	133 million

You can derive additional meaning from these numbers by re-ranking the nations per capita.

produced by TV Globo in Brazil and Televisa in Mexico. The Belgian broadcast company RTL, which once spent most of its programming dollars on imports like *Dallas* and *Dynasty*, now produces most of its own shows. The French TF-1 and Italian Rai Uno television services have cut back substantially on U.S. programs. The turnaround in Europe has been fueled not only by audience preferences for local material but also by a European Union policy that half of each nation's broadcast programming must originate within the EU.

There is also new competition, much of it well financed. In Europe the television service Canal One has teamed up with Bertelsmann of Germany to create a formidable competitor for the whole European audience. TVB in Hong Kong has its eye on dominating media fare to China, Southeast Asia and the Indian subcontinent. What once were easy pickings for U.S. media companies are now tough markets.

Although more media content is being originated in home countries, some critics say, "Don't be fooled." Shailaja Bajpai says that Indian TV producers clone U.S. television: "The American talk show has inspired Indian imitations. Never have so many Indians revealed so much about their private lives to such a wide audience. Every day a new show is planned. If nothing else, American television has loosened tongues (to say nothing of our morals). Subjects long taboo are receiving a good airing." Those Indian programs may be produced in India, but the concept is hardly Indian.

TRANSNATIONAL CULTURAL ENRICHMENT

Some scholars see transnational cultural flow in more benign terms than Herbert Schiller and his fellow cultural imperialism theorists. George Steiner has noted that European and American culture has been enriched, not corrupted, by the continuing presence of Greek mythology over 2000 years.

Sociologist Michael Tracey makes a similar point in a homey way: "I was born in a working-class neighbourhood called Oldham in the north of England. Before the First World War, Oldham produced most of the world's spun cotton. It is a place of mills and chimneys, and I was born and raised in one of the areas of housing—called St. Mary's—built to serve those mills. I recently heard a record by a local group of folk singers called the Oldham Tinkers, and one track was about Charlie Chaplin. This song was apparently very popular with local children in the years immediately after the First World War. Was that evidence of the cultural influences of Hollywood, a primeval moment of the imperialism of one culture, the subjugation of another? It seems almost boorish to think of it that way. Was the little man not a deep well of pleasure through laughter, a pleasure that was simply universal in appeal? Was it not Chaplin's real genius to strike some common chord, uniting the whole of humanity? Is that not, in fact, the real genius of American popular culture, to bind together, better than anything, common humanity?"

◼ Global Media Players

study<u>preview</u> **The first media companies to significantly extend their operations abroad were news agencies such as the Associated Press, Reuters and United Press. Today, companies that produce all kinds of media messages, not just news, are engaged in finding global markets.**

NEWS AGENCIES

Hundreds of agencies cover news around the world and sell their accounts to subscribing media organizations. Most of these are national and regional services. The primary global players are Associated Press, Reuters, Agence France-Presse and Interfax.

Associated Press The Associated Press is the largest news-gathering organization in the world, disseminating 20 million words and 1000-plus images a day. There are 8500 subscribers in 112 countries. The AP, based in New York, has 142 foreign bureaus in 72 countries. The AP is a nonprofit co-operative organization owned by daily newspapers.

media ONLINE

Associated Press The news any way you want it—read it, watch it or hear it.
www.ap.org

Reuters News and financial information.
www.reuters.com

Associated Press ◼ U.S.-based global news service; largest news-gathering organization in the world.

Reuters Reuters serves 6500 media organizations worldwide, including 290 in the United States and Canada. Altogether, counting subscribers to its financial and business news services, Reuters has 27 000 subscribers worldwide. The service is offered in 11 languages. There are 120 bureaus in 80 countries. U.S. video clients include CNN and NBC.

Agence France-Presse Paris-based **Agence France-Presse** was founded by Charles Havas in 1835. Today AFP is the third-largest global agency. AFP has 2000 people in 150 bureaus worldwide, including 850 full-time journalists. Text, photo, audio and video services are transmitted in Arabic, English, French, German, Spanish and Portuguese to 500 newspapers, 350 radio and 200 television clients and to 99 national news agencies that pass AFP stories on to more media outlets.

Interfax This Moscow-based news agency was founded as Tass in 1925. Today, reconstituted and renamed **Interfax**, the agency supplies reports in Russian, English, German, Spanish and Arabic. At its peak, the agency claimed 5500 media and nonmedia subscribers, but the disintegration of communism and the shriveling of Russian influence has meant inevitable declines.

VIDEO NEWS SERVICES

The major news networks—ABC, CBS, CNN, CBC, CTV, Fox and NBC—prefer to cover foreign stories with their own crews, but they also subscribe to global video services for stories and pictures that they miss. The largest news video suppliers are, not surprisingly, the world's two largest news services: New York–based Associated Press and London-based Reuters.

SYNDICATES

After Union recruiters swept through Baraboo, Wisconsin, and signed up the local boys for the Civil War, **Ansel Nash Kellogg** lacked the staff to get out his four-page Baraboo *Republic,* so he took to borrowing the inside pages of another newspaper. The practice not only saw Kellogg through a staffing crisis, but also sparked an idea to save costs by supplying inside pages at a fee to other short-handed publishers. By 1865 Kellogg was in Chicago providing ready-to-print material for newspapers nationwide. In journalism history Kellogg is remembered as the father of the newspaper **syndicate.**

In the 1880s **S.S. McClure** had a thriving syndicate, putting out 50 000 words a week in timeless features on fashion, homemaking, manners and literature. McClure and other syndicators charged subscribing newspapers a fraction of what each would have to pay to generate such material with its own staff. Features, poetry, opinion and serialized stories by the period's great literary figures, including Jack London, Rudyard Kipling, George Bernard Shaw, Robert Louis Stevenson and Mark Twain, became standard fare in many newspapers through syndication.

Today, syndicates seek international audiences, spreading expenses among more subscribers and building new revenue. Some syndicate material doesn't travel easily, like sophisticated humour columns and comic strips that reflect the traditions, experiences and values of a particular culture.

▛▖ Global Media Companies

study preview National origins of companies in the media business are blurring. Sony of Japan owns Columbia Pictures and many leading U.S. record labels under a subsidiary. Sony also owns a share of Time Warner. Bertelsmann of Germany is a big player in U.S. magazines and books. U.S. companies themselves have foreign stakes.

U.S.-BASED COMPANIES

Five U.S. media rivals have established themselves as major players in other countries.

- **Time Warner.** Time Warner, operating in 70-plus countries, is the world's largest media company, with a value ranging as high as $183 billion. Its CNN can reach a billion people in 212 countries. HBO Olé attracts legions of subscribers in Latin America. Warner Brothers' movies and TV shows are distributed worldwide. *Time* publishes editions in Europe, Latin America and the South Pacific.
- **Disney-ABC.** When Walt Disney laboured over his primitive animation for *Steamboat Willie* in 1928, he likely didn't dream that his name would forever be attached to a corporate giant. The huge acquisition of ABC in 1995 provided a domestic outlet for Disney Studio productions, which already had gone global. Theme parks in Tokyo, Hong Kong and Paris have added to Disney's world impact.
- **Viacom.** Viacom began as a syndication arm of CBS but a change in Federal Communications required it to be spun off. Ironically, Viacom made so much money recycling television shows that it acquired back CBS in 2001. Viacom's wildly profitable MTV can be tuned in at 400 million homes in 164 countries. Viacom's Paramount Pictures has a vault of 50 000 hours of television shows for international marketing.
- **News Corporation.** Beginning with an inherited newspaper in Adelaide, Australia, Rupert Murdoch built a successful chain, then expanded to Europe where he acquired the prestigious *Times* of London. Moving to the United States, Murdoch nabbed 20th Century Fox studios and created the Fox Television Network whose products are distributed by his BSkyB in Europe and STAR TV in Asia. Adding Murdoch's DIRECTV in 2003, there's scarcely a television set in the world that a News Corporation satellite can't reach.
- **NBC Universal.** In 2004, General Electric's NBC and Vivendi Universal Entertainment closed a merger that created the fifth-largest media conglomerate, NBC Universal. NBC's television network and cable channels, including Telemundo, joined with Universal's studios and theme parks, and Vivendi's A&M, Geffen, PolyGram and Motown labels. Wall Street figures net assets of the new company at $42 billion.

NON-U.S. COMPANIES

Once U.S. media companies held the commanding lead for overseas markets, but home-grown companies are pumping out more content all the time. Some of these companies have become global players themselves.

- **Bertelsmann.** The German company Bertelsmann established itself globally as a book and magazine company. It has 200 subsidiaries in 25 countries, many of them operating under the name they had when Bertelsmann acquired them. In the United States these include Random House, Bantam, Dell and Doubleday books. The company's U.S. interests, jointly owned with Sony since 2003, include RCA Records.
- **Hachette Filipacchi.** The French-Italian company Hachette Filipacchi publishes 74 magazines in 10 countries. This includes the 4.5 million circulation *Woman's Day,* which Hachette acquired when it bought the CBS magazine empire in 1988. Another Hachette magazine in the United States is the fashion magazine *Elle.*
- **Televisa.** Throughout Latin America, people watch soap operas, called *telenovelas.* Most of these originate from Televisa, a Mexican media giant.
- **TVB.** Hong Kong-based TVB has started an Asian television-satellite service. This company has plenty to put on the satellite. Its production runs about 6000 hours a year in both Cantonese and Mandarin.
- **TV Globo.** A Brazilian media company, TV Globo, true to its name, has developed a global audience. Its telenovelas air in all the Spanish-speaking and Portuguese-speaking countries and beyond, including China.
- **Pearson.** Once a British newspaper company, Pearson has sold its papers, except the *Financial Times,* to concentrate on book publishing. One subsidiary, Pearson Education, is the largest educational publisher in the United States. Pearson's trade-book imprints include Penguin.
- **Reed Elsevier.** An Anglo-Dutch conglomerate, Reed Elsevier owns the Lexis-Nexis online legal news reference service and publishes more academic journals than any other company. Worldwide, Reed has 36 000 employees. A major revenue source is library subscriptions to its online journals. The California state university library system alone pays $7 million to $8 million a year for Reed journals in an online format.

Time Warner Get a feel for this award-winning, global media and entertainment company.
www.timewarner.com/corp

Disney Check out upcoming movies, play games or plan a vacation to a Disney theme park.
http://disney.go.com

Viacom Learn more about this diverse, hugely successful entertainment company.
www.viacom.com

NBC Universal Take a sneak peak at NBC TV programs and movies.
www.nbcuni.com

Bertelsmann Media worldwide.
www.bertelsmann.com

Hachette Filipacchi The U.S. division.
www.hfmus.com/HachetteUSA/noflash/index.html

TVB Hong Kong satellite service.
www.tvb.com

TV Globo Brazilian media company.
http://tvglobointernacional.globo.com

Televisa Media giant from Mexico.
www.esmas.com/televisahome

Pearson Educating and entertaining all ages.
www.pearson.com

Reed Elsevier Providing information to professionals around the world.
www.reed-elsevier.com

Distinctive Media Systems

study preview National systems for operating mass media take many forms. Some are modest variations, like the British and Japanese methods to fund broadcasting. Dictatorships have wholly different infrastructures that determine content.

BRITAIN

Almost everybody has heard of the BBC, Britain's venerable public service radio and television system. Parliament created the British Broadcasting Corporation in 1927 as a government-funded entity that, despite government support, would have as much programming autonomy as possible. The idea was to avoid private ownership and to give the enterprise the prestige of being associated with the crown. The government appoints a 12-member board of governors, which runs BBC. Although the government has the authority to remove members of the board, it never has. BBC has developed largely independently of the politics of the moment, which has given it a credibility and stature that are recognized worldwide. The Beeb, as BBC is affectionately known, is financed through an annual licensing fee, about $230, on television receivers.

BBC is known for its global news coverage. It has 250 full-time correspondents, compared to CNN's 113. The Beeb's reputation for first-rate dramatic and entertainment programs is known among English-speaking people everywhere. The great issue today is whether the BBC should leave the government fold. Advocates of privatization argue that BBC could exploit its powerful brand name better if it were privatized. The privatization advocates say that BBC's government ties are keeping it from aggressively pursuing partnerships to make it a global competitor with companies like Time Warner and Rupert Murdoch's News Corporation. But continuing to do business as always, they say, will leave the Beeb in everybody else's dust.

INDIA

The world's largest democracy, India has a highly developed movie industry that took root by providing affordable entertainment to mass audiences when the country was largely impoverished. The industry, called **Bollywood**, a contrivance of its historic roots in Bombay and the U.S. movie capital Hollywood, is adapting as India moves rapidly out of its Third World past. Today India is becoming a model for new media applications, like Wi-Fi, as the country brings itself into modern times.

Bollywood ■ Nickname for India movie industry.

Bollywood The Indian movie industry, centred in Bombay and sometimes called Bollywood, pumps out an incredible 1200 movies a year. Although India has some internationally recognized moviemakers, most Bollywood productions are formulaic action movies that critics derisively label "curry westerns."

Bollywood At 85 cents a seat, people jam Indian movie houses in such numbers that some exhibitors schedule five showings a day starting at 9 a.m. Better seats sell out days in advance in some cities. There is no question that movies are the country's strongest mass medium. Even though per capita income is only $1360 a year, Indians find enough rupees to support an industry that cranks out 1200 movies a year, twice more than U.S. moviemakers. Most are B-grade formula melodramas and action stories. Screen credits often include a director of fights. Despite this, Indian movies are so popular that it is not unusual for a movie house in a Hindi-speaking area to be packed for a film in another Indian language that nobody in the audience understands. Movies are produced in 16 Indian languages.

Billboards, fan clubs and scurrilous magazines fuel the obsession with stars. Scholars Erik Barnouw and S. Krishnaswamy, in their book *Indian Film,* characterize the portrayals of stars as "mythological demigods who live on a highly physical and erotic plane, indulging in amours." With some magazines, compromising photos are a specialty.

A few Indian moviemakers have been recognized abroad for innovation and excellence, but they generally have an uphill battle against B-movies in attracting Indian audiences. Many internationally recognized Indian films, like those by Satyajit Ray, flop commercially at home.

In the late 1990s, Indian movies developed a cult following in the United States and Canada. The major Indian movie export market, however, was in Hindi-speaking parts of the world. In Sri Lanka, for example, whose language Sinhalese is closely related to Hindi, the domestic movie industry is overshadowed by imported Indian movies.

Wi-Fi India has taken a lead in linking remote villages with the rest of the world with wireless technology. Villagers and farmers who once had to walk several miles to pay their power bills now go to a "knowledge centre" as it's called—several rooms equipped with desktop computers, connected by Wi-Fi to the internet—and pay online. Such "knowledge centres" are being installed in 600 000 villages in a government-entrepreneurial program launched in 2005. Eventually, all 237 000 villages in India large enough to have a governing unit will be equipped. An Indian company named n-Logue has designed Wi-Fi kiosks for rural villages at $1200 a unit, complete with a computer, software, a digital camera, paper and a backup power supply. Kiosks can have ATM banking too.

JAPAN

Anyone who owns a television set in Japan can expect a knock on the door every couple of months. It is the collector from NHK, the Japan Broadcast Corporation, knocking to pick up a periodic $16 reception fee. This ritual occurs six times a year in 31 million doorways. The reception fee, required by law since 1950, produces $2.6 billion annually to support the NHK network.

NHK is a Japanese tradition. It went on the air in 1926, a single radio station, the first broadcast of which was the enthronement of Emperor Hirohito. Today, NHK operates three radio and two domestic television networks. It also runs Radio Japan, the national overseas shortwave service, which transmits 40 hours of programs a day in 21 languages.

The primary NHK television network, Channel One, offers mostly highbrow programming. NHK airs about 600 hours a year of British and U.S. documentaries and dramas from the BBC and PBS. The network prides itself on its news.

Most Japanese viewers, however, spend most of their television time with stations served by four networks, all with headquarters in Tokyo: Fuji, NHK, NTV and Tokyo Broadcasting System. A few independent stations complete Japan's television system. The commercial stations all offer similar fare: comedies, pop concerts and videos, quiz shows, sports and talk shows. In recent years, news has gained importance in attracting viewers and advertisers, encroaching on one of NHK's traditional strengths.

Models to help explain the world's great variety of mass media are important in this fast changing era of globalization. The most useful models focus on change—how economics, culture, technology and other factors influence media infrastructures and content in an interactive way. Models alone are insufficient to explain media policy in a global context. Economics are at the heart of understanding why mass media companies behave as they do.

Questions for Review

1. How has the ability of nations to control media content changed with new technologies?
2. What ideology do global media companies export?
3. What is the negative connotation of Herbert Schiller's term "cultural imperialism"?
4. How does media globalization work against indigenous and distinctive media content?
5. Is it a problem when values from dominant cultures subsume those of other cultures?
6. How does the continuum model bypass the bipolar model in sophistication?
7. How have global news agencies affected nations they cover for the rest of the world?
8. Where are the major global media companies based?

Questions for Critical Thinking

1. What does Thomas Friedman's Globalization 3.0 suggest about the mass media and the future of human society?
2. What can be expected if global consolidation of mass media companies continues?
3. Assess the view that "cultural imperialism" is a loaded term that misses an enriching aspect of transnational communication.
4. Does media globalization necessarily work against indigenous and distinctive media content?
5. Is human civilization moving toward a monolithic culture?
6. Use the subsystem model to explain the mass media in any developing country you choose.
7. Assess the criticism of some Third World leaders that news agencies like AP and Reuters are lackeys of the government in the country where they're based.
8. Why are the biggest global media companies based mostly in the United States and Europe?
9. Compare and contrast the U.S., British and Japanese systems of financing their national television networks.
10. What trends can you ascertain about media–government relations worldwide?

Deepening Your media LITERACY

What is the message of the Marlboro Man?

STEP 1 Write down how cultural intrusion differs from cultural imperialism.

Dig Deeper

STEP 2 A basic media literacy skill is to look beneath the surface of a media message. Consider a message such as the Marlboro Man, who has become an icon worldwide. The New Mexico Literacy Project has compiled a list of questions to deconstruct a media message. Use their questions to look more closely at the image of the Marlboro Man.

1. Who paid for the media? Why?
2. Who is being targeted?
3. What text, images or sounds lead you to this conclusion?
4. What is the literal meaning of the message?
5. What is the unstated or underlying message?
6. What kind of lifestyle is presented? Is it glamorized? If so, how?
7. What values are expressed?
8. What tools or techniques of persuasion are used?
9. What story is not being told?
10. In what ways is this a healthy media message? Or an unhealthy one? Or both?

What Do You Think?

STEP 3 Answer these questions:

1. Is it the responsibility of the company or country that exports a message like the Marlboro Man to make sure that it's a healthy message?
2. How much responsibility should be borne by the viewer?
3. What if the viewer doesn't have access to information about the health risks of smoking?
4. Is exporting the Marlboro Man cultural intrusion or cultural imperialism? Why?

Keeping Up to Date

Index on Censorship is published in London and provides monthly country-by-country status reports.

Scholarly journals that carry articles on foreign media systems, international communication and media responsibility include the *International Communication Bulletin, Journal of Broadcasting and Electronic Media, Journal of Communication* and *Journal and Mass Communication Quarterly.*

Professional journals that carry articles on foreign media systems and on media responsibility include *Columbia Journalism Review, Quill* and *American Journalism Review.*

Ongoing discussions on media responsibility also appear in the *Journal of Mass Media Ethics.*

For Further Learning

Herbert J. Altschull. *Agents of Power* (Longman, 1984).

J. Augment, P. Bross, R. Hiebert, O.V. Johnson and D. Mills. *Eastern European Journalism Before, During and After Communism* (Hampton, 1999).

Ben Bagdikian. *The Media Monopoly,* Fifth edition (Beacon, 1997).

Stephen P. Banks. *Multicultural Public Relations: A Social-Interpretive Approach,* Second edition (Iowa State University Press, 2000).

Chris Barker. *Television, Globalization and Cultural Identities* (Open Universities, 1999).

Eric Barnouw and S. Krishnaswamy. *Indian Film* (Columbia Univ. Press, 1963).

Carl L. Becker. *Freedom and Responsibility in the American Way of Life* (Vintage, 1945).

Isaiah Berlin. *Karl Marx: His Life and Environment* (Oxford University Press, 1939).

David Buckingham, Hannah Davies, Ken Jones and Peter Kelley. *Children's Television in Britain: History, Discourse and Policy* (British Film Institute, 1999).

Bernard Cohen. *The Press and Foreign Policy* (Princeton University Press, 1963).

Commission on Freedom of the Press. *A Free and Responsible Press* (University of Chicago Press, 1947).

James Curran, editor. *Media Organizations in Society* (Oxford University Press, 2000).

Frank Ellis. *From Glasnost to the Internet: Russia's New Infosphere* (St. Martin's, 1999).

Donna Evleth. *The Authorized Press in Vichy and German-Occupied France, 1940–1944: A Bibliography* (Greenwood, 1999).

Howard H. Frederick. *Global Communication and International Relations* (Wadsworth, 1993).

Thomas L. Friedman. *The World Is Flat: A Brief History of the 21st Century* (Farrar, Straus and Giroux, 2005).

Micah Garen and Marie-Hélène Carleton. *American Hostage: A Memoir of a Journalist Kidnapped in Iraq and the Remarkable Battle to Win His Release* (Simon & Schuster, 2005).

Urs E. Gattiker. *The Internet as a Diverse Community: Cultural, Organizational and Political Issues* (Earlbaum, 2001).

Leo A. Gher and Hussein Y. Amin, editors. *Civic Discourse and Digital Age Communication in the Middle East* (Greenwood, 2000).

Joseph Gibbs. *The Soviet Media in the First Phase of Perestroika* (Texas A&M University Press, 1999).

"Global Views on U.S. Media." *Media Studies Journal* (Fall 1995).

Emma Gray. "Glasnost Betrayed." *Media Studies Journal* (Spring-Summer 2000): 94–99.

Shelton A. Gunaratne, editor. *Handbook of the Media in Asia* (Sage, 2000).

William A. Hachten and Harva Hachten. *The World News Prism,* Fifth edition (Iowa State University Press, 1999).

Edward S. Herman and Robert W. McChesney. *The Global Media: The New Missionaries of Global Capitalism* (Cassell, 1997).

William E. Hocking. *Freedom of the Press: A Framework of Principle* (University of Chicago Press, 1947).

Wolfgang Hoffmann-Riem. *Regulating Media: The Licensing and Supervision of Broadcasting in Six Countries* (Guilford, 1996).

Frank Hughes. *Prejudice and the Press* (Devin-Adair, 1950).

L. Martin John and Anju Grover Chaudhary. *Comparative Mass Media Systems* (Longman, 1983).

Carla Brooks Johnston. *Winning the Global TV News Game* (Focal Press, 1995).

Jason Kirby. "Blood Splats and Bean Counters." *Maclean's* (January 29, 2007).

Jerry W. Knudson. "Licensing Journalists in Latin America: An Appraisal." *Journalism and Mass Communication Quarterly* (Winter 1996): 878–889.

Abbas Malek and Anandam P. Kavoori, editors. *The Global Dynamics of News: Studies in International News Coverage and News Agenda* (Ablex, 2000).

Marilyn Matelski. *Vatican Radio* (Praeger, 1995).

Robert W. McChesney. *Corporate Media and the Threat to Democracy* (Seven Stories Press, 1997).

John Merrill. *Global Journalism: Survey of International Communication* (Longman, 1995).

John C. Merrill. *The Imperative of Freedom: A Philosophy of Journalistic Autonomy* (Hastings House, 1974).

Ellen Mickiewicz. *Changing Channels: Television and the Struggle for Power in Russia,* Second edition (Duke University Press, 1999).

John C. Nerone, editor. *Last Rites: Revisiting Four Theories of the Press* (University of Illinois Press, 1995).

David D. Perlmutter. *Photojournalism and Foreign Policy: Icons of Outrage in International Crises* (Praeger, 1998).

Frank Rose. "Vivendi's High Wireless Act." *Wired* (December 2000): 318–333.

Herbert Schiller. *Mass Communications and American Empire* (Kelley, 1969).

Fred Siebert, Theodore Peterson and Wilbur Schramm. *Four Theories of the Press* (University of Illinois Press, 1956).

Tony Silvia, editor. *Global News: Perspectives on the Information Age* (Iowa State University Press, 2001).

Frank Smyth. "Danger Zone: When the Press Becomes the Target." *Quill* (December 2000): 58–59.

Colin Sparks with Anna Reading. *Communism, Capitalism and the Mass Media* (Sage, 1999).

Michael S. Sweeney. *Secrets of Victory: The Office of Censorship and the American Press and Radio in World War II* (University of North Carolina Press, 2001).

Joseph Robson Tanner. *English Constitutional Conflicts of the Seventeenth Century. 1603–1689* (Cambridge University Press, 1928).

Daya Kishan Thussu. *International Communication: Continuity and Change* (Arnold, 2000).

Daya Kishan Thussu, editor. *Electronic Empires: Global Media and Local Resistance* (Arnold, 1999).

Sun Xupei. *An Orchestra of Voices: Making the Argument for Greater Speech and Press Freedom in the People's Republic of China* (Greenwood, 2000).

Deep Throat Thirty-plus years after helping in the Watergate scandal revelations in *The Washington Post,* the retired Number Two man at the FBI, Mark Felt, identified himself as the knowledgeable insider source. The revelation renewed the ongoing debate on anonymous sources in the news but also emphasized the symbiotic relationship between the news media and the government.

Mass Media and Governance

Media in Theory

Does the News Media "Manufacture Consent?"

In their classic work, *Manufacturing Consent: The Political Economy of the Mass Media,* **Noam Chomsky** and **Edward Herman** argue that through gatekeeping, various filters create an environment whereby news is used as propaganda to keep the elite in power. In many ways, it echoes the work of Ben Bagdikian, whose theories on the effects of conglomeration were introduced in Chapter 1. According to Chomsky and Herman, the "propaganda model" limits diversity of opinion and thought in the news media, thereby "**manufacturing consent**" among media consumers by limiting debate on important social and political issues. It does so in the following ways:

- In these days of conglomeration, the members of the upper class of North America are also the primary owners of the North American mass media. More and more media are owned by fewer and fewer people. As a result, their point of view will be largely conservative. That, in turn, sets up a conservative agenda for news reporting.

- Most experts used by the media tend to be members of the elite themselves. According to Chomsky and Herman, this is because "government and corporate sources also have the great merit of being recognizable and credible by their status and prestige." This limits diversity of voices and opinion in the news media, which is not beneficial in a democracy.

Noam Chomsky ■ Believes the news media is an ideological apparatus for the elite in society.

Edward Herman ■ Wrote *Manufacturing Consent* with Noam Chomsky.

manufacturing consent A system limiting debate on political and social issues.

Antonio Gramsci ■ Italian theorist who expanded on Marxism to include ideas, not just economics.

hegemony ■ Coercion through consent.

Jürgen Habermas ■ German sociologist who believed that political ideas need to be debated.

public sphere ■ Where political ideas need to be debated.

Another variation of the effects of the news media comes from Italian cultural theory. **Antonio Gramsci** argued that the elite rule through a process called **hegemony**. Gramsci, a Marxist, maintained that class struggle isn't a conflict only based on economics; ideas are also involved. In 1995, Dominic Strinati offered this definition of hegemony: "Dominant groups in society, including fundamentally but not exclusively the ruling class, maintain their dominance by securing the 'spontaneous consent' of subordinate groups, including the working class, through the negotiated construction of a political and ideological consensus which incorporates both dominant and dominated groups." In other words, it isn't just that the ruling class dominates the lower classes, but the ruling class gets the lower classes to consent to be dominated. One of the ways that the elite influence the lower classes is through manipulation of the *ideas* communicated by the news media.

Another critique of the government's control of the news media comes from German sociologist **Jürgen Habermas**, who felt that true knowledge can be acquired only through the exchange of ideas. He argued that in the early days of mass media (the 1800s), people used to gather to read newspapers in coffee houses and discuss important political and social issues. He called this the **public sphere**. Only when issues are debated in public can anyone become truly informed. That doesn't happen anymore with the rise of mass media conglomerates. Media has now become a commodity—something to be bought and sold, rather than a tool for political information and debate. There is no more public sphere for real discourse.

There is a symbiotic relationship between the media and the government. It is through the news media that we learn about issues that face Canada and the world. The media are key in helping people sort through issues as part of the political process. Some argue that the media act as a watchdog on behalf of informed citizens in a democracy and help set the agenda for political debate. Others, like Chomsky, Gramsci and Habermas, see it as a tool for the ruling class to stay in power by controlling the messages about political matters.

■ Media Role in Governance

study<u>preview</u> **The news media are sometimes called the fourth estate or the fourth branch of government. These terms identify the independent role of the media in reporting on the government. The media act as a kind of watchdog on behalf of the citizens.**

FOURTH ESTATE

fourth estate ■ The press as a player in medieval power structures, in addition to the clerical, noble and common estates.

Edmund Burke ■ British member of Parliament who is sometimes credited with coining the term *fourth estate.*

Joseph Howe ■ Advocate of an "unshackled press."

Medieval English and French societies were highly structured into classes of people called *estates.* The first estate was the clergy. The second was the nobility. The third was the common people. After Gutenberg, the mass-produced written word began emerging as a player in the power structure, but it couldn't be pigeonholed as part of one or another of the three estates. In time the press came to be called the **fourth estate**. Where the term came from isn't clear, but **Edmund Burke**, a member of the British Parliament, used it in the mid-1700s. Pointing to the reporters' gallery, Burke said, "There sat a Fourth Estate more important by far than them all." The term remains for all journalistic activity today. The news media report on the other estates, ideally with roots in none and a commitment only to truth.

The role of the media as the "fourth estate" wasn't always the case. In the days after Confederation, newspapers in Canada were largely gazettes of business and government information. Some papers took political sides on issues, but they tended not to be too critical of the government of the day because of the consequences. Canadian media historian Wilfred Kesterton writes that "editors who refused to toe the official line risked prosecution, heavy fines, imprisonment, or worse—pro government thugs sometimes ransacked print shops and assaulted editors as authorities turned a blind eye."

That changed on New Year's Day, 1835, when **Joseph Howe** published "the letter" signed by "the people" in the *Novascotian*. In the letter, he accused the local police and the lieutenant-governor of corruption: "It is known that from the pockets of the poor and distressed, at least 1000 pounds are drawn yearly and pocketed by men whose services the country might very well spare." Howe was charged with seditious libel under the criminal code of the day for "wickedly, maliciously and seditiously desiring and intending to stir up and excite discontent among His Majesty's Subjects." During his six-hour defence, Howe invited the jurors to "leave an **unshackled press** as a legacy to your children." A jury acquitted him in only 10 minutes. The message to Canadian journalists was clear: Freedom of the press and intellectual freedom were important values in journalism. Canada's Fourth Estate was now an unshackled fourth estate that could not be controlled.

Media as Information Sources

study<u>preview</u> Most news media influence is through opinion leaders. Newspapers and magazines are especially important to these opinion leaders. For the public, television is the preferred source of national political news. For politically engaged people, talk radio and online media are also significant sources.

DIRECT VERSUS INDIRECT

Many people once saw a direct link between press reports and individual decision making. Today we know the linkage between the media and individuals generally is less direct. As discussed in Chapter 14, **Paul Lazarsfeld**'s pioneering studies on voter behaviour in 1940 and 1948 found most people rely on personal acquaintances for information about politics and governance. Lazarsfeld called this a **two-step flow** process, with **opinion leaders** relying heavily on the news media for information and ideas, and other people relying on the opinion leaders. In reality this is hardly a clinically neat process. The influence of opinion leaders varies significantly from issue to issue and even from day to day, and people who normally don't use the media much may do so at some points and then rely less on opinion leaders. As Lazarsfeld came to recognize the complexity of the process, he renamed it **multistep flow**.

In short, news coverage and media commentary have influence on the public, but usually it is through the intermediaries whom Lazarsfeld called opinion leaders. Lazarsfeld's observation is underscored every time network television reporters talk on-camera with political leaders and refer to the public in the third person as "they," as if *they* aren't even watching. Implicit in the third person is the reporters' and political leaders' understanding that their audience is made up more of opinion leaders than the body politic.

CITIZEN PREFERENCES

Which media do people use most for political news? Opinion leaders lean heavily on newspapers and magazines, which generally are more comprehensive and thorough than broadcast sources are. Not surprisingly, scholar Doris Graber found that better-educated people favour newspapers. Even so, there is no denying that television has supplanted newspapers as the primary source for national news for most people. For national coverage, the television networks present news attractively and concisely.

Media preference studies generally ask people to rank their preference, which can lead to a false conclusion that the second-ranked preference isn't relied on at all. While people may use television most, this hardly means that they don't read newspapers at all. The daily press in Canada turns out more than 5 million copies a day nationwide. The Canadian Newspaper Association says that half of all Canadian adults read a newspaper every day. Also, broadcast assignment editors look to newspapers and magazines, especially those with veteran political reporters and commentaries, for ideas on stories to pursue. It may be that TV and print are simply opposite sides of the same coin. As the University of Waterloo's Augie Fleras points out, "television and print represent alternative modes of persuasion. In theory, neither medium should be evaluated as superior, despit a common tendency to judge one by the standards of the other." In short, both can influence public opinion.

Media Effects on Governance

study<u>preview</u> Media coverage shapes what we think about as well as how to think about it. This means the media are a powerful linkage between the government and how people view their government. A negative aspect is the trend of the media to pander to transitory public interest in less substantive subjects, like scandals, gaffes and negative events.

AGENDA SETTING

A lot of people think the news media are powerful, affecting the course of events in godlike ways. It's true that the media are powerful, but scholars, going back to sociologist Paul Lazarsfeld in the 1940s and even Robert Park in the 1920s, have concluded that it's not in a direct tell-them-how-to-vote-and-they-will kind of way. Media scholars Maxwell McCombs and Donald Shaw cast media effects succinctly when they said the media don't tell people *what to think* but rather *what to think about*. This is a profound distinction. In covering a political campaign, explain McCombs and Shaw, the media choose which issues or topics to emphasize, thereby setting the campaign's agenda. "This ability to affect cognitive change among individuals," say McCombs and Shaw, "is one of the most important aspects of the power of mass communication." As discussed in Chapter 14 and 15, this has come to be called **agenda setting**.

agenda setting ■ Media tell people what to think about, not what to think.

Watergate Continuing coverage lends importance to an issue. A single story on a bribed senator might soon be forgotten, but day-after-day follow-ups can fuel ethics reforms. Conversely, if gatekeepers are diverted to other stories, a hot issue can cool overnight—out of sight, out of mind. Luckily, this did not happen in 1973. Had *The Washington Post* not doggedly followed up on a break-in at the Democratic Party's national headquarters in 1972, the public would never have learned that people around the Republican president, Richard Nixon, were behind it. *The Post* set the national agenda.

Monica Lewinsky People trust the news media to sort through the events of the day and make order of them. Lead stories on a newscast or those on Page 1 are expected to be the most significant. Not only does how a story is played affect people's agendas, but so do the time and space afforded it. For example, nobody would have spent much time pondering whether President Bill Clinton engaged in sexual indiscretions if David Brock, writing in *The American Spectator* in 1993, had not reported allegations by Paula Jones. Nor would the issue have reached a feverish level of public attention without Matt Drudge's 1997 report in his online *Drudge Report* about Monica Lewinsky. Lavish graphics can propel an item even higher.

Child Pornography Only if individuals are aware of an issue can they be concerned about it. Concern about the effects of child pornography became a major issue with media coverage of the Holly Jones case in Toronto. In 2004, Michael Briere pleaded guilty to the abduction, rape and murder of the 10-year-old girl. He blamed his addiction to child pornography as the reason he abducted and raped Jones. As a result, the issue of child pornography became a federal election issue. Shortly after Briere's conviction, police began to crack down on child porn.

CNN EFFECT

Television is especially potent as an agenda setter. For years, nobody outside Ethiopia cared much about a devastating famine. Not even after four articles in *The New York Times* was there much response. *The Washington Post* ran three articles, and the Associated Press distributed 228 stories—still hardly any response. The next year, however, disturbing videos aired by the CBC's Brian Stewart captured public attention and triggered a massive relief effort. In recent years many scholars looking at the agenda-setting effect of television vis-à-vis other media have focused on CNN, whose extensive coverage lends

A Failure of Government CNN deployed hundreds of staff to the Gulf Coast when Hurricane Katrina struck, documenting not only the disaster but the failure of the federal government to respond adequately. The coverage, including anchor Soledad O'Brien on the scene, kept the failure on the public agenda and forced President Bush to adjust his initially rosy claims about the federal response.

itself to study. As a result, the power of television to put faraway issues in the minds of domestic audiences has been labeled the **CNN Effect.**

FRAMING

Related to agenda setting and the CNN Effect is a process called **framing**, in which media coverage shapes how people see issues. Because the Pentagon allowed news reporters to accompany combat units in the Iraq War of 2003, there was concern that the war coverage might be decontextualized (see also Chapter 8 under War Zones: Combat Reporting). Critics foresaw coverage focusing on tactical encounters of the combat units, missing larger, strategic stories. In other words, highly dramatic and photogenic stories from combat units might frame the telling of the war story in terms of the minutiae of the conflict. Too, Pentagon war planners were aware that reporters living with combat units would, not unnaturally, see the story from the soldiers' perspective. The Pentagon, in fact, had carefully studied the 1982 war between Britain and Argentina, in which embedded British journalists were entirely reliant on the military not only for access to the battle zone but even for such basics as food. The resulting camaraderie gave a not-unnatural favourable twist to coverage. As it turned out, scholars who analyzed the coverage concluded that the framing from combat zones was largely, though not wholly, as the Pentagon had intended. The tone was favourable to the military and individual combat units. However, the reports from embedded reporters were packaged in larger-perspective accounts that also included material from war protesters, mostly in Europe, and the fractured diplomatic front.

From a Canadian perspective, framing is a common activity in politics. For years, Stephen Harper was framed by his opposition and the media as having a "hidden right wing agenda." In the 2006 Federal Election campaign, Conservative Party advertising hammered at inconsistencies in the comments of then Prime Minister Paul Martin. The goal was to frame Martin in the public mind as wavering. It seemed to work, as the label "Mr. Dithers" was soon applied to Martin—and it stuck.

Partisan framing is the easiest to spot. But news, though usually cast in a dispassionate tone, is also subject to framing. Framing cannot be avoided. Not everything about an event or issue can be compacted into a 30-second television story item or even a 3000-word magazine article. Reporters must choose what to include and what not to. Whatever a reporter's choices, the result is a framing of how the audience will see the reality.

PRIMING

Media coverage not only creates public awareness but can also trigger dramatic shifts in opinion. An example was the fate of the elder George Bush. In 1991 his approval ratings were at record highs. In 1992 the people thumped him out of office. What had happened? During the Persian Gulf War in 1991, the media put almost everything else on the back burner

CNN Effect ■ The ability of television, through emotion-raising video, to elevate distant issues on the domestic public agenda.

framing ■ Selecting aspects of a perceived reality for emphasis in a mass media message, thereby shaping how the audience sees the reality.

media ONLINE

CNN See the CNN Effect for yourself.
www.cnn.com

Brian Stewart Read about how this CBC reporter brought the issues of Ethiopia to the world.
www.cbc.ca/news/background/ethiopia/covering_famine.html

Bob Woodward

Reporters identify their sources in their stories to add credibility. Through "sourcing," as it's called, the news audience knows from whence information comes. Sourcing enables people to use their own judgment in assessing accuracy and significance. Sourcing is a fundamental taught in every journalism school. It is a vehicle that helps reporters keep a detached, neutral posture in their stories—except, ironically, for the nation's most respected reporter, Bob Woodward.

Woodward's 2003 *Bush at War,* written before the U.S. invasion of Iraq, followed an almost perennial string of Woodward books with significant revelations on government policymaking. As in earlier books, Woodward used a fly-on-the-wall perspective to tell his story. He detailed who said what at high-level meetings as if he had been there. He cited critical exchanges from chance encounters in hallways. He had quotations from internal memos.

His technique is to reconstruct what happened through countless interviews, picking up details secondhand and then testing them for accuracy with additional knowledgeable sources until he's satisfied he has it right. People open up to Woodward, confident that his sole agenda is seeking truth for the sake of telling truth and knowing that they can share information confidentially. He doesn't name off-the-record sources.

Woodward's reputation, and the technique too, goes back to his work in the early 1970s with fellow *Washington Post* reporter Carl Bernstein. They broke the Watergate scandal. Through relentless pursuit of information, undeterred even by a death threat, Woodward and Bernstein pieced together skullduggery in high places and eventually implicated President Richard Nixon, who resigned. Woodward and Bernstein had sources who would talk only if promised confidentiality. By not naming confidential sources but checking and rechecking information for accuracy, Woodward and Bernstein kept readers updated, expanding almost daily an understanding of what had happened in the Nixon White House. With every story more sources opened up to them, many confidentially.

Readers understood why Woodward and Bernstein broke the journalistic conventions of sourcing. Although Nixon supporters tried to discredit the stories, suggesting even that Woodward and Bernstein were concocting information, reader confidence in their accuracy grew with every revelation. Woodward carried that mantle of airtight accuracy into his later books. *The Brethren,* a 1979 work on the U.S. Supreme Court, coauthored with Scott Armstrong, took readers inside sealed conferences with telling insights into how the Court's opinions come to be. *The Commanders,* written after the first Gulf War, detailed strategic and tactical decision making in unmatched depth.

Bob Woodward

Confidential Sources Bob Woodward has followed through on his Watergate reporting of the early 1970s with breakthrough books about government decision making. To encourage insiders to talk, Woodward sometimes agrees not to divulge their names.

Although now an assistant managing editor at *The Washington Post,* Woodward cannot escape his reporting instincts. Knowing his reputation, sources come to him with stories. Many tips he passes on to *Post* reporters, but some he goes after himself. In the famously tight-lipped George W. Bush administration, Woodward had more access to the corridors of the White House than any regular White House reporter. When he called to ask for an interview, more often than not he got it. The reporters covering the White House daily were confined mostly to a press room suite. Even they found news in *Bush at War.*

to cover the war. The president's role in the coverage was as commander-in-chief. Primed by the coverage, the public gave Bush exceptionally favourable ratings. When the war ended, media coverage shifted to the economy, which was ailing, and the president was hardly portrayed heroically. His ratings plummeted, and in 1992 he lost a re-election bid.

In 1991 the media coverage created an environment that primed the public to see the president positively, and in 1992 the environment changed. It was a classic example of **priming**, the process in which the media affect the standard that people use to evaluate political figures and issues. This is hardly to say that the media manipulate the environments in which people see political figures and issues. No one, for example, would argue that the Persian Gulf War should not have been covered. However, the fact is that it was through the media that people were aware of the war and concluded the president was doing a great job.

MEDIA OBSESSIONS

Although critics argue that the media are politically biased, studies don't support this. Reporters perceive themselves as middle-of-the-road politically, and by and large they work to suppress personal biases. Even so, reporters gravitate toward certain kinds of stories to the neglect of others, and this flavours coverage.

Politics News reporters and editors have long recognized that people like stories about people, so any time an issue can be personified, so much the better. In Washington coverage this has meant focusing on the president as a vehicle for treating issues. A study of the *CBS Evening News* found that 60 percent of the opening stories featured the president. Even in nonelection years the media have a near-myopic fix on the White House. This displaces coverage of other important government institutions, like Congress, the courts, and state and local government.

Conflict Journalists learn two things about conflict early in their careers. First, their audiences like conflict. Second, conflict often illustrates the great issues by which society is defining and redefining its values. Take, for example, the ongoing debates on capital punishment, abortion or same-sex marriages. People get excited about these issues because of the fundamental values involved. This also makes them the subject of political discussion through the Canadian media.

Part of journalists' predilection for conflict is that conflict involves change—whether to do something differently. All news involves change, and conflict almost always is a signal to the kind of change that's most worth reporting. Conflict is generally a useful indicator of newsworthiness.

Scandals Journalists know too that their audiences like scandal stories—a fact that trivializes political coverage. Talking about coverage of Bill Clinton early in his presidency, political scientists Morris Fiorina and Paul Peterson said: "The public was bombarded with stories about Whitewater, Vince Foster's suicide, $200 haircuts, parties with Sharon Stone, the White House travel office, Hillary Clinton's investments, and numerous other matters that readers will not remember. The reason you do not remember is that, however important these matters were to the individuals involved, they were not important for the overall operation of government. Hence, they have been forgotten."

Canadian politics has also had its share of political scandals that were driven by media coverage. "Shawinigate" referred to the discovery that then Prime Minister Jean Chrétien might have used his influence not only as the MP for the riding of Shawinigan, but also as prime minister, to help the owners of the hotel Auberge Grand-Mere get a loan from the federal Business Development Bank. Although the federal ethics commissioner found no evidence of wrongdoing, the story was front-page news for many months. Then in 1999 came the federal sponsorship scandal that became known as "AdScam" or "Sponsorgate." Many politicians and bureaucrats were implicated in the scandal. Between the years of 1996 and 2004, the federal government spent money on advertising campaigns to help promote Canadian unity in Quebec. In 2004, federal auditor Sheila Fraser found that much of the money was misspent and unaccounted for. This led to the Gomery Commission in 2004.

Horse Races In reporting political campaigns, the news media obsess on reporting the polls. Critics say this treating of campaigns as **horse races** results in substantive issues being underplayed. Even when issues are the focus, as when a candidate announces a major policy position, reporters connect the issue to its potential impact in the polls.

priming ■ Process in which the media affect the standard that people use to evaluate political figures and issues.

horse race ■ An election campaign treated by reporters like a game—who's ahead, who's falling back, who's coming up the rail.

Brevity People who design media packages, such as a newspaper or newscast, have devised presentation formats that favour shorter stories. This trend has been driven in part by broadcasting's severe time constraints. Network anchors have complained for years that they have to condense the world's news into 45 minutes in their evening newscasts. The result: short, often superficial treatments. The short-story format shifted to many newspapers and magazines, beginning with the launch of *USA Today* in 1982. *USA Today* obtained extremely high story counts, covering a great many events by running short stories—many only a half-dozen sentences. The effect on political coverage has been profound.

The **sound bites** in campaign stories, the actual voice of a candidate in a broadcast news story, dropped from 47 seconds in 1968 to 10 seconds in 1988 and have remained short. Issues that require lengthy explorations, say critics, get passed up. Candidates, eager for airtime, have learned to offer quippy, catchy, clever capsules that are likely to be picked up rather than articulating thoughtful persuasive statements.

Some people defend brevity, saying it's the only way to reach people whose increasingly busy lives don't leave them much time to track politics and government. In one generalization, brevity's defenders note that the short attention span of the MTV generation can't handle much more than 10-second sound bites. Sanford Ungar, previously the communication dean at American University and now the president of Goucher College in Baltimore, Maryland, applauds the news media for devising writing and reporting styles that boil down complex issues so they can be readily understood by great masses of people. Says Ungar: "If *USA Today* encourages people not to think deeply, or not to go into more detail about what's happening, then it will be a disservice. But if *USA Today* teaches people how to be concise and get the main points across sometimes, they're doing nothing worse than what television is doing, and doing it at least as well."

■ Government Manipulation of Media

study<u>preview</u> **Many political leaders are preoccupied with media coverage because they know the power it can have. Over the years they have developed mechanisms to influence coverage to their advantage.**

INFLUENCING COVERAGE

Many political leaders stay up nights figuring out ways to influence media coverage. James Fallows, in his book *Breaking the News,* quoted a Clinton White House official as saying, "When I was there, absolutely nothing was more important than figuring out what the news was going to be. . . . There is no such thing as a substantive discussion that is not shaped or dominated by how it is going to play in the press."

The game of trying to outsmart the news media to help those in power set the agenda is nothing new. Theodore Roosevelt, at the turn of the 20th century, chose Sundays to issue many announcements. Roosevelt recognized that editors producing Monday newspapers usually had a dearth of news because weekends, with government and business shut down, didn't generate much worth telling. Roosevelt's Sunday announcements, therefore, received more prominent play in Monday editions. With typical bullishness, Roosevelt claimed that he had "discovered Mondays." Compared to how sophisticated government leaders have become at manipulating press coverage today, Roosevelt was simple, but effective.

Even Canada's first prime minister, Sir John A. Macdonald, was known to influence the media. In the book *Scrum Wars,* Allan Levine tells the story of a certain Lord Dufferin who was a speaker at McGill's Convocation in 1873. The speech was entirely in Greek. Despite the fact that none of the journalists in attendance understood Greek, the news media reported that Lord Dufferin's speech was "the purest ancient Greek without mispronouncing a word." When asked how the media knew that the speech was perfect, Macdonald replied that *he* had told them. While it was true that Macdonald didn't speak a word of Greek, he did know a little bit about politics.

Government influence on news media has also been the case in recent Canadian politics. For example, in 1997, during a demonstration at the APEC (Asia-Pacific Economic Cooperation) Summit held in Vancouver, the RCMP used pepper spray on protestors, even though it appeared to be a simple, peaceful protest. The media began to question if the Prime Minister's office was involved in the decision to use force. The CBC's Terry Milewski had arranged an interview with one of the protestors. In an email between the two, Milewski used the term "forces of darkness" to describe the government. Ottawa, looking to divert attention away from the incident itself, began to focus attention on Milewski. Pressure from the government resulted in Milewski being removed from the story. They had succeeded in turning attention away from questions about the Prime Minister's involvement with the RCMP to one of "biased" journalism.

SCRUMS

Scrums have been a staple of Canadian politics since the 1950s. Reporters, microphones and TV cameras surround politicians in the hallway outside of the House of Commons to ask questions about the issues raised during Question Period. Shortly after taking power in 2006, Stephen Harper introduced a new way of dealing with the news media. Instead of holding scrums on a regular basis, Harper's government tried to control the message as much as possible. Shanda Deziel, columnist for *Maclean's,* writes that "not in 30 years have the photographers had so little to work with. Trudeau, Mulroney, Chrétien and Martin all mugged in some way, but not Harper." The Prime Minister's office also wanted journalists to sign an "attendance sheet" in order to be able to ask questions during media conferences. Journalists balked at the idea; some even boycotted Harper's next few media conferences in protest.

> **scrum** ■ Members of the Parliamentary Press Gallery meet with politicians after Question Period.

TRIAL BALLOONS AND LEAKS

To check weather conditions, meteorologists send up balloons. To get an advance peek at public reaction, political leaders also float **trial balloons**. Nick Russell, in *Morals and the Media,* writes that during the 1960s, Prime Minister Diefenbaker would often have tea with Peter Dempson, the Ottawa Bureau Chief for the now defunct *Toronto Telegram*. At those meetings, the prime minister would "offer snippets of information, provided they were not directly attributed to him. If public reaction was adverse, Diefenbaker would simply dismiss it as press speculation."

> **trial balloon** ■ A deliberate leak of a potential policy, usually from a diversionary source, to test public response.

Trial balloons are not the only way in which the media can be used. Partisans and dissidents use **leaks** to bring attention to their opponents and people they don't much like. In leaking, someone passes information to reporters on the condition that he or she not be identified as the source. While reporters are leery of many leakers, some information is so significant and from such reliable sources that it's hard to pass up.

> **leak** ■ A deliberate disclosure of confidential or classified information by someone who wants to advance the public interest, embarrass a bureaucratic rival or supervisor, or disclose incompetence or skullduggery.

It's essential that reporters understand how their sources intend information to be used. It is also important for sources to have some control over what they tell reporters. Even so, reporter–source relationships lend themselves to abuse by manipulative government officials. Worse, the structures of these relationships allow officials to throttle what's told to the people. As political scientists Karen O'Connor and Larry Sabato said: "Every public official knows that journalists are pledged to protect the confidentiality of sources, and therefore the rules can be used to an official's own benefit—like, say, giving reporters derogatory information to print about a source without having to be identified with the source." In his work *The Newsmakers,* University of Calgary political science professor and media commentator David Taras refers to this practice as a "backchannel game, a tango between politicians and officials and reporters" that is likely inescapable. This game has been in play for many years. Paul Wells, writing in *Maclean's,* says that "Trudeau's cabinet leaked so badly the *Ottawa Citizen* ran a cartoon showing a reporter with a fake moustache sitting at the cabinet table." This manipulation is a regrettable, though unavoidable, part of the news-gathering process.

STONEWALLING

When Richard Nixon was under fire for ordering a cover-up of the Watergate break-in, he went months without a news conference. His aides plotted his movements to avoid even informal, shouted questions from reporters. He hunkered down in the White House in a classic example of **stonewalling**. Experts in the branch of public relations called political communications generally advise against stonewalling because people infer guilt or something to hide. Nonetheless, it is one way to deal with difficult media questions.

A variation on stonewalling is the **news blackout**. When U.S. troops invaded Grenada, the Pentagon barred the press. Reporters who hired runabout boats to get to the island were intercepted by a U.S. naval blockade. While heavy-handed, such limitations on media coverage do, for a limited time, give the government the opportunity to report what's happening from its self-serving perspective.

▛▖ Media–Government Issues

study<u>preview</u> Media coverage of politics raises many issues: How good a job is the media doing? What lessons can be learned from history? Does political advertising pander to emotional and superficial instincts?

CAMPAIGN ADVERTISING

Can candidates buy their way into office with advertising? While a candidate who vastly outspends another would seem to have an advantage, well-heeled campaigns can fail. For example, in presidential campaigns, no correlation has been established between winning and media spending. **Herbert Alexander**, a University of Southern California political scientist who tracks campaign spending, noted that George Bush outspent Bill Clinton $43 million to $32 million in 1992 and lost. Ross Perot also outspent Clinton, buying almost $40 million in media time and space. In 1988, however, Bush outspent Michael Dukakis $32 million to $24 million and won. The data point to campaign advertising as being only one of many variables in elections.

The fact remains, however, that a political campaign has a cost of admission. Candidates need media exposure, and a campaign without advertising would almost certainly be doomed.

It would be a mistake to conclude that political advertising has no effect. A major 1976 study by **Thomas Patterson and Robert McClure** concluded that 7 percent of the people in a 2700-person sample were influenced by ads on whether to vote for Richard Nixon or George McGovern for president. While that was a small percentage, many campaigns are decided by even slimmer margins. The lesson from the Patterson-McClure study is that political advertising can make a critical difference.

In Canada, broadcast election advertising is governed by the CRTC. According to the Commission, broadcasters "shall allocate time for the broadcasting of programs, advertisements or announcements of a partisan political character on an equitable basis to all accredited political parties and rival candidates represented in the election or referendum." On the surface, this would seem to be a fair practice. However, "equitable"doesn't mean "equal": but, generally, all candidates and parties are entitled to some coverage that will give them the opportunity to expose their ideas to the public.

CAMPAIGN COVERAGE

News coverage of the 1988 Bush–Dukakis presidential campaigns disappointed even media people. A forum of correspondents gave the coverage a C-minus report card. Lessons learned, postmortems were better for the 1992 and 1996 campaigns. Initial analysis of the 2000 coverage was favourable, in spite of the election night gaffe when the television networks called Florida prematurely for Al Gore and then for George W. Bush, contributing to the ensuing confusion over who was the actual winner. Even *The Globe and Mail* had to retract its November 8, 2000, headline that read "Bush Wins a Squeaker," when it appeared the irregularities in Florida still gave Al Gore a chance at winning. These are some of the lessons learned during that U.S. election:

- **Issues.** Reporters need to push for details on positions and ask tough questions on major issues, not accepting generalities. They need to bounce one candidate's position off other candidates, creating a forum of intelligent discussion from which voters can make informed choices.
- **Agenda.** Reporters need to assume some role in setting a campaign agenda. When reporters allow candidates to control the agenda of coverage, they become mere conduits for self-serving news releases and images from candidates. **Pseudo-events** with candidates, like visits to photogenic flag factories, lack substance. So do staged **photo ops**. Reporters need to guard against letting such easy-to-cover events squeeze out substantive coverage.
- **Interpretation.** Campaigns are drawn out and complicated, and reporters need to keep trying to pull together what's happened for the audience. Day-to-day spot news isn't enough. There also need to be explanations, interpretations and analyses to help voters see the big picture.
- **Inside coverage.** Reporters need to cover the machinery of the campaigns—who's running things and how. This is especially important with the growing role of campaign consultants. Who are these people? What history do they bring to a campaign? What agenda?
- **Polling.** Poll results are easy to report but tricky and inconsistent because of variations in methodology and even questions. News operations should report on competing polls, not just on their own. In tracking polls, asking the same questions over time for consistency is essential.
- **Instant feedback.** Television newsrooms have supplemented their coverage and commentary with email instant feedback from viewers. Select messages are flashed onscreen within minutes. In some programs a reporter is assigned to analyze incoming messages and identify trends. While all this makes for "good television," the comments are statistically dubious as indicators of overall public opinion. Too much can be read into them.
- **Depth.** With candidates going directly to voters in debates and talk-show appearances, reporters need to offer something more than what voters can see and hear for themselves. Analysis and depth add a fresh dimension that is not redundant to what the audience already knows.

LESSONS FROM RECENT CAMPAIGNS

Just as historians see the first television political commercials in 1952 swaying the election for Dwight Eisenhower, so may the campaign documentary of 2004 be seen as a new essential in political campaigns.

Campaign Movies Propagandist movie documentaries emerged as a potential campaign tool with **Michael Moore**'s Bush-bashing *Fahrenheit 9/11* in 2004. With slanted juxtapositioning of news and interview clips and scripting that frequently implied more than was said, *Fahrenheit* hit like a bombshell early in the campaign. The film opened on 900 screens five months before the election and grossed $23.9 million the first weekend, a record for a documentary. It played the movie-house circuit for weeks. One month ahead of the election, *Fahrenheit* was issued on DVD. The questions Moore framed dogged Bush the rest of the campaign.

Bloggers Political junkies created dozens of websites in 2004, many offering news, often slanted, but mostly commentary. Importantly, the sites had links to like-minded sites. These sites, called blogs as a shortened form of "web logs" because they are a kind of a personal journal or log, grew in importance as sources of information and ideas. The blogs, maintained by individuals, not media organizations, represented a kind of democratization in news coverage outside the structure of established news organizations. Although mostly amateurish, often one-person sideline operations, blogs scooped the major news media on occasion and led the way on some coverage.

Attack Ads The 2004 presidential campaign spawned **negative ads** and **attack ads** in unprecedented quantity. With little regard for facts or truth, Republicans loosely connected to the Bush campaign, under the banner of Swift Boat Veterans for Truth,

pseudo-event ■ A staged event to attract media attention, usually lacking substance.

photo op ■ Short for "photo opportunity." A staged event, usually photogenic, to attract media attention.

Michael Moore ■ Documentary producer whose *Fahrenheit 9/11* demonstrated the genre's potential in political campaigns.

Fahrenheit 9/11 ■ 2004 propagandist documentary that helped shape issues in 2004 presidential campaign.

negative ads ■ Political campaign advertising, usually on television, in which a candidate criticizes the opponent rather than emphasizes his or her platform.

attack ads ■ A subspecies of negative ads, especially savage in criticizing an opponent, many playing loose with context and facts.

ripped at the war-hero record of Democratic candidate John Kerry. Then there was the entry in a campaign advertising contest that likened George W. Bush to Hitler, which an anti-Bush group, Moveon.org, let sit on its website for days. Even the Stephen Harper Conservatives wasted little time in launching a series of negative ads aimed at Liberal leader Stéphane Dion that framed him as wishy-washy.

POLITICAL COVERAGE

How good a job is our news media doing as a watchdog or "fourth estate" that keeps tabs on our politicians? News coverage of politics has been the subject of disappointment among many, even media people. Canadian Anne McGrath claims that "the public sees media portrayals of government on television that reinforce the impression that politicians are negative, self-interested and arrogant." Her colleague at the University of Calgary, David Taras, writes that the news is "dominated by blood and gore crime stories, celebrity news, sports hype and the latest tidbits from the world of entertainment, while reports about political and social policies rarely grab the spotlight unless they feature high-octane confrontation or pathetic victims."

CHAPTER 17 Wrap-Up

No one denies that the news media are influential in governance and politics, but the influence generally is indirect through media-savvy opinion leaders. Even so, the media are powerful players in public life because they shape the public's agenda by reporting some issues and ignoring or downplaying others. The media also frame issues and prime how people see the issues. This is critical for media literacy.

Questions for Review

1. What does the term *fourth estate* mean?
2. How do the news media influence people on political issues?
3. How do media agenda-setting and priming work?
4. How do government leaders manipulate media coverage?
5. How good are the news media as a watchdog?
6. What do the ideas of Chomsky, Gramsci and Habermas have in common?

Questions for Critical Thinking

1. Who are opinion leaders in your life? How do they influence your views?
2. What personal values would influence you as a news reporter who sets public agendas and frames issues and primes how people see them?
3. What perils face a reporter who accepts information off the record from one source and later receives the same information on deep background from another source?

4. How can coverage of political campaigns be improved?
5. Can you think of instances where the news media might have manufactured *your* consent? How?

Deepening Your media LITERACY

Is the internet changing the government–media landscape?

STEP 1 Think about how a lack of electricity in Iraq might be reported by a U.S. television network, a Canadian newspaper and an Iraqi blogger.

Dig Deeper

STEP 2 If you were the press secretary for the president of the United States, how would you try to shape the media coverage of the issue of lack of electrical power in Iraq? Write a list of your ideas. Would your methods change for each kind of media? Would you try anything special for the blogger? What if the blogger were an American soldier stationed in Iraq?

What Do You Think?

STEP 3   Answer these questions:

1. How can the internet serve as a media watchdog?
2. How can you evaluate the credibility of internet blogs or political sites?
3. Can a blogger be an opinion leader? Or is an opinion leader someone who reads the blogs?
4. Who is setting the agenda: the blogger, the reader or the subject of the blog?

Keeping Up to Date

Professional journals that carry articles on media coverage of political issues and governance include *Columbia Journalism Review, Quill* and *American Journalism Review.*

Ongoing discussion on media responsibility also appears in the *Journal of Mass Media Ethics.*

For Further Learning

Eric Alterman. *When Presidents Lie: A History of Official Deception and Its Consequences* (Viking, 2004).

Ken Auletta. "Vox Fox." *New Yorker* (May 26, 2003): 58–73.

David Brock. *The Republican Noise Machine: Right-Wing Media and How It Corrupts Democracy* (Crown, 2004).

Noam Chomsky and Edward Herman. *Manufacturing Consent: The Political Economy of the Mass Media* (Pantheon, 1988).

Craig Crawford. *Attack the Messenger: How Politicians Turn You Against the Messenger* (Littlefield, 2005).

David Dadge. *Casualty of War: The Bush Administration's Assault on a Free Press* (Prometheus, 2004).

Claes H. de Vreese. "The Effects of Frames in Political Television News on Issue Interpretations and Frame Salience." *Journalism and Mass Communication Quarterly* (Spring 2004): 36–52.

Shanda Deziel. "Parliament Hill and the Press Gallery: One Big Unhappy Family." *Maclean's* (June 6, 2006).

James Fallows. *Breaking the News: How the Media Undermine American Democracy* (Vintage Books, 1997).

Augie Fleras. *Mass Communication in Canada* (Thomson Nelson, 2003).

Jürgen Habermas. *An Inquiry into a Category of Bourgeois Society* (MIT Press, 1991).

Dean Jobb. *Media Law for Canadian Journalists* (Emond Montgomery, 2006).

Allan Levine. *Scrum Wars: The Prime Ministers and the Media* (Dundurn Press, 1993).

Anne McGrath. "Media and Politics." In *Mediascapes* (Thomson Nelson, 2002).

Elizabeth M. Perse. *Media Effects and Society* (Erlbaum, 2001).

Michael Pfau, Michel Haigh, Mitchell Gettle, Michael Donnelly, Gregory Scott, Dana Warr and Elaine Wittenberg. "Embedding Journalists in Military Combat Units: Impact on Newspaper Story Frames and Tone." *Journalism and Mass Communication Quarterly* (Spring 2004): 74–88.

Stephen D. Reese, Oscar H. Grady Jr. and August E. Grant, editors. *Framing Public Life: Perspectives on Media and Our Understanding of the Social World* (Erlbaum, 2001).

Nick Russell. *Morals and the Media* (UBC Press, 2006).

Danny Schecter. *Embedded: Weapons of Mass Deception: How the Media Failed to Cover the War on Iraq* (Prometheus, 2003).

David Taras. *The Newsmakers: The Media's Influence on Canadian Politics* (Nelson Canada, 1990).

Mary Vipond. *The Mass Media in Canada* (James Lorimer and Company, 2000).

Stephen J. Wayne. *The Road to the White House, 2000* (Palgrave, 2001).

Paul Wells. "Without Enemies, Harper is Looking for Trouble." *Maclean's* (July 20, 2006).

Glossary

1-900 telephone numbers Used for phone-in surveys; respondents select themselves to participate and they pay for the call.

15 minutes CRTC limit on TV advertising per hour

384 Number of people in a properly selected sample for results to provide 95 percent confidence that results have less than 5 percent margin of error.

500-channel universe Fanciful term for the growth in media channels available in recent years.

60 percent Canadian content Level of Canadian content required by the CRTC.

A&R (artist and repertoire) Units of recording company responsible for talent.

ABC American Broadcasting Company. Built from ABC radio network. One of the Big Three over-the-air networks.

accepted practices What media do as a matter of routine, sometimes without considering ethics implications.

account executives Agency reps to clients.

acoustic recording Vibration-sensitive recording technology.

ad clutter So many competing ads that all lose impact.

adversarial public relations Attacking critics openly.

advertisements Messages intended to persuade people to buy.

advertising Unlike public relations, advertising seeks to sell a product or service.

advertising director Coordinates marketing and advertising.

advertorials Paid advertisements that state an editorial position.

Agence France-Presse Paris-based global news agency.

agenda setting Media tell people what to think about, not what to think.

aggressive stimulation Theory that people are inspired to violence from media depictions.

AGVOT Action Group on Violence on Television; helped develop programming codes for Canadian television.

Aird Commission First royal commission into Canadian broadcasting.

Alan Cross New music historian.

Albert Bandura Found media violence stimulated aggression in children.

Alien and Sedition Acts Discouraged criticism of government.

alienation Dissatisfaction with individual and cultural deviations from basic nature.

all-news radio A niche format that delivers only news and related informational content and commentary.

Allen DuMont Operated early fourth network.

Alliance Atlantis Canadian movie distributor.

alternative media Emerging, narrowly focused advertising vehicles.

alternative press Generally antiestablishment publication for a young alienated audience.

ambivalent media relations Mix of proactive, reactive and inactive media contacts.

American Research Institute Conducts movie prototype research.

amplification Spreading a message.

amplitude modulation AM

analog Broadcast transmission that uses a continuous, pulsing signal.

André Bazin French film critic who devised the term *auteur* for significant cutting-edge filmmakers.

Andrew Crisell Uses the ideas of semiotician Roland Barthes to analyze how radio meaning is created.

Andrew Hamilton Urged truth as defence for libel.

Ansel Nash Kellogg Founded the first syndicate.

Anson McKim Founded the first ad agency in Canada.

Antonio Gramsci Italian theorist who expanded on Marxism to include ideas, not just economics.

applied research Usefulness, usually economic, is apparent.

APR Indicates CPRS accreditation.

Arbitron International media and marketing research company.

Aristotle Advocate of the golden mean; defended portrayals of violence.

ARPANET Military network that preceded internet.

ASC Advertising Standards Canada, the self-regulatory body for advertising.

ASCAP Music licensing organization.

Associated Press U.S.-based global news service; largest news-gathering organization in the world.

Associated Press (AP) Co-op for gathering and distributing news.

Atom Egoyan Directs movies about personal uncertainty.

attack ads A subspecies of negative ads, especially savage in criticizing an opponent, many playing loose with context and facts.

audion tube Made voice transmission possible.

Audit Bureau of Circulations Checks newspaper circulation claims.

auteur A filmmaker recognized for significant and original treatments.

authentic performance Live with on-site audience.

autistic perception Synonym for selective perception.

bandwidth Space available in a medium, such as cable or the electromagnetic spectrum, to carry messages.

barrages Intensive repetition of ads.

Barry Diller Television entrepreneur who sees the mass media's financial future shifting to direct sales of products. He created early successful Fox programming.

basic communication model Shows sender, encoding, transmission, decoding, receiver.

BBM Nielsen Media Research Surveys TV and radio in Canada.

BDU Broadcast distribution undertakings. Technical name for cable companies and satellite providers.

Ben Bagdikian Critic of media consolidation.

Benjamin Day His penny newspaper, *The New York Sun,* brought advertising to a new level.

Benjamin Harris Published *Publick Occurrences.*

bias in communication Theory that media can have a bias for time and space.

Big Three ABC, CBS, NBC.

bipolar model Portrays extremes as opposites, such as libertarian and authoritarian political systems.

black music Folk genre from American black slave experience.

black weeks Periods when ratings are not conducted.

blog An amateur website, generally personal in nature, often focused on a narrow subject, such as politics. Short for "web log."

BMI Music licensing organization.

Board of Broadcast Governors (BBG) Forefather of the current CRTC.

Bob Woodward Bernstein's colleague in the Watergate revelations.

Bobo doll studies Kids seemed more violent after seeing violence in movies.

Bollywood Nickname for India movie industry.

books One-time, bound publications of enduring value on a single topic.

box office Fanciful term for revenue that a movie earns in exhibition.

brand A nongeneric product name designed to set the product apart from the competition.

brand image Spin put on a brand name.

brand manager Coordinates marketing and advertising for a specific brand.

breaking news Reports, often live, on events as they are occurring.

Brian Green Canadian journalism professor who defines news as "the significant, the unusual, that which affects us."

British Invasion Popularity in North America of the Beatles and other British acts.

Broadcasting Act Governs the CRTC and all broadcasters in Canada.

broadsheet A newspaper format with full-size pages; typically six columns wide and 22 or 24 inches long.

bunching Short-term ad campaign.

Butler ruling Supreme Court ruling that defined legal differences between obscenity and pornography.

C.S. Pierce Classified signs into different categories.

CAB Canadian Association of Broadcasters.

Canada Magazine Fund (CMF) Support for Canadian magazines through the Department of Canadian Heritage.

Canadian Broadcasting Corporation (CBC) Canada's national public television network. Began broadcasting in 1952.

Canadian Charter of Rights and Freedoms Basis for all laws, including media laws, in Canada.

Canadian Public Relations Society Professional public relations association.

Canadian Radio Broadcasting Act First statute governing broadcasting in Canada.

Canadian Recording Industry Association (CRIA) Canadian trade association of music recording companies.

Cancon Short form for Canadian content.

Canons of Journalism of the American Society of Newspaper Editors First media code, 1923.

CapCities Communications Owner of ABC before it was purchased by Disney.

Carl Bernstein *Washington Post* reporter who dug up Watergate.

catalytic theory Media violence is among factors that sometimes contribute to real-life violence.

categorical imperative Follow principles as if they had universal application.

cathartic effect People release violent inclinations by seeing them portrayed.

CATV Short for community antenna television. An early name for cable systems.

caveat emptor Buyer beware.

caveat venditor Seller beware.

CBFT First Canadian TV channel.

CBLT Second Canadian TV channel.

CBS Columbia Broadcasting System. Built from CBS radio network under William Paley. One of the Big Three over-the-air networks.

CBSC Canadian Broadcast Standards Council; self-regulatory body for Canadian radio and television broadcasters.

CD Short for "compact disc."

change model Shows the effect of mass media on numerous social variables and the effect of those variables on the media.

channel noise Interference during transmission.

Charles Darwin Devised survival-of-the-fittest theory.

chemical medium Underlying technology for movies is photographic chemistry.

Cherry Sisters Complainants in a case that barred performers from suing critics.

Chet Huntley and David Brinkley Headed first 30-minute network newscast.

CHFI Canada's first FM radio station.

cinéma vérité Truth or realism in movies. The basis for the documentary tradition.

Cineplex Entertainment LP Canada's largest theatre chain.

circulation Number of copies of a publication that circulate. Number of readers of a publication.

Classification and Rating Administration Board Rates movies on G, PG, PG-13, R, NC-17 scale.

Claude Shannon Devised a basic communication model, with Warren Weaver.

clickthrough A registered visit to an advertising site from a gateway elsewhere on the internet.

clickthrough fee A charge to advertisers when an online link to their ads is activated; also a fee paid to websites that host the links.

Clio Award Award for advertising creativity.

CNN Effect The ability of television, through emotion-raising video, to elevate distant issues on the domestic public agenda.

coaxial cable Heavy-duty landline for video signals.

code of ethics Statement that defines acceptable, unacceptable behaviour.

cognitive dissonance Occurs when people realize their values are inconsistent.

cohort analysis Demographic tool to identify marketing targets by common characteristics.

colonial period From the founding of the colonies to the American Revolution.

commission contract An advertising agency earns an agreed-upon percentage of what the advertising client spends for time and space, traditionally 15 percent.

communication Exchange of ideas, information.

compact disc Digital record format; now dominant.

compass model A looped model that juxtaposes traditional authoritarian and social responsibility models.

Competition Act Federal regulator of advertising in Canada.

compression Technology that makes a message more compact by deleting nonessential underlying code.

concentration of ownership Conglomeration and convergence of media into fewer and fewer hands.

concentric circle model Useful radiating model of the mass communication process.

confidence level Degree of certainty that a survey is accurate.

conglomeration Combining of companies into larger companies.

connotation Vehicle for cultural ideology and myth.

Conrad Black Founded the *National Post*.

consensible nature of news News organization second-guessing competition in deciding coverage.

consistency theory People choose media messages consistent with their individual views, values.

consumer magazines Sold on newsracks.

contemporary transmission Communication of cultural values to different cultures.

content-distribution model Divides functions of media companies into a creation category, such as producing a television program, and a distribution function, such as delivering the program on a cable system.

content analysis Measuring media content to establish a database for analysis.

contingency planning Developing programs in advance of an unscheduled but anticipated event.

continuum model A scale with authoritarianism at one end, libertarianism at the other and media systems at varying points in between.

convergence Early 21st-century model of media cross-ownership. Converged companies typically own print, broadcast, and internet holdings.

cool media Media that can be used passively.

copyright Protects intellectual property from theft.

Corning Glass Company that developed fibre optic cable.

corporate radio A disapproving term for programming engineered by radio chains for use in multiple markets.

counterculture newspapers Challenge, defy mainstream values.

CP The Canadian Press.

CPM Cost per thousand; a tool to determine the cost effectiveness of different media.

creative director Key person in ad campaigns.

crisis management Helping a client through an emergency.

CRTC Canadian Radio-television and Telecommunications Commission. It ensures that Canadians are seen and heard on Canadian media.

cultural imperialism One culture's dominance of another.

cumulative effects theory Theory that media influence is gradual over time.

CW network Network created in 2006 by merger of the WB and UPN.

cyber- Prefix for human connection via computers.

cyberpornography Indecency delivered by computer.

d-cinema Digitally filmed, edited, distributed and exhibited movies.

Dagenais ruling Rights need to be balanced.

Daniel Lord Priest who led a morality crusade against Hollywood.

dark fibre Excess telecommunication capacity available for data transfer.

Dave Nichol Canadian who was a store brand pioneer.

Davey Committee 1970 Royal Commission into media ownership.

David Brown Punished for criticizing the majority party.

David Cronenberg His films are the antithesis to Hollywood endings.

David Ogilvy Championed brand imaging.

David Rooney Believes that bias in journalism is inevitable.

David Sarnoff Head of RCA.

decoding Translating a symbolic message.

defamation False comments that harm a reputation.

defences for defamation Consent, truth, privilege, fair comment.

demassification Media focus on narrower audience segments.

demographics Characteristics of groups within a population being sampled, including age, gender, affiliations.

denotation Everyday meaning of the sign.

Denys Arcand Award-winning French-Canadian film director.

Depression Survivors Today's 80-something and 90-something generations.

desensitizing theory Tolerance of real-life violence grows because of media-depicted violence.

Desi Arnaz and Lucille Ball Introduced taping; led the television industry's move to Hollywood.

detribalization The removal of humankind from a natural, tribal state.

diamond seal Award for sales of 1 million units in Canada.

diaries Sampling technique in which respondents keep their own records.

diffusion of innovation Process through which news, ideas, values and information spread.

digital Broadcast transmission that sends signals in on-off data bits.

Digital Cinema Initiatives Joint movie studio project to identify an industry standard for d-cinema.

digital divide The economic distinction between impoverished groups and societal groups with the means to maintain and improve their economic well-being through computer access.

digital recording Recording and playback system using on-off binary code for sound.

direct-broadcast satellite Transmission from orbit to receiver; no TV station or cable system intermediary.

diversion function Media used as an entertainment source.

"Do unto others" Judeo-Christian principle for ethical behaviour.

documentary A video examination of a historical or current event or a natural or social phenomenon.

Don Ferguson Says Canadians need to see themselves reflected on Canadian TV.

Don Wolf Among the founders of *The Village Voice*.

dot-com A term for businesses that were started to capitalize on internet technology.

dot-com bubble Frenzied over investment in the telephone and internet infrastructure and also internet commerce in late 1990s.

dot-coms Commercial websites, so named because their web address ended with the suffix ".com."

Douglas Edwards Pioneer anchor.

drama credit CRTC incentive for production sector and Canadian channels.

DreamWorks Upstart movie studio, created in 1994 by David Geffen, Jeff Katzenberg and Steven Spielberg.

DualDisc Hybrid CD-DVD format introduced in 2005.

DuMont network Fourth network, operated 1950-1958.

Dwight Macdonald Said all pop art is kitsch.

dynamic routing Technology that makes every wireless device a vehicle for furthering a message along to its destination, rather than moving in a structured network.

Edmund Burke British member of Parliament who is sometimes credited with coining the term *fourth estate*.

Edward Bok Set media standards for ads.

Edward Herman Wrote *Manufacturing Consent* with Noam Chomsky.

Edward R. Murrow Reporter who criticized Joseph McCarthy.

Edwin Armstrong Invented FM as an alternative transmission method.

effect Result of mass communication.

effects studies Impact of media on society, of society on media.

egalitarianism Treat everyone the same.

electromagnetic spectrum Energy waves on which radio messages are piggybacked.

electronic delivery Sending news to readers' computer screens.

electronic media Recordings, radio, television or web, whose messages are stored electronically for transmission and retrieval.

Elisabeth Noelle-Neumann Leading cumulative effects theorist.

elitism Mass media should gear to sophisticated audiences.

elitists Focus on media responsibility to society.

embeds A 2003 Iraq war term for reporters accompanying, or embedded with, U.S. military combat units.

Emile Berliner His machine played discs that could be mass-produced.

encoding Putting something into symbols.

enlightened self-interest Mutually beneficial public relations.

environmental noise Interference at reception site.

equity contract An advertising agency is compensated with shares of stock in an advertising client.

Esquire First classy men's magazine.

ethnocentrism Seeing things on the basis of personal experience, values.

exhibition What movie houses do.

external public relations Gearing messages to outside organizations, constituencies, individuals.

F. Wayland Ayer Founded the first ad agency in America.

Fahrenheit 9/11 2004 propagandist documentary that helped shape issues in 2004 presidential campaign.

Federalist Papers Essays with diverse views on the form the new nation should take.

feedback Recipient's response to the sender.

Ferdinand de Saussure Swiss linguist.

fibre optic cable Glass strands capable of carrying data as light.

filters Receiver factor that impedes communication.

flacks Derisive word for public relations people.

flights Intensive repetition of ads.

flow Variation from day to day in significance of events worth covering.

flush factor Viewers leave during commercials to go to refrigerator, bathroom, etc.

focus groups Small groups interviewed in loosely structured ways for opinion, reactions.

Foster Hewitt First play-by-play announcer for Hockey Night in Canada.

fourth estate The press as a player in medieval power structures, in addition to the clerical, noble and common estates.

Fowler Commission Royal commission into television broadcasting in Canada.

Fox Network launched in 1986.

Fox News Channel Rupert Murdoch-owned cable news network.

framing Selecting aspects of a perceived reality for emphasis in a mass media message, thereby shaping how the audience sees the reality.

Frank Capra Hollywood movie director who produced powerful propaganda movies for U.S. war effort in World War II.

Frank Conrad Pioneer whose work led to KDKA.

Fred W. Friendly Partner of Edward R. Murrow; showed power of TV news through *See It Now* and other programs.

Frederic Ives Invented halftones in 1876.

Frederic Remington Illustrator sent by Hearst to find atrocities in Cuba.

free-standing inserts (FSIs) Preprinted advertising circulars inserted in newspapers.

freebie Gift for which the giver may expect favours in return.

frequency modulation FM

galvanic skin checks Monitor pulse, skin responses to stimuli.

garage bands Coined term for upstart performers without a studio contract.

Garth Jowett Believes Canada has always been dependent on Hollywood movies.

gatekeeper-regulator hybrids Media trade, professional groups.

gatekeepers Media people who influence messages en route.

General Electric Current NBC owner.

Genie Awards Canada's Oscars.

genres Broad thematic categories of media content.

geodemography Demographic characteristics by geographic area.

George Baer Epitomized offensive corporate paternalism in the 1890s.

George Brown Founded *The Globe and Mail*.

George Comstock Believes TV helps us become who we are.

George Eastman Devised celluloid film.

George Gallup Introduced probability sampling.

George Gerbner Speculated that democracy is endangered by media violence.

George Gilder Claims wordless society not on the horizon and that words do much to anchor meaning.

Gerald Levin Offered exclusive HBO programming to cable systems.

Gerald Tellis Dubious about TV ads.

global village Instantaneous connection of every human being.

gold record Award for sales of 1 million singles, 500 000 albums.

gold seal Award for sales of 50 000 units in Canada.

golden mean Moderation is the best course.

Grammy Award for excellence in music in the United States.

Greg Oliver Wrestling journalist.

group communication More than two people; in person.

growth period Second period in Canadian journalism; marked by expansion due to immigration following the War of 1812.

Guglielmo Marconi Produced the first wireless transmission. He is the father of telegraphy.

Hadley Cantril Concluded that there is less media effect than had been thought.

halftone A conversion of a photograph into tiny dots for reproduction on printing presses.

Harlequin Canadian publisher known for romances with cliché characters, settings and themes; the term is applied generically to pulp romances.

Harold Innis Canadian whose communication model was based on bias in communication.

Harold Lasswell Devised the narrative model. This mass communication model assumed powerful effects.

Harold Ross Pioneered the personality profile.

Harper's Weekly Pioneered magazine visuals.

Harry McMahan Dubious about ad creativity.

HBO Short for Home Box Office. First cable programming via satellite.

headline service Brief news stories.

hegemony Coercion through consent.

Henry Luce Magazine publisher known for *Time, Life, Sports Illustrated* and others.

Herb Schmertz Pioneered advertorials.

Herbert Alexander His studies have concluded that media advertising is only one of many variables in political campaigns.

Herbert Gans Concluded that journalists have mainstream values. Said social, economic and intellectual levels of audience coincide.

Herbert Schiller Saw Western cultures subsuming others.

high-, middle- and low-culture audiences Continuum identified by Herbert Gans.

high art Requires sophisticated taste to be appreciated.

highbrow, middlebrow and lowbrow Levels of media content sophistication that coincide with audience tastes.

hillbilly music Folk genre from rural Appalachian, Southern white experience.

historical transmission Communication of cultural values to later generations.

hit Tallied every time someone goes to a web page.

hometown daily Edited primarily for readers in a defined region.

homophyly A coding oneness that makes communication possible.

horse race An election campaign treated by reporters like a game—who's ahead, who's falling back, who's coming up the rail.

hot media Print media, which require more intimate audience involvement.

Howard Christenson Publishes *Broadcast Dialogue* magazine.

Hugh Hefner Adapted the personality profile to Q-and-A.

hypertext System for nonsequential reading.

hypertext markup language (HTML) Language that is used to code for web pages.

hypertext transfer protocol (HTTP) Coding that allows computers to talk with each other to read web pages.

hyping Intensive promotion to attract an audience during ratings periods.

iconoscope Zworykin's television vacuum tube.

icons Signs that look like what they signify.

image consulting Coaching individuals for media contacts.

image dissector Farnsworth's television vacuum tube.

Immanuel Kant Advocated the categorical imperative.

independent producers Movie production enterprises outside of the major studios.

index A sign that is connected to what it signifies.

indies Independently owned record-making companies; not part of Big Four.

infomercial Program-length broadcast commercial.

information boycott Severing ties with news media.

information pollution Media deluge people with information and no sense of order, priority.

informational filter Receiver's knowledge limits impede deciphering symbols.

infotainment Melding of media role as purveyor of information and entertainment.

institutional advertising Paid space and time to promote an institution's image, position.

integrated marketing communication Comprehensive program that links public relations, advertising.

Interfax Russian news agency.

internal public relations Gearing messages to inside groups, constituencies, individuals.

internalization Making sense of a decoded message.

internet A network of computer networks.

internet service provider (ISP) Company that charges a fee for online service.

internet site Where an institution establishes its web presence.

Internet2 A network consortium owned by research institutions for fast data transfer.

interpersonal communication Usually two people face to face.

interviews Face-to-face, mail or telephone survey technique.

intrapersonal communication Talking to oneself.

inverted pyramid Most important information first.

investigative reporting Enterprise reporting that reveals new information, often startling; most often these are stories that official sources would rather not have told.

iPod Brand name for Apple's handheld digital music device.

iTunes Online music store.

Ivy Lee Laid out fundamentals of public relations.

Izzy Asper Developed Global into Canada's third private TV network.

Jack An eclectic, somewhat unpredictable musical radio format.

Jack Trout Devised positioning.

Jackie Brenston Recorded "Rocket 88," first rock 'n' roll record, in 1951.

James Gordon Bennett New York newspaper publisher in 1830s; first to assign reporters to sports regularly.

Janet Cooke Classic case of representing fiction as truth.

jazz journalism 1920s, similar to yellow journalism.

Jean Valin Believes organizations are served best when they tell the truth.

Jim Vicary Made dubious subliminal advertising claims.

Johannes Gutenberg Inventor of printing press which, in turn, made mass media and advertising possible.

John Adams Federalist president.

John Bassett Founded CFTO Toronto, CTV's flagship station.

John Cameron Swayze Pioneer anchor.

John Campbell Published the first ad in the British colonies.

John D. Rockefeller Jr. Ivy Lee client who had been the target of public hatred.

John Dewey Advocate of pragmatism.

John Grierson Founder of the NFB.

John Kenneth Galbraith Advertising isn't about needs, it's about wants.

John Merrill Introduced the compass model, which showed that social responsibility and authoritarianism could be bedmates.

John Perry Barlow Believes copyright laws are archaic.

John Peter Zenger Defied authorities in *New-York Weekly Journal.*

John Rawls Advocated egalitarianism.

John Stuart Mill Advocated utilitarianism.

Jonathan Robbin Devised PRIZM geodemography system.

Joseph Howe Advocate of an "unshackled press."

Joseph Maxwell Introduced electrical recording in the 1920s.

Joseph Niépce French inventor of a light-sensitive photo process in 1826.

Joseph Pulitzer New York newspaper publisher in 1880s; organized the first newspaper sports department. Emphasized human interest in newspapers; later sensationalized.

Joshua Meyrowitz Noted that media have reduced generational, gender barriers.

Joyce Nelson Says public relations has two sides: the shadow and the persona.

junket Trip with expenses paid by someone who may expect favours in return.

Juno Award for excellence in music in Canada.

Jürgen Habermas German sociologist who believed that political ideas need to be debated.

Katherine Monk Developed a Canadian movie checklist.

KDKA First licensed commercial radio station in the United States. This Pittsburgh radio station pioneered sports broadcasting in 1920s.

Ken Soble and Al Bruner Dreamt of a Canadian superstation.

Kent Commission 1981 Royal Commission into newspaper ownership.

kitsch Pejorative word for trendy, trashy, low art.

leak A deliberate disclosure of confidential or classified information by someone who wants to advance the public interest, embarrass a bureaucratic rival or supervisor, or disclose incompetence or skullduggery.

Lee de Forest Inventor whose projects included the audion tube.

Legion of Decency Church listing of acceptable movies.

Leo Burnett Unique selling proposition doesn't need to be insulting.

libel A written defamation.

lightning news Delivered by telegraph.

Linda and Robert Lichter and Stanley Rothman Colleagues whose research indicates a liberal agenda in entertainment programming. They claim TV is reformist.

lobbyists Influence public policy, usually legislation or regulations.

local autonomy Independence from chain headquarters.

long-play (LP) 33 1/3-rpm microgroove discs that turned the recorded music industry into conceiving of its products as albums.

low art Can be appreciated by almost everybody.

lowest common denominator Messages for broadest audience possible.

Lumière brothers Opened the first movie exhibition hall.

Maclean's First Canadian newsmagazine.

magazine programs Investigative news programs, usually with three to four unrelated segments.

magazines Ongoing bound publications of continuing value with diverse topics.

mainstream media (MSM) Established media companies and products.

major studios Include Warner Brothers, Columbia, Universal, 20th Century Fox, Paramount, Disney, MGM.

make-goods Additional time that networks offer advertisers when ratings fall short of projections.

manufacturing consent A system limiting debate on political and social issues.

Marc Andreessen Invented the Netscape browser.

margin of error Percentage that a survey may be off the mark.

Mario Garcia Newspaper design expert who champions tabloid formats.

Marshall McLuhan Canadian who claimed the medium was the message. He blamed human alienation on mass-produced written word.

Martin Quigley Partner of Father Daniel Lord.

mass audiences Recipients of mass messages.

mass communication Many recipients; not face to face; a process.

mass communicators Message crafters.

mass media Vehicles that carry messages.

mass message What is communicated.

Maxwell McCombs and Donald Shaw Articulated agenda-setting theory.

media-induced passivity Media entice people away from social involvement.

media buyers Decide where to place ads.

media kit A packet provided to news reporters to tell the story in an advantageous way.

Media Metrix A service measuring internet audience size.

media plan Lays out where ads are placed.

media relations Using mass media to convey messages.

mediated message Adjusted to be effective when carried by the mass media.   208

Melvin DeFleur Scholar who concluded that mass communication theory has peaked.   262

merchandise tie-ins Studio deals to profit from merchandise carrying movie names and logos.

mesh networking The ad hoc network created for each single message to reach its destination; also called dynamic routing.

Michael Geist Canadian expert on how new technology is affecting Canadian law.

Michael McCabe Former head of Canadian Association of Broadcasters.

Michael Moore Documentary producer whose *Fahrenheit 9/11* demonstrated the genre's potential in political campaigns.

Michael Novak Believes TV is broad shaper of issues.

microwave relays Towers re-angle over-the-air signals to match the earth's curvature.

Millennials Generation X Baby Boomers Today's 40-something and 50-something generations.

minimalist effects theory Theory that media effects are mostly indirect.

misrepresentation Deception in gathering or telling information.

Moses Znaimer Believes TV reflects values and ideals.

Motion Picture Producers and Distributors of America (MPPDA) 1922 Hollywood attempt to establish moral code for movies.

Motion Picture Production Code 1930 Hollywood attempt to quiet critical moralists.

movable metal type Small blocks of type arranged into words, lines and pages.

MSNBC Cable news network owned by NBC and Microsoft.

muckraking Early 20th-century term for investigative reporting.

multiplexing Technology to transmit numerous messages simultaneously.

multistep flow Political information moves from the media to individuals through complex, ever-changing interpersonal connections.

Napster First online music-swapping software.

narcoticizing dysfunction People deceive themselves into believing they're involved when actually they're only informed.

narrative model Describes process in words, not schematic.

National Enquirer Magazine or newspaper?

National Geographic Introduced photography in magazines.

National Science Foundation Developed current internet to give scholars access to supercomputers.

NBC National Broadcast Company. Built from NBC radio network under David Sarnoff. One of the Big Three over-the-air networks.

negative ads Political campaign advertising, usually on television, in which a candidate criticizes the opponent rather than emphasizes his or her platform.

Nellie Bly Stunt reporter.

Netscape An internet browser that broadened web access widely.

new media Upstart media companies and media products resulting from new technology.

New York Daily News Founded 1919; its focus on the bizarre defined tabloid in public thinking as a word for sensationalism.

news Nonfiction reports on what people want or need to know.

news blackout When a person or institution decides to issue no statements despite public interest and also declines news media questions.

news hole Space for news in a newspaper after ads are inserted; also time in a newscast for news after ads.

newspaper chain Company that owns several newspapers.

newspapers Unbound publications, generally weekly or daily, with diverse, timely content.

NFB Canada's award-winning National Film Board.

Noam Chomsky Believes the news media is an ideological apparatus for the elite in society.

noise Impedes communication before message reaches receiver.

nonstop coverage News reporting geared to ever-present deadlines, as 24/7 formats.

Norman Mailer Among the founders of *The Village Voice*.

Norman McLaren Canadian innovator in animation.

nut Upfront distribution payment to exhibitor.

objective reporting Telling news without bias.

objectivity A concept in journalism that news should be gathered and told value-free.

obscenity Sexually explicit media depictions that the government can ban.

observational learning Theory that people learn behaviour by seeing it in real life, in depictions.

online advertising Provide messages to computers.

opinion leaders Media-savvy individuals who influence friends and acquaintances.

opinion surveys Seek audience reaction, views.

Orson Welles His radio drama cast doubt on powerful effects theory.

Ouimetoscope Canada's first movie house.

overnights Next-morning reports on network viewership.

P.T. Barnum Known for exaggerated promotion.

P3P A web protocol that allows users to choose a level of privacy. Short for Platform for Privacy Preferences Project.

Paramount Decision The landmark 1948 U.S. Supreme Court anti-monopoly decision which broke the major studios' hold on the U.S. movie industry.

parasocial interaction A false sense of participating in dialogue.

Parents' Music Resource Center Crusaded for labels on "objectionable" music.

partisan period From the American Revolution at least to the 1830s.

pass-along circulation All the people who see a periodical.

Pat Weaver Created NBC's *Tonight Show* and *Today*.

Paul Garrett Devised the notion of enlightened self-interest.

Paul Lazarsfeld Sociologist who concluded that media influence on voters generally is indirect. Found voters more influenced by other people than by mass media.

pay-per-view Cable companies charge subscribers for each program they watch.

Peak Viewing Period 7-11 p.m., seven days a week.

peer-to-peer sharing (P2P) Music-swapping software without a central server.

peer review A screening mechanism in which scholarly material is reviewed by leaders in a discipline for its merits, generally with neither the author nor the reviewers knowing each other's identity.

penetration Percentage of persons or households that a newspaper reaches in its circulation area.

penny papers Affordable by almost everyone.

penny press period One-cent newspapers geared to mass audience and mass advertising.

people meters Devices that track individual viewers.

performance contract An advertising agency earns expenses and an agreed-upon markup for the advertising client, plus bonuses for exceeding minimal expectations.

persistence of vision Retina's capability to retain an image briefly, allowing brain to fill in gaps between successive images.

personality profile In-depth, balanced biographical article.

Pete Williams Tilted news coverage by overwhelming the media with information during the Persian Gulf War.

Peter Desbarats Believes that Canadian journalism traditions are closely related to American traditions.

Peter Goldmark Inventor of long-play records.

Peter Harcourt Writes that Canadian movies reflect our own uncertainty.

Philo Farnsworth Invented technology that uses electrons to transmit moving images live.

Phonograph Trade name for the first recorder-playback machine.

photo op Short for "photo opportunity." A staged event, usually photogenic, to attract media attention.

physical filter Receiver's alertness impedes deciphering symbols.

pilot Prototype show for a series.

plagiarism Using someone else's work without permission or credit.

platinum record Award for sales of 2 million singles, 1 million albums.

platinum seal Award for sales of 100 000 units in Canada.

Playboy Widely imitated girlie/lifestyle men's magazine.

playlist A list of songs that a radio station plays.

podcasts Downloadable episodes of popular TV shows.

policy analysis Seeks implications of public policy, future effects.

political communication Advising candidates, groups on public policy issues, usually in elections.

pool system Reporters chosen on a rotating basis to cover an event to which access is limited.

pop art revisionism Pop art has inherent value.

popular art Art that tries to succeed in the marketplace.

population Group of people being studied.

populism Mass media should seek largest possible audiences.

populists Applaud media that attract a large following.

pornography Sexually explicit depictions that are protected from government bans.

positioning Targeting ads for specific consumer groups.

Postal Assistance Program (PAP) Discounted magazine mail rates for Canadian magazines.

Postwar Generation Today's 60-something generation.

Potter's Box Tool for sorting through the pros and cons of ethics questions.

powerful effects theory Theory that media have immediate, direct influence.

pragmatic ethics Judge acts by their results.

prescriptive ethics Follow the rules and your decision will be the correct one.

pressure groups Try to influence media messages, policies; include citizen groups, government agencies.

priming Process in which the media affect the standard that people use to evaluate political figures and issues.

principle of utility Best course bestows the most good for the most people.

Print Measurement Bureau Checks magazine circulation claims.

print media Books, magazines and newspapers.

private actions versus public morality Dichotomy that exposes discrepancies between behaviour and values.

PRIZM Identifies population characteristics by zip code.

pro-social Socialization perpetuates positive values.

proactive media relations Taking initiative to release information.

probability sampling Everyone in population being surveyed has an equal chance to be sampled.

process studies To understand the mass communication process.

product placement Writing a brand-name product into a television or movie script. When a manufacturer pays for its products to be used as props.

production Content-creation component of the movie industry.

promotion Promoting a cause, idea.

prototype research Checks response to product still in development.

prudence Applying wisdom, not principles, to an ethics situation.

pseudo-event A staged event to attract media attention, usually lacking substance.

psychographics Breaking down a population by lifestyle characteristics.

psychological filter Receiver's state of mind impedes deciphering symbols.

public domain Intellectual property that may be used without permission of the creator or owner.

public information One alternative word for public relations; others are public affairs, corporate communication.

public relations A management tool to establish beneficial relationships; messages intended to win support.

public relations agencies Companies that provide public relations services.

Public Relations Society of America Professional public relations association.

public sphere Where political ideas need to be debated.

publication bans Limitations on media freedom of speech.

publicity Brings public attention to something.

Publick Occurrences First colonial newspaper, Boston, 1690.

puffery Inflated claims.

pull media Messages requested by the receiver.

pulp fiction Quickly and inexpensively produced easy-to-read short novels.

push-pull model Some of the control in the communication process shifts to the receiver.

push media Messages sent to the receiver with or without prior consent.

quota sampling Demographics of the sample coincide with those of the whole population.

Radio-Television News Directors Association (RTNDA) Organization that believes the broadcasting of factual, accurately reported, and timely news and public affairs is vital.

Radio Marketing Bureau Claims radio is a perfect fit for modern life.

radio with pictures Simplistic definition of TV.

Ralph Potter Ethicist who devised the Potter's Box.

rap Rhythm-heavy music genre usually with rapid-fire, attitude-heavy lyrics.

ratings Measurements of broadcast audience size.

re-enactments Re-creating real events.

Reader Usage Measure (RUM) A tool developed by the magazine industry to score reader experience as a guide for designing magazines conceptually and for editing content.

reality programs Broadcast shows with a nonfiction basis.

Recording Industry Association of America (RIAA) Trade association of music recording companies.

redundancy Repetition of media messages.

Reginald Fessenden Canadian who broadcast the first radio program, 1906. Father of radio broadcasting.

regulators Nonmedia people who influence messages.

retribalization Restoring humankind to a natural, tribal state.

Reuters British-based global news agency.

rhythm and blues Distinctive style of black music that took form in the 1930s.

rice-roots reporting Uncensored field reporting from the Vietnam War.

risk investors Individuals and companies willing to put capital into ventures shunned by conservative financial institutions.

Robert Park Argued that media create awareness.

rock 'n' roll Genre marked by incessant beat with guitar as the dominant instrument.

rockabilly Hybrid of music in the black tradition and hillbilly music; precursor of rock 'n' roll. Emerged in the 1950s.

Roland Barthes French semiotician.

role modeling Basis for imitative behaviour.

Roone Arledge ABC television executive responsible for *Wide World of Sports* in 1961. Created ABC's *Monday Night Football*.

Rosser Reeves Devised unique selling proposition.

roving photographer Statistically unsound way to tap public opinion.

Rupert Murdoch Australian-born owner of the global company News Corporation. Created Fox network.

S.S. McClure Expanded syndicate concept.

Sam Phillips Pioneered rockabilly, rock 'n' roll; discovered Elvis Presley.

sample selection Process for drawing individuals to be interviewed.

sample size Number of people surveyed.

Samuel Morse Invented the telegraph.

Sarah Josepha Hale Founded first women's magazine.

satellite radio Delivery method of programming from a single source beamed to an orbiting satellite for transmission directly to individual end-users.

scribists Monks who copied books manually.

scrum Members of the Parliamentary Press Gallery meet with politicians after Question Period.

selective editing Misrepresentation through omission and juxtaposition.

selective exposure People choose some media messages over others.

selective perception People tend to hear what they want or expect to hear.

selective recall People recollect some events and messages for long term but not others.

selective retention Subconsciously, people retain some events and messages, not others.

semantic noise Sloppy message-crafting.

semiconductor Silicon chips that are used in digitization.

Seven Sisters Leading women's magazines.

Seymour Feshbach Found evidence for media violence as a release.

Shawn Fanning Inventor of Napster.

shelf life How long a periodical remains in use.

shock jock Announcer whose style includes vulgarities, taboos.

shopper An advertising paper without news.

signified Mental part of the sign.

signifier Physical part of the sign.

signs Creating meaning in communication.

slander A spoken defamation.

SOCAN Society of Composers, Authors and Music Publishers of Canada; music licensing organization.

social Darwinism Application of Darwin's survival-of-the-fittest theory to society.

socialization Learning to fit into society.

socialization function Media help people fit into society.

soft news Geared to satisfying audience's information wants, not needs.

sound bite The actual voice of someone in the news, sandwiched in a correspondent's report.

Spence Caldwell Initiator of the CTV network.

spiral of silence Vocal majority intimidates others into silence.

sponsored link Onscreen hot spot to move to an online advertisement.

sponsored magazine Generally non-newsrack magazine, often member-supported.

staffing Available staff resources to cover news.

staging news Creating an event to attract news media attention and coverage.

Stan Klees Founder of Cancon MAPL.

standard advertising unit (SAU) A trimmer newspaper broadsheet format with standardized dimensions; introduced in the 1980s.

Stanley Hubbard Satellite TV pioneer.

star system Helps raise the awareness of Canadian shows and stars.

statistical extrapolation Drawing conclusions from a segment of the whole.

status conferral Media attention enhances attention to people, subjects, issues.

stealth ads Advertisements, often subtle, in nontraditional, unexpected places.

stereotyping Using broad strokes to facilitate storytelling.

Steve Jobs Driving force behind Apple Computer revival, iPod, and iTunes.

Steve Maich *Maclean's* columnist with issues about the impact of the internet and the rhetoric surrounding it.

Steve Smith Proud supporter and producer of Canadian TV.

stimulation Stirs someone to communicate.

stonewall To refuse to answer questions, sometimes refusing even to meet with reporters.

store brands Products sold with a store brand, often manufactured by the retailer. Also called house brands and private labels.

straw poll Respondents select themselves to be polled; unreliable indicator of public opinion.

streaming Technology that allows playback of a message to begin before all the components have arrived.

studio A company that produces movies, sometimes also involved in distribution.

studio system A production-line movie production system devised by Hollywood in the 1920s.

subception Receiving subconscious messages that trigger behaviour.

subliminal advertising Ads that cannot be consciously perceived.

subsystem model Examines media in terms of originator and intended audience.

SurfWatch Software that intercepts indecent material.

surveillance function Media provide information on what's going on.

Susan Sontag Saw cultural, social value in pop art.

sweeps When broadcast ratings are conducted.

symbol A sign that has an arbitrary connection to what it signifies.

syndicates Provide low-cost, high-quality content to many news outlets.

syndicators Independent program producers and distributors.

tabloid A newspaper format with pages half the size of a broadsheet; typically five columns wide and 14 to 18 inches long; tab for short; not necessarily sensationalistic despite a connotation the term has acquired.

technological convergence Melding of print, electronic and photographic media into digitized form.

technological research To improve technology and find new technology.

telephone book journalism Emphasizing readers' names in articles.

Television Violence Monitoring Project Conducted contextual nonviolence studies and found less serious media depictions than earlier thought.

terrestrial radio Traditional name for over-the-air radio stations.

The Brass Check 1919 book that exposed newsroom corruption.

The Center for Media and Public Affairs Media research organization.

The Miracle case U.S. Supreme Court ruled that the First Amendment protected movies from censorship.

The New York Sun First penny newspaper, 1833.

The Village Voice Model for contemporary alternative press.

The War of the Worlds Novel that inspired a radio drama that became the test bed of the media's ability to instill panic.

Theodore Roosevelt Coined the term *muckraking*.

theoretical research Goal is to advance knowledge.

third-person effect One person overestimating the effect of media messages on other people.

Thomas Bohn Devised the concentric circle model, with Ray Hiebert, Donald Ungurait.

Thomas Edison Built the first audio recorder-playback machine.

Thomas Jefferson Anti-Federalist president.

Thomas Patterson and Robert McClure Effect of political advertising on voters is critical only in close campaigns.

Tim Berners-Lee Devised protocols, codes for the World Wide Web.

Time First American newsmagazine.

TiVo A television recording and playback device that allows viewers to edit out commercials. Also called a digital video recorder (DVR) or personal video recorder (PVR).

touring Live performances in highly promoted road trips; increasingly important revenue source for big-name performers.

trade journal Keeps members of profession or trade informed.

trailing Running shorter, smaller ads after campaign is introduced.

transmission Sending a message.

transplant period First period in Canadian journalism, in which newspapers or publishers from Britain and the United States were "transplanted" to Canada.

trial balloon A deliberate leak of a potential policy, usually from a diversionary source, to test public response.

truth A broad and accurate understanding.

two-step flow Media effect on individuals is through opinion leaders.

ultrawideband (UWB) Low-power Wi-Fi system that rides on existing frequencies licensed for other uses.

Ulysses James Joyce novel banned in the United States until 1930 court decision.

unique selling proposition (USP) Emphasizing a single feature.

United Artists Upstart artist-directed movie studio, started in 1919.

United Paramount Theaters Strengthened ABC in 1953 merger.

universal access Giving everyone the means to use the internet.

universal resource locator (URL) Address assigned to a page on the internet. Now known as a uniform resource locator.

unshackled press The idea that the press should be able to print the truth.

upfront Advance advertiser commitments to buy network advertising time.

Upton Sinclair Author of *The Brass Check*.

uses and gratifications studies Theory that people choose media that meet their needs, interests.

VALS Psychographic analysis by values, lifestyle, life stage.

veil of ignorance Making decisions with a blind eye to extraneous factors that could affect the decision.

virtual print fee Movie studio payment to theatres for showing a digital-format movie, as an offset for digital projection equipment.

visit Tallied for every person who visits a website.

visual literacy An understanding of images in order to interpret their meaning and significance.

Vladimir Zworykin RCA engineer who claimed to have invented television.

voice tracking A few announcers who prerecord music intros and outros for multiple stations to create a single personality for stations.

W.P. Davison Scholar who devised third-person effect theory.

Walter Cronkite Best-known television news anchor, now retired.

Walter Lippmann His book *Public Opinion* assumed powerful media effects in 1920s.

Warren Weaver Devised a basic communication model, with Claude Shannon.

Watergate Reporting of the Nixon administration scandal.

waves Intensive repetition of ads.

Webby A major award of excellence for websites.

webisodes Mini-movies, generally four minutes long, on the web; usually sponsored and sometimes with the advertiser as part of the storyline.

westward growth Third period in Canadian journalism: As Canadians moved west, so did the press.

whitewashing Covering up.

Wi-Fi Wireless fidelity technology.

Wilbur Schramm Concluded that television has minimal effects on children.

Wilfred Kesterton Canadian news historian.

Will Hays Led MPPDA.

William Caxton Printed the first advertisement.

William Dickson Developed the first movie camera.

William Gibson Sci-fi writer who coined the term *cyberspace*.

William Henry Vanderbilt Embodied the bad corporate images of the 1880s, 1890s with "The public be damned."

William McQuire Found most media violence research flawed.

William Paley Long-time CBS boss.

William Randolph Hearst Chain owner who dictated contents of all his newspapers. Built circulation with sensationalism.

Wilson Bryan Key Believes he sees subliminal advertising widely used.

World War II Veterans Today's 70-something and 80-something generations.

World Wide Web System that allows global linking of information modules in user-determined sequences.

XWA Canada's first radio station.

yellow period Late 1800s; marked by sensationalism.

Youth Criminal Justice Act Prohibits reporting on trials involving minors.

zapping Viewers record programs and eliminate commercial breaks.

'zine Magazine whose entire content—articles and ads—pitches a single product or product line.

zipping Viewers change television channels to avoid commercials.

Name Index

Subject Index

ethnic radio format, 85
ethnic newspapers, 44
European news model, 155
evaluating various media
    advertising, 202
    entertainment, 214
    internet, 140
    journalism, 166
    magazines, 54
    movies, 91, 109
    music, 71–72
    newspapers, 44
    radio, 86
    record companies, 71–72
evolving news models, 156
exhibition of movies, 96
exploratory reporting, 163
external public relations, 174

F

fair comment and criticism, 239
Federalist Papers, 149
feedback, 22
fibre-optic cables, 136
file sharing, 70
filters,
    informational, 27
    physical, 27
    psychological, 27
flackers, 183
focus groups, 229
folk music, 210
foreign ownership
    of magazines, 47
    Foreign Publishers Advertising Services Act,
        Bill C-55, 47
Fowler Commission, 240
FOX (network), 118
free standing inserts, 42
frequency modulation (FM), 79
Freidman globalization model, 294
Friends of Canadian Broadcasting, 287
fundraising, 176
Fundamentals in the Mass Communication
    Process
    Decoding, 24
    Encoding, 24
    Homophyly, 24
    Internalization, 24–25
    Stimulation, 23
    Transmission, 24

G

Gallup Poll, 221–223
galvanic skin checks, 220
gatekeepers, 25, 147, 156
    publication bans, 237
Genie Awards, 103
genres, 207–208
geography, and change model, 292
global communication, 294
    see also global mass media
Global-TV, 119

global mass media
    conglomeration, 294–296
    cultural intrusion, 297–299
    distinctive media systems,
        302–303
    effects, 296
    Friedman model, 294
    global media companies, 300–301
    global media players, 299–300
    globalization, effects of, 296
    internet and, 296
    models, 291–293
    nation states, 293
    timeline, 293
global media companies
    Bertelsmann, 301
    Disney-ABC, 301
    Hachette Filipacchi, 301
    NBC Universal, 301
    News Corporation, 301
    Pearson, 301
    Reed Elsevier, 301
    Televisa, 301
    Time Warner, 301
    TVB, 301
    TV Globo, 301
    Viacom, 301
global media models
    bipolar model, 291
    change model, 292
    compass model, 292
    continuum model, 291
    subsystem model, 292
global media players
    news agencies, 299
    syndicates, 300
    video news services, 300
global village, 278
globalization effects
    and the web, 296
    Canadian experience, 297
    corporate ideology, 296
    cultural subversiveness, 296
    latter day imperialism, 297
    non-downward media
        exchange, 297
    transnational cultural
        enrichment, 299
Globe and Mail, The, 40
gold record, 71
gold seal, 72
golden mean, 247
government manipulation of media
    influencing coverage, 314
    leaks, 315
    scrums, 315
    stonewalling, 316
    trial balloons, 315
Grammy Awards, 72
growth period of Canadian
    journalism, 153
Guide to Canadian News Media
    (Desbarats), 126, 152

Photo Credits

Chapter 11
p. 205 Paul Hawthorne/Getty Images; p. 208 Frank Micelotta/Getty Images; p. 213 ©1998 Copyrights ABC, Inc.; p. 215 Steve Allen/Getty Images; p. 216 AP/ Wide World Photos

Chapter 12
p. 219 Nielsen Media Research; p. 222 The Gallup Organization; p. 223 AP/Wide World Photos; p. 228 (top) AP/Wide World Photos, (bottom) The Arbitron Company, NY; p. 229 Douglas Burrows/ Getty Images

Chapter 13
p. 235 Electronic Frontier Foundation; p. 239 State Historial Society of Iowa – Iowa City; p. 242 CP Photo/ Tobin Grimshaw; p. 247 Corbis; p. 248 (top) North Wind Picture Archives, (bottom) North Wind Picture Archives; p. 249 (left) Courtesy Harvard News Office, (right) Bettmann/Corbis; p. 250 Office of Communications at Harvard Divinity School; p. 254 Mayita Mendex/Copyright 2003 *Newsday*. Reprinted with permission.

Chapter 14
p. 259 Culver Pictures; p. 266 A Band Apart/Miramax/ The Kobal Collection; p. 269 Bettmann/Corbis; p. 271 (left) Everett Collection, Inc., (right) © SCi ISales Curve Interactive Limited; p. 272 Kyle Cassidy/Annenberg School of Communication

Chapter 15
p. 277 CP/ Doug Ball; p. 280 AP/Wide World Photos; p. 281 (left) NYP Holdings, Inc., (right) Copyright 2005 by *The New York Times* Co.; p. 283 (left) Center for Media and Public Affairs, (right) Fredrich Cantor; p. 285 AP/Wide World Photos; p. 286 AP/Wide World Photos; p. 287 Courtesy friends.ca

Chapter 16
p. 291 Roberts Voets/CBS; p. 294 Win McNamee/Getty Images for *Meet the Press*; p. 295 James Knowler/ Reuters/Corbis; p. 297 SIO/UCSD Photo; p. 298 AP/Wide World Photos; p. 302 Courtesy of Video Sound, Inc., NJ

Chapter 17
p. 307 AP/Wide World Photos; p. 312 (left) Shawn Thew/AFP/Getty Images, (right) Alex Wong/Getty Images